Ninth Edition

Signs of Life in the U.S.A.

Readings on Popular Culture for Writers

Ninth Edition

Signs of Life in the U.S.A.

Readings on Popular Culture for Writers

Sonia Maasik
University of California, Los Angeles

Jack Solomon
California State University, Northridge

bedford/st.martin's
Macmillan Learning

Boston I New York

For Bedford/St. Martin's

Vice President, Editorial, Macmillan Learning Humanities: Edwin Hill
Senior Program Director for English: Leasa Burton
Program Manager, Readers and Literature: John E. Sullivan III
Marketing Manager: Joy Fisher Williams
Director of Content Development: Jane Knetzger
Developmental Editor: Sherry Mooney
Associate Content Project Manager: Matt Glazer
Workflow Manager: Lisa McDowell
Production Supervisor: Robert Cherry
Media Project Manager: D. Rand Thomas
Editorial Services: Lumina Datamatics, Inc.
Composition: Lumina Datamatics, Inc.
Photo Editor: Angela Boehler
Photo Researcher: Terri Wright
Permissions Editor: Angela Boehler
Senior Art Director: Anna Palchik
Cover Design: William Boardman
Cover Art/Cover Photo: Replica Statue of Liberty and roller coaster on exterior of New
    York-New York Hotel and Casino, Las Vegas, Nevada, USA / David Wall / Alamy
    Stock Photo; Muncie - Circa August 2016: Legacy McDonald's Hamburger Sign with
    Speedee / Jonathan Weiss / Alamy Stock Photo; Geological rock ridge in a California
    state park marks the San Andreas Fault Line / kenkisler / Shutterstock; Abraham
    Lincoln Memorial Sitting Chair famous Landmark Closeup Phrase Washington DC
    Monument / Hunter Bliss / Shutterstock; Route 66. Road sign of the more famous
    American road / Marco Mariani / Shutterstock.
Printing and Binding: LSC Communications

Manufactured in the United States of America.

2   1   0   9   8   7
f   e   d   c   b   a

For information, write: Bedford/St. Martin's, 75 Arlington Street, Boston, MA 02116

ISBN: 978-1-319-05663-6

Acknowledgments

*Text acknowledgments and copyrights appear at the back of the book on pages 569–73,
which constitute an extension of the copyright page. Art acknowledgments and copyrights
appear on the same page as the art selections they cover.*

Preface for Instructors

A funny thing happened on the way to the ninth edition of *Signs of Life in the U.S.A.*: Donald Trump — contrary to all of the projections that the latest in predictions markets technology could muster — was elected president of the United States. This gave us pause: not because we had any intention of turning our book into some sort of "Trump Reader," but because the election at once both verifies the fundamental premises of earlier editions of *Signs of Life* and promises to affect American culture in ways that it behooves the current edition to anticipate and address. And that is what we have strived to do, in as nonpartisan a manner as we can.

There are two basic ways in which the presidential election of Donald Trump bears out the guiding principles of this book. First, it exemplifies, in a particularly striking manner, the preeminent place of popular culture in contemporary American life. For Trump's road to the White House was paved in large part both by his success as a reality TV star and by his no-holds-barred employment of Twitter as a means to communicate with his followers. Not even the election of Ronald Reagan (himself a former entertainment figure) can really compare in this regard, because Reagan had spent years in the political arena — most notably as governor of California — before he went to Pennsylvania Avenue, and candidate Reagan had no social media available to maintain a 24/7 connection with voters. So 2016 really was different, reflecting the full coming of age of the power of pop culture.

But there is a second way in which the Trump presidency reflects what earlier editions of *Signs of Life* presumed and explored: the ever-growing ideological divide between two Americas—often called red state and blue state—is a theme that this book formally addressed in chapters devoted to the fundamental contradictions that have riven this nation from its inception. And if anyone has doubted the existence of this division, or felt that it was only a sideshow to a basically unified country, the Trump election, and more importantly its aftermath, loudly says otherwise. Americans have really seen nothing quite like this since the Civil War.

So, putting aside our own opinions about what could be called the "Election Heard Round the World," we have created this new edition of our book with our foundational assumptions not only strengthened but intensified: that American popular culture, no longer a mere cultural embellishment or ornament, now permeates almost everything we do, even as it reflects back to us what we are becoming as a society and who we are. Thus, if we wish to understand America today, we must learn to think critically about the vast panoply of entertainments and commodities that were once condescendingly dismissed as elements of "mass culture." And that is what *Signs of Life in the U.S.A.* has always been designed to teach your students to do.

Then and Now

The importance of thinking critically about popular culture has not always been apparent in the academic world. When the first edition of *Signs of Life* appeared, the study of popular culture was still embroiled in the "culture wars" of the late 1980s and early 1990s, a struggle for academic legitimacy in which the adherents of popular cultural studies prevailed so thoroughly that it now seems surprising that anyone ever objected to it at all. For today, the importance of understanding what Michel de Certeau has called "the practice of everyday life," and the value of using popular culture as a thematic ground for educating students in critical thinking and writing, is now taken for granted, as what was once excluded from academic study on the basis of a naturalized distinction between "high" and "low" culture is now an accepted part of the curriculum, widely studied in freshman composition classrooms as well as in upper-division undergraduate courses and graduate seminars.

But recognition of the importance that popular culture has assumed in our society has not been restricted to the academy. Increasingly, Americans are realizing that American culture and popular culture are virtually one and the same, and that whether we are looking at our political system, our economy, or simply our national consciousness, the power of popular culture to shape our lives is strikingly apparent. That's why, unlike most other popular culture texts, *Signs of Life* adopts an interpretive approach—semiotics—explicitly designed to analyze that intersection of ideology and entertainment that we call *popular culture*. We continue to make semiotics the guiding methodology behind *Signs of Life* because semiotics helps us, and our students, avoid the common pitfalls of an uncritical celebration of popular culture, or simple trivia swapping.

The Critical Method: Semiotics

The reception of the first eight editions of this text has demonstrated that the semiotic approach to popular culture has indeed found a place in America's composition classrooms. Instructors have seen that students feel a certain sense of ownership toward the products of popular culture and that using popular culture as a focus can help students overcome the sometimes alienating effects of traditional academic subject matter. More profoundly, the use of pop culture content in a composition class is a way of abiding by the fundamental principle that learning is a movement from the familiar to the unfamiliar, an assimilation of the unknown by way of the already known. Coming to your class with an established expertise in popular culture, your students will be all the more prepared to learn the university-level critical thinking and writing skills that their composition classes are designed to impart.

Reflecting the broad academic interest in cultural studies, we've assumed an inclusive definition of *popular culture* in this book. The seven chapters in *Signs of Life in the U.S.A.* embrace everything from the marketing and consumption of the products of mass production to the television programs and movies that entertain us. We came to choose semiotics as our approach to such subjects because it has struck us that, while students enjoy assignments that ask them to look at popular cultural phenomena, they often have trouble distinguishing between an argued interpretive analysis and the simple expression of an opinion. Some textbooks, for example, suggest assignments that involve analyzing a TV show or film, but they don't always tell a student *how* to do that. The semiotic method provides that guidance.

As a conceptual framework, semiotics teaches students to formulate cogent, well-supported interpretations. It emphasizes the examination of assumptions and of the way that linguistic and cultural codes shape our apprehension of the world. And, because semiotics focuses on how beliefs are formulated within a social and political context (rather than just judging or evaluating those beliefs), it's ideal for discussing sensitive or politically charged issues (like the 2016 presidential election). As an approach used in literature, linguistics, media and communications studies, anthropology, art and design coursework, sociology, law, and market research (to name only some of its more prominent field applications), semiotics has a cross-disciplinary appeal that makes it ideal for teaching a writing class to students from a variety of majors and disciplines. We recognize that semiotics has a reputation for being highly technical or theoretical; rest assured that *Signs of Life in the U.S.A.* does not require students or instructors to have a technical knowledge of semiotics. We've provided clear and accessible introductions that explain what students need to know.

We also recognize that adopting a theoretical approach may be new to some instructors, so we've designed the book to allow instructors to use semiotics with their students as much or as little as they wish. The book does not obligate instructors or students to spend a lot of time with semiotics — although we do hope you'll find the approach intriguing and provocative.

The Editorial Apparatus

With its emphasis on popular culture, *Signs of Life in the U.S.A.* should generate lively class discussion and inspire many kinds of writing and thinking activities. The General Introduction provides an overall framework for the book, acquainting students with the semiotic method they can use to interpret the topics raised in each chapter, while the section on "Writing about Popular Culture" provides a succinct guide to students for writing their papers, along with three sample student essays that demonstrate different approaches to writing critical essays on popular culture. The book's section on "Conducting Research and Citing Sources" offers an updated guide to the latest MLA-style conventions to help your students properly document the research they've done for their writing assignments, and three articles that guide students in the appropriate use of the Internet as a research tool.

Each chapter starts with a frontispiece — a provocative visual image related to the chapter's topic — and an Introduction that suggests ways to "read" the topic, provides model interpretations, and links the issues raised by the reading selections. Every Chapter Introduction also contains three types of boxed questions designed to stimulate student thinking on the topic. The Exploring the Signs questions invite students to reflect on an issue in a journal entry or other prewriting activity, while the Discussing the Signs questions trigger class activities such as debates, discussions, or small-group work. The Reading Online questions invite students to explore the chapter's topic on the Internet, both for research purposes and for texts to analyze.

Two sorts of assignments accompany each reading. The Reading the Text questions help students comprehend the selections, asking them to identify important concepts and arguments, explain key terms, and relate main ideas to one another and to the evidence presented. The Reading the Signs questions are writing and activity prompts designed to produce clear analytic thinking and strong persuasive writing; they often make connections among reading selections from different chapters. Most assignments call for analytic essays, while some invite journal responses, in-class debates, group work, or other creative activities. Complementing the readings in each chapter are images that serve as visual texts to be discussed. We also include a glossary of semiotic terms, which can serve as a ready reference to key words and concepts used in the Chapter Introductions. Finally, the Instructor's Manual (*Editors' Notes for* Signs of Life in the U.S.A.) provides suggestions for organizing your syllabus, encouraging student responses to the readings, and using popular culture and semiotics to teach your writing class.

What's New in the Ninth Edition

Popular culture evolves at a rapid pace, and the substantial revision required for the ninth edition of *Signs of Life in the U.S.A.* reflects this essential muta- bility. First, we have updated our readings, including more than thirty new selections focusing on issues and trends that have emerged since the last edi- tion of this book. We have also updated the exemplary topics in our Chapter Introductions, which are used to model the critical assignments that follow, and have adjusted the focus of some chapters to reflect the changing con- ditions of students' lives and the ways they consume popular culture. And, in light of the Trump election, we have restored to this edition our chapter on American contradictions: "American Paradox: Culture, Conflict, and Con- tradiction in the U.S.A." The way that students consume media has been revolutionized by digital and mobile technologies, and *Signs of Life in the U.S.A.* reflects this new reality, offering both an e-book version of the main text and a collection of reading comprehension quizzes for every reading in the book. These are available in LaunchPad Solo for Readers and Writers, a robust adaptable learning solution that can be packaged with *Signs of Life in the U.S.A.* for little to no cost.

Even as we revise this text to reflect current trends, popular culture con- tinues to evolve. The inevitable gap between the pace of editing and pub- lishing, on the one hand, and the flow of popular culture, on the other, need not affect the use of popular culture in the classroom, however. The readings in the text, and the semiotic method we propose, are designed to show stu- dents how to analyze and write critical essays about any topic they choose. That topic may have appeared before they were born, or it may be the latest box-office or prime-time hit to appear after the publication of this edition of *Signs of Life in the U.S.A.* Currently popular social media sites may well have been replaced by more recently arriving digital hangouts within the life span of this edition (indeed, Facebook obliterated MySpace shortly after the pub- lication of the sixth edition of this book), but such changes are opportuni- ties for further analysis, not obstacles. To put it another way, the practice of everyday life may itself be filled with evanescent fads and trends, but daily life is not itself a fad. As the vital texture of our lived experience, popular cul- ture provides a stable background against which students of every generation can test their critical skills.

Acknowledgments

The vastness of the terrain of popular culture has enabled many users of the eighth edition of this text to make valuable suggestions for the ninth edi- tion. We have incorporated many such suggestions and thank all for their comments on our text. We are also grateful to those reviewers who examined the book in depth: Robin Avner, Palomar College; Craig Bartholomaus, Metropolitan Community College - Penn Valley; Sharon Becker, Towson University; Maria Cahill, Husson University; Tammy Cherry, Florida State College Jacksonville; Wallace Cleaves, University of California at Riverside; Sharon Estes, Bucks County Community College; James Geasor, Queensborough Community College; Matthew Hidinger, Allan Hancock College; Marcia Holland, Indiana University South Bend; Elana Kent-Stacy, College of the Canyons; Dan Portillo, College of the Canyons; Rocco Versaci, Palomar College.

Finally, we'd like to give a special shout out to Eric Dinsmore of California State University, Northridge, whose suggestion that we have a look at the 2014 cinematic installment in the never-ending *Godzilla* franchise (along with providing us with the DVD) ended up making a direct contribution to our book.

If we have not included something you'd like to work on, you may still direct your students to it, using this text as a guide, not as a set of absolute prescriptions. The practice of everyday life includes the conduct of a classroom, and we want all users of the ninth edition of *Signs of Life in the U.S.A.* to feel free to pursue that practice in whatever way best suits their interests and aims.

Once again, we wish to thank heartily the people at Bedford/St. Martin's who have enabled us to make this new edition a reality. We especially want to thank our new editor, Sherry Mooney, whose always cheerful, diplomatic, and efficient assistance has kept this edition on course from start to finish. Matt Glazer and Andrea Cava ably guided our manuscript through the rigors of production, while Robert Cherry handled the numerous questions and details that arose during textbook development. Terri Wright expertly researched and obtained permissions for art, and Elaine Kosta cleared text permissions. Our thanks go as well to Kristin Ferraioli for her fine copyediting of this book.

With Bedford/St. Martin's, You Get More

At Bedford/St. Martin's, providing support to teachers and their students who use our books and digital tools is our top priority. The Bedford/St. Martin's English Community is now our home for professional resources, including Bedford *Bits*, our popular blog with new ideas for the composition classroom. Join us to connect with our authors and your colleagues at **community.macmillan.com** where you can download titles from our professional resource series, review projects in the pipeline, sign up for webinars, or start a discussion. In addition to this dynamic online community and book-specific instructor resources, we offer digital tools, custom solutions, and value packages to support both you and your students. We are committed to delivering the quality and value that you've come to expect from Bedford/St. Martin's, supported as always by the power of Macmillan Learning. To learn more about or to order any of the following products, contact your Bedford/St. Martin's sales representative or visit the Web site at **macmillanlearning.com**.

CHOOSE FROM ALTERNATIVE FORMATS OF SIGNS OF LIFE IN THE U.S.A.

Bedford/St. Martin's offers a range of affordable formats, allowing students to choose the one that works best for them.

- **Paperback.** To order the paperback edition, use ISBN 978-1-319-05663-6
- **Popular e-book formats.** For details of our e-book partners, visit **macmillanlearning.com/ebooks**.

SELECT VALUE PACKAGES

Add value to your text by packaging one of the following resources with *Signs of Life in the U.S.A.* To learn more about package options for any of the following products, contact your Bedford/St. Martin's sales representative or visit **macmillanlearning.com**.

LaunchPad Solo for Readers and Writers allows students to work on whatever they need help with the most. At home or in class, students learn at their own pace, with instruction tailored to each student's unique needs. *LaunchPad Solo for Readers and Writers* features:

- **Pre-built units that support a learning arc.** Each easy-to-assign unit is comprised of a pre-test check, multimedia instruction and assessment, and a post-test that assesses what students have learned about critical reading, the writing process, using sources, grammar, style, and mechanics. Dedicated units also offer help for multilingual writers.
- **Diagnostics that help establish a baseline for instruction.** Assign diagnostics to identify areas of strength and areas for improvement on topics related to grammar and reading and to help students plan a course of study. Use visual reports to track performance by topic, class, and student as well as comparison reports that track improvement over time.
- **A video introduction to many topics.** Introductions offer an overview of the unit's topic, and many include a brief, accessible video to illustrate the concepts at hand.
- **Twenty-five reading selections with comprehension quizzes.** Assign a range of classic and contemporary essays, each of which includes a label indicating Lexile level to help you scaffold instruction in critical reading.
- **Adaptive quizzing for targeted learning.** Most units include Learning-Curve, game-like adaptive quizzing that focuses on the areas in which each student needs the most help.
- **The ability to monitor student progress.** Use our gradebook to see which students are on track and which need additional help with specific topics.

- **Additional reading comprehension quizzes.** *Signs of Life in the U.S.A.* includes multiple-choice quizzes, which help you quickly gauge your students' understanding of the assigned reading. These are available in *LaunchPad Solo for Readers and Writers*.

Order ISBN 978-1-319-14989-5 to package *LaunchPad Solo for Readers and Writers* with *Signs of Life in the U.S.A.* at a significant discount. Students who rent or buy a used book can purchase access and instructors may request free access at **macmillanlearning.com/readwrite**.

Writer's Help 2.0 is a powerful online writing resource that helps students find answers whether they are searching for writing advice on their own or as part of an assignment.

- **Smart search.** Built on research with more than 1,600 student writers, the smart search in Writer's Help provides reliable results even when students use novice terms, such as *flow and unstuck*.
- **Trusted content from our best-selling handbooks.** Choose *Writer's Help 2.0, Hacker Version,* or *Writer's Help 2.0, Lunsford Version,* and ensure that students have clear advice and examples for all of their writing questions.
- **Diagnostics that help establish a baseline for instruction.** Assign diagnostics to identify areas of strength and areas for improvement on topics related to grammar and reading and to help students plan a course of study. Use visual reports to track performance by topic, class, and student as well as comparison reports that track improvement over time.
- **Adaptive exercises that engage students.** Writer's Help 2.0 includes LearningCurve, game-like online quizzing that adapts to what students already know and helps them focus on what they need to learn.
- **Reading comprehension quizzes.** *Signs of Life in the U.S.A.* includes multiple-choice quizzes, which help you quickly gauge your students' understanding of the assigned reading. These are available in Writer's Help 2.0.

Writer's Help 2.0 can be packaged with *Signs of Life in the U.S.A.* at a significant discount. For more information, contact your sales representative or visit **macmillanlearning.com/writershelp2**.

MACMILLAN LEARNING CURRICULUM SOLUTIONS

Curriculum Solutions brings together the quality of Bedford/St. Martin's content with our expertise in publishing original custom print and digital products. Developed especially for writing courses, our ForeWords for English program contains a library of the most popular, requested content in easy-to-use modules to help you build the best possible text. Whether you are considering creating a custom version of *Signs of Life in the U.S.A.* or incorporating our content with your own, we can adapt and combine the resources that work best for your course or program. Some enrollment minimums apply. Contact your sales representative for more information.

INSTRUCTOR RESOURCES

You have a lot to do in your course. Bedford/St. Martin's wants to make it easy for you to find the support you need — and to get it quickly.

Editor's Notes for Signs of Life in the U.S.A. is available as a PDF file that can be downloaded from **macmillanlearning.com**. Visit the Instructor Resources tab for *Signs of Life in the U.S.A.* In addition to chapter overviews and teaching tips, the instructor's manual includes sample syllabi, suggestions for classroom discussion, and possible responses for questions raised in the text.

Contents

"Frontier; opportunity; more. This has been the American trinity from the very start."

INTERNATIONAL CENTER FOR MEDIA AND THE PUBLIC AGENDA: *Students Addicted to Social Media*   *382*

"'Texting and IM-ing my friends gives me a constant feeling of comfort,' wrote one student. 'When I did not have those two luxuries, I felt quite alone and secluded from my life.'"

PAIRED READINGS: THE DIGITAL PANOPTICON

RONALD J. DEIBERT: *Black Code: Surveillance, Privacy, and the Dark Side of the Internet*   *386*

"Cyberspace is now an unavoidable reality that wraps our planet in a complex information and communications skin."

JOSEPH TUROW: *The Daily You: How the New Advertising Industry Is Defining Your Identity and Your Worth*   *394*

"Every day most if not all Americans who use the Internet, along with hundreds of millions of other users from all over the planet, are being quietly peeked at, poked, analyzed, and tagged as they move through the online world."

ERIN LEE: *How Effective Is Social Media Activism?*   *402*

"The only way to make a democracy work is to get off social media and do things in the real world."

BRIAN DUNNING: *Slacktivism: Raising Awareness*   *405*

"Raising awareness with Facebook 'Like' buttons certainly does no harm, but it's called slacktivism for a reason. By doing it, you're slacking. You're only making yourself feel good."

"Millennials, the term given for those born between 1980 and 2000, may be suffering from an identity crisis as they search for their authentic self."

"Post-racism, not post-racialism, should be our goal."

"Voters are angry about the economy, about race, about the 'establishment.' But knowing what voters are angry about doesn't necessarily tell us why they are angry."

"Americans are a 'positive' people. This is our reputation as well as our self image."

"Visceral and at times frightening narratives are running through our popular culture."

Ninth Edition

Signs of Life in the U.S.A.

Readings on Popular Culture for Writers

POPULAR SIGNS

*Or, Everything You Always
Knew about American Culture
(but Nobody Asked)*

American Civil War

In the summer and fall of 2016, Iron Man went to war against Captain America, Batman squared off against Superman, the war between the Lannisters and the Starks entered its sixth year, and Donald Trump captured the American presidency.

These events were not unrelated.

That is because, by the seventeenth year of the new millennium — and the ninth since the beginning of the Great Recession — America appeared to be splitting apart, and not simply along such traditional sectarian lines as Democrat versus Republican. We also saw Democrat versus Democrat (in the Clinton versus Sanders contest) and Republican versus Republican (as the existing party leadership largely turned its back on the Trump insurgency). Black Lives Matter contended not only with social injustice but with prior generations of civil rights activists; Western ranchers carried the American flag in their armed takeover of the Malheur National Wildlife Refuge; and five members of the Dallas Police Department were shot and killed as they provided security for a protest against police brutality.

At a time when social conflict in the nation had grown to proportions not seen since the 1960s, then, it was not at all surprising that America's popular culture would reflect it. Nor was it surprising that a well-known reality TV star would exploit that conflict to stage a successful presidential campaign. For in America today, popular culture isn't just about entertainment, and entertainment isn't simply a matter of leisure-time relaxation and recreation. In an era when digital technology can bring entertainment into the workplace, and work

1

can be performed while being entertained, the former demarcations between what French sociologist Henri Lefebvre called "everyday life" and "festival," or workaday and play, have crumbled, creating a world in which entertainment reflects reality, and reality is shaped by entertainment.

That is why we have written this book. Treating American popular culture as a system of **signs** that can tell us about who and where we are in our history, *Signs of Life in the U.S.A.* will teach you how to read — or interpret — these signs, while at the same time teaching you the critical thinking skills necessary to write strong university-level papers and arguments. Accordingly, each chapter in this book focuses upon a particular segment of popular culture and, by way of readings, images, and assignments, guides you through the process that will help you analyze the significance of the full range of our everyday lives, behaviors, and entertainments. We will return shortly in this Introduction to the signs of social disaffection that we find in contemporary popular culture, but first let's look at just what the phrase "popular culture" means and why it's important to think critically about it.

From Folk to For-Profit

Traditionally, popular, or "low," culture constituted the culture of the masses. It was set apart from "high" culture, which included classical music and literature, the fine arts and philosophy, and the elite learning that was the province of the ruling classes who had the money and leisure necessary to attain it — and who were often the direct patrons of high art and its creators. Low culture, for its part, had two main sides. One side, most notoriously illustrated by the violent entertainments of the Roman Empire (such as gladiatorial contests, public executions, and feeding Christians to lions) continues to be a sure crowd-pleaser to this day, as demonstrated by the widespread popularity of violent, erotic, and/or vulgar entertainment (can you spell *Jackass*?). The other side, which we can call "popular" in the etymological sense of being of the people, overlaps with what we now call "folk culture." Quietly existing alongside high culture, folk culture expresses the experience and creativity of the masses in the form of ballads, agricultural festivals, fairy tales, feasts, folk art, folk music, and so on. Self-produced by amateur performers, folk culture is exemplified by neighbors gathering on a modest Appalachian front porch to play their guitars, banjos, dulcimers, zithers, mandolins, and fiddles to perform, for their own entertainment, ballads and songs passed down from generation to generation.

Folk culture, of course, still exists. But for the past two hundred years, it has been dwindling, with increasing rapidity, as it becomes overwhelmed by a different kind of popular culture — a commercialized culture that, while still including elements of both the folk and the vulgar traditions, represents the outcome of a certain historical evolution. This culture, the popular culture that is most familiar today and that is the topic of this book, is a commercial,

Traditional high culture: Prima ballerina Misty Copeland poses in a New York City photo shoot.

for-profit culture aimed at providing entertainment to a mass audience. Corporate rather than communal, it has transformed entertainment into a commodity to be marketed alongside all the other products in a consumer society.

The forces that transformed the low culture of the past into contemporary popular culture arose during the industrial revolution of the late eighteenth century and its accompanying urbanization of European and American society. In particular, four essentially interrelated forces — industrialization, urbanization, capitalism, and electronic technology — shaped the emergence of the mass cultural marketplace of entertainments that we know today. To see how this happened, let's begin with the industrial revolution.

Prior to the industrial revolution, most Europeans and Americans lived in scattered agricultural settlements. While traveling entertainers in theatrical troupes and circuses might have visited the larger of these settlements, most people, especially those with little money, had little access to professional entertainment, and so had to produce their own. But with the industrial revolution, masses of people who had made their living through agriculture were compelled to leave their rural communities and move to the industrial towns and cities where employment was increasingly available. Populations began to concentrate in urban centers as the rural countryside emptied, leading to the development of mass societies.

With the emergence of these mass societies came the development of **mass culture**. For just as mass societies are governed by centralized systems of governance (as the huge expanse of the United States is governed by a federal government concentrated in Washington, DC), so, too, are mass cultures entertained by culture industries concentrated in a few locations (as the film and TV industries are concentrated in Hollywood and its immediate environs). Thanks to the invention of such technologies as the cinema, the phonograph, and the radio at the end of the nineteenth century, and of television and digital technology in the mid- to late-twentieth century, the means to disseminate centrally produced mass entertainments to a mass society became possible. Thus, whether you live in Boston or Boise, New York or Nebraska, the entertainment you enjoy today is produced in the same few locations and is the same entertainment (TV programs, movies, DVDs, or Netflix series) no matter where you consume it. This growth of mass culture has been fundamentally shaped by the growth of America's capitalist economic system, which has ensured that mass culture would develop as a for-profit industry.

To get a better idea of how the whole process unfolded, let's go back to that Appalachian front porch. Before electricity and urbanization, folks living in the backwoods of rural America needed to make their music themselves if they wanted it. They had no radios, phonographs, CD players, iPods, iPads, smartphones, or even electricity, and theaters with live performers were hard to get to and expensive. Under such conditions, the Appalachian region developed a vibrant folk music culture. But as people moved to cities like Pittsburgh and Detroit, where the steel and auto industries began to offer employment in the late nineteenth and early twentieth centuries, the conditions under which neighbors could produce their own music decayed, for the communal conditions under which folk culture thrived were broken down by the mass migration to the cities. At the same time, the need to produce one's own music declined as folks who had once plucked their own guitars and banjos could simply turn on their radios or purchase records to listen to professional musicians perform for them. Those musicians were contracted by recording companies that were in business to turn a profit, and their music, in turn, could be heard on the radio because corporate sponsors provided the advertising that made (and still makes) commercial radio broadcasting possible.

Thus, the folk music of the American countryside became *country music*. An amalgamation of the traditional songs that a predominantly Scots-Irish immigrant population brought over from the British Isles with such

Associated Press

Traditional folk culture in transition: Bill Monroe is known as the father of bluegrass music.

American traditions as "white" gospel music, cowboy songs, and rock 'n' roll, contemporary "country" preserves the rural working-class perspective of folk music even as it is performed by wealthy professionals. (Country music's working-class roots explain why it is so often filled with the broken romances and broken-down cars of the poor.)

So, the performance of folk music, once an amateur, do-it-yourself activity, became a professional, for-profit industry with passive consumers paying for their entertainment either by directly purchasing a commodity (for example, a CD or iTunes download) or by listening to the advertising that encourages them to purchase the products that sponsor their favorite radio programs. It's still possible, of course, to make one's own music, but most people find it easier and perhaps more aesthetically pleasing to listen to a professional recording. Today we are, in effect, constantly being trained to be the sort of passive consumers who keep the whole consumer-capitalist system going. Without that consumption, the economy might totally collapse.

This is hardly an exaggeration, for postindustrial capitalism is making popular culture all the more dominant in our society with every passing year. With the American economy turning further away from industrial production and increasingly toward the production and consumption of entertainment (including sports), entertainment has been moving from the margins of our cultural consciousness—as mere play or recreation—to its center as a major buttress of our economy. A constant bombardment of advertising (which, after all, is the driving force behind the financing of digital media, just as it was for radio and television a generation or two ago) continually prods us to consume the entertainments that our economy produces. That bombardment has been so successful that our whole cultural consciousness is changing: We are becoming more concerned with play than with work, even while *at* work. (Tell the truth now: Do you ever tweet, or post something to Tumblr or Instagram, during class?)

The result of the centuries-long process we have sketched above is the kind of culture we have today: an entertainment culture in which all aspects of society, including politics, and sometimes even the traditional elite arts, are linked by a common imperative to entertain. Indeed, as traditional high culture shrinks in social importance—having never had a mass audience to begin with and thus unable to compete effectively in a market economy—it has dwindled into becoming what might be called a "museum culture" (which is quietly marginalized and widely ignored). Popular culture has accordingly assumed its own "high" and "low" strata, with TV programs like *Orange Is the New Black* and *Game of Thrones* enjoying a kind of high cultural status, while *Duck Dynasty* profitably entertains at the low end.

Congressman Paul Ryan poses with *Duck Dynasty* stars Willie and Korie Robertson at the 2014 State of the Union address.

Pop Culture Goes to College

Far from being a mere recreational frivolity, a leisure activity we could easily dispense with, the popular culture of today constitutes the essential texture of our everyday lives. From the way we entertain ourselves to the goods and services that we produce and consume, we are enveloped in a popular cultural environment that we can neither do without nor escape, even if we wanted to. To see this, just try to imagine a world without the Internet, TV, movies, sports, music, shopping malls, or advertising. The study of popular culture has accordingly taken a prominent place in American higher education — not least in American composition classrooms, which have taken the lead in incorporating popular culture into academic study, both because of the subject's inherent interest value and because of its profound familiarity to most students. Your own expertise in popular culture means not only that you may know more about a given topic than your instructor, but that you can use that knowledge as a basis for learning the critical thinking and writing skills that your writing class is intended to teach you.

Signs of Life in the U.S.A., then, is designed to let you exploit your knowledge of popular culture so that you may grow into a better writer, whatever the subject. You can interpret the popularity of a TV program like *The Walking Dead*, for example, in the same manner as you would interpret, say, a short story, because *The Walking Dead*, too, constitutes a kind of sign. A **sign** is something, anything, that carries a meaning. The familiar red sign at an intersection, for instance, means exactly what it says: "STOP." But it also carries the implied message "or risk getting a ticket or into an accident." Words, too, are signs: you read them to figure out what they mean. You were trained to read such signs, but that training began so long ago that you may well take your ability to read for granted. Nevertheless, all your life you have been encountering and interpreting other sorts of signs. Although you were never formally taught to read them, you know what they mean anyway. Take the way you wear your hair. When you get your hair cut, you are not simply removing hair; you are making a statement, sending a message about yourself. It's the same for both men and women. Why was your hair short last year and long this year? Aren't you saying something with the scissors? In this way, you make your hairstyle into a sign that sends a message about your identity. You are surrounded by such signs. Just look at your classmates.

The world of signs could be called a kind of text, the text of America's popular culture. We want you to think of *Signs of Life in the U.S.A.* as a window onto that text. What you read in this book's essays and Chapter Introductions should lead you to study and analyze the world around you for yourself. Let the selections guide you to your own interpretations, your own readings, of the text of America.

In this edition of *Signs of Life in the U.S.A.*, we have chosen seven "windows" that look out onto separate, but often interrelated, segments of the American scene. In each chapter, we have included essays that help you think about a specific topic in popular culture and guide you to locate and analyze related examples of your own. Each chapter also includes an Introduction written to alert you to the kinds of signs you will find there, along with model analyses and advice on how to go about interpreting the topic that the chapter raises.

We have designed *Signs of Life in the U.S.A.* to reflect the many ways in which culture shapes our sense of reality and of ourselves, from the products we buy to the way culture, through such media as television and the movies, constructs our personal identities. This text thus introduces you to both the entertainment side and the ideological side of popular culture — and shows how the two sides are mutually dependent. Indeed, one of the major lessons you can learn from this book is how to find the ideological underpinnings of some of the most apparently innocent entertainments and consumer goods.

Signs of Life in the U.S.A. accordingly begins with a chapter called "Consuming Passions." Because America is a consumer culture, the environment in which the galaxy of popular signs functions is, more often than not, a consumerist one. This is true not only for obvious consumer products like clothes and cars but for traditionally nonconsumer items such as political candidates, who are often marketed like any other product. It is difficult to find anything in contemporary America that is not affected somehow by our consumerist ethos or by consumerism's leading promoter, the advertiser. Thus, the second chapter, "Brought to You B(u)y," explores the world of advertising, for advertising provides the grease, so to speak, that lubricates the engine of America's consumer culture. Because television and film are the sources of many of our most significant cultural products, we include a chapter on each. Chapters on the digital cloud, personal identity, and the paradoxical contradictions that condition so much of American life round out our survey of everyday life.

Throughout, the book invites you to go out and select your own "texts" for analysis (an advertisement, an app, a fashion fad, a TV show, and so on). Here's where your own experience is particularly valuable, because it has made you familiar with many different kinds of popular signs and their backgrounds, as well as with the particular popular cultural system or environment to which they belong.

The seven "windows" you will find in *Signs of Life in the U.S.A.* are all intended to reveal the common intersections of entertainment and ideology that exist in contemporary American life. Often what seems to be simply entertainment, like an action-adventure movie, can actually be quite political (consider the kerfuffle over *Star Wars: Episode VII–The Force Awakens*), while what *is* political can be cast as entertainment as well — as in *House of Cards*.

The point is that little in American life is merely entertainment; indeed, just about everything we do has a meaning, often a profound one.

The Semiotic Method

To find this meaning, to interpret and write effectively about the signs of popular culture, you need a method, and part of the purpose of this book is to introduce such a method to you. Without a methodology for interpreting signs, writing about them could become little more than producing descriptive reviews or opinion pieces. Although nothing is wrong with writing descriptions and opinions, one of your goals in your writing class is to learn how to write academic essays — that is, analytical essays that present theses or arguments that are well supported by evidence. The method we use in this book — a method known as **semiotics** — is especially well suited for analyzing popular culture. Whether or not you're familiar with this word, you already practice sophisticated semiotic analyses every day. Reading this page is an act of semiotic decoding (words and letters are signs that must be interpreted), but so is figuring out just what a friend means by wearing a particular shirt or dress. For a semiotician (one who practices semiotic analysis), a shirt, a haircut, a TV image, anything at all, can be taken as a sign, as a message to be decoded and analyzed to discover its meaning. Every cultural activity leaves a trace of meaning for semioticians, a kind of blip on the semiotic Richter scale for them to read and interpret, just as geologists "read" the earth for signs of earthquakes, volcanic activity, and other geological phenomena.

Many who hear the word *semiotics* for the first time assume that it is the name of a new and forbidding subject. But in truth, the study of signs is neither new nor forbidding. Its modern form took shape in the late nineteenth and early twentieth centuries through the writings and lectures of two men. Charles Sanders Peirce (1839–1914) was an American philosopher who first coined the word *semiotics*, while Ferdinand de Saussure (1857–1913) was a Swiss linguist whose lectures became the foundation for what he called *semiology* (which was later developed under the rubric of linguistic *structuralism*). Without knowing of each other's work, Peirce and Saussure established the fundamental principles that modern semioticians or semiologists — the terms are essentially interchangeable — have developed into the contemporary study of semiotics.

Reduced to its simplest principles, the semiotic method carries on Saussure's argument that the meaning of a sign lies, in part, in the fact that it can be *differentiated* from any other sign within the **system**, or **code**, to which it belongs. For example, in the traffic code, being able to distinguish the difference between green, red, and amber lights is essential to understanding the meaning of a traffic signal. But that's not all there is to it, because it is only within the code that green, red, and amber signify "go," "stop," and "caution." So, to interpret a traffic signal correctly, you need to be able to *associate* any particular red light you see with all other red traffic lights under the concept "stop" that the code assigns to it, and any green light with all other green lights under the concept "go," and so on.

But outside of the traffic code, the same colors can have very different meanings, always depending upon the system in which they appear. For example, in the codes of American politics, green signifies not only a political party but an entire worldview that supports environmentalist policies, while red, rather paradoxically, can signify either communist sympathies or the conservative politics of the so-called "red states," depending upon the context. Amber, for its part, has no significance within the codes of American politics.

The fact that the color red has gained this significance in the codes of American politics demonstrates the fact that systems, and the meanings encoded within them, can change — an important principle when you are interpreting signs of popular culture, because their meanings are constantly changing, unlike the more or less fixed signs of the traffic code. Here is where Peirce's contribution comes in, because while Saussure's structural semiology is static in its interpretational orientation, Peircean semiotics is dynamic, situating signs within *history* and thus enabling us to trace the ways in which meaning shifts and changes with time.

But neither Saussure nor Peirce applied their methodologies to signs of popular culture, so to complete our description of the semiotic method, we must turn to the work of French semiologist Roland Barthes (1915–1980), who, in his book *Mythologies* (1957), pioneered the semiotic analysis of everything from professional wrestling to striptease, toys, and plastics. It was Barthes, too, who established the political dimensions of semiotic analysis, revealing how phenomena that may look like mere entertainments can hold profound political or ideological significance. Since "politics" is something of a dirty word in our society, Barthes's politicization of pop culture may make you feel a little uneasy at first. You may even think that to find political meaning in popular culture is tantamount to reading something into it that isn't really there. But consider the way people responded to the 2016 reboot of the *Ghostbusters* franchise. A thoroughly goofy movie with impeccable *Saturday Night Live* credentials, the film attracted controversy before anyone even saw it, simply because the inaugural trailer revealed that the team this time would be all female, including three white scientists and one black transit worker. And all hell broke loose, as the politics of race and gender exploded across Twitter and Reddit.

In short, the political interpretation of popular culture, even when it is not conducted under the name of semiotics, is already a common practice. The semiotic method simply makes it explicit, pointing out that all social behavior is political because it always reflects some subjective or group interest. Such interests are encoded in the ideologies that express the values and opinions of those who hold them. Politics, then, is just another name for the clash of ideologies that takes place in any complex society where the interests of those who belong to it constantly compete with one another.

While not all signs of popular culture are politically controversial, careful analysis can uncover some set of political values within them, although those values may be subtly concealed behind an apparently apolitical facade. Indeed, the political values that guide our social behavior are often concealed behind images that don't look political at all. But that is because we have to look beyond what a sign of pop culture **denotes**, or directly shows, to what it **connotes**, or indirectly suggests. The **denotation** of a sign is its first level of meaning, and you have to be able to understand that meaning before you can move to the next level. The **connotation** of a sign takes you to its political or cultural significance.

Take, for instance, the depiction of the "typical" American family in the classic TV sitcoms of the 1950s and 1960s, which denoted images of happy, docile housewives in suburban middle-class families. At the time, most viewers did not look beyond their denotation, so to them those images looked "normal" or natural — the way families and women were supposed to be. The shows didn't seem a bit ideological. But to a feminist semiotician, the old sitcoms were in fact highly political, because from a feminist viewpoint the happy housewives they presented were really images designed to convince women that their place was in the home, not in the workplace competing with men. Such images — or signs — did not reflect reality; they reflected, rather, the interests of a patriarchal, male-centered society. That, in effect, was their connotation. If you disagree, then ask yourself why programs were called *Father Knows Best*, *Bachelor Father*, and *My Three Sons*, but not *My Three Daughters*. And why did few of the women characters have jobs or ever seem to leave the house? Of course, there was *I Love Lucy*, but wasn't Lucy a screwball whose husband, Ricky, had to rescue her from one crisis after another?

Such an interpretation reflects what the British cultural theorist Stuart Hall (1932–2014) called an *oppositional* reading. Such a reading of a cultural text like a sitcom challenges the "preferred reading," which would simply take the program at face value, accepting its representation of family life as normative and natural. The oppositional reading, on the other hand, proposes an interpretation that resists the normative view, seeking to uncover a political subtext that often contradicts any particular intended "message." The fact that so many cultural signifiers *appear* normative and natural, as transparent images of an apolitical social reality, can make oppositional reading look "unnatural" or like "reading into" your topic a meaning that isn't there. After all, isn't a sitcom simply a trivial entertainment that distracts viewers from the concerns of everyday life? But given the commercial foundation of our popular culture, the fact that something is entertaining is itself significant, because only those scripts that are calculated to be popular with a mass audience make it to the screen. In other words, popular culture appeals to audience desire, and so the fact that something is entertaining raises a fundamental semiotic

ABC/Photofest

The popular TV show *Leave It to Beaver*
(1957–1963) exemplified traditional family
values of the 1950s.

question: *Why* is it entertaining, and what does that say about those who are
entertained by it?

By looking for such broad signifiers of cultural consciousness and
desire, you will be moving back and forth between what might be called the
micro-semiotics of your immediate topic (that is, its specific signs and symbols)
to its *macro-semiotic* import, or overall cultural significance. The former cannot be separated from the latter, because to find the macro-semiotic meaning
of a cultural sign you must first explore its *micro-semiotic* details closely. Think
of it as exploring a forest while paying careful attention to the trees.

Abduction and Overdetermination

At this point you may be thinking that a semiotic analysis resembles sociological interpretation, and indeed cultural semiotics and sociology do resemble
each other. The differences are largely methodological. Sociology tends to be
highly statistical in its methodology, often working with case studies, surveys,
and other quantifiable evidence. Cultural semiotics primarily works by looking
at broad patterns of behavior and seeking what Charles Sanders Peirce called
abductive explanations for them. **Abduction** is the process of arriving at an
interpretation by seeking the most plausible explanation for something. No
one can absolutely prove a semiotic interpretation, but the more material you

can bring into your systems of related and differentiated signifiers, the more convincing your movement from denotation to connotation will be.

As you build up your interpretation of a cultural signifier, you can often find more than one explanation for it. Is that a problem? Are you just having trouble deciding on a single argument? No, because cultural signs are usually **overdetermined**; that is, they can have more than one cause or explanation (another word for this is *polysemous*). This is especially true for what we consider "rich" cultural signs — like such television programs as *Game of Thrones* and *The Walking Dead*, such movies as *Captain America: Civil War* and *Batman v Superman: Dawn of Justice*, and Donald Trump's march to the White House.

Interpreting Popular Signs: The War Against Everybody

The essential approach to interpreting signs of popular culture is to *situate signs within systems of related semiotic phenomena with which they can be associated and differentiated*. Being attuned to the history that provides the background for that system is equally essential. In taking this step, you are making the first movement from objective denotation to interpretive connotation.

So, let's look at the signs before us: *Game of Thrones*, *The Walking Dead*, *Captain America: Civil War*, *Batman v Superman: Dawn of Justice*, and the Donald Trump campaign. Combining elements of both fantasy and action-adventure storytelling, *Game of Thrones* and *The Walking Dead* can be situated in a system that includes such television series as *Star Trek* (in any of its incarnations), *Battlestar Galactica*, *Xena: Warrior Princess*, and *Buffy the Vampire Slayer*. *Captain America: Civil War* and *Batman v Superman: Dawn of Justice*, as action-adventure fantasies, belong to this system too, but they also, and more prominently, belong to the system of live-action superhero movies as adapted from superhero comic books and graphic novels. The fact that action-adventure fantasies of both kinds have been so popular in recent years is highly significant in itself and could be developed a great deal further in a more fully overdetermined interpretation. But for our purposes here we will simply note their enduring popularity in modern entertainment and thus their particular potential as cultural signifiers.

So, what do such entertainments denote? Boiled down to their essence, action-adventure fantasies dramatize violent conflicts between specially equipped, or superhumanly gifted, heroes and their opponents in a supernatural setting in which the stakes are enormous (or, as the television series *Heroes* put it, nothing less than "saving the world"). Such stories are the oldest in existence, and their **archetypal** popularity spans time and space, country and culture.

But when we look at *Game of Thrones* and *The Walking Dead* in this context, a striking **difference** appears, because in these two programs there aren't any truly clear-cut heroes — only antiheroes and villains, who are the worst people in the room — while in *Captain America: Civil War* and *Batman v*

A poster for the film *Captain America: Civil War* (2016).

Superman: Dawn of Justice, heroes who have been conventionally represented battling *only* worst-in-the-room opponents actually go at each other. And this difference prompts us to go back to the system in which these signs can be situated.

That system lets us see that they can be associated not only with action-adventure fantasies but with a host of morally hazy TV series and movies that erupted around the turn of the new millennium: shows like *The Sopranos, Mad Men, Breaking Bad, Dexter*, and *Sons of Anarchy*, along with such dark-visioned superhero movies as *Spiderman 3, The Dark Knight*, and *Deadpool*. Disrupting the traditional moral universe of popular entertainment with its clear divisions between good and evil, these antihero-featuring programs and films signified something new in the land.

It is at this point that we can look, abductively, for some interpretative explanations, thus moving from the denotations of our signs to their cultural connotations. To do this, we need to leave the system of related TV shows and movies for a moment and look at the larger historical context in which our signs appear.

The breaking down of America's simplified moral vision can be said to have begun in the 1960s, when the Vietnam War, the civil rights move-ment, and a widespread cultural revolution began to undermine confidence not only in the government but in American society itself. All forms of authority — including such institutions as education, mainstream religion, and the family — began to be questioned, with political leaders especially falling into disrepute after the Watergate scandal. More subtly, but perhaps just as effectively, a long-term decline in the economic status of the vast majority of

Americans set in, a decline that was accelerated by the advent of the Great Recession.

Breaking Bad, with its story line of a middle-class high school teacher turning to a life of crime in response to medical and economic stress, was an especially potent signifier of the lengths to which American viewers, invited to imagine themselves *as* Walter White, were willing to go as their own economic security crumbled. For while White *was* punished in the end, and revealed as a villain, not a mere antihero, for the many years that his story was told, viewers, under stress themselves, could at least vicariously imagine what it would be like to throw morality to the wind.

In other words, when we look at the system of antihero-themed programs we can abductively conclude that they expressed a post-'60s disillusionment in America. But we can find that disillusionment turning into outright rage in *Game of Thrones* and *The Walking Dead*, for here are worlds in which everyone is perpetually at war with everyone, where there is only violence and death without hope of salvation.

This rage can also be found expressed in *Captain America: Civil War* and *Batman v Superman: Dawn of Justice*, movies in which the ideological conflicts that divide Americans today are made explicit as they look for someone to blame for their suffering. Note how in *Captain America: Civil War* the battle between Captain America (and his Avenger allies) and Iron Man (and *his* Avenger allies) is essentially over the question of government regulation. Mirroring one of the key bones of contention between "blue-state" Democrats and "red-state" Republicans, the movie thus mediates actual political conflict in the way that professional wrestling does: rendering it a bit cartoonishly, perhaps, but, then, there was something a bit cartoonish about the shutting down of the entire federal government in 2013.

Something of the same sort occurs in *Batman v Superman: Dawn of Justice*. In this case, die-hard Batman fans are invited to view Superman as some sort of, well, *immigrant*, who has been making a mess of things. While there is a reconciliation of sorts between the two, a great deal of the plot compels the audience to take sides, just as it does in *Captain America: Civil War*, and just as Americans were passionately taking sides on such matters as immigration and government regulation and Donald Trump.

Thus, the most likely interpretation of the entire *Game of Thrones*, *Walking Dead*, *Captain America: Civil War*, and *Batman v Superman: Dawn of Justice* complex is that it expresses the same cultural forces that were behind the election of Donald Trump. To this can be added the Bernie Sanders presidential campaign, which introduced civil war into the Democratic Party, just as Trump did within the Republican Party as he became a voice of widespread economic and demographic discontent. Inviting Sanders supporters to join *him* in the wake of the Clinton nomination, Trump even attempted to extend the free-for-all: the spectacle of a battle of everybody against almost everybody.

The Classroom Connection

This analysis could be extended further, but we will leave that for you to consider for yourself. The key point is that while the popularity of any particular pop culture phenomenon is evanescent, what it *signifies* is not. Everything in an ever-shifting popular cultural terrain remains significant, just as all the historical events in an ever-changing world remain significant. In fact, performing an analysis of pop culture is essentially equivalent to writing interpretive history, but it is an interpretive history of the present.

Thus, semiotic analyses of popular culture are not different from the more conventional interpretive analyses you will be asked to perform in your college writing career. It is in the nature of all critical thinking to make connections and mark differences in order to go beyond the surface of a text or issue toward a meaning. The skills you already have as an interpreter of the popular signs around you — of images, objects, and forms of behavior — are the same skills that you develop as a writer of critical essays that present an argued point of view and the evidence to defend it.

Because most of us tend to identify closely with our favorite pop culture phenomena and have strong opinions about them, however, it can be difficult to adopt the same sort of analytic perspective toward popular culture that we do toward, say, texts assigned in a history or literature class. Still, this analytic perspective is what a semiotic interpretation requires: you need to set aside your aesthetic or fan-related opinions to pursue an interpretive argument with evidence to support it. It is not difficult to express an aesthetic opinion or a statement of personal preference, but that isn't the goal of analytic writing and critical thinking. Analytic writing requires that you marshal supporting evidence, just as a lawyer assembles evidence to argue a case. So, by learning to write analyses of our culture, by searching for supporting evidence to underpin your interpretive take on modern life, you are also learning to write critical arguments.

"But how," you (and perhaps your instructor) may ask, "can I know that a semiotic interpretation is correct?" Good question — it is commonly asked by those who object that a semiotic analysis might read too much into a subject. But then, it can also be asked by the writer of any interpretive essay, and the answer in each case is the same. No one can absolutely *prove* the truth of an argument in the human sciences; what you can do is *persuade* your audience by including pertinent evidence in an abductive reasoning process. In analyzing popular culture, that evidence comes from your knowledge of the system to which the object you are interpreting belongs. The more you know about the system, the more convincing your interpretations will be. And that is true whether you are writing about popular culture or about more traditional academic subjects.

Of Myths and Men

As we have seen, in a semiotic analysis we do not search for the meanings of things in the things themselves. Rather, we find meaning in the way we can relate things together through association and differentiation, moving from objective denotation to culturally subjective connotation. Such a movement commonly takes us from the realm of objective facts to the world of cultural values. But while values often *feel* like objective facts, from a semiotic perspective they are subjective points of view that derive from cultural systems that semioticians call *cultural mythologies*.

A cultural **mythology** is not some fanciful story from the past; indeed, if the word *mythology* seems confusing because of its traditional association with such stories, you may prefer to use the term "value system" or "ideology." Consider the value system that governs our traditional thinking about gender roles. Have you ever noticed how our society presumes that it is primarily the role of women — adult daughters — to take care of aging and infirm parents? If you want to look at the matter from a physiological perspective, it might seem that men would be better suited to the task: in a state of nature, men are physically stronger and so would seem to be the natural protectors of the aged. And yet, though our cultural mythology holds that men should protect the nuclear family, it tends to assign to women the care of extended families. It is culture that decides here, not nature.

But while cultural mythologies guide our behavior, they are subject to change. The cultural myths surrounding sexual relationships in America, for example, have changed dramatically in your lifetime. Not only do these myths no longer presume an orientation toward heterosexual marriage, but even the rules that once governed the American dating game are changing. Once, it was the role of the male to initiate proceedings (he calls) and for the female to react (she waits for the call). Similarly, the rules once held that it was the male's responsibility to plan the evening and pay the tab. Today, in the age of hookups and digital socializing, these rules may sound not simply antiquated but quaint.

A cultural mythology or value system, then, is a kind of lens that governs the way we view our world. Think of it this way: Say you were born with rose-tinted eyeglasses permanently attached over your eyes, but you didn't know they were there. Because the world would *look* rose colored to you, you would presume that it *is* rose colored. You wouldn't wonder whether the world might look otherwise through different lenses. But in the world, there are other kinds of eyeglasses with different lenses, and reality does look different to those who wear them. Those lenses are cultural mythologies, and no culture can claim to have the one set of glasses that reveals things as they really are.

The principle that meaning is not culture-blind, that it is conditioned by systems of ideology and belief that are codified differently by different cultures, is a foundational semiotic judgment. Human beings, in other words, construct their own social realities, so who gets to do the constructing becomes very important. Every contest over a cultural code is, accordingly, a contest for power, but the contest is usually masked because the winner generally defines its mythology as the truth, as what is most natural or reasonable. The stakes are high as myth battles myth, with truth itself as the highest prize.

This does not mean that you must abandon your own beliefs when conducting a semiotic analysis, only that you cannot take them for granted and must be prepared to argue for them with valid evidence. The need for such evidence suggests that while humans construct their own social realities, there is an extra-social reality that places limits on what human beings can construct (to take an uncontroversial example, a culture that insists that humans can fly unaided off cliffs is not going to exist for very long). This belief in an extra-social reality underlies the semiotic position of this book.

Thus, if you hold a contrary opinion on a topic, it is not enough to presuppose the innate superiority of your own perspective — to claim that anyone who disagrees with you is being "political" while you are simply telling the truth. This may sound heretical precisely because humans operate within cultural mythologies whose invisibility is guaranteed by the system. No mythology, that is to say, announces, "This is just a political construct or interpretation." Every mythology begins, "This is the truth." It is very difficult to imagine, from within the mythology, any alternatives. Indeed, as you read this book, you may find it upsetting to see that some traditional beliefs — such as "proper" roles of men and women — are socially constructed and not absolute. But the outlines of the mythology, the bounding (and binding) frame, can be discerned only by first seeing that it *is* a mythology, a constructed scaffolding upon which our consciousness and desires are constituted.

Getting Started

Mythology, like culture, is not static, and so the semiotician must always keep his or her eye on the clock, so to speak. History and the passing of time are constants in a constantly changing world. Since the earlier editions of this book, American popular culture has moved on. In this edition, we have tried to reflect those changes, but inevitably, further changes will occur in the time it takes for this book to appear on your class syllabus. That such changes occur is part of the excitement of the semiotic enterprise: There is always something new to consider and interpret. What does *not* change is the nature of semiotic interpretation — whatever you choose to analyze in the realm of American popular culture, the semiotic approach will help you understand it.

It's your turn now. Start asking questions, pushing, probing. That's what critical thinking and writing are all about, but this time you're part of the question. Arriving at answers is the fun part here, but answers aren't the basis of analytic thinking: questions are. Always begin with a question, a query, a hypothesis — something to explore. If you already knew the answer, you'd have no reason to conduct the analysis. We encourage you to explore the almost-infinite variety of questions that the readings in this book raise. Many come equipped with their own "answers," but you may (indeed you will and should) find that such answers raise further questions. To help you ask those questions, keep in mind the elemental principles of semiotics that we have just explored:

1. Cultural semiotics treats human behavior itself — not what people say about their behavior, but what they actually do — as **signs**.
2. The meaning of signs can be found not in themselves but in their relationships (both differences and associations) with other signs within a **system**. To interpret an individual sign, then, you must determine the general system to which it belongs.
3. Things have both **denotative** meanings (what they *are*) and **connotative** meanings (what they *suggest as signs*); semiotics moves beyond the denotative surface to the connotative significance.
4. Arriving at the connotative significance of a sign involves both **abduction** (a search for the most likely explanation or interpretation) and **overdetermination** (the multiple causes behind a cultural phenomenon).
5. What we call social "reality" is a human construct, the product of cultural **mythologies** or value systems that intervene between our minds and the world we experience. Such cultural myths reflect the values and ideological interests of their builders, not the laws of nature or logic.

Perhaps our first principle could be more succinctly phrased "Behavior is meaningful," and our second "Everything is connected," while our third advises "Don't take things at face value." More simply, always ask yourself, whenever you are interpreting something, "What's going on here?" In short, question *everything*. And one more reminder: signs are like weather vanes; they point in response to invisible historical winds. We invite you now to start looking at the weather.

WRITING ABOUT POPULAR CULTURE

Throughout this book, you will find readings on popular culture that you can use as models for your own writing or as subjects to which you may respond, assignments for writing critical essays on popular culture, and advice to help you analyze a wide variety of cultural phenomena. As you approach these readings and assignments, you may find it helpful to review the following suggestions for writing critical essays — whether on popular culture or on any subject — as well as some examples of student essays written in response to assignments based on *Signs of Life in the U.S.A.* Mastering the skills summarized and exemplified here should enable you to write the kinds of papers you will be assigned throughout your college career.

As you prepare to write a critical essay on popular culture, remember that you are already an expert in your subject. After all, simply by actively participating in everyday life, you have accumulated a vast store of knowledge about what makes our culture tick. Just think of all you know about movies, or the thousands upon thousands of ads you've seen, or the many messages you send whenever you post to Facebook or Instagram. Your very expertise in popular culture, ironically, may create a challenge simply because you might take your knowledge for granted. You might not think that your knowledge of popular culture can "count" as material for a college-level assignment, and it might not even occur to you to use it in an essay. But that knowledge is a great place for you to start. To write a strong essay, you need to do more than just "go with the flow" of your subject as you live it — instead, you need to consider it from a critical distance.

Using Active Reading Strategies

Your first step in developing a strong essay about any topic happens well before you sit down to write: You should make sure you accurately understand the reading selections your instructor has assigned. In other words, you want to engage in *active* reading — that is, you want to get more than just the "drift" of a passage. Skimming a selection may give you a rough idea of the author's point, but your understanding of it is also likely to be partial, superficial, or even downright wrong. And that's not a solid start to writing a good paper!

Active reading techniques can help you detect the nuances of how an author constructs his or her argument accurately and precisely. You should question, summarize, agree with, and/or refute the author's claims. In other words, imagine having a kind of *conversation* with the author. Studies have shown that such interactive learning simply works better than passive learning; if you read actively, you'll gain knowledge at a higher rate and retain it longer. With any reading selection, it can be helpful to read at least twice: first, to gain a general sense of the author's ideas and, second, to study more specifically how those ideas work together to form an argument. To read actively,

Active Reading Questions

- What is the author's *primary argument*? Can you identify a *thesis* statement, or is the thesis implied?
- What *key terms* are fundamental to that argument? If you are not familiar with the fundamental vocabulary of the selection, be sure to check a dictionary or encyclopedia for the word's meaning.
- What *evidence* does the author provide to support the argument? Is it relevant and specific? Does the author cite reliable, authoritative sources?
- What *underlying assumptions* shape the author's position? Does the author consider alternative points of view (counterarguments)?
- What *style* and *tone* does the author adopt?
- What is the *genre* of the piece? You need to identify what kind of writing you are responding to, because different genres have different purposes and goals. A personal narrative, for instance, expresses the writer's experiences and beliefs, but you shouldn't expect it to present a complete argument supported by documentation.
- Who is the *intended readership* of this selection, and does it affect the author's reasoning or evidence?

you can use formal discovery techniques, or what are called *heuristics*. One of the most famous heuristics is the journalist's "five Ws and an H": who, what, where, when, why, and how. By asking these six questions, a reporter can quickly unearth the essential details of a breaking story and draft a clear account of it. For your purposes, you can apply the preceding questions to reading selections you will discuss in your own essays.

As you read, write *annotations*, or notes, in your book. Doing so will help you both remember and analyze what you read. A pencil is probably the best memory aid ever invented. No one, not even the most perceptive reader, remembers everything — and let's face it, not everything that you read is worth remembering. Writing annotations as you read will lead you back to important points. And annotating helps you start analyzing a reading — long before you start writing an essay — rather than uncritically accepting what's on the page. If you are using an electronic version of this text, you can do the same with the highlighting and annotation tools available in most e-readers.

There's yet another reason to annotate what you read: You can use the material you've identified as the starting point for your journal notes and essays, and since it doesn't take long to circle a word or jot a note in the margin, you can save a great deal of time in the long run. We suggest that you *not* use a highlighter. While using a highlighter is better than using nothing — it can at least help you mark key points — writing *words* in your book goes much further in helping you analyze what you read. We've seen entire pages bathed in fluorescent-yellow highlighter, and that's of doubtful use in identifying the important stuff. Of course, if you simply can't bring yourself to mark up your book, write on sticky notes instead and put those in the margins.

So as you read, circle key words, note transitions between ideas, jot definitions of unfamiliar terms (you can probably guess their meaning from the context or look them up later), underline phrases or terms to research on a search engine such as Google, write short summaries of important points, or simply note where you're confused or lost with a question mark or a *huh?!* In fact, figuring out exactly what parts you do and don't understand is one of the best ways to tackle a difficult reading. Frequently, the confusing bits turn out to be the most interesting — and sometimes the most important. Responding to what you read *as* you read will help you become a more active reader — and will ultimately help you become a stronger writer.

Prewriting Strategies

Before you start writing, you'll find it useful to spend some time generating your ideas freely and openly: Your goal at this point is to develop as many ideas as possible, even ones that you might not actually use in your essay. Writing instructors call this process *prewriting*, and it's a step you should take when writing on any subject in any class, not just in your writing class. This textbook includes many suggestions for how you can develop your ideas; even if your instructor doesn't require you to use all of them, you can try them on your own.

These prewriting strategies will work when you are asked to respond to a particular reading or image. Sometimes, though, you may be asked to write about a more general subject. Your instructor may ask you to brainstorm ideas or to freewrite in response to an issue. You can use both strategies — brainstorming and freewriting — in your journal or on your own as you start working on an essay. *Brainstorming* is simply amassing as many relevant (and even some irrelevant) ideas as possible. Let's say your instructor asks you to brainstorm a list of popular toys used by girls and boys in preparation for an essay about the gendered designs of children's toys. Try to list your thoughts freely, jotting down whatever comes to mind. Don't censor yourself at this point. That is, don't worry if something is really a game rather than a toy, or if both boys and girls play with it, or if it is really an adult toy. Later on you can throw out any ideas that don't fit. What you'll be left with is a rich list of examples that you can then study and analyze. *Freewriting* works much the same way and is particularly useful when you're not sure how you feel about an issue. To freewrite, sit down and just start writing or typing, and don't stop until you've written for at least ten minutes. Let your ideas wander around your subject, working associatively, following their own path. As with brainstorming, you may produce some irrelevant ideas, but you may also arrive at a sharper picture of your beliefs.

Signs of Life in the U.S.A. frequently asks you to respond to a reading selection in a *journal* or *reading log*, sometimes directly and sometimes indirectly, as in suggestions that you write a letter to the author of a selection. In doing so, you're taking a first step in articulating your response to the issues and to the author's presentation of them. In asking you to keep a journal or a reading log, your instructor will probably be less concerned with your writing style than with your comprehension of assigned readings and your thoughtful responses to them. Let's say you're asked to write your response to Jessica Hagedorn's "Asian Women in Film: No Joy, No Luck" in Chapter 4. You should first think through exactly what Hagedorn is saying — what her point is — by asking the questions listed on pages 353–354 and by reviewing your annotations. Then consider how you feel about her essay. If you agree with Hagedorn's contention that films perpetuate outmoded stereotypes of Asian women, why do you feel that way? Can you think of films Hagedorn does not mention that reflect the gendered patterns she observes? Or do you know of films that represent Asian female characters positively? Suppose you're irritated by Hagedorn's argument: Again, why do you feel that way? Your aim in jotting all this down is not to produce a draft of an essay. It's to play with your own ideas, see where they lead, and even just help you decide what your ideas are in the first place.

If your instructor asks you to create your own topic, that freedom might actually make it harder to figure out where to start. Suppose you need to analyze an aspect of the film industry but can't decide on a focus. Here, the

Internet might help. You could explore a resource such as filmsite.org, a site divided into categories such as History, Genres, and Reviews. These categories can lead you to more specific links, such as "Film History – By Decade" and "Film Reviews – By Decade." With so many topics to choose from, you're bound to find something that interests you. In effect, you can go online to engage in *electronic brainstorming* about your topic.

One cautionary note: When going online to brainstorm, be sure to *evaluate the appropriateness of your sources* (see p. 57). Many sites are commercial and thus are intended more to sell a product or image than to provide reliable information. In addition, since anyone with the technological know-how can set up a Web site, some sites amount to little more than personal expression and need to be evaluated for their reliability, accuracy, and authenticity. Scrutinize the sites you visit carefully: Is the author an authority in the field? Does the site identify the author, at least by name and e-mail address? (Be wary of fully anonymous sites.) Does the site contain interesting and relevant links? If you find an advocacy site, one that openly advances a special interest, does the site's bias interfere with the accuracy of its information? Asking such questions can help ensure that your electronic brainstorming is fruitful and productive. If you are unsure of the validity of a site, you should check with your instructor.

You can also strengthen your argument if you consider the *history* of your subject. You might think this requires a lot of library research, but research may not be necessary if you are already familiar with the social and cultural history of your topic. If you know, for instance, that the baggy pants so popular among teens until recently were once ubiquitous among street-gang members, you know an important historical detail that goes a long way toward explaining their significance. Depending on your assignment, you might want to expand on your own historical knowledge and collect additional data about your topic, perhaps through surveys and interviews. If you're analyzing the ways people use social media to maintain personal relationships, for instance, you could interview some people from different age groups and genders, to get a sense of the range of people's habits. The material you gather through such interviews will be raw data, and you'll want to do more than just "dump" the information into your essay. Instead, see this material as an original body of evidence that you'll sort through (you probably won't use every scrap of information), study, and interpret in its own right.

Not all prewriting activities need be solitary, of course. In fact, *Signs of Life* includes lots of suggestions that ask you to work with other students, either in your class or across campus. We suggest such *group work* because much academic work is collaborative and collegial. A scientist conducting research, for instance, often works with a team; in addition, he or she may present preliminary findings at colloquia or conferences and may call or e-mail a colleague at another school to try out some ideas. There's no reason you can't benefit from the social nature of academic thinking as well. But be aware that in-class group work is by no means "busywork." The goal, rather, is to help you develop and shape your understanding of the issues and your attitudes toward them. If you're asked to study with three classmates how a product is packaged, for instance, you're starting to test Chris Arning's thesis in "What Can Semiotics Contribute to Packaging Design?" (Chapter 1), seeing how it applies or doesn't apply and benefiting from your peers' insights. By discussing packaging design with your peers, you are articulating, perhaps for the first time, what it might mean, and so are taking the first step toward writing a more formal analysis (especially if you receive feedback and comments from your class). Similarly, if you stage an in-class debate over the effectiveness of social media activism, you're amassing a storehouse of arguments, counterarguments, and evidence to consider when you write your own essay that either supports or refutes Brian Dunning's argument in "Slacktivism: Raising Awareness" (Chapter 5). As with other prewriting strategies, you may not directly use every idea generated in conversation with your classmates, but that's OK. You should find yourself better able to sort through and articulate the ideas that you do find valuable.

Developing Strong Arguments about Popular Culture

We expect that students will write many different sorts of papers in response to the selections in this book. You may write personal experience narratives, semiotic analyses, opinion pieces, research papers, and many others. We'd like to focus here on writing analytic essays because the experience of analyzing popular culture may seem different from that of analyzing other subjects. Occasionally we've had students who feel reluctant to analyze popular culture because they think that analysis requires them to trash their subject, and they don't want to write a "negative" essay about what may be their favorite film or TV program. Or a few students may feel uncertain because "it's all subjective." Since most people have opinions about popular culture, they say, how can any one essay be stronger than another?

While these concerns are understandable, they needn't be an obstacle to writing a strong analytic essay, whether on popular culture or any other topic. To avoid overt subjectivity, you should begin by setting aside your own personal tastes when writing an analysis, not because your preferences are unimportant, but because you need to be aware of your own attitudes and observations about your topic. An analysis of, say, *The Big Bang Theory* is not the same as a paper that explains "why I like (or dislike) this TV program." Instead, an analysis would explain how it works, what cultural beliefs and viewpoints underlie it, what its significance is, and so forth. And such a paper would not necessarily be positive or negative; it would seek to explain *how* the elements of the show work together to have a particular effect on its audience. If your instructor asks you to write a critical analysis or a critical argument, he or she is requesting neither a hit job nor a celebration of your topic.

For most of your college essays, you will probably be asked to make sure that your paper has a clear *thesis*. A thesis statement lays out the argument you intend to make and provides a scope for your essay. If you think of your thesis as a road map that your paper will follow, you might find that it is easier to structure your paper. A thesis for an essay on popular culture should follow the usual guidelines for any academic essay: It should make a debatable, interesting assertion (as opposed to a statement of fact or a truism); it should be demonstrable through the presentation of specific evidence; it should have a clear focus and scope; and it should spark your readers' interest. Additionally, a strong thesis statement will help you overcome any anxieties you might have about writing a strong analysis, because an effective thesis, rather than merely offering an opinion about a topic, also explains how you came to hold that opinion. The thesis statements in the sample student essays that begin on page 33 are annotated to help you see how they function in academic writing.

When your paper has a strong thesis, subjectivity becomes even less of a problem. That's because your analysis should be grounded in concrete demonstration. You're not simply presenting a personal opinion about your subject; rather, you're presenting a central insight about its significance, and you need to demonstrate it with logical, specific evidence. It's that evidence that will take your essay out of the category of being "merely subjective." You should start with your own opinion, but you will want to add to it lots of support that shows the legitimacy of that opinion. Does that sound familiar? It should, because that's what you need to do in any analytic essay, no matter what your subject matter happens to be.

When writing about popular culture, students sometimes wonder what sort of evidence they should use to support their points. Your instructor will probably give you guidelines for each assignment, but we'll provide some suggestions here. Start with your subject itself. You'll find it's useful to view your subject — whether it's an ad, a film, or anything else — as a text that you can "read" closely. That's what you would do if you were asked to analyze a poem: You would read it carefully, studying individual words, images, rhythm, and so forth, and those details would support whatever claims you want to make about the poem. Read your pop culture subject with the same care. If your instructor asks you to analyze a TV series, you should look at the details: What actors appear in the series, and what are their roles? What "story" does the program tell about its characters and the world in which they live? Is there anything missing from this world that you would expect to find? What are the *connotative* meanings behind the surface signs? Your answers to such questions could form the basis for the evidence that your essay needs.

Conducting a Semiotic Analysis

In an essay focused on a semiotic analysis, you can probe a wider range of questions about your subject, yielding even more specific evidence and arguments. You can start with some basic questions that we ask throughout the

Chapter Introductions in this book and that we summarize in the following list. As an example, let's apply these questions to the TV series *House*, still popular and significant even though it is now in reruns.

DENOTATIVE MEANINGS

What is a simple, literal description of your subject? You need to make sure you understand this basic definition before looking for "deeper meanings," because if you misunderstand the factual status of your subject, your analysis will probably get derailed. In the case of *House*, we find a story of a medical genius who, though he is his hospital's most successful diagnostician, is also rude, nasty, and practically dysfunctional in his personal life, suffering from an addiction to Vicodin and almost constant depression. The plots of *House* tend to exemplify the series's slogan, "Everybody lies," and often depict House's patients or their families as liars with dark secrets that they are concealing and that House eventually uncovers. Clearly, if we were to misidentify *House* as a documentary, we'd misconstrue it as a scathing political exposé of the U.S. medical system — but that doesn't feel right. *House* is no exposé.

CONNOTATIVE MEANINGS AND A SYSTEM OF RELATED SIGNS

After determining your subject's denotation, you should locate your subject within a larger system in order to determine its connotative meaning. Recall that a system is the network of related signs to which your topic belongs and that identifying the system helps to reveal its significance. This may sound hard to do, but it is through identifying a system that you can draw on your own vast knowledge of popular culture. So, in our analysis of *House*, we need to move from our denotative understanding of the series to its connotative

---

Questions for Conducting a Semiotic Analysis

- What is the **denotative** meaning of your subject? In other words, determine a factual definition of exactly what it is.
- What is your topic's **connotative** significance? To determine that, situate your subject in a system of related signs.
- What **associated** signs belong to that system?
- What **differences** do you see in those signs?
- What **abductive** explanation do you have for your observations? What is the most likely explanation for the patterns that you see?

significance. In order to make this move, we need to identify a system of related signs, in this case, we need to identify programs with which *House* is similar. In other words, to what genre of television programming does *House* belong? What conventions, goals, and motifs do shows in this genre share? What is the history of the genre? *House*, of course, belongs to the medical drama genre, which is distinct from, say, a sitcom, even though *House* does have certain comic elements that would allow us to classify it as a medical *dramedy*. The history of TV medical drama includes such programs as *Dr. Kildare* and *Ben Casey* in the 1960s; *Marcus Welby, M.D.*, and *Quincy, M.E.*, in the 1970s; *St. Elsewhere* and *ER* in the 1980s and beyond; and *Grey's Anatomy* and *Nip/Tuck* more recently. All these programs can be associated with *House* and testify to the enduring popularity of the genre.

DIFFERENCES WITHIN THE SYSTEM

But while the associations between these TV series demonstrate a popular interest in doctors and medical stories, there is still a striking difference to consider, a kind of dividing line marked by the series *St. Elsewhere*. Until *St. Elsewhere*, the main character of a medical drama was almost always a benevolent healer whose own personal life beyond the hospital was generally not a part of the story line (there were exceptions: Dr. Kildare once had a patient with whom he fell in love; Ben Casey had a somewhat edgy nature; and Jack Klugman's Quincy — a forensic pathologist whose mystery-solving abilities anticipate those of Gregory House — had plenty of attitude). But all in all, the physician protagonists of the earlier series maintained a general profile of almost superhuman benevolence; they were "official heroes," in Robert B. Ray's terms (see "The Thematic Paradigm," p. 303), caring for the innocent victims of disease.

St. Elsewhere changed that, and from that program onward (especially as developed by *ER*), the flaws in the lives and personalities of the main characters, the doctors, became much more prominent. The doctors were, in short, much more humanized — a shift in characterization that has led to the caustic, sometimes dysfunctional and lawbreaking Dr. House.

ABDUCTIVE EXPLANATIONS

At this point, we are ready to start interpreting, seeking abductive explanations for the shift. We can begin by identifying yet another system, this time by looking at the larger context of other television genres. If we look at this larger system, we can find in sitcoms, crime series, Westerns, and many other genres a shift similar to the one in the history of medical dramas. The difference between the family sitcoms of the 1950s and 1960s and those of the 1980s and beyond is well known, taking us from the happy families of the Cleavers and the Nelsons to the dysfunctional Bundys and Griffins. Similarly, it's a long way from Dick Tracy and *Dragnet*'s Joe Friday to the callous cops of *The Wire*. And it is a long way from *Gunsmoke* to *Justified*. Many other such differences could be mentioned, but we'll move on to our abductive interpretation.

The post–*St. Elsewhere* medical drama reflects a broader trend in American entertainment away from squeaky-clean TV protagonists to more "realistically" flawed ones, heroes who definitely have feet of clay. This trend reflects a cultural shift, the origins of which can be found in the cultural revolution of the 1960s, when American mass culture began a long process of disillusionment. After the Vietnam War and Watergate, increasingly cynical Americans were no longer predisposed to believe in human perfection, preferring a more "realistic" depiction of human beings with all their flaws visible.

Thus, we can now see *House* as part of a larger cultural trend in which the once-cherished, even revered, figure of the physician has been pulled off the pedestal and brought to earth along with everyone else. Heroes are still heroes (after all, Gregory House is just plain smarter than anyone else around him), but they are more like ordinary folks. They misbehave, get cranky, break rules. Even the victims of misfortune (patients in a medical drama) have been degraded, appearing no longer as the objects of our sympathy but as flawed people with dark secrets. *Everybody lies.* No one is innocent. To the disillusioned, *House*, with its all-too-human hero and cast, is an entertaining, if cynical, vision of the way things are — or at least of the way that large numbers of viewers think they are. Doctors (and cops, families, cowboys, and everyone else) have warts too, and, as a sort of anti–Marcus Welby, Gregory House entertains his audience by not being afraid to show his flaws to the world.

Reading Visual Images Actively

Signs of Life in the U.S.A. includes many visual images, some accompanied by questions for analysis. In analyzing images, you can develop the ability to identify specific telling details and evidence — a talent useful no matter what your subject matter may be. Because the semiotic method lends itself especially well to visual analysis, it is an excellent means for honing this ability. Here are some questions to consider as you look at images.

To see how we can apply these questions, let's look at a sample analysis of an advertisement for Lee jeans (see image on p. 31).

Appearance: Although this image is reproduced here in black and white, it originally appeared in color. The colors are muted, however, almost sepia-toned, and thus suggest an old-fashioned look.

Kind of image: This is a fairly realistic image, with a patina of rural nostalgia. A solitary woman, probably in her twenties or thirties, but perhaps older, is set against an empty natural expanse. She

Questions for Analyzing Images

- What is the **appearance of the image**? Is it black and white? Color? Is it in focus or is it blurry? Consider how the form in which the image is expressed affects its message. If an image is composed of primary colors, does it look fun and lively, for instance?

- What **kind of image** is it? Is it abstract, does it represent an actual person or place, or is it a combination of the two? If people are represented, who are they? Who does not appear? What are the people doing? Are they looking at each other, at the viewer, or away from the viewer?

- Who is the intended **audience** for the image? Is it an artistic photograph or a commercial work, such as an advertisement? If it is an ad, to what kind of person is it directed? Where is the ad placed? If the image is in a magazine, consider the audience for the publication. Do you need any background information to understand the image?

- What **emotions** does the image convey? Overall, is it serious, sad, funny? Is its expression of emotion, in your opinion, intentional? What emotional associations do you have with the image?

- If the image includes more than one element, what is the most prominent element in the **composition**? A particular section? A logo? Any writing? A person or group of people? A product? Why are some elements larger than others? How does each part contribute to the whole?

- Where does the image's **layout** lead your eye? Are you drawn to any specific part? What is the order in which you look at the various parts? Does any particular section immediately stand out?

- Does the image include **text**? If so, how do the image and the text relate to one another?

- Does the image call for a **response**? For instance, does it suggest that you purchase a product? If so, what claims does it make?

has a traditional hairstyle evocative of the 1950s or early 1960s and leads an old-fashioned bicycle with a wicker basket attached.

Audience: The intended audience for this jeans ad is most likely a woman in her late twenties or older. We see only the model's back, so she is faceless. That allows the viewer to project herself into the scene, and the nostalgic look suggests that the viewer could imagine herself at a younger time in her life. Note that the product is "stretch" jeans. There's no suggestion here, although it is often made in ads for other brands, that the jeans will enhance

The things that give a woman substance
will never appear on any "what's in/what's out" list.

Straight Leg STRETCH **Lee**

a woman's sexual appeal; rather, the claim is that the jeans are practical — and will fit a body beyond the teen years. Note the sensible hairstyle and shoes. For an interesting contrast, you might compare this ad to one for Diesel jeans.

Emotion: The woman's body language suggests individuality and determination; she's literally "going it alone." She's neither posing for nor aware of the viewer, suggesting that "what you see is what you get." And, perhaps, she doesn't particularly care what you think.

Composition and layout: The layout of the ad is carefully designed to lead your eye: The hill slopes down from top right toward middle left, and the bike draws your eye from bottom right to mid-left, with both lines converging on the product, the jeans. For easy readability, the text appears at the top against the blank sky.

Text: The message, "The things that give a woman substance will never appear on any 'what's in/what's out' list," suggests that Lee jeans are a product for women who aren't interested in following trends, but rather want a good, old-fashioned value — "substance," not frivolity.

Response: The manufacturer of Lee jeans would prefer, naturally, that the viewer of the ad buy the product. The viewer would identify with the woman wearing the jeans in the advertisement and be convinced that these practical (if not particularly cutting-edge) jeans would be a good purchase.

In sum, most fashion ads stress the friends (and often, mates) you will attract if you buy the product, but this ad presents "a road not taken," suggesting the American ideology of marching to the beat of a different drummer, the kind of old-fashioned individualism that brings to mind Robert Frost and Henry David Thoreau. The pastoral surroundings and the "old painting" effect echo artists such as Andrew Wyeth and Norman Rockwell. All these impressions connote lasting American values (rural, solid, middle American) that are meant to be associated with anti-trendiness and enduring qualities, such as individualism and practicality. And these impressions suggest the advertisers carefully and effectively kept the ad's semiotic messages in mind as they designed it.

Reading Essays about Popular Culture

In your writing course, it's likely that your instructor will ask you to work in groups with other students, perhaps reviewing one another's rough drafts. You'll find many benefits to this activity. Not only will you receive more feedback on your own in-progress work, but you will see other students' ideas and approaches to an assignment and develop an ability to evaluate academic writing. For the same reasons, we're including three sample student essays that satisfy assignments about popular culture. You may agree or disagree with the authors' views, and you might have responded to the assigned topics differently; that's fine. We've selected these essays because they differ in style, focus, and purpose and thus suggest different approaches to their assignments — approaches that might help you as you write your own essays about popular culture. We've annotated the essays to point out various argumentative, organizational, and rhetorical strategies. As you read the essays and the annotations, ask why the authors chose these strategies and how you might incorporate some of the same strategies into your own writing.

Essay 1

For this essay, UCLA theater major Elijah Green received a prompt that is often assigned in composition courses: write a textual analysis of one of the articles in *Signs of Life in the U.S.A.* His charge was to evaluate the author's reasoning and evidence, to examine the author's assumptions, and to consider whether there could be alternative readings of the evidence. In studying Alfred Lubrano's "The Shock of Education" (p. 543), Elijah finds some shortcomings in the author's reasoning and claims, even though he considers Lubrano's personal narrative to be "heartrending" overall. As you read Elijah's essay, notice how his critique goes beyond *what* the essay says and addresses *how* the text makes its argument. Whether you agree or disagree with his position, you should see that Elijah presents a clear judgment of Lubrano's essay.

Alfred Lubrano: The Shock of Myopia

In "The Shock of Education: How College Corrupts," Alfred Lubrano chronicles the formation of various fissures within his family during his college years that occurred because of the social mobility afforded him by his educational ascension. Beyond his own lived experience, Lubrano utilizes interviews — from others forced to "abandon their past" in the pursuit of education — and a supposedly renowned study on class to make the case that pursuing the American Dream has many grave implications for first-generation college students from lower-class backgrounds (543). Lubrano argues that while mobility does place its benefactors (in this case, college students) on a path to attain the American Dream, this freedom forces them to mold their "true" identities at school in a manner and climate that require them to cut ties with the world of their

Elijah summarizes Lubrano's main argument.

formative years. Heartrending though that graduation may be, Lubrano's argument whittles his vivid personal history down to a tidy narrative that neglects to interrogate the ways he might have capitalized on his learned insights to fortify his familial and community bonds. In forgoing a discussion of his personal role in widening the gulf between his two worlds, Lubrano misses the chance to engage adequately with the complex generational dynamics at play within and beyond the realm of his own experience. This leaves a gaping hole in his reasoning and claims — one that responsible thinkers should not overlook lest their cultural analysis succumb to the same weaknesses.

He moves to his thesis about the deficiencies he finds in the case that Lubrano makes to support his claims.

In critiquing his own cultural performance in respect to his generational placement, Lubrano says the following: "Mobility means discomfort" (544). With this comment, he posits that the members of his household are, in providing him with the opportunity for social mobility, at the peak of cultural performance by the standards of the working-class experience, while he is performing well by grinning and bearing the weight of the discomfort they are all enduring on his behalf. He tells of his learned self-censorship at family dinners and his deliberately studying in rooms separate from his family — all a part of the gradual shift that saw the "grammar of his heart" evolve to match that of his professors rather than his own parents as he entered the college environment (545). In his eyes, he and his family are experts on their own experience, because the members of each respective generation are properly adhering to the social codes of their class as they pursue the American Dream.

Elijah identifies one of Lubrano's key assumptions (that class roles are static).

However, Lubrano omits an analysis of the work he could have done to assuage the growing rift in his family unit. One wonders how much Lubrano's parents might have appreciated their son giving back to the community in ways that only someone with his unique exposure to vast educational resources might successfully actualize, such as mentoring the neighborhood youth. He shares his self-doubt, describing his high school as rife with students destined for "jobs in their parents' unions or secretaries' desks" (544). On account of his social status, Lubrano was conditioned to believe that he had minimal authority in crafting his transition to college life, but this was simply not the case. By accepting the idea that education and family must be kept separate to ensure academic

He then disputes that assumption.

success and gain social mobility, Lubrano failed to see how much of his heart seemed to be invested in both of those worlds and thus missed a chance to use his education as a force for good in his community. He believes that mobility implies the discomfort of its benefactors. But who is to say that discomfort shouldn't be reserved for the social forces that keep the working-class locked into a track that prevents them from claiming the tenets of the American Dream that promise upward mobility, or equity for all people in the pursuit of happiness? What was the purpose of his education if he wasn't willing to use it to enhance the world around him?

Elijah points out a possible consequence of Lubrano's assumptions.

An additional chink in the armor-like use of Lubrano's first-hand experience is this: he interviewed only subjects from his own generation. In doing so, he missed a valuable opportunity to chart how the so-called "Straddler struggle" has evolved with time. Do working-class students today, on the whole, have less trouble adjusting to the "status dissonance" they experience on college campuses, or are we worse off than when Lubrano was going through the system? (543) While it is worth noting that Lubrano wrote this essay in 1994 (before the Internet as the world now knows it), it is equally important to see that Lubrano did not enter the perspectives of the next generation — or even a retrospective look on his college experience from a later stage in his life, in some sort of follow-up piece — into a discourse with his own. Because of this myopic oversight, the reader is not led to consider, for instance, the increased connectivity of familial units in the Internet age, and how that may lessen (or intensify) the sense of isolation that clouded Lubrano's college experience.

The critique shifts to the evidence that Lubrano provides.

Elijah laments Lubrano's lack of a retrospective consideration of his college experience.

With the increased accessibility of personal communication devices, is there more or less pressure to communicate with family on a regular basis? How does that inform the way students are able to engage with their educations? Lubrano never lets us in on the secret. He cites the perspective of author Robert Rodriguez as one kindred to his own. Rodriguez is quoted as saying that he detested his parents' "shabbiness" and inability to access the new world he was entering (545). The reader can infer that the tether between Lubrano and Rodriguez's outlooks is that Lubrano felt similar claustrophobia at home and disdain for his family, relics of his former life. While that discomfort is understandable given the limited technical means of communication between Lubrano and his family, one wonders how that dynamic might play out differently when someone with access to their family at virtually all times of the day (i.e., a student with a cell phone) enters the picture. We are inundated with stories of long-distance boyfriends and, in the case of one Loretta Stec, communities that floundered in their efforts to cope with the people who were afforded access to higher education. These are all valid experiences that should be treated as such, but Lubrano never gives us the chance to see how those tales pan out. Is the next generation enduring these same hardships? Were Lubrano or Stec ever able to reconcile the realities of their disparate worlds? Without acknowledging these evolving attitudes, Lubrano's argument loses much of its credibility and becomes itself a relic of a time long behind us.

The succinct conclusion goes beyond simply restating previous points.

Though Lubrano offers many valuable insights into the complex struggles facing first-generation college students hailing from working-class families, his case that education only drives a wedge between those students and their families leaves a lot to be desired. The frame of his experience, as well as the interviews he conducted, constitute a vivid snapshot of only one period of time — each subject's college years — in only one generational configuration. By not acknowledging the shifts in attitudes of his chosen interviewees over time, as well as neglecting to interview students of the generations beyond his own, Lubrano crafts an argument that suffers greatly on the matter of credibility. He makes sweeping claims about the state of education, class relations, and even the American identity, yet fails to embrace the full dynamism of what American-ism or even working-class life has the potential to be. In the end, it is not the turbulence of working class students' ascension to higher education that proves particularly shocking, but Lubrano's own sense of myopia in his approach to his personal history.

Elijah signals closure by echoing a key word from his own title.

Works Cited

Lubrano, Alfred. "The Shock of Education: How College Corrupts." *Signs of Life in the U.S.A.: Readings on Popular Culture for Writers*. 9th ed., edited by Sonia Maasik and Jack Solomon, Bedford/St. Martin's, 2015, pp. 543–549.

Essay 2

In this essay, Amy Lin of UCLA argues that the Barbie doll, and all its associated products and marketing, essentially is a means for engendering a consumerist ethos in young girls who are the toy's fans. To do so, Lin relies on a range of sources, including articles in *Signs of Life in the U.S.A.*, academic and journalistic sources, and a corporate Web site that presents the panoply of Barbie products. Notice that Lin does not treat toysrus.com as a source of unbiased information about the products (that would amount to taking promotional material at face value); rather, she analyzes the Web site as evidence for her larger argument about consumerism. As you read Lin's essay, study how she uses her sources and integrates them into her own discussion.

Barbie: Queen of Dolls and Consumerism

In my closet, a plastic bag contains five Barbie dolls. A cardboard box beside my nightstand holds yet another, and one more box contains a Ken doll. Under my bed we find my Barbies' traveling walk-in closet, equipped with a light-up vanity and foldout chair and desk. We also find Doctor Barbie along with the baby, sticker Band-Aids, and sounding stethoscope with which she came. Under my sister's bed are their furniture set, including sofas, loveseats, flower vases, and a coffee table. A Tupperware container holds Ken's pants, dress shirts, and special boots (whose spurs make patterns when rolled in ink) in addition to Barbie's excess clothing that did not fit in the walk-in closet. In a corner of my living room sits the special holiday edition Barbie, outfitted in a gown, fur stole, and holly headband.

Amy's introduction is a visual anecdote that illustrates her argument about consumption.

These plastic relics prove that, as a young girl, I, like many other females, fell into the waiting arms of the Mattel Corporation. Constantly feeding the public with newer, shinier toys, the Barbie enterprise illustrates America's propensity for consumerism. Upon close examination, Barbie products foster materialism in young females through both their overwhelmingly large selection and their ability to create a financially carefree world for children, sending the message that excessive consumption is acceptable. This consequently perpetuates the misassumption that "the American economy [is] an endlessly fertile continent whose boundaries never need be reached" (Shames 81) among the American youth.

Amy articulates her thesis and refers to Laurence Shames's article as a context.

Search the term "Barbie" at toysrus.com, and you will receive 286 items in return — more than enough to create a blur of pinkish-purple as you scroll down the Web page. The Barbie enterprise clearly embraces "the observation that 'no natural boundary seems to be set to the efforts of man'" (Shames 78). In other words, humankind is, in all ways, ambitious; people will keep creating, buying, and selling with the belief that these opportunities will always be available. This perfectly describes the mentality of those behind Barbie products, as new, but unnecessary, Barbie merchandise is put on shelves at an exorbitant rate. At toysrus.com, for example, a variety of four different mermaids, eleven fairies, and two "merfairies" — products from the "Fairytopia-Mermaidia" line — find their place among the search results (*Toys*). Instead of inventing a more original or educational product, Mattel merges the mermaid world with the fairy world into "Fairytopia-Mermaidia," demonstrating the company's lack of innovation and care for its young consumers' development. Thus the corporation's main motivation reveals itself: profit. Another prime example found among the search results is the "Barbie: 12 Dancing Princesses Horse Carriage" (*Toys*), a more recent product in the Barbie family. The carriage, "in its original form, . . . can seat six princess dolls but . . . can expand to hold all 12 dolls at once" (*Toys*). The dolls, of course, do not come with it, forcing the child to buy at least one for the carriage to even be of any use. But that child will see the glorious picture of the carriage filled with all twelve dolls (which are inevitably on the box), and she will want to buy the remaining eleven. In addition, the product description states that the carriage "is inspired by the upcoming DVD release, Barbie in *The 12 Dancing Princesses*" (*Toys*). Essentially, one Mattel creation inspires another, meaning that the DVD's sole purpose is to give Mattel an excuse to create and market more useless merchandise.

Much of this, however, may have to do with branding, a strategy manufacturers utilize that ultimately results in "consumers transfer[ring] a favorable or unfavorable image from one product to others from the same brand" (Neuhaus and Taylor 419). In accordance with this strategy, all Barbie products must maintain a certain similarity so as not to "'confuse' potential customers . . . and thereby reduce demand for the products" (Sappington and Wernerfelt 280). This explains the redundancy found in much of

The corporate Web site is used not as a source of objective information but as evidence to support the thesis.

Amy moves to the larger marketing context.

Mattel's Barbie merchandise, since the sudden manufacturing of a radically different product could encourage the migration of consumers to another brand. But given that Barbie has become "the alpha doll" (Talbot 74) for girls in today's popular culture, young female consumers clearly associate only good things with Barbie. And who can blame them? Barbie has become a tradition handed down from mother to daughter or a rite of passage that most girls go through. In this way, excessive consumption and the effects of branding are handed down as well, as Barbie dolls are essentially their physical manifestations.

With a company as driven to produce and sell products as Mattel, consumers can expect to find increasingly ridiculous items on toy store shelves. One such product found at toysrus.com is "Barbie and Tanner" (*Toys*), Tanner being Barbie's dog. The doll and dog come with brown pellets that function both as dog food and dog waste, a "special magnetic scooper[,] and trash can" (*Toys*). Upon telling any post-Barbie-phase female about this product, she will surely look amazed and ask, "Are you kidding me?" Unfortunately, Tanner's movable "mouth, ears, head and tail" (*Toys*) and "soft[,] . . . fuzzy" coat will most likely blind children to the product's absurdity, instead enchanting them into purchasing the product. Another particularly hilarious item is the "Barbie Collector Platinum Label Pink Grapefruit Obsession" (*Toys*). The doll wears a "pink, charmeuse mermaid gown with deep pink chiffon wedges sewn into the flared skirt and adorned with deep pink bands that end in bows under the bust and at the hip" (*Toys*). And "as a . . . special surprise, [the] doll's head is scented with the striking aroma of pink grapefruit" (*Toys*). Finally, the doll is described as "an ideal tribute to [the] delightful [grapefruit] flavor" (*Toys*). The consumer will find it difficult to keep a straight face as he or she reads through the description, as it essentially describes a doll dedicated to a scent. The doll's randomness shows Mattel's desperation for coming out with new products. Eager to make profit, Barbie's designers, it seems, make dolls according to whatever whim that happens to cross their minds.

In the quest to make profit by spreading the consumerist mind-set, Barbie products even manage to commodify culture. Nowadays, Barbie dolls come in a variety of ethnicities. Take, for example, the "Diwali Festival Doll" from the "Barbie Dolls of the World"

The paragraph includes a rich array of concrete, specific detail.

Amy develops her argument by considering the cultural and ethnic angle.

A quick, short transition moves the reader to a broader consideration of Mattel's promotion of materialism.

Amy allows for a counterargument but then refutes it.

(*Toys*) line. Except for the traditional Indian apparel and dark hair, however, the doll could easily be mistaken for Caucasian. And what about Barbie's multiracial doll friends? They are reduced to mere accessories — disposable and only supplementary to Barbie, the truly important figure. Therefore, despite Mattel's attempts at identifying with a larger group of girls, an undeniable "aura of blondness still [clings] to the Mattel doll" (Talbot 82) because its attempts aim more toward creating a larger customer base than anything else.

But enough of dolls. Mattel has grown so large that it can expand its products beyond Barbie's mini-world. Consumers can easily find Barbie brand tennis shoes, rain boots, slippers, bicycles, and helmets. Many of Barbie's non-doll products even reflect the various fads among America's youth, such as video games, skateboards, scooters, guitars, and dance mats (in accordance with the popularity of the game, Dance Dance Revolution). Anne Parducci, Mattel's senior VP of Barbie Marketing, claims Mattel does this because it "want[s] to make sure . . . [it] capture[s] girls in the many ways they are spending their time now and in the future," that it "want[s] Barbie to represent a lifestyle brand for girls, not just a brand of toys" (Edut). This phenomenon, however, can simply be seen as Mattel trying to "infiltrat[e] girls' lives everywhere they go" (Edut). Either way, Mattel's actions allow materialism to develop at an early age, especially since it makes the latest "it" items more accessible to children. Those behind Barbie figure that if children are going to buy into the latest trends anyway, they might as well buy them from Mattel.

Since Barbie products promote the attitude of keeping up with society's crazes, they create a carefree fantasy world for children, obscuring the fact that Mattel's motivation is making money. The company knows that if it enchants children, those children will in turn convince their parents to buy the products for them. The company also knows that commercials are its best opportunities to do this. One recent Mattel commercial advertises the "Let's Dance Genevieve" doll, a doll also inspired by *The 12 Dancing Princesses* DVD that interacts with its owner in three ways: the doll "can dance to music for the girl," "teach the girl dance moves by demonstrating and using speech prompts," and "follow along with the girl's dance moves using special bracelets and a shoe accessory" (*Toys*). Girls dressed in ballerina attire give overly joyous reactions to the doll's behaviors, making the doll seem remarkably advanced when, really, the doll can only raise its arms and legs. In addition, computer graphic scenes from the movie run seamlessly into scenes of the girls playing with the doll, and one of these girls is even transposed onto a clip of the movie. This blurs the lines of reality and fantasy, encouraging young viewers to think that if they own the doll, they, too, can feel like "dancing princesses," that somehow the doll can transport its owner into a fairy-tale world. In actuality, young females will likely tire of the doll within weeks. The commercial even resorts to flattery, describing the doll and its owner as "two beautiful dancers." Finally, the commercial ends with inspirational lyrics, singing, "You can shine." This sort of "vaguely girl-positive" advertising only "wrap[s] the Mattel message — buy our products now!" (Edut). Together, all these advertising elements add up to a highly desirable product among young girls.

Barbie undoubtedly increases the materialistic tendencies in children, specifically females, Barbie's target audience. After all, since "Barbie dolls need new clothes and accessories more often than boys' action figures do," "young girls learn . . . very early" to "assume consumer roles" (Katz). Interestingly, "Barbie was an early rebel against the domesticity that dominated the lives of baby-boom mothers," as she shows no "car[e] for babies or children" or "visible ties to parents" (Cross 773). But ironically, instead of "[teaching] girls to shed [such] female stereotypes," Barbie simply created a new stereotype for females — the shopaholic persona — because "she prompted [young girls] to associate the freedom of being an adult with carefree consumption" (Cross 774). So the overall effect of Barbie's presence in children's lives is increased expectations for material possessions. Or, in other words, Barbie products cause "catalog-induced anxiety," a condition that can occur "from [viewing] catalogs themselves or from other forms of public exposure of the lives of the rich or celebrated, . . . mak[ing] what a typical person possesses seem paltry, even if the person is one of the many . . . living well by objective standards" (Easterbrook 404, 405). Given that Barbie is a fictitious character, Mattel can make her as beautiful, hip, and rich as it pleases. But what happens when little girls begin comparing their lives to that of Barbie? They think, "If Barbie gets to have such amenities, so should I." And toys like the "Barbie Hot Tub Party Bus" (*Target*) do not help the situation. The product description reads that the bus contains "all the comforts

References to Gary Cross's article buttress the essay's argument.

of home like a flat screen TV, dinette table, and beds" (*Target*).
Children will inevitably expect these luxuries that, for Barbie, are

Amy invokes Gregg Easterbrook as she explores the long-term implications of Mattel's promotion of consumerism.

merely givens in her doll utopia, causing discontent when they discover they cannot have everything they want. It may even reach the point where, "as . . . more material things become available and fail to" satisfy children, "material abundance . . . [can] have the perverse effect of instilling unhappiness — because it will never be possible to have everything that economics can create" (Easterbrook 402).

Amy signals closure by coming full circle, returning to her opening anecdote.

For my long-forgotten Barbie dolls, as for those of many older females, the dream house has stopped growing. In fact, the house has been demolished, leaving my dolls homeless. But this does not mean that women have escaped the effects of years of Barbie play as they have temporarily escaped the clutches of Mattel. (I say temporarily because even if a woman has outgrown Barbie, Mattel will suck her back in through her daughters, nieces, goddaughters, and granddaughters.) Since Barbie preaches the admissibility of hyperconsumption to females at a young age, women, unsurprisingly, "engage in an estimated 80% of all consumer spending" (Katz). Women, conditioned from all those trips to the toy store looking for the perfect party dress for Barbie or the perfect convertible to take her to that party, still find themselves doing this — just on a larger scale — in shopping malls. But perhaps men's consumerism is catching up.

By considering men's consumer habits and male dolls, Amy ends with a refreshing twist.

The recent "proliferation of metrosexuals" signals a rise in "straight young men whose fashion and grooming tastes have crossed over into areas once reserved for feminine consumption" (St. John 177, 174). Mattel, too, takes part in this phenomenon through the "reintroduc[tion] [of] the Ken doll," which now possesses a "new metrosexual look" (Talbot 79). Well, one thing is certain: Mattel continues its expansive construction on Barbie's ever-costly dream mansion, and knows that millions of little girls will do the same.

Works Cited

Cross, Gary. "Barbie, G.I. Joe, and Play in the 1960s." Maasik and Solomon, pp. 772–78.

Easterbrook, Gregg. "The Progress Paradox." Maasik and Solomon, pp. 400–407.

Edut, Ophira. "Barbie Girls Rule?" *Bitch: Feminist Response to Pop Culture*, 31 Jan. 1999, p. 16.

Geoffrey LLC. *Toys "R" Us*. 14 Nov. 2006, www.toysrus.com

Katz, Phyllis A., and Margaret Katz. "Purchasing Power: Spending for Change." *Iris,* 30 Apr. 2000, p. 36.

Maasik, Sonia, and Jack Solomon, editors. *Signs of Life in the U.S.A.: Readings on Popular Culture for Writers*, 7th ed., Bedford/St. Martin's, 2012.

Neuhaus, Colin F., and James R. Taylor. "Variables Affecting Sales of Family-Branded Products." *Journal of Marketing Research*, vol. 9, no. 4, 1972, pp. 419–22.

Sappington, David E. M., and Birger Wernerfelt. "To Brand or Not to Brand? A Theoretical and Empirical Question." *Journal of Business,* vol. 58, no. 3, 1985, pp. 279–93.

Shames, Laurence. "The More Factor." Maasik and Solomon, pp. 76–82.

St. John, Warren. "Metrosexuals Come Out." Maasik and Solomon, pp. 174–77.

Talbot, Margaret. "Little Hotties: Barbie's New Rivals." *New Yorker,* 4 Dec. 2006, pp. 74+.

Target Brands, Inc. *Target*. 14 Nov. 2006, www.target.com

Essay 3

Exemplifying a semiotic approach, Rose Sorooshian, a student at California State University, Northridge, explores the social and cultural conditions that led *The Walking Dead* to become one of America's most popular TV programs. The show became a hit not *despite* the difficult economic times in which it aired, she concludes, but *because* of those troubled times. Here, Sorooshian provides a fine reading of how a television program can be an articulate and potent sign of its time.

The Walking 99 Percent: An Analysis of *The Walking Dead* in the Context of the 2008 Recession

People have lost their homes and their jobs, and their standards of living are falling. People are fighting to survive, and these catastrophic events are not their fault. Yet somehow these events are affecting people more than they could possibly have imagined. This description could be the premise of the popular television show *The Walking Dead*, based on the series of graphic novels by the same name. Set in Georgia, the show follows Sheriff Rick Grimes, his wife, and their son, as well as a group of other survivors as they struggle to stay alive and maintain their humanity in the midst of a zombie apocalypse. However, this description also matches a real-life disaster that began in the United States in 2008 known as the Great Recession. A report from a Pew Research Center Survey describes the recent recession:

> Of the 13 recessions that the American public has endured since the Great Depression of 1929–33, none has presented a more punishing combination of length, breadth and depth than this one. A new Pew Research survey finds that 30 months after it began, the Great Recession has led to a downsizing of Americans' expectations about their retirements and their children's future; a new frugality in their spending and borrowing habits; and a concern that it could take several years, at a minimum, for their house values and family finances to recover. (Taylor)

Rose locates The Walking Dead in the historical context of the Great Recession.

Coming after a period of relatively stable economic times, the economic shock has created a great deal of fear and anger. And Americans are flocking to watch *The Walking Dead* in droves because they sense the parallels between the Great Recession and a zombie apocalypse. Though there have been cult-classic zombie movies in the past, never before has a zombie television show been so fervently embraced by such a widespread audience. What is the secret of its mainstream appeal, and what does the extreme popularity of *The Walking Dead* say about modern American society?

She poses a focusing question about the show's cultural significance.

One reason this show is so popular among a diverse audience is that today's TV viewers feel a strong connection between the characters' attempts to live through a zombie apocalypse and their own attempts to cope with modern life and, especially, their recent economic struggles. The zombie apocalypse depicted in *The Walking Dead* shares many similarities with the economic recession that America has been suffering since 2008. Both events affected everyone in the country, and not just a particular group. During both,

people lost homes, jobs, and a certain standard of living. People feel
like they are fighting just to survive and, most significantly, that
this catastrophe is not their fault, is beyond their control, and is
destroying their lives. Many feel that the government in some way
caused it, should have prevented it, and should take responsibility
for fixing it.

Rose links the characters' struggles with Americans' economic woes.

    Another reason for *The Walking Dead*'s popularity is that it
appeals to people who are highly critical of government entities
such as politicians, the military, and government agencies. This mistrust is reflected in one of the ways the show departs from previous
zombie movies. In most zombie movies, the protagonists' challenge
is something like "hold on until morning." That is, they have a set
amount of time they need to survive and then the government (the
military) will save them. Or, sometimes the challenge is to arrive
at a certain location where the government will take care of them.
However, in *The Walking Dead*, no encounter with any government
entity ends well. At the outset of the show, Rick is told that if he
can make it to Atlanta, the CDC (Centers for Disease Control) has a
base there that can help him. However, when he arrives, he finds
the city overrun with zombies, and when Rick and his companions,
including his wife and son, eventually do find the CDC compound,
it quickly becomes clear that the government will not be rescuing
anyone. All but one of the workers have either fled or committed
suicide. The government has failed to devise a cure for the virus that
is creating the zombies, and the building safety protocols almost
kill off the main cast of characters. In the end, one of their group
members and the last surviving CDC worker decide to stay behind
in the gas explosion that destroys the building, killing themselves
instead of continuing the struggle of living in the post-apocalyptic
world. That indicates how completely hopeless people are feeling. In
The Walking Dead, there is no magic cure, no government to come to
their rescue, no military to save them. They are on their own. This
parallel to the current economic environment is striking. People feel
abandoned by and afraid of their own government, left to fend for
themselves.

A compar- ison with other zombie movies points to a differ- ence within the system.

    Finally, the show's popularity spans across all demographics
because it is set in a total fantasy world open to one's own interpretation. In other words, viewers can choose to think of the "bad

guys," those responsible for the zombie apocalypse, as representing whomever they think are the bad guys in real life. As Leslie Savan states:

> Most of us watch because it's a terrific, suspenseful soap opera. But *TWD* also comes packed with a central metaphor—the zombie apocalypse—that can be used to explain just about every political point of view, whether right or left, pro-NRA or pro-gun control, small- or big-government, even pro-sequester or pro-stimulus. (Savan)

The Walking Dead airs on AMC, a TV channel that also broadcasts two other top-rated dramas: *Mad Men* and *Breaking Bad*. On the surface, these three shows could hardly seem more different. While *The Walking Dead* is a fairly standard horror show, *Mad Men* is a historical workplace drama set in the 1950s through 1960s in which most of the high-intensity moments come from whether or not an advertising deal will work out. And unlike both *Mad Men* and *The Walking Dead*, *Breaking Bad* is a modern-day reality show about a high school chemistry teacher who is diagnosed with terminal cancer and then begins dealing methamphetamine and becomes a drug lord. Although these three shows differ, they share the same attraction that makes them so popular today: All are chillingly realistic in their depiction of blood, guts, and a lot of naked skin. And this kind of realism is not exclusive to these three shows; most top television programs recently have followed this pattern, including comedies as well as dramas. *The Office*, *Parks and Recreation*, and *30 Rock* are three popular comedies that also present realistic portrayals of characters and situations. This becomes even more apparent in current fantasy and horror programs, including *The Walking Dead*, *Game of Thrones*, *Once upon a Time*, *Supernatural*, and *True Blood*, to name just a few. These shows tend to be very realistic in spite of their otherworldly concepts. Gone are the days of *Star Trek*'s shiny view of the future in which everything is clean and silver and everyone wears a uniform. TV's fantasy worlds are no longer clean, fun, or nice. They are dirty, trying, harsh places where people are cruel and life is difficult. In other words, they are just like reality but with zombies and vampires. People living through extremely difficult times, worrying about losing their jobs and their homes, can identify

Rose connects The Walking Dead *to other related TV programs.*

with the fear that monsters are threatening them. It seems very real to them, and they want their shows to display the same nitty-gritty realism they face in their lives. Anything less would seem superficial and irrelevant.

This realism also applies to the characters. Most of the protag- onists of previous decades were good, upstanding people: doctors, lawyers, fathers, and heroes. They were men, primarily, who did what they knew was right and stood for truth and justice. These days, however, those types of characters are viewed as old-fashioned, one-dimensional, and frankly silly. Instead, today's protagonists are flawed, sometimes immoral, characters, most of whom the aver- age viewer would not want to meet. Viewers identify with complex characters with a lot of wiggle room in their moral structures, such as a serial killer with a conscience, murderers who are also great fathers, sheriffs who disregard the law, and vampires who love and protect. According to Stephen Garrett in "Why We Love TV's Anti- heroes," "The heroes of today are radically different from those of two or three decades ago. They have evolved to represent a radically changed world" (319). Garrett goes on to state that in the past the difference between good and evil was clear, or, as he puts it, "There were never better baddies than the Nazis, and the causes, as well as the purposes, of the Second World War were crystal clear" (319). But now, Garrett explains, our wars are much less cut-and-dried. Conflicts now have "an element of moral ambiguity built into them" (319). Is it any wonder that, given such a change in our national moral compass, we would want television heroes who are likewise morally ambiguous? Gone are the days of the father character who comes home at five o'clock to pick up his pipe, listen to the prob- lems of the wife and children, and lay down a simple solution. Gone are the days of the doctors who can cure all ills, the lawyers who always follow the law, and the police officers who adhere firmly to their moral codes. Characters now must exist in some kind of moral gray area, or else they will seem irrelevant to today's viewers. *The Walking Dead* fills that need quite well.

Zombies are a popular cultural phenomenon right now. *The Walking Dead*, *Warm Bodies*, plus countless zombie events such as zombie walks and runs in which large groups of people get together and dress as zombies, all point to a societal fascination with the

The focus narrows to an interpre- tation of the characters.

Rose locates the show in the larger context of supernatural monster dramas.

concept of zombies. In fact, people seem interested in all kinds of undead beings. Vampires are, arguably, the most popular fantasy "creatures" right now, although contemporary vampires are no longer the monsters they once were. Vampires have become more human, more sympathetic, and much more sexy. Ever since another TV series, *Buffy the Vampire Slayer*, introduced the character of Angel as a sexy, brooding vampire with a soul, and with whom the title character, Buffy, was destined to fall in love, vampires have changed from bloodsucking monsters to bloodsucking heroes. As stated in *Signs of Life in the U.S.A.*, "To put it simply: Vampires are hot. From *True Blood* to *Twilight*, *The Vampire Diaries* to *The Gates*, contemporary popular culture is awash in vampire stories" (Maasik and Solomon 1). However, though vampires are still intensely popular, there appears to also be a continuing strong market for other types of supernatural monster drama, such as zombies.

The zombie movie has been a popular genre for decades, and the movie *Night of the Living Dead*, written and directed by George A. Romero, made zombie movies a staple of Hollywood. *The Walking Dead* has taken that popularity to a new level, however, because people facing their own fears and struggles seem to respond to the extremely realistic portrayal of the struggle of humans against zombies, who are, of course, a terrifying and perverted form of humans themselves. They reflect people's feelings of powerlessness and fear that they, their community, or their government will be "taken over" by evildoers. As Lee Roberts states, "The attraction of some to the zombie and the genre of films in which they appear represents an inner desire to place blame for society's misgivings on the establishment, i.e., big business, big government, etc., and use the zombie as the most logical outcome if the establishment were to be left unchecked by a complacent population" (Roberts).

Although *The Walking Dead*'s appeal may be that viewers strongly identify with characters who are fighting a battle against terrifying unknown forces, people who are insecure and fearful often cling to the known and even return to traditional behaviors and values. In a return to outdated gender roles, *The Walking Dead* portrays women as powerless and ineffective and men as strong and competent. Perhaps this indicates a desire on the part of the audience to go back to the 1950s, a more optimistic era when Americans

She argues that the show appeals to traditional values and explains why.

had great hopes of increasing affluence and an always-increasing standard of living, but it also means a return to a time when women were weak and subservient to men.

In this show, what little power the women may have is frequently stripped away. In a show in which characters rely heavily on weapons, the women lack the training to use them, but the men are portrayed as fully competent with various weapons and prevent the women from obtaining or holding on to them. In the second season, one of the male characters, Dale, decides that it is no longer prudent for Andrea, a young woman, to carry a gun. Although Dale holds no real authority over her and the gun is legally hers, Andrea barely protests Dale's confiscation of the gun. In fact, the only real fight she gives is asking for Shane, another male character, to back her up. Shane sides with Dale, saying that until everyone is trained in the use of guns, the fewer they have "floating around camp," the better ("What Lies Ahead"). Andrea accepts this with little argument. So, in a traditional and patriarchal way, the men get to decide who has the weapons and the men generally carry the weapons and protect the women and children. For a show set in a contemporary setting, this is strikingly old-fashioned. In addition, females in the show are generally incompetent. Andrea, while still in possession of her gun, does not know how to clean it herself and, when attacked by a zombie, has the entire thing in pieces. Instead of successfully staying quiet and hidden, she attracts the zombie's attention and must rely on Dale's weapon in order to save herself. Lori often says things that are viewed by the other characters as weak or ignorant. When the group stumbles upon a veritable gold mine of supplies in the form of a pileup of old cars, Lori emotionally tries to persuade them not to use the supplies by saying "This is a graveyard" ("What Lies Ahead"). The others simply ignore her (female) sentimentality. When hiding from a group of zombies, it is Sophia, a young girl, not Carl, her male counterpart, who attracts the attention of two zombies and has to run off into the woods to hide. And then only the male characters go out to search for her.

Specific details support her claim about traditional values.

Overall, this show reinforces very strong, traditional gender roles. The women are soft-spoken, weak, and mothering. They do not carry weapons, they are ineffectual fighters, and they require almost constant protection by the men. They worry about clothes and hygiene in spite of the terrors surrounding them. The show goes so far as to show a group of women washing clothes and gossiping while a man looks on as protection. The men, on the other hand, are strong and capable. They carry guns and other weapons and can take care of themselves (and the women). They rarely require help from others and never from a woman. They are the doers — they come up with the plans and put them into action. The women are carried along in their wake. Without the men, the women would not last a day. Without the women, the men would have a much easier time surviving. In a time when many people feel somewhat uncertain about gender roles, the show roots itself securely in a more comfortable (for some, anyway) past.

Rose returns to history as her essay draws to a close.

Both the Great Depression and the Great Recession began after years of economic prosperity, and the 2008 recession was the worst economic downturn since the Great Depression. But the entertainment choices during the 1930s were very different from those today. During the 1930s, Shirley Temple, a precocious child star, was the number one box office hit, and many found her movies to offer a temporary break from the misery and fear of the depressed economic state. "President Franklin Delano Roosevelt proclaimed that 'as long as our country has Shirley Temple, we will be all right'" ("Shirley Temple Black"). But now people seem to be looking for something else in their entertainment, immersing themselves in a terrifying zombie apocalypse. Why is this? Is it due to differences between the Great Depression and the Great Recession? According to National Public Radio, "Even though both events were momentous enough to earn the word 'great' as a modifier, they really are not comparable, according to recent research by economist Mark Vaughan, a fellow at the Weidenbaum Center on the Economy at Washington University in St. Louis" (qtd. in Geewax). Vaughn goes on to explain that the recent recession "pales in magnitude" with the Great Depression: "The Great Depression was painful in ways we can scarcely imagine now because we have grown so accustomed to having a government-funded safety net" (qtd. in Geewax).

In the 1930s, the public did not initially blame the government for the unemployment problem: This was prior to the passage of the Employment Act of 1946, which made the government responsible for maintaining high employment. In 2008, on the other hand, people felt betrayed and blamed the government and big business for the recession. During the Great Depression, people looked to entertainment as an escape from the frustrations of everyday life, while people today are, instead, looking for characters they can identify with as suffering victims being let down by the establishment and forced to take things into their own hands.

Rose encapsulates her answer to her opening question about the show's popularity.

The Walking Dead is a fairly well-written show with good acting and generally good special effects, and it tugs at emotional heartstrings and keeps the audience on the edge of their seats. But more than that, the show managed to come on the scene at just the perfect time when Americans were angry with government, angry with the establishment, and looking for a way to vent their frustrations. *The Walking Dead* is generic enough that all Americans can relate to it and, therefore, they can use it as a way to vicariously fight the recession without actually stepping out of their front doors.

Works Cited

Garrett, Stephen. "Why We Love TV's Antiheroes." Maasik and Solomon, pp. 318–21.

Geewax, Marilyn. "Did the Great Recession Bring Back the 1930s?" *NPR*, 11 July 2012, www.npr.org/2012/07/11/155991507 /did-the-great-recession-bring-back-the-1930s.

Maasik, Sonia, and Jack Solomon, editors. *Signs of Life in the U.S.A.: Readings on Popular Culture for Writers*, 7th ed., Bedford/St. Martin's, 2012.

Roberts, Lee. "Zombie Movie History: A Reference for Zombie Masters." *Best Horror Movies*, 2012, BestHorrorMovies.com. Accessed 6 May 2013.

Savan, Leslie. "Whose Side Is *The Walking Dead* On? *The Nation*, www .thenation.com/article/whose-side-walking-dead/. Accessed 6 May 2013.

"Shirley Temple Black." *The John F. Kennedy Center for the Performing Arts*, www.kennedy-center.org/. Accessed 6 May 2013.

Taylor, Paul, ed. "How the Great Recession Has Changed Life in America." *Pew Research Social & Demographic Trends*, 30 June 2010,

www.pewsocialtrends.org/2010/06/30/how-the-great
-recession-has-changed-life-in-america/. Accessed 6 May 2013.

"The Walking Dead (Season 1)." *Wikipedia*, 30 Apr. 2013,
en.wikipedia.org/wiki/The_Walking_Dead_(season_1). Accessed
6 May 2013.

"What Lies Ahead." *The Walking Dead*. Directed by Ernest Dickerson
and Gwyneth Horder-Payton. AMC, 16 Oct. 2011.

CONDUCTING RESEARCH AND CITING SOURCES

Your instructor may ask you to use secondary sources to support your analyses of popular culture. These sources may include a wide variety of published materials, from other essays (such as those featured in this book) to interviews you conduct to YouTube videos. When you write about popular culture, a host of sources are available to you to help lend weight to your arguments as well as help you develop fresh thinking about your topic.

The Internet age has afforded us innovative research opportunities, and with a wealth of information at your fingertips, it is up to you, the writer, to learn to determine which sources you should trust and which you should be suspicious of. As always, the library is a great place to begin. Research librarians continue to be excellent resources not only for finding sources for your papers, but for learning best practices for conducting research. It is more than likely that they are aware of resources at your disposal that you haven't considered, from academic databases like EBSCOhost to library catalogs to film and video archives.

The following selections offer additional help for conducting academically sound research online.

SCOTT JASCHIK

A Stand against Wikipedia

Increasingly, college faculty are concerned about the widespread use of Wikipedia in student research and writing. The problem, as faculty see it, is twofold. First, there is the problem of reliability. Wikipedia does strive to provide reliable information, but given the wide-open nature of the site — anyone can contribute — ensuring accuracy is not really possible. This leads to student work that can disseminate misinformation. Second, even where Wikipedia is accurate (and it can be an accurate source of information), it is, after all, an encyclopedia, and while encyclopedic sources may be suitable for background information, students performing college-level research should seek primary sources and academic-level secondary sources that they find on their own. The following article from insidehighered.com surveys the problems with Wikipedia as a research source as seen by college faculty from a number of universities.

As Wikipedia has become more and more popular with students, some professors have become increasingly concerned about the online, reader-produced encyclopedia.

While plenty of professors have complained about the lack of accuracy or completeness of entries, and some have discouraged or tried to bar students from using it, the history department at Middlebury College is trying to take a stronger, collective stand. It voted this month to bar students from citing the Web site as a source in papers or other academic work. All faculty members will be telling students about the policy and explaining why material on Wikipedia — while convenient — may not be trustworthy. "As educators, we are in the business of reducing the dissemination of misinformation," said Don Wyatt, chair of the department. "Even though Wikipedia may have some value, particularly from the value of leading students to citable sources, it is not itself an appropriate source for citation," he said.

The department made what Wyatt termed a consensus decision on the issue after discussing problems professors were seeing as students cited incorrect information from Wikipedia in papers and on tests. In one instance, Wyatt said, a professor noticed several students offering the same incorrect information, from Wikipedia. There was some discussion in the department of trying to ban students from using Wikipedia, but Wyatt said that didn't seem appropriate. Many Wikipedia entries have good bibliographies, Wyatt said. And any absolute ban would just be ignored. "There's the issue of freedom of access," he said. "And I'm not in the business of promulgating unenforceable edicts."

Wyatt said that the department did not specify punishments for citing Wikipedia, and that the primary purpose of the policy was to educate, not to be punitive. He said he doubted that a paper would be rejected for having a single Wikipedia footnote, but that students would be told that they shouldn't do so, and that multiple violations would result in reduced grades or even a failure. "The important point that we wish to communicate to all students taking courses and submitting work in our department in the future is that they cite Wikipedia at their peril," he said. He stressed that the objection of the department to Wikipedia wasn't its online nature, but its unedited nature, and he said students need to be taught to go for quality information, not just convenience.

The frustrations of Middlebury faculty members are by no means unique. 5 Last year, Alan Liu, a professor of English at the University of California at Santa Barbara, adopted a policy that Wikipedia "is not appropriate as the primary or sole reference for anything that is central to an argument, complex, or controversial." Liu said that it was too early to tell what impact his policy is having. In explaining his rationale — which he shared with an e-mail list — he wrote that he had "just read a paper about the relation between structuralism, deconstruction, and postmodernism in which every reference was to the Wikipedia articles on those topics with no awareness that there was any need to read a primary work or even a critical work."

Wikipedia officials agree — in part — with Middlebury's history department. "That's a sensible policy," Sandra Ordonez, a spokeswoman, said in an e-mail interview. "Wikipedia is the ideal place to start your research and get a global picture of a topic; however, it is not an authoritative source. In fact, we recommend that students check the facts they find in Wikipedia against other sources. Additionally, it is generally good research practice to cite an original source when writing a paper, or completing an exam. It's usually not advisable, particularly at the university level, to cite an encyclopedia." Ordonez acknowledged that, given the collaborative nature of Wikipedia writing and editing, "there is no guarantee an article is 100 percent correct," but she said that the site is shifting its focus from growth to improving quality, and that the site is a great resource for students. "Most articles are continually being edited and improved upon, and most contributors are real lovers of knowledge who have a real desire to improve the quality of a particular article," she said.

Experts on digital media said that the Middlebury history professors' reaction was understandable and reflects growing concern among faculty members about the accuracy of what students find online. But some worry that bans on citing Wikipedia may not deal with the underlying issues.

Roy Rosenzweig, director of the Center for History and New Media at George Mason University, did an analysis of the accuracy of Wikipedia for the *Journal of American History*, and he found that in many entries, Wikipedia was as accurate as or more accurate than more traditional encyclopedias. He said that the quality of material was inconsistent, and that biographical entries were generally well done, while more thematic entries were much less so. Like Ordonez, he said the real problem is one of college students using encyclopedias when they should be using more advanced sources. "College students shouldn't be citing encyclopedias in their papers," he said. "That's not what college is about. They either should be using primary sources or serious secondary sources."

In the world of college librarians, a major topic of late has been how to guide students in the right direction for research, when Wikipedia and similar sources are so easy. Some of those who have been involved in these discussions said that the Middlebury history department's action pointed to the need for more outreach to students. Lisa Hinchliffe, head of the undergraduate library and coordinator of information literacy at the University of Illinois at Urbana-Champaign, said that earlier generations of students were in fact taught when it was appropriate (or not) to consult an encyclopedia and why for many a paper they would never even cite a popular magazine or nonscholarly work. "But it was a relatively constrained landscape," and students didn't have easy access to anything equivalent to Wikipedia, she said. "It's not that students are being lazy today. It's a much more complex environment."

When she has taught, and spotted footnotes to sources that aren't appropriate, she's considered that "a teachable moment," Hinchliffe said. She said that she would be interested to see how Middlebury professors react when they get the first violations of their policy, and said she thought there could be positive discussions about why sources are or aren't good ones. That kind of teaching, she said, is important "and can be challenging." 10

Steven Bell, associate librarian for research and instructional services at Temple University, said of the Middlebury approach: "I applaud the effort for wanting to direct students to good quality resources," but he said he would go about it in a different way. "I understand what their concerns are. There's no question that [on Wikipedia and similar sites] some things are great and some things are questionable. Some of the pages could be by eighth graders," he said. "But to simply say 'don't use that one' might take students in the wrong direction from the perspective of information literacy."

Students face "an ocean of information" today, much of it of poor quality, so a better approach would be to teach students how to "triangulate" a source like Wikipedia, so they could use other sources to tell whether a given entry could be trusted. "I think our goal should be to equip students with the critical thinking skills to judge."

PATTI S. CARAVELLO

Judging Quality on the Web

When you conduct research on the Internet, you'll find a dizzying range of sources, from academic journals to government Web sites, from newspapers and popular magazines to blogs, wikis, and social networking and file-sharing sites. Having a plethora of sources at hand with just the click of a mouse has been a boon to researchers in all fields. But the very democratic basis of the Internet that makes all this information so readily available creates a challenge, for it comes with no guarantees of quality control. Indeed, it is incumbent upon you, the researcher, to determine the reliability of the Web sources that you use. The following article from the UCLA Library's Web site, "Judging Quality on the Web," lists criteria that will allow you to evaluate the usefulness and reliability of Internet sources.

Even after refining a query in a search engine, a researcher often retrieves a huge number of Web sites. It is essential to know how to evaluate Web sites for the same reasons you would evaluate a periodical article or a book: *to ascertain whether you can rely on the information, to identify its inherent biases or limitations, and to see how or whether it fits into your overall research strategy.*

A good (useful, reliable) Web site:

1. Clearly states the author and/or organizational **source** of the information
   Your task:
   - Consider the qualifications, other works, and organizational affiliation of the author
   - Look up the organization which produced the Web site (if it's unfamiliar) to identify its credentials, viewpoint, or agenda
   - If the source is an E-journal, discover whether it is refereed (reviewed by scholars before it is accepted for publication)

2. Clearly states the **date** the material was written and the date the site was last revised
   Your task:
   - If the information is not current enough for your purposes or the date is not given, look elsewhere

3. Provides **accurate** data whose parameters are clearly defined
   Your task:
   - Compare the data found on the Web site with data found in other sources (encyclopedias, reference books, articles, etc.) for accuracy, completeness, recency
   - Ask a librarian about other important sources to check for this information

4. Provides the **type and level** of information you need
   Your task:
   - Decide whether the level of detail and comprehensiveness, the treatment of the topic (e.g., scholarly or popular), and the graphics or other features are acceptable
   - If the site does not provide the depth of coverage you need, look elsewhere

5. Keeps **bias** to a minimum, and clearly indicates point of view
   Your task:
   - Be aware that producing a Web page does not require the checking and review that publishing a scholarly book requires; you might have retrieved nothing but someone's personal opinion on the topic
   - Appealing graphics can distract you from noticing even overt bias, so heighten your skepticism and examine the evidence (source, date, accuracy, level, links)

6. Provides live **links** to related high-quality Web sites
   Your task:
   - Click on several of the links provided to see if they are active (or if they give an "error" message indicating the links are not being maintained) and to see if they are useful
   - Check to see if the criteria are stated for selecting the links

7. In the case of **commercial** sites, keeps advertising separate from content, and does not let advertisers determine content
   Your task:
   - Look at the Web address: Sites that are commercial have *.com* in their addresses and might have advertising or offer to sell something. The *.com* suffix is also found in news sites (e.g., newspapers, TV networks) and personal pages (sites created by individuals who have purchased a domain name but who may or may not have a commercial or institutional affiliation)

8. Is clearly organized and **designed** for ease of use
   Your task:
   - Move around the page to see if its organization makes sense and it is easy to return to the top or to the sections you need
   - Decide whether the graphics enhance the content or detract from it

TRIP GABRIEL

For Students in Internet Age, No Shame in Copy and Paste

The Internet is an invaluable source for information about popular
culture, both because of its instant accessibility and because of its
ability to keep pace with the rapid turnover in popular fashions and
trends in a way that print-technology publication never can. But, as
is so often the case with the Internet, there is a downside to the matter. Because, as Trip Gabriel observes in this feature that originally
appeared in the *New York Times*, "concepts of intellectual property,
copyright, and originality are under assault in the unbridled exchange
of online information," the result is a pandemic of inadvertent,
and sometimes deliberate, plagiarism. Certainly in an era of group-
oriented writing — as on Wikipedia — traditional notions of individual authorship are being deconstructed, which makes it all the more
important that students learn in their writing classes what the conventions for documentation are and why they are still necessary. Trip
Gabriel is a longtime reporter, and former Styles editor, at the *New
York Times*.

At Rhode Island College, a freshman copied and pasted from a Web site's
frequently asked questions page about homelessness — and did not think he
needed to credit a source in his assignment because the page did not include
author information.

At DePaul University, the tip-off to one student's copying was the purple
shade of several paragraphs he had lifted from the Web; when confronted by
a writing tutor his professor had sent him to, he was not defensive — he just
wanted to know how to change purple text to black.

And at the University of Maryland, a student reprimanded for copying from Wikipedia in a paper on the Great Depression said he thought its
entries — unsigned and collectively written — did not need to be credited since
they counted, essentially, as common knowledge.

Professors used to deal with plagiarism by admonishing students to give credit
to others and to follow the style guide for citations, and pretty much left it at that.

But these cases — typical ones, according to writing tutors and officials 5
responsible for discipline at the three schools who described the plagiarism —
suggest that many students simply do not grasp that using words they did not
write is a serious misdeed.

It is a disconnect that is growing in the Internet age as concepts of intellectual property, copyright and originality are under assault in the unbridled
exchange of online information, say educators who study plagiarism.

Digital technology makes copying and pasting easy, of course. But that is the least of it. The Internet may also be redefining how students — who came of age with music file-sharing, Wikipedia and Web-linking — understand the concept of authorship and the singularity of any text or image.

"Now we have a whole generation of students who've grown up with information that just seems to be hanging out there in cyberspace and doesn't seem to have an author," said Teresa Fishman, director of the Center for Academic Integrity at Clemson University. "It's possible to believe this information is just out there for anyone to take."

Professors who have studied plagiarism do not try to excuse it — many are champions of academic honesty on their campuses — but rather try to understand why it is so widespread.

In surveys from 2006 to 2010 by Donald L. McCabe, a co-founder of the 10 Center for Academic Integrity and a business professor at Rutgers University, about 40 percent of 14,000 undergraduates admitted to copying a few sentences in written assignments.

Perhaps more significant, the number who believed that copying from the Web constitutes "serious cheating" is declining — to 29 percent on average in recent surveys from 34 percent earlier in the decade.

Sarah Brookover, a senior at the Rutgers campus in Camden, N.J., said many of her classmates blithely cut and paste without attribution.

"This generation has always existed in a world where media and intellectual property don't have the same gravity," said Ms. Brookover, who at 31 is older than most undergraduates. "When you're sitting at your computer, it's the same machine you've downloaded music with, possibly illegally, the same machine you streamed videos for free that showed on HBO last night."

Ms. Brookover, who works at the campus library, has pondered the differences between researching in the stacks and online. "Because you're not walking into a library, you're not physically holding the article, which takes you closer to 'this doesn't belong to me,'" she said. Online, "everything can belong to you really easily."

A University of Notre Dame anthropologist, Susan D. Blum, disturbed by 15 the high rates of reported plagiarism, set out to understand how students view authorship and the written word, or "texts" in Ms. Blum's academic language.

She conducted her ethnographic research among 234 Notre Dame undergraduates. "Today's students stand at the crossroads of a new way of conceiving texts and the people who create them and who quote them," she wrote last year in the book *My Word!: Plagiarism and College Culture*, published by Cornell University Press.

Ms. Blum argued that student writing exhibits some of the same qualities of pastiche that drive other creative endeavors today — TV shows that constantly reference other shows or rap music that samples from earlier songs.

In an interview, she said the idea of an author whose singular effort creates an original work is rooted in Enlightenment ideas of the individual. It is buttressed by the Western concept of intellectual property rights as secured by copyright law. But both traditions are being challenged.

"Our notion of authorship and originality was born, it flourished, and it may be waning," Ms. Blum said.

She contends that undergraduates are less interested in cultivating a 20 unique and authentic identity — as their 1960s counterparts were — than in trying on many different personas, which the Web enables with social networking.

"If you are not so worried about presenting yourself as absolutely unique, then it's O.K. if you say other people's words, it's O.K. if you say things you don't believe, it's O.K. if you write papers you couldn't care less about because they accomplish the task, which is turning something in and getting a grade," Ms. Blum said, voicing student attitudes. "And it's O.K. if you put words out there without getting any credit."

The notion that there might be a new model young person, who freely borrows from the vortex of information to mash up a new creative work, fueled a brief brouhaha earlier this year with Helene Hegemann, a German teenager whose best-selling novel about Berlin club life turned out to include passages lifted from others.

Instead of offering an abject apology, Ms. Hegemann insisted, "There's no such thing as originality anyway, just authenticity." A few critics rose to her defense, and the book remained a finalist for a fiction prize (but did not win).

That theory does not wash with Sarah Wilensky, a senior at Indiana University, who said that relaxing plagiarism standards "does not foster creativity, it fosters laziness."

"You're not coming up with new ideas if you're grabbing and mixing and 25 matching," said Ms. Wilensky, who took aim at Ms. Hegemann in a column in her student newspaper headlined "Generation Plagiarism."

"It may be increasingly accepted, but there are still plenty of creative people — authors and artists and scholars — who are doing original work," Ms. Wilensky said in an interview. "It's kind of an insult that that ideal is gone, and now we're left only to make collages of the work of previous generations."

In the view of Ms. Wilensky, whose writing skills earned her the role of informal editor of other students' papers in her freshman dorm, plagiarism has nothing to do with trendy academic theories.

The main reason it occurs, she said, is because students leave high school unprepared for the intellectual rigors of college writing.

"If you're taught how to closely read sources and synthesize them into your own original argument in middle and high school, you're not going to be tempted to plagiarize in college, and you certainly won't do so unknowingly," she said.

At the University of California, Davis, of the 196 plagiarism cases referred 30 to the disciplinary office last year, a majority did not involve students ignorant of the need to credit the writing of others.

Many times, said Donald J. Dudley, who oversees the discipline office on the campus of 32,000, it was students who intentionally copied — knowing it was wrong — who were "unwilling to engage the writing process."

"Writing is difficult, and doing it well takes time and practice," he said.

And then there was a case that had nothing to do with a younger generation's evolving view of authorship. A student accused of plagiarism came to Mr. Dudley's office with her parents, and the father admitted that he was the one responsible for the plagiarism. The wife assured Mr. Dudley that it would not happen again.

Synthesizing and Citing Sources

One of the questions you might ask yourself as you write is, "How many sources do I need?" Your instructor may give you guidance, but questions of exactly when you need to employ the support of other authors is up to you. Synthesis in academic writing refers to the incorporation of sources into your writing. As you develop your arguments, you will want to look at your sources and consider how what they say interacts with your own opinions. Do you see any similarities between what you want to write and what your sources say, or will you be faced with the task of discussing how your sources don't see your topic the way you do? Think of your paper as a conversation between you and your sources. As you write, ask yourself where you and your sources agree and disagree, and make sure you account for this in your paper. You might want to ask yourself the following questions:

- Have I used my sources as evidence to support any claims I'm making?
- Have I considered any counterarguments?
- Have I taken care to characterize my sources in a way that is fair and accurate?
- When I have finished my draft, have I reconsidered my thesis in light of the source material I've used? Do I need to change my thesis to reflect any new discoveries I've made?

Finally, you will want to make sure you have properly documented any sources you use in your papers. When you write an essay and use another author's work — whether you use the author's exact words or paraphrase them — you need to cite that source for your readers. In most humanities courses, writers use the system of documentation developed by the Modern Language Association (MLA). This system indicates a source in two ways: (1) notations that briefly identify the sources in the body of your essay and (2) notations that give fuller bibliographic information about the sources at the end of your essay. The notations for some commonly used types of sources are illustrated in this chapter. For documenting other sources, consult a writing handbook or the *MLA Handbook*, Eighth Edition (New York: Modern Language Association of America, 2016).

In-Text Citations

In the body of your essay, you should signal to your reader that you've used a source and indicate, in parentheses, where your reader can find the source in your list of works cited. You don't need to repeat the author's name in both your writing and in the parenthetical note.

SOURCE WITH ONE AUTHOR

Patrick Goldstein asserts that "Talk radio has pumped up the volume of our public discourse and created a whole new political language — perhaps the prevailing political language" (16).

SOURCE WITH TWO AUTHORS

Researchers have found it difficult to study biker subcultures because, as one team describes the problem, "it was too dangerous to take issue with outlaws on their own turf" (Hooper and Moore 368).

INDIRECT SOURCE

In discussing the baby mania trend, *Time* claimed, "Career women are opting for pregnancy and they are doing it in style" (qtd. in Faludi 106).

List of Works Cited

At the end of your essay, include a list of all the sources you have cited in parenthetical notations. This list, alphabetized by author, should provide full publication information for each source; you should indicate the date you accessed any online sources.

The first line of each entry should begin flush left. Subsequent lines should be indented half an inch (or five spaces) from the left margin. Double-space the entire list, both between and within entries.

Nonelectronic Sources

BOOK BY ONE AUTHOR

Whitehead, Colson. *The Underground Railroad*. Doubleday, 2016.

BOOK BY TWO AUTHORS

Stiglitz, Joseph E., and Bruce C. Greenwald. *Creating a Learning Society: A New Approach to Growth, Development, and Social Progress*. Columbia UP, 2015.
(Note that only the first author's name is reversed.)

BOOK BY THREE OR MORE AUTHORS

Cunningham, Stewart, et al. *Media Economics*. Palgrave Macmillan, 2015.

WORK IN AN ANTHOLOGY

Corbett, Julia B. "A Faint Green Sell: Advertising and the Natural World." *Signs of Life in the U.S.A.: Readings on Popular Culture for Writers*, 9th ed., edited by Sonia Maasik and Jack Solomon, Bedford/St. Martin's, 2017. p. 209.

ARTICLE IN A WEEKLY MAGAZINE

Grossman, Lev. "A Star Is Born." *Time*, 2 Nov. 2015, pp. 30+.

(A plus sign is used to indicate that the article is not printed on consecutive pages; otherwise, a page range should be given: 16–25, for example.)

ARTICLE IN A MONTHLY MAGAZINE

Kunzig, Robert. "The Will to Change." *National Geographic*, Nov. 2015, pp. 32–63.

ARTICLE IN A JOURNAL

Matchie, Thomas. "Law versus Love in *The Round House*." *Midwest Quarterly*, vol. 56, no. 4, Summer 2015, pp. 353–64.

PERSONAL INTERVIEW

Chese, Charlie. Personal interview. 28 Sept. 2017.

Electronic Sources

FILM OR DVD

Scott, Ridley, director. *The Martian*. Performances by Matt Damon, Jessica Chastain, Kristen Wiig, and Kate Mara, Twentieth Century Fox, 2015.

Ghostbusters. Directed by Paul Feig, performances by Kristen Wiig, Melissa McCarthy, Kate McKinnon, Leslie Jones, Sony Pictures, 2016.

TELEVISION PROGRAM

The Daily Show with Trevor Noah. Comedy Central, 3 Feb. 2017.

SOUND RECORDING

Adele. "Hello." 25, XL, 2015.

E-MAIL

Katt, Susie. "Interpreting the Mall." Message to the author. 29 Sept. 2017.

ARTICLE IN AN ONLINE REFERENCE BOOK

Hall, Mark. "Facebook (American Company)." *The Enyclopaedia Britannica*, 30 Nov. 2015, www.britannica.com/topic/Facebook.

ARTICLE IN AN ONLINE JOURNAL

Boetzkes, Amanda. "Resource Systems, the Paradigm of Zero-Waste, and the Desire for Sustenance." *Postmodern Culture*, vol. 26, no. 2, January 2016. Project MUSE, doi:10.1353/pmc.2016.0008.

ARTICLE IN AN ONLINE MAGAZINE

Mele, Nicco and Neiman Reports. "Television Is Having Its Moment." *Salon*, 14 Nov. 2016, www.
salon.com/2016/11/14/telivision-is-having-its-moment/.

ONLINE BOOK

Euripides. *The Trojan Women*. Translated by Gilbert Murray, Oxford University Press, 1915.
Internet Sacred Text Archive, 2011, www.sacred-texts.com/cla/eurip/troj_w.htm.

ONLINE POEM

Geisel, Theodor. "Too Many Daves." *The Sneetches and Other Stories*. Random House, 1961.
Poetry Foundation, 2015, www.poetryfoundation.org/poem/171612.

PROFESSIONAL WEB SITE

National Council of Teachers of English. *National Council of Teachers of English*.
2014, www.ncte.org/.

PERSONAL HOME PAGE

Stallman, Richard. Home page, 2016, stallman.org/.

POSTING TO A DISCUSSION LIST

Yen, Jessica. "Quotations within Parentheses (Study Measures)." *Copyediting-L*, 18 Mar. 2016,
list.indiana.edu/sympa/arc/copyediting-l/2016-03/msg00492.html.

ONLINE SCHOLARLY PROJECT

Peter S. Donaldson, director. *MIT Global Shakespeares*. Massachusetts Institute of Technology,
2010. globalshakespeares.mit.edu/#.

WORK FROM A DATABASE SERVICE

Macari, Anne Marie. "Lyric Impulse in a Time of Extinction." *American Poetry Review*, vol. 44,
no. 4, July/Aug. 2015, pp. 11–14. *General OneFile*, go.galegroup.com/.

YOUTUBE OR OTHER ONLINE VIDEO

vlogbrothers. "Compassion, Weakness, and the 2016 Election." *YouTube*, 14 Oct. 2016, www.
youtube.com/watch?v=BC7JRRlZHHI.

PHOTOGRAPH OR WORK OF ART

Bradford, Mark. *Let's Walk to the Middle of the Ocean*. 2015, Museum of Modern Art, New York.
Clough, Charles. *January Twenty-First*. 1988–89, Joslyn Art Museum, Omaha, www.joslyn.
org/collections-and-exhibitions/permanent-collections/modern-and-contemporary/
charles-clough-january-twenty-first/.

1

CONSUMING PASSIONS

The Culture of American Consumption

The CCI

The CCI is one of the most avidly watched broadcasts in America, and, no, it isn't a television crime series. Based on the monthly Consumer Confidence Survey, as issued by The Conference Board (a private, nonprofit organization that, in its own words, "is a global, independent business membership and research association working in the public interest"), the Consumer Confidence Index (CCI) charts the mood of American consumers. When the index goes up, the stock market goes up; when it goes down, the stock market goes down with it.

What does this have to do with popular culture? The short answer is "everything" because American popular culture is grounded in consumption, whether we're considering the direct purchase of goods and services; the enjoyment of music, movies, and television; or simply the use of a smartphone or other digital devices and all that they offer you. That's why your Facebook page, Instagram account, and Snapchat activities are free; it's why commercial television and radio are free as well. Such media are free because they're underwritten by advertising and marketing expenditures made by companies that want to sell you something. While movies, for their part, are usually not free, they themselves are commodities to be consumed through the purchase of theater tickets, DVDs, cable subscriptions, Netflix or Redbox accounts, and so on. Music, too, is a commodity, whether consumed via download, CD, or vinyl (yes, there has been a small resurgence of that most venerable of music technologies). In short, American popular culture is grounded in a consumer society, and that's why this chapter appears first in this book.

The fact that ours is a consumer society has profound cultural implications. Perhaps the most critical is the way that consumerism has redirected middle-class values, once grounded in thrift, self-denial, and hard work (as descended from the Protestant work ethic), toward a new consciousness devoted to instant gratification, luxury, and pleasure. Once the preserve of a tiny leisure-class minority, such values have not simply transformed America from a producer to a consumer society. Ultimately, they have also come to endanger the very environment in which we live for the simple reason that the current levels of consumption in America are simply not environmentally sustainable.

But there's little chance that America's consumerist consciousness will be abating in the foreseeable future because consumption is not only a source of economic activity and personal pleasure; it is also a form of communication. That is to say, our possessions aren't simply objects, they're **signs** — from the out-and-out status symbols whose purpose is to convey your place in the social hierarchy, to the clothes you wear, the music you listen to, and even the smartphone you choose to buy — all of which convey to others what sort of person you are and what your values may be. Like all signs, they get their meaning from the cultural **systems**, or **codes**, within which they appear, and their meanings can change as history reworks the systems that define them. To see how, let's look at a consumer trend that has been in fashion for many years and looks to continue for quite some time to come.

The Skinny on Skinny Jeans

Once again, it all begins with a **difference**: in this case, baggy versus skinny.

From the 1980s through the 1990s and into the early 2000s, baggy jeans were the jean style of choice for many young Americans, especially boys and men. That changed sometime early in the new millennium, when decidedly tight jeans exploded into popularity for both men and women. In itself, such a difference would appear to be meaningless, but when systematically situated within the history of blue jeans and the meanings that jeans have conveyed over the years, this difference becomes significant — in fact, rather complicatedly significant.

So let's look at some history. Blue jeans first appeared in the nineteenth century when Levi Strauss tailored durable denim cloth into trousers for the miners in the California Gold Rush. As such, their **denotation** was simply the pants themselves. But given their use by men engaged in heavy manual labor, those trousers came to **connote**, or signify, "working-class clothing," with cowboys being the most glamorous of their wearers. By the 1950s, however, blue jeans began to bear an additional class significance as "casual wear" for middle-class Americans. But whether they connoted working-class or casual middle-class wear, by the mid-twentieth century blue jeans were still regarded as unsuitable for formal middle-class attire, either in school or on the job.

LEVI'S
AMERICA'S FINEST
OVERALL
SINCE 1850

RUGGED as the
men who wear 'em!

GO TO YOUR RODEO—AMERICA'S OWN EXCITING SPORT

Image Courtesy of The Advertising Archives

During the countercultural revolution of the 1960s, American baby boomers self-consciously adopted blue jeans as a kind of uniform in defiance of middle-class proscriptions, often wearing them as a sign of solidarity with the working class. Jeans became so identified with the counterculture that Charles Reich, in his popular 1970 book *The Greening of America*, argued that denim bell-bottoms were a symbol of the Age of Aquarius, signifying a free and free-wheeling new generation that had overturned the middle-class values of the past. Eventually, however, as happens so often in American consumer culture, what was once a symbol of defiance soon settled down into a simple fashion statement, and by the 1970s, blue jeans signified little more than "fashionable clothing" for work or play. This fashion statement paved the way for the emergence of designer jeans, like Jordache and Chic, which were worn very tight by both men and women and were styled to enhance a person's sex appeal.

In the latter part of the 1970s, however, blue jeans began to assume yet another significance when members of some punk rock and New Wave bands introduced a new jeans alternative. The jacket art for Blondie's album *Parallel Lines* provides a good illustration: The male band members all wear narrowly tailored black jeans, tapered down tightly at the ankle. What is more, one member of the group wears bright red Converse sneakers, while another wears one black Converse sneaker and one red one. The sleek new look was "hipster" rather than sexy, with a retro vibe that recalled a Beat-era fashion from the 1950s — a sartorial allusion that, as we shall see in a moment, has important resonances with today's skinny jeans trend.

Discussing the Signs of Consumer Culture

Make a categorized list of the fashion styles worn by your classmates. Be sure to note details, such as styles of shoes, jewelry, backpacks, or sunglasses, as well as broader trends. Next, discuss what the clothing choices say about individuals. What messages are people sending about their personal identity? Do individual students agree with the class's interpretations of their clothing choices? Can any distinctions be made by gender, age, or ethnicity? Then discuss what the fashion styles worn by the whole class signify: Is a group identity projected by class members?

By the mid-1980s, however, blue jeans took an entirely new direction with the widespread popularity of extravagantly oversized, or baggy, jeans. Replacing the loose athletic sweat suits that were popular during the break-dancing era, baggy jeans were a signifier of the evolution of rap/hip-hop and urban street fashion. Part of a uniform that then included backward-facing ball caps and untied Nike basketball sneakers, baggy jeans were often worn "sagging," in a further reference to the growing pop cultural influence of the black street gangs who began it all — an influence that, merging with gangsta rap in the 1990s, emerged as a dominant fashion system that endured for well over twenty years. Then, as usually happens with fashions originally intended to be subversive, the whole thing simmered down into just another teen clothing preference without any real significance.

All of these changes take us closer to the present. In the early 2000s, the look that Blondie had resurrected from the 1950s came to be adopted by various post-punk, indie, and otherwise "alternative" bands, like the Kings of Leon. As a result, skinny jeans re-entered the fashion system big time, projecting a new image, or connotative significance, that was quite different from the "street gang" imagery of the baggy jean era. In short, skinny jeans became "hip," where hip meant "coffee shop–indie" and/or "alternative hipster."

At this point in the history of blue jeans, then, something socially profound happened: the cut of your jeans assumed a pronounced racial significance, especially when combined with your musical preferences. That is to say, hipsters wearing skinny jeans also tended to embrace a "white-coded" alternative musical spectrum, while wearers of baggy jeans tended to prefer "black-coded" hip-hop musical forms, especially gangsta rap. This difference in overall cultural styles was not without its conflicts, however, conflicts that boiled to the surface in 2009 when rappers New Boyz released a video for "You're a Jerk" — a single from their significantly titled album *Skinny Jeanz and a Mic*. Highlighting skinny jeans and brightly colored Converse sneakers (both of which echoed that Blondie album cover), this video initially attracted some very angry commentary on YouTube. Since these comments aren't reprintable here, let's just say that along with the positive fan responses, in 2009 there were a lot of hostile accusations that the New Boyz were "murdering" hip-hop . . . and more.

The crux of the matter went back to those baggy jeans, which had become such an enduring signifier of African American street culture. One may say that it was a question of authenticity, with "skinny over baggy" signifying to some black consumers a kind of fashion betrayal. Interviews with the members of New Boyz and other figures in the jerkin' scene in 2009 clearly indicate that they were quite aware of what they were doing. While they retained many of the traditional signifiers of hip-hop culture through their music, their break-dance-grounded dancing, their wearing of baseball caps (though adjusted in new ways), and their wearing of sagging skinny jeans, they explicitly distinguished themselves from the gangsta subculture, speaking to interviewers of the "positive" attractions of such things as entrepreneurialism. Given that their skinny jeans had origins in such white-coded fashions as punk (significantly, a hairstyle seen among jerkers was called the "frohawk") and New Wave, the New Boyz thus not only adopted a white-coded fashion statement but also reversed a pattern in American youth culture that usually features white youth adopting and adapting the signifiers of black youth. Hence the hostile reaction. Indeed, at the time, one black fan of skinny jeans remarked to a reporter that he swapped his skinny jeans for baggy ones before returning home in order to avoid getting into trouble in his neighborhood.

But that was then, and fashion history rolls on. A survey of the more recent YouTube comments accompanying the "New Boyz 'You're a Jerk' OFFICIAL Music Video HD Extended" version reveals that the whole matter has lost its sting. One commenter places it in the "distant" past ("my daddy use to always try to do this dance lols whole house be shakin"), while another simply says "wonderful." But still, one quietly unhappy holdover from the old days remarks: "I am still angry at them for introducing dudes to skinny pants . . . sigh," he or she writes.

And so, once again, time has softened the edges of a once-edgy fashion signifier, for just as baggy jeans came eventually to signify little more than a popular youth fashion choice, so, too, have skinny jeans become so pervasive today that they have lost much of their "hipster" connotation and usually signify nothing more than "I'm wearing what every other Millennial is wearing."

Disposable Decades

As the above discussion demonstrates, when analyzing a consumer sign you will often find yourself referring to particular decades in which certain popular fads and trends were prominent, because the decade in which a given style appears may be an essential key to the system that explains it. Have you ever wondered why American cultural trends seem to change with every decade? Or, why is it so easy to speak of the 1960s or the 1970s or the 1980s and immediately recognize the popular styles that dominated each decade? Have you ever looked at the style of a friend and thought, "Oh, she's so seventies"? Can you place platform shoes or bell-bottoms at the drop of a hat? A change in the calendar always seems to herald a change in style in a consuming culture. But why?

The decade-to-decade shift in America's pop culture and consumer identity goes back a good number of years. It's still easy, for example, to distinguish the 1920s of F. Scott Fitzgerald's Jazz Age from the wrathful 1930s of John Steinbeck. The 1950s, an especially connotative decade, raise images of ducktail haircuts and poodle skirts, drive-in culture and Elvis, family sitcoms and white-bread innocence, while the 1960s are known for acid rock, hippies, the student revolution, and back-to-the-land communes. We remember the 1970s as a pop cultural era divided among disco, Nashville, and preppiedom, with John Travolta, truckers, and Skippy and Muffy as dominant pop icons. The boom-boom 1980s gave us Wall Street glitz and the yuppie invasion. Indeed, each decade since World War I — which, not accidentally, happens to coincide roughly with the rise of modern advertising and mass production — seems to carry its own consumerist style.

It's no accident that the decade-to-decade shift in consumer styles coincides with the advent of modern advertising and mass production, because it was mass production that created a need for constant consumer turnover in the first place. Mass production, that is, promotes stylistic change because with so many products available, a market must be created to consume all of them, and this means constantly consuming *more*. To get people to keep buying all the new stuff, you have to convince them that the stuff they already have is passé. Why else do fashion designers completely change their lines each year? Why do car manufacturers annually change their color schemes and body shapes when the previous year's model seemed good enough? Why does each new incarnation of the Apple iPhone introduce so many different colors and features? The new colors and designs aren't simply functional improvements (though they are marketed as such); they are inducements to go out and replace what you already have to avoid appearing out of fashion. Just think: If you could afford to buy any car or phone you want, what would it be? Would your choice a few years ago have been the same?

Mass production, then, creates consumer societies based on the constant creation of new products that are intended to be disposed of the next product year. But something happened along the way in the establishment of our consumer culture: We began to value consumption more than production. Shoppers storm the doors as the Christmas buying season begins earlier and earlier every year. Listen to the economic news: Consumption, not production, is relied upon to carry America out of its economic downturns. When Americans stop buying, our economy grinds to a halt. Consumption lies at the center of our economic system now, constituting some two-thirds of our economic activity, and the result has been a transformation in the very way we view ourselves.

> ### Exploring the Signs of Consumer Culture
>
> "You are what you buy." In your journal, freewrite on the importance of consumer products in your life. How do you respond to being told your identity is equivalent to the products you buy? Do you resist the notion? Do you recall any instances when you have felt lost without a favorite object? How do you communicate your sense of self to others through objects, whether clothing, books, food, home decor, electronic goods, or something else?

A Tale of Two Cities

It has not always been thus in America, however. Once, Americans prided themselves on their productivity. In 1914, for example, the poet Carl Sandburg boasted of a Chicago that was "Hog Butcher for the World, / Tool Maker, Stacker of Wheat, / Player with Railroads and the Nation's Freight Handler." One wonders what Sandburg would think of the city today. From the South Side east to the industrial suburb of Gary, Indiana, Chicago's once-proud mills and factories rust in the winter wind. At the Chicago Mercantile Exchange, trade today is in commodity futures, not commodities.

Meanwhile, a few hundred miles to the northwest, Bloomington, Minnesota, buzzes with excitement. For there stands the Mall of America, a colossus of consumption so large that it contains within its walls a seven-acre Nickelodeon Universe theme park, with lots of room to spare. You can find almost anything you want in the Mall of America, but most of what you find won't have been manufactured in America. The proud tag "Made in the U.S.A." is an increasingly rare item. It's a long way from Sandburg's Chicago to the Mall of America, a trip that traverses America's shift from a producer to a consumer economy. This shift is not simply economic; it is behind a cultural transformation that is shaping a new mythology in which we define ourselves, our hopes, and our desires.

Ask yourself right now what your own goals are in going to college. Do you envision a career in law, or medicine, or banking and finance? Do you want to be a teacher, an advertising executive, or a civil servant? Or maybe you are preparing for a career in an Internet-related field. If you've considered any of these careers, you are contemplating what are known as service jobs. While essential to society, none of them actually produces anything. If you've given thought to going into some facet of traditional manufacturing, on the other hand, you are unusual because America offers increasingly fewer opportunities in that area and little prestige. The prestigious jobs are in law and medicine and in high-tech operations like Google and CRISPR, a fact that is easy to take for granted. But ask yourself: "Does it have to be so?"

To live in a consumer culture is not simply a matter of shopping or career choice, however; it is also a matter of being. Often aligned with the preeminent American mythology of personal freedom, the freedom to consume *what* you want *whenever* you want it has become — thanks in large part to mobile digital technology — a defining value of modern American life: a human right, not a mere pleasure or convenience. You are what you buy, and what you buy fulfills what you are. And in case you forget this, a constant drumbeat of advertising and marketing schemes exhorts you to go out and buy something, replacing the freedom to march to the beat of a different drummer with the freedom to buy.

When the Going Gets Tough, the Tough Go Shopping

In a cultural system where our identities are displayed in the products we buy, it accordingly behooves us to pay close attention to what we consume and why. From the cars we drive to the clothes we wear, we are enmeshed in a web of consumption. As students, you are probably freer to choose the images you wish to project through the products you consume than most other demographic groups in America. This claim may sound paradoxical: After all, don't working adults have more money than starving students? Yes, generally. But the working world places severe restrictions on the choices employees can make in their clothing and grooming styles, and even automobile choice may be restricted (real estate agents, for example, can't escort their clients around town in Kia Souls). And even in the era of the Zuckerberg hoodie, applicants for white-collar positions are still best advised to adopt the codes of corporate business wear, with its emphasis on necktied and dark-hued sobriety. On campus, however, you can be pretty much whatever you want to be, which is why your own daily life provides you with a particularly rich field of consumer signs to read and decode.

Reading Consumer Culture Online

Log on to one of the many home shopping networks or auction sites such as Shop at Home (shopathome.com) or eBay (ebay.com), or visit the site of a retail store that you have visited in its brick-and-mortar version. Analyze both the products sold and the way they are marketed. Who is the target audience, and what images and values are used to attract this market? How does the marketing compare to non-electronic sales pitches, such as displays in stores and magazines or TV advertising? Does the electronic medium affect your behavior as a consumer? How do you account for any differences in electronic and traditional marketing strategies?

So go to it. By the time you finish reading this book, a lot will have changed. Look around. Start reading the signs.

The Readings

As this chapter's lead essay, Laurence Shames's "The More Factor" offers a historical context for American consumer culture, relating America's frontier history to our ever-expanding desire for more goods and services. Anne Norton and Malcolm Gladwell follow with a paired set of readings on the ways in which retailers seek to maximize sales by designing the shopping environment to influence consumers' buying behavior, with Norton providing semiotic analyses of shopping malls and mail-order catalogs and Gladwell reporting on the measures that brick-and-mortar store managers take to encourage spending. Next, Michael Pollan exposes some of the less-than-sunny realities behind the idealized narratives of the organic foods industry, while Jon Mooallem explores the world of self-storage facilities in an era when consumption is outstripping many Americans' ability to house all their stuff. Chris Arning takes us into the world of packaging, revealing the place of semiotics on the front lines of high-stakes brand positioning and marketing. James A. Roberts's survey of status consumption and the paradox of diminishing returns is followed by Steve McKevitt's exposé of the ways in which technology and psychology intersect in the consumer marketplace. The chapter concludes with Troy Patterson's breakdown of the complex semiotics of the "hoodie," a kind of case study that leads in to Thomas Frank's revelation of how corporate America has turned consumption into a hip signifier of inauthentic rebellion: a "commodification of dissent."

LAURENCE SHAMES

The More Factor

A bumper sticker popular in the 1980s read, "Whoever dies with the most toys wins." In this selection from *The Hunger for More: Searching for Values in an Age of Greed* (1989), Laurence Shames shows how the great American hunger for more — more toys, more land, more opportunities — is an essential part of our history and character, stemming from the frontier era when the horizon alone seemed the only limit to American desire. Shames is both a fiction author and journalist who has contributed to such publications as *Playboy, Vanity Fair, Manhattan, inc.,* and *Esquire.*

1

Americans have always been optimists, and optimists have always liked to speculate. In Texas in the 1880s, the speculative instrument of choice was towns, and there is no tale more American than this.

What people would do was buy up enormous tracts of parched and vacant land, lay out a Main Street, nail together some wooden sidewalks, and start slapping up buildings. One of these buildings would be called the Grand Hotel and would have a saloon complete with swinging doors. Another might be dubbed the New Academy or the Opera House. The developers would erect a flagpole and name a church, and once the workmen had packed up and moved on, the towns would be as empty as the sky.

But no matter. The speculators, next, would hire people to pass out handbills in the Eastern and Midwestern cities, tracts limning the advantages of relocation to "the Athens of the South" or "the new plains Jerusalem." When persuasion failed, the builders might resort to bribery, paying people's moving costs and giving them houses, in exchange for nothing but a pledge to stay until a certain census was taken or a certain inspection made. Once the nose count was completed, people were free to move on, and there was in fact a contingent of folks who made their living by keeping a cabin on skids and dragging it for pay from one town to another.

The speculators' idea, of course, was to lure the railroad. If one could create a convincing semblance of a town, the railroad might come through it, and a real town would develop, making the speculators staggeringly rich. By these devices a man named Sanborn once owned Amarillo.[1]

---

[1] For a fuller account of railroad-related land speculation in Texas, see F. Stanley, *Story of the Texas Panhandle Railroads* (Borger, Tex.: Hess Publishing Co., 1976).

But railroad tracks are narrow and the state of Texas is very, very wide.   5
For every Wichita Falls or Lubbock there were a dozen College Mounds or
Belchervilles,[2] bleached, unpeopled burgs that receded quietly into the dust,
taking with them large amounts of speculators' money.

Still, the speculators kept right on bucking the odds and depositing empty
towns in the middle of nowhere. Why did they do it? Two reasons — reasons
that might be said to summarize the central fact of American economic history and that go a fair way toward explaining what is perhaps the central
strand of the national character.

The first reason was simply that the possible returns were so enormous
as to partake of the surreal, to create a climate in which ordinary logic and
prudence did not seem to apply. In a boom like that of real estate when the
railroad barreled through, long shots that might pay one hundred thousand to
one seemed worth a bet.

The second reason, more pertinent here, is that there was a presump-
tion that America would *keep* on booming — if not forever, then at least longer
than it made sense to worry about. There would always be another gold rush,
another Homestead Act, another oil strike. The next generation would always
ferret out opportunities that would be still more lavish than any that had gone
before. America *was* those opportunities. This was an article not just of faith,
but of strategy. You banked on the next windfall, you staked your hopes and
even your self-esteem on it, and this led to a national turn of mind that might
usefully be thought of as the habit of more.

A century, maybe two centuries, before anyone had heard the term *baby
boomer*, much less *yuppie*, the habit of more had been instilled as the operative
truth among the economically ambitious. The habit of more seemed to suggest that there was no such thing as getting wiped out in America. A fortune
lost in Texas might be recouped in Colorado. Funds frittered away on grazing
land where nothing grew might flood back in as silver. There was always a
second chance, or always seemed to be, in this land where growth was destiny
and where expansion and purpose were the same.

The key was the frontier, not just as a matter of acreage, but as idea. Vast,   10
varied, rough as rocks, America was the place where one never quite came to
the end. Ben Franklin explained it to Europe even before the Revolutionary
War had finished: America offered new chances to those "who, in their own
Countries, where all the Lands [were] fully occupied . . . could never [emerge]
from the poor Condition wherein they were born."[3]

So central was this awareness of vacant space and its link to economic
promise that Frederick Jackson Turner, the historian who set the tone for much
of the twentieth century's understanding of the American past, would write
that it was "not the constitution, but free land . . . [that] made the democratic

---

[2]T. Lindsay Baker, *Ghost Towns of Texas* (Norman, Okla.: University of Oklahoma Press, 1986).
[3]Benjamin Franklin, "Information to Those Who Would Remove to America," in *The
Autobiography and Other Writings* (New York: Penguin Books, 1986), 242.

type of society in America."[4] Good laws mattered; an accountable government mattered; ingenuity and hard work mattered. But those things were, so
to speak, an overlay on the natural, geographic America that was simply *there*,
and whose vast and beckoning possibilities seemed to generate the ambition
and the sometimes reckless liberty that would fill it. First and foremost, it was
open space that provided "the freedom of the individual to rise under conditions of social mobility."[5]

Open space generated not just ambition, but metaphor. As early as 1835,
Tocqueville was extrapolating from the fact of America's emptiness to the
observation that "no natural boundary seems to be set to the efforts of man."[6]
Nor was any limit placed on what he might accomplish, since, in that heyday
of the Protestant ethic, a person's rewards were taken to be quite strictly pro-
portionate to his labors.

Frontier; opportunity; more. This has been the American trinity from the
very start. The frontier was the backdrop and also the raw material for the
streak of economic booms. The booms became the goad and also the justification for the myriad gambles and for Americans' famous optimism. The optimism, in turn, shaped the schemes and visions that were sometimes noble,
sometimes appalling, always bold. The frontier, as reality and as symbol, is
what has shaped the American way of doing things and the American sense
of what's worth doing.

But there has been one further corollary to the legacy of the frontier, with
its promise of ever-expanding opportunities: Given that the goal — a realistic goal for most of our history — was *more*, Americans have been somewhat
backward in adopting values, hopes, ambitions that have to do with things
other than more. In America, a sense of quality has lagged far behind a sense
of scale. An ideal of contentment has yet to take root in soil traditionally
more hospitable to an ideal of restless striving. The ethic of decency has been
upstaged by the ethic of success. The concept of growth has been applied
almost exclusively to things that can be measured, counted, weighed. And the
hunger for those things that are unmeasurable but fine — the sorts of accomplishment that cannot be undone by circumstance or a shift in social fashion,
the kind of serenity that cannot be shattered by tomorrow's headline — has
gone largely unfulfilled, and even unacknowledged.

2

If the supply of more went on forever, perhaps that wouldn't matter very 15
much. Expansion could remain a goal unto itself, and would continue to

---

[4]Frederick Jackson Turner, *The Frontier in American History* (Melbourne, Fla.: Krieger, 1976
[reprint of 1920 edition]), 293.
[5]Ibid., 266.
[6]Tocqueville, *Democracy in America.*

generate a value system based on bulk rather than on nuance, on quantities of money rather than on quality of life, on "progress" itself rather than on a sense of what the progress was for. But what if, over time, there was less more to be had?

That is the essential situation of America today.

Let's keep things in proportion: The country is not running out of wealth, drive, savvy, or opportunities. We are not facing imminent ruin, and neither panic nor gloom is called for. But there have been ample indications over the past two decades that we are running out of more.

Consider productivity growth — according to many economists, the single most telling and least distortable gauge of changes in real wealth. From 1947 to 1965, productivity in the private sector (adjusted, as are all the following figures, for inflation) was advancing, on average, by an annual 3.3 percent. This means, simply, that each hour of work performed by a specimen American worker contributed 3.3 cents worth or more to every American dollar every year; whether we saved it or spent it, that increment went into a national kitty of ever-enlarging aggregate wealth. Between 1965 and 1972, however, the "more-factor" decreased to 2.4 percent a year, and from 1972 to 1977 it slipped further, to 1.6 percent. By the early 1980s, productivity growth was at a virtual standstill, crawling along at 0.2 percent for the five years ending in 1982.[7] Through the middle years of the 1980s, the numbers rebounded somewhat — but by then the gains were being neutralized by the gargantuan carrying costs on the national debt.[8]

Inevitably, this decline in the national stockpile of more held consequences for the individual wallet.[9] During the 1950s, Americans' average hourly earnings were humping ahead at a gratifying 2.5 percent each year. By the late seventies, that figure stood just where productivity growth had come to stand, at a dispiriting 0.2 cents on the dollar. By the first half of the eighties, the Reagan "recovery" notwithstanding, real hourly wages were actually moving backward — declining at an average annual rate of 0.3 percent.

Compounding the shortage of more was an unfortunate but crucial demo-   20
graphic fact. Real wealth was nearly ceasing to expand just at the moment when the members of that unprecedented population bulge known as the baby boom were entering what should have been their peak years of income expansion. A working man or woman who was thirty years old in 1949 could expect to see his or her real earnings burgeon by 63 percent by age forty. In

---

[7]These figures are taken from the Council of Economic Advisers, *Economic Report of the President*, February 1984, 267.

[8]For a lucid and readable account of the meaning and implications of our reservoir of red ink, see Lawrence Malkin, *The National Debt* (New York: Henry Holt and Co., 1987). Through no fault of Malkin's, many of his numbers are already obsolete, but his explanation of who owes what to whom, and what it means, remains sound and even entertaining in a bleak sort of way.

[9]The figures in this paragraph and the next are from "The Average Guy Takes It on the Chin," *New York Times*, 13 July 1986, sec. 3.

1959, a thirty-year-old could still look forward to a gain of 49 percent by his or her fortieth birthday.

But what about the person who turned thirty in 1973? By the time that worker turned forty, his or her real earnings had shrunk by a percentage point. For all the blather about yuppies with their beach houses, BMWs, and radicchio salads, and even factoring in those isolated tens of thousands making ludicrous sums in consulting firms or on Wall Street, the fact is that between 1979 and 1983 real earnings of all Americans between the ages of twenty-five and thirty-four actually declined by 14 percent.[10] The *New York Times*, well before the stock market crash put the kibosh on eighties confidence, summed up the implications of this downturn by observing that "for millions of bread-winners, the American dream is becoming the impossible dream."[11]

Now, it is not our main purpose here to detail the ups and downs of the American economy. Our aim, rather, is to consider the effects of those ups and downs on people's goals, values, sense of their place in the world. What happens at that shadowy juncture where economic prospects meld with personal choice? What sorts of insights and adjustments are called for so that economic ups and downs can be dealt with gracefully?

Fact one in this connection is that, if America's supply of more is in fact diminishing, American values will have to shift and broaden to fill the gap where the expectation of almost automatic gains used to be. Something more durable will have to replace the fat but fragile bubble that had been getting frailer these past two decades and that finally popped — a tentative, partial pop — on October 19, 1987. A different sort of growth — ultimately, a growth in responsibility and happiness — will have to fulfill our need to believe that our possibilities are still expanding.

The transition to that new view of progress will take some fancy stepping, because, at least since the end of World War II, simple economic growth has stood, in the American psyche, as the best available substitute for the literal frontier. The economy has *been* the frontier. Instead of more space, we have had more money. Rather than measuring progress in terms of geographical expansion, we have measured it by expansion in our standard of living. Economics has become the metaphor on which we pin our hopes of open space and second chances.

The poignant part is that the literal frontier did not pass yesterday: it has not existed for a hundred years. But the frontier's promise has become so much a part of us that we have not been willing to let the concept die. We have kept the frontier mythology going by invocation, by allusion, by hype.

It is not a coincidence that John F. Kennedy dubbed his political program the New Frontier. It is not mere linguistic accident that makes us speak of Frontiers of Science or of psychedelic drugs as carrying one to Frontiers of Perception. We glorify fads and fashions by calling them Frontiers of Taste.

25

---

[10]See, for example, "The Year of the Yuppie," *Newsweek*, 31 December 1984, 16.
[11]"The Average Guy."

Nuclear energy has been called the Last Frontier; solar energy has been called the Last Frontier. Outer space has been called the Last Frontier; the oceans have been called the Last Frontier. Even the suburbs, those blandest and least adventurous of places, have been wryly described as the crabgrass frontier.[12]

What made all these usages plausible was their being linked to the image of the American economy as an endlessly fertile continent whose boundaries never need be reached, a domain that could expand in perpetuity, a gigantic playing field that would never run out of room and on which the game would get forever bigger and more filled with action. This was the frontier that would not vanish.

It is worth noting that people in other countries (with the possible exception of that other America, Australia) do not talk about frontier this way. In Europe, and in most of Africa and Asia, "frontier" connotes, at worst, a place of barbed wire and men with rifles, and at best, a neutral junction where one changes currency while passing from one fixed system into another. Frontier, for most of the world's people, does not suggest growth, expanse, or opportunity.

For Americans, it does, and always has. This is one of the things that sets America apart from other places and makes American attitudes different from those of other people. It is why, from *Bonanza* to the Sierra Club, the notion or even the fantasy of empty horizons and untapped resources has always evoked in the American heart both passion and wistfulness. And it is why the fear that the economic frontier — our last, best version of the Wild West — may finally be passing creates in us not only money worries but also a crisis of morale and even of purpose.

3

It might seem strange to call the 1980s an era of nostalgia. The decade, after 30 all, has been more usually described in terms of coolness, pragmatism, and a blithe innocence of history. But the eighties, unawares, were nostalgic for frontiers; and the disappointment of that nostalgia had much to do with the time's greed, narrowness, and strange want of joy. The fear that the world may not be a big enough playground for the full exercise of one's energies and yearnings, and worse, the fear that the playground is being fenced off and will no longer expand — these are real worries and they have had consequences. The eighties were an object lesson in how people play the game when there is an awful and unspoken suspicion that the game is winding down.

It was ironic that the yuppies came to be so reviled for their vaunting ambition and outsized expectations, as if they'd invented the habit of more, when in fact they'd only inherited it the way a fetus picks up an addiction in the womb.

---

[12]With the suburbs again taking on a sort of fascination, this phrase was resurrected as the title of a 1985 book — *Crabgrass Frontier: The Suburbanization of America*, by Kenneth T. Jackson (Oxford University Press).

The craving was there in the national bloodstream, a remnant of the frontier, and the baby boomers, described in childhood as "the luckiest generation,"[13] found themselves, as young adults, in the melancholy position of wrestling with a two-hundred-year dependency on a drug that was now in short supply.

True, the 1980s raised the clamor for more to new heights of shrillness, insistence, and general obnoxiousness, but this, it can be argued, was in the nature of a final binge, the storm before the calm. America, though fighting the perception every inch of the way, was coming to realize that it was not a preordained part of the natural order that one should be richer every year. If it happened, that was nice. But who had started the flimsy and pernicious rumor that it was normal?

READING THE TEXT

1. Summarize in a paragraph how, according to Shames, the frontier functions as a symbol of American consciousness.

2. What does Shames mean when he says, "Open space generated not just ambition, but metaphor" (para. 12)?

3. What connections does Shames make between America's frontier history and consumer behavior?

4. Why does Shames term the 1980s "an era of nostalgia" (para. 30)?

5. Characterize Shames's attitude toward the American desire for more. How does his tone reveal his personal views on his subject?

READING THE SIGNS

1. Shames asserts that Americans have been influenced by the frontier belief "that America would *keep* on booming" (para. 8). Do you feel that this belief continues to be influential into the twenty-first century? Write an essay arguing for your position.

2. Shames claims that, because of the desire for more, "the ethic of decency has been upstaged by the ethic of success" (para. 14). In class, form teams and debate the validity of Shames's claim.

3. **CONNECTING TEXTS**   Read or review Steve McKevitt's "Everything Now" (p. 123). Using Maslow's hierarchy of needs (p. 126), write an essay illustrating, refuting, or complicating the proposition that "the hunger for more" is driven by the fact that "our *needs* have been fulfilled and so, for the first time ever, we have an economy that is almost entirely devoted to the business of satisfying our *wants* instead" (para. 3).

4. In an essay, argue for or refute the proposition that the "hunger for more" that Shames describes is a universal human trait, not simply an American one.

---

[13]Thomas Hine, *Populuxe* (New York: Alfred A. Knopf, 1986), 15.

ANNE NORTON

The Signs of Shopping

> Shopping malls are more than places to shop, just as mail-order
> catalogs are more than simple lists of goods. Both malls and cata-
> logs are coded systems that not only encourage us to buy but, more
> profoundly, help us construct our very sense of identity, as in the
> J. Peterman catalog that "constructs the reader as a man of rugged
> outdoor interests, taste, and money." In this selection from *Republic
> of Signs* (1993), Anne Norton, a professor of political science at the
> University of Pennsylvania, analyzes the many ways in which malls
> and catalogs sell you what they want by telling you who you are.
> Norton's other books include *Alternative Americas* (1986) and *On the
> Muslim Question* (2013).

Shopping at the Mall

The mall has been the subject of innumerable debates. Created out of the
modernist impulse for planning and the centralization of public activity, the
mall has become the distinguishing sign of suburban decentralization, spring-
ing up in unplanned profusion. Intended to restore something of the lost unity
of city life to the suburbs, the mall has come to export styles and strategies to
stores at the urban center. Deplored by modernists, it is regarded with affection only by their postmodern foes. Ruled more by their content than by their
creators' avowed intent, the once sleek futurist shells have taken on a certain
aura of postmodern playfulness and popular glitz.

The mall is a favorite subject for the laments of cultural conservatives and
others critical of the culture of consumption. It is indisputably the cultural
locus of commodity fetishism. It has been noticed, however, by others of a
less condemnatory disposition that the mall has something of the mercado,
or the agora, about it. It is both a place of meeting for the young and one of
the rare places where young and old go together. People of different races
and classes, different occupations, different levels of education meet there. As
M. Pressdee and John Fiske note, however, though the mall appears to be a
public place, it is not. Neither freedom of speech nor freedom of assembly
is permitted there. Those who own and manage malls restrict what comes
within their confines. Controversial displays, by stores or customers or the
plethora of organizations and agencies that present themselves in the open
spaces of the mall, are not permitted. These seemingly public spaces conceal
a pervasive private authority.

The mall exercises its thorough and discreet authority not only in the regulation of behavior but in the constitution of our visible, inaudible, public discourse. It is the source of those commodities through which we speak of our identities, our opinions, our desires. It is a focus for the discussion of style among peripheral consumers. Adolescents, particularly female adolescents, are inclined to spend a good deal of time at the mall. They spend, indeed, more time than money. They acquire not simple commodities (they may come home with many, few, or none) but a well-developed sense of the significance of those commodities. In prowling the mall they embed themselves in a lexicon of American culture. They find themselves walking through a dictionary. Stores hang a variety of identities on their racks and mannequins. Their window displays provide elaborate scenarios conveying not only what the garment is but what the garment means.

A display in the window of Polo provides an embarrassment of semiotic riches. Everyone, from the architecture critic at the *New York Times* to kids in the hall of a Montana high school, knows what *Ralph Lauren* means. The polo mallet and the saddle, horses and dogs, the broad lawns of Newport, Kennebunkport, old photographs in silver frames, the evocation of age, of ancestry and Anglophilia, of indolence and the Ivy League, evoke the upper class. Indian blankets and buffalo plaids, cowboy hats and Western saddles, evoke a past distinct from England but nevertheless determinedly Anglo. The supposedly arcane and suspect arts of deconstruction are deployed easily, effortlessly, by the readers of these cultural texts.

Walking from one window to another, observing one another, shoppers, especially the astute and observant adolescents, acquire a facility with the language of commodities. They learn not only words but a grammar. Shop windows employ elements of sarcasm and irony, strategies of inversion and allusion. They provide models of elegant, economical, florid, and prosaic expression. They teach composition.   5

The practice of shopping is, however, more than instructive. It has long been the occasion for women to escape the confines of their homes and enjoy the companionship of other women. The construction of woman's role as one of provision for the needs of the family legitimated her exit. It provided an occasion for women to spend long stretches of time in the company of their friends, without the presence of their husbands. They could exchange information and reflections, ask advice, and receive support. As their daughters grew, they would be brought increasingly within this circle, included in shopping trips and lunches with their mothers. These would form, reproduce, and restructure communities of taste.

The construction of identity and the enjoyment of friendship outside the presence of men was thus effected through a practice that constructed women as consumers and subjected them to the conventions of the market-place. Insofar as they were dependent on their husbands for money, they were dependent on their husbands for the means to the construction of their identities. They could not represent themselves through commodities without the funds men provided, nor could they, without money, participate in the community of women that was realized in "going shopping." Their identities were made contingent not only on the possession of property but on the recognition of dependence.

Insofar as shopping obliges dependent women to recognize their dependence, it also opens up the possibility of subversion.[1] The housewife who shops for pleasure takes time away from her husband, her family, and her house and claims it for herself. Constantly taught that social order and her private happiness depend on intercourse between men and women, she chooses the company of women instead. She engages with women in an activity marked as feminine, and she enjoys it. When she spends money, she exercises an authority over property that law and custom may deny her. If she has no resources independent of her husband, this may be the only authority over property she is able to exercise. When she buys things her husband does not approve — or does not know of — she further subverts an order that leaves control over property in her husband's hands.[2]

Her choice of feminine company and a feminine pursuit may involve additional subversions. As Fiske and Pressdee recognize, shopping without buying and shopping for bargains have a subversive quality. This is revealed, in a form that gives it additional significance, when a saleswoman leans forward and tells a shopper, "Don't buy that today, it will be on sale on Thursday." Here solidarity of gender (and often of class) overcome, however partially and briefly, the imperatives of the economic order.

Shoppers who look, as most shoppers do, for bargains, and salespeople who warn shoppers of impending sales, see choices between commodities as something other than the evidence and the exercise of freedom. They see covert direction and exploitation; they see the withholding of information and the manipulation of knowledge. They recognize that they are on enemy terrain and that their shopping can be, in Michel de Certeau's[3] term, a "guerrilla raid." This recognition in practice of the presence of coercion in choice challenges the liberal conflation of choice and consent.

Shopping at Home

Shopping is an activity that has overcome its geographic limits. One need no longer go to the store to shop. Direct mail catalogues, with their twenty-four-hour

---

[1] Nuanced and amusing accounts of shopping as subversion are provided in John Fiske's analyses of popular culture, particularly *Reading the Popular* (Boston: Unwin Hyman [now Routledge], 1989), pp. 13–42.

[2] See R. Bowlby, *Just Looking: Consumer Culture in Dreiser, Gissing, and Zola* (London: Methuen, 1985), p. 22, for another discussion and for an example of the recommendation of this strategy by Elizabeth Cady Stanton in the 1850s.

[3] **Michel de Certeau** (1925–1986) French social scientist and semiotician who played an important role in the development of contemporary cultural studies. –EDS.

phone numbers for ordering, permit people to shop where and when they please. An activity that once obliged one to go out into the public sphere, with its diverse array of semiotic messages, can now be done at home. An activity that once obliged one to be in company, if not in conversation, with one's compatriots can now be conducted in solitude.

The activity of catalogue shopping, and the pursuit of individuality, are not, however, wholly solitary. The catalogues invest their commodities with vivid historical and social references. The J. Peterman catalogue, for example, constructs the reader as a man of rugged outdoor interests, taste, and money.[4] He wears "The Owner's Hat" or "Hemingway's Cap," a leather flight jacket or the classic "Horseman's Duster," and various other garments identified with the military, athletes, and European imperialism. The copy for "The Owner's Hat" naturalizes class distinctions and, covertly, racism:

> Some of us work on the plantation.
> Some of us own the plantation.
> Facts are facts.
> This hat is for those who own the plantation.[5]

Gender roles are strictly delineated. The copy for a skirt captioned "Women's Legs" provides a striking instance of the construction of the gaze as male, of women as the object of the gaze:

> Just when you think you see something, a shape you think you recognize, it's gone and then it begins to return and then it's gone and of course you can't take your eyes off it.
>
> Yes, the long slow motion of women's legs. Whatever happened to those things at carnivals that blew air up into girls' skirts and you could spend hours watching.[6]

"You," of course, are male. There is also the lace blouse captioned "Mystery": "lace says yes at the same time it says no."[7] Finally, there are notes of imperialist nostalgia: the Shepherd's Hotel (Cairo) bathrobe and white pants for "the bush" and "the humid hell-holes of Bombay and Calcutta."[8]

---

[4] I have read several of these. I cite *The J. Peterman Company Owner's Manual No. 5*, from the J. Peterman Company, 2444 Palumbo Drive, Lexington, Ky. 40509.

[5] Ibid., p. 5. The hat is also identified with the Canal Zone, "successfully bidding at Beaulieu," intimidation, and LBOs. Quite a hat. It might be argued against my reading that the J. Peterman Company also offers the "Coal Miner's Bag" and a mailbag. However, since the descriptive points of reference on color and texture and experience for these bags are such things as the leather seats of Jaguars, and driving home in a Bentley, I feel fairly confident in my reading.

[6] Ibid., p. 3. See also pp. 15 and 17 for instances of women as the object of the male gaze. The identification of the gaze with male sexuality is unambiguous here as well.

[7] Ibid., p. 17.

[8] Ibid., pp. 7, 16, 20, 21, 37, and 50.

It may no longer be unforgivable to say that the British left a few good things behind in India and in Kenya, Singapore, Borneo, etc., not the least of which was their Englishness.[9]

As Paul Smith observes, in his reading of their catalogues, the Banana Republic has also made capital out of imperial nostalgia.[10]

The communities catalogues create are reinforced by shared mailing lists. The constructed identities are reified and elaborated in an array of semiotically related catalogues. One who orders a spade or a packet of seeds will be constructed as a gardener and receive a deluge of catalogues from plant and garden companies. The companies themselves may expand their commodities to appeal to different manifestations of the identities they respond to and construct. Smith and Hawken, a company that sells gardening supplies with an emphasis on aesthetics and environmental concern, puts out a catalogue in which a group of people diverse in age and in their ethnicity wear the marketed clothes while gardening, painting, or throwing pots. Williams-Sonoma presents its catalogue not as a catalogue of things for cooking but as "A Catalog for Cooks." The catalogue speaks not to need but to the construction of identity.

The Nature Company dedicates its spring 1990 catalogue "to trees," endorses Earth Day, and continues to link itself to the Nature Conservancy through posters and a program in which you buy a tree for a forest restoration project. Here, a not-for-profit agency is itself commodified, adding to the value of the commodities offered in the catalogue.[11] In this catalogue, consumption is not merely a means for the construction and representation of the self, it is also a means for political action. Several commodities are offered as "A Few Things You Can Do" to save the earth: a string shopping bag, a solar battery recharger, a home newspaper recycler. Socially conscious shopping is a liberal practice in every sense. It construes shopping as a form of election, in which one votes for good commodities or refuses one's vote to candidates whose practices are ethically suspect.

READING THE TEXT

1. What does Norton mean when she claims that the suburban shopping mall appears to be a public place but in fact is not?
2. What is Norton's interpretation of Ralph Lauren's Polo stores?
3. How is shopping a subversive activity for women, according to Norton?
4. How do mail-order catalogs create communities of shoppers, in Norton's view?

[9]Ibid., p. 20.

[10]Paul Smith, "Visiting the Banana Republic," in *Universal Abandon?* ed. Andrew Ross for *Social Text* (Minneapolis: University of Minnesota Press, 1988), pp. 128–48.

[11] *The Nature Company Catalog*, The Nature Company, P.O. Box 2310, Berkeley, Calif. 94702, Spring 1990. See pp. 1–2 and order form insert between pp. 18 and 19. Note also the entailed donation to Designs for Conservation on p. 18.

READING THE SIGNS

1. Visit a local shopping mall, and study the window displays, focusing on stores intended for one group of consumers (teenagers, for example, or children). Then write an essay in which you analyze how the displays convey what the stores' products "mean."

2. Bring a few product catalogs to class, and in small groups compare the kinds of consumer "constructed" by the cultural images and allusions in the catalogs. Do you note any patterns associated with gender, ethnicity, or age group? Report your group's interpretations to the whole class.

3. **CONNECTING TEXTS**   Interview five women of different age groups about their motivations and activities when they shop in a mall. Use your results as evidence in an essay in which you support, refute, or complicate Norton's assertion that shopping constitutes a subversive activity for women. To develop your ideas, consult Jia Tolentino's "How 'Empowerment' Became Something for Women to Buy" (p. 180).

4. Select a single mail-order catalog, and write a detailed semiotic interpretation of the identity it constructs for its market.

5. Visit the Web site for a major chain store (for instance, urbanoutfitters.com or anthropologie.com), and study how the site "moves" the consumer through it. How does the site induce you to consume?

UNDERSTANDING SHOPPING

MALCOLM GLADWELL
The Science of Shopping

Ever wonder why the season's hottest new styles at stores like the Gap are usually displayed on the right at least fifteen paces in from the front entrance? It's because that's where shoppers are most likely to see them as they enter the store, gear down from the walking pace of a mall corridor, and adjust to the shop's spatial environment. Ever wonder how shop managers know this sort of thing? It's because, as Malcolm Gladwell reports here, they hire consultants like Paco Underhill, a "retail anthropologist" and "urban geographer" whose studies (often aided by hidden cameras) of shopping behavior have become valuable guides to store managers looking for the best ways to move the goods. Does this feel just a little Orwellian? Read on. A staff writer for the *New Yorker*, in which this selection first appeared, Gladwell has also written *The Tipping Point* (2000) and *David and Goliath* (2013).

Human beings walk the way they drive, which is to say that Americans tend to keep to the right when they stroll down shopping-mall concourses or city sidewalks. This is why in a well-designed airport travellers drifting toward their gate will always find the fast-food restaurants on their left and the gift shops on their right: people will readily cross a lane of pedestrian traffic to satisfy their hunger but rarely to make an impulse buy of a T-shirt or a magazine. This is also why Paco Underhill tells his retail clients to make sure that their window displays are canted, preferably to both sides but especially to the left, so that a potential shopper approaching the store on the inside of the sidewalk — the shopper, that is, with the least impeded view of the store window — can see the display from at least twenty-five feet away.

Of course, a lot depends on how fast the potential shopper is walking. Paco, in his previous life, as an urban geographer in Manhattan, spent a great deal of time thinking about walking speeds as he listened in on the great debates of the nineteen-seventies over whether the traffic lights in midtown should be timed to facilitate the movement of cars or to facilitate the movement of pedestrians and so break up the big platoons that move down Manhattan sidewalks. He knows that the faster you walk the more your peripheral vision narrows, so you become unable to pick up visual cues as quickly as someone who is just ambling along. He knows, too, that people who walk fast take a surprising amount of time to slow down — just as it takes a good stretch of road to change gears with a stick-shift automobile. On the basis of his research, Paco estimates the human downshift period to be anywhere from twelve to twenty-five feet, so if you own a store, he says, you never want to be next door to a bank: potential shoppers speed up when they walk past a bank (since there's nothing to look at), and by the time they slow down they've walked right past your business. The downshift factor also means that when potential shoppers enter a store it's going to take them from five to fifteen paces to adjust to the light and refocus and gear down from walking speed to shopping speed — particularly if they've just had to navigate a treacherous parking lot or hurry to make the light at Fifty-seventh and Fifth.

Paco calls that area inside the door the Decompression Zone, and something he tells clients over and over again is never, ever put anything of value in that zone — not shopping baskets or tie racks or big promotional displays — because no one is going to see it. Paco believes that, as a rule of thumb, customer interaction with any product or promotional display in the Decompression Zone will increase at least thirty percent once it's moved to the back edge of the zone, and even more if it's placed to the right, because another of the fundamental rules of how human beings shop is that upon entering a store — whether it's Nordstrom or K Mart, Tiffany or the Gap — the shopper invariably and reflexively turns to the right. Paco believes in the existence of the Invariant Right because he has actually verified it. He has put cameras in stores trained directly on the doorway, and if you go to his office, just above Union Square, where videocassettes and boxes of Super-eight film from all his work over the years are stacked in plastic Tupperware containers practically up to the ceiling, he can show you reel upon reel of grainy entry-way video — customers striding in the door, downshifting, refocusing, and then, again and again, making that little half turn.

Paco Underhill is a tall man in his mid-forties, partly bald, with a neatly trimmed beard and an engaging, almost goofy manner. He wears baggy khakis and shirts open at the collar, and generally looks like the academic he might have been if he hadn't been captivated, twenty years ago, by the ideas of the urban anthropologist William Whyte. It was Whyte who pioneered the use of time-lapse photography as a tool of urban planning, putting cameras in parks and the plazas in front of office buildings in midtown Manhattan, in order to determine what distinguished a public space that worked from one that didn't. As a Columbia undergraduate, in 1974, Paco heard a lecture on Whyte's work and, he recalls, left the room "walking on air." He immediately read everything Whyte had written. He emptied his bank account to buy cameras and film and make his own home movie, about a pedestrian mall in Poughkeepsie. He took his "little exercise" to Whyte's advocacy group, the Project for Public Spaces, and was offered a job. Soon, however, it dawned on Paco that Whyte's ideas could be taken a step further — that the same techniques he used to establish why a plaza worked or didn't work could also be used to determine why a store worked or didn't work. Thus was born the field of retail anthropology, and, not long afterward, Paco founded Envirosell, which in just over fifteen years has counselled some of the most familiar names in American retailing, from Levi Strauss to Kinney, Starbucks, McDonald's, Blockbuster, Apple Computer, AT&T, and a number of upscale retailers that Paco would rather not name.

When Paco gets an assignment, he and his staff set up a series of video 5 cameras throughout the test store and then back the cameras up with Envirosell staffers — trackers, as they're known — armed with clipboards. Where the cameras go and how many trackers Paco deploys depends on exactly what the store wants to know about its shoppers. Typically, though, he might use six cameras and two or three trackers, and let the study run for two or three days, so that at the end he would have pages and pages of carefully annotated tracking sheets and anywhere from a hundred to five hundred hours of film. These days, given the expansion of his business, he might tape fifteen thousand hours in a year, and, given that he has been in operation since the late seventies, he now has well over a hundred thousand hours of tape in his library.

Even in the best of times, this would be a valuable archive. But today, with the retail business in crisis, it is a gold mine. The time per visit that the average American spends in a shopping mall was sixty-six minutes last year — down from seventy-two minutes in 1992 — and is the lowest number ever recorded. The amount of selling space per American shopper is now more than double what it was in the mid-seventies, meaning that profit margins have never been narrower, and the costs of starting a retail business — and of failing — have never been higher. In the past few years, countless dazzling new retailing temples have been built along Fifth and

Madison Avenues — Barneys, Calvin Klein, Armani, Valentino, Banana Republic, Prada, Chanel, NikeTown, and on and on — but it is an explosion of growth based on no more than a hunch, a hopeful multimillion-dollar gamble that the way to break through is to provide the shopper with spectacle and more spectacle. "The arrogance is gone," Millard Drexler, the president and C.E.O. of the Gap, told me. "Arrogance makes failure. Once you think you know the answer, it's almost always over." In such a competitive environment, retailers don't just want to know how shoppers behave in their stores. They *have* to know. And who better to ask than Paco Underhill, who in the past decade and a half has analyzed tens of thousands of hours of shopping videotape and, as a result, probably knows more about the strange habits and quirks of the species *Emptor americanus* than anyone else alive?

Paco is considered the originator, for example, of what is known in the trade as the butt-brush theory — or, as Paco calls it, more delicately, *le facteur bousculade* — which holds that the likelihood of a woman's being converted from a browser to a buyer is inversely proportional to the likelihood of her being brushed on her behind while she's examining merchandise. Touch — or brush or bump or jostle — a woman on the behind when she has stopped to look at an item, and she will bolt. Actually, calling this a theory is something of a misnomer, because Paco doesn't offer any explanation for why women react that way, aside from venturing that they are "more sensitive back there." It's really an observation, based on repeated and close analysis of his videotape library, that Paco has transformed into a retailing commandment: A women's product that requires extensive examination should never be placed in a narrow aisle.
    Paco approaches the problem of the Invariant Right the same way. Some retail thinkers see this as a subject crying out for interpretation and speculation. The design guru Joseph Weishar, for example, argues, in his magisterial *Design for Effective Selling Space*, that the Invariant Right is a function of the fact that we "absorb and digest information in the left part of the brain" and "assimilate and logically use this information in the right half," the result being that we scan the store from left to right and then fix on an object to the right "essentially at a 45 degree angle from the point that we enter." When I asked Paco about this interpretation, he shrugged, and said he thought the reason was simply that most people are right-handed. Uncovering the fundamentals of "why" is clearly not a pursuit that engages him much. He is not a theoretician but an empiricist, and for him the important thing is that in amassing his huge library of in-store time-lapse photography he has gained enough hard evidence to know how often and under what circumstances the Invariant Right is expressed and how to take advantage of it.
    What Paco likes are facts. They come tumbling out when he talks, and, because he speaks with a slight hesitation — lingering over the first syllable in, for example, "re-tail" or "de-sign" — he draws you in, and you find yourself truly hanging on his words. "We have reached a historic point in American history," he told me in our very first conversation. "Men, for the first time, have

begun to buy their own underwear." He then paused to let the comment sink in, so that I could absorb its implications, before he elaborated: "Which means that we have to *totally* rethink the way we sell that product." In the parlance of Hollywood scriptwriters, the best endings must be surprising and yet inevitable; and the best of Paco's pronouncements take the same shape. It would never have occurred to me to wonder about the increasingly critical role played by touching — or, as Paco calls it, petting — clothes in the course of making the decision to buy them. But then I went to the Gap and to Banana Republic and saw people touching, and fondling and, one after another, buying shirts and sweaters laid out on big wooden tables, and what Paco told me — which was no doubt based on what he had seen on his videotapes — made perfect sense: that the reason the Gap and Banana Republic have tables is not merely that sweaters and shirts look better there, or that tables fit into the warm and relaxing residential feeling that the Gap and Banana Republic are trying to create in their stores, but that tables invite — indeed, symbolize — touching. "Where do we eat?" Paco asks. "We eat, we pick up food, on tables."

Paco produces for his clients a series of carefully detailed studies, totalling   10 forty to a hundred and fifty pages, filled with product-by-product breakdowns and bright-colored charts and graphs. In one recent case, he was asked by a major clothing retailer to analyze the first of a new chain of stores that the firm planned to open. One of the things the client wanted to know was how successful the store was in drawing people into its depths, since the chances that shoppers will buy something are directly related to how long they spend shopping, and how long they spend shopping is directly related to how deep they get pulled into the store. For this reason, a supermarket will often put dairy products on one side, meat at the back, and fresh produce on the other

Sports apparel for sale at a NikeTown store in Chicago.

side, so that the typical shopper can't just do a drive-by but has to make an entire circuit of the store, and be tempted by everything the supermarket has to offer. In the case of the new clothing store, Paco found that ninety-one percent of all shoppers penetrated as deep as what he called Zone 4, meaning more than three-quarters of the way in, well past the accessories and shirt racks and belts in the front, and little short of the far wall, with the changing rooms and the pants stacked on shelves. Paco regarded this as an extraordinary figure, particularly for a long, narrow store like this one, where it is not unusual for the rate of penetration past, say, Zone 3 to be under fifty percent. But that didn't mean the store was perfect — far from it. For Paco, all kinds of questions remained.

Purchasers, for example, spent an average of eleven minutes and twenty-seven seconds in the store, nonpurchasers two minutes and thirty-six seconds. It wasn't that the nonpurchasers just cruised in and out: in those two minutes and thirty-six seconds, they went deep into the store and examined an average of 3.42 items. So why didn't they buy? What, exactly, happened to cause some browsers to buy and other browsers to walk out the door?

Then, there was the issue of the number of products examined. The purchasers were looking at an average of 4.81 items but buying only 1.33 items. Paco found this statistic deeply disturbing. As the retail market grows more cutthroat, store owners have come to realize that it's all but impossible to increase the number of customers coming in, and have concentrated instead on getting the customers they do have to buy more. Paco thinks that if you can sell someone a pair of pants you must also be able to sell that person a belt, or a pair of socks, or a pair of underpants, or even do what the Gap does so well: sell a person a complete outfit. To Paco, the figure 1.33 suggested that the store was doing something very wrong, and one day when I visited him in his office he sat me down in front of one of his many VCRs to see how he looked for the 1.33 culprit.

It should be said that sitting next to Paco is a rather strange experience. "My mother says that I'm the best-paid spy in America," he told me. He laughed, but he wasn't entirely joking. As a child, Paco had a nearly debilitating stammer, and, he says, "since I was never that comfortable talking I always relied on my eyes to understand things." That much is obvious from the first moment you meet him: Paco is one of those people who looks right at you, soaking up every nuance and detail. It isn't a hostile gaze, because Paco isn't hostile at all. He has a big smile, and he'll call you "chief" and use your first name a lot and generally act as if he knew you well. But that's the awkward thing: He has looked at you so closely that you're sure he does know you well, and you, meanwhile, hardly know him at all.

This kind of asymmetry is even more pronounced when you watch his shopping videos with him, because every movement or gesture means something to Paco — he has spent his adult life deconstructing the shopping experience — but nothing to the outsider, or, at least, not at first. Paco had to keep stopping the video to get me to see things through his eyes before I began to understand. In one sequence, for example, a camera mounted high on the wall outside the changing rooms documented a man and a woman shopping for a pair of pants for what appeared to be their daughter, a girl in her mid-teens. The tapes are soundless, but the basic steps of the shopping dance are so familiar to Paco that, once I'd grasped the general idea, he was able to provide a running commentary on what was being said and thought. There is the girl emerging from the changing room wearing her first pair. There she is glancing at her reflection in the mirror, then turning to see herself from the back. There is the mother looking on. There is the father — or, as fathers are known in the trade, the "wallet carrier" — stepping forward and pulling up the jeans. There's the girl trying on another pair. There's the primp again. The twirl. The mother. The wallet carrier. And then again, with another pair. The full sequence lasted twenty minutes, and at the end came the take-home lesson, for which Paco called in one of his colleagues, Tom Moseman, who had supervised the project.

"This is a very critical moment," Tom, a young, intense man wearing little round glasses, said, and he pulled up a chair next to mine. "She's saying, 'I don't know whether I should wear a belt.' Now here's the salesclerk. The girl says to him, 'I need a belt,' and he says, 'Take mine.' Now there he is taking her back to the full-length mirror." 15

A moment later, the girl returns, clearly happy with the purchase. She wants the jeans. The wallet carrier turns to her, and then gestures to the sales-clerk. The wallet carrier is telling his daughter to give back the belt. The girl gives back the belt. Tom stops the tape. He's leaning forward now, a finger jabbing at the screen. Beside me, Paco is shaking his head. I don't get it — at least, not at first — and so Tom replays that last segment. The wallet carrier tells the girl to give back the belt. She gives back the belt. And then, finally, it dawns on me why this store has an average purchase number of only 1.33. "Don't you see?" Tom said. "*She wanted the belt.* A great opportunity to make an add-on sale . . . *lost!*"

Should we be afraid of Paco Underhill? One of the fundamental anxieties of the American consumer, after all, has always been that beneath the pleasure and the frivolity of the shopping experience runs an undercurrent of manip-ulation, and that anxiety has rarely seemed more justified than today. The practice of prying into the minds and habits of American consumers is now a multibillion-dollar business. Every time a product is pulled across a supermarket checkout scanner, information is recorded, assembled, and sold to a market-research firm for analysis. There are companies that put tiny cam-eras inside frozen-food cases in supermarket aisles; market-research firms that feed census data and behavioral statistics into algorithms and come out with complicated maps of the American consumer; anthropologists who sift through the garbage of carefully targeted households to analyze their true consumption patterns; and endless rounds of highly organized focus groups and questionnaire takers and phone surveyors. That some people are now tracking our every shopping move with video cameras seems in many respects the last straw: Paco's movies are, after all, creepy. They look like the surveillance videos taken during convenience store holdups — hazy and soundless and slightly warped by the angle of the lens. When you watch them, you find yourself waiting for something bad to happen, for someone to shoplift or pull a gun on a cashier.

The more time you spend with Paco's videos, though, the less scary they seem. After an hour or so, it's no longer clear whether simply by watching people shop — and analyzing their every move — you can learn how to control them. The shopper that emerges from the videos is not pliable or manipulable. The screen shows people filtering in and out of stores, petting and moving on, abandoning their merchandise because checkout lines are too long, or leaving a store empty-handed because they couldn't fit their stroller into the aisle between two shirt racks. Paco's shoppers are fickle and headstrong, and are quite unwilling to buy anything unless conditions are perfect — unless the belt is presented at *exactly* the right moment. His theories of the butt-brush and petting and the Decompression Zone and the Invariant Right seek not to make shoppers conform to the desires of sellers but to make sellers conform to the desires of shoppers. What Paco is teaching his clients is a kind of slavish devotion to the shopper's every whim. He is teaching them humility.

READING THE TEXT

1. Summarize in your own words the ways that retailers use spatial design to affect the consumer's behavior and buying habits.

2. What is Gladwell's tone in this selection, and what does it reveal about his attitudes toward the retail industry's manipulation of customers?

3. What effect does Gladwell's description of Paco Underhill's background and physical appearance have on the reader?

4. Why does Paco Underhill's mother say that he is "the best-paid spy in America" (para. 13)?

READING THE SIGNS

1. **CONNECTING TEXTS**   Visit a local store or supermarket, and study the spatial design. How many of the design strategies that Gladwell describes do you observe, and how do they affect customers' behavior? Use your observations as the basis for an essay interpreting the store's spatial design. To develop your ideas further, consult Anne Norton's "The Signs of Shopping" (p. 83).

2. In class, form teams and debate the proposition that the surveillance of consumers by retail anthropologists is manipulative and unethical.

3. Visit the Web site of a major retailer and analyze its design. How is the online "store" designed to encourage consuming behavior?

4. **CONNECTING TEXTS**   Write an essay in response to Gladwell's question "Should we be afraid of Paco Underhill?" (para. 17). To develop your ideas, consult Joseph Turow's "The Daily You: How the New Advertising Industry Is Defining Your Identity and Your Worth" (p. 394).

MICHAEL POLLAN
Supermarket Pastoral

One of the signs of society's increasing sensitivity to the environment, and to the lives of the animal species whose misfortune it is to be part of the human food chain, is the growth of the organic foods movement. So successful has this movement been — supporting the emergence of such grocery store chains as Whole Foods Market and Sprouts — that it has spawned an elaborate marketing technique that Michael Pollan calls "Supermarket Pastoral": "a most seductive literary form, beguiling enough to survive in the face of many discomfiting facts." These facts include the fundamental contradiction at the heart of the narrative, which is that the organic foods movement has become fully industrialized and that its tales of wholly "natural" ingredients and happy free-ranging hens gloss over a lot of synthetic additives and penned-up, soon-to-be-slaughtered chickens. Michael Pollan is the author of *The Omnivore's Dilemma* (2006), from which this selection is taken. His most recent book, *Cooked: A Natural History of Transformation* (2013), continues his explorations into the world of food.

Supermarket Pastoral

I enjoy shopping at Whole Foods nearly as much as I enjoy browsing a good bookstore, which, come to think of it, is probably no accident: Shopping at Whole Foods is a literary experience, too. That's not to take anything away from the food, which is generally of high quality, much of it "certified organic" or "humanely raised" or "free range." But right there, that's the point: It's the evocative prose as much as anything else that makes this food really special, elevating an egg or chicken breast or bag of arugula from the realm of ordinary protein and carbohydrates into a much headier experience, one with complex aesthetic, emotional, and even political dimensions. Take the "range-fed" sirloin steak I recently eyed in the meat case. According to the brochure on the counter, it was formerly part of a steer that spent its days "living in beautiful places" ranging from "plant-diverse, high-mountain meadows to thick aspen groves and miles of sagebrush-filled flats." Now a steak like that has got to taste better than one from Safeway, where the only accompanying information comes in the form of a number: the price, I mean, which you can bet will be considerably less. But I'm evidently not the only shopper willing to pay more for a good story.

   With the growth of organics and mounting concerns about the wholesomeness of industrial food, storied food is showing up in supermarkets everywhere these days, but it is Whole Foods that consistently offers the most cutting-edge grocery lit. On a recent visit I filled my shopping cart with eggs "from cage-free vegetarian hens," milk from cows that live "free from unnecessary fear and distress," wild salmon caught by Native Americans in Yakutat, Alaska (population 833), and heirloom tomatoes from Capay Farm ($4.99 a pound), "one of the early pioneers of the organic movement." The organic broiler I picked up even had a name: Rosie, who turned out to be a "sustainably farmed" "free-range chicken" from Petaluma Poultry, a company whose "farming methods strive to create harmonious relationships in nature, sustaining the health of all creatures and the natural world." Okay, not the most mellifluous or even meaningful sentence, but at least their heart's in the right place.

In several corners of the store I was actually forced to choose between subtly competing stories. For example, some of the organic milk in the milk case was "ultrapasteurized," an extra processing step that was presented as a boon to the consumer, since it extends shelf life. But then another, more local dairy boasted about the fact they had said no to ultrapasteurization, implying that their product was fresher, less processed, and therefore more organic. This was the dairy that talked about cows living free from distress, something I was beginning to feel a bit of myself by this point.

This particular dairy's label had a lot to say about the bovine lifestyle: Its Holsteins are provided with "an appropriate environment, including shelter and a comfortable resting area, . . . sufficient space, proper facilities and the company of their own kind." All this sounded pretty great, until I read the story of another dairy selling raw milk — *completely* unprocessed — whose "cows graze green pastures all year long." Which made me wonder whether the first dairy's idea of an appropriate environment for a cow included, as I had simply presumed, a pasture. All of a sudden the absence from their story of that word seemed weirdly conspicuous. As the literary critics would say, the writer seemed to be eliding the whole notion of cows and grass. Indeed, the longer I shopped in Whole Foods, the more I thought that this is a place where the skills of a literary critic might come in handy — those, and perhaps also a journalist's.

WORDY LABELS, point-of-purchase brochures, and certification schemes are supposed to make an obscure and complicated food chain more legible to the consumer. In the industrial food economy, virtually the only information that travels along the food chain linking producer and consumer is price. Just look at the typical newspaper ad for a supermarket. The sole quality on display here is actually a quantity: tomatoes $0.69 a pound; ground chuck $1.09 a pound; eggs $0.99 a dozen — special this week. Is there any other category of product sold on such a reductive basis? The bare-bones information travels in both directions, of course, and farmers who get the message that consumers care only about price will themselves care only about yield. This is how a cheap food economy reinforces itself.

One of the key innovations of organic food was to allow some more information to pass along the food chain between the producer and the consumer — an implicit snatch of narrative along with the number. A certified organic label tells a little story about how a particular food was produced, giving the consumer a way to send a message back to the farmer that she values tomatoes produced without harmful pesticides or prefers to feed her children milk from cows that haven't been injected with growth hormones. The word "organic" has proved to be one of the most powerful words in the supermarket: Without any help from government, farmers and consumers working together in this way have built an $11 billion industry that is now the fastest growing sector of the food economy.

Yet the organic label itself — like every other such label in the supermarket — is really just an imperfect substitute for direct observation of how a food is produced, a concession to the reality that most people in an industrial society haven't the time or the inclination to follow their food back to the farm, a farm which today is apt to be, on average, fifteen hundred miles away. So to bridge that space we rely on certifiers and label writers and, to a considerable extent, our imagination of what the farms that are producing our food really look like. The organic label may conjure an image of a simpler agriculture, but its very existence is an industrial artifact. The question is, what about the farms themselves? How well do they match the stories told about them?

Taken as a whole, the story on offer in Whole Foods is a pastoral narrative in which farm animals live much as they did in the books we read as children, and our fruits and vegetables grow in well-composted soils on small farms much like Joel Salatin's. "Organic" on the label conjures up a rich narrative, even if it is the consumer who fills in most of the details, supplying the hero (American Family Farmer), the villain (Agribusinessman), and the literary genre, which I've come to think of as Supermarket Pastoral. By now we may know better than to believe this too simple story, but not much better, and the grocery store poets do everything they can to encourage us in our willing suspension of disbelief.

Supermarket Pastoral is a most seductive literary form, beguiling enough to survive in the face of a great many discomfiting facts. I suspect that's because it gratifies some of our deepest, oldest longings, not merely for safe food, but for a connection to the earth and to the handful of domesticated creatures we've long depended on. Whole Foods understands all this better than we do. One of the company's marketing consultants explained to me that the Whole Foods shopper feels that by buying organic he is "engaging in authentic experiences" and imaginatively enacting a "return to a utopian past with the positive aspects of modernity intact." This sounds a lot like Virgilian pastoral, which also tried to have it both ways. In *The Machine in the Garden* Leo Marx writes that Virgil's shepherd Tityrus, no primitive, "Enjoys the best of both worlds — the sophisticated order of art and the simple spontaneity of nature." In keeping with the pastoral tradition, Whole Foods offers what Marx terms "a landscape of reconciliation" between the realms of nature and culture, a place where, as the marketing consultant put it, "people will come together through organic foods to get back to the origin of things" — perhaps by sitting down to enjoy one of the microwaveable organic TV dinners (four words I never expected to see conjoined) stacked in the frozen food case. How's that for having it both ways?

Of course the trickiest contradiction Whole Foods attempts to reconcile is the one between the industrialization of the organic food industry of which it is a part and the pastoral ideals on which that industry has been built. The organic movement, as it was once called, has come a remarkably long way in the last thirty years, to the point where it now looks considerably less like a movement than a big business. Lining the walls above the sumptuously stocked produce section in my Whole Foods are full-color photographs of local organic farmers accompanied by text blocks setting forth their farming philosophies. A handful of these farms — Capay is one example — still sell their produce to Whole Foods, but most are long gone from the produce bins, if not yet the walls. That's because Whole Foods in recent years has adopted the grocery industry's standard regional distribution system, which makes supporting small farms impractical. Tremendous warehouses buy produce for dozens of stores at a time, which forces them to deal exclusively with tremendous farms. So while the posters still depict family farmers and their philosophies, the produce on sale below them comes primarily from the two big corporate organic growers in California, Earthbound Farm and Grimmway Farms,* which together dominate the market for organic fresh produce in America. (Earthbound alone grows 80 percent of the organic lettuce sold in America.)

As I tossed a plastic box of Earthbound prewashed spring mix salad into my Whole Foods cart, I realized that I was venturing deep into the belly of the industrial beast Joel Salatin had called "the organic empire." (Speaking of my salad mix, another small, beyond organic farmer, a friend of Joel's, had told me he "wouldn't use that stuff to make compost" — the organic purist's stock insult.) But I'm not prepared to accept the premise that industrial organic is necessarily a bad thing, not if the goal is to reform a half-trillion-dollar food system based on chain supermarkets and the consumer's expectations that food be convenient and cheap.

And yet to the extent that the organic movement was conceived as a critique of industrial values, surely there comes a point when the process of industrialization will cost organic its soul (to use a word still uttered by organic types without irony), when Supermarket Pastoral becomes more fiction than fact: another lie told by marketers.

---

*Grimmway Farms owns Cal-Organic, one of the most ubiquitous organic brands in the supermarket.

The question is, has that point been reached, as Joel Salatin suggests? Just how well does Supermarket Pastoral hold up under close reading and journalistic scrutiny?

About as well as you would expect anything genuinely pastoral to hold up in the belly of an $11 billion industry, which is to say not very well at all. At least that's what I discovered when I traced a few of the items in my Whole Foods cart back to the farms where they were grown. I learned, for example, that some (certainly not all) organic milk comes from factory farms, where thousands of Holsteins that never encounter a blade of grass spend their days confined to a fenced "dry lot," eating (certified organic) grain and tethered to milking machines three times a day. The reason much of this milk is ultrapasteurized (a high-heat process that damages its nutritional quality) is so that big companies like Horizon and Aurora can sell it over long distances. I discovered organic beef being raised in "organic feedlots" and organic high-fructose corn syrup — more words I never expected to see combined. And I learned about the making of the aforementioned organic TV dinner, a microwaveable bowl of "rice, vegetables, and grilled chicken breast with a savory herb sauce." Country Herb, as the entrée is called, turns out to be a highly industrialized organic product, involving a choreography of thirty-one ingredients assembled from far-flung farms, laboratories, and processing plants scattered over a half-dozen states and two countries, and containing such mysteries of modern food technology as high-oleic safflower oil, guar and xanthan gum, soy lecithin, carrageenan, and "natural grill flavor." Several of these ingredients are synthetic additives permitted under federal organic rules. So much for "whole" foods. The manufacturer of Country Herb is Cascadian Farm, a pioneering organic farm turned processor in Washington State that is now a wholly owned subsidiary of General Mills. (The Country Herb chicken entrée has since been discontinued.)

I also visited Rosie the organic chicken at her farm in Petaluma, which   15
turns out to be more animal factory than farm. She lives in a shed with twenty thousand other Rosies, who, aside from their certified organic feed, live lives little different from that of any other industrial chicken. Ah, but what about the "free-range" lifestyle promised on the label? True, there's a little door in the shed leading out to a narrow grassy yard. But the free-range story seems a bit of a stretch when you discover that the door remains firmly shut until the birds are at least five or six weeks old — for fear they'll catch something outside — and the chickens are slaughtered only two weeks later.

Reading the Text

1. Pollan begins the selection with his own tale of a shopping trip to Whole Foods. Why do you think he includes personal experience? What effect does it have on your response as a reader?

2. Explain in your own words what Pollan means by "Supermarket Pastoral" (para. 8).

3. How do "wordy labels, point-of-purchase brochures, and certification schemes" (para. 5) affect a consumer's shopping behavior in a store like Whole Foods, according to Pollan?

4. Explain how, in Pollan's view, the organic food business has become industrialized.

5. How do you characterize Pollan's tone in this selection? How does it affect your response to his position?

READING THE SIGNS

1. **CONNECTING TEXTS**　Visit a Whole Foods outlet, or another retailer that is promoted as organic, green, or alternative, and study the products, interior décor, and claims made about how items are sourced. Consider whether your observations combine to create a Supermarket Pastoral narrative. In an essay, write an argument that outlines the narrative that your store tells, whether it be Supermarket Pastoral or something else. To develop your ideas, consult Julia B. Corbett's "A Faint Green Sell: Advertising and the Natural World" (p. 209). Alternatively, conduct the same sort of analysis of a more typical supermarket. Do you see similar strategies at work there? How might you explain any differences you may detect?

2. Adopt the perspective of a Whole Foods manager, and write a response to Pollan's critique of the store chain. How would the manager defend the chain against the claim that it offers "'a landscape of reconciliation' between the realism of nature and culture" (para. 9)?

3. **CONNECTING TEXTS**　Study the packaging of one or more items available at a store like Whole Foods or Sprouts. Using Chris Arning's "What Can Semiotics Contribute to Packaging Design?" (p. 111) as a critical framework, analyze how the packaging works not simply as a container but as a collection of signs created by marketers. What signs does your chosen packaging use, and what do they signify?

4. Write an essay that supports, opposes, or complicates the proposition that industrial organic is a better alternative to "a half-trillion-dollar food system based on chain supermarkets and the consumer's expectations that food be convenient and cheap" (para. 11).

5. In small groups, analyze the various eateries available on your campus, studying the "food narrative" that they convey to students. To what extent do you see the Supermarket Pastoral as a dominant narrative? Do other narratives appear? Use your group's observations to support your own essay analyzing how food is marketed to students. Try to account for your findings.

Credit Card Barbie

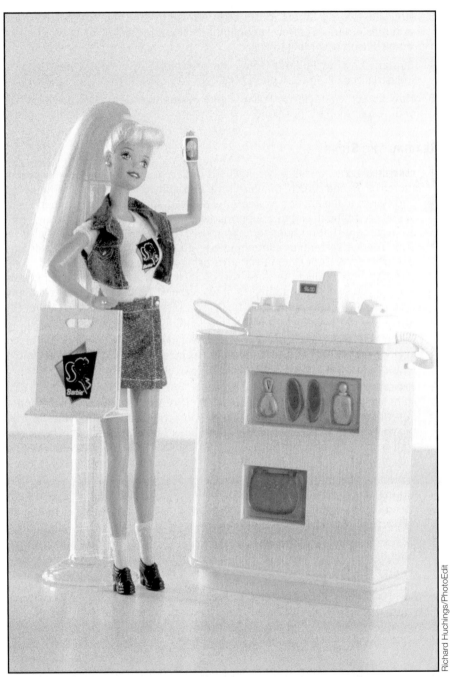

Reading the Signs

1. Why might girls enjoy playing with a Barbie who shops rather than engaging her in some other kind of activity?

2. Do you think that having Barbie use a credit card to purchase cosmetics has an effect on the girls who play with the doll? If so, what are those effects?

JON MOOALLEM
The Self-Storage Self

The Great Recession emptied a lot of homes as their owners were cast into the abyss of foreclosure, but in doing so it filled a lot of storage facilities with the piles of things — some of them mere junk, some of them priceless possessions — that most of us accumulate in our lives. In this feature article for the *New York Times Magazine*, Jon Mooallem visits some of the ordinary folk who have found themselves needing self-storage units in the wake of broken careers, broken engagements, broken marriages, or simply disrupted lives. And the things they hold on to, paying sizable fees to store stuff that often appears to be little better than trash, may be surprising — until we remember that our possessions are an important measure of our lives. Jon Mooallem is a contributing writer for the *New York Times Magazine* and is the author of *Wild Ones: A Sometimes Dismaying, Weirdly Reassuring Story about Looking at People Looking at Animals in America* (2013).

Statewide Self Storage spreads out near Highway 4 in Antioch, Calif., a suburban community between San Francisco and Sacramento. It's a phalanx of long, low-slung buildings separated by wide driveways and lined with red doors. The complex houses 453 storage units and is wedged between a car dealership and a Costco.

It was the last afternoon in May, and the sun seared all the concrete and corrugated steel. Statewide's gate opened, and a man named Jimmy Sloan made for the far corner of the property. Sloan, who dresses and styles his hair like James Dean, is a part-owner of the Harley-Davidson repair shop nearby. He rolled open the door of a 10-by-30-foot unit, the largest Statewide offers. It was his ex-fiancée's but still leased under his name, and packed with, among other things, a particleboard shelving unit, some wicker items, a microwave oven, a box labeled "Mickey's Hornet Neon," a floor lamp, a television and a wooden child's bed standing on its end on a desk. It was hard to tell how deep the inventory went. "She hasn't seen most of this stuff in six years," Sloan said.

For five years, he stored most of it above the garage of his house. But he had to borrow on the house to keep the bike shop running, and last year, feeling in over his head, he opted to sell the house and downsize before he fell behind and risked foreclosure. "Pretty much got out of that house at zero — didn't make a penny on it," he told me with the kind of ascetic pride that wouldn't have made any sense before our economically crippled era. Sloan's fiancée insisted he rent a storage unit and move everything over the garage into it for her. So he did. Then they split up.

He kept paying the rent on the unit for almost a year — $217 every month. But Sloan finally lost his patience and told her: "You know, we're not even together anymore. This stuff's gotta go." Everything here, he told me, was worth less than what he had paid to store it. "Storage is always a bad investment, any way you look at it," he said. The rent was her responsibility now. But the former future Mrs. Jimmy Sloan never paid Statewide. By now, it seemed likely that the managers would end up auctioning off the contents of the unit in accordance with state law. That was fine with Jimmy Sloan. But he wanted to get in first and make sure that his late father's collection of hunting knives and die-cast toy tractors, which he'd lost track of, weren't mixed in there. And so, to regain access, he'd just walked into the office and paid Statewide what was owed: $460. He'd counted out the cash unresentfully, like a man retrieving his dog from a neighbor's house for the 10th or 11th time.

"That stuff is Happy Meal junk," he now said, pointing to a see-through 5 Rubbermaid bin in the storage unit's brickwork of boxes. It was full of brightly colored plastic toys and a pair of hot pink sunglasses that belonged to his ex-fiancée's children. "The kids broke it, played with it once. It wasn't even for Christmas," he said.

Sloan had not started rummaging for his dad's knife and tractor collections in earnest; he was still pecking at the concretion's surface, not tunneling into it. But already he'd found a Marilyn Monroe poster and a souvenir road sign for James Dean Boulevard and set them near the door. They were his, from his old living room. He had forgotten about them and wanted to take them home. Soon, he peeled back the top of a huge bin. Inside, I could see a VHS cassette of "American Pie" and a black-and-white toy football with the logo of the Oakland Raiders. "Look at that!" Sloan said suddenly. "A Raider football!" He put it next to the poster and the road sign. Apparently it, too, was just appealing enough to hang on to.

The Self Storage Association, a nonprofit trade group, estimates that since the onset of the recession, occupancies at storage facilities nationwide are down, on average, about 2 or 3 percent. It's not a cataclysmic drop but enough to disorient an industry that has always considered itself recession-resistant, if not outright recession-proof. But the collapsing economy created an opportunity, and in some cases an ultimatum, for Americans to reassess the raft of obligations and the loads of stuff we accumulated before things went wrong.

We've been making difficult decisions, and for a lot of us, that has involved rolling up the door of a storage unit and carting property in or out. The storage industry's expansion in the first flush years of this decade was both enabled by, and helped enable, the extreme consumption that defined America then. The people coming through the gates now are defining who we will be when this turmoil is over.

The first modern self-storage facilities opened in the 1960s, and for two decades storage remained a low-profile industry, helping people muddle through what it terms "life events." For the most part, storage units were meant to temporarily absorb the possessions of those in transition: moving, marrying or divorcing, or dealing with a death in the family. And the late 20th century turned out to be a golden age of life events in America, with peaking divorce rates and a rush of second- and third-home buying. At the same time, the first baby boomers were left to face down the caches of heirlooms and clutter in their parents' basements.

Across America, from 2000 to 2005, upward of 3,000 self-storage facilities went up every year. Somehow, Americans managed to fill that brand-new empty space. It raises a simple question: where was all that stuff before? "A lot of it just comes down to the great American propensity toward accumulating stuff," [industry veteran Tom] Litton explained. Between 1970 and 2008, real disposable personal income per capita doubled, and by 2008 we were spending nearly all of it — all but 2.7 percent — each year. Meanwhile, the price of much of what we were buying plunged. Even by the early '90s, American families had, on average, twice as many possessions as they did 25 years earlier. By 2005, according to the Boston College sociologist Juliet B. Schor, the average consumer purchased one new piece of clothing every five and a half days.

Schor has been hacking intrepidly through the jumble of available data [10] quantifying the last decade's consumption spree. Between 1998 and 2005, she found, the number of vacuum cleaners coming into the country every year more than doubled. The number of toasters, ovens and coffeemakers tripled. A 2006 U.C.L.A. study found middle-class families in Los Angeles "battling a nearly universal overaccumulation of goods." Garages were clogged. Toys and outdoor furniture collected in the corners of backyards. "The home-goods storage crisis has reached almost epic proportions," the authors of the study wrote. A new kind of customer was being propelled, hands full, into self-storage.

Consider our national furniture habit. In an unpublished paper, Schor writes that "anecdotal evidence suggests an 'Ikea effect.'" We've spent more on furniture even as prices have dropped, thereby amassing more of it. The amount entering the United States from overseas doubled between 1998 and 2005, reaching some 650 million pieces a year. Comparing Schor's data with E.P.A. data on municipal solid waste shows that the rate at which we threw out old furniture rose about one-thirteenth as fast during roughly the same period. In other words, most of that new stuff — and any older furniture it displaced — is presumably still knocking around somewhere. In fact, some seven million American households now have at least one piece of furniture in their storage units. Furniture is the most commonly stored thing in America.

The marketing consultant Derek Naylor told me that people stockpile furniture while saving for bigger or second homes but then, in some cases, "they don't want to clutter up their new home with all the things they have in storage." So they buy new, nicer things and keep paying to store the old ones anyway. Clem Tang, a spokesman for Public Storage, explains: "You say, 'I paid $1,000 for this table a couple of years ago. I'm not getting rid of it, or selling it for 10 bucks at a garage sale. That's like throwing away $1,000.'" It's not a surprising response in a society replacing things at such an accelerated rate — this inability to see our last table as suddenly worthless, even though we've just been out shopping for a new one as though it were.

"My parents were Depression babies," Litton told me, "and what they taught me was, it's the accumulation of things that defines you as an American, and to throw anything away was being wasteful." The self-storage industry reconciles these opposing values: paying for storage is, paradoxically, thrifty. "That propensity toward consumption is what fueled the world's economy," Litton said. The self-storage industry almost had to expand; it grew along with the volume of container ships reaching our ports.

By 2007, a full 15 percent of customers told the Self Storage Association they were storing items that they "no longer need or want." It was the third-most-popular use for a unit and was projected to grow to 25 percent of renters the following year. The line between necessity and convenience — between temporary life event and permanent lifestyle — totally blurred. "There's a lot of junk stored in our properties," Ronald L. Havner Jr., Public Storage's chief executive, told a symposium in New York. But really, there's no way of knowing exactly who is still [storing their possessions], what they've got locked up and how they feel about it — and, more important, how those complicated feelings might change if the psychology of the American consumer is substantially reshaped in a recovery.

Tom Litton, for example, still keeps four storage units himself, at two facilities, all of them 10-by-30 units. I asked what's inside. "I have a canoe, I have a vending machine, I have a drill press," Litton began. His old lawn mower was in one. (He got a bigger, riding lawn mower when he bought a ranch in wine country.) "I've got some of my old clothes that I probably wouldn't wear anyway," he continued, and some trophies from college. "I also have some old cassette tapes that I produced." The cassettes are like audiobooks, he explained — tutorials on how to get into the storage industry and succeed. He made them before the storage-facility building boom ended a couple of years ago. "They didn't sell," Litton said, "so they're all in storage now." 15

One afternoon in late May, a woman slouched inside one of Statewide's narrow hallways, reorganizing the innards of her unit. She said her name was Elizabeth — no last name given, since, as she told me, "this is not a high-self-esteem moment." Most everything here belonged to Elizabeth's parents, who entered assisted living last year, and she needed to clear it out to cut expenses.

She was keeping an eye out for particular family memorabilia, but otherwise it was a long, beleaguering purge. "Just stuff? Like my mother's kitchen stuff?" she told me. "Whatever."

Boxed haphazardly inside the closet-size space was, as she put it, 53 years of married life. An empty pill bottle and an egg carton lingered on the little bit of visible floor space. "I got rid of all the furniture," Elizabeth said, except her own drafting table, which, she pointed out, had wound up against the rear wall. She was an architect, accomplished but out of work ("Architecture is dead, dead, dead, dead," she explained) and was attacking this project with a conspicuously architect-ish methodology.

She had brought with her dozens of new, perfectly uniform white boxes, each bearing the Harry Potter logo in one of several colors. They lined the hallway behind her, still flattened. "When the books come out, there's just hundreds and hundreds of these boxes at every bookstore," she said. "I just went around and got them." She repacked and erected a tidy column of Harry Potter boxes in one corner of the unit. She turned a few others, tops folded inward, into a kind of bookshelf. "This was when *The Half-Blood Prince* came out," Elizabeth said. "They stack really nicely." She was going to transfer these boxes, full of the few things worth saving, into a storage unit she recently rented in a nearby town. That unit housed most of what Elizabeth owned. Forced to leave her parents' old house and unable to afford a place of her own, she had moved in with a friend about eight months ago. As far as the storage industry was concerned, then, all the contemporaneous chaos of Elizabeth's and her parents' lives ultimately amounted to a wash: one old unit was being vacated, one new one was being rented.

In fact, since last year, owners around the country have reported quickening rates of both move-outs and move-ins, making any occupancy rate — the industry's fundamental yardstick — feel kind of arbitrary, like the momentary averaging-out of a blur of activity, with no single, dominant trend (or maybe even logic) behind it. At Statewide, for example, those like Elizabeth renting smaller units — traditionally the backbone of the business — have been steadily leaving. "All I hear is, 'I can't afford it anymore,'" says Joe Dopart, who manages Statewide along with his daughter Amy and his wife, Evie, a retired schoolteacher. At the same time, though, Statewide's larger units — mostly empty for years — are now completely full. "Every single one, practically, has a foreclosure in it," Amy told me. Others were being rented by endangered businesses, like a coffee shop and a tea room whose owners were forced to shutter their storefronts in Antioch's struggling historic downtown and move everything into storage while they plotted their next moves.

The upshot, while this traffic runs both ways in the background, is that 20 Statewide has remained about 88 percent full — about two or three points lower than last summer, right in line with the national estimate. But that may obscure a more meaningful shift. By shaking up the composition of renters, and their reasons for renting, the recession could be quietly tilting the character of American storage closer to what it was originally: a pragmatic solution to a sudden loss of space, rather than a convenient way of dealing with, or putting off dealing with, an excess of stuff.

Of course, some people don't fit entirely into one category or the other. I found people who had been foreclosed on at most of the storage places I hung around at, and I met many more who were forced to walk away from places they were renting. Among them were two teenage brothers, Luis Jaramillo and Nikolas Aceves, in the city of Stockton, an hour from Sacramento, whose family was about to scatter to relatives' houses in surrounding towns. And Jason Williams, a 38-year-old father of three who was filling a unit with furniture before he and his family moved in with his stepmother.

On one of my first mornings at Statewide, Evie Dopart introduced me to Danielle Johnson, who worked at Dollar Tree and was also studying criminal justice. After her husband left to serve in Iraq, she couldn't afford the rent on their house in Oakland. So she locked everything but her clothes and schoolbooks in storage and moved in with her grandma. "It's O.K.," she assured me, "I'll get another one someday." She meant another house. That was a year ago. Her husband was now stationed in Kentucky, but if Johnson pulled out of school to join him, she would have to repay her student loans immediately and would end up with nothing. "Well," she told me, "I'm just going to finish, and I'll have my degree. He can wait." She seemed incapable of not putting a good face on the situation. "Actually," she told me and Evie, "it's kind of cool living with Grandma. Home-cooked meals are awesome, and no one makes them like Grandma does."

"Your family's Italian, right?" Evie asked.

"No, we're redneck, though," Johnson said with a big smile. "And I mean rednecks make some really good food. Gosh! My grandma's biscuits and gravy are screaming."

Virtually no one I asked, at any level of the business, took seriously the idea that this recession would produce a sea change in who uses self-storage and why. In an industry whose freewheeling success has been so closely tied to the evolving character and prosperity of our society, it can be hard to even talk about storage's future without getting philosophical or patriotic.   25

"I really think there's a spirit that things will turn around," Jim Chiswell, a Virginia-based consultant to the industry, told me. "I believe that my children — and both my children are proving it already — they're going to have more at the end of their lifetimes, and more success, than I've had. And so will their children. I don't believe the destiny of this country as a beacon of freedom and hope is over. And I believe there will be more growth, and more people wanting to have things and collect things." Tom Litton put it another way: "The good news is that your age group" — I'm 31 — "has the same propensity for accumulating crap that I have. You guys got introduced to it in college, and you actually think you really need storage. You see storage the way that we all see cable and Internet access."

Maybe the recession really is making American consumers serious about scaling back, about decluttering and de-leveraging. But there are upward of

51,000 storage facilities across this country — more than seven times the number of Starbucks. Storage is part of our national infrastructure now. And all it is, is empty space: something Americans have always colonized and capitalized on in good times, and retreated into to regroup when things soured. It's tough to imagine a product more malleable to whatever turns our individual life stories take, wherever we're collectively heading.

But where are we now? Of all the storage units I toured, one sticks out as being most emblematic of this particular moment. It belonged to Terry Wallace, a 59-year-old veteran with white streaks in his hair and a broad, shaggy moustache who, when I stumbled across his 10-by-30 at a Storage PRO in Stockton, was sitting in a leather office chair, working at his desk under the open door, like a notary in a storefront. Some open mail and a Herman Wouk novel were pushed aside, and the desk was covered with stacks of quarters, the ones celebrating the 50 states. Wallace was sorting them, state by state, into empty prescription-pill bottles. "I've got 'em all," he said, astounded. "I've got all 50." Then he invited me in.

A folded-up Nordic Track leaned against the desk, and a bucket of fire axes sat behind him. (After serving as a helicopter mechanic in Vietnam, Wallace worked as a back-country firefighter in Yosemite.) But otherwise, the unit looked warehouselike. Stacked, labeled boxes stretched down either side of the deep, rectangular space with a snug but passable aisle between. This was everything Wallace owned, except the truck parked outside. A year ago, he was living in an apartment in Carson City, Nev., funneling the entire $1,200 he collected in retirement benefits and disability directly into his rent and alimony payments every month. "So I started doing a lot of credit-card stuff," he said. Soon he was $30,000 in debt.

Wallace hated living in a city anyway, "so because of my debt crisis and my marriage crisis and everything, I moved everything into storage and I just live out of my truck," he told me, resting his hands on his gut. That was June 15, 2008. At first, he rented a second unit across the way and spent a few months sorting, giving away items he didn't need to an organization for homeless veterans. "You can call me homeless," he told me. "But I'm not goofing around. I've got money, but I just want to get this debt down." 30

It was like a cleansing: the storage unit cost about $200 a month. But aside from gas, truck payments and food (he had several boxes of meals-ready-to-eat stocked here), it was his only major expense. He had cut out rent, cable, phone and electricity, and purged all the unnecessary fees from his bank statements. For the last year, he had been camping a lot and driving around the West visiting ex-firefighter friends. He saw a woman in Antioch occasionally. "It's feeling good," he said, "and it's working. That's the thing: it's working. Debts are down to almost zippo right now." He figured he'd be done by Thanksgiving.

For a decade at least, storage has been a mechanism allowing Americans to live beyond our means. Wallace was using his unit as a center of gravity, to pull his financial life back within reach. He had even started saving, he told me, and was looking into a small condo in a suburb near Lake Tahoe. "It's not my style or anything," he said; he'd prefer something more secluded — bigger, and with land. "But I could do that." He missed sleeping in his own bed.

He also missed his music collection — and the books and rare coins he had collected. Also, his pins. "Little pins, like flag pins," he explained. "I've got veterans pins, and I've got Rose Parade pins, and pins that I got at fairs." He missed his stuff. "Hey," he said as I left. "I'll call you when I'm getting ready to load the truck."

READING THE TEXT

1. How does Mooallem's opening anecdote about repair-shop owner Jimmy Sloan's visit to his Statewide Self Storage unit set a tone for the rest of the selection?

2. According to Mooallem, how has the Great Recession affected the self-storage industry?

3. Synthesize in your own words the various reasons that customers rely upon self-storage facilities.

4. What does sociologist Juliet B. Schor mean by the "Ikea effect" (para. 11)?

5. What does storage industry consultant Tom Litton mean by saying young people have "the same propensity for accumulating crap that I have. . . . [They] see storage the way that we all see cable and Internet access" (para. 26)?

READING THE SIGNS

1. In a journal entry, contemplate your own and/or your family's possessions. If you needed to scale back what you own, how would you decide what to dispose of, keep, store, or sell? What would your choices indicate about your priorities and interests?

2. **CONNECTING TEXTS** Write an essay in which you evaluate the validity of Tom Litton's claim that "it's the accumulation of things that defines you as an American" (para. 13). To develop your ideas, consult Laurence Shames's "The More Factor" (p. 76) and the Introduction to Chapter 1, "Consuming Passions: The Culture of American Consumption" (p. 67).

3. **CONNECTING TEXTS** In "Everything Now" (p. 123), Steve McKevitt argues that our current consumption habits are "enormously wasteful: a huge and unnecessary drain on the world's dwindling natural resources" (para. 22). In an essay, write an argument that assesses the extent to which Americans' propensity for accumulating material objects contributes to that drain. Does storing items actually reduce the need to produce more, or does it serve to enable the production of more waste?

4. Despite the economic woes suffered by many of the people interviewed in this article, industry consultant Tom Litton remains confident about America's economic future. What is the basis of his confidence? Write an essay in which you demonstrate, refute, or modify his position.

CHRIS ARNING
What Can Semiotics Contribute to Packaging Design?

Usually, semiotic analyses are conducted from the perspective of the *receiver* of a message — as when we analyze an advertisement, a television show, or any other phenomenon of popular culture. But as semiotician Chris Arning demonstrates in his description of how semiotics can help brand owners maximize their profits, the focus can be reversed to analyze the *sending* of the message. And in the case of product packaging, that message lies in the physical elements of the package itself, which, much like many advertisements, may say less about the product than it does about the emotions of the consumers who are expected to buy it. With the product's outside being just as (if not more) important than its inside, Arning suggests, it behooves marketers to carefully craft the signals that their products send, and that means paying attention to the semiotics of packaging design. Chris Arning is the founder of Creative Semiotics Ltd, a semiotics consulting firm, as well as of the Semiotic Thinking Group on LinkedIn, and teaches classes on Brands and Meaning at the University of Warwick.

Consumers shop for meaning, not stuff.

—LAURA OSWALD

This is certainly true of brand communication and no less true of packaging. As a brand owner, do you know what messages you transmit through the cues embedded in your pack design replicated millions of times? Consumers see packaging as an integral part of a product's value proposition. This includes the language conveyed on packs, the materials used and the graphical schema employed including colours, typography and symbols.

Psychotherapist Louis Cheskin spent most of his life investigating how design elements impacted people's perceptions of value, appeal, and relevance. He also discovered that most people could not resist transferring their feelings towards the packaging to the product itself. His most famous achievement was turning Marlboro cigarettes into a 'man's' cigarette from its original appeal to women. At the time its unique product differentiation was a red wrapper, to hide lipstick marks. Because more men than women were smokers, Cheskin convinced Phillip Morris that they would have more success by appealing to men. Cheskin's recommendations were to redesign the package to denote masculinity, whilst keeping the red colour.

His recommendations underlie everything from the 'Man-Sized Flavour' advertising campaign and the now iconic packaging (resembling a medal), to the masculine and virile Marlboro Man himself. The Marlboro Man sported tattoos to give him a rugged back-story and often appeared as a cowboy on horseback (the predominant image that has survived today).

We have lived through an age of mass affluence and during this time, packaging has undergone a mass wave of so-called 'premiumisation' across all sectors, with even cleaning products like Fairy Liquid getting in on the act. In such a context, packaging in the UK and elsewhere is no longer just a container, but a manifesto for brand communication. For some consumers, it is even fetishistic. This means that the bar for what is considered quality has been raised. We expect charming and emotionally engaging packaging as part of the overall product proposition, and in certain categories it is even a brand discriminator.

Plastic versus glass, rotund versus rectilinear, puce versus cobalt: the devil 5 is in the detail, and these details can be critical to the success of packaging. Whilst pack designers are technically competent and have a knack for aesthetics, it is sometimes necessary to have a more in-depth understanding of how to express brand distinction in pack communication. This is where semiotics comes in to play.

So, what is semiotics? Semiotics is the study of meaning and communication. It can inject rigour and more rationality into design processes, making us more mindful of our choices. Residing in academic research, mainly in disciplines such as linguistics, media studies and sociology, the application of semiotics has taken off in the commercial world and provided enormous value in the area of brand packaging. More and more, the use of semiotics research is penetrating the sphere of packaging design, giving brands a tremendous head start in communicating core values, personality and brand positioning to the market. So what can semiotics contribute to packaging design? Mega multi-nationals such as Procter & Gamble (P&G) and Unilever were asking this question five years ago. These days semiotics is a part of their vocabulary and insight budget. The interest in the 'S' word is now spreading among brand developers, designers, advertisers and packaging experts, making it worthwhile to take a closer look at what the semiotics research approach is all about.

The British writer J.G. Ballard once remarked that he could read the respective political ideologies of Britain and the USA inscribed into the front grill designs of Rolls Royce (parliamentary, monarchical) and Cadillacs (democratic, presidential). Whilst semiotics is not always that grandiose in interpretation, it does make links from the material detail to the ideas these details are likely to trigger in the minds of consumers encountering brand packs on a shelf—it is a powerful interpretive tool.

Consumers intuitively read and respond to the codes contained in brand communication, especially in brand packaging. For example, consider the packaging of personal care products containing lavender and how it has changed over time. Dated or clichéd packaging of lavender conveyed the symbolic code of 'grannies floral'—pale mauve labelling, italicised old-world fonts and lavender sprig designs used as borders. The images conveyed the message that this product is best kept in white linens and lingerie drawers. The dominant design of packaging lavender today has shifted from nostalgic old world notions to expressing the code of authenticity. Use of labels with images of lavender, overt use of pale purple for package and copy that states it is lavender — all convey a message that reads, "I am really lavender." The more emergent expression of lavender in personal care is shifting toward the key benefit of lavender, namely its role in aromatherapy and relaxation. Packaging design is more evocative, using explicit language such as 'relax, unwind, calm down.' The colour palette embraces dark purple to emphasise deep relaxation and the word 'lavender' is not always stated on pack. Understanding these semiotic codes and patterns of change does more than provide interesting historical dimensions. The codes create confident foundations for brands to be relevant, contemporary, and, above all else, appealing to consumers. By considering semiotics, a brand has a greater ability to pitch its packaging execution at exactly the right angle for consumers to read the desired message.

For example, the Courvoisier bottle conveys value through metaphors of opulence. As with many premium luxury items, it is as much an *objet d'art* to be contemplated, as it is a commodity to be consumed. The effect is achieved through solidity of material, flamboyant fluting of its bottle shape and other such extravagant features. As a cognac, it is squat and rotund, which evokes the lavishness of 16th century France where the drink originated. Arguably it is about possessing an object of beauty and identifying with an object of power and prestige — both anchored by the prominent Napoleon emblem. Many fast-moving consumer goods categories are also subject to what is called code convergence (where dominant graphical schemas tend to imitate category leaders and become more homogeneous over time), so packaging designers are pushed even further to innovate whilst still respecting product category norms.

Applied semiotics in brand strategy and design can help bring awareness that meaning, and therefore perceived value, is generated via the differences that exist between brands within a category and that signs change according to the prevailing culture. This market intelligence can be a key competitive advantage, particularly in mature, cluttered product categories. This understanding can be strategic, e.g. how the changing meanings of gold vs. bronze (via their connotations in art and other areas) affect their optimal use on pack; or tactical, e.g. how the choice of font typeface can convey the right impression and inflect meaning.

In practice, there are typically four main uses of semiotics methodology in package design:

- brand understanding
- inspiration
- evaluation, and
- global intelligence.

Brand Understanding

This is a very common area for a semiotics investigation. It is usually triggered by a brand review, to understand the rules or 'codes' of a category in order to sharpen communication and become more differentiated. For instance, when a well-known Swiss chocolate manufacturer recognised the need to become more suited to the UK market, it undertook a brand audit. The first step was to show the connotations of propriety and stuffy conservatism and the positioning of chocolate as a confectionary item. This was conveyed via the use of glossy materials, rectilinear neo-classical motifs and other outdated signifiers going as far as the fussy scoring of chocolate tablets. The second step was to show the trajectory of change in the chocolate category towards more organic motifs, rougher, pulped materials and a move away from *fin-de-siècle* refinement, towards an inter-cultural awareness and how this was being reflected in and on pack. The third step was to suggest some ways that the brand could incorporate some of the new, emergent codes into the design brief.

In a more recent project, a company, for NPD purposes, needed to understand the codes of beauty serums used in packaging material and formulation. The analysis revealed that some of the codes used in the serums, which included the use of the golden ratio and contour bias in pack design, conveyed a deft sense of symmetry and perfection. There was also a strong brand value association communicated via emotional design. Semiotics also revealed intertextual links between serums and the mythology of elixirs as life giving essence. Semiotics, like a serum itself, delivered a succinct, concentrated and easily absorbed dose of market intelligence that helped in the decision-making process.

Brand Inspiration

Semiotics leverages nuanced understanding of cultural change, aesthetic theory and lateral thinking to be a powerful hypotheses-generating engine. For instance, if we wanted to communicate the more emergent, leading-edge expressions of "naturalness" in a pack design for a cosmetics product, the initial analysis would involve understanding the cultural connotations of naturalness. Some questions that would be explored are: What does natural mean to us today? How is it different from three years ago? How do other categories communicate natural in their packaging? What are the new ways of communicating natural in cosmetics packaging? The semiotics research would decode the meanings of natural in a wider cultural context and within the cosmetics category.

Back in 2005, Wrigley's commissioned a semiotics study to feed into an innovation workshop to develop concepts for a new gum for young adults. The result was '5 gum,' a sensation in its category, which has enjoyed great commercial success and numerous industry awards. In this case, the semiotic   15 insight showed that there was a stark discrepancy between the codes used within the gum market (fiddly, childish packs with primary colour cartoon graphics) and the market for US teens which was increasingly mature, ironic and enamoured of darker themes like the occult and extreme sports. Following the semiotic research, Wrigley's decided to translate some of this danger and mystique into the pack design for the new product.

Brand Evaluation

Semiotics can help assess and adjudicate between different strategic options for packaging, helping to fast-track the design and development process. In a recent study, a leading semiotics consultancy was asked to help a client develop new packaging for a premium yogurt brand that would have an increased price point. Using applied semiotic research, the consultancy derived a model and list of criteria including pack shape, material, haptic cues, graphic schema, layout, color and gradation from a rubric of similar projects to help the client achieve a solid competitive advantage.

Global Intelligence

Simplicity is not as simple as it used to be. At least, this was the conclusion drawn from a study looking at so-called 'simple' packaging. The trouble is that 'simple' cannot be equated with 'basic' anymore: it is more about 'managed complexity' and what counts as optimal varies significantly across markets. Of course, there is a set of universal rules regarding what counts as simplicity. Visual tricks such as symmetry, the law of thirds, golden ratio and contour bias that create a pleasing visual impression operate within the realm of neuroaesthetics. It seems, however, that hard-wired ideas are themselves subject to regional variation and inflection too — indeed 'simplicity' turns out to be almost as subject to variation as notions such as authenticity and other diffuse marketing terms. The American economist, Professor Theodore Levitt, famous for popularising the term 'globalization' was only half right. The world has become globalized and there is more standardization, but the keynote of design is hybridization between global design idiom and local motifs. In certain enclaves of consumer society, parochial tastes stubbornly persist and food packaging is one such niche.

Global Food Packaging

For a global food brand wanting to reconnect with notions such as simplicity, this is not an easy task when semiotics shows such a wide global variation in pack codes. For example, in Mexico, the baroque and riotous colors rule supreme, high color saturation; negligible color contrast and ornamentation are favoured. By contrast in Japan, a Zen-inflected subtlety and restraint with a generous use of white space dominate. In the UK, revivalist motifs and a return to thrift prevail and in France notions of regionality and *terroir* are the main focus. In India, simplicity per se is not a resonant term and seems only to be signified in food through proxies like spiritual purity or motherly love. In general, in developing markets, references to simplicity run up against a desire to flee poverty and taste abundance and packaging seems to reflect that paradox. These are the sorts of differences that applied use of semiotics can bring to a design team's attention.

The use of semiotic research can assist in developing effective packaging solutions, whether acting as a spring board for brand innovation and new product development; harmonising the appearance of the brand across markets; refreshing and/or updating the look of a brand; determining what signs and symbols the category is accessing, and ensuring a solid competitive advantage. It provides a toolkit for utilizing signs and symbols in terms of pack format (shape, size, texture), color, labelling and copy. It can also help determine what enhances or detracts from the emergent expressions of a particular trait or ingredient and how this links back to what is emerging in society.

Not intended to be prescriptive, semiotics provides a direction for packaging design innovation and implementation that is rooted in the wider culture. It can give brands the confidence to see beyond faddish and seasonal trends. It can be used as a guide in constructing packaging with both relevant and contemporary meaning that truly communicates the brand's personality and values for achieving successful brand growth. 20

Semiotics helps to bring to the fore the relationship between meaning and value, the influence of the competitive context and cultural changes. Semiotics can help create new opportunities, provide critical market intelligence for forays into new product categories and is vital in accounting for global variation.

READING THE TEXT

1. What does Arning mean by saying that "packaging has undergone a mass wave of so-called 'premiumisation' across all sectors" (para. 4)?

2. In your own words, what are the four uses of semiotics in packaging design, and how does each use operate?

3. Why does the increasing globalization of consumer culture make semiotics an especially useful tool in packaging design, in Arning's view?

4. Summarize how the significance of lavender has evolved in the packaging of personal care products, as Arning describes it.

5. What is "code convergence" in packaging design, according to Arning (para. 9)?

READING THE SIGNS

1. In your journal, write your own reponse to Laura Oswald's opening quotation: "Consumers shop for meaning, not stuff." Have you ever purchased a product simply because you liked the packaging? What did you like about the packaging, and how did it contribute to your sense of identity?

2. Bring one product package to class; preferably, as a class, choose from a few similar product categories (personal hygiene, say, or bottled water), so that all students bring items from those categories. In class, give a brief presentation in which you interpret your package. After all students have presented, compare the different messages the packages send to consumers.

3. Visit a popular retail store, such as Urban Outfitters or Victoria's Secret, and study the ways the store uses packaging to create, as Laura Oswald puts it, "a meaning" that targets its typical market. Be thorough in your observations, studying everything from the store's shopping bags to its perfume or cologne packages to its clothing labels. Use your findings as evidence for an essay in which you analyze the image the store creates for itself and its customers.

4. **CONNECTING TEXTS**   Visit a store with an explicit political theme, such as The Body Shop or Whole Foods Market, and write a semiotic analysis of the packaging you see in the store. To develop your ideas, consult Michael Pollan's "Supermarket Pastoral" (p. 96) and Julia B. Corbett's "A Faint Green Sell: Advertising and the Natural World" (p. 209).

5. Study the product packaging that is visible to a visitor to your home or dorm room and write an analysis of the messages that packaging might send to the visitor.

6. **CONNECTING TEXTS**   Select a consumer product that has iconic packaging and research the evolution of the packaging designs. Use your findings as a jumping-off point to analyze semiotically the history of this product's packages. In what ways do the packages serve as signs of their time? To develop your ideas, read Kalle Oskari Mattila's "The Age of the Wordless Logo" (p. 194).

JAMES A. ROBERTS
The Treadmill of Consumption

Once, "keeping up with the Joneses" was a neighborhood affair; now, thanks to modern mass media, it's a matter of "keeping up with the Kardashians" — that is, competing with the rich and famous in a never-ending spiral of status consumption. James A. Roberts's analysis of the compulsion to signify "social power through conspicuous consumption" is a sobering read for anyone who has ever gone into debt just to have a snazzier cell phone, like GoldVish's million-dollar white-gold and diamond offering. A professor of marketing at Baylor University, Roberts is the author of *Shiny Objects: Why We Spend Money We Don't Have in Search of Happiness We Can't Buy* (2011), from which this selection is taken.

Using material possessions to exhibit status is commonplace in today's consumer culture. We may not know our neighbors, but we feel compelled to make sure they know that we're people of value. As humans we rely on visual cues such as material possessions to convey our status to others and to ascertain the status of people we don't know. The quest for status symbols influences both kids and adults, although the objects we choose to display may differ with age. (Cell phones may be an exception that spans all age groups.)

For young people, cell phones are seen as necessities, not luxuries. A teen or even preteen without a cell phone feels set apart, on the outside looking in. This is in part because cell phones are a way to stay tightly connected with others (text messaging "blind," with cell phone in the pocket, is one of my favorites); however, cell phones are also important fashion statements and social props. For young people, cell phones are second only to cars as symbols of independence. Many teens see cell phones as an extension of their personality, and phone manufacturers and service providers, knowing this, give them many options to express their inner selves — ways to personalize their ringtone, change their "wallpaper," and customize their "skin," for example, as well as add many apps and accessories.

Adults, especially men, are also susceptible to the status appeal of cell phones. Researchers in the United Kingdom studied the use of cell phones after reading newspaper stories about nightclubs in South America that required patrons to check their phones at the door. Club managers found, the stories reported, that many checked phones were props — not working cell phones. To learn more about whether and how people were using their cell phones as social props, the researchers studied cell phone use in upscale pubs in the UK. What they found is most interesting: men and women used their cell phones in different manners. While women would leave their phone in their purse until they needed it, men were more likely to take their phone out of their pocket or briefcase and place it on the counter or table in view of all. Furthermore, like peacocks strutting with their plumage in full display to attract a mate, men spent more time tinkering with and displaying their phone when the number of men relative to women in the pub increased.[1]

As long as consumers attempt to signal their social power through conspicuous consumption, the levels required to make a visible statement of power will continue to rise. If person A buys a new car, person B has to buy a better car to compete; and then person A has to buy a boat as well — and so on.

[1] John E. Lycett and Robin I. M. Dunbar, "Mobile Phones as Lekking Devices among Human Males," *Human Nature* 11, no. 1 (2000): 93–104.

But once basic needs are met there's no additional happiness with additional purchases. The process of moving ahead materially without any real gain in satisfaction is often called "the treadmill of consumption." That treadmill is a barrier to raising your level of happiness, because it causes you to quickly adapt to good things by taking them for granted.

Research has shown that humans are very flexible. We tend to get used to new circumstances in our lives — including financial circumstances, both good and bad — and we make such mental shifts quickly. Economic gains or losses do give us pleasure or pain, but the effects wear off quickly. When our situation improves, having more money or possessions almost instantaneously becomes the new "normal." As our store of material possessions grows, so do our expectations.

Many researchers have likened this process to drug addiction, where the addict continually needs more and more of the drug of choice to achieve an equivalent "high." This means that acquiring more possessions doesn't take us any closer to happiness; it just speeds up the treadmill. I regret to say that there is a great deal of evidence supporting the existence — and potential harm — of the treadmill of consumption.

If the treadmill didn't exist, people with more possessions would be happier than those "less fortunate" souls who own less. But this simply isn't the case. The "less fortunate" are, for the most part, just as happy as those with more stuff. Big purchases and the piling up of material possessions hold little sway over happiness. Probably the most discouraging proof for this statement can be found in the study of lottery winners. An integral component of the shiny-objects ethos is quick riches. What better way to catapult yourself past your neighbors than to strike it rich with the lottery, right? If you foresee nothing but a lifetime of fun and sun for lottery winners, you're wrong. A study of twenty winners found that they were no happier a few years after their good fortune; in fact, some were even less happy than before they bought their winning ticket.[2] If the lottery can't pull us out of our current torpor, what hope is there for a raise at work, a flat-screen (plasma) television, an iPhone, or a new car (surely the new Lexus would be an exception)?

Consuming for Status

One important reason that consumers buy products is to satisfy social needs. Many of us spend a large proportion of our disposable income on so-called status items, and this trend is on the rise as we continue to embrace the shiny-objects ethos. "Wait a minute," some of you might be saying; "hasn't the current economic crisis stemmed the tide of status consumption?" My response to that question is that it never has in the past. Sure, we might mind

---

[2]Philip Brickman et al., "Lottery Winners and Accident Victims: Is Happiness Relative?" *Journal of Personality and Social Psychology* 36, no. 8 (1978): 917–27.

our financial p's and q's during the actual crisis, but we have always returned to our profligate ways once we've navigated our way through the economic doldrums.

You need look no further back than the early 2000s, when the Internet bubble burst and the stock market tanked. It wasn't long until our spending picked up again, and with a renewed vengeance. That's precisely what brought us where we are today. Similar economic corrections in the 1970s, '80s, and '90s produced the same results: we tightened our financial belts only to loosen them when the clouds receded. It's really a lot like yo-yo dieting. Each time after we fall off the financial wagon we're a little worse off than the time before. Apparently as consumers we tend to suffer from short-term memory loss!

Pursuing materialistic ideals is a competitive and comparative process — hence the expression "keeping up with the Joneses." And today, with daily twenty-four/seven media coverage of the lifestyles of the rich and famous, our competition is no longer limited to our neighborhood. Bill and Melinda Gates and the sultan of Brunei have replaced Joe and Irma down the street as our points of reference. To achieve a position of social power or status, one must exceed this expanding community norm. Even the superrich aren't happy. There's always someone with a bigger home or fancier yacht — or, heaven forbid, a prettier wife. Yes, we even use other humans as chattel in our attempt to secure our position in the social hierarchy! The result of all this social posturing is no end to our wants and little improvement in our satisfaction, despite an ever-increasing consumption of goods. And Madison Avenue knows it: after price, status is the principal theme of most advertising.

Status consumption has been defined as "the motivational process by which individuals strive to improve their social standing through conspicuous consumption of consumer products that confer or symbolize status to the individual and to surrounding significant others."[3] It is our attempt as consumers to gain the respect, consideration, and envy from those around us. Status consumption is the heart and soul of the consumer culture, which revolves around our attempts to signal our comparative degree of social power through conspicuous consumption. If you don't buy into status consumption yourself, you certainly know people who do. They go by many names, but "social climbers" and "status seekers" will do for now. Climbers and seekers work to surround themselves with visible evidence of the superior rank they claim or aspire to. Most of us, to some degree, are concerned with our social status, and we try to make sure others are aware of it as well.

Status consumption began in the United States as a way for members of the upper crust to flaunt their wealth to each other. Over the past century the practice has trickled down to the lower rungs of the economic ladder.

10

---

[3]Jacqueline Eastman et al., "The Relationship between Status Consumption and Materialism: A Cross Cultural Comparison of Chinese, Mexican, and American Students," *Journal of Marketing Theory and Practice*, Winter 1997, 52–66, 58.

Can You Hear Me Now?

I thought I had found the ultimate status symbol when I came across Motorola's new $2,000 Aura cell phone. The avant-garde Aura sports 700-plus individual components, a stainless-steel housing, and a front plate that takes the manufacturer a month to create. Add to this list the world's first handset with a circular display (great color and resolution!), a sixty-two-carat sapphire crystal lens, a multimedia player, stereo Bluetooth, and much, much more.

My amazement over Motorola's Aura was short-lived, however. I lost interest when I heard about the $1 million — yes, $1 million — cell phone from GoldVish (a Swiss company). The phone is made of eighteen-carat white gold and is covered with diamonds. Bluetooth? Of course. How about a two-gigabyte memory, eight-megapixel camera, MP3 player, worldwide FM radio, and e-mail access? Not to worry if a million is a bit rich for you: GoldVish has made available several other phones for around $25,000 — no doubt delivered in plain brown-paper packaging to avoid any embarrassment associated with buying a cheaper model.[4]

People are willing to go into debt to buy certain products and brands — let's say a $2,500 Jimmy Choo handbag — because these status symbols represent power in our consumer culture. Cars, for example, are an expensive but easy way to tell the world you've made it; there's no mistaking which are the most expensive. The problem is that nearly everyone else is upgrading to the latest model as well, so no real increase in status occurs — another example of the treadmill of consumption. Fortunately — note the irony there — our consumer culture, with its vast array of products, allows us many other opportunities to confer status upon ourselves. Media mogul Ted Turner put it this way: "Life is a game. Money is how we keep score."[5]

Status consumers are willing to pay premium prices for products that are perceived to convey status and prestige. A high-end Patek Philippe watch is a good example of a product that is — and is blatantly marketed as — a quintessential status symbol. One of Patek's advertising slogans is, "You never really own a Patek Philippe. You merely look after it for the next generation." Trust me; you're buying it for yourself. Despite the manufacturer's claims to the contrary, a Patek Philippe does not keep better time than the myriad of cheaper alternatives on the market; on the contrary, it serves

---

[4]Darren Murph, "Motorola Intros Avant-Garde $2,000 Aura, Markets It Like a Rolex," October 21, 2008, www.endgadget.com, accessed October 21, 2008.

[5]Ted Turner quote, www.quotegarden.com, accessed November 15, 2009.

primarily as an unambiguous symbol of status. To many people, owning a Patek signals that you've made it. To me, however, it sends the signal that you've forgone a golden opportunity to do good with the money spent so lavishly on a very expensive watch. It's a zero-sum game no matter how much money you make.

And, of course, Patek Philippe watches are only one of a myriad of examples I could use to document our preoccupation with status consumption. What about Lucky Jeans, bling (it's shiny), Hummer automobiles (maybe one of the more blatant cries for help), iPhones, fifty-two-inch plasma TVs, $3,000 Chihuahua lap dogs (think Paris Hilton), McMansions, expensive rims for your car tires, anything couture, Gulfstream jets, Abercrombie & Fitch and Hollister clothes (for teens and preteens) — even drinking water! No consumer product category has been left untouched. Even the most banal, everyday products have been branded — think $2,000 fountain pens.

Today, status is conveyed more often through ownership of status prod-   15
ucts than through personal, occupational, or family reputation. This is particularly true in large, impersonal metropolitan areas, where people can no longer depend on their behavior or reputation to convey their status and position in society.

READING THE TEXT

1. Define in your own words what Roberts means by "the treadmill of consumption."

2. How have the mass media affected the desire for status symbols, according to Roberts?

3. What explanation does Roberts give for his claim that economic downturns have a minimal effect on the pursuit of material goods?

4. In your own words, explain Roberts's concept of the "shiny-objects ethos" (para. 7).

READING THE SIGNS

1. In your journal, explore what items count as status symbols in your own circle of friends (these do not need to be the sort of high-end items that Roberts mentions but could be particular brands of jeans, handbags, shoes, or electronic devices). What appeal do these items have for you? Does acquiring them make you happy? If so, how long does that feeling last? If not, why not?

2. **CONNECTING TEXTS**   Roberts assumes that the treadmill of consumption is irreversible, that we will inevitably "continue to embrace the shiny-objects ethos" (para. 8). Discuss this assumption in class. If you agree, what evidence can you advance to support Roberts's claim? If you do not, what economic or social evidence can you find to refute his belief? Use the class discussion as a springboard for your own essay on this topic. To develop your ideas, you might consult Laurence Shames's "The More Factor" (p. 76) and Steve McKevitt's "Everything Now" (p. 123).

3. In what ways does television, especially reality TV programming, encourage the shiny-objects ethos? Select one show, such as *Keeping Up with the Kardashians*, and analyze the way in which it stimulates the desire to buy products that convey prestige and status.

STEVE McKEVITT
Everything Now

Paradoxically, although today people in developed societies have more consumer choices, 24/7 access to a global cornucopia of goods, and (thanks to generous credit availability) more sheer *stuff*, many report feelings of unhappiness, especially when it comes to the stress triggered by working to pay for all that stuff. But while work indeed contributes to that unhappiness, Steve McKevitt argues in this selection that much of it can be credited to massive marketing campaigns designed to convince us that if we only buy this product or that service, we will be happy. Combining psychology with the technological ability to bombard us around the clock with clever advertisements designed to convince us that our every *want* is actually a *need*, current marketing strategies keep us unhappy in order to move the goods. A marketing consultant and author of the book *Everything Now* (2013, from where this selection comes), McKevitt is working on a PhD at the University of Sheffield.

You can never get enough of what you don't need to make you happy.
　　　　　　　—ERIC HOFFER, philosopher and social writer

What do you want?

Whether you are looking for motor cars, mobile phones, holidays or simply what to have for lunch, the range of options available to you can be genuinely overwhelming. With nothing more than a broadband Internet connection, you can enjoy immediate and unfettered access to millions of books, newspapers and magazines; thousands of movies and TV shows and almost the entire canon of recorded music. Many lifetimes' worth of content, all of it available at the click of a mouse. Whatever it is you want, you can have it. Everything Now.

We are living through a time of endless choices and unlimited convenience. We now take for granted the ubiquity of goods and services that can be instantly accessed, but the 24/7 society we live in — where everything is available practically all the time — is a recent achievement. Everything Now did not happen by chance or overnight. It is the culmination of a deliberate and concerted 30-year drive to increase choice and convenience for everyone. Those of us lucky enough to be living in the developed world today are, on average, healthier, wealthier, longer lived and better educated than at any other point in history. Our *needs* have been fulfilled and so, for the first time ever, we have an economy that is almost entirely devoted to the business of satisfying our *wants* instead. The question is: with so much effort dedicated to giving us what we want, why aren't we happier or, at the very least, worrying less and enjoying life more? . . .

People do not buy technology, what they buy is functionality. Consumers do not purchase stereos, DVD players and mobile phones because they want the items for themselves, but because they want to listen to music, watch movies, and keep in touch with family and friends. The same is true of computers. But in this case there is much more functionality, so people end up buying computers for many different reasons — to work, play games, browse the Internet, edit movies, create magazines and so on. To do this they need to run software. To gain a competitive edge within a crowded market, software publishers were creating products crammed with features and optimised to run most effectively on the fastest machines available at the time of their release.

This was especially true for computer games, which, because of their rich   5
graphics, placed the heaviest demands upon the hardware. If consumers wanted to derive the most functionality from the latest software — in the case of my games, experience the smoothest animation, highest resolution, and most spectacular visuals — they would need the fastest computer, which would almost certainly contain one of [Intel's] microprocessors.

However, as Intel's business model demonstrated, it would only be the fastest computer for a maximum of three months. The pace of this process was so rapid that [Intel VP of Marketing] Manfred could be confident that even the best computer available today would not be able to cope with the latest software being published three years hence. The pursuit of functionality — our games — could be used to force consumers to invest in Intel's new technology. Intel was not only creating faster microprocessors, it was also creating the demand for them.

Intel may be a master of the art, but it is certainly not the only company in the business of inventing wants as well as products. Manfred is correct: wants are very different to needs. "Want versus Need" is one of the most basic concepts in economics. A need is something we have to have — like food, sleep or water. A want is something we would like to have — like a Big Mac, a Tempur mattress or a bottle of Evian. You might think that you cannot survive without your BlackBerry or your BMW, but you can. It might even be the case that you do need a phone to carry out your work and a car to get around in, but what brand it is and, to a large extent, what features it has are really just wants.

Needs are rational and permanent. We have always needed — and will always need — food, water and shelter. The solution may change, but the problem is always the same, you can't create new needs. Wants, on the other hand, are emotional, ephemeral and ever changing. Just because you want something today doesn't mean you will want it tomorrow, always want it, or ever want it again. For example, back in 1981, everybody wanted a Rubik's Cube, it was the world's most popular toy, but it is unlikely to ever repeat this feat in the future. This transience creates an opportunity for anyone who is trying to sell us something — whether that's a product, a service or even an idea — and they can invent wants for us as well as the means to assuage them.

In 1976, a year with one of the hottest summers on record, almost nobody drank bottled water in the UK (unless they went on holiday "abroad"); we spent less than £200,000 on just 3 million litres of the stuff. Today, each of us drinks an average of 33 litres per year, spending a total of £1.4 billion. We do this despite the fact that tap water is essentially an identical product that is as widely and freely available as it was in 1976.

Manufacturing wants for things like bottled water is what keeps us in a 10 permanent state of dissatisfaction, because only by making us unhappy with what we have today is it possible to persuade us to pay for something that will make us happy tomorrow. In the case of bottled water, its success depended on us becoming dissatisfied with drinking tap water. The basis of this dissatisfaction is usually emotional rather than rational, it doesn't require hard evidence — all that is needed, perhaps, is promoting a notion that bottled water tastes better or using language to suggest it is somehow healthier than tap water. In Intel's case, the continual introduction of new microprocessors means that purchasing a new computer will only briefly appease the existing want for maximum functionality. Likewise, once upon a time, you may have yearned for an iPhone Mk1, but now, several upgrades later with that model nothing more than a distant memory, you've become dissatisfied with your current handset, and can't wait for the opportunity to forsake it for next year's version. It is simple and, as ever-increasing sales of bottled water, personal computers and mobile phones testifies, it has been extremely effective.

Maslow's Hierarchy of Needs is a theory of developmental psychology which describes the phases of human growth. It is often portrayed as a pyramid, with the biggest, most basic needs at the bottom (air, food, water), then safety issues (health, employment, property), moving up through relationships and esteem (achievement, confidence, respect), reaching self-actualisation at the top (morality, creativity and problem solving).

Maslow believed that these needs play a major role in motivating behaviours in Western societies where the individual is paramount. Basic biological, physiological and safety needs will always take priority over the need for respect or self-expression, but once they have been satisfied, the needs higher up the pyramid become increasingly important. As one set of needs is assuaged, focus moves to those on the next level up the pyramid. Everything Now is an extreme example of an individualistic society, hence our tendency is to be egocentric, focusing on the improvement of one's self and circumstances, with self-actualisation at the zenith.

For example, tackling obesity and associated issues of low self-esteem is a priority in the UK and USA, where food is cheap and plentiful, but in places where food is expensive and in short supply, these problems simply don't exist. There are few branches of Weight Watchers in the Third World and no need, at present, for Western governments to develop famine-relief strategies to feed their own people. . . .

Yes we are still innovating, but we are doing so in small steps, not the giant leaps we once were. [John] Smart makes a very interesting observation about the areas in which innovation is taking place:

> Certain types of innovation saturation might now appear to be occurring because our accelerating technological productivity is beginning to intersect with an effectively fixed number of human needs . . . We may observe that as the world develops and we all climb higher on Maslow's hierarchy of relatively fixed needs, those who already have sufficient housing, transportation, etc., are now pursuing innovations on the most abstract, virtual, and difficult-to-quantify levels, like social interaction, status, entertainment, and self-esteem.

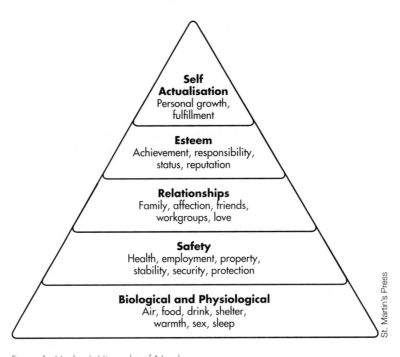

Figure 1. Maslow's Hierarchy of Needs

It is because we don't really need anything anymore that the focus of   15
innovation has itself turned to addressing our wants instead. As Maslow
demonstrates, once needs are taken care of, wants can be just as powerful
drivers. This is all well and good if we know what it is that we want, but most
of the time we don't. Nor do the things we want necessarily have to be good,
either for ourselves or for the rest of society. Some people want to smoke, to
take drugs or, as a more extreme example, to commit crimes. Needs require
rational decision-making. However, the evidence is that decisions about wants
are driven entirely by our emotions and these feelings can be so strong that
they cause us to overrule or simply ignore rational objections. This combination makes us highly suggestible: easily persuaded by things that engage our
sympathies, willing to be told what it is that we want, and then to act upon
that information, regardless of the consequences. We should also consider
that the people empathising with us — the ones engaging our sympathies and
then telling us what it is that we want — are often trying to hawk us a solution
as well.

You can find examples of this everywhere. Just look at an everyday product, like toothpaste. We need toothpaste to ensure our teeth and gums remain
healthy. On average, people with healthy teeth live longer and tend to lead
healthier lives than those who lose their teeth prematurely. Visit your local
supermarket and you'll find around 120 different brands of toothpaste to
choose from. Some promise fresher breath, others whiter teeth, others healthier gums. There will be brands for sensitive teeth, for people with fillings or
cavities, there will be gels, pastes and powders, but despite this welter of
options, each and every one will be virtually identical chemically; essentially
the same thing, packaged and positioned in dozens of slightly different ways.
The same is true whatever the category, from soap to soap operas. Scratch
beneath the surface of Everything Now's apparently endless choice at any
point and what you will find is hundreds of virtually identical products. Toothpaste is really just toothpaste.

Nobody needs to have 120 different varieties of intrinsically indistinguishable products like toothpaste or soap to choose from, and you may argue that
nobody wants them either, but these "choices" are offered in a much more
subtle way. Where once there was a category called soap, now there are soaps
for dry skin, greasy skin, sensitive skin; there is strong soap, gentle soap; soap
in a bar, in a bottle, in a jar or from a dispenser; liquid soap, foam soap, hard
soap, scented soap, simple soap, plain soap, soft soap and soap on a rope.
Now all you have to do is choose one.

Things can't go on like this. And that's not some liberal cri de coeur, I
mean it literally: they can't. Whatever your views are on climate change, you
have to at least concede that we are not going to be able to rely on fossil fuels
forever. If we carry on at the current rate of consumption — some 85 million
barrels of oil a day, burning through the fossil record at the rate of 20 million
years, every year — then we're going to run out sooner rather than later. Well,
I'm all for screwing in low-energy light bulbs, buying locally produced peas

and only drinking European wine, if that's what it takes to save the planet, yet I can't help thinking that, in the face of the thousands of freight carriers that are making their way to these shores slowly, but inexorably, from China and India to deliver their precious cargoes of Christmas cracker gifts and trinkets, these Herculean efforts might not suffice!

And even if we do discover substantial new reserves of oil and gas to ensure we can be supplied with miniature screwdriver sets and mini playing cards for the next 200 years, there still aren't enough resources for everyone to live as wastefully as we do in the developed world. We are currently using 1.5 times the world's gross annual product every year, which requires us to draw on an inevitably limited and dwindling stockpile of natural resources to make up the shortfall. But even as we burn through 50 percent more than we produce, over-fishing, over-farming, over-watering and deforesting as we go, competition for these diminishing resources is increasing as the huge economies in Brazil, Russia, India and China (the so-called BRIC nations) and those in the rest of Southern Asia and South America become stronger. This means that even if those miniature screwdriver sets are still available, they're going to be a lot more expensive. And I do mean a lot more. Economists expect food prices to double in the next 20 years in real terms. Remember, this is the case even if we ignore climate change, which, I'll concede, is a bit like ignoring a herd of elephants in your living room. . . .

The world we live in today no longer needs either stone knappers or 20 rocket-scientists. It requires people to work out how the music industry can make money from file sharing; how Sunday newspaper executives can convince new readers that 500,000 words of content is worth the price of a cup of coffee; how TV channels can survive without relying on advertising revenue. It needs marketers and creative thinkers who can persuade millions of other people that This Brand is exclusively for them, that the next version of this film/TV/video game franchise is really the best one ever, or that some website helps us get closer to the things we love. It needs people who can develop products that are slightly better than the previous version, who can identify tiny gaps in crowded markets, who can think up new ways to package, deliver or sell the same things. It needs people who can find innovative ways of managing finance, who can manipulate the money markets, exploit political boundaries and economic loopholes, who can persuade people to leverage their assets, or to liquidate, re-mortgage, plough-back or reinvest, or just to keep their capital moving. But most of all it needs people who can work out ways of getting all of the above to us as soon as we want it. And of course, we want it now.

Inventors are innovating as much now as they ever have, it's just that they are solving problems that won't necessarily be rewarded with patents. The inventors are busy doing other things. Not necessarily brilliant things either. For every iPad there is a Chicken Nugget — but both are, in their own way, elegant solutions to problems people didn't know that they had.

Everything Now is enormously wasteful: a huge and unnecessary drain on the world's dwindling natural resources. By skewing our motivation it has entirely displaced the process of innovation. This is the real cost of changing our focus to wants instead of needs. Everything Now is making it almost impossible for us to address any genuinely big problems we face in the long term. We are not just demand-led, but are busily creating the demands themselves. We have become so obsessed with inventing and meeting the wants of the individual in the short term that attention has become diverted from the real challenges of meeting fundamental human needs of the future: energy and food supply, changing climate, population growth and the sustainable use of natural resources.

SOURCES

Bott, David (Director of Innovation Programmes, UK Government Technology Strategy Board), "Challenge = Opportunity" The 9th Roberts Lecture, University of Sheffield, 18 October 2011.
Davies, John, "Debt Facts and Figures July 2011," Credit Action, July 2011.
Purdy, L., "The Dissatisfaction Syndrome," Publicis, May 2002.

READING THE TEXT

1. Summarize in your own words the distinctions between "wants" and "needs," according to McKevitt.

2. What is the logic behind Maslow's hierarchy of needs?

3. How does the marketing of products such as computers and bottled water convince consumers that these items are "needs," not "wants," as McKevitt explains?

4. After describing the world of "Everything Now," McKevitt says, "Things can't go on like this. . . . I mean it literally: they can't" (para. 18). Why does he believe this?

5. What effect has the wide variety of consumer choices had on the relative happiness of people today, according to McKevitt?

READING THE SIGNS

1. In your journal, write your own response to McKevitt's opening quotation from Eric Hoffer: "You can never get enough of what you don't need to make you happy."

2. In class, make a list of all the consumer products that you and your classmates need, and then a list of what you want. What differences, if any, are there between the lists? If you have difficulty categorizing a product as a need or a want, how do you explain that difficulty?

3. **CONNECTING TEXTS**   Using McKevitt's selection as a critical perspective, write an essay analyzing the results of the University of Maryland research study described in "Students Addicted to Social Media" (p. 382). Do you think the

students reported on in that selection would categorize their electronic devices as needs or wants? Where would you locate those devices on Maslow's hierarchy of needs? Alternatively, use McKevitt's essay as a framework for analyzing the ways teens consume social media as described in danah boyd's "It's Complicated: MySpace vs. Facebook" (p. 437).

4. Study current advertisements (either print or online) for bottled water. Do today's ads reflect McKevitt's claim that "only by making us unhappy with what we have today is it possible to persuade us to pay for something that will make us happy tomorrow" (para. 10)?

TROY PATTERSON
The Politics of the Hoodie

The "hoodie" has come a long way from the days when it was just a utilitarian sweatshirt worn by athletes, farmers, and construction workers. In the 1980s, rappers turned it into an essential accessory of urban street style. Then, in the new millennium, Mark Zuckerberg turned it into a signifier of laid-back postindustrial chic in the digital age, on the one hand, and the shooting death of Trayvon Martin transformed it into an emblem of black oppression, on the other. In short, the hoodie is now a complex semiotic system in its own right, whose history and widely branching meanings are surveyed in this article by Troy Patterson, a contributing writer for the *New York Times Magazine*, in which this reading originally appeared.

On a recent night, shopping online for a light jacket or a cotton sweater — some kind of outerwear to guard my body against a springlike breeze — I clicked on the "new arrivals" page of the website of a popular retailer and encountered, unexpectedly, another instance of the complex oddity of race. Here, projecting catalog-model cordiality in the sterile space of an off-white backdrop, was a young black man in a hoodie.

On the street, a black guy in a hoodie is just another of the many millions of men and boys dressed in the practical gear of an easygoing era. Or he should be. This is less an analysis than a wish. The electric charge of the isolated image — which provokes a flinch away from thought, a desire to evade the issue by moving on to check the sizing guide — attests to a consciousness of the hoodie's recent history of peculiar reception. In a cardigan or a crew neck, this model is just another model. In the hoodie, he is a folk demon and a scapegoat, a political symbol and a moving target, and the system of signs that weighs this upon him does not make special distinctions for an Italian cashmere hoodie timelessly designed in heather gray.

Watching Beyoncé's recent video for "Formation," with its set piece showing a black child in a hooded sweatshirt disarming a rank of riot police with his dance moves, most Americans grasped the outfit as a rhetorical device serving a dreamlike declaration about protest and civil rights. During the N.F.L. playoffs, football fans saw the quarterback Cam Newton, the locus of a running dialogue about blackness, wear hoodies to interviews, and they read tweets that called him a "thug" for it. The boxing movie *Creed* — starring Michael B. Jordan opposite Sylvester Stallone, who made the hoodie a fixture in *Rocky* (1976) — features rousing scenes of Jordan jogging across Philadelphia in a gray hoodie. The transfer of the garment from the old white champ to the young black contender plays as an echo of the film's broader racial politics.

At the computer, prodded out of the rhythm of browsing, I tried to imagine the meetings that led to this catalog model being placed in this hoodie, in the vacuum of commercial space. Beyond the usual earnest discussion of the styling of his pushed-up sleeves and the asymmetrical dangle of his drawstrings, there had to have been delicate conversations, informed by H.R. policy and P.C. etiquette, straightforward aesthetic concerns and knotty social ones. It is impossible that the production designers were ignorant of the ghost of Trayvon Martin, the unarmed 17-year-old fatally shot four years ago while wearing much the same thing. Did the model present a distraction from the reality on the streets? Did the art director start feeling somehow guilty for even considering such a question? The choice to put the kid in the picture must count as a modest political act, given the rich absurdity of the codes pertaining to a harmless piece of clothing.

The hooded sweatshirt emerged as a pop political object after decades of   5
mundane hard work. In the 1930s, the company now known as Champion Athletic Apparel began turning them out to keep football players warm on the sidelines, also attracting business from men who operated backhoes and cherry pickers and forklifts — the forefathers of style for the guys who top their hoods with hard hats turned backward.

But the hoodie did not warrant enough consideration to earn its diminutive nickname until after it was processed by B-boys, graffiti artists, and break dancers in the '80s. Youth culture did the work of tugging it from the sphere of sportswear, where clothing exists to enhance performance, into the world of street wear, where clothing is performance in itself. By the 1990 release of the video for "Mama Said Knock You Out," with LL Cool J styled as a boxer in his corner, his lips visible beneath a hood that shielded his eyes, the hoodie had accomplished its transformation into an element of style.

Like their peers in the suburbs, bundled up on BMX bikes or skateboarding in sweatshirts with the logo of Thrasher magazine, a generation of hip-hop kids found the hoodie suitable for the important adolescent work of taking up space and dramatizing the self. There was and is a theater of the hood: pulling it up with a flourish, tugging it down to settle in its energetic slouch. The hood frames a dirty look, obscures acne and anxiety, masks headphones in study hall, makes a cone of solitude that will suffice for an autonomous realm. And if, in its antisurveillance capacity, the hood plays with the visual rhetoric of menace, it is heir to a tradition in teen dressing stretching back to the birth of the teenager, when he arrived fully formed in leather jacket and bluejeans. The cover of the Wu-Tang Clan's first album catches the mood: Members of the group wear black hoodies and white masks, as if to abduct the listener into a fantasy of ninja stealth.

But this was just a prologue to an era in which the hoodie became at once an anodyne style object and a subject of moral panic, its popularity and its selective stigmatization rising in proportion. A glance at almost any police blotter, or a recollection of the forensic sketch of the Unabomber, will confirm the hoodie as a wardrobe staple of the criminal class, and this makes it uniquely convenient as a proxy for racial profiling or any other exercise of enmity. The person itching to confirm a general bias against hip-hop kids or crusty punks imputes crooked character to the clothing itself.

Which brings you to the transcript of the 911 call made by Trayvon Martin's killer. Dispatcher: "Did you see what he was wearing?" George Zimmerman: "Yeah. A dark hoodie, like a gray hoodie." Trivial details can bear serious import. Surely there would have been demonstrations after the killing and the killer's acquittal regardless of what the victim wore. As it happened, those demonstrators — legislators on chamber floors, marchers in the street — picked up the sweatshirt as an emblem, donning hoods in solidarity. Instantly a symbol aggrieved at having to be one, the hoodie was jolted into a curious space: Where the basic hoodie means to defend against the elements, the protest hoodie seeks to offend the right people. In the paranoid view of stodgy shopkeepers, the hoodie is to be feared for extinguishing individuality; in its politicized life, it mutes identity to signal alliance, not unlike a resistance group's uniform.

All that potential subtext is attached to a generally evocative item of cloth-   10 ing. The white working-class hoodie still glows with the Rocky Balboa ideal of grit and tenacity. The yoga-class hoodie is sold on a promise of snuggly virtue that may explain why in Saskatchewan they call the thing a "bunny hug." The tech-sector hoodie made default by Facebook's Mark Zuckerberg carries on the garment's proud juvenile tradition of informality and defiance. Once perceived as an affront to professionalism, it has since settled in as a convention.

In January, there emerged a debate in the business press regarding the rituals of dress in the tech industry and their relationship to the field's hospitableness to women. The argument proceeded in an article on Quartz headlined "The Subtle Sexism of Hoodies" and in counterarguments suggesting, for instance, that "hoodies represent a rejection of old ideas and an openness to new ones." I was struck by the ready acceptance of the notion that a Silicon Valley hoodie was not just a prerequisite in its field, like Gucci loafers on Wall

Street, but also a costume of dominance. Its visual strength abets its powers as a cultural marker, needing just a nudge to create its own contexts.

You must have seen a sitcom or TV commercial in which black actors wear hoodies in new millennial colors — mustard, maroon — to portray coders. In a current General Electric ad, for example, the costume functions as characterization, and the cheery color of the cotton somehow trumps that of the skin in terms of mass iconography. But the ascent of casual wear does not quite disguise the unchanging strictness of social codes, and the hood continues to frame matters of class and race in ways that tend to satisfy the interest of power. The lingering question of the hoodie is simply: Who enjoys the right to wear one without challenge?

READING THE TEXT

1. Patterson does not use the word "semiotics" in his essay, but he essentially is providing a semiotic reading of the hoodie. In class, discuss the various ways in which his article uses semiotic techniques to explain the significance of the hoodie.

2. Summarize in your own words the hoodie's evolution from a practical clothing item to one that bears charged political meanings that are racially coded.

3. Patterson opens his essay by describing an online clothing retailer's ad showing a young black man modeling a cashmere hoodie. Why does Patterson assert that "there had to have been delicate conversations, informed by H.R. policy and P.C. etiquette, straightforward aesthetic concerns and knotty social ones" (para. 4) among the ad's creators?

4. Explain in your own words how the Trayvon Martin shooting turned the hoodie into an "emblem" intended "to offend the right people" (para. 9).

READING THE SIGNS

1. In class, brainstorm other clothing categories that may have a political or class significance (the business suit and blue jeans are just two of many possibilities). Select one of these categories and write your own semiotic interpretation of that category. You may find it useful to conduct some research on the history of your topic.

2. In an essay, propose your own response to Patterson's concluding statement: "The lingering question of the hoodie is simply: Who enjoys the right to wear one without challenge?" (para. 12). To develop your ideas, you might conduct an online survey of some of the groups Patterson mentions (hip-hop artists, high-tech workers, social activists) to discern the current symbolic significance of the hoodie. You might also do a survey of clothing retailers (online or brick and mortar) to see how this item is being marketed, for whom, and in what price ranges.

3. Patterson says that "the hoodie is to be feared for extinguishing individuality; in its politicized life, it mutes identity to signal alliance" (para. 9). Select a group that uses clothing to signal its identity (the military, scouting

organizations, even sororities and fraternities are some that come to mind), and write an argumentative essay in which you weigh the extent to which the group's uniforms encourage uniformity or bonding.

4. Randomly observe students at your school congregating in a public place (say, the student union building). Then write a semiotic interpretation of the fashion trends you observe. What patterns of fashion preference do you see? Do they align with gender or racial characteristics? Are there current fashion trends that you don't see?

5. Write an essay in which you support, oppose, or complicate the stance that the adoption of the hoodie as corporate wear is an instance of what Thomas Frank calls "commodifying" an alternative or countercultural position. To develop your ideas, read Frank's "Commodify Your Dissent" (below).

THOMAS FRANK

Commodify Your Dissent

"Sometimes You Gotta Break the Rules." "This is different. Different is good." "The Line Has Been Crossed." "Resist the Usual." If you are guessing that these defiant declarations must come from the Che Guevara / Jack Kerouac Institute of World Revolution and Extreme Hipness, you're in for a surprise, because they are actually advertising slogans for such corporations as Burger King, Arby's, Toyota, Clash Clear Malt, and Young & Rubicam. Just why huge corporations are aping the language of the Beats and the 1960s counterculture is the centerpiece of Thomas Frank's thesis that the countercultural idea has become "an official aesthetic of consumer society." Commodifying the decades-long youth habit of dissenting against corporate America, corporate America has struck back by adopting the very attitudes that once meant revolution, Frank believes, thus turning to its own capitalist uses the postures of rebellion. Indeed, when Apple can persuade you to buy a computer because its guy is just plain *cooler* than some IBM nerd, there may be no way out. Frank is the author of *Commodify Your Dissent: Salvos from the Baffler* (with Matt Weiland, 1997), from which this selection is taken. His most recent book, *Listen, Liberal: Or, What Ever Happened to the Party of the People?* was published in 2016.

The public be damned! I work for my stockholders.
— WILLIAM H. VANDERBILT, 1879

Break the rules. Stand apart. Keep your head. Go with your heart.
— TV commercial for Vanderbilt perfume, 1994

Capitalism is changing, obviously and drastically. From the moneyed pages of the *Wall Street Journal* to TV commercials for airlines and photocopiers we hear every day about the new order's globe-spanning, cyber-accumulating ways. But our notion about what's wrong with American life and how the figures responsible are to be confronted haven't changed much in thirty years. Call it, for convenience, the "countercultural idea." It holds that the paramount ailment of our society is conformity, a malady that has variously been described as over-organization, bureaucracy, homogeneity, hierarchy, logocentrism, technocracy, the Combine, the Apollonian.[1] We all know what it is and what it does. It transforms humanity into "organization man," into "the man in the gray flannel suit." It is "Moloch[2] whose mind is pure machinery," the "incomprehensible prison" that consumes "brains and imagination." It is artifice, starched shirts, tailfins, carefully mowed lawns, and always, always, the consciousness of impending nuclear destruction. It is a stiff, militaristic order that seeks to suppress instinct, to forbid sex and pleasure, to deny basic human impulses and individuality, to enforce through a rigid uniformity a meaningless plastic consumerism.

As this half of the countercultural idea originated during the 1950s, it is appropriate that the evils of conformity are most conveniently summarized with images of 1950s suburban correctness. You know, that land of sedate music, sexual repression, deference to authority, Red Scares, and smiling white people standing politely in line to go to church. Constantly appearing as a symbol of arch-backwardness in advertising and movies, it is an image we find easy to evoke.

The ways in which this system are to be resisted are equally well understood and agreed-upon. The Establishment demands homogeneity; we revolt by embracing diverse, individual lifestyles. It demands self-denial and rigid adherence to convention; we revolt through immediate gratification, instinct uninhibited, and liberation of the libido and the appetites. Few have put it more bluntly than Jerry Rubin did in 1970: "Amerika says: Don't! The yippies say: Do It!" The countercultural idea is hostile to any law and every establishment. "Whenever we see a rule, we must break it," Rubin continued. "Only by breaking rules do we discover who we are." Above all rebellion consists of a sort of Nietzschean antinomianism,[3] an automatic questioning of rules, a rejection of whatever social prescriptions we've happened to inherit. Just Do It is the whole of the law.

The patron saints of the countercultural idea are, of course, the Beats, whose frenzied style and merry alienation still maintain a powerful grip

---

[1]**Apollonian** An allusion to the god Apollo, a term for rational consciousness. –Eds.

[2]**Moloch** An ancient idol to whom children were sacrificed, used by Allen Ginsberg as a symbol for industrial America in his poem "Howl." –Eds.

[3]**Nietzschean antinomianism** An allusion to the German philosopher Friedrich Nietzsche's challenging of conventional Christian morality. –Eds.

on the American imagination. Even forty years after the publication of *On the Road*, the works of Kerouac, Ginsberg, and Burroughs remain the sine qua non of dissidence, the model for aspiring poets, rock stars, or indeed anyone who feels vaguely artistic or alienated. That frenzied sensibility of pure experience, life on the edge, immediate gratification, and total freedom from moral restraint, which the Beats first propounded back in those heady days when suddenly everyone could have their own TV and powerful V-8, has stuck with us through all the intervening years and become something of a permanent American style. Go to any poetry reading and you can see a string of junior Kerouacs go through the routine, upsetting cultural hierarchies by pushing themselves to the limit, straining for that gorgeous moment of original vice when Allen Ginsberg first read "Howl" in 1955 and the patriarchs of our fantasies recoiled in shock. The Gap may have since claimed Ginsberg and *USA Today* may run feature stories about the brilliance of the beloved Kerouac, but the rebel race continues today regardless, with ever-heightening shit-references calculated to scare Jesse Helms, talk about sex and smack that is supposed to bring the electricity of real life, and ever-more determined defiance of the repressive rules and mores of the American 1950s — rules and mores that by now we know only from movies.

But one hardly has to go to a poetry reading to see the countercultural   5
idea acted out. Its frenzied ecstasies have long since become an official aesthetic of consumer society, a monotheme of mass as well as adversarial culture. Turn on the TV and there it is instantly: the unending drama of consumer unbound and in search of an ever-heightened good time, the inescapable rock 'n' roll soundtrack, dreadlocks and ponytails bounding into Taco Bells, a drunken, swinging-camera epiphany of tennis shoes, outlaw soda pops, and mind-bending dandruff shampoos. Corporate America, it turns out, no longer speaks in the voice of oppressive order that it did when Ginsberg moaned in 1956 that *Time* magazine was

> always telling me about responsibility. Business-
> men are serious. Movie producers are serious.
> Everybody's serious but me.

Nobody wants you to think they're serious today, least of all Time Warner. On the contrary: the Culture Trust is now our leader in the Ginsbergian search for kicks upon kicks. Corporate America is not an oppressor but a sponsor of fun, provider of lifestyle accoutrements, facilitator of carnival, our slang-speaking partner in the quest for that ever-more apocalyptic orgasm. The countercultural idea has become capitalist orthodoxy, its hunger for transgression upon transgression now perfectly suited to an economic-cultural regime that runs on ever-faster cyclings of the new; its taste for self-fulfillment and its intolerance for the confines of tradition now permitting vast latitude in consuming practices and lifestyle experimentation.

Consumerism is no longer about "conformity" but about "difference." Advertising teaches us not in the ways of puritanical self-denial (a bizarre notion on the face of it), but in orgiastic, never-ending self-fulfillment. It counsels not rigid adherence to the tastes of the herd but vigilant and constantly updated individualism. We consume not to fit in, but to prove, on the surface at least, that we are rock 'n' roll rebels, each one of us as rule-breaking and hierarchy-defying as our heroes of the '60s, who now pitch cars, shoes, and beer. This imperative of endless difference is today the genius at the heart of American capitalism, an eternal fleeing from "sameness" that satiates our thirst for the New with such achievements of civilization as the infinite brands of identical cola, the myriad colors and irrepressible variety of the cigarette rack at 7-Eleven.

As existential rebellion has become a more or less official style of Information Age capitalism, so has the countercultural notion of a static, repressive Establishment grown hopelessly obsolete. However the basic impulses of the countercultural idea may have disturbed a nation lost in Cold War darkness, they are today in fundamental agreement with the basic tenets of Information Age business theory. . . .

Contemporary corporate fantasy imagines a world of ceaseless, turbulent change, of centers that ecstatically fail to hold, of joyous extinction for the craven gray-flannel creature of the past. Businessmen today decorate the walls of their offices not with portraits of President Eisenhower and emblems of suburban order, but with images of extreme athletic daring, with sayings about "diversity" and "empowerment" and "thinking outside the box." They theorize their world not in the bar car of the commuter train, but in weepy corporate retreats at which they beat their tom-toms and envision themselves as part of the great avant-garde tradition of edge-livers, risk-takers, and ass-kickers. Their world is a place not of sublimation and conformity, but of "leadership" and bold talk about defying the herd. And there is nothing this new enlightened species of businessman despises more than "rules" and "reason." The prominent culture-warriors of the right may believe that the counterculture was capitalism's undoing, but the antinomian businessmen know better. "One of the t-shirt slogans of the sixties read, 'Question authority,'" the authors of *Reengineering the Corporation* write. "Process owners might buy their reengineering team members the nineties version: 'Question assumptions.'"

The new businessman quite naturally gravitates to the slogans and sensibility of the rebel sixties to express his understanding of the new Information World. He is led in what one magazine calls "the business revolution" by the office-park subversives it hails as "business activists," "change agents," and "corporate radicals." . . . In television commercials, through which the new American businessman presents his visions and self-understanding to the public, perpetual revolution and the gospel of rule-breaking are the orthodoxy of the day. You only need to watch for a few minutes before you see one of

these slogans and understand the grip of antinomianism over the corporate
mind:

> Sometimes You Gotta Break the Rules — Burger King
> If You Don't Like the Rules, Change Them — WXRT-FM
> The Rules Have Changed — Dodge
> The Art of Changing — Swatch
> There's no one way to do it. — Levi's
> This is different. Different is good. — Arby's
> Just Different From the Rest — Special Export beer
> The Line Has Been Crossed: The Revolutionary New Supra — Toyota
> Resist the Usual — the slogan of both Clash Clear Malt and Young &
>   Rubicam
> Innovate Don't Imitate — Hugo Boss
> Chart Your Own Course — Navigator Cologne
> It separates you from the crowd — Vision Cologne

In most, the commercial message is driven home with the vanguard iconography of the rebel: screaming guitars, whirling cameras, and startled old timers
who, we predict, will become an increasingly indispensable prop as consumers require ever-greater assurances that, Yes! You are a rebel! Just look at how
offended they are! . . .

The structure and thinking of American business have changed enormously in   10
the years since our popular conceptions of its problems and abuses were formulated. In the meantime the mad frothings and jolly apolitical revolt of Beat,
despite their vast popularity and insurgent air, have become powerless against
a new regime that, one suspects, few of Beat's present-day admirers and prac-
titioners feel any need to study or understand. Today that beautiful countercultural idea, endorsed now by everyone from the surviving Beats to shampoo
manufacturers, is more the official doctrine of corporate America than it is a
program of resistance. What we understand as "dissent" does not subvert,
does not challenge, does not even question the cultural faiths of Western business. What David Rieff wrote of the revolutionary pretensions of multiculturalism is equally true of the countercultural idea: "The more one reads in academic multiculturalist journals and in business publications, and the more one
contrasts the speeches of CEOs and the speeches of noted multiculturalist academics, the more one is struck by the similarities in the way they view the
world." What's happened is not co-optation or appropriation, but a simple
and direct confluence of interest.

READING THE TEXT

1. In your own words, define what Frank means by "countercultural idea"
    (para.1) and its commodification.

2. How does Frank explain the relationship between the countercultural idea and conformity?

3. How were the Beats early progenitors of today's countercultural ideas, according to Frank?

4. In what ways does Frank believe that modern business has co-opted the countercultural idea?

5. How do you characterize Frank's tone in this selection? Does his tone enhance or detract from the forcefulness of his argument?

READING THE SIGNS

1. Analyze some current advertising in a magazine, on the Internet, or on television, determining whether the advertisements employ the countercultural idea as a marketing ploy. Use your observations as the basis for an essay in which you assess whether the countercultural idea and the associated "iconography of the rebel" (para. 9) still prevail in advertising, as Frank suggests.

2. In class, brainstorm a list of today's cultural rebels, either marketing characters or real people such as actors or musicians, and discuss why these rebels are considered attractive to their intended audience. Use the class discussion as a springboard for your own essay in which you analyze how the status of cultural rebels is a sign of the mood of modern American culture.

3. Write an essay in which you agree, disagree, or modify Frank's contention that marketing no longer promotes conformity but, rather, promotes "never-ending self-fulfillment" and "constantly updated individualism" (para. 6).

4. Visit a youth-oriented store such as Urban Outfitters, and analyze its advertising, product displays, exterior design, and interior decor. Write an essay in which you gauge the extent to which the store uses the iconography of the rebel as a marketing strategy.

5. Study a current magazine focused on business or on modern technology, such as *Bloomberg Businessweek*, *Business 2.0*, or *Wired*. To what extent does the magazine exemplify Frank's claim that modern business eschews conformity and embraces rebellion and rule breaking? Alternatively, you might analyze some corporate Web sites, preferably several from companies in the same industry. Keep in mind that different industries may have very different corporate cultures; the values and ideals that dominate high tech, for instance, may differ dramatically from those in finance, entertainment, or social services.

2

BROUGHT TO YOU B(U)Y

The Signs of Advertising

A Tale of Two Puppies

Something was oddly familiar about the GoDaddy commercial that ran during Super Bowl XLIX...that is, until it was pulled from the broadcast due to audience outcry. The ad begins with an image of a pickup tooling along a country road with a box full of golden retriever puppies in the truck bed. The vehicle hits a bump, and one of the puppies is thrown out onto the road, where he finds himself alone and abandoned in the wilderness. With emotional music playing in the background (reminiscent of the haunting soundtrack of the movie *Hachi: A Dog's Tale*), the puppy makes his way home, through storm and peril, to a lovely farmhouse where his owner happily greets him — only to pack him off into a delivery van because she's just sold him online thanks to using GoDaddy. The ad ends with the puppy's bewildered expression just before the van's door slams shut.

Now, let's go back a year to Super Bowl XLVIII, and Budweiser's "Puppy Love" commercial. This ad begins by showing an image of a horse ranch with a sign out front that reads "Warm Springs Puppy Adoption." As Passenger's song "Let Her Go" plays in the background, the ad creates a visual narrative about a yellow lab puppy who is great friends with the ranch's Clydesdales and takes every opportunity he can to escape from the ranch house to visit their stables. One day the puppy is adopted, but as the car is taking him away, the Clydesdales surround it and "rescue" him, so to speak. The puppy then leads all the horses back to the ranch, where he is rapturously welcomed by his original owners. The concluding image of the puppy playing with one of the horses reassures the audience that he won't be adopted out again.

We begin this chapter with these two ads because they offer particularly good opportunities for learning how to perform semiotic analyses of advertisements. To begin with, both ads are famous. For its part, the GoDaddy ad was pulled from the Super Bowl XLIX lineup after unprecedented viewer protest — a move that, apparently, has never happened before — while the Budweiser "Puppy Love" ad is, according to the TV news sources that reported on the GoDaddy debacle, the fourth-most shared Super Bowl ad of all time. Famous ads, especially those created for the Super Bowl commercial breaks with the knowledge that the whole world will be watching, and which, accordingly, enjoy unusually large production budgets and are often crafted (like the much-celebrated Macintosh *1984* commercial) to be broadcast only during a single Super Bowl, are *designed* to be culturally significant. In addition, with the GoDaddy ad expecting its viewers to recognize it as a parody of the "Puppy Love" commercial, and the "Puppy Love" ad itself clearly alluding to the popular *Puppy Bowl* show (aired every Super Bowl Sunday), as well as to a history of dogs-promoting-beer ads, the two commercials make explicit the usually implicit **systems of association and difference** that are critical to semiotic interpretation. Finally, through analyzing the public response to the two ads, a clear **sign** of American consciousness and values emerges. Let's look at how to find it.

As we have explained in the Introduction to this book, the semiotic analysis of a cultural sign moves from the **denotation** of a sign to its **connotation**. This chapter begins with brief denotative descriptions of the two ads we are analyzing. In each case, we find bucolic country settings, beautiful farmhouses and horse barns, country roads, wholesome-looking blonde women ranchers, and adorable puppies. But there is a striking **difference** between the narrative denotations of the two ads, because the one denotes a heart-warming story of a puppy finding happiness in his original home, while the other ends abruptly (even shockingly) in a puppy being thrust into exile. Of course, this difference was no accident: It was deliberately engineered by the creators of the GoDaddy ad, who clearly assumed that the ad's viewers would associate it with the previous year's "Puppy Love" ad. For its part, the "Puppy Love" ad was intended to appeal to its audience's love for dogs and horses, to its pre-existing knowledge of the Budweiser Clydesdales (which have been selling beer for generations), and to its probable attraction to Animal Planet's annual *Puppy Bowl* show. The GoDaddy ad creators were counting on this same set of audience interests in order to create their parody of "Puppy Love," for without it the joke would be lost.

As you can see, then, both ads belong to the same system of associations and differences, with both referring to a history of commercials (from Budweiser's Spuds MacKenzie to Stroh's Alex in the 1980s) and dog stories (the GoDaddy ad strongly suggests *Lassie Come Home* as well as *Hachi: A Dog's Tale*). And furthermore, both ads allude to an American value system in which dogs are beloved (a long time ago there was a joke that the best-selling book in America would be a story about Abraham Lincoln's doctor's dog). But in spite of this shared set of **associations**, there is that crucial difference between the two ads that points to significance. To determine what that significance is, we can do some **abductive** reasoning.

This is easy for the Budweiser commercial: Far and away the most likely explanation for why "Puppy Love" was created the way it was lies precisely in its appeal to American "puppy love" generally. We can now add to that (remember, semiotic significance is usually **overdetermined**, or can have multiple explanations) the American **mythology** of the rural "heartland" — of the clean and morally pure country where people (the characters in the Budweiser ads are somewhat glamorized versions of "good country folks") lead wholesome, animal-loving lives. Such an ad was clearly intended to make its audience associate Budweiser beer, a product that's hardly wholesome, with the sort of traditional values that Super Bowl audiences can be expected to have.

But there's a hitch — as happens so often when analyzing signs of pop culture. We can find this only in a very careful reading of "Puppy Love," which reveals, in a very brief shot in the opening scene, a pen full of identical lab puppies. The fact that these puppies are purebred labs suggests that the "Warm Springs Puppy Adoption" ranch is no ordinary animal rescue operation: It looks all too much like a puppy mill. This contradiction in the ad's sentimental logic is important because, while the general audience for "Puppy Love" may have missed it, the creators of the GoDaddy ad evidently did not. And this leads to our abductive interpretation of what *they* were thinking.

As we have seen, it is clear that the GoDaddy ad creators meant to parody "Puppy Love." But why, given the depth of America's affection for puppies, would anyone want to disturb that affection? Surely no one would want to have a product or service associated with unhappiness or anger. That's not the way ads work. But if we look at *another* system to which the GoDaddy ad belongs (but *not* "Puppy Love"), we can see what was likely going through the minds of its creators. This system can be called the self-reflexive tradition of advertising. This tradition, best exemplified by a long series of Energizer Bunny commercials, features ads that openly parody other ads. The purpose of such parody is to appeal to their intended viewers' suspicions about the integrity of advertising while making them feel good about an ad that dramatizes such suspicions in a comic way (Gain detergent's ads featuring Ty Burrell in 2016 are especially striking in this regard). Thus, by appealing to their viewers' pleasure at seeing a funny commercial that mocks other commercials promoting similar products, self-reflexive ads move the goods by substituting a feeling unrelated to the product for the product itself. Indeed, most ads work that way.

Identifying *this* system thus enables us to interpret abductively what the GoDaddy advertisers had in mind. As a self-reflexive ad, it appeals to its audience's suspicions of marketing ploys — suspicions that the GoDaddy creators evidently assumed that its target market — sophisticated business people who sell their wares online via Web sites — would harbor. In other words, GoDaddy assumed that the audience of its ad would see that the joke was on Budweiser.

Discussing the Signs of Advertising

Bring to class an ad from a newspaper, magazine, or commercial Web site, and in small groups discuss your semiotic reading of it. Be sure to ask, "Why am I being shown this or being told that?" How do the characters in the ad function as signs? What sort of people don't appear as characters? What cultural myths are invoked in this ad? What relationship do you see between those myths and the intended audience of the publication? Which ads do your group members respond to positively, and why? Which ads doesn't your group like?

It's also possible that the GoDaddy ad creators saw the contradiction in "Puppy Love" that we have described, and assumed that their sophisticated target viewers would be happy to see that contradiction made explicit in its own parody of the ad. But the whole thing blew up in their faces, because while viewers *did* see that the GoDaddy ranch was a puppy mill, and *did* see that they were supposed to find that funny (as a parody of "Puppy Love"), many didn't find it funny at all. Instead, missing the subtle but semiotically probable point that the ad was parodying the puppy mill hints in "Puppy Love," outraged viewers lit up Twitter with scandalized denunciations of anyone who would think that puppy mills were funny. So, finding himself with a lot of egg on his face (and out a lot of cash), GoDaddy's CEO went public with an apology, and withdrew the ad, promising to do better in the future.

What we learn from this rather entertaining moment in advertising history is that it's not a good idea to toy with some values. Americans will commodify just about anything, but most do not tolerate cruelty to animals in their entertainment. Have you ever noticed that violence to people in movies and on TV is more or less unrestricted, but you rarely see violence against animals? And when you do, the perpetrator (as in *Fatal Attraction*) is thus signified as a total villain. In our opinion, this says something very nice about us as Americans. And it also says that you cannot count on Super Bowl viewers to be highly trained semioticians.

And Here's the Pitch

The preceding analysis is intended to illustrate how advertisements, too, are **signs** of cultural desire and consciousness. Indeed, advertising is not just show-and-tell. In effect, it's a form of behavior modification, a psychological strategy designed not only to inform you about products but also to persuade you to buy them by making associations between the product and certain

---

Exploring the Signs of Advertising

Select one of the products appearing in the "Portfolio of Advertisements" (in this chapter), and design in your journal an alternative ad for that product. Consider what different images or cast of characters you could include. What different **mythologies** — and thus, different values — could you use to pitch this product? Then freewrite on the significance of your alternative ad. If you have any difficulty imagining an alternative image for the product, what does that say about the power of advertising to control our view of the world? What does your choice of imagery and cultural myths say about you?

---

pleasurable experiences or emotions that may have nothing to do with the product at all — like sex, or a promise of social superiority, or a simple laugh. Indeed, in no other area of popular culture can we find a purer example of the deliberate movement from objective **denotation** (the pictorial image of a product that appears in an ad) to subjective **connotation** (the feeling that the advertiser associates with the product), thereby transforming *things* into signs.

No one knows for sure just how effective a given ad campaign might be in inducing consumer spending by turning objects into signs, but no one's taking any chances either, as the annual increase in advertising costs for the Super Bowl reveals: At last count, a thirty-second spot averaged $4.5 million. And it's the promise of ever-increasing advertising revenues that's turned Google into the darling of Wall Street. As James B. Twitchell has written, America is indeed an "ad culture," a society saturated with advertising.

The Semiotic Foundation

There is, perhaps, no better field for semiotic analysis than advertising, for ads work characteristically by substituting signs for things, and by reading those signs, you can discover the values and desires that advertisers seek to exploit. It has long been recognized that advertisements substitute images of desire for the actual products, selling images of fun, popularity, or sheer celebrity — promising a gratifying association with the likes of LeBron James if you get your next burger from McDonald's. Automobile commercials, for their part, are notorious for selling not transportation but fantasies of power, prestige, and sexual potency.

By substituting desirable images for concrete needs, modern advertising seeks to transform desire into necessity. You need food, for example, but it takes an ad campaign to convince you through attractive images that you need a Big Mac. Your job may require you to have a car, but it's an ad that persuades you that a Land Rover is necessary for your happiness. If advertising worked otherwise, it would simply present you with a functional profile of a product and let you decide whether it will do the job.

From the early twentieth century, advertisers have seen their task as the transformation of desire into necessity. In the 1920s and 1930s, for example, ads created elaborate story lines designed to convince readers that they needed this mouthwash to attract a spouse or that caffeine-free breakfast drink to avoid trouble on the job. In such ads, products were made to appear not only desirable but absolutely necessary. Without them, your very survival as a socially competent being would be in question. Many ads still work this way, particularly "guilt" ads that prey on your insecurities and fears. Deodorants and mouthwashes are still pitched in such a fashion, playing on our fear of smelling bad in public. Can you think of any other products whose ads play on guilt or shame? Do you find them to be effective?

The Commodification of Desire

Associating a logically unrelated desire with an actual product (as in pitching beer through sexual come-ons) can be called the **commodification** of desire. In other words, desire itself becomes the product that the advertiser is selling. This marketing of desire was recognized as early as the 1950s in Vance Packard's *The Hidden Persuaders*. In that book, Packard points out that by the 1950s America was well along in its historic shift from a producing to a consuming economy. The implications for advertisers were enormous. Since the American economy was increasingly dependent on the constant growth of consumption, as discussed in the Introduction to Chapter 1, manufacturers had to find ways to convince people to consume ever more goods. So, they turned to the advertising mavens on Madison Avenue, who responded by creating ads that persuaded consumers to replace perfectly serviceable products with "new and improved" substitutions within an overall economy of planned design obsolescence.

America's transformation from a producer to a consumer economy also explains why, while advertising is a worldwide phenomenon, it is nowhere as prevalent as it is here. Open a copy of *Vogue*. It is essentially a catalog, where scarcely a page is without an ad. Indeed, marketers themselves call this plethora of advertising "clutter" that they must creatively "cut through" each time they design a new ad campaign. The ubiquity of advertising in our lives points to an economy in which people are constantly pushed to buy, as opposed to economies like China's, which despite recent rises in consumer interest, continues to emphasize constant increases in production. And desire is what opens the wallet.

While the basic logic of advertising may be similar from era to era, the content of an ad, and hence its significance, differs as popular culture changes. This is why a thorough analysis of a specific advertisement should include

Reading Advertising Online

Many viewers watch the Super Bowl as much for the commercials as for the football game; indeed, the ads shown during the Super Bowl now have their own pregame public-relations hype and, in many a media outlet, their own postgame analysis and ratings. Visit *Advertising Age*'s report on the most recent Super Bowl (www.adage .com), and study the ads and the commentary about them. What images and styles predominate, and what do the dominant patterns say about popular taste? What does the public's avid interest in Super Bowl ads say about the power of advertising and its role in American culture?

a historical survey of ads by the same company (and even from competing companies) for the same product, examining the *differences* that point to significance. (The Internet has made this task much easier, as enormous archives of both print and television ads can be found on Web sites such as YouTube and vintageadbrowser.com; a simple search of ads will produce all sorts of relevant images and information.)

Looking at ads from different eras reveals just what was preoccupying Americans at different historical periods. Advertising in the 1920s, for instance, focused especially on its market's desires for improved social status. Ads for elocution and vocabulary lessons appealed to working- and lower-middle-class consumers, who were invited to fantasize that buying the product or service could help them enter the middle class. Meanwhile, middle-class consumers were invited to compare their enjoyment of the sponsor's product with that of the upper-class models shown happily slurping the advertised coffee or purchasing the advertised vacuum cleaner. Of course, things haven't changed that much since the 1920s. Can you think of any ads that use this strategy today? How often are glamorous celebrities called in to make you identify with their "enjoyment" of a product?

One particularly amusing ad from the 1920s played on America's fear of communism in the wake of the Bolshevik revolution in Russia. "Is your washroom breeding Bolsheviks?" asks a print ad from the Scott Paper Company. The ad's lengthy copy explains how your bathroom might be doing so: If your company restroom is stocked with inferior paper towels, it says, discontent will proliferate among your employees and lead to subversive activities. RCA Victor and Campbell's Soup, we are assured, are no such breeding grounds of subversion, thanks to their contracts with Scott. You, too, can join the good fight against communism by buying Scott towels, the ad suggests.

The New Marketing

With all the advertising out there, it is getting harder for advertisers to get our attention, or keep it, so they are constantly experimenting with new ways of getting us to listen. For years now, advertisers who are out to snag the youth market have staged their TV ads as if they were music videos — complete with rapid jump cuts, rap or rock music, and dizzying montage effects — to grab the attention of their target audience and to cause their viewers to associate the product with the pleasures of music videos. Self-conscious irony is also a popular technique to overcome the ad-savvy sophistication of generations of consumers who have become skeptical of advertising ploys.

Then there is the marketing strategy known as "stealth advertising," whereby companies pay people to do things like sit in Starbucks and play a game on a smartphone; when someone takes an interest, they talk about how cool the game is, and ask others to take their photo with this really cool smartphone — and by the way, they say, isn't this a really cool smartphone? The trick here is to advertise a smartphone without having people actually know they're being marketed to — just what the ad doctor ordered for advertising-sick consumers.

Then there are those stealth ads that appear on such Web sites as BuzzFeed and Yahoo!. Interspersed among the actual news headlines are corporate-sponsored "headlines" that are really advertisements in disguise: advotainment, if you will. By masking the ad in the form of the content for which you went to the Web site in the first place, such a marketing strategy updates for the digital era the television trick of turning commercials into, say, sitcoms to accompany actual sitcoms.

But most profoundly, those with products and services to sell are increasingly coming to rely on marketing strategies based on data mining (a polite term for online spying) rather than attention getting. That is, by purchasing information about our online behavior from such titans as Facebook and Google, would-be advertisers attempt to determine just which consumers would be most susceptible to their ads. If you post on your Facebook page that you are planning a long trip, for example, you will immediately find airline ads on your screen. If you conduct a Google search for watches, ads for watches suddenly appear on other sites you visit.

Many people do not mind this sort of marketing surveillance and in fact regard it as a way of receiving relevant product information more efficiently than the traditional hit-or-miss advertising approach. For such consumers, the convenience offered by online data mining offsets its invasiveness. For others, especially after the revelation in 2013 of the scale of the National Security Administration's phone and Internet surveillance, the corporate invasion of their privacy is more alarming. Whatever your personal take on the matter happens to be, there is no question that personal privacy has been a major casualty of a digital culture that is mostly underwritten by the advertising revenues that flow from data mining.

As the years pass and the national mood shifts with the tides of history, new advertising techniques will surely emerge. So look around and ask yourself, as you're bombarded with advertising, "Why am I being shown *that*, or being told *this*?" Or cast yourself as the director of an ad, asking yourself what you would do to pitch a product; then look at what the advertiser has done. Pay attention to the way an ad's imagery is organized, its precise denotation. Every detail counts. Why are these colors used, or why is the ad in black and white? Why are cute stuffed animals chosen to pitch toilet paper? What are those people doing in that perfume commercial? Why the cowboy hat in an ad for jeans? Look, too, for what the ad doesn't include: Is it missing a clear view of the product itself, or an ethnically diverse cast of characters? In short, when interpreting an ad, transform it into a text, going beyond what it denotes to what it connotes — to what it is trying to insinuate or say.

Populism versus Elitism

American advertising tends to swing in a pendulum motion between the status-conscious ads that dominated the 1920s and the more populist approach of decades like the 1970s, when *The Waltons* was a top TV series and country music and truck-driving cowboys lent their popular appeal to Madison Avenue. This swing between elitist and populist approaches in advertising reflects a basic division within the American dream itself, a mythic promise that at once celebrates democratic equality and encourages you to rise above the crowd, to be better than anyone else. Sometimes Americans are more attracted to one side than to the other, but there is bound to be a shift back to the other side when the thrill wears off. Thus, the populist appeal of the 1970s (even disco had a distinct working-class flavor: recall John Travolta's character in *Saturday Night Fever*) gave way to the elitist 1980s, and advertising followed. Products such as Gallo varietal wines, once considered barely a step up from jug wine, courted an upscale market, while Michelob Light promised beer fans that they "could have it all." Status advertising was all the rage in that glitzy, go-for-the-gold decade.

The 1990s brought in a different kind of advertising that was neither populist nor elitist but was characterized by a cutting, edgy humor. This humor was especially common in dot.com ads that typically addressed the sort of young, irreverent, and rather cocky souls who were the backbone of what was then called the "New Economy" and is now called "Web 1.0." More broadly, edgy advertising appealed to twentysomething consumers who were coveted by the marketers who made possible such youth-oriented TV networks as Fox and the WB. Raised in the *Saturday Night Live* era, such consumers were accustomed to cutting humor and were particularly receptive to anything that smacked of attitude, and in the race to get their attention, advertisers followed with attitude-laden advertising.

The new millennium has seen an increasing tendency of advertising that focuses on demographically targeted markets. Such *niche marketing* is not new, but it has been intensified both by the growth of digital media and by the number of subscription television sources that cater to an enormous variety of viewer categories. Once upon a time, TV advertisers had only three networks to choose from: ABC, CBS, and NBC and their affiliates. In those days, TV commercials were constructed to appeal to a relatively undifferentiated (though primarily white and middle-class) national audience. Today, with audiences identifying their tastes, and even identities, through their cable choices and online behavior, advertisers tailor their ads much more specifically, choosing images and strategies designed to appeal to particular demographics and even to particular individuals. This development appears to be breaking up America's "common culture" into an atomized one. What effect this change may be having on our society could prove to be one of the most important semiotic questions of all.

The Readings

Jack Solomon begins the chapter with a semiotic analysis of American advertising, highlighting the ways in which conflicting mythologies of populism and elitism are exploited to push the goods. A paired set of readings by James B. Twitchell and Steve Craig follows, revealing the elaborate psychological profiling schemes by which marketers categorize potential consumers and the gender-coded formulas that can be found in TV commercials. Next, Jia Tolentino deplores the ways in which the call for women's empowerment has been sidetracked into ad campaigns for everything from paper towels to underwear, while Alex Mayyasi reveals the "calculated, highly progressive ad campaign" by which Subaru of America reimaged its line as being cars for lesbians. Jessica Contrera is next up with a survey of the "mortifyingly" inept efforts of political campaign managers to entice millennials to vote, and Kalle Oskari Mattila explains why, and how, text is disappearing from corporate logos as part of a "debranding" effort to entice consumers back to the corporations they mistrust. Juliet B. Schor then surveys the ways in which marketers try to turn kids into cool customers — perhaps somewhat ahead of their actual years — while Stephanie Miller reports on "gamification": "the practice of applying game mechanics to non-game environments to motivate people and change behavior." Julia B. Corbett concludes the readings with a look at marketers who seek to cash in on the "lucrative market of 'green consumers.'" The chapter then presents a "Portfolio of Advertisements" for you to decode for yourself.

1. The advertisement on page 151 tells a story. What is it? You might start with the title of the ad.

2. To whom is the ad directed? What emotions does it play on? Be sure to provide evidence for your answers. What are the "dearest possessions" the ad refers to?

3. This ad originally appeared in 1914. If you were to update it for a magazine today, what changes would you make? Why?

JACK SOLOMON

Masters of Desire: The Culture of American Advertising

When the background music in a TV or radio automobile commercial is classical, you can be pretty certain that the ad is pitching a Lexus or a Mercedes. When it's country western, it's probably for Dodge or Chevy. English accents are popular in Jaguar ads, while a good western twang sure helps move pickup trucks. Whenever advertisers make use of status-oriented or common-folk-oriented cultural cues, they are playing on one of America's most fundamental contradictions, as Jack Solomon explains in this cultural analysis of American advertising. The contradiction is between the simultaneous desire for social superiority (elitism) and social equality (populism) that lies at the heart of the American dream. And one way or another, it offers a good way to pitch a product. Solomon, a professor of English at California State University, Northridge, is the author of *The Signs of Our Time* (1988), from which this selection is taken. He is also coeditor with Sonia Maasik of both *California Dreams and Realities* (2005) and this textbook.

> Amongst democratic nations, men easily attain a certain equality of condition; but they can never attain as much as they desire.
>
> — ALEXIS DE TOCQUEVILLE

On May 10, 1831, a young French aristocrat named Alexis de Tocqueville arrived in New York City at the start of what would become one of the most famous visits to America in our history. He had come to observe firsthand the institutions of the freest, most egalitarian society of the age, but what he found was a paradox. For behind America's mythic promise of equal opportunity, Tocqueville discovered a desire for *unequal* social rewards, a ferocious competition for privilege and distinction. As he wrote in his monumental study, *Democracy in America*:

> When all privileges of birth and fortune are abolished, when all professions are accessible to all, and a man's own energies may place

him at the top of any one of them, an easy and unbounded career seems open to his ambition. . . . But this is an erroneous notion, which is corrected by daily experience. [For when] men are nearly alike, and all follow the same track, it is very difficult for any one individual to walk quick and cleave a way through the same throng which surrounds and presses him.

Yet walking quick and cleaving a way is precisely what Americans dream of. We Americans dream of rising above the crowd, of attaining a social summit beyond the reach of ordinary citizens. And therein lies the paradox.

The American dream, in other words, has two faces: the one communally egalitarian and the other competitively elitist. This contradiction is no accident; it is fundamental to the structure of American society. Even as America's great myth of equality celebrates the virtues of mom, apple pie, and the girl or boy next door, it also lures us to achieve social distinction, to rise above the crowd and bask alone in the glory. This land is your land and this land is my land, Woody Guthrie's populist anthem tells us, but we keep trying to increase the "my" at the expense of the "your." Rather than fostering contentment, the American dream breeds desire, a longing for a greater share of the pie. It is as if our society were a vast high-school football game, with the bulk of the participants noisily rooting in the stands while, deep down, each of them is wishing he or she could be the star quarterback or head cheerleader.

For the semiotician, the contradictory nature of the American myth of equality is nowhere written so clearly as in the signs that American advertisers use to manipulate us into buying their wares. "Manipulate" is the word here, not "persuade"; for advertising campaigns are not sources of product information, they are exercises in behavior modification. Appealing to our subconscious emotions rather than to our conscious intellects, advertisements are designed to exploit the discontentments fostered by the American dream, the constant desire for social success and the material rewards that accompany it. America's consumer economy runs on desire, and advertising stokes the engines by transforming common objects — from peanut butter to political candidates — into signs of all the things that Americans covet most.

But by semiotically reading the signs that advertising agencies manufacture to stimulate consumption, we can plot the precise state of desire in the audiences to which they are addressed. Let's look at a representative sample of ads and what they say about the emotional climate of the country and the fast-changing trends of American life. Because ours is a highly diverse, pluralistic society, various advertisements may say different things depending on their intended audiences, but in every case they say something about America, about the status of our hopes, fears, desires, and beliefs.

We'll begin with two ad campaigns conducted by the same company that bear out Alexis de Tocqueville's observations about the contradictory nature of American society: General Motors' campaigns for its Cadillac and Chevrolet lines. First, consider an early magazine ad for the Cadillac Allanté. Appearing as a full-color, four-page insert in *Time*, the ad seems to say "I'm special — and   5 so is this car" even before we've begun to read it. Rather than being printed on the ordinary, flimsy pages of the magazine, the Allanté spread appears on glossy coated stock. The unwritten message is that an extraordinary car deserves an extraordinary advertisement, and that both car and ad are aimed at an extraordinary consumer, or at least one who wishes to appear extraordinary compared to ordinary citizens.

Ads of this kind work by creating symbolic associations between their product and what the consumers to whom they are addressed most covet. It is significant, then, that this ad insists that the Allanté is virtually an Italian rather than an American car; as its copy runs, "Conceived and Commissioned by America's Luxury Car Leader — Cadillac" but "Designed and Handcrafted by Europe's Renowned Design Leader — Pininfarina, SpA, of Turin, Italy." This is not simply a piece of product information, it's a sign of the prestige that European luxury cars enjoy in today's automotive marketplace. Once the luxury car of choice for America's status drivers, Cadillac has fallen far behind its European competitors in the race for the prestige market. So the Allanté essentially represents Cadillac's decision, after years of resisting the trend toward European cars, to introduce its own European import — whose high cost is clearly printed on the last page of the ad. . . .

American companies manufacture status symbols because American consumers want them. As Alexis de Tocqueville recognized a century and a half ago, the competitive nature of democratic societies breeds a desire for social distinction, a yearning to rise above the crowd. But given the fact that those who do make it to the top in socially mobile societies have often risen from the lower ranks, they still look like everyone else. In the socially immobile societies of aristocratic Europe, generations of fixed social conditions produced subtle class signals. The accent of one's voice, the shape of one's nose, or even the set of one's chin immediately communicated social status. Aside from the nasal bray and uptilted head of the Boston Brahmin, Americans do not have any native sets of personal status signals. If it weren't for his Mercedes-Benz and Manhattan townhouse, the parvenu Wall Street millionaire often couldn't be distinguished from the man who tailors his suits. Hence, the demand for status symbols, for the objects that mark one off as a social success, is particularly strong in democratic nations — stronger even than in aristocratic societies, where the aristocrat so often looks and sounds different from everyone else.

Status symbols, then, are signs that identify their possessors' place in a social hierarchy, markers of rank and prestige. We can all think of any number of status symbols — Rolls-Royces, Beverly Hills mansions, even shar-pei puppies (whose rareness and expense has rocketed them beyond Russian wolfhounds as status pets and has even inspired whole lines of wrinkle-faced stuffed toys) — but how do we know that something *is* a status symbol? The explanation is quite simple: When an object (or puppy!) either costs a lot of money or requires influential connections to possess, anyone who possesses it must also possess the necessary means and influence to acquire it. The object itself really doesn't matter, since it ultimately disappears behind the presumed social potency of its owner. Semiotically, what matters is the signal it sends, its value as a sign of power. One traditional sign of social distinction is owning a country estate and enjoying the peace and privacy that attend it. Advertisements for Mercedes-Benz, Jaguar, and Audi automobiles thus frequently feature drivers motoring quietly along a country road, presumably on their way to or from their country houses.

Advertisers have been quick to exploit the status signals that belong to body language as well. As Hegel observed in the early nineteenth century, it is an ancient aristocratic prerogative to be seen by the lower orders without having to look at them in return. Tilting his chin high in the air and gazing down at the world under hooded eyelids, the aristocrat invites observation while refusing to look back. We can find such a pose exploited in an advertisement for Cadillac Seville in which we see an elegantly dressed woman out for a drive with her husband in their new Cadillac. If we look closely at the woman's body language, we can see her glance inwardly with a satisfied smile on her face but not outward toward the camera that represents our gaze. She is glad to be seen by us in her Seville, but she isn't interested in looking at *us*!

Ads that are aimed at a broader market take the opposite approach. If   10 the American dream encourages the desire to "arrive," to vault above the mass, it also fosters a desire to be popular, to "belong." Populist commercials accordingly transform products into signs of belonging, utilizing such common icons as country music, small-town life, family picnics, and farmyards. All of these icons are incorporated in GM's Heartbeat of America campaign for its Chevrolet line. Unlike the Seville commercial, the faces in the Chevy ads look straight at us and smile. Dress is casual; the mood upbeat. Quick camera cuts take us from rustic to suburban to urban scenes, creating an American montage filmed from sea to shining sea. We all "belong" in a Chevy.

Where price alone doesn't determine the market for a product, advertisers can go either way. Both Johnnie Walker and Jack Daniel's are better-grade whiskies, but where a Johnnie Walker ad appeals to the buyer who wants a mark of aristocratic distinction in his liquor, a Jack Daniel's ad emphasizes the down-home, egalitarian folksiness of its product. Johnnie Walker associates itself with such conventional status symbols as sable coats, Rolls-Royces, and black gold; Jack Daniel's gives us a Good Ol' Boy in overalls. In fact, Jack Daniel's Good Ol' Boy is an icon of backwoods independence, recalling the days of the moonshiner and the Whisky Rebellion of 1794. Evoking emotions quite at odds with those stimulated in Johnnie Walker ads, the advertisers of Jack Daniel's transform their product into a sign of America's populist tradition. The fact that both ads successfully sell whisky is itself a sign of the dual nature of the American dream. . . .

Populist advertising is particularly effective in the face of foreign competition. When Americans feel threatened from the outside, they tend to circle the wagons and temporarily forget their class differences. In the face of the Japanese automotive "invasion," Chrysler runs populist commercials in which Lee Iacocca joins the simple folk who buy his cars as the jingle "Born in America" blares in the background. Seeking to capitalize on the popularity of Bruce Springsteen's *Born in the USA* album, these ads gloss over Springsteen's ironic lyrics in a vast display of flag-waving. Chevrolet's Heartbeat of America campaign attempts to woo American motorists away from Japanese automobiles by appealing to their patriotic sentiments.

The patriotic iconography of these campaigns also reflects the general cultural mood of the early to mid-1980s. After a period of national anguish in the wake of the Vietnam War and the Iran hostage crisis, America went on a patriotic binge. American athletic triumphs in the Lake Placid and Los Angeles Olympics introduced a sporting tone into the national celebration, often making international affairs appear like one great Olympiad in which America was always going for the gold. In response, advertisers began to do their own flag-waving.

The mood of advertising during this period was definitely upbeat. Even deodorant commercials, which traditionally work on our self-doubts and fears of social rejection, jumped on the bandwagon. In the guilty sixties, we had ads like the Ice Blue Secret campaign with its connotations of guilt and shame. In the feel-good Reagan eighties, Sure deodorant commercials featured images of triumphant Americans throwing up their arms in victory to reveal — no wet marks! Deodorant commercials once had the moral echo of Nathaniel Hawthorne's guilt-ridden *The Scarlet Letter*; in the early eighties they had all the moral subtlety of *Rocky IV*, reflecting the emotions of a Vietnam-weary nation eager to embrace the imagery of America Triumphant. . . .

Live the Fantasy

By reading the signs of American advertising, we can conclude that America is a nation of fantasizers, often preferring the sign to the substance and easily enthralled by a veritable Fantasy Island of commercial illusions. Critics of Madison Avenue often complain that advertisers create consumer desire, but semioticians don't think the situation is that simple. Advertisers may shape consumer fantasies, but they need raw material to work with, the subconscious dreams and desires of the marketplace. As long as these desires remain unconscious, advertisers will be able to exploit them. But by bringing the fantasies to the surface, you can free yourself from advertising's often hypnotic grasp.

I can think of no company that has more successfully seized upon the subconscious fantasies of the American marketplace — indeed the world marketplace — than McDonald's. By no means the first nor the only hamburger chain in the United States, McDonald's emerged victorious in the "burger wars" by transforming hamburgers into signs of all that was desirable in American life. Other chains like Wendy's, Burger King, and Jack-In-The-Box continue to advertise and sell widely, but no company approaches McDonald's transformation of itself into a symbol of American culture.

McDonald's success can be traced to the precision of its advertising. Instead of broadcasting a single "one-size-fits-all" campaign at a time,

McDonald's pitches its burgers simultaneously at different age groups, different classes, even different races (Budweiser beer, incidentally, has succeeded in the same way). For children, there is the Ronald McDonald campaign, which presents a fantasy world that has little to do with hamburgers in any rational sense but a great deal to do with the emotional desires of kids. Ronald McDonald and his friends are signs that recall the Muppets, *Sesame Street*, the circus, toys, storybook illustrations, even *Alice in Wonderland*. Such signs do not signify hamburgers. Rather, they are displayed in order to prompt in the child's mind an automatic association of fantasy, fun, and McDonald's.

The same approach is taken in ads aimed at older audiences — teens, adults, and senior citizens. In the teen-oriented ads we may catch a fleeting glimpse of a hamburger or two, but what we are really shown is a teenage fantasy: groups of hip and happy adolescents singing, dancing, and cavorting together. Fearing loneliness more than anything else, adolescents quickly respond to the group appeal of such commercials. "Eat a Big Mac," these ads say, "and you won't be stuck home alone on Saturday night."

To appeal to an older and more sophisticated audience no longer so afraid of not belonging and more concerned with finding a place to go out to at night, McDonald's has designed the elaborate "Mac Tonight" commercials, which have for their backdrop a nightlit urban skyline and at their center a cabaret pianist with a moon-shaped head, a glad manner, and Blues Brothers shades. Such signs prompt an association of McDonald's with nightclubs and urban sophistication, persuading us that McDonald's is a place not only for breakfast or lunch but for dinner too, as if it were a popular off-Broadway nightspot, a place to see and be seen. Even the parody of Kurt Weill's "Mack the Knife" theme song that Mac the Pianist performs is a sign, a subtle signal to the sophisticated hamburger eater able to recognize the origin of the tune in Bertolt Brecht's *Threepenny Opera*.

For yet older customers, McDonald's has designed a commercial around the   20
fact that it employs a large number of retirees and seniors. In one such ad, we see an elderly man leaving his pretty little cottage early in the morning to start work as "the new kid" at McDonald's, and then we watch him during his first day on the job. Of course he is a great success, outdoing everyone else with his energy and efficiency, and he returns home in the evening to a loving wife and a happy home. One would almost think that the ad was a kind of moving "help wanted" sign (indeed, McDonald's *was* hiring elderly employees at the time), but it's really just directed at consumers. Older viewers can see themselves wanted and appreciated in the ad — and perhaps be distracted from the rationally uncomfortable fact that many senior citizens take such jobs because of financial need and thus may be unlikely to own the sort of home that one sees in the commercial. But realism isn't the point here. This is fantasyland, a dream world promising instant gratification no matter what the facts of the matter may be.

Practically the only fantasy that McDonald's doesn't exploit is the fantasy of sex. This is understandable, given McDonald's desire to present itself as a family restaurant. But everywhere else, sexual fantasies, which have

always had an important place in American advertising, dominate the advertising scene. You expect sexual come-ons in ads for perfume or cosmetics
or jewelry — after all, that's what they're selling — but for room deodorizers?
In a magazine ad for Claire Burke home fragrances, for example, we see a
well-dressed couple cavorting about their bedroom in what looks like a cheery
preparation for sadomasochistic exercises. Jordache and Calvin Klein pitch
blue jeans as props for teenage sexuality. The phallic appeal of automobiles,
traditionally an implicit feature in automotive advertising, becomes quite
explicit in a Dodge commercial that shifts back and forth from shots of a
young man in an automobile to teasing glimpses of a woman — his date — as
she dresses in her apartment.

The very language of today's advertisements is charged with sexuality.
Products in the more innocent fifties were "new and improved," but everything in the eighties is "hot!" — as in "hot woman," or sexual heat. Cars are
"hot." Movies are "hot." An ad for Valvoline pulses to the rhythm of a "heat
wave, burning in my car." Sneakers get red hot in a magazine ad for Travel Fox
athletic shoes in which we see male and female figures, clad only in Travel Fox
shoes, apparently in the act of copulation — an ad that earned one of *Adweek*'s
annual "badvertising" awards for shoddy advertising.

The sexual explicitness of contemporary advertising is a sign not so much
of American sexual fantasies as of the lengths to which advertisers will go to
get attention. Sex never fails as an attention-getter, and in a particularly competitive, and expensive, era for American marketing, advertisers like to bet
on a sure thing. Ad people refer to the proliferation of TV, radio, newspaper,
magazine, and billboard ads as "clutter," and nothing cuts through the clutter
like sex.

By showing the flesh, advertisers work on the deepest, most coercive
human emotions of all. Much sexual coercion in advertising, however, is a
sign of a desperate need to make certain that clients are getting their money's worth. The appearance of advertisements that refer directly to the pre-
fabricated fantasies of Hollywood is a sign of a different sort of desperation:
a desperation for ideas. With the rapid turnover of advertising campaigns
mandated by the need to cut through the "clutter," advertisers may be hard
pressed for new ad concepts, and so they are more and more frequently turning to already-established models. In the early 1980s, for instance, Pepsi-Cola
ran a series of ads broadly alluding to Steven Spielberg's *E.T.* In one such ad,
we see a young boy, who, like the hero of *E.T.*, witnesses an extraterrestrial
visit. The boy is led to a soft-drink machine where he pauses to drink a can of
Pepsi as the spaceship he's spotted flies off into the universe. The relationship
between the ad and the movie, accordingly, is a parasitical one, with the ad
taking its life from the creative body of the film. . . .

Madison Avenue has also framed ad campaigns around the cultural pres- 25
tige of high-tech machinery. This is especially the case with sports cars, whose
high-tech appeal is so powerful that some people apparently fantasize about
being sports cars. At least, this is the conclusion one might draw from a

Porsche commercial that asked its audience, "If you *were* a car, what kind of car would you be?" As a candy-red Porsche speeds along a rain-slick forest road, the ad's voice-over describes all the specifications you'd want to have if you *were* a sports car. "If you were a car," the commercial concludes, "you'd be a Porsche."

In his essay "Car Commercials and *Miami Vice*," Todd Gitlin explains the semiotic appeal of such ads as those in the Porsche campaign. Aired at the height of what may be called America's "myth of the entrepreneur," these commercials were aimed at young corporate managers who imaginatively identified with the "lone wolf" image of a Porsche speeding through the woods. Gitlin points out that such images cater to the fantasies of faceless corporate men who dream of entrepreneurial glory, of striking out on their own like John DeLorean and telling the boss to take his job and shove it. But as DeLorean's spectacular failure demonstrates, the life of the entrepreneur can be extremely risky. So rather than having to go it alone and take the risks that accompany entrepreneurial independence, the young executive can sub-stitute fantasy for reality by climbing into his Porsche — or at least that's what Porsche's advertisers wanted him to believe.

But there is more at work in the Porsche ads than the fantasies of corpo-rate America. Ever since Arthur C. Clarke and Stanley Kubrick teamed up to present us with HAL 9000, the demented computer of *2001: A Space Odyssey*, the American imagination has been obsessed with the melding of man and machine. First there was television's *Six Million Dollar Man*, and then mov-ieland's *Star Wars*, *Blade Runner*, and *Robocop*, fantasy visions of a future dom-inated by machines. Androids haunt our imaginations as machines seize the initiative. *Time* magazine's "Man of the Year" for 1982 was a computer. Robot-built automobiles appeal to drivers who spend their days in front of computer screens — perhaps designing robots. When so much power and prestige is being given to high-tech machines, wouldn't you rather be a Porsche?

In short, the Porsche campaign is a sign of a new mythology that is emerging before our eyes, a myth of the machine, which is replacing the myth of the human. The iconic figure of the little tramp caught up in the cogs of industrial production in Charlie Chaplin's *Modern Times* signified a humanis-tic revulsion to the age of the machine. Human beings, such icons said, were superior to machines. Human values should come first in the moral order of things. But as Edith Milton suggests in her essay "The Track of the Mutant," we are now coming to believe that machines are superior to human beings, that mechanical nature is superior to human nature. Rather than being threat-ened by machines, we long to merge with them. *The Six Million Dollar Man* is one iconic figure in the new mythology; Harrison Ford's sexual coupling with an android is another. In such an age it should come as little wonder that computer-synthesized Max Headroom should be a commercial spokesman for Coca-Cola, or that Federal Express should design a series of TV ads featur-ing mechanical-looking human beings revolving around strange and powerful machines.

Fear and Trembling in the Marketplace

While advertisers play on and reflect back at us our fantasies about every-thing from fighter pilots to robots, they also play on darker imaginings. If dream and desire can be exploited in the quest for sales, so can nightmare and fear.

The nightmare equivalent of America's populist desire to "belong," for example, is the fear of not belonging, of social rejection, of being different. Advertisements for dandruff shampoos, mouthwashes, deodorants, and laun-dry detergents ("Ring around the Collar!") accordingly exploit such fears, bullying us into consumption. Although ads of this type were still around in the 1980s, they were particularly common in the fifties and early sixties, reflecting a society still reeling from the witch-hunts of the McCarthy years. When any sort of social eccentricity or difference could result in a public denunciation and the loss of one's job or even liberty, Americans were keen to conform and be like everyone else. No one wanted to be "guilty" of smelling bad or of having a dirty collar.

"Guilt" ads characteristically work by creating narrative situations in which someone is "accused" of some social "transgression," pronounced guilty, and then offered the sponsor's product as a means of returning to "innocence." Such ads, in essence, are parodies of ancient religious rituals of guilt and atonement, whereby sinning humanity is offered salvation through the agency of priest and church. In the world of advertising, a product takes the place of the priest, but the logic is quite similar.

In commercials for Wisk detergent, for example, we witness the drama of a hapless housewife and her husband as they are mocked by the jeering voices of children shouting "Ring around the Collar!" "Oh, those dirty rings!" the housewife groans in despair. It's as if she and her husband were being stoned by an angry crowd. But there's hope, there's help, there's Wisk. Cleans-ing her soul of sin as well as her husband's, the housewife launders his shirts with Wisk, and behold, his collars are clean. Product salvation is only as far as the supermarket. . . .

If guilt looks backward in time to past transgressions, fear, like desire, faces forward, trembling before the future. In the late 1980s, a new kind of fear commercial appeared, one whose narrative played on the worries of young corporate managers struggling up the ladder of success. Representing the nightmare equivalent of the elitist desire to "arrive," ads of this sort cre-ated images of failure, story lines of corporate defeat. In one ad for Apple computers, for example, a group of junior executives sits around a table with the boss as he asks each executive how long it will take his or her depart-ment to complete some publishing jobs. "Two or three days," answers one nervous executive. "A week, on overtime," a tight-lipped woman responds. But one young up-and-comer can have everything ready tomorrow, today, or yes-terday, because his department uses a Macintosh desktop publishing system. Guess who'll get the next promotion?

30

For other markets, there are other fears. If McDonald's presents senior citizens with bright fantasies of being useful and appreciated beyond retirement, companies like Secure Horizons dramatize senior citizens' fears of being caught short by a major illness. Running its ads in the wake of budgetary cuts in the Medicare system, Secure Horizons designed a series of commercials featuring a pleasant old man named Harry — who looks and sounds rather like Carroll O'Connor — who tells us the story of the scare he got during his wife's recent illness. Fearing that next time Medicare won't cover the bills, he has purchased supplemental health insurance from Secure Horizons and now securely tends his roof-top garden. . . .

The Future of an Illusion

There are some signs in the advertising world that Americans are getting fed up with fantasy advertisements and want to hear some straight talk. Weary of extravagant product claims and irrelevant associations, consumers trained by years of advertising to distrust what they hear seem to be developing an immunity to commercials. At least, this is the semiotic message I read in the "new realism" advertisements of the eighties, ads that attempt to convince you that what you're seeing is the real thing, that the ad is giving you the straight dope, not advertising hype.

You can recognize the "new realism" by its camera techniques. The lighting is usually subdued to give the ad the effect of being filmed without studio lighting or special filters. The scene looks gray, as if the blinds were drawn. The camera shots are jerky and off-angle, often zooming in for sudden and unflattering close-ups, as if the cameraman were an amateur with a home video recorder. In a "realistic" ad for AT&T, for example, we are treated to a monologue by a plump stockbroker — his plumpness intended as a sign that he's for real and not just another actor — who tells us about the problems he's had with his phone system (not AT&T's) as the camera jerks around, generally filming him from below as if the photographer couldn't quite fit the equipment into the crammed office. "This is no fancy advertisement," the ad tries to convince us, "this is sincere."

An ad for Miller draft beer tries the same approach, re-creating the effect of an amateur videotape of a wedding celebration. Camera shots shift suddenly from group to group. The picture jumps. Bodies are poorly framed. The color is washed out. Like the beer it is pushing, the ad is supposed to strike us as being "as real as it gets."

Such ads reflect a desire for reality in the marketplace, a weariness with Madison Avenue illusions. But there's no illusion like the illusion of reality. Every special technique that advertisers use to create their "reality effects" is, in fact, more unrealistic than the techniques of "illusory" ads. The world, in reality, doesn't jump around when you look at it. It doesn't appear in subdued gray tones. Our eyes don't have zoom lenses, and we don't look at things with our heads cocked to one side. The irony of the "new realism" is that it is more unrealistic, more artificial, than the ordinary run of television advertising.

But don't expect any truly realistic ads in the future, because a realistic advertisement is a contradiction in terms. The logic of advertising is entirely semiotic: It substitutes signs for things, framed visions of consumer desire for the thing itself. The success of modern advertising, its penetration into every corner of American life, reflects a culture that has itself chosen illusion over reality. At a time when political candidates all have professional image-makers attached to their staffs, and the president of the United States can be an actor who once sold shirt collars, all the cultural signs are pointing to more illusions in our lives rather than fewer — a fecund breeding ground for the world of the advertiser.

READING THE TEXT

1. Describe in your own words the paradox of the American dream, as Solomon sees it.

2. In Solomon's view, why do status symbols work particularly well in manipulating American consumers?

3. Why, in Solomon's view, has McDonald's been so successful in its ad campaigns?

4. What is a "guilt" ad (para. 31), according to Solomon, and how does it affect consumers?

5. What relationship does Solomon find between the "new realism" (para. 35) of some ads and the paradoxes of the American dream?

READING THE SIGNS

1. **CONNECTING TEXTS**   The American political scene has changed since the late 1980s, when this essay was first published. Do you believe the contradiction between populism and elitism that Solomon describes still affects American advertising and media? In an analytic essay, argue your case. Be sure to discuss specific media examples. To develop your ideas, you might consult Jeffrey Fleishman's "How an Angry National Mood Is Reflected in Pop Culture" (p. 531).

2. **CONNECTING TEXTS**   In television advertising, the most coveted market is the 18 to 49 age group, a cohort that often includes what James B. Twitchell ("What We Are to Advertisers," p. 163) describes as "experiencers" and "strivers." To what extent do the TV ads you watch display a populist or elitist ethos? Or do you find that the ads do not harbor class sensitivity? How do you explain your observations?

3. Bring to class a general-interest magazine (such as *People* or *O: The Oprah Magazine*), and in small groups study the advertising. Do the ads tend to have an elitist or a populist appeal? What relationship do you see between the appeal you identify and the magazine's target readership? Present your group's findings to the class.

4. In class, brainstorm a list of status symbols common in advertising today. Then discuss what groups they appeal to and why. Can you detect any patterns based on gender, ethnicity, or age?

5. Visit your college library, and locate an issue of a popular magazine from an earlier decade, such as the 1930s or 1940s. Then write an essay in which you compare and contrast the advertising found in the early issue with that in a current issue of the same publication. What similarities and differences do you find in the myths underlying the advertising, and what is the significance of these similarities and differences?

CREATING CONSUMERS

JAMES B. TWITCHELL
What We Are to Advertisers

Are you a "believer" or a "striver," an "achiever" or a "struggler," an "experiencer" or a "maker"? Or do you have no idea what we're talking about? If you don't, James Twitchell explains it all to you in this selection in which the psychological profiling schemes of American advertising are laid bare. For like it or not, advertisers have, or think they have, your number, and they will pitch their products according to the personality profile they have concocted for you. And the really spooky thing is that they're often right. A prolific writer on American advertising and culture, Twitchell's books include *Adcult USA: The Triumph of Advertising in American Culture* (1996).

Mass production means mass marketing, and mass marketing means the creation of mass stereotypes. Like objects on shelves, we too cluster in groups. We find meaning together. As we mature, we move from shelf to shelf, from aisle to aisle, zip code to zip code, from lifestyle to lifestyle, between what the historian Daniel Boorstin calls "consumption communities." Finally, as full-grown consumers, we stabilize in our buying, and hence meaning-making, patterns. Advertisers soon lose interest in us not just because we stop buying but because we have stopped changing brands.

The object of advertising is not just to brand parity objects but also to brand consumers as they move through these various communities. To explain his job, Rosser Reeves, the master of hard-sell advertising like the old Anacin ads, used to hold up two quarters and claim his job was to make you believe they were different, and, more importantly, that one was better than the other. Hence, at the macro level the task of advertising is to convince different sets of consumers — target groups — that the quarter they observe is somehow different in meaning and value than the same quarter seen by their across-the-tracks neighbors.

In adspeak, this is called *positioning*. "I could have positioned Dove as a detergent bar for men with dirty hands," David Ogilvy famously said, "but I chose to position it as a toilet bar for women with dry skin." Easy to say, hard to do. But if Anheuser-Busch wants to maximize its sales, the soccer mom driving the shiny Chevy Suburban must feel she drinks a different Budweiser than the roustabout in the rusted-out Chevy pickup.[1]

The study of audiences goes by any number of names: psychographics, ethnographics, macrosegmentation, to name a few, but they are all based on the ineluctable principle that birds of a feather flock together. The object of much consumer research is not to try to twist their feathers so that they will flock to your product, but to position your product in such a place that they will have to fly by it and perhaps stop to roost. After roosting, they will eventually think that this is a part of their flyway and return to it again and again.

Since different products have different meanings to different audiences,   5
segmentation studies are crucial. Although agencies have their own systems for naming these groups and their lifestyles, the current supplier of much raw data about them is a not-for-profit organization, the Stanford Research Institute (SRI).

The "psychographic" system of SRI is called acronomically VALS (now VALS2+), short for Values and Lifestyle System. Essentially this schematic is based on the common-sense view that consumers are motivated "to acquire products, services, and experiences that provide satisfaction and give shape, substance, and character to their identities" in bundles. The more "resources" (namely money, but also health, self-confidence, and energy) each group has, the more likely they will buy "products, services, and experiences" of the group they associate with. But resources are not the only determinant. Customers are also motivated by such ineffables as principles, status, and

---

[1] Cigarette companies were the first to find this out in the 1930s, much to their amazement. Blindfolded smokers couldn't tell what brand they were smoking. Instead of making cigarettes with different tastes, it was easier to make different advertising claims to different audiences. Cigarettes are hardly unique. Ask beer drinkers why they prefer a particular brand and invariably they tell you: "It's the taste," "This goes down well," "This is light and refreshing," "This is rich and smooth." They will say this about a beer that has been described as their brand, but is not. Anheuser-Busch, for instance, spent three dollars per barrel in 1980 to market a barrel of beer; now they spend nine dollars. Since the cost to reach a thousand television households has doubled at the same time the audience has segmented (thanks to cable), why not go after a particular market segment by tailoring ads emphasizing, in different degrees, the Clydesdales, Ed McMahon, Beechwood aging, the red and white can, dates certifying freshness, the spotted dog, the Eagle, as well as "the crisp, clean taste." While you cannot be all things to all people, the object of advertising is to be as many things to as many segments as possible. The ultimate object is to convince as many segments as possible that "This Bud's for you" is a sincere statement.

action. When SRI describes these various audiences, they peel apart like this (I have provided them an appropriate car to show their differences):

- Actualizers: These people at the top of the pyramid are the ideal of every-one but advertisers. They have "it" already, or will soon. They are sophisti-cated, take-charge people interested in independence and character. They don't need new things; in fact, they already have their things. If not, they already know what "the finer things" are and won't be told. They don't need a new car, but if they do they'll read *Consumer Reports*. They do not need a hood ornament on their car.

- Fulfilled: Here are mature, satisfied, comfortable souls who support the sta-tus quo in almost every way. Often they are literally or figuratively retired. They value functionality, durability, and practicality. They drive something called a "town car," which is made by all the big three automakers.

- Believers: As the word expresses, these people support traditional codes of family, church, and community, wearing good Republican cloth coats. As consumers they are predictable, favoring American products and recogniz-able brands. They regularly attend church and Walmart, and they are trans-ported there in their mid-range automobile like an Oldsmobile. Whether Oldsmobile likes it or not, they do indeed drive "your father's Oldsmobile."

Moving from principle-oriented consumers who look inside to status-driven consumers who look out to others, we find the Achievers and Strivers.

- Achievers: If consumerism has an ideal, here it is. Bingo! Wedded to their jobs as a source of duty, reward, and prestige, these are the people who not only favor the establishment but are the establishment. They like the concept of prestige. Not only are they successful, they demonstrate their success by buying such objects as prestigious cars to show it. They like hood ornaments. They see no contradiction in driving a Land Rover in Manhattan.

- Strivers: A young Striver is fine; he will possibly mature into an Achiever. But an old Striver can be nasty; he may well be bitter. Since they are unsure of themselves, they are eager to be branded as long as the brand is elevating. Money defines success and they don't have enough of it. Being a yuppie is fine as long as the prospect of upward mobility is possible. Strivers like foreign cars even if it means only leasing a BMW.

[And then there] are those driven less by the outside world but by their desire to participate, to be part of a wider world.

- Experiencers: Here is life on the edge — enthusiastic, impulsive, and even reckless. Their energy finds expression in sports, social events, and "doing something." Politically and personally uncommitted, experiencers are an advertiser's dream come true as they see consumption as fulfillment and are willing to spend a high percent of their disposable income to attain it. When you wonder about who could possibly care how fast a car will accel-erate from zero to sixty m.p.h., they care.

- Makers: Here is the practical side of Experiencers; they like to build things and they experience the world by working on it. Conservative, suspicious, respectful, they like to do things in and to their homes, like adding a room, canning vegetables, or changing the oil in their pickup trucks.

- Strugglers: Like Actualizers, these people are outside the pale of materialism not by choice, but by low income. Strugglers are chronically poor. Their repertoire of things is limited not because they already have it all, but because they have so little. Although they clip coupons like Actualizers, theirs are from the newspaper. Their transportation is usually public, if any. They are the invisible millions.

As one might imagine, these are very fluid categories, and we may move through as many as three of them in our lifetimes. For instance, between ages 18 and 24 most people (61 percent) are Experiencers in desire or deed, while less than 1 percent are Fulfilled. Between ages 55 and 64, however, the Actualizers, Fulfilled, and Strugglers claim about 15 percent of the population each, while the Believers have settled out at about a fifth. The Achievers, Strivers, and Makers fill about 10 percent apiece, and the remaining 2 percent are Experiencers. The numbers can be broken down at every stage allowing for marital status, education, household size, dependent children, home ownership, household income, and occupation. More interesting still is the ability to accurately predict the appearance of certain goods in each grouping. SRI sells data on precisely who buys single-lens reflex cameras, who owns a laptop computer, who drinks herbal tea, who phones before five o'clock, who reads the *Reader's Digest*, and who watches *Beavis and Butthead*.

When one realizes the fabulous expense of communicating meaning for a product, the simple-mindedness of a system like VALS2 + becomes less risible. When you are spending millions of dollars for a few points of market share for your otherwise indistinguishable product, the idea that you might be able to attract the owners of socket wrenches by shifting ad content around just a bit makes sense. Once you realize that in taste tests consumers cannot tell one brand of cigarettes from another — including their own — nor distinguish such products as soap, gasoline, cola, beer, or what-have-you, it is clear that the product must be overlooked and the audience isolated and sold.

READING THE TEXT

1. What do marketers mean by "positioning" (para. 3), and why is it an important strategy to them?

2. What does the acronym VALS stand for, and what is the logic behind this system?

3. Why do marketers believe that the "product must be overlooked and the audience isolated and sold" (para. 8), according to Twitchell?

4. Why does Twitchell explain that the VALS2 + categories are "fluid" (para. 7)?

READING THE SIGNS

1. Write a journal entry in which you identify where you fit in the VALS2 + system. Conversely, explain why none of the categories describe you. What is your attitude toward being stereotyped by marketers?

2. In class, discuss whether the categories of consumers defined by the VALS2 + paradigm are an accurate predictor of consumer behavior. Use the discussion as the basis of an essay in which you argue for or against the proposition that stereotyping consumer lifestyles is an effective way of marketing goods and services.

3. Study the VALS2 + paradigm in terms of the values it presumes. To what extent does it presume traditionally American values such as individualism? Use your analysis to formulate an argument about whether this marketing tool is an essentially American phenomenon.

4. **CONNECTING TEXTS**   Using the VALS2 + paradigm, analyze the consumption habits of the interviewees described in Jon Mooallem's "The Self-Storage Self" (p. 103). Do they fit neatly into the paradigm, or do their patterns of consumption call for a revision of it? Use your findings as the basis of an essay in which you assess the usefulness of the paradigm.

5. **CONNECTING TEXTS**   Twitchell, Malcolm Gladwell ("The Science of Shopping," p. 88), and Joseph Turow ("The Daily You: How the New Advertising Industry Is Defining Your Identity and Your Worth," p. 394) all describe marketing research strategies. Read these selections, and write an argument that supports, opposes, or modifies the proposition that marketers have misappropriated research techniques for manipulative, and therefore ethically questionable, purposes.

CREATING CONSUMERS

STEVE CRAIG

Men's Men and Women's Women

Men and women both drink beer, but you wouldn't guess that from the television ads that pitch beer as a guy beverage and associate beer drinking with such guy things as fishing trips, bars, and babes. Conversely, both men and women can find themselves a few pounds overweight, but you wouldn't know that from the ads, which almost always feature women, as they are intended to appeal to women dieters. In this selection, Steve Craig provides a step-by-step analysis of four TV commercials, showing how advertisers carefully craft their ads to appeal, respectively, to male and female consumers. A professor in the department of radio, television, and film at the University of North Texas, Craig has written widely on television, radio history, and gender and media.

Gender and the Economics of Television Advertising

The economic structure of the television industry has a direct effect on the placement and content of all television programs and commercials. Large advertisers and their agencies have evolved the pseudo-scientific method of time purchasing based on demographics, with the age and sex of the consumer generally considered to be the most important predictors of purchasing behavior. Computers make it easy to match market research on product buying patterns with audience research on television viewing habits. Experience, research, and intuition thus yield a demographic (and even psychographic) profile of the "target audience." Advertisers can then concentrate their budgets on those programs which the target audience is most likely to view. The most economical advertising buys are those in which the target audience is most concentrated (thus, the less "waste" audience the advertiser must purchase) (Barnouw, 1978; Gitlin, 1983; Jhally, 1987).

Good examples of this demographic targeting can be seen by contrasting the ads seen on daytime television, aimed at women at home, with those on weekend sports telecasts. Ads for disposable diapers are virtually never seen during a football game any more than commercials for beer are seen during soap operas. True, advertisers of some products simply wish to have their commercials seen by the largest number of consumers at the lowest cost without regard to age, sex, or other demographic descriptors, but most consider this approach far too inefficient for the majority of products.

A general rule of thumb in television advertising, then, is that daytime is the best time to reach the woman who works at home. Especially important to advertisers among this group is the young mother with children. Older women, who also make up a significant proportion of the daytime audience, are generally considered less important by many advertisers in the belief that they spend far less money on consumer goods than young mothers.

Prime time (the evening hours) is considered a good time to reach women who work away from home, but since large numbers of men are also in the audience, it can also be a good time to advertise products with wider target audiences. Weekend sports periods (and, in season, "Monday Night Football") are the only time of the week when men outnumber women in the television audience, and therefore, become the optimum time for advertising products and services aimed at men.

Gendered Television, Gendered Commercials

In his book *Television Culture* (1987, Chs. 10, 11), John Fiske discusses 5 "gendered television," explaining that the television industry successfully designs some programs for men and others for women. Clearly, program producers and schedulers must consider the target audience needs of their clients (the advertisers) in creating a television program lineup. The gendering of programming allows the industry to provide the proper audience for advertisers by constructing shows pleasurable for the target audience to watch, and one aspect of this construction is in the gender portrayals of characters.

Fiske provides the following example:

> Women's view of masculinity, as evidenced in soap operas, differs markedly from that produced for the masculine audience. The "good" male in the daytime soaps is caring, nurturing, and verbal. He is prone to making comments like "I don't care about material wealth or professional success, all I care about is us and our relationship." He will talk about feelings and people and rarely express his masculinity in direct action. Of course, he is still decisive, he still has masculine power, but that power is given a "feminine" inflection. . . . The "macho" characteristics of goal centeredness, assertiveness, and the morality of the strongest that identify the hero in masculine television, tend here to be characteristics of the villain. (p. 186)

But if the programming manipulates gender portrayals to please the audience, then surely so must the commercials that are the programs' reason for being. My previous research (Craig, 1990) supports the argument that advertisers also structure the gender images in their commercials to match the expectations and fantasies of their intended audience. Thus, commercials portraying adult women with children were nearly four times more likely to appear during daytime soap operas than during weekend sports (p. 50). Daytime advertisers exploit the image of women as mothers to sell products to mothers. Likewise, during the weekend sports broadcasts, only 18 percent of the primary male characters were shown at home, while during the daytime ads, 40 percent of them were (p. 42). For the woman at home, men are far more likely to be portrayed as being around the house than they are in commercials aimed at men on weekends.

Gendered commercials, like gendered programs, are designed to give pleasure to the target audience, since it is the association of the product with a pleasurable experience that forms the basis for much American television advertising. Yet patriarchy conditions males and females to seek their pleasure differently. Advertisers therefore portray different images to men and women in order to exploit the different deep-seated motivations and anxieties connected to gender identity. I would now like to turn to a close analysis of four television commercials to illustrate some of these differing portrayals. Variations in how men and women are portrayed are especially apparent when comparing weekend and daytime commercials, since ads during these day parts almost completely focus on a target audience of men or women respectively.

Analysis of Four Commercials

In order to illustrate the variation of gender portrayal, I have chosen four commercials. Each was selected to provide an example of how men and women are portrayed to themselves and to the other sex. The image of men and women in commercials aired during weekend sports telecasts I call "Men's Men" and "Men's Women." The portrayals of men and women in commercials aimed at women at home during the daytime hours I call "Women's Men" and "Women's Women." Although there are certainly commercials aired during these day parts that do not fit neatly into these categories, and even a few that might be considered to be counter-stereotypical in their gender portrayals, the commercials and images I have chosen to analyze are fairly typical and were chosen to permit a closer look at the practices revealed in my earlier content analysis. Further, I acknowledge that the readings of these commercials are my own. Others may well read them differently.

Men's Men

I would first like to consider two commercials originally broadcast   10
during weekend sports and clearly aimed at men. (These and the other commercials I will discuss were broadcast on at least one of the three major networks. I recorded them for analysis during January 1990.)

COMMERCIAL 1: ACURA INTEGRA (:30)

> MUSIC: Light rock guitar music runs throughout. Tropical elements (e.g., a steel drum) are added later.

A young, white, blond, bespectacled male wearing a plain sweatshirt is shown cleaning out the interior of a car. He finds an old photograph of himself and two male companions (all are young, slender, and white) posing with a trophy-sized sailfish. He smiles. Dissolve to what appears to be a flashback of the fishing trip. The three men are now seen driving down the highway in the car (we now see that it is a new black Acura Integra) in a Florida-like landscape. We see a montage of close-ups of the three men inside the car, then a view out the car window of what looks to be the Miami skyline.

> ANNOUNCER (male): "When you think about all the satisfaction you get out of going places . . . why would you want to take anything less . . ."

Dissolve to a silhouette shot of a young woman in a bathing suit walking along the beach at sunset.

> ANNOUNCER: ". . . than America's most satisfying car?"

On this last line, the three young men are seen in silhouette knee-deep in the water at the same beach, apparently watching the woman pass. One of the men drops to his knees and throws his arms up in mock supplication. A montage of shots of the three men follows, shots of a deep-sea fishing boat intercut with shots of the first man washing the car. The montage ends with the three posing with the trophy sailfish. The screen flashes and freezes and becomes the still photo seen at the first shot of the commercial. The final shot shows a long shot of the car, freshly washed. The first man, dressed as in the first shot, gives the car a final polish and walks away. The words "Acura" and "Precision Crafted Performance" are superimposed over the final shot.

ANNOUNCER: "The Acura Integra."

This ad, which ran during a weekend sports telecast, has a number of features that makes it typical of many other commercials aimed at men. First, it is for an automobile. My previous research found that 29 percent of the network commercials telecast in the weekend time period were for cars and other automotive products (compared to only 1 percent during the daytime sample) (Craig, 1990, p. 36). In our culture, automobiles are largely the male's province, and men are seen by the automotive industry as the primary decision makers when it comes to purchases. Further, cars are frequently offered as a means of freedom (literally so in this ad), and escapism is an important component in many weekend ads (only 16 percent of weekend ads are set at home compared to 41 percent of daytime ads) (p. 43).

Second, with the exception of a brief silhouette of the woman on the beach, there are no women in this commercial. Camaraderie in all-male or nearly all-male groupings is a staple of weekend commercials, especially those for automobiles and beer. Again, my earlier research indicates that fully one-third of weekend commercials have an all-adult male cast (but only 20 percent of daytime commercials have an all-adult female cast) (p. 36).

The escapism and male camaraderie promised in this commercial are simply an extension of the escapism and camaraderie men enjoy when they watch (and vicariously participate in) weekend sports on television. Messner (1987) suggests that one reason for the popularity of sports with men is that it offers them a chance to escape from the growing ambiguity of masculinity in daily life.

> Both on a personal/existential level for athletes and on a symbolic/ideological level for spectators and fans, sport has become one of the "last bastions" of male power and superiority over — and separation from — the "feminization" of society. The rise of football as "America's number-one game" is likely the result of the comforting *clarity* it provides between the polarities of traditional male power, strength, and violence and the contemporary fears of social feminization. (p. 54)

The Acura commercial acts to reinforce male fantasies in an environment of clear masculinity and male domination. Men's men are frequently portrayed as men without women. The presence of women in the commercials might serve to threaten men's men with confusing uncertainty about the nature of masculinity in a sexist, but changing, society (Fiske, 1987, pp. 202–209, offers an extended psychoanalytic explanation of the absence of women in masculine television). On the other hand, the absence of women must *not* suggest homosexuality. Men's men are clearly heterosexual. To discourage any suspicions, the Acura ad portrays three (rather than two) men vacationing together.

It is also at least partly for this reason that the single quick shot in which the woman *does* appear in this commercial is important. She is nothing more than an anonymous object of desire (indeed, in silhouette, we cannot even see her face), but her presence both affirms the heterosexuality of the group while at the same time hinting that attaining sexual fulfillment will be made easier by the possession of the car. Men's men have the unchallenged freedom of a fantasized masculinity — to travel, to be free from commitment, to seek adventure.

15

Men's Women

COMMERCIAL 2: MILLER BEER (:30)

We see the interior of a cheap roadside cafe. It is lit with an almost blinding sunlight streaming in the windows. A young couple sits in a far booth holding hands. A young, blond waitress is crossing the room. A silent jukebox sits in the foreground. At first we hear only natural sounds. We cut to a close-up from a low angle from outside the cafe of male legs as they enter the cafe. The legs are clad in blue jeans and cow-boy boots. As the man enters, we cut to a close-up of the blond waitress looking up to see the man. We see a close-up of the man's body as he passes the silent jukebox. As if by magic, the jukebox begins to play the rhythm and blues number "I Put a Spell on You." We see the couple that was holding hands turn in surprise. The man in the booth's face is unlit and we can see no features, but the woman is young with long blond hair. She looks surprised and pulls her hand away from the man's. We cut to an extreme close-up of the waitress's face. It is covered with sweat. As she watches the man pass, a smile appears on her face. She comes over to take the man's order. The camera takes the man's point of view.

MAN: "Miller Genuine Draft."
WAITRESS: "I was hopin' you'd say that."

We see a shot of a refrigerator door opening. The refrigerator is filled with sweating, backlit bottles of Miller beer. We then see a close-up of the man holding a bottle and opening it magically with a flick of his thumb (no opener). A montage of shots of the product amid blowing snow follows this. The sounds of a blizzard are heard.

ANNOUNCER: "Cold filtered. Never heat pasteurized. Miller Genuine Draft. For those who discover this real draft taste . . . the world is a *very* cool place."

On this last line we see close-ups of the woman in the booth and the waitress. Wind is blowing snow in their faces and they are luxuriating in the coolness. The waitress suddenly looks at the camera with shocked disappointment. We cut to an empty seat with the man's empty beer bottle rocking on the table. The music, snow, and wind end abruptly. We see the man's back as he exits the cafe. The final shot is of the waitress, elbow propped on the counter, looking after the man. The words "Tap into the Cold" are superimposed.

When women do appear in men's commercials, they seldom challenge the primary masculine fantasy. Men's women are portrayed as physically attractive, slim, and usually young and white, frequently blond, and almost always dressed in revealing clothing. Since most men's commercials are set in locations away from home, most men's women appear outside the home, and only infrequently are they portrayed as wives. There are almost always hints of sexual availability in men's women, but this is seldom played out explicitly. Although the sexual objectification of women characters in these ads is often quite subtle, my previous content analysis suggests that it is far more common in weekend than in daytime ads (Craig, 1990, p. 34). Men's women are also frequently portrayed as admirers (and at times, almost voyeurs), generally approving of some aspect of product use (the car he drives, the beer he drinks, the credit card he uses).

In these respects, the Miller ad is quite typical. What might have been a simple commercial about a man ordering and drinking a beer becomes an elaborate sexual fantasy, in many respects constructed like a porn film. The attractive, eager waitress is mystically drawn to the man who relieves her bored frustrations with an orgasmic chug-a-lug. She is "hot" while he (and the beer) is "*very* cool." But once he's satisfied, he's gone. He's too cool for conversation or commitment. We never see the man's face, but rather are invited, through the use of the point-of-view shot, to become a participant in the mystic fantasy.

There is, of course, considerable tongue-in-cheek intent in this ad. Males know that the idea of anonymous women lusting after them, eager for sex without commitment, is fantasy. But for many men, it is pleasurable fantasy, and common enough in weekend commercials. The main point is that the product has been connected, however briefly, with the pleasure of this fantasy. The physical pleasure of consuming alcohol (and specifically cold Miller beer) is tied to the pleasurable imaginings of a narrative extended beyond that which is explicitly seen.

One industry executive has explained this advertising technique. Noting the need for "an imaginary and motivating value" in ads, Nicolas (1988) argues that:

> Beyond the principle of utility, it becomes more and more important to associate a principle of pleasure to the value. The useful must be linked to the beautiful, the rational to the imaginary, the indispensable to the superfluous. . . . It is imperative that the image be seductive. (p. 7)

Although some research has documented changes in gender portrayals 20 in television advertising over the past few years (e.g., Bretl & Cantor, 1988; Ferrante et al., 1988), such conclusions are based on across-the-schedule studies or of prime time rather than of specifically gendered day parts. While avoiding portraying women as blatant sex objects is doubtless good business in daytime or prime time, it would almost certainly inhibit male fantasies such as this one, commonly seen during weekend sports. The man's woman continues to be portrayed according to the rules of the patriarchy.

The next two commercials were originally aired during daytime soap operas. They represent Madison Avenue's portrayal of women and men designed for women.

Women's Women

COMMERCIAL 3: WEIGHT WATCHERS (:30)

The opening shot is a quick pan from toe to head of a young, thin, white woman with dark hair. She is dressed in a revealing red bathing suit and appears to be reclining on the edge of a pool. Her head is propped up with a pillow. She is wearing sunglasses and smiling.

ANNOUNCER (woman, voice-over): "I hate diets . . . but I lost weight fast with Weight Watchers' new program."

We see the same woman sitting at a dining table in a home kitchen eating a meal. She is wearing a red dress. The camera weaves, and we briefly glimpse a man and two small children also at the table. Another close-up of the woman's body at the pool. This time the camera frames her waist.

ANNOUNCER: "And I *hate* starving myself."

We see the same family group eating pizza at a restaurant. More close-ups of the woman's body at poolside.

ANNOUNCER: "But with their new 'fast and flexible' program I don't have to."

Shot of the woman dancing with the man, followed by a montage of more shots of the family at dinner and close-ups of the woman at poolside.

ANNOUNCER: "A new food plan lets me live the way I want . . . eat with my family and friends, still have fun."

Close-up shot of balance scales. A woman's hand is moving the balance weight downward.

ANNOUNCER: "And in no time . . . *here I am!*"

Shot of the woman on the scales. She raises her hands as if in triumph. The identical shot is repeated three times.

ANNOUNCER: "Now there's only one thing I hate . . . not joining Weight Watchers sooner."

As this last line is spoken, we see a close-up of the woman at the pool. She removes her sunglasses. The man's head comes into the frame from the side and kisses her on the forehead.

This commercial portrays the woman's woman. Her need is a common one in women's commercials produced by a patriarchal society — the desire to attain and maintain her physical attractiveness. Indeed, my previous research indicates that fully 44 percent of the daytime ads sampled were for products relating to the body (compared with only 15 percent of the ads during weekend sports). In this ad, her desire for an attractive body is explicitly tied to her family. She is portrayed with a husband, small children, and a nice home. It is her husband with whom she dances and who expresses approval with a kiss. Her need for an attractive body is her need to maintain her husband's interest and maintain her family's unity and security. As Coward (1985) has written:

> Most women know to their cost that appearance is perhaps the crucial way by which men form opinions of women. For that reason, feelings about self-image get mixed up with feelings about security and comfort. . . . It sometimes appears to women that the whole possibility of being loved and comforted hangs on how their appearance will be received. (p. 78)

But dieting is a difficult form of self-deprivation, and she "hates" doing it. Implicit also is her hatred of her own "overweight" body — a body that no longer measures up to the idealized woman promoted by the patriarchy (and seen in the commercial). As Coward explains:

> . . . advertisements, health and beauty advice, fashion tips are effective precisely because somewhere, perhaps even subconsciously, an anxiety, rather than a pleasurable identification [with the idealized body], is awakened. (p. 80)

Weight Watchers promises to alleviate the pain of dieting at the same time it relieves (or perhaps delays) the anxiety of being "overweight." She can diet and "still have fun."

A related aspect is this ad's use of a female announcer. The copy is written   25 in the first person, but we never see the model speaking in direct address. We get the impression that we are eavesdropping on her thoughts — being invited to identify with her — rather than hearing a sales pitch from a third person. My earlier research confirmed the findings of other content analyses that female voice-overs are relatively uncommon in commercials. My findings, however, indicated that while only 3 percent of the voice-overs during weekend sports were by women announcers, 16 percent of those during daytime were. Further, 60 percent of the women announcers during daytime were heard in commercials for body-related products (Craig, 1990, p. 52).

Women's Men

COMMERCIAL 4: SECRET DEODORANT (:30)

We open on a wide shot of a sailing yacht at anchor. It is sunrise and a woman is on deck. She descends into the cabin. Cut to a close-up of the woman as she enters the cabin.

WOMAN: "Four bells. Rise and shine!"

A man is seen in a bunk inside the cabin. He has just awakened. Both he and the woman are now seen to be young and white. She is thin and has bobbed hair. He is muscular and unshaven (and a Bruce Willis look-alike).

MUSIC: Fusion jazz instrumental (UNDER).
MAN (painfully): "Ohhhh . . . I can't move."
WOMAN: "Ohhhhh. I took a swim — breakfast is on — I had a shower. Now it's *your turn*."

As she says this, she crosses the cabin and places a container of Secret deodorant on a shelf above the man. The man leans up on one elbow then falls back into bed with a groan.

MAN: "Ahhh, I can't."

She pulls him back to a sitting position then sits down herself, cradling him in her arms.

WOMAN: "Come onnn. You only changed *one* sail yesterday."
MAN (playfully): "Yeah, but it was a *big* sail."

Close-up of the couple. He is now positioned in the bed sitting with his back to her. He leans his head back on her shoulder.

WOMAN: "Didn't you know sailing's a sport? You know . . . an active thing."
MAN: "I just don't get it. . . . You're so together already. . . . Um. You smell great."
WOMAN: "Must be my Secret."

She looks at the container of Secret on the shelf. The man reaches over and picks it up. Close-up of the Secret with the words "Sporty Clean Scent" visible on the container.

MAN: "Sporty clean?"
WOMAN: "It's new."
MAN: "Sounds like something I could use."
WOMAN: "Unnnnn . . . I don't think so. I got it for me."

She takes the container from him and stands up and moves away. He stands up behind her and holds her from behind.

WOMAN: "For these close quarters . . . ?"
MAN: "Well, close is good."

He begins to kiss her cheek.

WOMAN: "I thought you said you couldn't move."

She turns to face him.

MAN: "I was saving my strength?"
WOMAN: "Mmmm."

We dissolve to a close-up of the product on the shelf.

ANNOUNCER (woman): "New Sporty Clean Secret. Strong enough for a man, but pH-balanced for an active woman."

This commercial portrays the woman's man. He's good looking, sensitive, romantic, and he appreciates her. What's more, they are alone in an exotic location where he proceeds to seduce her. In short, this commercial is a 30-second romance novel. She may be today's woman, be "so together," and she may be in control, but she still wants him to initiate the love-making. Her man is strong, active, and probably wealthy enough to own or rent a yacht. (Of course, a more liberated reading would have her as the owner of the yacht, or at least sharing expenses.) Yet he is also vulnerable. At first she mothers him, holding him in a Pietà-like embrace and cooing over his sore muscles. Then he catches her scent — her Secret — and the chase is on.

As in the Weight Watchers commercial, it is the woman's body that is portrayed as the source of the man's attraction, and it is only through maintaining that attraction that she can successfully negotiate the relationship. Although at one level the Secret woman is portrayed as a "new woman" — active, "sporty," self-assured, worthy of her own deodorant — she still must rely on special (even "Secret") products to make her body attractive. More to the point, she still must rely on her body to attract a man and fulfill the fantasy of security and family. After all, she is still mothering and cooking breakfast.

Once again, the product is the source of promised fantasy fulfillment — not only sexual fulfillment, but also the security of a caring relationship, one that allows her to be liberated, but not too liberated. Unlike the women of the Acura and Miller's commercials who remained anonymous objects of desire, the men of the Weight Watchers and Secret commercials are intimates who are clearly portrayed as having relationships that will exist long after the commercial is over.

Conclusion

Gender images in television commercials provide an especially intriguing field of study. The ads are carefully crafted bundles of images, frequently designed to associate the product with feelings of pleasure stemming from deep-seated fantasies and anxieties. Advertisers seem quite willing to manipulate these fantasies and exploit our anxieties, especially those concerning our gender identities, to sell products. What's more, they seem to have no compunction about capitalizing on dehumanizing gender stereotypes to seek these ends.

A threat to patriarchy is an economic threat, not only to men who may   30
fear they will have their jobs taken by women, but also in a more fundamental way. Entire industries (automotive, cosmetics, fashion) are predicated on the assumption that men and women will continue behaving according to their stereotypes. Commercials for women therefore act to reinforce patriarchy and to co-opt any reactionary ideology into it. Commercials for men need only reinforce masculinity under patriarchy and, at most, offer men help in coping with a life plagued by women of raised conscience. Betty Friedan's comments of 1963 are still valid. Those "deceptively simple, clever, outrageous ads and commercials" (p. 270) she wrote of are still with us. If anything, they have become more subtle and insidious. The escape from their snare is through a better understanding of gender and the role of mass culture in defining it.

WORKS CITED

Barnouw, E. (1978). *The sponsor*. New York, NY: Oxford.

Bretl, D. J., & Cantor, J. (1988). The portrayal of men and women in U.S. television commercials: A recent content analysis and trends over 15 years. *Sex Roles, 18*(9/10), 595–609.

Coward, R. (1985). *Female desires: How they are sought, bought and packaged*. New York, NY: Grove.

Craig, S. (1990, December). *A content analysis comparing gender images in network television commercials aired in daytime, evening, and weekend telecasts*. (ERIC Document Reproduction Service Number ED329217)

Ferrante, C., Haynes, A., & Kingsley, S. (1988). Image of women in television advertising. *Journal of Broadcasting & Electronic Media, 32*(2), 231–237.

Fiske, J. (1987). *Television culture*. New York, NY: Methuen.

Friedan, B. (1963). *The feminine mystique*. New York, NY: Dell.

Gitlin, T. (1983). *Inside prime time*. New York, NY: Pantheon.

Jhally, S. (1987). *The codes of advertising: Fetishism and the political economy of meaning in the consumer society*. New York, NY: St. Martin's.

Messner, M. (1987). Male identity in the life course of the jock. In M. Kimmel (Ed.), *Changing men* (pp. 53–67). Newbury Park, CA: Sage.

Nicolas, P. (1988). From value to love. *Journal of Advertising Research, 28*, 7–8.

READING THE TEXT

1. How, according to John Fiske, is television programming gendered?

2. Why is male camaraderie such a common motif in "men's men" advertising, according to Craig?

3. What roles do women tend to play in the two types of commercials aimed at men? What roles do men tend to play in the two types of commercials aimed at women?

4. Why does Craig believe that "a threat to patriarchy is an economic threat" (para. 30)?

READING THE SIGNS

1. In class, discuss whether you agree with Craig's interpretations of the four commercials that he describes. If you disagree, what alternative analysis do you propose?

2. The four commercials Craig analyzes aired in 1990. View some current commercials broadcast during daytime and sports programs. Use your observations as the basis for an argument about whether the gendered patterns in advertising that Craig outlines exist today. If the patterns persist, what implications do they have for the tenacity of gender codes? If you see differences, how can you account for them?

3. Write an essay in which you support, refute, or modify Craig's belief that gendered advertising of the sort he describes is "dehumanizing" (para. 29).

4. Watch TV programs that are not overtly geared toward one gender, such as prime-time scripted drama or network news. To what extent does the advertising that accompanies these shows fit Craig's four categories of gender portrayal? How do you account for your findings? Alternatively, watch a program that is largely geared toward female viewers, such as *Orange Is the New Black*, and analyze the advertising for this show.

5. **CONNECTING TEXTS** Enter the debate over the origins of gender identity: Is it primarily biologically determined or largely socially constructed? Write an essay in which you advance your position; you can develop your ideas by consulting Aaron Devor's "Gender Role Behaviors and Attitudes" (p. 474) and Deborah Blum's "The Gender Blur: Where Does Biology End and Society Take Over?" (p. 480).

JIA TOLENTINO

How "Empowerment" Became Something for Women to Buy

The women's movement has changed a lot in America, but one marketing habit that it hasn't been able to change is the inexhaustible capacity of the advertising industry to turn everything — even social revolution — into an ad campaign. So, just as Madison Avenue's Virginia Slims campaign once presented cigarette smoking as an act of feminist defiance, "empowerment" marketing today is only harming women, as Jia Tolentino argues in this essay for the *New York Times Magazine*. Indeed, it ultimately restricts women's choices to accumulating wealth and flaunting their sex appeal. But there has to be more to life than being Kim Kardashian or Sheryl Sandberg, doesn't there? Jia Tolentino is a deputy editor at *Jezebel*.

At my day job as an editor at a women's website, I receive a daily mess of emails promoting random products and activities as "empowering." Recent offerings include the Pure Barre workout, divorce, Miley Cyrus, attention deficit hyperactivity disorder, ancient Egyptian sex rites, leggings, sending nude photos, receiving nude photos, declining to send or receive nude photos, doing stand-up comedy and purchasing full-bottomed lingerie. The mix of things presumed to transmit and increase female power is without limit yet still depressingly limiting.

"Empowerment" wasn't always so trivialized, or so corporate, or even so clamorously attached to women. Four decades ago, the word had much more in common with Latin American liberation theology than it did with "Lean In." In 1968, the Brazilian academic Paulo Freire coined the word "conscientization," empowerment's precursor, as the process by which an oppressed person perceives the structural conditions of his oppression and is subsequently able to take action against his oppressors.

Eight years later, the educator Barbara Bryant Solomon, writing about American black communities, gave this notion a new name, "empowerment." It was meant as an ethos for social workers in marginalized communities, to discourage paternalism and encourage their clients to solve problems in their own ways. Then in 1981, Julian Rappaport, a psychologist, broadened the concept into a political theory of power that viewed personal competency as fundamentally limitless; it placed faith in the individual and laid at her feet a corresponding amount of responsibility too.

Sneakily, empowerment had turned into a theory that applied to the needy while describing a process more realistically applicable to the rich.

The word was built on a misaligned foundation; no amount of awareness can change the fact that it's the already-powerful who tend to experience empowerment at any meaningful rate. Today "empowerment" invokes power while signifying the lack of it. It functions like an explorer staking a claim on new territory with a white flag.

Enter the highly marketable "women's empowerment," neither practice   5 nor praxis, nor really theory, but a glossy, dizzying product instead. Women's empowerment borrows the virtuous window-dressing of the social worker's doctrine and kicks its substance to the side. It's about pleasure, not power; it's individualistic and subjective, tailored to insecurity and desire. The new empowerment doesn't increase potential so much as it assures you that your potential is just fine. Even when the thing being described as "empowering" is personal and mildly defiant (not shaving, not breast-feeding, not listening to men, et cetera), what's being marketed is a certain identity. And no matter what, the intent of this new empowerment is always to sell.

Aerie, the lingerie brand of American Eagle, increased its sales by 26 percent in the last quarter of 2015 primarily on the strength of its "#AerieReal" campaign, which eschews Photoshop and employs models of a slightly larger size — and is described as "empowering" as if by legal mandate. Dove, the Patient Zero of empowerment marketing, has lifted its sales to the tune of $1.5 billion with its "#RealBeauty" campaign, cooked up by executives who noticed that few women like to call themselves beautiful and saw in that tragic modesty a great opportunity to raise the profile of the Dove brand.

When consumer purchases aren't made out to be a path to female empowerment, a branded corporate experience often is. There's TEDWomen ("about the power of women"), the Forbes Women's Summit ("#RedefinePower") and Fortune's Most Powerful Women Conference (tickets are $10,000).

This consumption-and-conference empowerment dilutes the word to pitch-speak, and the concept to something that imitates rather than alters the structures of the world. This version of empowerment can be actively disempowering: It's a series of objects and experiences you can purchase while the conditions determining who can access and accumulate power stay the same. The ready participation of well-off women in this strategy also points to a deep truth about the word "empowerment": that it has never been defined by the people who actually need it. People who talk empowerment are, by definition, already there.

So women's empowerment initiatives begin to look increasingly suspicious. In 2013, Kate Losse, a former speechwriter for Mark Zuckerberg, criticized Sheryl Sandberg's Lean In initiative for locating disempowerment in women's "presumed resistance to their careers rather than companies' resistance to equal pay." A company's sudden emphasis on empowerment is often a sign of something to atone for. Searching online for the word, I kept being served two advertisements by Google. The first was for Brawny paper towels, tagged #StrengthHasNoGender; the other was for Goldman Sachs ("See how Goldman is committed to helping women succeed"). Brawny is a holding of the Koch Brothers, who have spent millions of dollars funding anti-abortion initiatives; Goldman Sachs is, well, Goldman Sachs.

I am right in this word's target demographic, being young, female, edu- 10 cated and upwardly mobile. I work at a women's website. I love raises and underwear and voting. And still, I have never said "empowerment" sincerely or heard it from a single one of my friends. The formulation has been diluted to something representational and bloodless — an architectural rendering of a building that will never be built.

But despite its nonexistence in honest conversation, "empowerment" goes on thriving. It's uniquely marketable, like the female body, which is where women's empowerment is forced to live. On March 8, International Women's Day, Kim Kardashian posted an essay on the topic to her subscription-only website, in response to the backlash over a naked selfie she had posted — criticism leveled mainly by women who drink their empowerment a different way.

"I am empowered by my body," she wrote. "I am empowered by my sexuality." Quickly, her focus turned global: "I hope that through this platform I have been given, I can encourage the same empowerment for girls and women all over the world."

On that day, corporate empowerment came to a teleological summit in the hands of Kardashian, who's not as different from Sheryl Sandberg as she may seem. Like Sandberg, Kardashian is the apotheosis of a particular brand of largely contentless feminism, a celebratory form divorced from material politics, which makes it palatable — maybe irresistible — to the business world.

The mistake would be to locate further empowerment in choosing between the two. Corporate empowerment — as well as the lightweight, self-exculpatory feminism it rides on — feeds ravenously on the distracting performance of identity, that buffet of false opposition. Sandberg and Kardashian are perceived by most to be opposites, two aesthetically distinct brands fighting for our allegiance, when each has pioneered a similar, punishingly individualistic, market-driven understanding of women's worth, responsibility and strength. In the world of women's empowerment, they say the same thing differently: that our radical capability is mainly our ability to put money in the bank.

READING THE TEXT

1. Summarize in your own words the evolution of the word "empowerment," as Tolentino describes it.

2. Why does Tolentino claim that, as a sales pitch, "empowerment can be actively disempowering" (para. 8)?

3. What does Tolentino mean when she asserts that "[Kim] Kardashian is the apotheosis of a particular brand of largely contentless feminism, a celebratory form divorced from material politics, which makes it palatable — maybe irresistible — to the business world" (para. 13)?

4. Why do you think Tolentino uses the rhetorical strategy of referring to her own identity as "being young, female, educated and upwardly mobile. I work at a women's website. I love raises and underwear and voting" (para. 10)? What effect does her self-reference have on a reader's response to her argument?

READING THE SIGNS

1. Study instances of the American Eagle or Dove ad campaigns that Tolentino describes. Write an essay arguing whether the ads you examine are indeed empowering women or are simply a new twist on advertising's tendency to objectify women's bodies.

2. Tolentino does not mention "Real Beauty Sketches," Dove's experiment in which forensic artist Gil Zamora first draws a sight-unseen woman based on her own self-description and then draws the same woman based on a stranger's description of her. The goal is to show women that they are "more beautiful" than they assume. Watch some of these sketches on YouTube, and then write an essay in which you critique the videos. How do you think Tolentino would respond to them? Do you believe that they are problematic, as she considers the original "Real Beauty" ad campaign to be?

3. Conduct your own online search for "empowerment" advertising, and evaluate the ads you find in light of Tolentino's critique. To what extent do they illustrate her claim that "a company's sudden emphasis on empowerment is often a sign of something to atone for" (para. 9)?

4. **CONNECTING TEXTS**   Write an essay in which you support, oppose, or modify Tolentino's assertion that Sheryl Sandberg and Kim Kardashian "say the same thing differently: that our radical capability is mainly our ability to put money in the bank" (para. 14). To develop your ideas, consult Thomas Frank, "Commodify Your Dissent" (p. 134).

5. In an essay, support, refute, or complicate the proposition that empowerment ads represent a healthy change in advertising directed at women consumers.

ALEX MAYYASI

How Subarus Came to Be Seen as Cars for Lesbians

Advertising campaigns are, in effect, complex semiotic analyses performed in reverse. That is, rather than reading ads to determine what they're trying to say and do to their audiences, marketing semioticians often read the behavior of their target audiences to determine what to put in their ads. And in this in-depth analysis for the *Atlantic*, Alex Mayyasi shows how the marketers for Subaru of America did just that: They interpreted the behavior of lesbian consumers in order to devise an ad campaign that successfully revamped the image of Subarus into "cars for lesbians." Alex Mayyasi is a writer at Priceonomics.

How do you advertise a car that journalists describe as "sturdy, if drab"?

That was the question faced by Subaru of America executives in the 1990s. After the company's attempts to reinvigorate sales — by releasing its first luxury car and hiring a hip ad agency to introduce it to the public — failed, it changed its approach. Rather than fight larger car companies over the same demographic of white, 18- to 35-year-olds living in the suburbs, executives decided to market their cars to niche groups — such as outdoorsy types who liked that Subarus could handle dirt roads.

In the 1990s, Subaru's unique selling point was that the company increasingly made all-wheel drive standard on all its cars. When the company's marketers went searching for people willing to pay a premium for all-wheel drive, they identified four core groups who were responsible for half of the company's American sales: teachers and educators, health-care professionals, IT professionals, and outdoorsy types.

Then they discovered a fifth: lesbians. "When we did the research, we found pockets of the country like Northampton, Massachusetts, and Portland, Oregon, where the head of the household would be a single person — and often a woman," says Tim Bennett, who was the company's director of advertising at the time. When marketers talked to these customers, they realized these women buying Subarus were lesbian.   5

"There was such an alignment of feeling, like [Subaru cars] fit with what they did," says Paul Poux, who later conducted focus groups for Subaru. The marketers found that lesbian Subaru owners liked that the cars were good for outdoor trips, and that they were good for hauling stuff without being as large as a truck or SUV. "They felt it fit them and wasn't too flashy," says Poux.

Subaru's strategy called for targeting these five core groups and creating ads based on its appeal to each. For medical professionals, it was that a Subaru with all-wheel drive could get them to the hospital in any weather conditions. For rugged individualists, it was that a Subaru could handle dirt roads and haul gear. For lesbians, it was that a Subaru fit their active, low-key lifestyle.

Although it was easier to get senior management on board with making ads for hikers than for lesbians, the company went ahead with the campaign anyway. It was such an unusual decision — and such a success — that it helped push gay and lesbian advertising from the fringes to the mainstream. People joke about lesbians' affinity for Subarus, but what's often forgotten is that Subaru actively decided to cultivate its image as a car for lesbians.

And it did so at a time when few companies would embrace or even acknowledge their gay customers. Talking with people involved in Subaru's 1990s marketing campaign, the constant refrain is how different the environment was back then. "I can't emphasize enough that this was before there was any positive discussion [of LGBT issues]," says Tim Bennett. Gay causes seemed to be on the losing side of the culture war: The Clinton Administration had just instituted its "Don't Ask, Don't Tell" policy regarding homosexuality in the military, and in 1996, Congress would pass the Defense of Marriage Act.

Pop culture had also yet to embrace the LGBT cause. Mainstream movies and TV shows with gay characters — like *Will & Grace* — were still a few years away, and few celebrities were openly gay. When Ellen Degeneres became a rare exception in 1997, and her character in the show *Ellen* came out as gay in an episode of the sitcom, many companies pulled their ads. "We don't think it is a smart business decision to be advertising in an environment that is so polarized," a spokesperson for Chrysler explained after the company pulled its ads. "The environment around this is so angry we feel we lose no matter what we do."

At that time, gay-friendly advertising was largely limited to the fashion and alcohol industries. When a 1994 IKEA ad featured a gay couple, the American Family Association, a nonprofit, mounted boycotts, and someone called in a (fake) bomb threat on an IKEA store.

As Poux explains, the attitude of most businesses toward LGBT advertising was: "Why would you do something like that? You'd be known as a gay company." In the 1990s, Poux worked at Mulryan/Nash, an agency that specialized in the gay market. Early in his career, he made cold calls to ask companies for their business. "All the rules of marketing went out the window at this fear" of marketing to gays and lesbians, he says. "People would choke up on the phone. It was tough."

It was in this context that Subaru's marketing team hired Mulryan/Nash and pitched Subaru's Japanese management on ads for lesbian customers. Writing in the *Huffington Post*, the reporter Ron Dicker captured some of the cultural confusion that followed:

> When one Subaru ad man . . . proposed the gay-targeting ads in talks with Japanese executives, the executives hurriedly looked up "gay" in their dictionaries. Upon reading the definition, they nodded at the idea enthusiastically. Who wouldn't want happy or joyous advertising?

"It was certainly a learning process for everybody," says Bennett. While Bennett, who is gay, didn't reveal his sexual orientation for fear of overshadowing the effort, he nonetheless recalls holding company meetings with names along the lines of "Who Are Gays and Lesbians?"

A 50-year-old conglomerate like Fuji Heavy Industries, the parent company of Subaru, is not normally where one would look for a leader in social progress. But the corporate environment did have its advantages. For starters, there was a great business case for the marketing campaign. Subaru was struggling, and its niche marketing campaign was its plan for redemption. The internationalism of global business also helped. Subaru of America knew it had to support its gay and lesbian employees if it wanted to appeal to lesbian customers, so they scheduled a meeting with a senior Japanese executive to make the case for domestic partnership benefits. Bennett and his colleagues had prepared to argue their case at length, but the meeting lasted 20 seconds. The executive, who had worked for Subaru in Canada, already knew about benefits for same-sex couples. "He said, 'Yeah that's fine. We did that in Canada years ago. Anything else?'" says Bennett. "It was the easiest thing we did."

By 1996, Subaru ads created by the Mulryan/Nash ad agency were appearing both in gay publications and mainstream media. Although the marketing team worried about conservatives mounting a boycott, Subaru developed a public stance: Since the company sold cars to, in the company's words, a "diverse and well educated" group of people, their customers wouldn't be offended by the ads.

Inside Subaru of America, though, not everyone was united on the effort. There was public backlash, and Bennett says the campaign survived only because their team really cared about the project and had the support of a cohort of straight allies in the company.

And the Subaru company line did have some truth to it. In response to the ads, Subaru received letters from a grassroots group that accused the carmaker of promoting homosexuality. Everyone who penned a letter said they'd never buy a Subaru again. But the marketing team quickly discovered that none of the people threatening a boycott had ever bought a Subaru. Some of them had even misspelled "Subaru." Like nerds who grow up to confront their bullies, Subaru executives came to realize that the people opposing the acknowledgement of gays and lesbians were not as imposing as they seemed.

One of the reasons that, these days, the carmaker's role in cultivating its lesbian-friendly image is less well known is that so many straight people were blind to the subtext of the advertisements.

For its first Subaru ads, Mulryan/Nash hired women to portray lesbian couples. But the ads didn't get good reactions from lesbian audiences. What worked were winks and nudges. One campaign showed Subaru cars that had license plates that said "Xena LVR" (a reference to *Xena: Warrior Princess*, a TV show whose female protagonists seemed to be lovers) or "P-TOWN" (a moniker for Provincetown, Massachusetts, a popular LGBT vacation spot). Many ads had taglines with double meanings. "Get Out. And Stay Out" could refer to exploring the outdoors in a Subaru — or coming out as gay. "It's Not a Choice. It's the Way We're Built" could refer to all Subarus coming with all-wheel-drive — or LGBT identity. "Each year we've done this, we've learned more about our target audience," John Nash, the creative director of the ad agency told the website *AdRespect*. "We've found that playful coding is really, really appreciated by our consumers. They like deciphering it."

The delight among niche audience groups in "decoding" the hints in Subaru ads surprised the marketing team — and in the case of its gay-friendly ads, so did straight audiences' ignorance. While many gay and lesbian consumers loved the shoutouts in the license plates, straight people would only

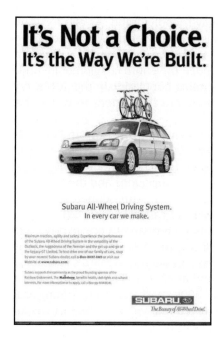

notice features like a bike rack. Poux, who helped come up with the license-plate idea, says he held focus groups with straight audiences where he'd show ads featuring gay couples. Even after an hour of talking about gay issues, they'd think a man was shopping with his uncle.

In articles at the time, Subaru executives said they felt uncertain about the "intrigue" created by the perception of "secret coding." But Poux says there was some comfort in the fact that the gay marketing went under the radar. As more companies began marketing to LGBT audiences, such coding — which fell under the category of the new marketing term "gay vague" — became a way for companies to reach queer audiences with minimal risk of a conservative backlash.

That said, Subaru did not hide its support of gay and lesbian customers. While Volkswagen played coy about whether an ad perceived as gay-friendly really portrayed a gay couple, Subaru sponsored events like gay-pride parades, partnered with the Rainbow Card, a credit card that instead of cash back offered donations to gay and lesbian causes, and hired Martina Navratilova, a former tennis pro and a lesbian, to appear in Subaru ads.

Navratilova's role in Subaru's ads came with a certain poignance. She had been outed against her will, and while she spoke honestly about her sexual orientation, she had lamented that gay athletes had "to hide in the closet to sell [themselves] to Madison Avenue." For her to become the face of a car company during her retirement, says the Rainbow Card co-creator Pam Derderian, was a beautiful, fullcircle moment.

Subaru's gay and lesbian focused marketing campaign was a hit, and the company's efforts continue today. In focus groups and online polls, gay and lesbian consumers consistently choose Subaru vehicles as their favorite cars or Subaru as the most gay-friendly brand. As one focus-group participant put it, "Martina Navratilova is a spokesperson. What more do you want?"

That reputation has translated into financial success, and Subaru's parent company recently rebranded the entire conglomerate under the Subaru name due to the carmaker's surging popularity. In the 2010s, only Tesla grew faster than Subaru, which led Subaru's president to worry that Subaru could get "too big."

Lesbians buying Subaru cars did not singlehandedly resurrect the carmaker, but the gay market was one of the best for Subaru. The carmaker tracked the effectiveness of its niche marketing by partnering with 40 or 50 organizations — like outdoor associations and the Rainbow Card — to offer discounts on Subaru cars. Every year, Tim Bennett says, the LGBT organizations were in the top five in terms of cars sold.

Subaru was not the first company to create advertisements for gay and lesbian consumers, but it was the first major company in the United States to do it so transparently and consistently. Subaru's lesbian-focused ad campaign was widely discussed, and its success helped spur growth in gay and lesbian marketing. By the early 2000s, marketers were writing articles that called gays and lesbians an "underserved market" and "perfect consumers."

For some, though, it was an uncomfortable embrace. The perception of the gay market as a goldmine relied on the misperception that all gay people were well-off and part of dual-earner households without children. A number of academics criticized corporate America's embrace of the LGBT community: While companies wanted the profits that came from marketing a gay sense of style, they focused on upper-class and white gay identities — rarely gay people of color or those unable to afford medical treatment for HIV/AIDS.

But according to Derderian, that perspective underestimates the intelligence of LGBT consumers. To show that Subaru cared about its gay and lesbian customers, she says, the carmaker supported causes that they cared about. Through its sponsorship of the Rainbow Card, Subaru contributed millions of dollars to HIV/AIDS research and LGBT causes that helped both their customers and people who couldn't afford a Subaru.

Moreover, Derderian, like many LGBT people who see a company pitching to the gay market, vetted firms interested in sponsoring the Rainbow Card by looking into the policies they had for their employees, like benefits for same-sex partners. This led to a trend of companies making their internal policies more gay-friendly when they wanted to advertise to gay customers. When Ford created gay-friendly ads, it revised its policies for its more than 100,000 employees.

In a sense, all Subaru did was notice a group of customers who often felt unwelcome and invisible, and create ads for them. But it was a big deal at the time. While companies' involvement in causes are almost always driven by an interest in the bottom line, it's heartening that the origins of lesbians' stereotypical affinity for Subarus is not a cynical marketing campaign, but a progressive one.

READING THE TEXT

1. What was the predominant social attitude toward the LGBT (lesbian, gay, bisexual, and transgender) community in the 1990s, according to Mayyasi?

2. Why did Subaru embark on niche marketing campaigns in the late 1990s, and what impact did it have on the company's sales?

3. What is "playful coding" in advertising, and why do some marketers employ it for gay consumers?

4. How did gay and straight consumers respond to Subaru ads, and what may explain the differences?

READING THE SIGNS

1. In an essay, support, oppose, or complicate Mayyasi's assumption that the Subaru ads aimed at gay consumers were not based primarily on stereotypes about this consumer group. To develop your ideas, read Michael Hulshof-Schmidt's blog entry "What's in an Acronym?" (p. 489).

2. Study some current online ads for Subaru, and analyze the ways they construct a consumer's identity. Do you see evidence that the ads continue to use the niche marketing strategy that Mayyesi describes? Use your findings as the basis for an analysis of current Subaru advertising techniques.

3. **CONNECTING TEXTS**   Adopt the perspective of John Sherman ("The New Normative: Queer Politics in *The Outs*," p. 259), and write a response to Mayyesi's claim that the Subaru's marketing campaign to LGBT consumers is "progressive" (para. 31).

4. In class, brainstorm other groups that might enjoy "secret coding" in ads, and conduct an online search to determine how widespread this strategy is. In an essay, focus on one of the groups and analyze the ads you find. Do they use secret coding in the same way that Subaru used it for gay audiences? How do you account for any differences you might find?

JESSICA CONTRERA

Most Young People Don't Vote. Condescending to Them Isn't Helping

It's not a cliché that Americans between the ages of 18 and 30 tend to vote in far smaller numbers than their elders do. But it *is* a cliché, and a rather dumb one at that, Jessica Contrera believes, to encourage young people to vote by approaching them with get-out-the-vote videos "filled with lewd innuendoes, sly suggestions and incessant repetition of the number 69." Still, that's what a lot of voting drive campaigns do to attract young voters, showering them with pop culture references and sexual allusions that "are so off that they are remembered not for their positive impact but for their ability to induce cringes." C'mon baby boomers, grow up! Jessica Contrera is a staff writer at the *Washington Post*, where this selection originally appeared.

The video is filled with lewd innuendoes, sly suggestions and incessant repetition of the number 69. It's narrated by a young woman and man who keep saying things like "insert" and "on top" and "niiice."

They're not talking about sex. They're talking about voting.

This is the premise of an actual public service announcement aimed at getting millennials to vote this year. Released this month from the news start-up Mic, the advertisement is based on the premise that, according to Pew Research Center, 69 million millennials and 69 million baby boomers are eligible to vote this year — hence, the excuse for some sex jokes. The video squeezes in other pertinent statistics and actual information about issues of interest to young people, but they're sandwiched between cheesy, suggestive jokes.

"Sometimes it seems like [baby boomers] are afraid to try new positions," a narrator says, "but we're ready to *go down* on history."

The #69TheVote campaign is Mic's response to young voters' historically   5
abysmal turnout rates. It's a problem campaigns and civic organizations have been grappling with for decades — at least as far back as 1956, when the Eisenhower campaign ran a television ad featuring a young woman declaring "I'm a college girl, voting for the first time!"

Despite the notable uptick in young voters when President Obama was first elected, less than 20 percent of young people under 30 showed up to the polls for the 2014 midterm elections. It was the lowest youth turnout rate recorded in a federal election, according to CIRCLE, a Tufts University center on voting research.

But many efforts to lure the youngsters to the polls — with marketing campaigns that attempt to *speak their language* — have been memorably mortifying.

"Come this November, just don't *blow* it . . . Unless you're into that," the narrators for that #69theVote PSA utter with what sounds like a wink and a smirk.

"This doesn't make voting look cooler," wrote one YouTube commenter. "It just makes sex look worse."

Cory Haik, Mic's chief strategy officer (and a former *Washington Post*   10 employee), explained, "We wanted to get people's attention" with the video. "I think you have to get in their face in some kind of way, make something that breaks out, which is really hard to do." And "several thousand" people clicked through on the campaign's link to register to vote, she said.

As with any voting bloc, there's a fine line between speaking directly to millennials' interests and awkward, blatant pandering. Candidates and campaigns want to engage young people on their level, but one emoji too many and the message reads like a note from a mom who just learned to text.

They want to show young people they're fluent in pop culture, but the Hillary Clinton campaign could only play Rachel Platten's pop hit "Fight Song" so many times before it became a joke among the reporters and staff who can never get the tune out of their heads. (The song "represents how Hillary Clinton will never give up, and she will do everything she can to make sure families get ahead and stay ahead," the campaign's director of millennial media defensively told Yahoo News last week.)

Efforts to woo young voters picked up steam in 1992, when Bill Clinton became the first presidential candidate to appear on MTV, which launched a voting activism program, "Choose or Lose," that same year. He talked about being a Leo and his first rock-and-roll experience, "going nuts over Elvis Presley," while wearing what the *New York Times* called "an awful-looking flowered necktie."

Rock the Vote, meanwhile, had recently formed, and it enlisted Madonna for an ad in which she wrapped herself in an American flag while hamming it up with some buff backup dancers. Then it found its signature formula: Line up a dizzying number of celebrities, drop them in front of a neutral background and have them name-drop the issues that will get people to vote.

According to one study that tracked voting in the places Rock the Vote ads   15 ran, they actually did increase turnout by a few percentage points.

And then there are the efforts to talk directly to young voters that are so off that they are remembered not for their positive impact but for their ability to induce cringes.

Take "Crush on Obama," the viral music video of 2007, created by the YouTube channel Barely Political. The spoofy slow jam certainly got buzz, with "Obama Girl" Amber Lee Ettinger cooing and writhing over her fondness for the then-senator from Illinois. But Obama later said the song upset his daughters.

This election cycle, a 31-year-old rapper known as Aspiring Mogul gifted the world with the Ben Carson rap, which rhymed "Carson" with "awesome" and promised that "if we want to get American back on track, we gotta vote Ben Carson, a matter of fact." The campaign spent $150,000 to air the song on the radio in Atlanta, Miami and Detroit.

Carson later said he was "horrified" by the song.

Even established hip-hop stars have struggled with their outreach efforts.   20
In 2004, Sean "Diddy" Combs launched a "Vote or Die" campaign — which
quickly inspired a *South Park* parody in which Combs stalks and threatens to
kill a reluctant voter.

That same year, Norman Lear's voting advocacy group "Declare Yourself"
created an ad mimicking the then-popular MTV show *Pimp My Ride.* The PSA
was called "Phat Ride." It had shiny hub caps, scantily clad ladies and a black
guy in gold chains saying, "Yo what's up, player?" Then a man screws his own
mouth shut, symbolically silencing his own opinions.

Exactly the motivation you needed to get out and vote, right?

The swing-and-misses aren't just limited to presidential races, of course.
Take the "Say Yes to the Candidate" videos that ran on behalf of 2014 GOP
candidates including Florida Gov. Rick Scott and Pennsylvania Gov. Tom Corbett. In a surprisingly on-point imitation of TLC's *Say Yes to the Dress,* young,
beautiful women shop for their perfect wedding gowns. The Republican candidates represent the sleek, affordable dresses, while the Democratic competitors are expensive frumpy messes.

"Rick Scott is becoming a trusted brand," the blushing bride says as she
checks her rear end in a mirror.

As Stephen Colbert summed it up at the time: "This ad shows that the   25
modern GOP finally understands the real concerns of women: weddings!"

American University professor Jennifer Lawless, author of "Running from
Office: Why Young Americans are Turned Off to Politics" said that video is the
best example of a "mortifying" effort to talk to young women. And yet. . . .

"I'm sitting here, years later, remembering it," she said. "If an ad like that
generates more mainstream attention. . . . It is putting a conversation about
voting in popular culture, and that has its benefits."

So maybe Clinton should keep on playing "Fight Song," no matter how
many people roll their eyes. Lately, her youth-outreach tactics have included
snapping selfies with Kim Kardashian, selling T-shirts emblazoned with the
word "Yaaas" and dropping references to Pokémon Go.

When the hosts of a hip-hop morning radio show told her she was pandering, she asked, "Is it working?"

Donald Trump seems less concerned with specifically targeting young vot-   30
ers. Considering the low rates at which young people vote, and the polls that
show Clinton trouncing Trump in voters under 35, his campaign may have
decided its efforts are better spent with older voters.

As Trump said to one young protester in his audience this month:

"Go home to mom. And your mother is voting for Trump!"

READING THE TEXT

1. According to Contrera, what assumptions do get-out-the-vote campaigns
    aimed at young people make about their target audience?

2. Summarize in your own words the history of attempts to capture the attention of young voters since the early 1990s.

3. What are the differences between the approaches Hillary Clinton and Donald Trump used in the 2016 presidential campaign? How does Contrera implicitly explain them?

4. Explain why the title of this article calls political campaigns aimed at young voters "condescending."

READING THE SIGNS

1. Visit Mic or Rock the Vote online, and study current attempts to involve young voters in political campaigns. Use your observations as the basis for an essay in which you argue whether the messages you view are "speaking directly to millennials' interests" or are "awkward, blatant pandering" (para. 11).

2. In small groups, brainstorm strategies for a voting campaign targeting young people that would be the opposite of condescending. Share your ideas with the class. Which of your classmates' suggestions, if any, are both respectful of millennials' intelligence and values *and* genuinely effective in motivating their audience's political involvement?

3. Read James B. Twitchell's "What We Are to Advertisers" (p. 163), focusing on his discussion of how marketers create identities for consumers. With that discussion in mind, write an essay in which you define the identity that "condescending" and "mortifying" political campaigns create for millennials.

4. Watch online several campaigns aimed at young voters that promoted Hillary Clinton's 2016 presidential run. In an essay, analyze the appeals that these campaigns make to their viewers. To what extent do you feel that they speak to their viewers' interests effectively?

5. Given Donald Trump's success in the 2016 presidential election, write an essay that evaluates Contrera's assessment of his campaign's appeals to young voters. Are there any topics that you think Contrera might have considered more or has neglected to raise? Could she have predicted the importance of those topics?

KALLE OSKARI MATTILA
The Age of the Wordless Logo

What do you do when you are a large corporation trying to sell stuff to consumers who don't like large corporations? Why, of course, you try to conceal the fact that you *are* a corporation. And this strategy, as Kalle Oskari Mattila explains in this piece for the *Atlantic*, is exactly what is going on as corporations from MasterCard to McDonalds modify their logos to remove all textuality from them. What is left are spare, wordless images. "The advertising industry likes to call this type of marketing 'authentic,'" Mattila remarks; advertising scholars call it "debranding." We think it's "sneaky." Mattila is a graduate student in the nonfiction MFA writing program at Columbia University.

MasterCard unveiled its new logo earlier this summer, and as far as rebrandings go, the tweaks were subtle: The company kept its overlapping red and yellow balls intact, and moved its name, which was previously front and center, to beneath the balls, while making the text lowercase. With increasing frequency, MasterCard said, it would do away with using its name in the logo entirely. The focus would be more on the symbol than the words.

MasterCard's move reflects a wider shift among some of the most widely recognized global brands to de-emphasize the text in their logos, or remove it altogether. Nike was among the first brands to do this, in 1995, when its swoosh began to appear with the words "Just Do It," and then without any words at all. Apple, McDonald's, and other brands followed a similar trajectory, gravitating toward entirely textless symbols after a period of transition with logos that had taglines like "Think Different" or "I'm lovin' it."

This shift is ostensibly in accordance with a more streamlined approach to design, as well as certain features of the modern economy: Symbols work better than long names on computer screens and apps, and they allow for greater flexibility if a company wants to dabble in multiple industries at once. For instance, names like Starbucks Coffee and MasterCard are tied to specific products in ways that symbols are not, which can be a disadvantage at a time

when it's perfectly plausible for a company that makes phones to make cars too. Additionally, visual cues can travel across borders more easily, because they eliminate the need for translation.

But perhaps the most powerful impetus for these slimmed-down logos is that it's increasingly more difficult to reach buyers when so many of them are skeptical of big corporations. A recent survey by the public-relations firm Cohn & Wolfe found that four-fifths of global consumers now consider brands neither open nor honest. "Consumers are jaded about advertising in a way they weren't several decades ago," says Adam Alter, an associate professor of marketing at New York University's Stern School of Business, via email. "It is harder to appeal to them than it used to be, and they tend to see through overt marketing pitches." That has in turn led to a new arsenal of branding tactics. "Companies have had to learn subtlety," Alter says.

Among that arsenal is what's called "debranding" or "decorporatizing" — a   5 strategy based on paring down that can only be deployed by the most identifiable of brands. Some marketers believe that debranding can make global brands appear "less corporate" and "more personal" to consumers. Nameless logos can evoke more personal and immediate reactions — which is important in a media environment with plenty of possible distractions and diversions. "Researchers have demonstrated that the use of visual imagery (vs. verbal imagery) in advertising increases consumers' attention and challenges them to interpret and understand the ad's message in a more active manner than words do," wrote Jill J. Avery, a senior lecturer at Harvard Business School, in an email. "This process of interpretation or 'elaboration' produces a higher quantity of mental images and, in many cases, a more personalized understanding of the ad's message." In short, it is easier to make associations based on two bright, primary-colored balls than it is with the word MasterCard.

The need to get personal and friendly is particularly germane to young people, the target market of many global consumer-product enterprises. It's likely that this factored into MasterCard's decision to rebrand. As an increasing number of consumers — especially younger ones — prefer to make transactions on their phones rather than using cash or cards, and shy away from racking up credit-card debt, one worry for MasterCard's investors is that the company hasn't fully broken into the mobile-payments market yet. By contrast, PayPal — another brand that carried out a visual refresh a few years ago in which it de-emphasized its name on its logo — enjoys a substantial Millennial user base, a good portion of which is loyal to Venmo, a popular mobile-payment app it acquired.

The benefits of debranding can be huge. One of the most successful executions of it has been the "Share a Coke" promotion, for which Coca-Cola replaced its name on bottles with people's first names, like Sarah and David, and other everyday monikers, like Mom and Dad. The campaign increased Coca-Cola's U.S. sales by more than 2 percent and, in doing so, helped reverse more than 10 years of decline in Coke consumption in the U.S.

The advertising industry likes to call this type of marketing "authentic." Cohn & Wolfe compiles an annual list of the "world's most authentic brands," drawing on surveys of nearly 12,000 consumers in 14 countries. This year's Top 20 includes Paypal and MasterCard, as well as Coca-Cola. Authenticity, of course, is a funny thing when it comes to marketing: Asserting one's authenticity feels, well, inauthentic. At a time when consumers are placing more and more importance on companies that feel genuine rather than corporate, it makes all too much sense that marketers would start trying to make it more difficult to distinguish between the two.

READING THE TEXT

1. According to Mattila, why are many corporations moving to wordless logos?
2. In your own words, what is the goal of "debranding" or "decorporatizing" a brand?
3. What does the word "authentic" mean in today's advertising parlance?

READING THE SIGNS

1. In an essay, support, refute, or modify Mattila's claim that "Authenticity . . . is a funny thing when it comes to marketing: Asserting one's authenticity feels, well, inauthentic" (para. 7). Base your argument on an analysis of specific ad campaigns.

2. **CONNECTING TEXTS**   Select a mass market consumer product that has been sold for at least three decades, and research the history of its identifying logo and packaging. Use your results as the basis for an essay in which you analyze how the product's image has evolved over the years. What sort of reactions does the logo and packaging elicit from consumers? How might you account for any changes that you observe? To develop your ideas, consult Chris Arning's "What Can Semiotics Contribute to Packaging Design?" (p. 111).

3. In class, brainstorm the features that a genuinely "authentic" ad campaign should have, then examine your results. What characteristics do those features share, and how often do you see them in current advertising? If your class has difficulty producing a list, what does that say about the class's attitudes toward advertising and its strategies?

4. Most colleges and universities sport their own logos, often accompanied by mascots or other figures, images that act as a sign of your campus. Research the history of your school's logo, analyzing the identity it creates for your school. Has the logo evolved over the years? If so, how and how might any changes you see reflect an evolution in the character of your school?

JULIET B. SCHOR

Selling to Children: The Marketing of Cool

Being cool isn't just an attitude — it's a consumer lifestyle. As Juliet B. Schor describes the situation in this selection from her book *Born to Buy* (2005), the marketing of edgy, sexy, violent, and subversive images of coolness has moved from teen and young-adult advertising to children's advertising. Closely related to what Thomas Frank calls the "commodification of dissent," cool marketing to kids has created a "feedback loop," whereby advertisers study youth behavior to see what kids respond to, while the kids study advertisements to see what's cool and what's not. A professor of sociology at Boston College, Schor is the author of numerous books on American consumption.

The Marketing of Cool

Cool has been around for decades. Back in the fifties, there were cool cats and hipsters. In the sixties, hippies and the Beatles were cool. But in those days, cool was only one of many acceptable personal styles. Now it's revered as a universal quality — something every product tries to be and every kid needs to have.[1] Marketers have defined cool as the key to social success, as what matters for determining who belongs, who's popular, and who gets accepted by peers. While there is no doubt that the desire for social acceptance is a central theme of growing up, marketers have elevated it to the sine qua non of children's psyches. The promotion of cool is a good example of how the practices of marketing to teens, for whom social acceptance is even more important, have filtered down to the children's sphere. In a recent survey of 4,002 kids in grades 4 through 8, 66 percent reported that cool defines them.[2] Part of why is that cool has become *the* dominant theme of children's marketing.

Part of the genius of cool is its versatility. Cool isn't only about not being a dork. Cool takes on many incarnations. It can incorporate dork and jock, if necessary. It can be driven by neon or primary colors; it's retro or futuristic, techno or natural. Today, Target is cool. Yesterday it was the Gap. Good-bye Barney. Hello Kitty. By the time you read these words, today's cool will not be. But although cool is hard to pin down, in practice it centers on some recurring themes, and these themes are relentlessly pushed by marketers in the

[1] For a now-classic account of cool-hunting, see Gladwell (1997), reprinted in Schor and Holt (2000).

[2] A recent survey in which 66 percent of kids say cool defines them is from the KidID survey of JustKid Inc. Data provided to the author and presented by Wynne Tyree at KidPower 2002.

conception and design of products, packaging, marketing, and advertising. At every step, these principles apply.

One theme is that cool is socially exclusive, that is, expensive. In an earlier era, cheap stuff dominated kids' consumer worlds, mainly because they didn't have much money. They bought penny candy, plastic toys, and cheap thrills. In those days, the functional aspects of products were paramount, such as the fact that the toy is fun to play with or the candy tastes good. Social symbolism and status weren't wholly absent, but they were far less important. Now that kids have access to so much more money, status and its underlying values of inequality and exclusion have settled at the heart of the kid consumer culture. Branding expert Martin Lindstrom reports that for tweens, the brand took over from function as the main attraction of products in the 1990s.[3] From video games, to apparel, to that ubiquitous symbol of status, the athletic shoe, kids' products have upscaled, in the process becoming both more unaffordable and more desirable. Gene Del Vecchio, former Ogilvy and Mather executive and author of *Creating Ever-Cool: A Marketer's Guide to a Kid's Heart*, is more candid than most others about the exclusionary nature of cool: "Part of cool is having something that others do not. That makes a kid feel special. It is also the spark that drives kids to find the next cool item."[4] When Reebok introduced its computerized Traxtar shoe, it was banking on a message of "superiority" ("I have Traxtar and you don't"), according to the people who designed the program.[5] The shoe became the top seller in its category, a notable accomplishment given its significantly higher price. Marketers convey the view that wealth and aspiration to wealth are cool. Material excess, having lots of money, career achievement, and a lifestyle to go with it are all highly valued in the marketing world's definition of what's hot and what's not. Living modestly means living like a loser.

Cool is also associated with being older than one's age.[6] Marketers and advertisers take this common desire of kids and play into it in a variety of ways. They put a few older kids in ads that are targeted to younger kids. They have young kids in ads morph into older kids or into adults. They use adult celebrity endorsers for products or brands that kids buy. They depict fantasy worlds in which a young kid sees himself or herself grown up. Cool is also associated with an antiadult sensibility, as ads portray kids with attitude, outwitting their teachers and tricking their parents. Finally, cool is about the taboo, the dangerous, the forbidden other. Among advertisers, *edgy* has been

---

[3]On the shift from function to brand as the main attraction, see Lindstrom (2003), p. 82.

[4]Gene Del Vecchio quote "part of cool" is from Del Vecchio (1997), p. 121.

[5]On Traxtar marketing and its success, see Siegel et al. (2001), pp. 179–190.

[6]On kids wanting to be older than they are, this is what Paul Kurnit had to say in our interview: "Emulation and aspiration work up, but only to a certain point. So if you capture six to eleven year olds, your bull's-eye is probably the eleven year old boy. . . . If you're looking for the eleven year old boy you're probably in a commercial casting a twelve or thirteen year old boy."

and remains the adjective of the moment — not "over the edge," because that is too dangerous, but "at the edge," "pushing the edge."

Edgy style has associations with rap and hip-hop, with "street" and African American culture. In the 1990s, ads aimed at white, middle-class Americans began to be filmed in inner-city neighborhoods with young black men as the stars. The ads made subtle connections to violence, drugs, criminality, and sexuality — the distorted and stereotypical images of young black men that have pervaded the mainstream media. As Harvard University's Douglas Holt wrote in 1999 in a paper we coauthored, "Street has proven to be a potent commodity because its aesthetic offers an authentic threatening edginess that is very attractive both to white suburban kids who perpetually recreate radical youth culture in relation to their parents' conservative views about the ghetto, and to urban cultural elites for whom it becomes a form of cosmopolitan radical chic. . . . We now have the commodification of a virulent, dangerous 'other' lifestyle. . . . Gangsta."[7]

The story of how street came to be at the core of consumer marketing began more than thirty years ago. Chroniclers of the marketing of "ghetto" point to the practices of athletic shoe companies, starting with Converse in the late 1960s and, more recently, Nike and its competitors. The shoe manufacturers intentionally associated their product with African American athletes, giving free shoes to coaches in the inner cities, targeting inner-city consumers in their research, attaching their brand to street athletics and sociability.[8] They also developed a practice dubbed "bro-ing" by industry insiders, that is, going to the streets to ask the brothers which designs deserve the moniker of cool. Apparel companies, beginning with Tommy Hilfiger, became active in this world, giving rap stars and other prominent tastemakers free samples of their latest styles.[9] While the connection to inner-city life may sound like a contradiction with the idea that cool is exclusive and upscale, it is partially resolved by the fact that many of the inner-city ambassadors of products are wealthy, conspicuous consumers such as rap stars and athletes driving fancy cars and living luxurious lifestyles.

Eventually soft drink companies, candy manufacturers, culture producers, and many others that sell products to teens and kids would be on the street, trying desperately to get some of that ineluctable cool to rub off on their brand. As advertiser Paul Kurnit explains, "What's going on in white America today is [that] the inner city is very much a Gold Standard. We've got lots of white kids who are walking around, emulating black lifestyle."[10] Of course, mere association with ghetto style is not a guarantee of success. Some campaigns have been flat-footed with their mimicry. Others lack basic credibility, such as preppy tennis shoe K-Swiss, which tried to position itself as a street brand.

---

[7]Douglas Holt quote on street as a potent commodity is from Holt and Schor (1998).
[8]On sneaker marketing in the inner city, see Vanderbilt (1998), ch. 1.
[9]On Hilfiger, see Smith (1997) and Spiegler (1997).
[10]Paul Kurnit quote from his interview with O'Barr (2001).

The brands that have been skilled at this approach are those with images that are more plausibly and authentically connected to it.

Although many aspects of African American culture have had a long historical association with cool such as jazz and sartorial styles, as well as a legacy of contributions to popular culture, what's happening now is unique. Never before have inner-city styles and cultural practices been such a dominant influence on, even a primary definer of, popular culture. The process is also no longer one of mainstreaming, in which a cultural innovation from the margins is incorporated into the larger culture. Rather, in the words of Douglas Holt again, "It is now the local, authentic qualities of Street culture that sell. Instead of black cultural products denuded of their social context, it is now primarily the context itself — the neighborhood, the pain of being poor, the alienation experienced by black kids. These are the commodifiable assets." The other new development is the role of large corporations in the movement of styles and cultural forms from the ghetto to the suburb. The process no longer develops through an organic movement as it once did. Instead, cool hunters manage the process of cultural transmission. Another novel aspect is the evolution of a back-and-forth dynamic between the companies and the grass roots, with cool-hunting and street marketing creating what media critics have called a feedback loop.

The feedback loop is a sharp departure from decades past, when consumers blindly followed where advertisers led. In Holt's words, marketers once possessed a monopoly on "cultural authority," in which they set the tone and agenda, and consumers eagerly looked to them to learn what to wear, eat, drive, and value.[11] That cultural authority has virtually disappeared. Its demise can be traced to the backlash against advertising that originally emerged in the 1950s with the popularity of books such as John Kenneth Galbraith's *The Affluent Society* and Vance Packard's *The Hidden Persuaders*.[12] By the 1960s, some of the most successful marketers were those who took their cues from consumers. Since, then, advertisers have increasingly attempted to figure out what people already value and let those findings direct ads. With youth, the process has gone a step further, because they know the advertisers are relying on them, and consciously play to their influence. That's the feedback idea, which has been identified by observers such as Douglas Kellner, Holt, and Douglas Rushkoff. As Rushkoff explains, in a plea to the industry: "It's turned into a giant feedback loop: you watch kids to find out what trend is 'in,' but the kids are watching you watching them in order to figure out how to act. They are exhibitionists, aware of corporate America's fascination with their every move, and delighting in your obsession with

---

[11]On the cultural authority of marketers, see Holt (2002).
[12]On these issues, see Kellner (1998), Holt (2002), and Frank (1997) on the backlash against advertisers and the subsequent marketing of cool.

their tastes."[13] Although there's a democratic veneer to the feedback loop, that perspective obscures the fact that giant businesses orchestrate, control, and profit from the process. Furthermore, kids are increasingly pulling outrageous and even dangerous stunts to get themselves noticed by the great big marketing machine.

Originally, the marketing of edgy was a teen and young adult develop-   10
ment. Now it too has trickled down to the children's market, though with some adjustments. Kid advertisers had to become far more discriminating, screening out what had become an anything-goes ethic. By way of illustration, consider the heroin-chic fashion photography of the mid-1990s. At that time cool hunters routinely included drugs, including hard ones, on their lists of what's hot and what's not. As one now-famous accounting from a cool-hunter publication that appeared in the *New Yorker* had it: "In San Francisco it's Nike, heroin, and reggae; in Chicago, Jungle music, Tag watches, and drugs."[14] Similarly, in kids' ads, violent images are more restricted, although this is less the case in movie ads, video games, and on the Web. The situation is similar with sexuality, exploitative racial imagery, and certain antisocial themes, all of which are prominent in cultural forms for teens and young adults. While going edgy can almost guarantee cool, it can also jeopardize a brand that depends on maintaining its wholesome image. Advertisers calibrate the degree of edginess and strive to go as far as, but not beyond what, a brand's image can tolerate.

Kids Rule: Nickelodeon and the Antiadult Bias

What else is cool? Based on what's selling in consumer culture, one would have to say that kids are cool and adults are not. Fair enough. Our country has a venerable history of generational conflict and youth rebellion. But marketers have perverted those worthy sentiments to create a sophisticated and powerful "antiadultism" within the commercial world.[15]

This trend also has a history. Advertising agencies have been co-opting youth rebellion for years, beginning with Bill Bernbach's embrace of the counterculture in Volkswagen ads in the 1960s, a development insightfully chronicled in Thomas Frank's *The Conquest of Cool*. More recently, the entity most responsible for the commercial exploitation of youth rebellion has been Viacom. The trend began with MTV and its teen audience, as the enormously popular network capitalized on teen desires to separate from and rebel against

---

[13]The feedback loop is explored in the PBS special *Merchants of Cool*, available online at pbs.org/frontline/shows/cool/. Douglas Rushkoff quote from his essay "The Pursuit of Cool: Introduction to Anti-Hyper-Consumerism," available online at http://www.rushkoff.com/essay/sportswearinternational.html.

[14]On cool-hunters' lists of what's hot and what's not, see Gladwell (1997), from which these items are drawn.

[15]For an early recognition of the rise of antiadultism, see Nader (1996).

their parents.[16] MTV allowed teens to immerse themselves in an increasingly separate culture, with its own fashions, language, and attitudes. Over time, some of that sensibility has trickled down to Nickelodeon's younger target.

Nickelodeon was founded in 1979 as a cable network, but it has since become a transcendent brand identity, selling a wide array of products and a relationship with kids. Nickelodeon would eventually dominate children's media. Nickelodeon's audience outpaces all other kid-oriented networks by a wide margin. At 80 percent, its household penetration tops the children's cable networks.[17] As I write these words, it is enjoying its best ratings year ever, surging far above the competition. The Nickelodeon Web site is the number one children's online destination. Its magazines boast 1.1 million subscribers and 6.3 million readers.[18] Nickelodeon is shown in 158 countries. Incredibly enough, given its limited demographic target, Nickelodeon has become one of the nation's most profitable networks.[19] In the process, it has remade children's programming and advertising.

Early on, Nickelodeon earned a reputation for offering quality shows. Its graphics were visually arresting, and the content was fresh. In comparison to the tired world of program-length commercials, that is, shows whose primary purpose is to sell products, Nickelodeon's offerings stood out. The network has also benefited from its recognition that children are a diverse group in terms of race and ethnicity, family type, and age. On the revenue side, Nickelodeon has made hay with the insight that children are a major influence market for parental purchases. A senior executive explained their stance: "The whole premise of our company was founded on serving kids, and what we've found is that when you do good things for kids, it happens to be good for business."[20]

The secret of Nickelodeon's success is its core philosophy: *kids rule.* In everything that they do, Nickelodeon tries to take the child's perspective. The network has positioned itself as kids' best friend, on their side in an often-hostile environment. Donna Sabino, director for research and development at Nickelodeon's Magazine Group, explained the thinking to me: "It's hard to be a kid in an adult world. The adult world doesn't respect kids. Everywhere else adults rule; at Nick kids rule."[21] The Nickelodeon worldview is that

15

---

[16]On the sale of youth rebellion to teens, see Nader (1996), ch. 4 and conclusion.

[17]Nickelodeon's ratings are from *Kidscreen* magazine (2002), p. 33. On weekdays in 2002, Nickelodeon commanded a 2.7 audience share, a full point above the Cartoon Network; on Saturday mornings, its 4.2 share was 1.2 points higher than the number two.

[18]The 1.1 million subscribers and 6.3 million readers from June 2003 data provided by Donna Sabino to the author.

[19]On Nickelodeon's profitability, see Carter (2002). MTV Networks, to which Nickelodeon belongs, earned more than $3 billion in revenue in 2002. The statistic of 158 countries is also from this source.

[20]"Whole premise of our company" quote by Lisa Judson, senior vice president of programming and executive creative director, cited in Hood (2000).

[21]Sabino quote beginning "It's hard to be a kid" and thirteen criteria from interview with the author, July 2001.

childhood has gotten tough. "Kids are experiencing increased pressure for achievement and activity. They don't have enough time for homework, they're overscheduled." Nickelodeon gives them what they need: "funny, happy, empowering." There are thirteen criteria a program must have to pass muster at the network, including good quality, a kid-centered message, humor, and edgy visual design. In theory, these are good criteria. But in practice, when kid-centric and edgy come together, what often results is attitude — an antiauthoritarian us-versus-them sensibility that pervades the brand.

Nickelodeon is not unique in its positioning. The world of children's marketing is filled with variants of the us-versus-them message. A prominent example is the soft drink Sprite, one of the most successful youth culture brands.[22] One witty Sprite ad depicted an adolescent boy and his parents on a road trip. The parents are in the front seat singing "Polly wolly doodle all the day," the epitome of unnerving uncool. He's in the back, banging his head on the car window in frustration, the ignominy of being stuck with these two losers too much to bear. "Need a CD player?" the ad asks.

A Fruit-to-Go online promotion tells kids that "when it comes to fashion class, your principal is a flunkie." A spot for Sour Brite Crawlers has a group of tween boys in an elevator going into gross detail about how they eat this gummy worm candy, eventually sickening the adults and forcing them to flee. The creators of the spot consider it "a great example . . . where tweens demonstrate their superiority of the situation with control over the adults."[23]

Adults also enforce a repressive and joyless world, in contrast to what kids and products do when they're left in peace. Consider a well-known Starburst classroom commercial. As the nerdy teacher writes on the board, kids open the candy, and the scene erupts into a riotous party. When the teacher faces the class again, all is quiet, controlled, and dull. The dynamic repeats itself, as the commercial makes the point that the kid world, courtesy of the candy, is a blast. The adult world, by contrast, is drab, regimented, BORRRR-inggg.

A study of 200 video game ads produced between 1989 and 1999 revealed a similar approach. Researchers Stephen Kline and Greig de Peuter report themes of boy empowerment through "oedipal rebellion" and rejection of home environments depicted as boring suburban spaces. "Nintendo ads," they write, "often construct the gamer as under siege by the adultified world while promising the young male gamers 'empowerment' and 'control' in an unlimited virtual world."[24] This attitude pervades the company's marketing strategy as well. As one Nintendo marketer explained, "We don't market to parents. . . . We market to our target group, which is teens

[22]On Sprite's success positioning itself as a youth brand, see *Merchants of Cool*, program 1911, *Frontline*. Available at www.pbs.org/wgbh/pages/frontline/shows/cool/etc/script.html.

[23]The Sour Brite Crawlers example is from Siegel et al. (2001), p. 61.

[24]"Nintendo ads" from Kline and de Peuter (2002), p. 265.

and tweens. . . . The parental seal of approval, while it is something that we like, it is not something that we actively encourage in our marketing because that might say to the kids that we're boring."[25]

A related theme in some kid advertising is to promote behavior that is annoying, antisocial, or mischievous. There's usually a playful quality to these spots, as in the various ads involving stealing candy at the movies. Julie Halpin of the Gepetto Group explains the strategy they used for Kids Foot Locker: "We wanted to be able to show them the empowerment they could have with the shoes. . . . What's really fun about a new pair of sneakers is a lot of the things that kids do that are really mischievous: squeaking on the floor, giving each other flat tires, writing little messages underneath. . . . Sales during the advertising period were about 34 percent higher than they were the previous year."[26]

Industry insiders and outsiders confirm the antiadultism in much of today's youth advertising. As one marketer explained to me: "Advertisers have kicked the parents out. They make fun of the parents. . . . We inserted the product in the secret kid world. . . . [It's] secret, dangerous, kid only."[27] Media critic Mark Crispin Miller makes a similar point: "It's part of the official advertising worldview that your parents are creeps, teachers are nerds and idiots, authority figures are laughable, nobody can really understand kids except the corporate sponsor. That huge authority has, interestingly enough, emerged as the sort of tacit superhero of consumer culture. That's the coolest entity of all."[28]

Similar trends can be found in programming. Journalist Bernice Kanner notes that "television dads — and to a lesser extent moms — once portrayed as loving and wise are now depicted as neglectful, incompetent, abusive or invisible. Parenthood, once presented as the source of supreme satisfaction on TV, is now largely ignored or debased." It's "parents as nincompoops."[29] After 9/11, Holly Gross, then of Saatchi and Saatchi Kid Connection, counseled companies that although "families *are* reconnecting and kids and parents *do* wish for more time together . . . that doesn't mean the tender moments must be shared in *your* marketing communication . . . some parents are just *sooooo* embarrassing." She advises going "parent-free" to market to tweens.[30]

[25]Nintendo marketer quote on targeting kids directly is from Kline and de Peuter (2002), p. 266.

[26]Halpin quote from an interview with her at Reveries, available online at http://www.reveries.com/reverb/kids_marketing/halpin/index.html.

[27]"Advertisers have kicked the parents out" quote from Mary Prescott (pseudonym), interview with the author, July 2001.

[28]Crispin Miller quote from *Merchants of Cool* transcript, cited above.

[29]Television dads quote from Kanner (2002), p. 45, and parents as nincompoops on p. 56. See also Hymowitz (1999), ch. 4, for a discussion of antifamilial attitudes in television.

[30]Holly Gross quote from Gross (2002b).

Marketers defend themselves against charges of antiadultism by arguing that they are promoting kid empowerment. Social conservatives, however, see treachery in the ridicule of adults. Wherever one comes down on this debate, it's important to recognize the nature of the corporate message: kids and products are aligned together in a really great, fun place, while parents, teachers, and other adults inhabit an oppressive, drab, and joyless world. The lesson to kids is that it's the product, not your parent, who's really on your side.

Age Compression

One of the hottest trends in youth marketing is age compression — the practice of taking products and marketing messages originally designed for older kids and targeting them to younger ones. Age compression includes offering teen products and genres, pitching gratuitous violence to the twelve-and-under crowd, cultivating brand preferences for items that were previously unbranded among younger kids, and developing creative alcohol and tobacco advertising that is not officially targeted to them but is widely seen and greatly loved by children. "By eight or nine they want 'N Sync," explained one tweening expert to me, in the days before that band was eclipsed by Justin Timberlake, Pink, and others.

Age compression is a sprawling trend. It can be seen in the import of television programming specifically designed for one year olds, which occurred, ironically, with Public Broadcasting's *Teletubbies*. It includes the marketing of designer clothes to kindergarteners and first graders. It's the deliberate targeting of R-rated movies to kids as young as age nine, a practice the major movie studios were called on the carpet for by the Clinton administration in 2000. It's being driven by the recognition that many children nationwide are watching MTV and other teen and adult programming. One of my favorite MTV anecdotes comes from a third-grade teacher in Weston, Massachusetts, who reported that she started her social studies unit on Mexico by asking the class what they knew about the country. Six or seven raised their hands and answered, "That's the place where MTV's Spring Break takes place!" For those who haven't seen it, the program glorifies heavy partying, what it calls "booty-licious girls," erotic dancing, wet T-shirt contests, and binge drinking.

Nowhere is age compression more evident than among the eight- to twelve-year-old target. Originally a strategy for selling to ten- to thirteen-year-olds, children as young as six are being targeting for tweening. And what is that exactly? Tweens are "in-between" teens and children, and tweening consists mainly of bringing teen products and entertainment to ever-younger audiences. If you're wondering why your daughter came home from kindergarten one day singing the words to a Britney Spears or Jennifer Lopez song, the answer is that she got tweened. Tween marketing has become a major focus of the industry, with its own conferences, research tools, databases, books, and specialty firms. Part of why tweening is so lucrative is that

25

it involves bringing new, more expensive products to this younger group. It's working because tweens have growing purchasing power and influence with parents. The more the tween consumer world comes to resemble the teen world, with its comprehensive branding strategies and intense levels of consumer immersion, the more money there is to be made.[31]

READING THE TEXT

1. Explain in your own words what constitutes "cool" in children's advertising, according to Schor.
2. How has "street" culture influenced consumer marketing, as Schor explains it?
3. What does researcher Douglas Holt mean by his claim that "the neighborhood, the pain of being poor, the alienation experienced by black kids . . . are the commodifiable assets" (para. 8) exploited in advertising?
4. What does the term "age compression" (para. 24) mean, in your own words?

READING THE SIGNS

1. Perform a semiotic analysis of an advertisement from any medium directed at children. What signifiers in the ad are especially addressed to children? To what extent do you see evidence of "cool marketing"? Consider such details as colors, music, voice track, the implied narrative of the ad, and its characters and their appearance.
2. Conduct an in-class debate over whether advertising to young people should be more strictly regulated. To develop support for your team's position, watch some TV programs aimed at children or teens and the advertising that accompanies them.
3. **CONNECTING TEXTS**   Read or reread James B. Twitchell's "What We Are to Advertisers" (p. 163), and write an essay in which you analyze whether Twitchell's assertion that "mass marketing means the creation of mass stereotypes" (para. 1) applies to child or tween consumers.
4. Using Thomas Frank's perspective in "Commodify Your Dissent" (p. 134) as a critical framework, analyze a suite of ads aimed at tweens and discuss the extent to which the ads "commodify" coolness and edginess. Ads that promote popular clothing, such as jeans, can be especially rich objects of analysis.

---

[31]On the idea of the tween and its evolution from earlier categories of sub- and preteen, see Cook and Kaiser (2003).

STEPHANIE MILLER

The Power of Play: Gamification Can Change Marketing

Times change, and advertisers have to change with them or they won't stay in business. So when, by the year 2011, it became apparent that millennial consumers spent a lot of their time playing games on their smartphones, marketing professionals decided that they needed to get with the program and start turning advertising into a game itself. The technique is called "gamification," and in this report for TopRight Partners, Stephanie Miller tells us some of the ways in which it is done. So hang on, and get ready for more gamification campaigns, such as Domino's Pizza's "Pizza Hero" mobile app, which lets you shake your smartphone so it can pick your toppings for you. Stephanie Miller is a writer for ClickZ, DMNews, and many other marketing publications.

Marketing is increasingly returning to its roots: Arresting attention by creating a fun distraction. One way to grab attention, empower social sharing and help people have fun is to "gamify" your marketing.

Gamification — the practice of applying game mechanics to non-game environments to motivate people and change behavior — has been tested seriously by marketers since 2011, and is now mainstream. "Gamification aims to inspire deeper, more engaged relationships and to change behavior, but it needs to be implemented thoughtfully," said Brian Burke, research vice president at Gartner in this press release. "Successful and sustainable gamification can convert customers into fans, turn work into fun, or make learning a joy."

Gartner and other vendors emphasize the need to motivate, engage and reward audiences to play. In the course of that play — be it customers or internal sales or other employee teams — people will discover new products, learn about their own interests and skills, and become ambassadors for the game (and hopefully, the brand that makes it happen).

The folks at M2 Research found that effective gamification can increase marketing exposure and engagement by 100 percent–150 percent. They recommend elements of a great game include: Strategy (The Play Proposition), Creativity (The Mechanics of Play), Communication, Reward, Virality (Share-ability). An early decision that marketers must make for a true game is the player relationship — competitive or collaborative. Or, if your brand allows it, perhaps neither — as demonstrated by the great Pizza Hero mobile app feature from Domino's Pizza. It's inspired by gaming, but not forced into a construct. Its simple pizza slot machine feature allows you to just shake your smartphone and the app will pick the toppings.

Before you leap headfirst into the mobile app phantasmagoria, note that 5 mobile analytics firm Localytics has found that 26 percent of apps are only used once after being downloaded. The Domino's portfolio of mobile apps is one that combines brand, business, and the customer experience — the essential elements for a big digital win.

As with any customer engagement strategy, it's all about context. The TopRight Customer BuyWay™ methodology always starts with a rich understanding of customers' needs, wants, and expectations of the brand, across all channels. I don't know that you can start out thinking, "We need a mobile app game." Start out thinking about customer engagement — what will motivate people to engage with the brand and solution? What content will provide utility, guidance and assistance with some real challenge? When the answer is, "Play a fun game to learn more" or "Interact with other customers to increase loyalty," then the answer might be a new gamified mobile app. The crux is providing an experience that delights.

Games do not have to be an app. Interactive elements with gaming features can work well in ecommerce when there is already brand loyalty. Clothing company Moosejaw gamified the way they engage loyal customers by offering items for low prices that went up throughout the day creating a sense of urgency for consumers to buy. They also included ways for consumers to score better deals by inviting friends and posting socially. The company reports that when the tool was launched, in less than 15 minutes, Quikly sold over five hundred $10 Moosejaw gift cards. Consumers then took those $10 gift cards and, on average, made purchases of $66, a 560 percent return on investment.

Give your games meaning, and your customers will have the motivation to engage. If the games are relevant and fun, and the players are challenged at different skills levels, they will build sustained momentum. As you can see from Domino's and Moosejaw, gaming can be less about chance and reward levels and more about sales, too. Getting the game on for your marketing can be an effective way to move the business to the #TopRight.

READING THE TEXT

1. Explain in your own words what "gamification" means.

2. What are the criteria for successful gamification, according to Miller?

3. Why does Miller say "As with any customer engagement, it's all about context" (para. 6).

4. Miller's intended audience is marketing professionals. How does that audience affect her tone in this selection?

READING THE SIGNS

1. **CONNECTING TEXTS**   Adopt the perspective of retail anthropologist Paco Underhill in Malcolm Gladwell's "The Science of Shopping" (p. 88), and write an evaluation of gamification as a marketing strategy. Alternatively, write your evaluation from the perspective of Joseph Turow ("The Daily You: How the New Advertising Industry Is Defining Your Identity and Worth," p. 394).

2. In an essay, support, refute, or complicate the proposition that having ordinary consumers "become ambassadors for the game (and hopefully, the brand that makes it happen)" (para. 3) is an ethically dubious practice, especially because they are often unaware that they are being so used.

3. **CONNECTING TEXTS**   As a motivational technique, gamification targets people's desires for rewards and pleasure in an effort to engage their loyalty. Read Steve McKevitt's "Everything Now" (p. 123), and write an essay in which you locate gamification in the spectrum of needs and wants that he describes. To develop your ideas, you might visit online loyalty programs and examine how they "convert customers into fans" (para. 2).

4. **CONNECTING TEXTS**   Gamification techniques have been used to promote not just commercial products but also social causes. Research one or two gamified campaigns, such as Free Rice, Recyclebank, and Foldit, and analyze the appeals made to the target audience. To what extent do these campaigns constitute useful activism, on the one hand, or a variant of "slacktivism," on the other. You might read Brian Dunning's "Slacktivisim: Raising Awareness" (p. 405) and Erin Lee's "How Effective Is Social Media Activism?" (p. 402) to develop your essay.

JULIA B. CORBETT
A Faint Green Sell: Advertising and the Natural World

Though "green" marketing and advertising is not as prevalent today as it was in the 1980s and 1990s, advertisers still exploit natural imagery to move the goods. Believing, however, that "the business of advertising is fundamentally 'brown'" and that "therefore the idea of advertising being 'green' and capable of supporting environmental values is an oxymoron," Julia B. Corbett sets out to analyze and categorize the ways in which advertising exploits nature, from treating it as a commodity to presenting nature as something that exists solely for the pleasure of human beings. All these strategies, Corbett concludes, perpetuate "an anthropocentric, narcissistic relationship" with the natural world. In other words, beautiful mountain ad backgrounds do not mean that you should go out and buy an SUV. Julia B. Corbett is a professor of communication at the University of Utah.

In the 1980s, advertisers discovered the environment. When a revitalized environmental movement helped establish environmentalism as a legitimate, mainstream public goal (Luke, 1993), corporate America quickly capitalized on a lucrative market of "green consumers" (Ottman, 1993; Zinkham & Carlson, 1995).

Marketers not only could create new products and services, they could also reposition existing ones to appear more environmentally friendly. What resulted was a flood of advertisements that focused on green product attributes, touting products as recyclable and biodegradable and claiming them good or safe for the environment. Increases in this genre were remarkable, with green print ads increasing 430 percent and green television ads increasing 367 percent between 1989 and 1990 (Ottman, 1993). The total number of products claiming green attributes doubled in 1990 to 11.4 percent from the previous year ("Selling green," 1991).

Virtually all of the existing research on so-called green advertising was conducted during this boom. Green advertising was defined by researchers as product ads touting environmental benefits or corporate green-image ads (Banerjee, Gulas, & Iyer, 1995; Shrum, McCarty, & Lowrey, 1995). Researchers also targeted and segmented green consumers (Ottman, 1993) and tested their motivations (Luke, 1993). Green appeals were categorized (Iyer & Banerjee, 1993; Obermiller, 1995; Schuhwerk & Lefkoff-Hagius, 1995) and consumer response to green ads analyzed (Mayer, Scammon, & Zick, 1993; Thorson, Page, & Moore, 1995).

By the late 1990s, advertisers announced the end of the green-ad boom. *Advertising Age* reported that as the country headed into the thirtieth anniversary of Earth Day, green positioning had become more than just a non-issue — it was almost an anti-issue (Neff, 2000). Marketers were launching a whole new class of disposable products from plastic storage containers to dust mops. There was a perceived decline in controversy over anti-green products such as disposable diapers, toxic batteries, and gas-guzzling SUVs (sport utility vehicles). In addition, only 5 percent of new products made claims about recyclability or recycled content, and the explosion of e-tailing added boxes, styrofoam peanuts, and air-puffed plastic bags to the waste stream. Green product ads in prime-time television, which never amounted to more than a blip, virtually disappeared by 1995, reflecting "the television tendency to get off the environmental bandwagon after it had lost its trendiness" (Shanahan & McComas, 1999, p. 108).

But Shanahan and McComas noted that their study — like virtually all research published during the green-ad boom — did not consider the most prevalent use of the environment in advertising: when nature functions as a rhetorically useful backdrop or stage. Using nature merely as a backdrop — whether in the form of wild animals, mountain vistas, or sparkling rivers — is the most common use of the natural world in advertisements. For all but the most critical message consumers, the environment blends into the background. We know that an advertisement for a car shows the vehicle outdoors and that ads for allergy medications feature flowers and "weeds." The environment per se is not for sale, but advertisers are depending on qualities and features of the non-human world (and our relationship to it) to help in the selling message. When the natural world is so depicted, it becomes a convenient, culturally relevant tool to which meanings can be attached for the purpose of selling goods and services. Although this intentional but seemingly casual use of the environment in advertising is by far the most common, it is the least studied by researchers.

Nature-as-backdrop ads also are notable for their enduring quality. 5 Although the number of ads that focus on product attributes such as "recyclable" may shift with marketing trends and political winds, nature has been used as a backdrop virtually since the dawn of advertising. The natural world was depicted in early automobile ads ("see the USA in your Chevrolet") and Hamms Beer commercials ("from the land of sky-blue water") and continues to be a prominent feature in the advertising landscape. Nature-as-backdrop ads, therefore, provide an important record of the position of the natural world in our cultural environment and, as such, deserve scrutiny.

Advertisements are a special form of discourse because they include visual signals and language fragments (either oral or written) that work together to create messages that go beyond the ability of either individually. This essay undertakes a critical analysis of the symbolic communicative discourse of advertising, viewing nature-as-backdrop ads as cultural icons of environmental values embedded in our social system. When ads present the environment with distorted, inauthentic, or exaggerated discourse, that discourse has the potential to foster inauthentic relationships to nature and influences the way we perceive our environment and its value to us.

Schudson (1989) argued that ads have special cultural power. In addition to being repetitive and ubiquitous, ads reinforce messages from primary institutions in the social system, provide dissonance to countering messages, and generally support the capitalistic structure that the advertising industry was created to support. This essay will discuss how the ad industry developed, how ads work on us, and how ads portray the natural world. It will argue, according to environmental theories such as deep ecology (Bullis, 1996; Naess, 1973), that the "green" in advertising is extremely faint by examining and developing six related concepts:

1. The business of advertising is fundamentally "brown"; therefore, the idea of advertising being "green" and capable of supporting environmental values is an oxymoron.

2. Advertising commodifies the natural world and attaches material value to non-material goods, treating natural resources as private and possessible, not public and intrinsic.

3. Nature-as-backdrop ads portray an anthropocentric, narcissistic relationship to the biotic community and focus on the environment's utility and benefit to humans.

4. Advertising idealizes the natural world and presents a simplified, distorted picture of nature as sublime, simple, and unproblematic.

5. The depiction of nature in advertising disconnects and estranges us from what is valued, yet at the same time we are encouraged to reconnect through products, creating a circular consumption.

6. As a ubiquitous form of pop culture, advertising reinforces consonant messages in the social system and provides strong dissonance to oppositional or alternative messages.

The "Brown" Business of Advertising

1. The business of advertising is fundamentally "brown"; therefore, the idea of advertising being "green" and capable of supporting environmental values is an oxymoron.

Advertisements are nothing new to this century or even previous ones. There are plentiful examples in literature, including the works of Shakespeare, that peddlers have long enticed buyers by advertising (in print or orally) a good's attributes and associated meanings. After World War II, however, advertising found a firm place in the worldview of Americans. According to Luke (1993), after 1945, corporate capital, big government, and professional experts pushed practices of a throw-away affluent society onto consumers as a purposeful political strategy to sustain economic growth, forestall mass discontent, and empower scientific authority. Concern for the environment was lacking in the postwar prosperity boom, at least until the mid-1960s when Rachel Carson sounded the alarm over chemicals and the modern-day environmental movement was born (Corbett, 2001).

To help alert consumers to new mass-produced goods, a new type of show called the "soap opera" was created for the relatively recent phenomenon of television. These daytime dramas were created for the sole purpose of delivering an audience of homemakers to eager manufacturers of household products, including soap. Advertisers realized that advertising on soap operas would help to establish branding, or creating differing values for what are essentially common, interchangeable goods such as soap.

Essentially, advertising was viewed as part of the fuel that would help keep a capitalist economy burning. Capitalism is a market system that measures its success by constant growth (such as the gross national product and housing starts), a system that many environmentalists recognize as ultimately unsustainable. You might even say that advertising developed as the culture that would help solve what some economists view as the central problem of capitalism: the distribution of surplus goods (Twitchell, 1996). Schudson (1989) concluded, "Advertising is capitalism's way of saying 'I love you' to itself." In a capitalist economy, advertising is a vital handmaiden to consumption and materialism. In the words of the author of *Adcult*, Americans "are not too materialistic. We are not materialistic enough" (Twitchell, 1996, p. 11).

The development of mass media, particularly radio and television, played an important role in delivering audiences to advertisers. By the mid-1980s, half of U.S. homes had cable, and the burgeoning number of channels allowed advertisers to target more specific audience segments. Advertisers and media programmers engage in a dance to fill each other's needs, each having a vested interest in constructing certain versions of the world and not others. According to Turow (1999), "the ad industry affects not just the content of its own campaigns but the very structure and content of the rest of the media system" (p. 194). At the same time, media develop formats and tones for their outlets and programming deemed to be most acceptable to the audiences that they hope marketers find most attractive. What this means for programming is that the upscale twenty-something audience — the most appealing segment to advertisers — will find itself represented in more media outlets than older men and women to whom only a small number of highly targeted formats are aimed. According to researchers of the green marketing boom, the segments of the population most committed to the environment do not belong to this twenty-something group (Ottman, 1993).

It is precisely the ability of advertisers and media programmers to tell some stories and not others that gives these entities power. "When people read a magazine, watch a TV show, or use any other ad-sponsored medium, they are entering a world that was constructed as a result of close cooperation between advertisers and media firms" (Turow, 1999, p. 16). Because all media provide people with insights into parts of the world with which they have little direct contact, media representations of the natural world to a largely urbanized population are highly significant. They show us, over and over again, where we belong in the world and how we should treat it. Yet, representations of the natural world are crafted for the sole purpose of selling certain audiences to advertisers.

The close cooperation between advertisers and media firms is understandable given advertising's financial support of media. For newspapers and some magazines, at least 50 percent of their revenue is from advertising; ad support approaches 100 percent for much of radio and television. By some estimates, advertisers spent $27 billion on support to television, $9 billion on radio, $46 billion on daily newspapers, and about $7 billion on consumer magazines (Turow, 1999, p. 13).

Given advertising's purpose of selling audiences to advertisers, is it even possible for any form of advertising — whether product ads or nature-as-backdrop ads — to be "green"? Dadd and Carothers (1991) maintained that a truly green economy would require all products to be audited and analyzed from cradle to grave for their environmental effects. Effects could include the resources used and pollution generated in the product's manufacture, energy used to produce and transport the product, the product's role in the economic and social health of the country of origin, investment plans of the company, and final disposal of product.

Applying this standard at the most basic level connotes it is an oxymoron to label marginally useful or necessary products (and the ads that promote them) as "green" or somehow good for the environment. Can an advertisement that encourages consumption of a product (or patronage of a company that produces the product) ever be green with a capital G? In his attempt to reconcile a brown industry with green ideals, Kilbourne (1995) identified three levels of green in advertisements. But even at the lowest level (defined as ads promoting a small "techno-fix" such as biodegradability) the message is still that "consuming is good, more is better, and the ecological cost is minimal" (p. 15). If an ad recognizes finite resources, it nevertheless views the environment purely as a resource, not as possessing intrinsic, non-economic value. Kilbourne concluded that from a purely ecological position, a truly Green ad is indeed an oxymoron: "the only Green product is the one that is not produced" (p. 16). Other researchers have likewise tried to categorize the green in advertisements (Banerjee et al., 1995). Adapting the deep and shallow ecology concepts of Naess (1973) to advertisements, they concluded that very few ads were "deep" — 2 percent of television and 9 percent of print — defined by the researchers as discussing environmental issues in depth and mentioning actions requiring more commitment.

However, these attempts to make advertising fit a green framework simply illustrate how ideologically opposed advertising and environmental values are. Because advertising is the workhorse of capitalism and supports continually increased production, it is ideologically contrary to environmentalism, which recognizes that ever-increasing growth and consumption are inherently unsustainable. It matters not whether an ad boasts of recyclability or quietly features pristine mountain meadows in the background; the basic business of advertising is brown. Perhaps the only truly Green product is not only one not produced, but also one not advertised.

Nature as Commodity

2. Advertising commodifies the natural world and attaches material value to non-material goods, treating natural resources as private and ownable, not public and intrinsic.

Have you ever viewed a single advertisement and then rushed out to buy that product? Probably not. That is not the way that advertising generally works on us, especially not for national consumer goods. Advertising scholars argue that ads cannot create, invent, or even satisfy our desires; instead, ads channel and express current desires with the hope of exploiting them.

You may disagree that ads cannot create desires, particularly if you have ever found yourself yearning for a product that six months ago you did not know existed or that you "needed." But even if ads do not greatly corrupt our immediate buying habits, they can gradually shape our values by becoming our social guides for what is important and valued. According to Benton (1995), advertising displays values and signals to people what our culture thinks is important. Advertising is not capable of inventing social values, but it does a masterful job at usurping and exploiting certain values and not others. The prominent (though not monopolistic) role of advertising in the symbolic marketplace is what gives advertising "a special cultural power"

(Schudson, 1989). In the words of one scholar, "Advertising is simply one of a number of attempts to load objects with meaning . . . it is an ongoing conversation within a culture about the meaning of objects" (Twitchell, 1996, p. 13).

The rhetorical challenge for an advertiser, then, is to load one product (even though numerous similar ones exist) with sufficient meaning so that the product appears able to express a desire. The natural world is full of cultural meaning with which to associate products, thereby attaching commodity value to qualities that are impossible to own. By borrowing and adapting well-known, stereotypical portrayals of nature, advertising is able to associate water with freshness and purity and weather as fraught with danger. If, for example, an ad wants to attach the value of "safety" to one particular car, it might demonstrate the car's ability to dodge "dangerous" elements of nature, such as falling rocks. On the other hand, if the ad wants to convey a truck's durability, it could just as easily attach a very different meaning to the same resource and say the truck is "like a rock." Neither product guarantees that you can buy safety or durability; both product ads merely expressed a consumer desire for them by associating a non-material good with a material one.

Animals in particular provide cultural shorthand for advertising. Animals, as popular symbols of the nonhuman environment, are a way for advertisers to link the perceived "personality" and stereotyped cultural value of the animal to the product (Phillips, 1996). In car advertising alone, ads compare vehicles to rams, eagles, wolves, cougars, falcons, and panthers. Some ads go so far as to portray the vehicle as an animal itself. An individual needs no direct experience with untamed environs to know what an eagle or cougar represents and is valued for.

The portrayal of animals in advertising need not be authentic or realistic for us to ascertain the value they represent. In a television commercial, two raccoons are peering inside a brightly lit living room window, "singing" a song from *My Fair Lady*. As the camera moves beyond the raccoons into the living room — where it appears the residents are not home — it focuses on the rocker-recliner. The raccoons sing, "All I want is a room somewhere, far away from the cold night air. Warm hands, warm feet . . ."

In this ad, the rocker-recliner you are enticed to buy has no direct or obvious connection to the natural world, but animals are very much part of the overall persuasive message. We are able to overlook the anthropomorphized singing raccoons because we have enough shared cultural meaning about raccoons and their behavior. We can decipher that these cute, mischievous "bandits" would like to "break in" to this warm room far away from the cold night air and maybe even snooze in that rocker. The intrinsic value of raccoons as a species has been usurped and exploited to demonstrate the comfort and desirability of a certain brand of chair.

Even if the original function of advertising was to market simple products 25 such as soap, advertising now functions to market feelings, sensations, and lifestyles. According to advertisers, the consumption of an object often has more to do with its meaning than with its actual use (Twitchell, 1996).

Discrete objects — whether cold medicine or fabric softener — are easier to sell if they are associated with social and personal meaning. The purpose of an ad is not to stress that the product functions properly, but that consumption of it will cure problems (Lasch, 1978), whether loneliness, aging, or even a desire to connect with the natural world. Advertising channels our psychological needs and ambitions into consumptive behaviors (Pollay, 1989). Price (1996) concluded that the success of the store The Nature Company depends "not so much [on] what nature is as what nature means to us" (p. 189).

Take for example a series of print and television ads for a particular SUV that labeled the vehicle as "the answering machine for the call of the wild." The print version tells us that "nature calls out for us" but with the vehicle's leather-trimmed seats, "civilization's never very far away." In television versions, we see the vehicle traveling over rugged terrain (but not the woman driving it) while an answering machine plays numerous messages from a worried mother and boyfriend to the woman who has escaped into the wild.

These ads do not focus on all the ways that this vehicle is superior to all the other very similar SUVs out there. The ads give us no reason to believe that the repair record, safety rating, price, or other important product attributes are somehow superior. Instead, these ads are selling meanings and values associated with the natural world. This product will reconnect you with "the wild," which appears to be missing in your life, and it will help you escape from your troubles and relationships. A rugged environment (yet one somehow made safer and more civilized by this SUV) is portrayed as the best place to find peace and this vehicle will take you there. (An ad for a very different type of product used the same slogan in a different way: "Radio Shack is answering the call of the wild with two-way personal radios." In the ad, "renowned wildlife expert" Jim Fowler uses the radio in a remote-looking location. "No matter where the wild calls you, you'll be ready to answer.")

Some scholars insist that advertising appeals primarily to personal dissatisfactions in our lives and insecurities over the ways and pace in which we live, not to our personal needs. In doing so, ads are carriers of anxiety that serve only to alienate us further (Lasch, 1978). In the SUV ads, the driver is not portrayed as using the vehicle for personal need, but for escape from relationship problems to an environment that is depicted as being free of all problems.

The rhetorical argument of commodification leads us to believe that we can solve problems and dissatisfactions with a purchase. We buy the peace and escape — represented by the wilderness and promised by the product — even though the product is incapable of fulfilling that promise. The intent of advertising, says Pollay (1989), is to preoccupy society with material concerns and to see goods as a path to happiness and a solution to problems (which is very brown thinking). In many of the appeals of nature-as-backdrop ads, the advertisements attempt to associate material goods with nonmaterial qualities that have disappeared from many people's lives, qualities such as solitude, wilderness, lush landscapes, free-flowing water, and clean air.

In a print ad for L.L. Bean, we see a man wading across calm, milky blue waters to a small sailboat in early morning light. The caption reads, "Don't mistake a street address for where you actually live." Apparently this man cannot "live" in his everyday life — which we assume takes place in a far less serene setting — but must leave it to achieve qualities it lacks. Yet another SUV ad promises, "Escape. Serenity. Relaxation." Pristine mountain vistas and sparkling waters (usually devoid of people) allow us to romanticize about a life lost or connections broken. When such adventures are tied in such a way to products, that connection materializes a way of experiencing the natural world.

Commodification of what are essentially public resources — like milky   30 blue waters — encourages us to think of resources as private and possessible. Ads may invoke public values of family, friendship, and a common planet as part of their message, but these values are put to work to sell private goods, a very capitalist principle. The satisfaction derived from these goods, even those that appear inherently collective such as water, is depicted as invariably private. This encourages "the promotion of a social order in which people are encouraged to think of themselves and their private worlds" (Schudson, 1989, p. 83), a very anthropocentric and narcissistic perspective. The environment, in many respects, doesn't function well as private space.

For the Pleasure of Humans

3. Nature-as-backdrop ads portray an anthropocentric, narcissistic relationship to the biotic community and focus on the environment's utility and benefit to humans.

Another common feature in advertising appeals that utilize the natural world is self-absorption and narcissism. The word derives from Narcissus, a youth in Greek mythology who fell in love with his own reflection in a pool. The way in which advertising portrays this universal emotional type is as self-absorbed, self-righteous, and dependent on momentary pleasures of assertion. Narcissism in advertising often takes the form of outdoor adventure, as in this print ad: Two pickup trucks are parked on an expansive, rolling sand dune. In the open bed of each truck, a young man in a wet suit appears to be wind-surfing — through the manipulation of computer graphics. Water splashes around them in the air and onto the sand. The caption says the trucks are "built fun tough" and have "gallons of attitude." Of course we know this picture to be fake (although a similar juxtaposition of desert and water exists in human-made Lake Powell), but the picture tells us that these men are in it for the fun, for the adventure.

A narcissist is most concerned with pleasing himself or herself at the expense of others, and if we extend the analogy, at the expense of the environment. In terms of environmental ideology, a narcissist would be anthropocentric, believing that his or her own outdoor pleasure comes before that of other species and their needs. Ads that show people "conquering" natural elements are expressing me-first anthropocentrism. According to Lasch (1978), our culture is marked by an exaggerated form of self-awareness and mass narcissism, finely attuned (with the help of advertising) to the many demands of the narcissistic self.

Another example is a television ad that shows a young boy working through the pages of a puzzle book. He reads aloud, "Help the knight reach the castle," and with his crayon follows the winding path safely past the dragon to the castle. On the next page he reads, "Help the Jeep Wrangler reach the fishing hole." "Hmm," he says, grins, and makes a noise like a truck revving up. He draws a line straight across the puzzle book landscape, across two mountain ranges, a deep valley, and a patch of quicksand, ignoring the cleared path. As he smiles smugly, the announcer tells us that a Jeep is "more fun than you imagine."

Yet another truck commercial begins in a deserted mountain valley at twilight. Next, a gigantic booted foot with a spur crashes to the ground, reverberating all in sight. We then see that the foot belongs to a cowboy the size of Paul Bunyan. The message is that the human is essentially larger than life, dominating the entire landscape and all within it, as Bunyan did. Such exaggerated domination intentionally positions humans at the top of a pyramid, instead of belonging equally to a biotic community.

Nature as Sublime

4. Nature-as-backdrop ads idealize the natural world and present a simplified, distorted picture of nature as sublime, simple, and unproblematic.

As much as ads intentionally distort reality (in images such as wind-surfing in a truck or singing raccoons), they also present reality as it should be, a reality that is worth desiring and emulating (and owning). If you have backpacked or camped, you know that slapping mosquitoes, getting dirty, getting wet, and sweating are often part of the package. Such a real outdoor experience is unlikely to be depicted in advertisements (unless the product is for something like insect repellent). Instead, ads subordinate reality to a romanticized past, present, or even future. "Real" in advertising is a cultural construct: "The makers of commercials do not want what is real but what will seem real on film. Artificial rain is better than 'God's rain' because it shows up better on film or tape" (Schudson, 1989, p. 79). Advertisers do not intend to capture life as it really is, but intend instead to portray the "ideal" life and to present as normal and everyday what are actually relatively rare moments, such as a phenomenal sunset or a mosquito-less lake.

A great many nature-as-backdrop ads present the natural world as sublime, a noble place inspiring awe and admiration. As an exercise, my students draw their interpretation of a sublime place in nature, and invariably, similar elements appear in their pictures: snow-capped mountain peaks towering

35

above pine trees and a grassy or flower-filled meadow, through which a clear creek or river flows. Sometimes, large mammals such as deer graze in the meadow. Humans are rarely present.

According to Oravec (1996), the sublime is a literary and artistic convention that uses a prescribed form of language and pictorial elements to describe nature, and that in turn encourages a specific pattern of responses to nature. Artistically, sublime representations can include blurring, exaggeration of detail, and compositional elements such as a foreground, middle ground, and frame. Settings are frequently pastoral or wild with varying amounts of human presence. There is a self-reflexive nature to the positioning, with the observer feeling both within a scene and also outside it, viewing the scene (and reflexively, the self) from a higher or more distant (and morally outstanding) perspective.

Oravec (1996) has called the sublime the founding trope in the rhetoric of   40
environmentalism: "Sublimity has remained a touchstone or grounding for our public conception of nature and, through nature, of the environment" (p. 68). As a conventional linguistic device, the sublime represents and encodes our understanding of the natural world. Because the sublime is associated with what is "natural," "the sublime connotes an authenticity and originality that is part of its very meaning; yet like rhetoric itself, it has a long-standing reputation for exaggeration and even falsehood" (p. 69).

The sublime is as much a part of advertising as it is of the artistic and literary realms. Advertising presents the natural world as pristine, simple, and not endangered, yet depictions are always contrived and often created. What appears as real rain is artificial, what looks like a natural wildlife encounter is contrived, and what appears entirely natural was created with computer animation and digital manipulation. The artificial seamlessly approximates the real in the sublime world of advertising.

Numerous vacation advertisements depict people in sublime settings, such as thin and tan couples on pristine white sand beaches, or peacefully cruising under sunny skies amid glaciers and whales. Vacationers in this idealized world never encounter anything other than perfect environmental conditions and enjoy these sublime locations unfettered by crowds.

A host of pharmaceutical ads likewise enlist nature backdrops as rhetoric for the sublime. One ad for an arthritis medication takes place in a pastoral setting assumed to be a park. The sun is shining, the park is empty except for the actors, there is no litter or noise, and even the dogs are exceedingly friendly and behaved. In another ad for what is presumed to be a mood-enhancer, a woman strolls slowly along a pristine, deserted beach in soft light, a contented smile on her face. In these instances, the sublime backdrop doubly represents the sublime state the person will achieve upon taking the medication. Many of these ads rely so heavily on the power of sublime meaning that the actual purpose of the drug is not stated, only assumed.

Other commercials depict the sublime after a product has changed problematic nature into idealized nature. Numerous ads for lawn care products and allergy medications first portray nature in a state of chaos or war, needing to be tamed and brought under control. One television ad for lawn chemicals showed a small army of men and supplies descending from the sky to tame and tackle nature. Some allergy commercials depict the flowers and weeds physically attacking people. But ah, after the product is introduced, unproblematic and peaceful nature returns.

When humans are introduced into sublime scenes, their representation is also idealized. Just as nature is presented as reality-as-it-should-be, people are presented as-they-should-be in a limited number of social roles. Therefore, people in ads are primarily attractive, young or middle-aged, vibrant, and thin, or they are celebrities with those qualities. The environments in which they live, whether inside or outside, are also limited to idealized conditions; no one has dirty houses or unkempt lawns, and no one travels through dirty city streets, encounters polluted rivers, or finds abused landscapes. In the world of advertising, there are no poor people, sick people, or unattractive people, and sometimes there are no people at all. For example, most car ads do not show anyone actually driving the vehicle through the tinted windows, and you hear only the disembodied voice of the announcer. The social roles played by advertising actors are easily identifiable — the businessperson, the grandmother, the teenager — but the actors are anonymous as individual people and portray only social roles tailored to specific demographic categories. The flat, abstract, idealized, and sometimes anonymous world of advertising "is part of a deliberate effort to connect specific products in people's imagination with certain demographic groupings or needs or occasions" (Schudson, 1989, p. 77).

Of course you recognize pieces of this idealized presentation of people and their environments, just as you recognize the utterly impossible pieces — a car parked on an inaccessible cliff or polar bears drinking Coke. We are not stupefied by a natural world that is unrealistic and idealized in advertising: in fact, we expect it.

A Natural Disconnect

5. The depiction of nature in advertising disconnects and estranges us from what is valued, and we attempt to reconnect through products, creating a circular consumption.

Some critics believe that advertising may be more powerful the less people believe it and the less it is acknowledged. According to Schudson (1989), ads do not ask to be taken literally and do not mean what they say, but "this may be the very center of their power" (p. 87). While we are being exposed to those 3,000 ads a day, we may carry an illusion of detachment and think them trivial and unimportant. According to some theories, though, it is very possible to "learn" without active involvement, a so-called sleeper effect. This myth of immunity from an ad's persuasion may do more to protect our self-respect than help us comprehend the subtleties and implications of their influence (Pollay, 1989). Although we may not think an ad speaks to us, its slogan may suddenly pop into our vocabulary — just do it, it does a body good, got milk? We may be unaware and uninvolved in front of the television, but the message of the ad may prove important at purchase time. According to Pollay (1989), advertising does more than merely stimulate wants; it plays a subtle role in changing habits.

Take the habit of drying your clothes, an activity that for many people throughout the world involves pinning clothes to a line in the backyard or between buildings. When I was a girl, I loved sliding between clean sheets dried outside on the clothesline and drinking in the smell. How do many people get that same outside-smell nowadays? They get it with detergents and fabric softeners with names like "mountain air" and "springtime fresh" or with similarly scented dryer sheets. Although perceived convenience and affordable dryers no doubt helped change our clothes-drying habits, where did we learn to associate the smell of outdoors with purchased products? Advertising.

The message in these product ads is that the artificial smell is somehow   50 easier or superior or even just equivalent to the real smell in the natural world. It not only commodifies something of value from the natural world, it gradually disconnects us from that thing of value. The more successfully ads teach us to associate natural qualities such as fresh air with products, the more disconnected we become from what was originally valued. The more estranged from the original thing of value, the more we may attempt to reconnect through products that promise an easy replacement. When we become so estranged from the natural world that we attempt to reconnect through products, a circular consumptive pattern is created — which supports the capitalist economy that advertising was created to support. If advertising tells us that non-saleable qualities of the outdoors such as fresh air and natural smells are easy to bring inside, need we worry about the condition of the real world?

Just as advertising can change habits, it can help create rituals and taboos. A good example of a taboo largely created by advertising is litter. Through national advertising campaigns begun decades ago, litter was labeled as an environmental no-no. While cleaning up litter makes for a visually appealing environment, the automobiles from which the trash is generally tossed cause far more environmental harm than almost all types of litter.

Advertising also works to create rituals. A ritual is created when we make inert, prosaic objects meaningful and give them symbolic significance. Mistletoe means little to us as a parasitic evergreen, but it is loaded with significance as a holiday ritual about kissing. Whales mean more to us as communicative, spiritual symbols of the deep than for their inherent value and place in ocean ecosystems. Price (1996) concluded that Native American fetishes and baskets, which have been ritualized by nonnative populations (and appropriated by advertising), "associate nature nearly interchangeably with indigenous peoples" (p. 189). In a similar way, once a species or animal has been so ritualized, it precludes a more complete and accurate knowing of it and disconnects us.

Advertising, directly and subtly, idealizes and materializes a way of experiencing the world, including the natural world. It promotes products as the simple solutions to complex dilemmas by tapping into our dissatisfactions and desires. If you feel disconnected to the natural world, you can "solve" that with mountain-scented laundry products, bear fetishes, and whale audiotapes, but these purchases only increase the estrangement. If you need to escape modern life yet want to feel safe and civilized while doing so, you can simply solve that by taking a rugged SUV into the wilderness.

Yet environmental dilemmas are anything but simple, and wilderness is a good example. A print ad features a four-wheel-drive car crossing a spar-kling, boulder-strewn stream and announces, "Coming soon to a wilderness near you." In this idealized portrayal, there is no mud being stirred up from the bottom of the stream, no dirt of any kind on the car, and of course, there is no visible driver. But in addition, "wilderness" is a rare commodity that rarely exists "near you," and by its very definition, includes few people and even fewer developed signs of people. In wilderness with a capital W, cars and all motorized equipment are forbidden. Setting aside an area as wilder-ness involves contentious negotiations and land-use trade-offs. But whether formally designated or not, experiencing wilderness is not the simple matter of materialization and driving a certain kind of car.

Another example of advertising portraying a complex environmental issue as simple and uncomplicated is the depiction of water. We see it bab-bling down brooks in beverage commercials, refreshing someone in a soap commercial, quenching thirst in ads for water filters and bottled water. Pure, clean, healthy — but simple? More than half the world's rivers are drying up or are polluted. Agricultural chemicals have seeped into many U.S. underground aquifers. Oil, gas, and a host of herbicides and pesticides wash off streets and lawns into waterways. Political and legal fights are waged over dams, diver-sions, and water rights. A host of bacterial contaminants have threatened water supplies and public health in major U.S. cities, and traces of antibiotics and other prescription drugs have been detected in some municipal water supplies. Clean water is definitely not a simple environmental issue. 55

Advertising Does Not Stand Alone

6. As a ubiquitous form of popular culture, advertising reinforces consonant messages in the social system and provides strong dissonance to oppositional or alternative messages.

For any societal element to wield power, it must exist in concert with other social institutions in a way that is mutually reinforcing. Advertising is layered on top of other cultural elements and bound up with other institu-tions, from entertainment and popular culture to corporate America and manufacturing. Each element is heteroglossic, continually leaking into other sectors, with advertising slogans showing up in both casual conversation and political speeches. The very ubiquitousness of advertising — extending beyond regular media buys to include placing products in movies, sponsoring sporting events, and the full-length infomercial — ensures its power and influence in numerous places and institutions.

For an example of this interwoven character of advertising and consumption with other elements of society, consider plastics recycling. We routinely see ads touting how certain products are recyclable or made from recycled items. Currently, the plastics industry is running an advertising campaign that reminds us of all the wonderful ways that plastic contributes to our lives. That means that multiple corporate public relations departments and public relations agencies are involved in getting mileage from the recycling issue. Public relations and advertising personnel have regular contact with media people in both the advertising and editorial sides, and the boundaries between news and advertising functions are becoming increasingly blurred (Stauber & Rampton, 1995). Meanwhile, giant corporate conglomerates have become the norm, putting journalists under the same corporate roof as advertisers and the very companies they attempt to scrutinize. For example, if a television station is owned by General Electric and is also receiving thousands of dollars in revenue from an ad campaign about the value of plastics, there is dissonance — whether acknowledged or not — for those TV reporters covering a story about environmental impacts and energy used to recycle plastic.

The hallowed halls of education are not immune from commercial messages, including those about plastic. Captive youngsters are a tempting market: more than 43 million kids attend schools and even elementary-age children exert tremendous spending power, about $15 billion a year (McNeal, 1994). Ads cover school buses, book covers, and scoreboards, and corporate flags fly next to school flags. The Polystyrene Packaging Council, like other corporations, has supplied "supplemental educational materials" free of charge to K–12 classrooms. Their "Plastics and the Environment" lesson teaches that plastics are great and easily recycled, even though most plastics are not recyclable for lack of markets. Consumers Union evaluated this lesson as "highly commercial and incomplete with strong bias. . . . [T]he disadvantages of plastics . . . are not covered" (Zillions, 1995, p. 46). Another critic noted that when teachers use such materials, "American students are introduced to environmental issues as they use materials supplied by corporations who pollute the soil, air, and water" (Molnar, 1995, p. 70).

Beyond communication and education, legal sectors also get involved in advertising claims about recycled and recyclable plastic, and politicians know it is wise to support recycling as a generalized issue. Some municipalities sponsor curbside pick-up programs for plastic, and trash haulers and manufacturers run businesses dependent on recycling plastics. Recycling plastics not only creates new business opportunities, it also is philosophically consistent with a capitalist economy that is based on ever-increasing consumption. After all, the message of recycling is not to reduce or avoid consumption but essentially to consume something again. According to one critic in *Harper's*, 60 oftentimes the new product created from recycled plastics is "the perfect metaphor for everything that's wrong with the idea of recycling plastics. It's ugly as sin, the world doesn't need it, and it's disposable" (Gutin, 1992, p. 56).

The vested interest of so many powerful social institutions makes it that much harder to separate the influence of one from another — such as advertising from news media — and to effect significant social change. It also makes the ubiquitous, repetitive messages of advertising reinforced and in a sense replicated, free of charge. Individuals or groups with oppositional messages about plastics would have to contend with what seems a united front about the place, if not the value, of plastic.

Working Together

Obviously, the six concepts presented here work in concert. Here is one final example of an ad that considers them together.

First, the visual of this television ad: A waterfall flows over the driver's seat of a car and a tiny kayaker (in relation to the size of the car seat) spills down the face of the falls. The scene quickly shifts to the kayaker (full-sized now and paddling away from us) amid glaciers. The next scene takes us into the car's back cargo area — still covered with water — and two orca whales breach in front of the kayaker, who pauses mid-stroke. (In all of these shots, we have never seen the kayaker's face; when he paddles away, his head is covered in a fur-lined parka that looks "native.") The next shot is a close-up of a paddle dipping into water shimmering with the colors of sunset and above the words "Discover Chevy Tahoe." The last scene shows the unoccupied vehicle parked on the edge of a stream in front of snow-covered mountain peaks. The accompanying audio includes Native American–sounding drum beats and a mixed chorus singing a chant-like, non-English song. Over this music, we hear the voice of a male announcer who quotes a passage from John Muir about how a person needs silence to get into the heart of the wilderness away from dust, hotels, baggage, and chatter.

The meanings that these elements convey to us are multiple. Peace, serenity, at-oneness with nature, and a return to a simple yet sublime "native" existence are part of the promise of this vehicle. Native drums, whales, glaciers, paddling through still waters, and even the deep ecologist Muir are powerful, idealized, and ritualized symbols that are employed to market a feeling and a sensation. The seamless juxtaposition of scene both inside and outside the vehicle conveys that nature is transported effortlessly for you to experience these things directly, without leaving the safety and luxury of your car. The vehicle is the commodity to aid your escape to this sublime place, a place depicted as real yet entirely contrived, with kayakers spilling over car seats. The entire promise is one of self-gratification, helping the driver/kayaker travel to this idealized wilderness. Yet, if you truly want to heed John Muir's advice, silence is needed to get into the heart of the wilderness, not a noisy car. Hence if you buy into (pun intended) the vehicle being the solution (and not existing instead in your own life or soul), the result is further estrangement from the very thing desired and valued. Advertising, as a primary support system for a capitalist economy, can only transfer meaning and express latent desires — not deliver on any of these promises.

REFERENCES

Banerjee, S., Gulas, C. S., & Iyer, E. (1995). Shades of green: A multidimensional analysis of environmental advertising. *Journal of Advertising, 24,* 21–32.

Benton, L. M. (1995). Selling the natural or selling out? Exploring environmental merchandising. *Environmental Ethics, 17,* 3–22.

Bullis, C. (1996). Retalking environmental discourses from a feminist perspective: The radical potential of ecofeminism. In J. G. Cantrill & C. L. Oravec (Eds.), *The symbolic earth: Discourse and our creation of the environment* (pp. 123–148). Lexington, KY: University Press of Kentucky.

Corbett, J. B. (2001). Women, scientists, agitators: Magazine portrayal of Rachel Carson and Theo Colborn. *Journal of Communication, 51,* 720–749.

Dadd, D. L., & Carothers, A. (1991). A bill of goods? Green consuming in perspective. In C. Plant & J. Plant (Eds.), *Green business: Hope or hoax?* Philadelphia, PA: New Society Publishers (pp. 11–29).

Fink, E. (1990). Biodegradable diapers are not enough in days like these: A critique of commodity environmentalism. *EcoSocialist Review, 4.*

Gutin, J. (1992, March–April). Plastics-a-go-go. *Harper's, 17,* 56–59.

Iyer, E., & Banerjee, B. (1993). Anatomy of green advertising. *Advances in Consumer Research, 20,* 484–501.

Kilbourne, W. E. (1995). Green advertising: Salvation or oxymoron? *Journal of Advertising, 24,* 7–20.

Lasch, C. (1978). *The culture of narcissism.* New York, NY: W. W. Norton.

Luke, T. W. (1993). Green consumerism: Ecology and the ruse of recycling. In J. Bennett & W. Chaloupka (Eds.), *In the nature of things: Languages, politics and the environment* (pp. 154–172). Minneapolis, MN: University of Minnesota Press.

Mayer, R. N., Scammon, D. L., & Zick, C. D. (1993). Poisoning the well: Do environmental claims strain consumer credulity? *Advances in Consumer Research, 20,* 698–703.

McNeal, J. U. (1994, February 7). Billions at stake in growing kids market. *Discount Store News, 41.*

Molnar, A. (1995). Schooled for profit. *Educational Leadership, 53,* 70–71.

Naess, A. (1973). The shallow and the deep, long-range ecology movement: A summary. *Inquiry, 16,* 95–100.

Neff, J. (2000, April 10). It's not trendy being green. *Advertising Age, 16.*

Obermiller, C. (1995). The baby is sick / the baby is well: A test of environmental communication appeals. *Journal of Advertising, 24,* 55–70.

Oravec, C. L. (1996). To stand outside oneself: The sublime in the discourse of natural scenery. In J. G. Cantrill & C. L. Oravec (Eds.), *The symbolic earth: Discourse and our creation of the environment* (pp. 58–75). Lexington, KY: University Press of Kentucky.

Ottman, J. A. (1993). *Green marketing: Challenges and opportunities for the new marketing age.* Lincolnwood, IL: NTC Business Books.

Phillips, B. J. (1996). Advertising and the cultural meaning of animals. *Advances in Consumer Research, 23,* 354–360.

Pollay, R. W. (1989). The distorted mirror: Reflections on the unintended consequences of advertising. In R. Hovland & G. B. Wilcox (Eds.), *Advertising in Society* (pp. 437–476). Lincolnwood, IL: NTC Business Books.

Price, J. (1996). Looking for nature at the mall: A field guide to the Nature Company. In W. Cronon (Ed.), *Uncommon ground: Rethinking the human place in nature*, (pp. 186–203). New York, NY: W. W. Norton.

Schudson, M. (1989). Advertising as capitalist realism. In R. Hovland & G. B. Wilcox (Eds.), *Advertising in society* (pp. 73–98). Lincolnwood, IL: NTC Business Books.

Schuhwerk, M. E., & Lefkoff-Hagius, R. (1995). Green or non-green? Does type of appeal matter when advertising a green product? *Journal of Advertising, 24*, 45–54.

Selling green. (1991, October). *Consumer Reports, 56*, 687–692.

Shanahan, J., & McComas, K. (1999). *Nature stories: Depictions of the environment and their effects*. Cresskill, NJ: Hampton Press.

Shrum, L. J., McCarty, J. A., & Lowrey, T. M. (1995). Buyer characteristics of the green consumer and their implications for advertising strategy. *Journal of Advertising, 24*, 71–82.

Stauber, J., & Rampton, S. (1995). *Toxic sludge is good for you! Lies, damn lies, and the public relations industry*. Monroe, ME: Common Courage Press.

Thorson, E., Page, T., & Moore, J. (1995). Consumer response to four categories of "green" television commercials. *Advances in Consumer Research, 22*, 243–250.

Turow, J. (1999). *Breaking up America: Advertisers and the new media world*. Chicago, IL: University of Chicago Press.

Twitchell, J. B. (1996). *Adcult USA: The triumph of advertising in American culture*. New York, NY: Columbia University Press.

Zillions: For Kids from Consumer Reports (1995). *Captive kids: Commercial pressures on kids at school*. New York, NY: Consumers Union Education Services.

Zinkham, G. M., & Carlson, L. (1995). Green advertising and the reluctant consumer. *Journal of Advertising, 24*, 1–6.

READING THE TEXT

1. Define in your own words "nature-as-backdrop" ads.

2. How, according to Corbett, did advertising become "part of the fuel that would help keep a capitalist economy burning" (para. 11)?

3. Why does Corbett claim, "commodification of what are essentially public resources — like milky blue waters — encourages us to think of resources as private and possessible" (para. 30)? Why does she think such commodification is problematic?

4. In your own words, define the term "sublime."

5. How can some ads using nature as a backdrop be considered to reflect our narcissism?

6. Why does Corbett have concerns regarding ad campaigns for plastics recycling, which is usually considered an environmentally conscious venture?

READING THE SIGNS

1. In an essay, write your own argument in response to Corbett's speculative question: "Is it even possible for any form of advertising — whether product ads or nature-as-backdrop ads — to be 'green'?" (para. 15).

(Continued on page 227)

Portfolio of Advertisements

READING THE SIGNS

Consider these questions as you analyze the advertisements on the following pages.

1. This ad for the Bose Sound-Link Mini speaker reflects a change in the way that people listen to music. What is that change, and how is Bose responding to it through this ad?

2. This ad for Buffalo Exchange promotes an attitude as well as a lifestyle. What is that attitude, and how does it reflect what Thomas Frank calls the "commodification of dissent"?

3. An ad for a trade organization rather than a particular brand, this pitch for California Walnuts is intended to resemble a certain kind of movie poster. What is the kind of movie alluded to here, and why do you think it was chosen to spearhead this campaign?

4. This ad for Playdead's video game Limbo contains a typical image from the game itself but otherwise very little information as to what the product being advertised is. What is the ad designer taking for granted about the audience for this ad? How might a fan of the game respond differently to the ad than someone unfamiliar with it?

5. This ad for Sanuk sandals contains numerous images, most of which are not of sandals. What are those images, and what do they say about the presumed lifestyles and desires of the target market for the product?

6. This ad contains a mixture of populist and elitist appeals. What are those appeals, and how do they combine to sell watches?

7. This online ad for Air Canada played on tensions surrounding the 2016 US election season. What presumptions about its viewers does this ad make? How might those presumptions backfire?

Bose Corporation

Buffalo Exchange, LTD

CALIFORNIA WALNUTS

NATURAL DEFENDERS OF THE HUMAN BODY™

The harder you live, the more you need powerful, portable California Walnuts.
They're rich in the essential plant-based omega-3 fatty acid ALA.

And the American Heart Association certifies foods, including walnuts, for the
contribution they can make to an overall heart-healthy diet.

*Supportive but not conclusive research shows that eating 1.5 ounces of walnuts per day, as part of a low saturated fat and low cholesterol diet and not resulting in increased caloric intake, may reduce the risk of coronary heart disease." (FDA) One ounce of walnuts provides 18g of total fat, 2.5g of monounsaturated fat, 13g of polyunsaturated fat including 2.5g of alpha-linolenic acid — the plant-based omega-3 fatty acid and 3.68mmol of antioxidants.

WALNUTS.ORG   FACEBOOK.COM/CAWALNUTS   TWITTER.COM/CAWALNUTS

American
Heart
Association
CERTIFIED
Meets Criteria For
Heart-Healthy Food

Per one ounce serving.
See heartcheckmark.org/guidelines

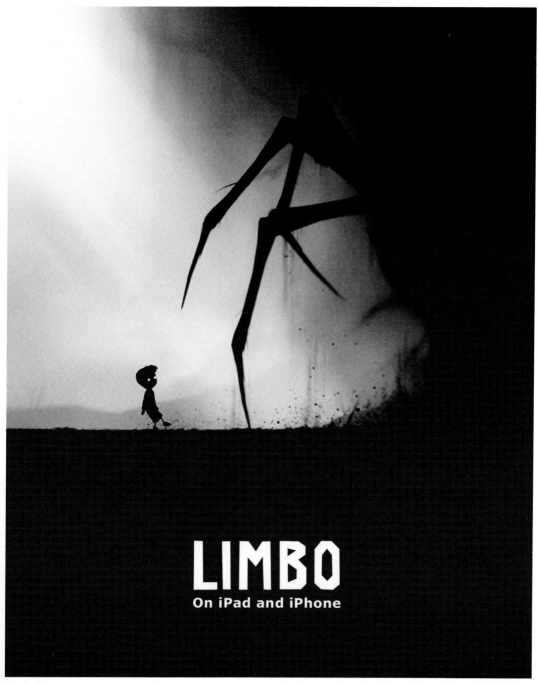

LIMBO
On iPad and iPhone

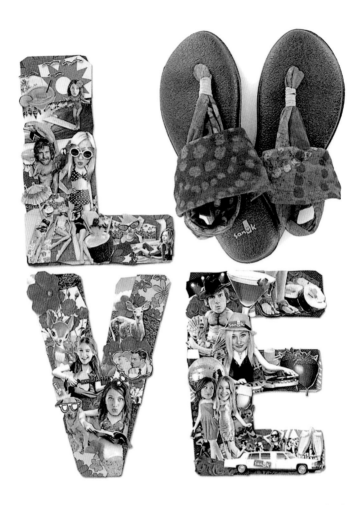

SANDALS ARE FOR: LAUGHTER, LOVE AND LATE NIGHTS.

YOGA MAT SANDALS

Deckers Outdoor Corporation as the brand Sanuk®

THE LONG TRADITION OF DETROIT WATCHMAKING HAS JUST BEGUN.

WATCHES WILL BE MADE IN DETROIT FOR DECADES TO COME, BUT WE WILL NEVER MAKE THIS ONE AGAIN. RESERVE **THE RUNWELL**, AN EXTREMELY LIMITED SINGLE EDITION OF THE FIRST HANDMADE WATCH FROM THE MOTOR CITY.

SHINOLA.COM

SHINOLA
DETROIT

Where American is made.™

Shinola

AMERICANS SEARCHING:

How can I move to Canada?

1,367,902

AIR CANADA

2. Study some travel magazines, focusing on the advertising. To what extent is nature presented as "sublime" or as a backdrop? Use your observations to demonstrate, refute, or complicate the contention that presenting nature as "unproblematic" can have a dangerous effect on our environmental consciousness.

3. Select a single ad that uses nature as a backdrop, and conduct an in-depth analysis of it. As a critical framework, use the six reasons advertising can be "faint green" that Corbett outlines on pages 212–224.

4. Adopting the perspective of Laurence Shames ("The More Factor," p. 76), write an essay in which you argue whether the "faint green" advertising Corbett describes is an expression of the American desire for "more."

5. **CONNECTING TEXTS**   Corbett asserts that "attempts to make advertising fit a green framework simply illustrate how ideologically opposed advertising and environmental values are" (para. 17). In class, form teams and debate this assertion. Use the debate as a jumping-off point for your own essay in which you explore your own response. Teams might also want to consult Michael Pollan's "Supermarket Pastoral" (p. 96).

6. Study advertisements for companies that produce oil, plastics, or chemicals. Do they use nature as a backdrop, as Corbett describes, or is nature presented in a different way? Use your observations to describe and critique the techniques such companies use to present a positive public image. As an alternative, do the same with automobile advertising, focusing on ads for SUVs (you might study a magazine such as *Car and Driver* or consult promotional material on auto companies' Web sites). Or study advertising that promotes alternative-fuel vehicles, such as the Prius, Volt, or Leaf.

3

ON THE AIR
Television and Cultural Forms

Litchfield Is the New Mayberry

Television isn't always television anymore. It's Netflix, and Hulu, and Apple TV, and an ever-growing host of new players who are disrupting the traditional medium for televised entertainment — the "box" — and replacing it with digital alternatives. The effects of this technological revolution go well beyond the transformation of the way we watch "television" because, following in the footsteps of such subscription broadcasters as HBO and Showtime, which don't have to rely on advertising revenue to conduct their business, streaming TV providers are free of many of the restrictions that commercial sponsorship continues to hold over television content. Enjoying less vulnerability to consumer boycotts than their traditional network predecessors, streaming and cable sources alike can dare to go where TV never went before and one of the most striking signifiers of this new freedom, paradoxically enough, can be found in a highly popular Netflix series about a prison.

With programs such as *The L Word* and *The Sopranos* preceding it, *Orange Is the New Black* (based on the memoir of the same name by Piper Kerman) would not appear to be particularly remarkable. With its explicit sexuality — gay and straight — and no-holds-barred story lines, this Netflix blockbuster probably appears to be nothing new to you and, thus, not especially significant. To see its full significance, you need to perform a **semiotic** analysis, complete with the construction of a semiotic **system** of relevant **associations** and **differences**. Since the semiotic analysis of any television series involves the same procedure, we will describe the outlines of such an analysis here, moving subsequently to an analysis of a single episode of *Orange Is the*

229

New Black to help you write your own analyses not only of this program but of any series you choose.

When constructing a semiotic system within which to situate and contextualize a television series, you want to begin by categorizing precisely what kind of show it is. There are dramatic series, sitcoms, soap operas, game shows, unscripted programs (reality TV, or RTV), and so on. Among these broad varieties of programs we find categories such as crime, family, Westerns, professional (including medical, law, and business-based programs), action adventure, relationship (shows like *Girls* and *Sex and the City*), and other types. Thus you can have a dramatic crime series (*CSI*), a family sitcom (*Leave It to Beaver*), a war comedy (*M*A*S*H*), a medical drama (*ER*) and others with a large number of permutations (consider how *The Sopranos* was simultaneously a crime and a family drama).

In recent years, one television genre, the *dramedy*, has been especially popular. Mixing comedy and drama, dramedic hits include *House, M.D.* (a medical dramedy) and *Desperate Housewives* (a dramedic soap opera). *Orange Is the New Black* belongs to this category, as well as to another, relatively rare programming type that could be called the prison program (examples of this genre include HBO's *Oz,* an Australian series called *Wentworth* — a revival of an earlier program called *Prison Block H* that is rather similar to *Orange Is the New Black* — and a British series called *Bad Girls*). As you can see, categorizing a TV program can take a good deal of thought and research. You want to look into the history of the kind of program you are analyzing and see how your chosen series relates to that history. The more completely, and accurately, you can categorize your series, the stronger your analysis will be.

Say, for example, you are analyzing an animated family sitcom like *South Park* or *The Simpsons*. Your system would include such shows as *Father Knows Best, Leave It to Beaver, The Dick Van Dyke Show*, *The Flintstones*, and *Married with Children*. All of these shows can be associated with *South Park* and *The Simpsons*, but there are also some crucial differences. Like *Married with Children*, but unlike all the other shows listed here, *South Park* and *The Simpsons* feature what are commonly called dysfunctional families, just like *Family Guy, Malcolm in the Middle*, and a host of dysfunctional family sitcoms that sprang up in the late 1980s and bourgeoned in the 1990s. The difference between the dysfunctional family sitcoms and the traditional ones points to a profound change in American attitudes toward family life itself. Reflecting an era of high divorce rates, and a growing, often feminist-illuminated, audience resistance to the patriarchal propaganda promulgated in the golden age of family sitcoms during the 1950s and 1960s, the dysfunctional family sitcoms have proven to be an enduring sign of our times.

So, what about *Orange Is the New Black*? There aren't very many American prison-based dramedies to compare it to, but we can still see something of importance through a brief comparison. The heading of this chapter section alludes to one such show: *The Andy Griffith Show*. Situated in Mayberry, an idealized southern village, that program focused on a country sheriff who contends with local criminals and runs the local jail. But, of course, the whole thing never gets much naughtier than a spit-wad fight in an elementary school cafeteria: and that's precisely the point. It's a long stretch from Mayberry to Litchfield, longer in its way than the cultural divide between *Father Knows Best* and *Family Guy*. What grittily realistic prison programming does exist (*Oz* is the best example) is male-based, not female. And *Orange Is the New Black* is, in the main, a woman's show.

For this reason, despite its association with the Australian *Wentworth*, the gender difference that marks *Orange Is the New Black* indicates that we would do well to look beyond the prison genre to the relationship category, programs that explore complex and intimate connections among women.

The resemblance to *The L Word* is immediately apparent in the opening sequence of "The Chickening," the episode of *Orange Is the New Black* that we have chosen to analyze in detail. In the language of movie ratings, it is explicit and involves nudity — essentially, it portrays a lesbian sexual interlude. It's not surprising, then, that the central relationship of the series, which is between Piper and Alex (*not* Piper and Larry), inscribes a connection to *The L Word* as well. And here we find another sign.

Today, it may be hard to see just what a difference it is to find a mainstream American TV series that focuses on lesbian relationships. As late as 1997, when Ellen DeGeneres came out as a lesbian on her ABC series *Ellen*, consumer boycotts of the program's sponsors were threatened; now, when transgender issues have taken center stage of the nation's sexuality-based controversies, that controversy seems almost quaint. Still, Ellen DeGeneres broke ground, and she broke the ice. So, the fact that "The Chickening" (albeit on Netflix, not network TV) could begin with the kind of scene that it does is itself a sign of just how far America has come in matters of human sexuality.

More evidence that *Orange Is the New Black* is more of a relationship or (perhaps more accurately) a sisterhood program — one that goes well beyond the more heterosexually oriented sisterhood series *Sex and the City* — than it is a prison series lies once again in a crucial difference. The traditional prison show focuses on either the innocence of its protagonist (*The Fugitive* is one instance) or the protagonist's attempts to escape (*The Prisoner* is a good example). In contrast, *Orange Is the New Black*'s protagonist is unquestionably guilty, so that is not a concern. Nor, really, is escape a desperate goal for the prisoners. At least in the show's first year, Litchfield is a minimum-security prison with such "country club" amenities as yoga classes and rather verdant grounds into which Piper can take her morning cup of tea and read a book. In fact, the main plot point of "The Chickening" begins with Piper spotting a chicken wandering on the grounds while she sips her tea and enjoys the autumn foliage. Becoming an obvious symbol in the episode, that chicken also becomes a device around which the rather loosely structured story line can be organized.

And that story line raises another element in the system to which *Orange Is the New Black* belongs. Loosely plotted story lines, which continue from episode to episode without any attempt at closure, have become increasingly popular in recent years, forming a system of **postmodern** series from *Twin Peaks* to *The X-Files* to *Lost*. Like *Lost*, *Orange Is the New Black* is filled with flashbacks intended to reveal a little more of the backstories of the ensemble cast, but it never fills in all the blanks at once. To know fully what's going on, the audience must tune in to every episode, but with new twists developing every time around, the story line remains wide open (as in *Desperate Housewives*, which might be called a postmodern soap opera).

So, we might say that *Orange Is the New Black* is a sisterhood-themed postmodern soap opera, breaking old barriers to what can be represented on television and exploring new horizons of human being.

This takes us back to that chicken. Like Herman Melville's novel *Moby-Dick*, "The Chickening" draws explicit attention to the symbolism of an animal, in this case a chicken (one character named Red, who is especially obsessed with it, is even referred to as "Ahab" in the episode) without telling the viewer what that symbolism is. We *are* told the chicken's "story": the women believe that it is the sole survivor of a chicken massacre outside the fence that has come to haunt, as it were, the prison. But beyond this general significance, the inmates offer up a number of particular interpretations. To Red, for example, the chicken is a symbol of power, and she wants to cook and eat it to absorb that power. To the Latina prisoners, it is a symbol of forbidden fruits and money (they think it is filled with $1000 worth of heroin). To the black prisoners, the chicken is a symbol of forbidden sweets (they think it is filled with candy). And to the prison warden (a man who, like most men in the show, is an exemplar of abusive patriarchal authority), the chicken is a myth that stirs up Litchfield's prison population and makes the women more difficult to control.

The episode ends with Piper chasing the chicken through the yard, but just as she seems to have trapped it, the chicken rather magically appears *outside* the prison fence, and the final shot shows Piper *inside* the fence gazing at something she cannot attain for herself. Does this mean that the chicken simply signifies "freedom"? That certainly seems to be one of its meanings, but the differences among the various inmates as to the chicken's significance suggest that the matter is more complicated than that. So, we need to dig a little further.

It *is* significant that the chicken is a hen and not a rooster (at least so the bird appears), for while the women of Litchfield interpret it differently, they share a sense that the chicken represents something desired but out of reach (while the male warden would like to see the whole legend of the chicken suppressed). With its open-ended symbolism, the chicken is thus expressly addressed to a female viewership, symbolizing whatever the viewer most desires but cannot quite attain.

We can now return to the overall significance of *Orange Is the New Black*. Belonging to a system of sisterhood television programs, the series pushes new boundaries of what it means to be a woman and how that can be represented on TV. Far edgier than *Sex and the City* and *Desperate Housewives*, the show escapes from the conventional gender stereotypes that circumscribe these associated programs—in which heterosexual relationships, dieting, and fashion take up so much of the characters' time—to explore dimensions of women's experience that have hitherto been more or less taboo on American television. Ironically, this greater freedom of expression is set within the context of a prison story, which may be the most profound point of all: that only within the confines of a women's prison can a contemporary woman explore who she is.

Writing about Television

We began this chapter with a semiotic analysis of both a television series as a whole and a single episode of it to show how you can look at television programs in the same way that you can look at any cultural phenomenon: as a series of signs, or signifiers, of the society that consumes them. But while you might find writing about television familiar from high school assignments in which you wrote about a favorite program—perhaps in a summary-writing exercise, a descriptive essay, or an opinion piece about what made a particular program your favorite—writing semiotic interpretations of TV shows is a different task. Although you still need to rely on your skills in description and

Enjoy it or not, *Game of Thrones* provides enormous potential for cultural analysis.

summarization in writing semiotic analyses of TV, you should put aside your personal opinions of a show (that is, whether you like it or not) to construct interpretive arguments about its cultural significance.

Television offers an especially rich field of possible writing topics, ranging from a historical analysis of a whole category, or genre, of TV programming, or of a general trend, to an interpretation of a single TV show episode — or all of these topics combined. Whatever approach to television you take, however, you will probably need to do some research. No one can be expected to know about all the TV programs (from both the past and the present) that can be associated with and differentiated from any particular show that you're analyzing, so you should plan to find reliable sources to help you contextualize whatever program you are interpreting.

From Symbols to Icons

When writing about TV, keep in mind that the ubiquity of televised (or digitized) images in our lives represents a shift from one kind of sign system to another. As Marshall McLuhan pointed out over fifty years ago in *The Gutenberg Galaxy* (1962), Western culture since the fifteenth century has defined itself around the printed word — the linear text that reads from left to right and top to bottom. The printed word, in the terminology of the American founder of semiotics, Charles Sanders Peirce, is a **symbolic sign**, one whose meaning is entirely arbitrary or conventional. A symbolic sign means what it does because those who use it have decided so. Words don't look like what they mean. Their significance is entirely abstract.

Not so with a visual **image**, which does resemble its object and is not entirely arbitrary. Although a photograph is not literally the thing it depicts and may reflect a good deal of staging and manipulation by the photographer, we often respond to it as if it were an innocent reflection of the world. Peirce called such signs "icons," using this term to refer to any sign that visually resembles what it means. The way you interpret an **icon**, then, differs from the way you interpret a symbol or word. The interpretation of words involves your cognitive capabilities; the viewing of icons is far more sensuous, more a matter of vision than cognition. The shift from a civilization governed by the paradigm of the book to one dominated by the image accordingly involves a shift in the way we "read" our world, as the symbolic field of the printed page yields to the iconic field of the screen.

The change from a symbolic, or word-centered, world to an iconic universe filled with visual images carries profound cultural implications. For while we *can* read visual images actively and cognitively (which, of course, is the whole point of this book), the sheer visibility of icons tempts us to receive them uncritically and passively. Icons look so much like the realities they refer

---

Discussing the Signs of Television

With your class, choose a current television program, and all watch the same episode (either individually as "homework" or together while you're in class). Interpret the episode semiotically. What values and cultural myths does the show project? What do the commercials broadcast during the show say about its presumed audience? Go beyond the episode's surface appeal or "message" to look at the particular images it uses to tell its story, always asking, "What is this program *really* saying?"

---

to that it's easy to forget that icons, too, are signs: images that people construct to carry **ideological** meanings.

Consider, for example, the image of the American family as presented in the classic situation comedies of the 1950s and 1960s. White, suburban, and middle class, these families signified an American ideal that glorified patriarchal authority. Even *I Love Lucy*, a sitcom showcasing Lucille Ball, reinforced masculine privilege through such plotlines as Lucy's attempt to market her own line of "Vitameatavegamin" dietary supplements, an endeavor which, the show implied, was predestined to end in disaster due to female business incompetence. The advent of such "dysfunctional" family sitcoms as *Married with Children*, which undermined *male* authority and competence, thus signified a profound difference, a rejection of the old patriarchal values.

And Now a Word from Our Sponsors

Whatever show you choose to analyze, remember why it's on TV in the first place: to make money. In the early history of the medium in America, this was accomplished solely through commercial sponsorship. Viewers received free television content, but at the expense not only of having to watch the advertisements that accompanied the show but also in becoming subject to the restrictions that sponsors could influence over that content. Always on the alert for possible audience objection to controversial topics, TV's commercial sponsors have placed quite a number of limits on what can, and can't, be aired on television programming.

Network TV still has these limitations, but with the advent of cable and streaming television media that are paid for by consumer subscription, a

---

Exploring the Signs of Television: Viewing Habits

In your journal, explore your television-viewing habits and how the way you have watched TV has changed over time. When and why do you usually watch television? Have you transitioned from watching shows with your family or friends to watching them alone on a computer? Do you watch shows when they are broadcast, or do you watch them via Netflix, Hulu, or DVR on your own time? Do you think of watching television as a social activity? If so, write about how the diverse technical options for watching television have complicated this notion. If not, what place does watching television occupy in your life?

---

lot of the barriers have come down. Leading the way into ever more daring programming with *The Sopranos*, HBO, for example, not only continues to push the boundaries of allowable sexual and violent content but has also stimulated such later content providers as Netflix, whose hit series, *Orange Is the New Black* (with which we began this chapter by analyzing) seems to be competing with HBO to see just where the limits may (or may not) lie. We've come a long way since Ricky and Lucy slept in separate beds, sheathed from neck to toe in conservative pajamas so no potential product consumers would be offended by the sight of a married couple in bed together.

Still, the majority of viewers watch commercially sponsored programs, and the advertising that accompanies such programs can provide a good deal of useful information as to who their intended audiences may be. Why is the nightly news often sponsored by over-the-counter painkillers, for example? Why is daytime TV, especially in the morning, typically accompanied by ads for vocational training schools? Why are youth-oriented prime-time shows filled with fast-food commercials, while family programs have a lot of car ads?

Your analysis of a single episode of a television program can also usefully include a survey of where the show fits in what cultural studies pioneer Raymond Williams called the "flow" of an evening's TV schedule. Flow refers to the sequence of TV programs and advertisements, from, say, the 5:00 news, through the pre-prime-time 7:00 to 8:00 slot, through prime time and on through to the 11:00 news and the late-night talk shows. What precedes your program? What follows? Can you determine the strategy behind your show's scheduling?

Reality Bites

With the full return of scripted television — a veritable renaissance of creativity that has seen TV eclipse film as a source of high-art popular culture — reality TV has lost some of its luster in recent years, but it still generates a lot of programming, and its special stars — from the Kardashian/Jenner clan to the Robertsons to *The Apprentice* host who went on to win the presidential election in 2016 — continue to loom large over the cultural landscape. But its significance has changed over the years, and it accordingly merits a brief look here, beginning with an overview of its history.

One might say that reality television began in 1948 with Allen Funt's *Candid Camera*, which featured the filming of real people (who didn't know they were on camera) as they reacted to annoying situations concocted by the show's creators. The show's attraction lay in the humor viewers could enjoy by watching other people get into minor jams. There is a name for this kind of humor that comes from psychoanalytic theory: schadenfreude, or taking pleasure in the misfortunes of others, as when we laugh at someone slipping on a banana peel. And we shall see that this appeal from the early days of reality TV is very much a part of the genre's popularity today.

After *Candid Camera* came the 1970s PBS series *An American Family*. In this program, a camera crew moved in with a suburban family named the Louds and filmed them in their day-to-day lives. The Louds were not contestants and there were no prizes to be won. The program was conceived as an experiment in cinema verité to see if it was possible for television to be authentically realistic. The experiment was a bit of a failure, however, as the Loud family members began to act out for the camera. The result was the eventual dissolution of the Louds as a family unit and a general uneasiness about such experiments.

The next and probably most crucial step was when MTV launched *The Real World* in 1992. Like *An American Family*, *The Real World* (and similar programs like *Big Brother*) attempts to be realistic, with its constant camera recording a group of people living in the same house. Unlike *An American Family*, however, *The Real World* is a fantasy that caters to young-adult viewers, who can imagine themselves living in glamorous circumstances and vicariously enjoy the experience of becoming instant TV stars. That there is a certain tampering with reality in *The Real World*, a deliberate selection of participants based upon their appearance and how they can be cast into often-contrived romances as well as conflicts, constitutes a contradiction that differentiates *The Real World* from *An American Family* and leads us to the dawning of the reality revolution.

The astounding success of the inaugural versions of *Who Wants to Marry a Multi-Millionaire?* and *Survivor* established reality TV's full coming-of-age. In both programs, we can see strong traces of what made their pioneering predecessors popular. But through their introduction of a game show element, complete with contestants competing for huge cash prizes, a whole new dimension was added with new layers of significance in an even more **over-determined** fashion. Reality programs that include a game show dimension offer their viewers the vicarious chance to imagine themselves as being in the shoes of the contestants (after all, in principle, anyone can get on a game show) and winning lots of money. There's an element of schadenfreude here as well, if viewers take pleasure in watching the losers in game show competitions. But by adding the real-life element of marriage to the mix, *Who Wants to Marry a Multi-Millionaire?* (and its descendants) brought an extra dimension of humiliation, not to mention voyeurism, to the genre. It's one thing to be caught on camera during the emotional upheaval of competing for large cash prizes, but it's quite another to be in an erotic competition, and lose, with millions watching you.

While game shows usually feature some sort of competition among the contestants, the *Survivor* series took such competition to a new level by compelling its contestants to engage in backstabbing conspiracies as they clawed their way to the top. (The 2006 season even introduced an element of racial conflict by forming tribes according to race.) It isn't enough for tribe to compete against tribe; there has to be intratribal backbiting and betrayal as well. Such a subtext constitutes a kind of grotesque parody of American capitalism itself, in which the cutthroat competition of the workplace is moved to the wilderness.

A lot of RTV still exists to evoke a kind of freak show appeal (shows like *Jersey Shore, Here Comes Honey Boo Boo, My Super Sweet 16,* and the on-again-off-again-on-again *Toddlers and Tiaras*), inviting its viewers to sneer at its central figures, but a good deal of RTV today expresses the values and desires of its highly segmented audiences, not its hostilities. From *Duck Dynasty*, which appealed to rural — and generally conservative — Americans, to *Dancing with the Stars* and various other talent show–themed programs that, in the tradition of *American Idol,* address a host of **mass cultural** fantasies, RTV often presents its audiences with visions of their versions of an ideal life. Even working-class Americans have found truck drivers (*Ice Road Truckers*) and commercial fishing crews (*Deadliest Catch*) to identify with, and home owners and home buyers can choose from a plethora of do-it-yourself programs to help them purchase and maintain their houses.

In this respect, then, we can see how RTV has followed an evolutionary path that is quite similar to that of digital technology, because whether we get our content from a TV set or a computer, RTV enables us to customize our viewing down to the most granular details of our lifestyles and values. The medium that once pulled America together, if only by compelling everyone to watch the same limited programming on the same limited number of networks, is now, paradoxically enough, helping to pull things asunder as the multitudinous choices of network, cable, and digital TV draw us ever further into our own self-mirroring echo chambers wherein we may find only

---

Reading about TV Online

The Internet has given rise to a number of popular sites for TV criticism and community discussion, including tvworthwatching.com. Using a search engine, find a forum devoted to your favorite TV show and take notes on how the community of fans interacts. What about the show you've chosen most interests fans? What topics are most popular or most contested? Does the conversation stick to television, or does it veer into discussions of users' personal lives? Are you drawn to participate? Using the forum as a microcosm, reflect on how television might be considered a social adhesive. How do the fans of TV shows use the Internet to bond over the show and with one another?

---

our own realities. And it is within such an environment that we may find yet another explanation for a country that appears to be coming apart at the seams.

The Readings

We begin this chapter's readings with an essay by Neal Gabler suggesting that having contributed to the atomization of American society, "TV has learned how to compensate for the increasing alienation it seems to induce" by filling its schedule with shows saturated with inauthentic "flocks" of friends and family relationships. A paired set of readings by Anna Keszeg and Claire Miye Stanford on women's television follows, with Keszeg situating *Girls* in a system that includes *Sex and the City* while exploring the semiotics of the characters' fashion choices and Stanford analyzing the feminist dimensions of ABC's *Nashville*. John Sherman's review of *The Outs* celebrates the show's refusal to focus on gay characters *just* because they are gay, while Olivia Goldhill explores the televisual worldview of Trump nation. Nick Serpe's trenchant analysis of such reality TV shows as *Repo Games*, *Pawn Stars*, and *Storage Wars* is next, revealing the depths to which RTV will go in a bad economy to maintain profits. Emily Nussbaum then takes us to Westeros, the setting for a "sophisticated cable drama about a patriarchal subculture." Massimo Pigliucci steps up to the lectern with a philosophical analysis of *The Big Bang Theory*'s ongoing critique of scientism, which is as accessible as the series he analyzes, and Clara McNulty-Finn closes the chapter with a survey of the social mediated evolution of rap/hip-hop from the 1990s into the second decade of the new millennium.

NEAL GABLER
The Social Networks

Remember *Friends*, that sprightly comedy in which no one ever seemed to be alone? Or *Sex and the City*, wherein busy Manhattan professional women always seemed to have time to share a glass of water and some lettuce? Indeed, even today, wherever you look on television, Neal Gabler notes in this essay that originally appeared in the *Los Angeles Times*, you are certain to see "lots of folks spending the better part of their day surrounded by their friends and family in happy conviviality." Yet oddly enough, this sort of programming is appearing "at a time when it is increasingly difficult to find this kind of deep social interaction anyplace but on TV." Clearly, Gabler suggests, television is providing some sort of compensation for the social atomization that it itself has contributed to, and thus, all the simulated conviviality, while being a pleasant "dream," is "pure wish fulfillment," indeed, rather "phony," and, perhaps, sad. Neal Gabler is a well-known analyst and historian of American cinema and popular culture.

With the new television season upon us, here are a few things you are virtually certain to see again and again and again: lots of folks spending the better part of their day surrounded by their friends and family in happy conviviality; folks wandering into the unlocked apartments and homes of friends, family, and neighbors at any time of the day or night as if this were the most natural thing in the world; friends and family sitting down and having lots of tearful heart-to-hearts; Little League games, school assemblies, and dance recitals, all attended by, you guessed it, scads of friends and family.

You're going to be seeing these scenes repeatedly because the basic unit of television is not the lone individual or the partnership or even the nuclear family. The basic unit of television is the flock — be it the extended family of brothers and sisters, grandfathers and grandmothers, nieces, nephews, and cousins, or the extended circle of friends, and, rest assured, it is always a circle. On television friends never come in pairs; they invariably congregate in groups of three or more.

That television has become quite possibly the primary purveyor in American life of friendship and of the extended family is no recent blip. Over the last twenty years, beginning with *Seinfeld* and moving on through *Friends*, *Sex and the City,* and more recently to *Desperate Housewives*, *Glee*, *The Big Bang Theory*, *How I Met Your Mother*, *Cougartown*, and at least a half-dozen other shows, including this season's newbies *Raising Hope* and *Better with You*, television has become a kind of friendship machine dispensing groups of people in constant and intimate contact with one another, sitting around in living rooms, restaurants, and coffee shops, sharing everything all the time. You might even say that friendship has become the basic theme of television, certainly of broadcast television, though cable has its own friendship orgies like *Men of a Certain Age*, *My Boys*, and *It's Always Sunny in Philadelphia*. Friendship is what television is about.

What makes this so remarkable is that it has been happening at a time when it is increasingly difficult to find this kind of deep social interaction anyplace but on TV. Nearly a decade ago, Harvard professor Robert Putnam observed in his classic *Bowling Alone* that Americans had become more and more disconnected from one another and from their society. As Putnam put it, "For the first two-thirds of the twentieth century a powerful tide bore Americans into ever deeper engagement in the life of their communities, but a few decades ago — silently, without warning — that tide reversed and we were overtaken by a treacherous current." It was a current that pulled Americans apart.

Moreover, the current that Putnam observed has, according to more   5 recent studies, only intensified in the last decade. One study found that Americans had one-third fewer nonfamily confidants than they had twenty years earlier, and 25 percent had no one in whom to confide whatsoever. Another study of 3,000 Americans found that on average they had only four close social contacts, but these included family members like one's own spouse. This decline in real friendships may account in part for the dramatic rise of virtual friendships like those on social-networking sites where being "friended" is less a sign of personal engagement than a quantitative measure of how many people your life has brushed and how many names you can collect, but this is friendship lite. Facebook, in fact, only underscores how much traditional friendship — friendship in which you meet, talk, and share — has become an anachronism and how much being "friended" is an ironic term.

Among the reasons Putnam cited for the increasing atomization in American life were economic pressures and anxieties; women entering the workplace in full-time employment by necessity and thus disengaging from their friends and neighbors; metropolitan sprawl, which meant more time spent commuting, greater social segregation, and the disruption of community boundaries; and last but by no means least, the rise of television itself, especially its splintering influence on later generations who have grown up addicted to the tube. It is no secret that watching television is not exactly a communal activity. Rather, we often use it to fill a communal void. But instead of bringing comfort, it seems only to remind us of our alienation. In Putnam's view, based on several studies, "TV is apparently especially attractive for people who feel unhappy, particularly when there is nothing else to do."

It's not that we prefer television to human contact. The laugh track attests that most people don't really want to be alone in front of their TV sets. They want to be part of a larger community. Yet another study indicates that TV provides a sort of simulacrum of community because the relationship between the TV viewer and the people he or she watches on the screen competes with and even substitutes for physical encounters with real people. It is Facebook with hundreds of "friends" but without any actual contact with any of them, only the virtual contact of watching.

But what none of these theories of television has noticed is that TV has learned how to compensate for the increasing alienation it seems to induce. And it compensates not by letting us kill time with "friends" on-screen but by providing us with those nonstop fantasies of friendship, which clearly give us a vicarious pleasure. Watch *Seinfeld* or *Friends* or *Sex and the City* or *Community* or *Men of a Certain Age* — the list is endless — and you'll see people who not only are never ever alone but people whose relationships are basically smooth, painless, uninhibited and deeply, deeply intimate — the kind of friendships we may have had in college but that most of us can only dream about now. How many adults do you know who manage to hang out with their friends every single day for hour after hour?

Or watch the incomparable *Modern Family* or *Brothers and Sisters* or *Parenthood* and you'll see big, happy family gatherings with lots of bonhomie and jokes and an outpouring of love. On the last there seems to be a huge extended family dinner every other night where most families would be lucky to have one such get-together each year at Thanksgiving. And don't forget those school assemblies, already mentioned, which everyone in the family takes off work to attend en masse or the weekend birthday parties where attendance is also compulsory.

One feels a little churlish pointing out how phony most of this intimacy is.   10
After all, these shows, even one as observant as *Modern Family*, aren't about realism. They aren't about the genuine emotional underpinnings of friendship or family, and they certainly aren't about the rough course that almost every relationship, be it with a friend or family member, takes — the inevitable squabbles, the sometimes long and even permanent ruptures, the obtuseness, the selfishness, the reprioritization, the expectations of reciprocity, the drifting apart, the agonizing sense of loneliness even within the flock. These shows are pure wish fulfillment. They offer us friends and family at one's beck and call but without any of the hassles. It is friendship as we want it to be.

For the fact is that we miss the friendships we no longer have, and we know that Facebook or e-mails cannot possibly compensate for the loss. So we sit in front of our television sets and enjoy the dream of friendship instead: a dream where we need never be alone, where there are a group of people who would do anything for us, and where everyone seems to understand us to our very core, just like Jerry and George, Chandler and Joey, Carrie and her girls, or the members of the McKinley High glee club. It is a powerful dream, and it is one that may now be the primary pleasure of television.

READING THE TEXT

1. Summarize in your own words what Gabler means by saying, "The basic unit of television is the flock" (para. 2).

2. How does Robert Putnam's research on friendship in America inform Gabler's argument?

3. Why does Gabler say that "being 'friended' is an ironic term" (para. 5)?

4. How does Gabler use concession to strengthen his argument?

5. In your own words, explain what Gabler means by "simulacrum of community" (para. 7)?

READING THE SIGNS

1. Write an argumentative essay in which you assess the validity of Gabler's claim that "instead of bringing comfort, [television] seems only to remind us of our alienation" (para. 6). To support your argument, you might interview friends or acquaintances about their reasons for watching television.

2. In an essay, analyze an episode of one of the friend-heavy TV programs that Gabler mentions, such as *The Big Bang Theory*, *Glee*, or *Modern Family*. To what extent does it confirm Gabler's assertion that "these shows are pure wish fulfillment" (para. 10)?

3. Write an essay in which you support, oppose, or complicate Gabler's belief that Facebook offers "friendship lite" (para. 5). To develop your ideas, read "Students Addicted to Social Media" (p. 382).

4. **CONNECTING TEXTS**   Adopting Gabler's perspective, analyze the friendships and interpersonal relations depicted in Lena Dunham's *Girls*. To what extent do they replicate or deviate from the ones represented in the shows Gabler discusses? How do you think Gabler would explain any differences you see among these TV shows? To develop your ideas, read Anna Keszeg's "What Their Clothes Tell Us about Those Girls" (below).

SIGNIFYING WOMEN ON TV

ANNA KESZEG
What Their Clothes Tell Us about Those Girls

Do clothes make the Girl? Not quite, Anna Keszeg suggests in this philosophical analysis of the sartorial significance of the fashion choices of the protagonists of *Girls*, TV's millennialist answer to *Sex and the City*. For while that earlier series about four adult women in New York does reflect the ways in which "the biological and social functions of dress play a decisive role" in a woman's life, the "sophomoric" logic expressed by the fashion choices of the "twenty-something teenagers" in *Girls* is far more equivocal. Still experimenting with their lives, these young women are playing with conventional fashion codes, not conforming to them, and the result is a lot of "equivocation" and confusion. Anna Keszeg is a lecturer in the Department of Communication, Public Relations, and Advertising at Babe-Bolyai University in Romania.

According to Dr. Michael Carter, noted historian of clothing, fashion theory begins with nineteenth-century Scottish philospher Thomas Carlyle's novel about the philosophy of clothing, *Sartor Resartus* ('The Tailor Retailored'). In a fashion (pun intended) similar to Carlyle's, TV shows can use clothes as metaphors of individual personalities and their ways of thinking.

The Foursome of Romantic Sitcoms

Before there was *Girls*, there was *Sex and the City*, which utilized a similar format: offer four perspectives on fashion and dress to exemplify four distinct clothing philosophies of urban culture.

In the making of the first *Sex and the City* movie, stylist Patricia Field explains the clothing culture of each character: the fashionable uptown chic of Carrie, the sexually explicit and dirty chic of Samantha, the sweet preppy style of Charlotte, and the androgynous career gal look of Miranda.

While the stylist sees all those fashion habits in terms of brands, designers, and accessories, let's accept the challenge to define them in terms of fashion theories. And I'll keep with simple associations: I'll use Roland Barthes for Carrie, Thomas Carlyle for Samantha, Herbert Spencer for Charlotte, Thorstein Veblen and Georg Simmel for Miranda.

Roland Barthes spoke about the fashion system as a set of signs and 5 meanings connected to all clothing habits similar to a language capable of expressing facts and meanings about the whole world. Thomas Carlyle uses the clothing metaphor to describe the moral depravity of humanity. Herbert Spencer considers that there is an end to fashion evolution in the principle of equity and reason. Thorstein Veblen and Georg Simmel defend the classic sociological view that dress expresses achieved or idealized social status or belonging.

The fashion system of Barthes applies to Carrie because there is meaning in each of her outfits: they are like academic texts full of invisible footnotes referring to collections, fashion anecdotes, codified information and professional savoir-faire. For Samantha, Miranda, and Charlotte the classic sociological and contextual fashion theories are inter-connectivity operative: the sexually explicit dress of Samantha is the other side of Charlotte's moderate womanhood in the Protestant tradition of classic elegance. And in the case of Miranda the theorists of trickle-down clothing well express her professionalism.

In those three cases the biological and social functions of dress play a decisive role. In non-professional settings, people use clothing to identify with a particular group or subculture. Doing so legitimizes even shocking or freaky choices, while assuring an easiness of self-expression. There are only two problems with the appropriation of fashion in this way: its cost, and the difficulty of choosing a well-developed wardrobe. Even if it's expensive and difficult to organize and understand, fashion is a very reassuring factor in the life of *Sex and the City*'s protagonists and the well-being of characters is related to their success in managing to be always well-dressed. The fashion system is good as it is.

Same Sign of Four?

It's easy to see the four main characters of *Sex and the City* as two-dimensional stereotypes (or fashion archetypes), but doing so is not so easy with the four main characters of *Girls*. This is so in part because the characters bear problematic relations to the protagonists of the older sitcom. When Jessa moves to Shoshanna in the pilot of the series, there is a *Sex and the City* poster on the wall (Shosh is a huge *Sex and the City* fan: "seeing *Sex and the City* is a necessity like being on Facebook.")

Jessa had never seen an episode of the series and Shosh — in her usual never-caring-about-the-other's-answer-style — gives her account of how the four "girls" relate to their *Sex and the City* counterparts. She states, "You're funny because you're definitely like a Carrie with Samantha aspects and Charlotte's hair. It's like a very good combination. I think I'm definitely a Carrie at heart, but like sometimes. . . . sometimes Samantha kind of comes out, and then when I'm at school I try to put on my Miranda-hat." Shoshanna is the least intellectual of the four girls, and as such is the only one who would define herself in terms of *Sex and the City*. The other "girls" have more complicated relations to the fashion system.

The cast of *Girls*.

Unlike *Sex and the City*, *Girls* is not a series about gender roles and women's biographies, it's more about growing up and experiencing adulthood. And even with an emphasis on the female characters, the sitcom is working on the ethos of *the* or *a* generation and not on the symbolic values of big city womanhood. The clothing culture has to be rethought in the frame of adult self-definition and of new models of consumption: Jessa exemplifies desires from sensual pleasure and immediate gratification. Marnie exemplifies a struggle to grow up, and is often out of control. Shoshanna, by contrast, is largely in control — she's focused on her education, and is ambitious. Hannah exemplifies the radical otherness of her own life-experience. (She tells her parents while asking for their financial support: "I don't want to freak you out but I think I may be the voice of my generation." After seeing their underwhelmed faces, she changes it to "*A* voice of *a* generation.")

In *Sartor Resartus*, Thomas Carlyle tells us that the dress of the western culture makes visible the differences between the natural order of things and the non-natural human existence. These differences constitute a main feature of his pessimistic and morally condemning views on fashion. For some, this attitude fell into disfavor around the middle of the twentieth century. At that time, dress culture, in many ways, became about the adequate relation between the natural order of personality and non-natural order of society.

For the characters in *Sex and the City*, being a single woman in New York is uneasy; there are problems with the social roles of women. For the characters on *Girls*, the focus is on the difficulty of the complications associated with being an adult. Somehow grown-up roles become unnatural and it is difficult to become content. Let's say, then, that all the patterns of the relation to dress proposed by former clothing philosophies (fashion as social status, fashion as expression of sexual power, fashion as expression of individuality and fashion as symbolic system) have to be damaged. Let's look to new models to illustrate the fashion statements of our four "girls."

The Girls' Fashions

In the *Seinfeld* episode, "The Jacket," Kramer says to Jerry upon seeing Jerry's new suede jacket: "That's more you than you've ever been."

Marnie has never made a wrong fashion choice: she has the perfect break-up-with-Charlie outfit (think of something along the lines of Carrie's post-wedding-break-up wardrobe here), she has perfect dinner outfits, she has perfect day-at-the-beach wear, and perfect doing-something-morally-dubious outfits. Marnie's clothes are in perfect harmony with her desired social status, and she believes that the perfect dresses will perfectly show one's status and personality ("Jessa, I put you in the lighthouse because it's bohemian.")

It's a fashion world without failure. Her fashion territory is that of pure social representation.

And while Marnie (in her own mind) is the perfect "cool person" with whom other "cool people" can't wait to work, nothing in her life matches with that conception of coolness: no cool working place, no cool boyfriend, and she loses contact even with her best friends. We see the social system of clothes in complete freefall — at least for the time being, Marnie's fashion choices are out of sync with who she really is.   15

For Jessa, fashion is the art of self-expression. Specifically, she's expressing her life as a heroin addict. She adopts the very European style tradition of an Yves Saint-Laurent. She asserts, "Down with the Ritz — long live the street." Jessa's attitude smacks (pun intended) of the struggling of western civilization with its outcast others: non-western cultures, tribes, peasants, and the working class. (While traveling to Marnie's weekend house, Jessa insists on sitting in the back of the bus for "political reasons.") And, as in the case of the sixties-seventies trickle-up fashion revolutions, a bohemian-guilty feeling will always be part of her ensemble.

Jasper, Jessa's rehab-connection, uses the "people like us" term for describing themselves, and that strong conscience of undeniable otherness is the main feature of Jessa's fashion choices. Everything is classy because she is the one who wears it — Jessa has confidence. (Even when donning a geisha-dress with big floral print mixed up with UGGs.)

As for the bubbly Shoshanna, there is a Krameresque side of her fashion-comportment. What William Irwin said of Kramer — the "K man" — that he is "par excellence the aesthetic stage of Kierkegaardian human existence," works for Shoshanna Shapiro too. What she finds interesting and pleasurable is constantly changing, and what's even more: without any consequence. Equivocation is always the answer! Even if it's always something tricky in her choices, she manages keeping them up by negating them. All dressing issues are like her famous equivocations, Shosh states, "I think it's time to unchoose some of those choices." And in that girly pink room there is space for very elaborate fashion decisions, later asserting, "I feel like my bandana collection is like my most developed collection." Oh, Em. Effing. Gee. It's like bandana is the new shoe.

Negating Fashion in the Terrible Twos

Finally we arrive at Hannah. As one might expect, things are getting more complicated with her. Her narrative voice always keeps changing because Hannah is, in her own words, "busy with trying to become who she is." We might need a little help here. And we'll seek it again from Jerry Seinfeld. Again, quoting the episode "The Jacket," in his opening comedy routine monologue, Jerry says, "I hate clothes, okay? I hate buying them. I hate picking them out of my closet. I can't stand every day trying to come up with little outfits for myself. I think eventually fashion won't even exist. It won't. I think eventually we'll all be wearing the same thing. 'Cause anytime I see a movie or a TV show where there's people from the future or another planet, they're all wearing the same thing. Somehow they decided, 'This is going to be our outfit. One-piece silver jumpsuit, V-stripe, and boots. That's it.'" Jerry's attitudes on clothing fit Hannah to a tee (pun intended).

In the eighth episode of the first season of *Girls* ("Weirdos Need Girlfriends Too") we encounter an iconic pair of pyjamas: a cream one-piece sleeper with buttons on the front for boys and girls equally. Hannah seems pretty comfortable in it; she even leaves the house with them on (this appears to be a subtle allusion to the many pyjama-on-the-streets-scenes from *Sex and the City*). There's truly something symptomatic about those pyjamas: it's a form of dress beyond the standard consumption circle. It represents efforts to rethink the whole system of fashion. The procedure of inventing it is completely childish, anarchic and radical: clothing needs only one feature to be validated and this is its functionality. Those pyjamas are the complete negation of the fashion industry — as a child would negate its existence. Because it's too hard to pick clothes out of the closet, it's too hard to fill the closet, it's too hard even going shopping.

Adam invented what Jerry dreamed about — what I call a "sophomoric dress." It's a clothing piece which reinvents the whole set of attitudes toward clothing and fashion: the social status is unimportant, the age, the gender and the individuality equally, but there are so many benefits that come with it that those losses are worth it: you can get fat in it, you can sleep in it, it's colorless and it doesn't even require boots.

But inventing that uniform doesn't annihilate all clothing. They need to be reinvented in that sophomoric frame. For Hannah there's not even one piece of proper clothing, which is obvious. Somehow she decided that she has a whole range of dresses and accessories created by the fashion system that she uses as a fashion-illiterate; she hasn't a clue about the meaning of dress and the rules of using it. So she has to start from the beginning: she picks up every single piece of clothing and walks around in it like the first human who had worn it. And there's always something wrong with her appearance. As Jessa puts it to Marnie, "have you ever noticed when she gets dressed up and she puts on a good dress and nice shoes and she does her lipstick and then she leaves her forehead shiny? It's like you came so far, wash your forehead."

During the whole series Hannah never speaks about her fashion choices: it's as if her entire clothing system has an inner evaluation principle, which avoids critics (or attempts to do so). And here we see a connection with Elaine Benes of *Seinfeld*, who is an excellent mate for the three boys of the *Seinfeld* series until her fashion choices come to light. In the episode "The Shoes," the Botticelli shoes of Elaine become the main source of drama. Elaine apparently doesn't like it when anyone talks about her shoes, nor does she like to think about them. But when she's forced to give them away, she decides to lose them instead. It's the same with Hannah: even totally neglecting the fashion system (she seems to work very hard on doing so), she still has a huge wardrobe and spends a lot of time preparing her manicure and inventing interesting patterns and combinations. The complete negation and the intense involvement are equally strong components of her attitude toward fashion. There is a kind of ambiguity in her attitude.

This ambiguity is the basis of the sophomoric attitude: smart and wise, and foolish and dull, all at the same time. And what that attitude has gained over time from its invention in the Judd Apatow movies and in *Seinfeld,* is the extraordinary self-confidence of the characters who adopt it. We can call this "the perseverance of the sophomoric." If in *Seinfeld* and in most of Apatow's movies it was explicit but presented only like an exception, in *Girls* it's a whole bunch of folks who are alike, a whole sophomoric society. This is why they have to come up with a new fashion system, emotional theory, social hierarchy, and dating habits. The sophomoric logic is that of Shoshanna's failed argumentation. It's the logic of equivocation.

But how can we apply the rules of critical thinking—formal and informal logical fallacies—to a dress? Jenn Rogien, costume designer, provides the basis. Let's take the famous example of her favorite costume joke of the series: Hannah's *GQ* colleague Joe wears, during Hannah's first work day, the same shirt as Hannah wore during one of Season One's group portraits. This is what we could call a wardrobe equivocation. *Girls* logic is all about that transformational attitude: you heard a story and you heard it like many times with little differences and then you make it work for you—pick a sense that only works for you (or for an unrepresentative minority) and use it like it's a universal given. Like Jenni Konner, writer and producer on *Girls*, does it even on Twitter, "I am in Tokyo and almost everyone is Shoshanna." 25

Twenty-Something Teenagers

Rousseau and nineteenth-century educational philosophy enjoyed a childish innocence. As for us, we decided to fall for teenagers. Because their seriousness about their innocence is so much more interesting. With *Girls* we have the whole culture and the whole world reinvented by the teenage attitude of those twenty-six-year-old adults.

It has been said that the conflicts of the second half of the twentieth century were gender-based, and the first epoch of the emerging twenty-first century are based on generational differences. In his 1923 essay *The Problem of Generations*, Karl Mannheim defined the generations as "important agents of social change." *Girls* nicely exemplifies that phenomenon. As dresses have to be reinvented, filled with content and appropriated, so do adult life histories. It's always difficult to think about *Girls*, because each affirmation is somehow part of an uneasy adulthood that lies at the heart of each protagonist's problems.

As radical feminists often hold, only a woman can speak in the name of and about womanhood. Similarly, for the sophomoric generation only the sophomoric perspective works. And this perspective is based on the main logical structure of the show: the equivocation, a form of logical fallacy that involves interchanging those definitions. It's the same in the case of Kaspar Hauser, who was a cultural curiosity in the nineteenth century because of his innate method of logical thinking. And if his arguments were used to rethink the academic logic of his epoch, Hannah Horvath is our Kaspar Hauser who keeps on developing her equivocations.

Consider some exemplary moments from the series, which bring to light this logic of equivocation. Shoshanna states, "Basically it's been a very sexually adventurous time for me. I'm alternating nights of freedom with nights of academic focus. So at the end of my senior year I will have had both experiences while also still being super-well-prepared for the professional world."

Hannah seemingly goes through periods or phases in which self-contained   30
psychological episodes play out. She had her period of mental illness, she had periods of crisis and depression, and she's experienced professional burnout, all while she's in her first serious relationship and experiencing her first serious job.

And, finally, we have Adam who is wise and advises the others. "You might just need to face up to the fact that you're just not meant for a job in the traditional sense." Later he states, "Holding on to toxic relationships keeps us from growing." Hannah sums up Adam as follows, "I'd say in some ways he's the most mature person I've ever met and in other ways he's not yet been born." And if Adam's sentences make sense, we have all the necessary elements for the correct interpretation of his statements: we just have to laugh at his actions.

This is what *Girls* is putting clearly in front of us: there has to be a lot of equivocation behind social conventions, if it's so easy to misinterpret them. Their sophomoric attitude to life and culture is so comfortable to watch, because after all — like Jessa — we don't like women telling other women what to do, or how to do it, or when to do it. Nor do we like anybody to tell us these things. What about wardrobe and fashion issues? All of our clothes are finally back in business.

READING THE TEXT

1. In your own words, summarize how the "fashion theories" of Roland Barthes, Thomas Carlyle, Herbert Spencer, Thorstein Veblen, and Georg Simmel match the personalities of the four lead characters in *Sex and the City*.

2. According to Keszeg, how do the four lead characters in *Girls* differ from those in *Sex and the City*?

3. What fashion metaphors apply to *Girls*'s four main characters, in Keszeg's view?

4. What does Keszeg mean by the term "sophomoric dress" (para. 21) and how does it apply to Hannah?

5. Why does Keszeg call the clothing choices of the *Girls* characters "equivocal"?

READING THE SIGNS

1. In your journal, write a semiotic analysis of your own clothing choices, especially as they relate to gender. What sartorial signs do you typically wear, and for what occasions? Are there any clothing choices you refuse to sport, and if so, why? Overall, what messages does your wardrobe send about your personality and ways of thinking?

2. In class, brainstorm a list of women-centered TV programs, ones that are part of the same semiotic system as *Girls*. In your own essay, use Keszeg's essay as an interpretive model and write an analysis of the metaphorical significance of clothing in one or two of these programs. Be sure to discuss how the shows you focus on either resemble or differ from others in the system.

3. **CONNECTING TEXTS**   Taking a lead from Keszeg's discussion of clothing choices in *Girls*, write an analysis of how fashion works as a metaphor in a male-focused TV show. How do you account for any differences in the significances you see in your male-focused program? To develop your ideas, consult Aaron Devor, "Gender Role Behaviors and Attitudes" (p. 474).

4. Although the clothing choices in a prison series like *Orange Is the New Black* are obviously limited, both the show's name and flashback scenes involve careful choices of clothing. Write an essay in which you analyze the semiotics of clothing in *Orange Is the New Black*. To develop your ideas, consult the Introduction to this chapter.

SIGNIFYING WOMEN ON TV

CLAIRE MIYE STANFORD

You've Got the Wrong Song: Nashville *and Country Music Feminism*

Ever since Tammy Wynette counseled women to "Stand By Your Man," no matter what abuse he dishes out, country music has hardly been noteworthy for its feminist spirit. Such a background makes the country music–themed series *Nashville* all the more remarkable, Claire Miye Stanford argues in her review of the program, which she regards as "one of the most feminist television shows on television." In fact, for Stanford, *Nashville* resists simple political categorization and instead mixes femininity and feminism in the Dolly Parton tradition. Claire Miye Stanford is a freelance writer who has written for *The Millions*, *The Rumpus*, *Good*, and the *Los Angeles Review of Books*, in which this reading first appeared.

Both femininity and feminism have become harder and harder to define in 2013. In regard to the first, there are as many examples of femininity in the world as there are people (not just biological women) who embody them. As for the second, the term "feminism" is now so loaded with meaning, confusion, and incorrect associations that it has become all too common, especially among young women, to disavow the term entirely.

Into this complex terminology, enter Rayna James (Connie Britton) and Juliette Barnes (Hayden Panettiere), the lead characters of ABC's *Nashville*, created by former Nashville resident Callie Khouri. Khouri is a film veteran who wrote 1991's *Thelma & Louise*, a feminist classic that also won her the Academy Award for best original screenplay (typically a heavily male-dominated category). In its first season, the show has explored what it means to be both feminine and feminist in the world of country music and television.

Ultimately, any female-driven television show has to contend with these two concepts — whether that treatment is overt or more indirect, if only because every female-driven show will ultimately contend with the characters' love lives and how they interact with men (since their romantic interests are, almost always, male). But what stands out about *Nashville*, among all female-driven television shows, is that it places these omnipresent questions in unique contexts: professional, rather than personal, in the frame of a highly gendered genre, industry, city, and region.

But can a show that is so ostensibly interested in the "feminine" — in sexual and romantic relationships, in motherhood and daughterhood, in short skirts and spangly tops and big hair — also be feminist? That same question has been asked time and time again about country music itself, long considered a bastion of heteronormative, gendered songs about pick-up trucks. Historically, most feminist ire lands squarely on the shoulders of country music legend Tammy Wynette, and her biggest hit, 1968's "Stand By Your Man," in which Wynette advises the listener to forgive your man and, for that matter, to be "proud" of him, even when he's off having "good times / doing things that you don't understand." Whether these things that "you don't understand" are cheating, boozing, gambling, or other unsavory activities is not entirely clear, but still, Wynette counsels the listener to stand by him "'cause after all he's just a man"; in other words, he can't help it, it's in his Man Nature to mistreat you.

There are countless other songs, less famous than Wynette's, with the same degrading message, but critics keep circling back to "Stand By Your Man" as a kind of shorthand for anti-feminist doctrine in country music, and, to a greater extent, life in general. In 1992, Hillary Clinton referred to the song when responding to allegations of then-presidential-hopeful Bill's extramarital affairs. "I'm not sitting here some little woman standing by my man like Tammy Wynette," she said in a *60 Minutes* interview. (In a whole other layer of feminist rhetoric, Clinton was pressured into apologizing to Wynette only

5

days later by legions of country music fans who said it was an unfair comparison.)

Still, plenty of female country musicians have serious feminist chops, using their lyrics to take on political feminist issues from birth control and abortion to equal pay and spousal abuse. Loretta Lynn's 1975 song, "The Pill," is the first major song to mention oral contraceptives; more recently, Neko Case's 2002 song, "Pretty Girls," examines the judgment that comes with abortion. Other songs — about disappointment in marriage and motherhood, about not being slut-shamed for wearing a short skirt, about hitting your cheating husband upside the head with a cast-iron skillet — are not as overtly political, but still deal with realities of female experience head-on, without conforming to gender norms or social conventions.

Of all female country musicians, Dolly Parton presents the most interesting example of the tension that exists between femininity and feminism. Her 1980 classic hit, "9 to 5," is set to a catchy beat but makes a political point about being an ambitious woman in a discriminatory workplace. Lesser known, her 1968 song "Just Because I'm a Woman" took on sexual hypocrisy and double standards way before "slut-shaming" was even an established phrase. But these days, Parton is often discounted as an artist — and as a feminist — made into a punch line about breast implants and plastic surgery; even when she is held up as a feminist icon, the argument often comes with a tone of questioning surprise and an acknowledgment that her big hair, big breasts, and tiny waist make her a less-than-obvious feminist heroine.

In their music on the show, both Rayna and Juliette fall firmly in the Dolly Parton camp of female country music star; while their songs are not overtly political or feminist — no abortion or birth control talk here — they are very much about women standing on their own, standing up for themselves, and being respected. Juliette's hits include "Telescope," which warns a cheating lover that she knows full well what he's up to; "Boys and Buses," advising that chasing after boys is a waste of time; and "Undermine," a heartfelt ballad about how it's harder — but more worthwhile — to achieve something on your own than to undermine someone else. Rayna's songs, tinged with more experience, are more downcast, but they, too, advocate for standing one's ground: "Buried Under" tells the story of a woman grappling with finding out her lover's long-buried secrets; in "No One Will Ever Love You," the singer insists that her love is the best love the listener will ever find, and he should accept it.

Of all *Nashville*'s songs, the song that Juliette and Rayna fictionally "co-wrote" does the most to situate them within the world of women in country music. Titled "Wrong Song," the song is a fiery duet, addressed to a lying, cheating man, and in classic Rayna/Juliette fashion, it stands up for the woman, saying that she won't stand for that. But "Wrong Song" goes a step further than the usual woman-power advocacy, adding a meta-layer of commentary on country music (and music in general), turning the song into a defiant take on expectations for country music and female narratives in general. The song begins with a series of conditional ifs, setting up the typical country-song scenario — man drinks too much, does foolish thing, woman misses him and forgives him:

> If you think you're gonna hear
> how much I miss you
> If you're needing to feel better 'bout yourself
> If you're waiting to hear me
> say I forgive you
> 'Cause tequila turned you into someone else

The song then slows down, ever so slightly, as it winds up to the chorus, meanwhile deploying the Tammy Wynette shorthand for the disempowered woman, the country music stereotype who stands by her man no matter what he does:

> If you're looking for one more chance
> A little stand by your man

And then there comes the booming chorus, both women's voices coming together for the coup de grace, calling out all those songs before it for so easily forgiving wayward men, and also calling out the listener himself for expecting that they would forgive him, just because they are country music singers, just because they are ladies. If you think you're getting the stereotypical female narrative of passivity and forgiveness (à la "Stand By Your Man"), they tell the listener, then you've got the wrong song and the wrong girl:

> You've got the wrong song
> Coming through your speakers
> This one's about a liar and a cheater
> Who didn't know what he had
> 'till it was gone
> You've got the wrong girl
> Cause I've got your number
> I don't know what kind of spell
> you think I'm under
> This ain't a feel-good,
> 'Everything's fine' sing-along
> You've got the wrong song

This song, this performance, is the epitome of *Nashville* womenhood: active, empowered, and take-charge. But this song is more than just a statement on behalf of the characters. In one catchy chorus, it takes on the music industry and its demands on female artists, and then goes a step further by putting that examination on television, a similar crucible of issues concerning money, sexuality, female image, and power.

As characters, Rayna and Juliette are strong women, still rare on televi- 10 sion, but not impossible to find. As a show, though, *Nashville* — in its unapologetically pure focus on female characters, its self-aware examination of the struggles of female artists, and its critique of male-dominated industries — is one of the most feminist television shows on television.

Still, neither Rayna nor Juliette is a feminist, or, at least, we've never heard them say that they are. *Nashville* has never dropped the F-bomb, surely afraid of alienating part of its audience. As the show goes on, however, and as both Rayna and Juliette give more and more fictional interviews to television talk shows and magazines, the absence of the word "feminist" becomes a more glaring omission; after all, media love to ask women to define themselves in terms of feminism, especially strong, powerful women.

But that kind of definitive stance — feminist or not feminist — doesn't interest *Nashville*. The show is focused on individual characters rather than overarching labels, in showing how strong, powerful women live their strong, powerful lives. There are men on *Nashville*, too, but they are pretty much ineffectual; any success they have comes, directly or indirectly, as a result of their partnerships with the show's various women. Indeed, every woman on the show — not just Rayna and Juliette — is portrayed as a strong woman; they may have their faults, but all of them, from up-and-comer Scarlett O'Connor to Rayna's sister Tandy to more minor characters like the managers and political wives, have ambition, drive, and agency, as well as a self-possessed dignity that leaves no question about who is in control.

There is only one notable exception to this otherwise consistently empowered cast of female characters: the needy, conniving, and man-reliant Peggy Kenter, who has an affair with Rayna's husband and leaks Rayna's subsequent divorce to the tabloids. In both her demeanor and her actions, Peggy appears like a caricature of a helpless female, as if a reminder of all the ghosts of stereotypical soapy female characters past. Peggy is also notably the only character whose situation is presented without a trace of compassion; the show, it would seem, has no sympathy for a woman like Peggy — a woman who belongs in a different kind of world, on a different kind of show.

In fact, even though *Nashville* is billed as a primetime soap, it is much better described as a workplace drama, where the workplace is the country music mainstage. Along with reproductive rights, women's advancement and equal treatment in the workplace is one of the last — and most persistent — issues for feminism, a fact that makes *Nashville*'s portrait of this very particular workplace all the more interesting from a feminist point of view.

As in a workplace drama, we see the way the women express themselves 15 in front of others, but we also see what happens when the stage curtain is pulled back, and how that empowerment translates to both their personal lives and their behind-the-scenes business decisions. And it's in this offstage life that the show truly uses Rayna and Juliette to explore questions of feminism, especially when it looks at the challenges a woman faces when she insists on being in control of her own life.

These challenges are different for Rayna and Juliette, who are at distinct stages in both their career and personal life. For Rayna, married with two daughters, they manifest as a question of how to balance her career ambitions with being a good ("good") mother, daughter, and wife (and eventually ex-wife). Rayna never feels guilty about any of the decisions she makes related to her career; she misses her daughters when she is on the road, but she does not feel guilty or ashamed that she has left them with their (very loving) father. On the flipside, when her father has a heart attack, she flies back to Nashville immediately and says she might have to cancel that night's concert, but those decisions are made without agony, without any drama over where to put family and where to put career. This departure from female guilt over the intersection of professional and domestic priorities is refreshing.

Rayna also faces the challenge of how to stay relevant as a female artist and performer in her forties, an age our society deems over the hill. Again, the show defies the stereotypical storyline — one that might end in a middle-age crisis, substance abuse, or plastic surgery — and gives the character of Rayna the dignity of a real person, taking on a real professional challenge. Rayna has to work even harder to stay relevant; there is no such thing as resting on laurels, especially for a female celebrity over the age of thirty. And, as always, Rayna rises to the challenge, writing more songs, evolving her sound, taking more risks, going on tour. When faced with a challenge, Rayna does not break down; she steels herself and takes it on, and she succeeds — not by chance or wiles, but by hard work and force of will.

For Juliette — young, hot, and unattached — the challenges are different. More than anything, Juliette wants to be taken seriously: by her record label, by her employees, by her colleagues, by reviewers, by her fans. Her youth is a major part of her problem: her male-dominated world (her boss at the label, her manager, her roadies, her band, the predominately male reviewers) do not want to take her seriously. But, even more problematic for a young woman like Juliette is her attitude. She knows what she wants, and she does what she wants without thinking of the consequences.

Juliette's behavior is not always perfect, but her slips in judgment are exacerbated by her gender and her age, and these mistakes drive the show's examination of social and professional double standards. Were Juliette a man, she would be described as "driven" and "demanding" when she fires her manager or changes her set list at the last minute; instead, since she is a woman, she is seen as irrational. Were she a man, she would be called a "bad boy" for her brushes with the law and her late nights clubbing; since she is a woman, this behavior threatens to ruin her career and her image. When Juliette's ex-boyfriend blackmails her over a sex tape he secretly filmed, the show takes on one of the most gendered celebrity scandals: a sex tape for a male celebrity means almost nothing, but becomes part of a woman's permanent record.

Even when exploring the rivalry between Rayna and Juliette — one of ²⁰
Nashville's central plotlines — the show treats the women with sophistication
and dignity, making it clear from the start that it's a professional rivalry. It
would be ideal if all women — or, for that matter, all people — could support
each other even in competition, but in the world in which Rayna and Juliette
operate, that isn't an option. This kind of competition is particularly endemic
to women and particularly brutal, but professional competition transcends gender. Record labels only have so much promotional money to put behind artists;
magazines only have so many pages to dedicate to female country music stars.
In the plotline that will wrap up this season, Rayna and Juliette are both nominated for Female Country Music Artist of the Year. This turn of events is a brilliant move by the show in that it brings their competition to the forefront.

The show's recognition of this contest — and also the way the rivalry
unfolds — again defies the typical portrayal of female envy. The very fact
that competition is the major plot point of the show recognizes that women
can compete in the first place — that women don't always "play nice," that a
woman can want to be number one. Beyond that initial recognition, the rivalry
itself is handled with sophistication and dignity. Other than a few snippy comments in the first few episodes when the show was finding its footing, both
women are refreshingly direct (the gendered thing to say here would be that
they aren't catty) about their relationship. Other than a few offhand statements, neither of them really talks about the other behind her back; when one
of them is frustrated or angry at the other, she says so to her rival's face.

Most refreshingly, the competition stays entirely in the professional
sphere. When Juliette is confronted with a giant billboard of Rayna's face as a
celebrity endorsement, she does not react by commenting on Rayna's appearance or her age; she is pissed, but she is pissed because she wants an endorsement deal and a billboard of her own. When Rayna is forced to fly on Juliette's
plane, she is also unhappy, but mostly about the fact that she doesn't have
her own jet. Even when Juliette beds Rayna's long-ago love, the story focuses
more on both women wanting him as a bandleader and songwriter — in a professional capacity — than a sexual or romantic rivalry.

In fact, in a brilliantly self-aware move, this season's closing plotline
about Rayna and Juliette's award rivalry perfectly appropriates real-world
media commentary about the show itself. When the show debuted in the
fall, *Nashville*'s creator Khouri and stars Connie Britton and Hayden Panettiere
both had to spend a lot of time (an inordinate amount of time) telling interviewers that the show was not about a "catfight" between the two women. In
a recent episode, as Britton's Rayna and Panettiere's Juliette walked a red carpet together, reporters ask them how it feels to compete and Rayna, echoing
Britton's real-life remarks, tells them, "If you're expecting a catfight, you're
not going to get it."

Not only does this statement provide a new meta-commentary on female-
driven narratives, but also continues the themes established in "Wrong Song"
of defying traditional expectations for women, both for the way women act

and the way women are represented — and represent themselves. In other words, if viewers come to *Nashville* looking for the same old soapy female tropes — catfights, bitchiness, seduction, backstabbing — then they've got the wrong show.

READING THE TEXT

1. According to Stanford, how do the fictional *Nashville* characters Rayna James and Juliette Barnes compare with real-life country music stars Tammy Wynette and Dolly Parton?

2. Why does Stanford claim that the word "'feminism' is now so loaded with meaning, confusion, and incorrect associations that it has become all too common, especially among young women, to disavow the term entirely" (para. 1)?

3. Summarize in your own words the conventional motifs of mainstream country music. In what ways does *Nashville* depart from the genre's conventions?

4. What does Stanford mean by saying that "Wrong Song" adds "a meta-layer of commentary on country music (and music in general)" (para. 9)?

READING THE SIGNS

1. In class, list on the board the connotations class members attach to the word "feminism." What do you think the sources of these connotations may be? Do you detect any differences between male and female students; if so, how do you account for them?

2. In an essay, argue for your own response to Stanford's question about *Nashville*: "Can a show that is so ostensibly interested in the 'feminine' . . . also be feminist?" (para. 4). As an alternative, focus your argument on a different program that features women characters, such as *Orange Is the New Black*.

3. Using Stanford's critique of femininity and feminism as a critical framework, analyze some songs popularized by current real-life country music artists such as Carrie Underwood or Miranda Lambert. As an alternative, conduct a survey of country music lyrics by both male and female performers, and write an essay analyzing the gender politics implicit in these lyrics.

4. Write a semiotic analysis of a music superstar such as Lady Gaga, who is overtly political in her public persona and actions. In what ways might your object of analysis reflect "the themes established in 'Wrong Song' of defying traditional expectations for women, both for the way women act and the way women are represented — and represent themselves" (para. 24)?

5. Adopting Stanford's perspective, analyze the gender dynamics you see in a different show that focuses on Southern female characters, *Here Comes Honey Boo Boo*. To what extent does this show replicate or defy "the same old soapy female tropes" (para. 24)? To develop your ideas, watch one or two episodes of the show.

JOHN SHERMAN

The New Normative: Queer Politics in The Outs

Is it possible to create a television series that features gay protagonists and yet is not a "gay" program? For John Sherman, the answer
is "yes," and the evidence is the Vimeo drama *The Outs* — a crowd-
funded indie breakout that follows the lives of Brooklyn men who
just happen to be gay. This, Sherman suggests in a review that first
appeared in the *Los Angeles Review of Books*, is what TV in a post-
heteronormative society can look like, and he likes it a lot. John
Sherman is a freelance writer in Brooklyn.

I first found *The Outs* late one night a few years ago, amid a deep internet
dive for queer web series. Netflix's "Gay & Lesbian" offerings tend toward
low-budget American softcore and tragically star-crossed foreign coming-out
stories (and I'd already watched most of them anyway), so when I came
upon *The Outs*, a beautifully shot, sharply written comedy set in Brooklyn
about a pair of ex-boyfriends — Mitchell (creator, director, and co-writer Adam
Goldman) and Jack (Hunter Canning) — and their friends — notably Oona
(series co-writer Sasha Winters) — I watched all seven episodes of the first
season in a giddy, insomniac vigil.

Web series in general are a way to find underfunded people making interesting work, and they often offer more diversity, of both narrative and subject
matter, than even the second-string original-programming slate of most online
streaming services. *The Outs* was funded through a Kickstarter, but despite
its DIY bona fides it feels remarkably like a television series, complete with a
playlist-worthy soundtrack. The second season of *The Outs*, six half-hour episodes, premiered March 30 on Vimeo On Demand as part of the site's original
programming debut. This boost has added some truly lovely B-roll, but otherwise admirably retains the texture of the first.

A standout scene from the first season, in an episode called "Over It,"
takes place at a late-night, hole-in-the-wall diner where four of the characters
sit sipping coffee in a cramped booth. Mitchell is arguing with Paul (known
for most of the first season only as "Scruffy," played by Tommy Heleringer)
about President Obama's famously "evolving" position on same-sex marriage:
Mitchell defends it, Paul decries it, while Jack coyly recuses himself. Their conversation turns to hate speech (Mitchell: "Some asshole called me a 'faggot' at
Whole Foods"), and the question of what to do in the face of it, and the table
is again divided.

It's a classic *Sex and the City* setup: a table, an issue, a difference of
opinion. In *Sex and the City*, the varied experience of sexually liberated and

professional womanhood is sufficient to support a range of opinion; in *The Outs*, Goldman has created a show with sufficient depth to support conflicting notions of sexual and identity politics, a complexity rarely afforded to queer characters onscreen. That four college-educated gay men living above the poverty line in Brooklyn might feel differently about any number of issues — not simply Bernie versus Hillary, but issues that might not occur, or not even occur not to have occurred, to a heterosexual audience — is at least as revolutionary as the idea that four professional women in Manhattan 20 years ago might not agree on threesomes or the ethics of fake orgasms.

Given its setting and the demographic of its protagonists (twentysome- 5 thing), it may be tempting to compare it to any number of shows — to call it, for instance, a male *Sex and the City*, a Brooklyn *Looking*, a gay *Girls*, a less gainfully employed *Will & Grace* — but its closest TV relative may be *Broad City*. Both series began as self-funded passion projects of their creators and stars, and both have since been vaulted to distribution deals, publicity, and production budgets. Both are driven by the writing, humor, and politics of their creators, and both take identity politics as a given; no less than being an empowered woman, being openly queer, whether in 2016, or 2012, or 1987, or 1969, is inherently political. Perhaps the greatest similarity, though, is both shows' web-native scrappiness, which can see beyond the limitations of the medium. Neither is content merely to follow in the footsteps of its predecessors.

The Outs fills a unique place in the television landscape even as it winkingly transcends it, consistently introducing low-hanging plot points, considering them, and declining to indulge. In one episode in the second season, Mitchell is in sudden need of a roommate. Jack offers gingerly to move in, to which Mitchell responds with exhausted repulsion, "Jesus, God, no, please . . . I mean, thank you, that's very sweet of you, but that's just, like, the worst possible, cheesiest, television version of our lives. It doesn't make any sense" — a meta nod to what might have been a plot-point layup on a different show, like *Friends* or *Will & Grace* (on which almost exactly that happened at least once).

The relationships on *The Outs* are queer in a way that challenges the popular image of a same-sex relationship, both for romantic partners and friends. Whereas the boundaries of Will and Jack's friendship on *Will & Grace* were defined by their mutual sexual repulsion — as though that might be the only reason for two gay men *not* to sleep together — the friendship between Mitchell and Jack is devoid of sexual tension because of their history and their mutual growth. They're ex-boyfriends with emotional benefits.

For a show set in the post-DOMA United States, on the heels of *Obergefell v. Hodges*, talk of same-sex marriage is notably — though not inexplicably — absent. A rare mention occurs in the third episode, when Mitchell's British boyfriend Rob sighs in exasperation over a health insurance debacle and suggests just getting married so he can get a green card. "Let's just get married. Then I'll be a citizen and you can be my 'baby-daddy,' or wha'ever. And then everything will work itself out. Yeah?" Mitchell answers simply, "Alrighty," and spoons him comfortingly. This view of marriage as a practical solution — for the sake of health insurance, of all things — is generational as much as it is an instance of gay cynicism about traditionally exclusive civic institutions, but to see it so nonchalantly on display is noteworthy, and of a piece with a certain strain of young, queer cognoscenti.

But even to call cynicism about same-sex marriage "noteworthy" — or to call ambivalence "cynicism" — is an observation steeped in a view of gay life as aspiring to necessarily normative achievements. These characters live in the same United States as the rest of us, with the same multiplicity of sentiment around what it means to get gay-married, from anti-assimilationist dissenters to more traditional, solitaire-engagement-ring romantics. More than any other series I've seen, *The Outs* deals in these deeper cuts of queer politics in rants about tone-deaf pro-gay tweets and nonnormative notions of sexual fealty, evidence of a collective self-examination and an anti-assimilatory politics that challenges the normative, family-friendly, two-men-and-a-baby gayness that has dominated queer representation in pop culture.

This is the norm of the anti-norm, the queer self that questions normative   10
virtues without necessarily challenging them as invalid. *The Outs* represents a plurality of queer politics with a greater breadth than in a show in which gay characters are shunted off to the side or fettered by the traditional boundaries of same-sex relationships and parenthood. *The Outs* exists in a world of marriage equality, and doubtless couldn't be so casual without it, even as it presses against the walls of normativity, increasingly within reach.

The Outs blends tenets of modern queer thought with an almost imperceptible flourish: at least twice in the series, same-sex couples make reference to group sex, or to having been with other people, without making it a topic of discussion. No one is surprised or upset, and the conversation simply moves forward. In the universe of *The Outs*, and in a contemporary, urban, millennial milieu, such asides have the potency of an on-screen bong — an ordinary feature of life, signifying nothing, really. Without speaking against the values of marriage and family, and all the things the marriage-equality movement has put forth as cardinal queer virtues, *The Outs* contains characters who, without crises of self-love or -interest, go about life in loving relationships that may or may not include men on the side or threesome sex with mysterious strangers that later become fun stories to tell at happy hour.

This manner of talking about gay sex and relationships is refreshingly blasé, and it subtly quashes the parallel visions of gay men as *Modern Family* minstrels and debaucherous perverts living in sex communes, as well as the gawker's urge to delve into specifics. There is no inherent morality to sex, and the only character whose sexual choices are questioned is Oona, the lone straight woman, and she questions them herself.

The Outs is an example of what will hopefully, eventually, one day be commonplace: it's a show featuring gay characters that isn't *about* being gay. The characters of *The Outs* can hear the subway from inside their apartments, they show up at the door when a friend is in crisis, they worry about making rent; their apartments may be a few Airbnb clicks nicer than most people's I know, but they have roommates, they make booty calls, and some of them are men who date men. The New York City they live in is one I recognize, a fact that, perhaps even more than the characters' experiences, politics, or sexuality, breathes real life into the show and its characters.

READING THE TEXT

1. What is the significance of the title *The Outs*?

2. According to Sherman, what is the difference between a gay TV show and one that features gay characters?

3. How does the production history of *The Outs* reflect the contemporary landscape of television?

4. What does Sherman mean by saying that *The Outs* represents "the norm of the anti-norm" (para. 10)?

READING THE SIGNS

1. Watch an episode of *The Outs*, and write an essay in which you agree, disagree, or modify Sherman's claim that the program's characters "are queer in a way that challenges the popular image of a same-sex relationship, both for romantic partners and friends" (para. 7).

2. **CONNECTING TEXTS**   Compare *The Outs* to a heterosexual "relationship" show like *New Girl*. To what extent does your comparison reveal that *The Outs* indeed exemplifies "the new normative"? To develop your analysis, consult Neal Gabler's "The Social Networks" (p. 240).

3. Write an analysis in which you compare *The Outs* with another gay-themed show like *The L Word*. To what extent do the shows feature gay characters but not focus on their being gay?

4. Read Michael Hulshof-Schmidt's "What's in an Acronym?: Parsing the LGBTQQIP2SAA Community" (p. 489). Adopting his perspective, write an essay in which you support, refute, or modify Sherman's contention that "*The Outs* fills a unique place in the television landscape even as it winkingly transcends it" (para. 6).

OLIVIA GOLDHILL

Trump Supporters Are Living in a Reality Shaped by Television

In this era of "alternative facts" and "fake news," it's beginning to appear that Americans are living in "alternative realities." And according to Olivia Goldhill, this just might be attributable to the way we consume the news. In short, reality looks different depending upon whether one learns about it on television or via print media, according to Harvard political theorist Danielle Allen. And since supporters of Donald Trump tend to watch their news rather than read it, their views of the world are profoundly different from those who read, say, the *Washington Post*. The result, as Goldhill succinctly puts it, is that "Half the nation consistently fails to understand the other half because the US is a nation divided between those who watch the news and those who read it." Does the fact that Allen's observation first appeared in the *Washington Post*, and now in this book, mean that the division between TV people and text people is doomed to persist? Or will Fox News online bridge the gap? Stay tuned. Olivia Goldhill is a "weekend writer" at Quartz, in which this text originally appeared.

Donald Trump's enduring popularity has surprised just about everyone. And no wonder, argues Harvard political theorist Danielle Allen. Half the nation consistently fails to understand the other half because the US is a nation divided between those who watch the news and those who read it. The conversations on the two different media are starkly different, she says, making it increasingly difficult for those who read news to understand the perspective of those who watch it, and vice versa.

Those who read news and analysis are largely out of touch with the narratives that shape TV news, and the viewers who watch it. "My hypothesis is that, as of summer 2015, the conversations in TV and radio land were barely visible within text-based journalism," she wrote in a *Washington Post* article on the subject.

Trump, Allen says, is a television candidate.

"He was already in the world of television conversation. That's the genre that he fits in and that's what he appeals to," she says. "You have to switch hats from the expectations and standards of a reading context to the expectations and standards of a television-watching context. That's all you need to know for understanding why he's appealing."

Allen believes that Trump's anti-political correctness rhetoric makes far 5 more sense in the context of TV, where there's often criticism of elites and professional sectors.

Television also tends to have a greater focus on the potential dangers of crime and terrorism than print media. "TV news spends a lot more time on chasing bad guys and reporting on bad guys than print media does," says Allen. Indeed, studies have shown that those who watch a large amount of TV are more likely to feel a greater threat from crime, and that the crime shown on TV is more violent and dangerous than real-world crime.

Not only does Trump better fit the narratives that often shape TV news, he also suits the language of television. Allen believes that the linguistic complexity of TV news is several grades below that of print news. And so Trump, whose speeches are at a fourth-grade level, is quite literally speaking the language of television.

Trump knows his supporters are not reading erudite columns on politics, and so he consciously presents himself as a TV candidate, argues Allen. He's shown disdain for the rhetoric and practice of print media and, when he first launched his campaign, his website had no policy papers on it. "All it had on it were short video statements from Trump," she says. "He knew he was after a watching audience, not a reading one."

In general, she says, the divide between watching and reading news is sharp. "People are consuming stuff either in a written or in a TV form and, for the most part, it's not a matter of going back and forth between them," she adds.

Allen believes the divide between those who read and watch news is so 10 strong that she would "guess" those who watch news are more likely to be Trump supporters and those who read news are more likely to be Clinton supporters. "That's roughly the same as saying that people with college degrees are more likely to support Clinton and people without them are more likely to support Trump," she adds.

To those who find Trump reprehensible, it might seem the only possible explanation for his popularity is that his supporters live in a different reality. Allen's argument gives credence to this theory. Trump supporters live in a world shaped by television discussions, not print ones. The only way to understand this alternate reality is to start watching more TV.

READING THE TEXT

1. Explain in your own words Danielle Allen's distinction between the "expectations and standards of a reading context" and "the expectations and standards of a television-watching context" (para. 4).

2. Why does Allen believe that Donald Trump "suits the language of television" (para. 7)?

3. What does Goldhill mean by concluding the article by saying "The only way to understand this alternate reality is to start watching more TV" (para. 11)?

4. How does television encourage anti-politically correct views, according to Allen?

Reading the Text

1. **CONNECTING TEXTS**   In addition to print news and television, many people get their news from social media and other online sources, but Goldhill doesn't mention these options. In an essay addressed to Goldhill, write an argument that outlines how these other news sources might have affected the outcome of the 2016 presidential election. To develop your ideas, consult the International Center for Media and the Public Agenda's "Students Addicted to Social Media" (p. 382) and Jeffrey Fleishman's "How an Angry National Mood Is Reflected in Pop Culture" (p. 531).

2. Conduct surveys with a demographically mixed group who voted in the 2016 presidential election, asking not simply who their presidential choice was but, more broadly, how they received news about the candidates and how often they sought such news. Then, based on your results, write an essay in which you evaluate Danielle Allen's "guess" that "those who watch news are more likely to be Trump supporters and those who read news are more likely to be Clinton supporters" (para. 10).

3. Select a current news story that includes violence or crime, and then analyze both print and television coverage of the story. In an essay, argue whether your analysis supports, refutes, or complicates the assumption that television news has "a greater focus on the potential dangers of crime and terrorism than print media" (para. 6).

4. Watch two or three of Donald Trump's campaign speeches (you might visit YouTube) and do a linguistic analysis of your choices. Write an essay in which you respond to the contention that "Trump, whose speeches are at a fourth-grade level, is quite literally speaking the language of television" (para. 7).

NICK SERPE

Reality Pawns: The New Money TV

When the going gets tough, reality TV gets nasty. Such is the conclusion that Nick Serpe draws in this review of such RTV shows as *Repo Games*, "one of the vilest reality shows in the history of American television," as Serpe puts it. Pulling no punches, Serpe explores the ways in which the Great Recession has been exploited by RTV producers who have found that debt and down-and-outedness make for entertaining fare in such programs as *Pawn Stars* and *Storage Wars*, gritty shows that, like *Repo Games*, reap profits out of other people's losses. Nick Serpe is the online editor of *Dissent: A Quarterly of Politics and Culture*, from which this selection is taken.

Repo Games, one of the vilest reality shows in the history of American television, premiered on Spike in 2011 with no fanfare and a simple premise, delivered in a voiceover intro: "Nobody wants to meet the repo man. But when this repo man comes, you'll get the chance to ditch those late notices for good." A little more than a minute later, we see a man built like a professional wrestler pull up in front of a woman's house, along with a camera crew that rushes into her driveway like a SWAT team. The owner's "REPO REPORT" then flashes across the screen: "Name: Wallace. Age: 44, Vehicle: '96 Dodge Caravan. Intel: Her weave alone will whoop your ass." Heavy metal plays in the background. A tow truck backs in under the van, which Wallace does not appreciate, and then the wrestler, co-host Tom DeTone, proceeds to describe the situation in which Wallace now finds herself: Tom is going to repo her car, but if she can answer three of five trivia questions right, the car will be hers, and fully paid off. The tow rig lifts the back of the car when she gets answers wrong and brings it down when she gets them right. With six family members watching on, Wallace prevails. She dances with Tom and then boasts in the post-game interview, "I ain't going to even fucking look for a job now."

The next contestant, a skinny, shirtless stoner living at his mom's, has a similar message when he wins: "Guess what I learned, America: if you don't pay your bill, somebody else will."

The last contestant, a woebegone fifty-eight-year-old man, grovels when he loses: "Even though I lost, you guys gave me an opportunity to save my car and I appreciate that, because in this time and age not many people would even do that." Tom responds, "Wish you all the best, John, and I wish I could pay off everybody's car. It's just not possible."

Even in "this time and age" — years into a hollow economic recovery built atop an already hollowed-out economy, more than a decade after the ascendance of American reality television — and even given the very low bar of taste set by Spike, I expected to find some online traces of outrage at the cruelty, exploitation, and heavy-handed stereotypes on display in *Repo Games*. All I could find was a commentary in the *American Thinker*, a conservative website, speculating that "the numerous stupid and vulgar contestants" on the show were typical Obama voters. In depicting these people seemingly cast from a Tea Partier's nightmare — the lazy welfare queen, the languid video-gamer mooching off the 'rents, the emasculated, aging white man who "never should've gotten this far" — the show "inadvertently [veered] from goofy entertainment into trenchant social commentary."

Reality television, though almost never considered serious, was seriously considered in its early days, and the attention was mostly negative. Some early precursors, such as MTV's *The Real World* (1992–present), which brought a group of young strangers together under one roof for a few months, earned begrudging respect for their occasionally frank depictions of stigmatized subjects. But the ethical tone and artistic qualities of reality TV seemed to be set by *Who Wants to Marry a Multi-Millionaire?*, a one-night special aired on Fox in February 2000. *Multi-Millionaire* was like a beauty pageant that collided with a high-stakes *Dating Game*: women were paraded on stage for a rich man, seen only in silhouette, who would pick a lucky winner and marry her right then and there. The National Organization of Women denounced the show, as did the bride in numerous interviews. (It turns out that a restraining order had been filed against the man by a former girlfriend, not to mention that he wasn't that rich after all.) The marriage was annulled in April. By the summer, American versions of *Survivor* and *Big Brother*, both European imports, had premiered and won huge audiences. These series featured "normal" people, competing for prizes and for their fifteen minutes of fame. They set the standards — confessional interviews, fierce competition, oblivious narcissism, casting designed to foster conflict, semi-scripted scenes — that would define the genre.

Critics worried about what had opened the reality TV floodgates. Perhaps it was the seductive intimation that anyone could be (briefly) famous — and that the skeptical audience probably deserved it more than the charmless cut-throats who auditioned successfully. Perhaps the viewing public was growing so detached, so impatient with clichés and inured to fictional cruelty, that they hungered for something realer. Maybe we'd watched so much television that we were all acting like TV characters anyway; someone just had to put the cameras in front of us. Or was the rest of TV already so bad that anything novel was welcome?

If you were reading the tea leaves of popular taste, you would find a lot to get upset about. But focusing only on viewers reinforces the idea that TV programming is driven by what consumers want. There's no doubt that reality TV would have remained a very marginal phenomenon without a willing audience, but it wouldn't have spread the way it did — with proliferating subgenres colonizing the whole TV landscape — were it not for the economics of producing these shows. According to Charles B. Slocum, assistant executive director of the Writers Guild of America, West:

> In virtually every line of the production budget, reality-based programming is cheaper than traditional programming. Not as much equipment is needed, and it's cheaper. There is a smaller crew. There are fewer paid performers. There are fewer sets. The economic role of reality-based programming is to permit a network to cost-average down the price of programming across the entire primetime schedule.

And, as a strike this spring by writers on the show *Fashion Police* brought to public attention, reality writers are predominantly nonunionized, with wages and benefits that reflect this fact. Even if entertainment execs weren't terrified of the Internet pushing down their bottom lines, cheap and titillating programming was a no-brainer.

The cultural panic over reality programming faded as the genre became a permanent and profitable TV fixture. In the meantime, a relatively small group of intelligent and well-crafted television dramas, from *The Sopranos* to *Breaking Bad*, became critical darlings, arguably marking the first time the medium has surpassed mainstream American cinema as an art form.

As a result, more recent developments in reality TV, including some of the most popular cable shows of the last five years, have attracted less attention. Critics have taken note of the rise of so-called blue-collar TV — where "blue collar" means burly fishermen (*Deadliest Catch*) and loggers (*Ax Men*) risking their lives to take care of their families — and the related "redneck" subgenre, featuring, for example, Cajuns with thick accents hunting swamp alligators (*Swamp People*). *Repo Games* also follows people doing their jobs — the co-hosts are supposedly both actual repo men — but it is part of a different phenomenon: the money-crazed, market-idealizing reality show, immersed in a funhouse version of the culture of debt and credit.

Although consumer debt was holding the American economy together for 10 decades before the recession laid it bare, these shows are a distinctly postrecession phenomenon. They thrive on foreclosed property and unpaid bills; they promote a bargain-basement ethos where everything has a price, and where discovering and comparing those prices is a source of pleasure. These shows are competitive in the way that much reality TV is, but the competitions are embedded in actual economic practice. These shows are the popular idea of the free market, writ small.

Two shows define this subgenre more than any other: *Pawn Stars*, which premiered on the History Channel in the summer of 2009, and A&E's *Storage Wars*, launched in December 2010. These remarkably formulaic programs set viewing records on their respective channels and inspired cable TV execs to run dozens of imitators.

Pawn Stars depicts the goings-on at a Las Vegas pawn shop that caters both to people making ends meet at the end of the month and to habitual gamblers. Most of the store's transactions are pawns, offered at the industry's typically high interest rates. Most of the customers depicted on the show, however, resemble the people who bring heirlooms to *Antiques Roadshow*, if slightly gruffer. And most of the transactions depicted are sales and purchases, not loans. (The producers defend the absence of the typical pawn customer by appealing to the unique character of this pawn shop, to the repeat customers' desire for privacy, and to audience sensibilities.)

In its structure, *Pawn Stars* is in fact a lot like *Antiques Roadshow*, the old PBS standby. Both ride on the fantasy that treasure might be lurking in anyone's attic. But the differences between *Roadshow* and what History Channel executives are calling "artifactual entertainment" are telling. The pawn shop setting (unlike *Roadshow*'s convention hall set-up) tells us that we're here for business, and lends the show at least the pretense of documentary. The PBS series features dozens of experts in various fields, while on *Pawn Stars* the assessors are mainly in the family business: Richard Harrison the patriarch, his son Rick (the show's star), Rick's son Corey, and Corey's friend Austin "Chumlee" Russell. They sometimes call on specialist "friends" in town to assess or restore particular items, and they frequently go to shooting ranges to test antique weapons, such as a nineteenth-century cannon shown on the first episode. *Pawn Stars* also attempts to signify youthfulness (successfully, as evidenced by its high under-thirty-five viewer ratings) with generic hard-rock interludes and souped-up graphics.

Despite its alleged factual and historical content, *Pawn Stars* is character driven. The Harrisons and Chumlee bicker and mock each other more or less constantly, in scenes that seem scripted to varying extents. The arguments are presented as a tough-guy façade covering a warm, family-friendly core. These men make their living by driving down what their customers ask for, but they have to put food on their tables, too, and pay all those employees we don't see on camera. Their homespun manner, their fascination with historical artifacts and the moment of discovery, the fact that we don't see their private homes (a very rare sight in the entire subgenre) or any truly desperate clientele — all of it makes the pawn biz seem like an honest one: usury with a human face. There aren't any complex debt vehicles or international price-fixing scandals at this lender, and the simple profit calculus is literally shown on screen: projected sale price minus purchase price equals projected profit. When the Harrisons and their staff won the National Pawnbrokers Association "Pawnbroker of the Year" award in 2010, the organization claimed they had improved the public image of pawn shops more in one year than the NPA's publicity team had over decades.

On *Storage Wars*, naked economic warfare takes a more central role, but the family unit and flights of whimsy intervene to prevent the characters from looking like complete sociopaths. The show features a husband and wife duo who auction off storage units whose owners are delinquent in their payments. Various characters who want to resell the contents try to intimidate and frustrate each other as they compete for the units. The winners dig through their lockers and assign unverified prices to the items inside. On the first season, there's Dave, a brash man with a secondhand business big enough that he brings a team of men with him to carry off his hauls; Jarrod and Brandi, another husband-and-wife pair, who run a struggling consignment shop; Barry, a dilettante collector who employs various outlandish tricks (for instance, using a little person on stilts) to gain advantage; and Darrell, a perpetually sunburned and doltish man who, along with his son, is on the hunt for the "wow factor." One participant warns that "once we get through those gates, there is [sic] no friends, and there is no professional courtesy. It's every man for himself, and may the best man win," and at the end of each episode, the day's winner is declared according to self-reported profits. But despite the fierce bidding, the show's tone is light-hearted, even ironic.

Pawn Stars and *Storage Wars* launched an entire subgenre, with various epigones on cable channels including TLC, Lifetime, Discovery, Travel, Spike, and of course History and A&E. There are direct franchise spin-offs, such as *Cajun Pawn Stars* and *Storage Wars: Texas*, related shows such as *American Restoration* (which features an antique restorer frequently consulted on *Pawn Stars*), and a host of imitators. On *American Pickers*, two friends travel around the country dropping in on old farmers and hoarders to make on-the-spot deals on salvaged antiques. On *Barter Kings*, the hosts do away with cash altogether, transforming a small and inexpensive item into something grand through a series of in-kind trades with people they meet through Craigslist. Other shows transplant the auction idea into other settings, like *Baggage Battles* (unclaimed luggage at airports), *Container Wars* (unclaimed commercial shipping containers), *Texas Car Wars* (semi-junked hotrods), and *Flip Men* and *Property Wars* (foreclosed houses). On *Picker Sisters* and *Pawn Queens*, there are women.

One of the most notable of the debt-and-credit reality TV shows released in the wake of *Pawn Stars* and *Storage Wars* is *Hardcore Pawn*, truTV's most popular show and the inspiration for its own spin-offs, such as *Hardcore Pawn: Chicago* and the deranged *Combat Pawn*. Although it is clearly an attempt to cash in on the popularity of *Pawn Stars*, the show's producers and writers have set out to differentiate themselves from their relatively staid predecessor. Like the other shows in the subgenre, *Hardcore Pawn* extols the small-business owner, depends on a familial cast to drive the action ("We disagree more than regular employees, but we have each other's back"), and is full of scripted scenes that strain credulity. But *Hardcore Pawn* trades on its grit and volatility. The Harrisons appear to make money by playing with toys, while the Golds have captured the pugilistic atmosphere of *The Jerry Springer Show*, replete with bleeped-out cursing, fights broken up by large security guards, and a stripper pole (all on the first episode).

Despite the obvious fakery, the Detroit pawn shop owned by Les Gold, a third-generation pawnbroker working with his children Seth and Ashley, appears to have real customers who are about as happy as you would expect customers at a pawn shop—let alone a pawn shop in Detroit—to be. And as Les proudly states, "We don't call the experts, we are the experts." The customers lie and get lied to, and they are indeed desperate. "We're not *Antiques Roadshow*," Les told an interviewer, claiming *Hardcore Pawn* shows "how the *other* other half lives," a reverse image *Lifestyles of the Rich and Famous*. (David Paulin, author of the *American Thinker* commentary, explicitly draws a comparison between the people on *Repo Games* and the poor depicted in Michael Harrington's *The Other America*, all of whom he sees as suffering more from a lack of middle-class values than a lack of money.) "The draw that truTV has really focused on was the reality of what goes on in a real pawn shop with real people,"[*] Gold told

---

[*]truTV's motto is "Not Reality. Actuality," and its reality programming is consistently a couple of steps beyond credibility; some of its shows, including another repo show, *Operation Repo*, are filmed like reality shows but feature completely reconstructed scenes. The trajectory of truTV, which used to be Court TV (spell "court" backward, drop the "oc," and you get something like the truth), mirrors a number of other cable channels. The History Channel has dropped its standard historical content in favor of reality fare and picked up a slogan to reflect the change: "History: Made Every Day." TLC, which used to stand for "The Learning Channel," now stands for "TLC," and A&E (previously "Arts & Entertainment") is now just "A&E," presenting "Real Life. Drama."

an interviewer for the *Detroit Free Press*. Again, its claim to depicting real life is laughable. But the show might actually present what the typical petit bourgeois believes is typical of the working poor, either jocular deference or outrageous hijinks.

Watched in close succession, these cash-crazed shows reveal a number of common tropes. They portray an unforgiving social landscape, where taking risks at others' expense is the way to get ahead. They recommend crude psychological techniques for closing the sale: trick your auction competition into dropping too much money on a bad unit, encourage people selling their goods to name a price before you do, leverage their personal problems to encourage a less-than-ideal trade, and never be afraid to get the better deal. They rely on family and childhood friends to provide some centripetal moral force and invoke "the economy" and "the times" to explain why people are willing to do what they do. They express awe in the face of old, undiscovered, and abandoned riches, and nostalgia for a simpler capitalism. And beneath the veneer of small-town, small-business, conservative ethics, you can find the preening personalities, petty feuds, platitudes, and falsities that have characterized the bulk of reality television.

Some of the suspicious scenes are obvious and expected. Struggling actors are cast into the parts of longtime assistants to the experts; the first "reveal" of a locked-up, foreclosed house begins with a camera already inside; a piece of dialogue is filled with zingers that could only have been written beforehand; transactions that could have taken place online are dramatized on location; shop owners implement harebrained schemes to squeeze a couple extra bucks.

But a lawsuit issued last fall by Dave Hester, possibly the most despised character on *Storage Wars*, after he was fired, charged that producers "salted" storage lockers with rare, expensive, and antique items before they went on the block. Allegedly, some of the items already belonged to the winner before the sale, and at other times goods were supplied by a large Los Angeles antiques store. The auctions themselves, Hester claims, were often staged, with producers giving extra money to contestants they wanted to win a particular locker. Parts of the far-reaching suit (as of this writing) have been dismissed by the Los Angeles Superior Court, and A&E denies his allegations. But given the unbelievable rate at which bidders find unbelievable items on the show, it's hard to believe that Hester is just making it up. Some committed, online amateur sleuths (like the person behind www.storagewarsisfake .com) have made a cause of finding inconsistencies in this show and other reality-cash programs that back up his claims.

One of the biggest revelations in the lawsuit was an incidental one: at the time the suit was issued, Hester was earning $25,000 per episode, plus numerous bonuses. The real cash was never in buying abandoned storage units, but in making the auctions an exciting venue of social conflict for TV. On online message boards, people claiming to have attended these auctions in the past write that they have given up: huge crowds now show up and lose lots of money in the elusive pursuit of the baseball card collections, rare coins, celebrity memorabilia, and bizarre antiques that frequently pop up on *Storage Wars* and its competitor shows. Others have reported their disappointment upon visiting the Harrisons' pawn shop in Las Vegas, where the main business now appears to be selling *Pawn Stars* tchotchkes.

This isn't to deny that the market in buying foreclosed properties, and in pawning and selling secondhand goods, has boomed in the post-recession years. As Richard Harrison told the *Las Vegas Sun*, "[Y]ou have to understand that 17 to 20 percent of people in the United States don't have an active checking account or any bank affiliation, and this is a place where they can get a loan." The same arguments are made by the booming payday loan industry and others in the quick-cash credit business. They can get away with charging usurious rates — what scholars have called "the cost of being poor" — because they satisfy a need that other institutions, from banks to employers to government programs, aren't meeting.

Are these shows also satisfying a need? Busted-economy reality TV wouldn't exist if it weren't cheap to make, and it may be popular for any number of the scary-seeming reasons that reality TV in general is popular. But it also seems like a coming out for a number of predatory business practices that seem refreshingly frank in the wake of a financial crisis that people are told is too complicated for them to understand. For an audience primed on the language of individual bootstrapping and grave threats to the free market, these shows may seem practically heartwarming.

Rick Harrison made his politics explicit in recent months. In an interview on the *Mark Levin Show*, a program hosted by one of the most popular right-wing radiomen this side of Rush Limbaugh, Harrison assailed the state for not granting him a permit to film a *Pawn Stars* segment on government land (they blamed, falsely, he believed, the sequester for the permit denial) and attacked Obamacare for hurting employers. After beginning to make an interesting if ill-informed point about how small banks were treated poorly by the Obama administration while the big banks were bailed out, Harrison revealed a simpler, more sinister endgame: "We have the government that's down on business, down on business, people with money. I know someone else who did that. His name was Lenin. I mean he blamed the banks, aka the Jews, he blamed the intelligentsia. Let's reeducate everybody." 25

This sort of statement is a commonplace in right-wing U.S. politics, and, along with Rick Santelli's infamous screed against "loser" homeowners who couldn't keep up with their mortgages, constitutes the worldview of the Tea Party Right: the beleaguered middle against the underclass and its elite allies. But coming from the *Pawn Stars* star, the statement brought to mind an exchange from the film *Repo Man*, Alex Cox's 1984 punk classic. Bud, played by Harry Dean Stanton, tells his repo trainee Otto (Emilio Estevez), "Credit is a sacred trust, it's what our free society is founded on. Do you think they give a damn about their bills in Russia?"

OTTO: They don't pay bills in Russia, it's all free.

BUD: All free? Free my ass. What are you, a fuckin' commie? Huh?

OTTO: No, I ain't no commie.

BUD: Well, you better not be. I don't want no commies in my car. No Christians either.

These shows and the seedy corner of the economy they depict aren't just about winners and losers, but strivers and failures, the bold and the broken. In this universe, there are simply some people on the right side of the asymmetrical information divide, and others born to be conned. And there is no mutual aid without interest.

READING THE TEXT

1. What reasons does Serpe provide to support his claim that the growth of reality TV was largely *not* audience driven?

2. Summarize in your own words the history of reality TV, as Serpe presents it.

3. What is the appeal of *Pawn Stars* and *Storage Wars*, according to Serpe?

4. What connection does Serpe see between "busted-economy reality TV" (para. 24) and right-wing politics in America?

5. How do producers of shows like *Storage Wars* manipulate events to make the program more entertaining and less realistic, according to Serpe?

READING THE SIGNS

1. In class, discuss the tone of Serpe's article. To what extent does that tone enhance or reduce its effectiveness?

2. Watch one of the programs that Serpe discusses, and conduct your own analysis of it. Does the show use any of the "common tropes" (para. 19) that Serpe mentions? Is it a "funhouse version of the culture of debt and credit" (para. 9)?

3. Write an essay in which you support, refute, or complicate Serpe's link between right-wing politics and the popularity of "debt-and-credit" reality TV shows.

4. In the 1950s, the show *Queen for a Day* also focused on people in economic distress. Research *Queen for a Day*, and write an analysis comparing it to a program like *Repo Games*. In what way are the shows similar? How do you account for any differences?

5. **CONNECTING TEXTS**   Read Jon Mooallem's "The Self-Storage Self" (p. 103), and compare the real-life lives of self-storage users with the lives of those depicted on reality TV programs like *Storage Wars*. Use your comparison as the basis for an essay in which you argue for the appropriateness of the word "reality" in RTV.

EMILY NUSSBAUM

The Aristocrats: The Graphic Arts of Game of Thrones

In one sense, HBO's smash hit series *Game of Thrones*, like the novels it's based on, turns the past upside down, transforming J.R.R. Tolkien's magical Middle Earth into the wholly nightmarish Westeros. But when it comes to television history, the show is very much in the tradition of such programs as *The Sopranos* and *Mad Men*, dramas set within patriarchal subcultures. The result, Emily Nussbaum observes in this review for the *New Yorker*, is a show that features "copious helpings of pay-cable nudity, much of it in scenes that don't strictly require a woman to display her impressive butt dimples as the backdrop for a monologue about kings." Emily Nussbaum is the television critic for the *New Yorker*.

For critics, sorting through television pilots is an act of triage. Last year, when "Game of Thrones" landed on my desk, I skimmed two episodes and made a quick call: we'd have to let this one go. The HBO series, based on the best-selling fantasy books by George R. R. Martin, looked as if it were another guts-and-corsets melodrama, like "The Borgias," or that other one. In the première, a ten-year-old boy was shoved out of a tower window. The episode climaxed with what might be described as an Orientalist gang rape / wedding dance. I figured I might catch up later, if the buzz was good.

It was the right decision, even if I made it for the wrong reason. "Game of Thrones" is an ideal show to binge-watch on DVD: with its cliffhangers and Grand Guignol dazzle, it rewards a bloody, committed immersion in its foreign world — and by this I mean not only the medieval-ish landscape of Westeros (the show's mythical realm) but the genre from which it derives. Fantasy — like television itself, really — has long been burdened with audience condescension: the assumption that it's trash, or juvenile, something intrinsically icky and low. Several reviews of "Game of Thrones" have taken this stance, including two notable writeups in the *Times*: Ginia Bellafante sniffed that the show was "boy fiction" and Neil Genzlinger called it "vileness for voyeurism's sake," directed at "Dungeons & Dragons types."

It's true that "Game of Thrones" is unusually lurid, even within the arms race of pay cable: the show is so graphic that it was parodied on "Saturday Night Live," with a "behind-the-scenes" skit in which a horny thirteen-year-old boy acted as a consultant. To watch it, you must steel yourself for baby-stabbing, as well as rat torture and murder by molten gold. But, once I began sliding in disks in a stupor, it became clear that, despite the show's Maltese vistas and asymmetrical midriff tops, this was not really an exotic property. To the contrary, "Game of Thrones" is the latest entry in television's most esteemed category: the sophisticated cable drama about a patriarchal subculture. This phenomenon launched with "The Sopranos," but it now includes shows such as "Deadwood," "Mad Men," "Downton Abbey," and "Big Love." Each of these acclaimed series is a sprawling, multi-character exploration of a closed, often violent hierarchical system. These worlds are picturesque, elegantly filmed, and ruled by rigid etiquette — lit up, for viewers, by the thrill of seeing brutality enforced (or, in the case of "Downton Abbey," a really nice house kept in the family). And yet the undergirding strength of each series is its insight into what it means to be excluded from power: to be a woman, or a bastard, or a "half man."

The first season of "Game of Thrones" built up skillfully, sketching in ten episodes a conflict among the kingdoms of Westeros, each its own philosophical ecosystem. There were the Northern Starks, led by the gruffly ethical Ned Stark and his dignified wife, Catelyn, and their gruffly ethical and dignified children. There were the Southern Lannisters, a crowd of high-cheekboned beauties (and one lusty dwarf, played by the lust-worthy Peter Dinklage), who form a family constellation so twisted, charismatic, and cruel that it rivals "Flowers in the Attic" for blond dysfunction. Across the sea, there were the Dothraki, a Hun-like race of horseman warriors, whose brutal ruler, Drogo, took the delicate, unspellable Daenerys as a bride. A teen girl traded like currency by her brother, Daenerys was initiated into marriage through rape; in time, she began to embrace both that marriage and her desert queenhood. (Although the cast is mostly white, the dusky-race aesthetics of the Dothraki sequences are headclutchingly problematic.) By the finale, she was standing naked in the desert — widowed, traumatized, but triumphant, with three baby dragons crawling over her like vines. (This quick summary doesn't capture the complexity of the series' ensemble, which rivals a Bosch painting: there's also the whispery eunuch Spider; a scheming brothel owner named Littlefinger; and a ketchup-haired sorceress who gives birth to shadow babies.)

In the season's penultimate episode, the show made a radical move: it   5
killed off the protagonist. On a public stage, Ned Stark was beheaded, on the orders of the teenage sadist King Joffrey, a sequence edited with unusual beauty and terror — birds fluttering in the air, a hushed soundtrack, and a truly poignant shot from Ned's point of view, as he looked out toward his two daughters. This primal act suggested the limits of ethical behavior in a brutalized universe, and also dramatized the show's vision of what aristocracy means: a succession of domestic traumas, as each new regent dispatches threats to his bloodline. (Or, as Joffrey's mother, Cersei, puts it, kinghood means "lying on a bed of weeds, ripping them out one by one, before they strangle you in your sleep.") It demonstrated, too, a willingness to risk alienating its audience.

This season, early episodes have suggested the outlines of a developing war, hopping among a confusing selection of Starks, semi-Starks, and members of the Baratheon clan. (There are so many musky twenty-something men with messy hair that a friend joked they should start an artisanal pickle factory in Red Hook.) Greater than the threat of war is the danger that, in time, the television adaptation may come to feel not so much epic as simply elephantine. Still, the most compelling plots remain those of the subalterns, who are forced to wield power from below. These characters range from heroic figures like the tomboy Arya Stark to villains like Littlefinger, but even the worst turn out to have psychic wounds that complicate their actions. If the show has a hero, it's Tyrion (Dinklage), who is capable of cruelty but also possesses insight and empathy, concealed beneath a carapace of Wildean wit. So far, his strategic gifts have proved more effective than the torture-with-rats approach. Power is "a trick, a shadow on the wall," the eunuch tells Tyrion. "And a very small man can cast a very large shadow."

Then, of course, there are the whores. From the start, the show has featured copious helpings of pay-cable nudity, much of it in scenes that don't strictly require a woman to display her impressive butt dimples as the backdrop for a monologue about kings. (The most common fan idiom for these sequences is "sexposition," but I've also seen them referred to as "data humps.") These scenes are at once a turn-on and a turn-off. At times, I found myself marvelling at the way that HBO has solved the riddle of its own economic existence, merging "Hookers at the Point" with quasi-Shakespearean narrative. In the most egregious instance so far, Littlefinger tutored two prostitutes in how to moan in fake lesbianism for their customers, even as they moaned in fake lesbianism for us—a real Uroboros of titillation.

Viewed in another light, however, these sex scenes aren't always so gratuitous. Like "Mad Men," "Game of Thrones" is elementally concerned with the way that meaningful consent dissolves when female bodies are treated as currency. War means raping the enemy's women; princesses go for a higher price, because their wombs are the coin of the realm, cementing strategic alliances. It helps that the narrative is equally fascinated by the ways in which women secure authority, and even pleasure, within these strictures, and that in the second season its bench of female characters has got even deeper—among them, a seafaring warrior princess, a butch knight, and Tyrion's prostitute girlfriend.

"Game of Thrones" is not coy about the way the engine of misogyny can grind the fingers of those who try to work it in their favor. An episode two weeks ago featured a sickening sequence in which King Joffrey ordered one prostitute—a character the audience had grown to care about—to rape another. The scenario might have been scripted by Andrea Dworkin; it seemed designed not to turn viewers on but to confront them with the logical endgame of this pornographic system. It echoed a very similar line-crossing moment in "The Sopranos," when Ralphie beat a pregnant Bada Bing girl to death. But while the scene may have been righteous in theory, in practice it was jarring, and slightly incoherent, particularly since it included the creamy nudity we've come to expect as visual dessert.

As with "True Blood," the show's most graphic elements — the cruel ones,   10
the fantasy ones, and the cruel-fantasy ones — speak to female as well as male
viewers. (One of the nuttiest quotes I've ever read came from Alan Ball, "True
Blood"'s showrunner, who said that a focus group had revealed that men
watched his series for the sex and women for the romance. Please.) But there is
something troubling about this sea of C.G.I.-perfect flesh, shaved and scentless
and not especially medieval. It's unsettling to recall that these are not merely
pretty women; they are unknown actresses who must strip, front and back,
then mimic graphic sex and sexual torture, a skill increasingly key to attaining
employment on cable dramas. During the filming of the second season, an
Irish actress walked off the set when her scene shifted to what she termed
"soft porn." Of course, not everyone strips: there are no truly explicit scenes of
gay male sex, fewer lingering shots of male bodies, and the leading actresses
stay mostly buttoned up. Artistically, "Game of Thrones" is in a different class
from "House of Lies," "Californication," and "Entourage." But it's still part of
another colorful patriarchal subculture, the one called Los Angeles.

READING THE TEXT

1. Describe in your own words the genre to which Nussbaum categorizes *Game of Thrones*: "the sophisticated cable drama about a patriarchal subculture" (para. 3).

2. According to Nussbaum, how does *Game of Thrones* resemble shows like *Mad Men* and *The Sopranos*?

3. What does Nussbaum mean by saying "the most compelling plots remain those of the subalterns, who are forced to wield power from below" (para. 6)?

4. In your own words, describe Nussbaum's attitude toward the violence, nudity, and sex scenes in *Game of Thrones*.

5. Why does Nussbaum conclude that "there is something troubling about this sea of C.G.I.-perfect flesh, shaved and scentless and not especially medieval" (para. 10)?

READING THE SIGNS

1. **CONNECTING TEXTS**   Using Jeffrey Fleishman's "How an Angry National Mood Is Reflected in Pop Culture" (p. 531), analyze how *Game of Thrones* reflects current American attitudes toward class and power. To develop your ideas further, consult Michael Parenti's "Class and Virtue" (p. 354).

2. In class, discuss how Nussbaum's review article, published in the *New Yorker*, differs from a scholarly analysis of a mass media product. For comparison, you might compare it to Anna Keszeg's or Massimo Pigliucci's essays, both of which are scholarly articles, in this chapter.

3. In class, brainstorm the system of "sword and sorcery" productions (*Lord of the Rings* is just one that comes to mind). In your own essay, locate *Game of Thrones* within this system and analyze how it both resembles and differs

from the other entertainments in the system. What is the most crucial difference that you identify, and what does that difference signify?

4. Watch a current or more recent episode of *Game of Thrones*. In an analytic essay, assess the extent to which the episode you choose demonstrates Nussbaum's assertion that "the undergirding strength of each series is its insight into what it means to be excluded from power: to be a woman, or a bastard, or a 'half man'" (para. 3).

MASSIMO PIGLIUCCI

The One Paradigm to Rule Them All: Scientism and The Big Bang Theory

Mash up *Friends* with *Seinfeld*, toss in a dash of *Son of Flubber*, and what do you get? *The Big Bang Theory*, TV's perennial Nielsen chart-topper. And one of the things that makes this hit series so popular, Massimo Pigliucci argues in this philosophical analysis of the show, is its persistent, and hilarious, takedowns of "scientism": that is, the belief that science has all the answers to life, the universe, and everything. For while the goofy geniuses of *The Big Bang Theory* do know an awful lot about, say, connecting every electrical device in their apartments to the Internet, they don't always have a lot of simple common sense, which is where human capabilities beyond scientific acumen come in. And that's the point. Massimo Pigliucci is a former evolutionary biologist turned philosophy professor at the City University of New York's Lehman College and Graduate Center, who is the author of *Nonsense on Stilts: How to Tell Science from Bunk* (2010).

Why is *The Big Bang Theory* so funny? Some fans think it's the writing; others, the acting; still others, the directing. Different aspects of the show no doubt work together on multiple levels. This essay explores one way in which the various facets — writing, acting, directing — come together to make us laugh. The characters of Sheldon Cooper, Leonard Hofstadter, Howard Wolowitz, and Rajesh "Raj" Koothrappali are so funny (in part) due to their extremely "scientistic" worldviews, entirely framed by their practice of science. The humor manifests as their scientific approach unfolds in everyday life. They, of course, invariably fail at various mundane tasks, in sharp contrast with their nonintellectual but much more pragmatic neighbor Penny. In this way, art teaches us something about life. Through the lens of *The Big Bang Theory*, we can see how attempts to develop a thoroughgoing scientistic worldview are bound to fail, calling for more balanced approaches to understanding the world around us.

The Data

In "The Hamburger Postulate," Leonard Hofstadter finally decides to ask his equally nerdy colleague, Leslie Winkle, to go out on a date:

> LEONARD: Leslie, I would like to propose an experiment. . . . I was thinking of a bio-social exploration with a neuro-chemical overlay.
> LESLIE: Wait, are you asking me out?
> LEONARD: I was going to characterize it as a modification of our colleagues slash friendship paradigm with the addition of a date-like component, but we don't need to quibble over terminology.

Leslie suggests they simplify things a bit, as in any good scientific experiment, by skipping the actual date and going straight to the kissing stage. This will determine empirically what sort of neuro-chemical arousal they get from the experience and hence determine whether they wish, in fact, to begin dating. Leslie reports that Leonard's kiss produces absolutely no arousal in her, ending their experiment and Leonard's inquiry. Having agreed with the parameters, he quietly leaves the lab a bit wistful.

It's "Anything Can Happen Thursday Night" from "The Hofstadter Isotope," and the guys are — gasp — considering going out to a bar to pick up women. Leonard quickly comes back to Earth, muttering, "C'mon, Howard, the odds of us picking up girls in a bar are practically zero." Undaunted, Wolowitz replies, "Oh, really? Are you familiar with the Drake equation?" Sheldon unflinchingly recites the formula for the Drake equation, used to calculate the odds of finding an extraterrestrial civilization with whom to communicate.[1] "Yeah, that one!" Howard quickly injects and continues:

> You can modify it to calculate our chances of having sex by changing the formula to use the number of single women in Los Angeles, the number of those who might find us attractive, and what I call the Wolowitz coefficient: Neediness, times Stress, squared. In crunching the numbers I came up with a conservative 5,812 potential sex partners within a 40 mile radius.

[1] The actual equation looks like this: $N = R * fp * ne * fl * fi * fc * L$. Where N is the number of civilizations in our galaxy with whom communication is possible; R is the average galactic rate of star formation per year; fp is the fraction of stars with planets; ne is the average number of potentially life-sustaining planets per star; fl is the fraction of planets actually developing life; fi is the further fraction developing intelligent life; fc is the fraction of civilizations developing communication technology; and L is the length of time these civilizations produce detectable signals. You can play with the equation yourself here: <www.activemind.com/Mysterious/Topics/SETI/drake_equation.html> .

Leonard muses that he must be joking. Stone-faced, Howard replies, "I'm a horny engineer, Leonard, I never joke about math or sex."

In "The Friendship Algorithm," Sheldon endeavors to develop a scientific approach to acquiring friends. He proceeds to demonstrate the power of the algorithm over the phone, trying to convince the irksome Barry Kripke to spend time with him. Sheldon, however, soon gets stuck in an infinite loop caused by the structure of his own algorithm. Howard notices this and promptly strolls over to Sheldon's whiteboard to modify the procedure, thereby helping Sheldon achieve his goal. Placing his hand over the phone, Sheldon muses, "A loop counter, and an escape to the least objectionable activity. Howard, that's brilliant. I'm surprised you saw that." Slowly making his way back to his chair, Howard rhetorically and sarcastically asks, "Gee, why can't Sheldon make friends?"

These examples illustrate the attempt to reduce complex social skills to simple matters of logic, of the kind that might be implemented in a computer program. Once we are finished chuckling at Sheldon, Howard, Leonard, or Raj, the inevitable reaction is: dating or making friends simply isn't that cut and dried. This, in turn, leads us to ask: why even try to apply scientific methodologies to complex social interactions? Why think that science holds all of the answers?

The Background

Science is indisputably the most effective way human beings have developed to understand — and even control, to a point — the natural world. It used to be a branch of philosophy, until the scientific revolution of the seventeenth century. Galileo and Newton thought of themselves as "natural philosophers," and the very term *scientist* was coined by the philosopher William Whewell as recently as 1834, in analogy with the word *artist*. The root of the term, however, is the Latin *scientia*, which means knowledge broadly construed, not only in the sense of what we today consider scientific knowledge.

Scientism is the idea that science can and should be expanded to every domain of human knowledge or interest, including the social sciences and the humanities, or alternatively the idea that the only kind of knowledge really worth having is that provided by the natural sciences. The appeal of scientism may derive from another important idea that is fundamental to the practice of science: reductionism. Reductionism is a basic and very successful approach common to the physical and biological sciences, articulated by René Descartes (1596–1650) in his *Meditations on First Philosophy*. Descartes was interested in establishing firm epistemic foundations for mathematics, philosophy, and science. To this end, he proffered four principles that he discovered on which to build a successful science. The second and third principles summarized the practice of reductionism:

The second, to divide each of the difficulties under examination into as many parts as possible, and as might be necessary for its adequate solution. The third, to conduct my thoughts in such order that, by commencing with objects the simplest and easiest to know, I might ascend by little and little, and, as it were, step by step, to the knowledge of the more complex; assigning in thought a certain order even to those objects which in their own nature do not stand in a relation of antecedence and sequence.[2]

The "divide and conquer" strategy (second principle), coupled with the "building from the bottom up" (third principle) approach, are exactly how physics has been able to subsume the entire domain of chemistry, and why molecular biology has been such a successful science since the discovery of the structure of DNA as recently as 1953. It is this triumph of the Cartesian method that has made reductionism a staple of the way science is done today.

Moreover, there is an intuitive appeal to reductionism and, by extension, to scientism, because of the common acknowledgment — among both scientists and philosophers — that the world is made of the same kind of basic stuff, be it quarks or superstrings. From this, it is tempting to conclude that a complete understanding of the world can be arrived at by simply studying the basic stuff of the universe carefully. Of course, science — particularly physics — is the discipline that studies the basic stuff of the universe. Perhaps this kind of thinking fuels the heated discussion between Leslie and Sheldon about string theory and loop quantum gravity in "The Codpiece Topology." If a complete understanding of everything depends on exploring the basic stuff of the universe, it is very important that you are studying the correct basic stuff.

The Ramifications

The term *scientism* is almost never used in a positive sense; rather, it is ordinarily meant as an insult, usually hurled by (some) philosophers and humanists at scientists who seem to trespass on territory that does not belong to them. True, Howard's attempt to mathematically quantify the delicate art of human dating is amusing, as is Leslie and Leonard's experiment. And Sheldon's attempt at friendship is simply comical. Yet what accounts for the animosity associated with scientism?

Consider that staunchly valuing a scientific approach to things may hamper our ability to see the "bigger picture." These days, for instance, our society

10

---

[2]In case you are really curious, here are the first and the fourth; "The first was never to accept anything for true which I did not clearly know to be such; that is to say, carefully to avoid precipitancy and prejudice, and to comprise nothing more in my judgment than what was presented to my mind so clearly and distinctly as to exclude all ground of doubt." And: "The last, in every case to make enumerations so complete, and reviews so general, that I might be assured that nothing was omitted."

seems to be in the thrall of a quantification frenzy: we wish to measure (and compare) people's intelligence or learning or happiness by using simple, linear scales that afford us a feeling of precision and scientific accuracy. The risk, of course, is that we may miss the structure (and beauty?) of the forest because we are focused on counting the individual trees, discounting the importance of anything that is not amenable to a scientific-quantifying approach (think again of Sheldon's friendship algorithm) or straitjacketing complex phenomena (such as intelligence, learning, or happiness) into easily digestible numbers that make our decisions and our entire worldview much simpler than they would otherwise be.

Even Sheldon seems to get close to understanding this point during a conversation with his sister Missy in "The Pork Chop Indeterminacy." Introducing her to the rest of the gang, he says, "She is my twin sister, she thinks she is funny, but frankly I've never been able to see it." Missy knowingly replies, "That's because you have no measurable sense of humor, Shelly." Without skipping a beat, Sheldon rhetorically asks, "How exactly would one measure a sense of humor? A humor-mometer?" The delightful play on the term *measurable* shows that Missy, and not Sheldon, has a sense of humor exactly because humor resists quantifiable analysis.

Too much emphasis on science also risks becoming a sterile end, in and of itself, as in this exchange from "The Cooper-Hofstadter Polarization," where the boys proudly show Penny a new piece of software that Howard developed, which allows people from all over the world to take control of Leonard and Sheldon's apartment's fixtures:

LEONARD: See?
PENNY: No.
SHELDON: [impatiently] Someone in Szechuan province, China, is using his computer to turn our lights on and off.
PENNY: Oh, that's . . . handy. Ahem, here is a question: why?

When the four scientists answer, in unison, "Because we can," Penny shakes her head in exasperation. The exercise is fascinating to the boys because it shows that it can be done, even though there are much better (but less "scientific") ways of accomplishing the same goal. Penny would simply have them use the light switch (or, at most, buy a universal remote from Radio Shack.)

Philosophers who criticize scientistic approaches to human problems seek to highlight the ethical issues raised by a science-based view of everything. When we attempt to reduce, or reinterpret, the humanities and our everyday experience in scientific terms, we not only are bound to miss something important, we also risk dehumanizing our own and other people's existence, possibly even becoming callous about the dangers of doing certain types of science on the ground that the latter represents in itself the highest conceivable goal. For instance, since the Large Hadron Collider (LHC), the world's highest energy particle accelerator, has gone into service near Geneva (Switzerland), there has been discussion of the possible dangers posed by some of the experiments planned for the facility. The controversy is briefly featured in "The Pork Chop Indeterminacy." Leonard informs Raj, "Some physicists are concerned that if the Supercollider actually works, it will create a black hole and swallow up the earth, ending life as we know it." Raj unsympathetically answers, "What a bunch of crybabies."

True, there doesn't seem to actually be any measurable (!) risk of a black hole suddenly materializing inside the LHC and destroying the Earth, but science does have a long history of questionable effects on human life, from the tragedy of the eugenic movement (which from 1909 through the 1960s was responsible for the forced sterilization of sixty thousand individuals deemed to be genetically "unfit" in the United States) to the invention of nuclear weapons and the development of biological warfare. So an argument can be made that we shouldn't necessarily carry out certain types of scientific research just "because we can," as the boys explained to Penny. Science needs the guidance of external disciplines — such as ethics — as well as a serious engagement with public discourse to avoid eugenics-type Frankenstein scenarios. Yet this assumes the very thing that a scientistic approach denies: that meaningful rational discourse is possible or relevant outside of science itself.

Even if scientists know best, should science be used to improve the human condition without the explicit consent of the people whose lives are affected, in order to achieve the alleged improvement? And what constitutes an "improvement" in our existence, anyway? This question is implicitly posed in "The Gothowitz Deviation," when Leonard discovers that Sheldon is using positive reinforcement (a behavioral control technique devised by B. F. Skinner) with Penny — giving her chocolate every time she does something he likes:

LEONARD: You can't train my girlfriend like a lab rat.

SHELDON: Actually, it turns out I can.

LEONARD: Well, you shouldn't.

SHELDON: There is just no pleasing you, is there, Leonard? You weren't happy with my previous approach in dealing with her, so I decided to employ operant conditioning techniques. . . . I'm just tweaking her personality, sanding off the rough edges, if you will.

LEONARD: No, you are not sanding Penny!

SHELDON: Oh c'mon, you can't tell me that you are not intrigued by the possibility of building a better girlfriend.

The exchange is hilarious, but the underlying issue — the interplay between science at all costs and a consideration of extrascientific ethical values — has led to some horrifying outcomes, even in recent history. One of the most notorious cases is the Tuskegee syphilis experiment, conducted in Tuskegee, Alabama, between 1932 and 1972. Doctors working with the U.S.

government began a study of 399 black men affected by syphilis, as well as an additional 201 used as controls, without telling the men in question that they had the disease. More crucially, once an effective cure became available — with the development of penicillin in the mid-1940s — the researchers knowingly withdrew treatment from the subjects. The study continued for decades and was terminated only because of a leak to the press, with the resulting controversy eventually leading to federal legislation to regulate scientific research that affected human subjects, as well as to the establishment of the Office for Human Research Protections.[3]

The Analysis

So, what exactly is the problem with scientism, and what solutions are available to us? The answers to these two questions are actually among the several comedic premises that make *The Big Bang Theory* work so well as a show: respectively, the tendency of scientists to overreach, and the push back we can generate by applying some common sense (along with, perhaps, good philosophical reflection). Again, there should be no question that science is by far the best toolbox that humanity has come up with to discover how the world works. Science also needs much defending, as it has been under increasing attack recently, with large portions of Americans denying the theory of evolution, rejecting the notion of anthropogenic climate change, or believing that somehow vaccines cause autism.[4] As Carl Sagan aptly put it in his *The Demon-Haunted World*, a classic collection of essays about pseudoscience and assorted nonsense, science is like a very precious candle in the dark, which deserves our respect and requires our protection.

Yet it should be equally clear that science has a proper domain of application (however large). This implies that there are areas where science doesn't belong or it is not particularly informative or has nothing to do with what we really want. One of the benefits of *The Big Bang Theory* is its effectiveness in demonstrating this point, especially through many of the lighthearted exchanges between Penny and Sheldon.

One such exchange is particularly relevant to the debate about scientism. In "The Work Song Nanocluster," Sheldon volunteers to help Penny make her new "Penny Blossom" business enterprise become as profitable as possible. A bit surprised, Penny asks, "And you know about that stuff?" Sheldon, slightly scoffing, answers, "Penny, I'm a physicist. I have a working

20

---

[3]Disturbingly, however, some federal agencies can still engage in human research without consent, via a presidential executive order, presumably under the increasingly all-encompassing excuse of "national security."

[4]For a fuller discussion of the relationship between science and pseudoscience, see my own *Nonsense on Stilts: How to Tell Science from Bunk* (Chicago: University of Chicago Press, 2010).

knowledge of the entire universe and everything it contains." Rather annoyed, Penny asks a question to test Sheldon's hypothesis: "Who's Radiohead?" This time skipping many beats, Sheldon musters, "I have a working knowledge of the *important* things in the universe." This is a near perfect example of the fallacy of scientism: physicists may one day be successful in arriving at a theory of everything, but "everything" has a very specific and limited meaning here, referring to the basic building blocks of the universe. It does not follow, either epistemologically or ontologically, that one can then simply apply the Cartesian method to work one's way up from superstrings to the cultural significance of Radiohead.[5] Moreover, Sheldon is offering a not-so-implicit value judgment here. Yet one could reasonably ask, why is theoretical physics the only important mode of discourse? Or, more to the point, how could Sheldon prove or justify this position within science alone? Value judgments, again following David Hume, seem distinct from scientific discourse exactly because what is or can be done is no sure guide to what ought to be done.

Moreover, it is downright pernicious for science, as well as for society at large, when prominent scientists such as Stephen Hawking declare an entire field of inquiry (philosophy) dead. Hawking does so, while at the same time engaging in some (bad) philosophical reasoning throughout his book, particularly when he comments on the very nature of science — a classic domain of study for philosophy. Or consider again Sam Harris, who wrote an entire tome about how science can provide us with values, rejecting without argument one of the most fundamental distinctions made by philosophers, the one between empirical facts and values.[6] Harris does this while at the same time making a very particular (and entirely unacknowledged) set of philosophical choices right at the beginning of his book, such as taking onboard a consequentialist ethical philosophy as the basis for his ideas about human happiness.

---

[5]Epistemology is the branch of philosophy that deals with what we can know, while ontology is the branch that attends to the existence of things. In this context, reductionism may be ontologically insufficient to explain reality, if it turns out that there are truly novel ("emergent") phenomena at higher levels of complexity that cannot be directly reduced to lower levels. Even if ontologically feasible, reductionism surely does not work epistemologically, because it would make for an unwieldy account of reality above the quantum level. For instance, while engineers certainly agree that a bridge is, ultimately, made of quarks (ontology), attempting to describe its macroscopic physical properties by developing a detailed quantum mechanical model of it (epistemology) would be sheer folly.

[6]To be fair, even some philosophers, such as W. V. O. Quine, have questioned the existence of a sharp distinction between facts and values, but they have done so within strict limits and based on careful arguments. Harris, instead, simply thinks that philosophical arguments are capable only of increasing the degree of boredom in the universe and accordingly dismisses them out of hand—an exceedingly anti-intellectual attitude exhibited by a self-styled public intellectual.

A much more reasonable view, I think, is that natural science, social science, philosophy, literature, and art each must have a respected place at the high table of societal discourse, because they are all necessary — and none sufficient — for human flourishing. Or, as it was so beautifully put in "The Panty Piñata Polarization,"

> SHELDON: Woman, you are playing with forces beyond your Ken.
> PENNY: Yeah, well, your Ken can kiss my Barbie.

Philosophically, I can see no better way to articulate the message: sometimes, science is just not the point, and it certainly isn't the only point.

READING THE TEXT

1. Explain in your own words the meaning of "scientism."
2. In what ways does *The Big Bang Theory* satirize scientism?
3. What dangers does Pigliucci find in a belief in scientism?
4. Describe Pigliucci's attitude toward *The Big Bang Theory*. What evidence can you provide to support your description?
5. In offering his reading of *The Big Bang Theory*, Pigliucci refers to episodes in scientific history (such as the Tuskegee syphilis experiement) and to real-life scientists (such as Stephen Hawking). What effect do these sorts of references have on your response to his essay?

READING THE SIGNS

1. In class, brainstorm TV shows and films that feature scientists. Use the class's list as a starting point for your own essay in which you analyze semiotically the popular image of scientists in modern entertainment. Do you find any differences in this image depending on genre (science fiction, comedy, or drama, for instance)? If so, what do they signify?
2. Write an essay in which you support, refute, or qualify Pigliucci's thesis that *The Big Bang Theory* is a a critique of scientism.
3. In an essay, write your own response to Pigliucci's opening question: "Why is *The Big Bang Theory* so funny?" (para. 1).
4. Watch several episodes of *The Big Bang Theory*, with at least one from the show's early years and another that is recent. Write an essay in which you describe the evolution of the show. What changes do you identify, and what do they signify?
5. Write an essay in which you support, oppose, or complicate Pigliucci's contention that "when we attempt to reduce, or reinterpret, the humanities and our everyday experience in scientific terms, we not only are bound to miss something important, we also risk dehumanizing our own and other people's existence, possibly even becoming callous about the dangers of doing certain types of science on the ground that the latter represents in itself the highest conceivable goal" (para. 14).

CLARA McNULTY-FINN
The Evolution of Rap

> Rap has come a long way since DJs Kool Herc and Hollywood began experimenting with funk and disco in the 1970s. Arguably the most popular of popular musical genres today, rap/hip-hop continues to evolve, and in this survey of its evolution from the 1990s into the new millennium, Clara McNulty-Finn looks at the changes that have taken place in the era of social networking. The "gangsta rap" era has become the anything-goes age, in which "successful hip-hop artists rap about everything from thrift shopping to the sheer excess of their lifestyles." Clara McNulty-Finn is a writer and editor for the *Harvard Political Review*.

Even those unfamiliar with the genre can recognize that rap and hip-hop are not what they used to be. A pre-2005 hip-hop or rap hit can be easily distinguished from a track released in the past decade, and artists who have gotten into the game within the last ten years bear little similarity to what was the norm for '90s-era rappers.

Earlier hip-hop music has a distinct tone with a relatively consistent theme of "hood politics," a term referenced by Nas in his 2002 hit "One Mic." Meanwhile, the artists themselves maintained strict "gangster" personas: most of the genre's biggest names, such as The Notorious B.I.G. and Jay-Z, were known drug dealers and many were convicted criminals.

Just a decade later, some of the most successful rap hits relay messages formerly unheard of in the genre while the artists themselves come from a variety of backgrounds. Rappers such as Macklemore have hits about formerly taboo subjects like homosexuality, and artists such as Drake, a former Canadian child actor, prove that being a "thug" is no longer a pre-requisite to success. In fact, in an interview with ABC, Drake confessed that he was once described as "the furthest thing from hood."

Indeed, everything from the definition of mainstream hip-hop to the function of record labels to the personas of the artists themselves has evolved over the past decade. While some aspects of this evolution are obvious, it is in the subtleties of these changes that the inextricable link between social and musical development is revealed. The hip-hop/rap genre, despite having garnered a reputation of violence and misogyny, is a uniquely genuine voice amidst the development of our culture.

Lyrics and Society

Perhaps the most striking difference between 1990s hip-hop and more modern tracks is the lyrics. In general, hip-hop in the previous decade had a relatively narrow focus. Songs were less about an artist's success and more about his or her rise to it; even the most financially successful rappers wrote about violence, crime, and living in poverty. According to Rauly Ramirez, manager of Billboard's Hip-Hop chart, '90s rappers "would create this persona," portraying themselves as thugs and gangsters because that was "the character [they] had to be to succeed." The necessity for an artist to create and maintain this character led to a common theme among rap songs in the '90s. Rap was the story of the ghetto life and the anthem of gangsters, which prevented hip-hop from joining pop and rock in the mainstream.

Those who did listen to hip-hop, however, found that even as artists were carefully constructing their persona, there was honesty in their lyrics. Poppa Sims, a lyricist associated with the major record label Bad Boy Records, emphasized that in writing openly about violence and drugs, '90s hip-hop artists forced listeners to consider the "underlying reasons behind these things . . . it was survival." Indeed, the early era of rap publicized the notion that poverty begets crime. On his 2002 debut album "Gangster and a Gentleman," artist Styles P claimed that after a childhood of abuse and poverty, "the best thing that happened" to him was breaking into the crack industry because he was finally "gettin' everything that [he] was askin' about."

While, a decade later, rap lyrics still tell an artist's story, each rapper has a different one; artists no longer need to write about the "ghetto life" to be signed by a major record label. The definition of who a rapper can be, and what stories hip-hop can tell, has broadened indefinitely since the mid-2000s. Ramirez pinpoints the origins of this transition to the release of Kanye West's 2004 debut album, "The College Dropout." Rather than focusing on drug dealing or violence or living on the streets, the album addressed religion, West's pursuit of music, and as he says on the track "Breathe In Breathe Out," his desire to "say something significant."

In the years following the release of Kanye's first album, more and more rappers moved away from "gangsta rap" and towards developing their individuality as artists. Today's most successful hip-hop artists rap about everything from thrift shopping to the sheer excess of their lifestyles. Even as sexuality increasingly perpetuates mainstream hip-hop, artists are less afraid to present a softer side to relationships as well. In J Cole's 2013 hit "Power Trip," the sole reference to drug usage was the line "love is a drug, like the strongest stuff ever" and Drake, whose album "Take Care" topped the Hip-Hop/Rap Charts in 2012, confessed in "Shot for Me" that he "never cheated, for the record." Indeed, contrary to the themes of aggression and illegality that perpetuated earlier hip-hop, many of today's biggest artists have taken a gentler approach towards romance even amidst the genre's misogynistic reputation.

Social Media and the Internet

The Internet, and in particular the role of social media, has become an irrefutable reflection of societal development. Websites like Tumblr and Facebook, where users can express themselves by publishing photos or writing blog posts, seem to emphasize a fresh pursuit of individuality and self-expression. Meanwhile, a person's ability to share these updates with "followers" or "friends" suggests a simultaneous desire to achieve a sense of community. According to WAJZ-FM program director J Will, it is this rising relevance of social media sites that bears responsibility for many of the stylistic developments within the hip-hop genre.

Prior to the rise of social media, an artist's sole means of establishing a   10
fan base was to capture the attention of a record label. With only a few major labels in the business, this reliance on agents contributed to the streamlined message seen in '90s rap lyrics. But as emerging rap artist Miles From Nothing puts it, "we're in an era where artists don't need agents. If they know how to use sites like SoundCloud and YouTube, they can get themselves out there." Ramirez agrees, admitting that in many respects social media outlets have replaced the function of A&R scouts, who ordinarily are responsible for recruiting artists to different record labels.

Not having to uphold the expectations of a record label allows artists to craft their own message while still finding success. Immortal Technique is one rapper whose albums underscore the effects of this artistic freedom. Immortal Technique, who has released five albums since 2002, has not signed with a record label, giving him the freedom to rap about controversial political and social issues. In his 2008 album "The 3rd World," for example, he raps that the United States government "[calls] us terrorists after they ruined our countries . . . and that's not socialist mythology, this is urban warfare." While not all unsigned artists choose to pursue such controversial themes, they are able to create a loyal fan base through social media and music sharing sites while maintaining complete control over the music they're producing.

Even as sites like YouTube allow rappers more freedom in constructing their messages, social media outlets like Twitter and Instagram give listeners an entirely new level of access to their favorite artist's daily life. Will suggests that, because we live in an Internet-infused world "where people want to connect with one another," we crave a sincerity-driven connection with rap artists. As the barriers between these artists and their fans break away, honesty has become an integral part of a record's success and an artist's longevity. It used to be "very much about painting a picture," Ramirez notes. "Now it's about being yourself."

Underground Versus the Mainstream, Then and Now

The rise of the Internet age affected one other crucial aspect of the hip-hop genre. With social media providing increased visibility for artists, what constitutes a mainstream rapper, and the relationship between artists and radio stations, has changed completely. Underground '90s rap, according to Ramirez, stuck to politically and socially conscious messages as opposed to "the [gangster] theme that perpetuated a lot of mainstream hip-hop." While

'90s mainstream artists signed with major labels and maintained a "thug" persona, underground groups such as Public Enemy spat lyrics like "how the hell can a color be no good for a neighborhood," a line from their 2000 track "Who Stole the Soul."

Fast forward a decade and, with the aid of social media, there is no longer a single theme for mainstream hip-hop artists. As Will puts it, mainstream music has become about "how well [a track's] message resonates with the typical person." The more universal a song, the larger an audience it will reach; now that hip-hop has become more accepted by the masses, the potential for rap artists to make it big is even greater.

That being said, even artists who avoid the mainstream by remaining independent of any major record label can still find financial success. Of the 75 rap albums that topped the Billboard Rap charts since 2010, nearly 15 percent were produced by artists considered outside of the mainstream. However, despite the fact that underground rappers now have the potential to succeed financially, because they rap about themes that appeal only to a loyal niche of listeners, Will admits that "the chance of their music actually making it onto radio is unlikely."

The hip-hop that does play on the radio is different from '90s rap not only in message but in sound. Ally Reid, station manager at FLY 92.3, says that she has seen an increase in collaboration between hip-hop artists and vocalists from other genres. "There are genres that used to exist," she observes, listing rap and pop as examples, but "a lot of those boundaries have really . . . broken away." Ramirez agrees, adding that "the songs that fly up to the top of the rap charts . . . are a blending of the genres. They're the most digestible." Hip-hop artists who do choose to sign with major labels such as Columbia or Republic Records are encouraged to find pop artists to sing catchy hooks, or add more of a dance beat to their record, in order to achieve success on a mainstream scale.

What Hasn't Changed

Of course, some aspects of the genre haven't changed. As Poppa Sims puts it, in addition to a commitment to honest communication, an artist's "longevity comes from the fact that [he or she] put in real, hard work." Most of today's biggest rappers, such as Eminem, Jay-Z and Lil Wayne, debuted in the '90s era of rap, and have since worked to establish their own record labels and production companies while continuing to record in order to secure their footholds in the music industry.

But this type of decades-long success is also dependent on an artist's commitment to telling their story and maintaining a consistent message, even if it requires doing more of the production legwork to avoid the inherent limitations of signing with a label. If a rapper can't get people to "familiarize themselves with who they are, then they're easily forgotten," Sims attests. An artist's success, therefore, is contingent upon his or her sincerity across albums. Ramirez cites artist 50 Cent as an example of how damaging a lack of honesty can be. "He defined a very strong persona early on," Ramirez says, but people just "wanted to see him as a person." Because 50 never adapted to the demand for sincerity in hip-hop music, he remains removed from the comparative success of fellow "mainstream" artists.

There seems to be a general agreement that these basic strategies for success won't be changing anytime soon. Ramirez predicts that as long as social media remains relevant, "doors will continue to open . . . for different characters and different styles," and it will become even easier for new artists to break into the game and for rappers to find success independently. More and more hip-hop artists are finding their way into the mainstream as well. Will attributes this to more listeners "opening up their ears to the genre, and understanding that this is just another way people are communicating." As it continues to evolve alongside the development of social media and the Internet, rap will only strengthen its foothold in the music world. In the words of Will, "hip hop is here to stay."

READING THE TEXT

1. Summarize in your own words how the lyrics of hip-hop/rap have changed since the early 1990s.

2. According to McNulty-Finn, how has the rise of social media affected the evolution of hip-hop/rap?

3. What, in McNulty-Finn's view, distinguishes mainstream hip-hop that receives radio play from "underground," often self-produced music?

4. What evidence does McNulty-Finn provide to support her contention that "the hip-hop/rap genre, despite having garnered a reputation of misogyny, is a uniquely genuine voice amidst the development of our culture" (para. 4)?

READING THE SIGNS

1. Write a journal entry in which you brainstorm your favorite musical artists, whether their music is rap or another genre. Then discuss why you are attracted to these artists. What do your musical choices say about your identity?

2. In class, conduct a debate on whether hip-hop/rap is, as McNulty-Finn contends, "a uniquely genuine voice amidst the development of our culture" (para. 4). To support your team's position, be sure to garner evidence drawn from both the early days of hip-hop/rap and current incarnations of the genre.

3. Write an essay in which you support, oppose, or modify Rauly Ramirez's belief that Kanye West was pivotal in defining what a rapper could be. To support your thesis, ground your analysis in readings of both West's songs and their accompanying videos.

4. Rap has long been embraced by non-black performers and audiences. Write an essay on the effect that rap's acceptance "by the masses" (para. 14), as McNulty-Finn puts it, has had on the genre.

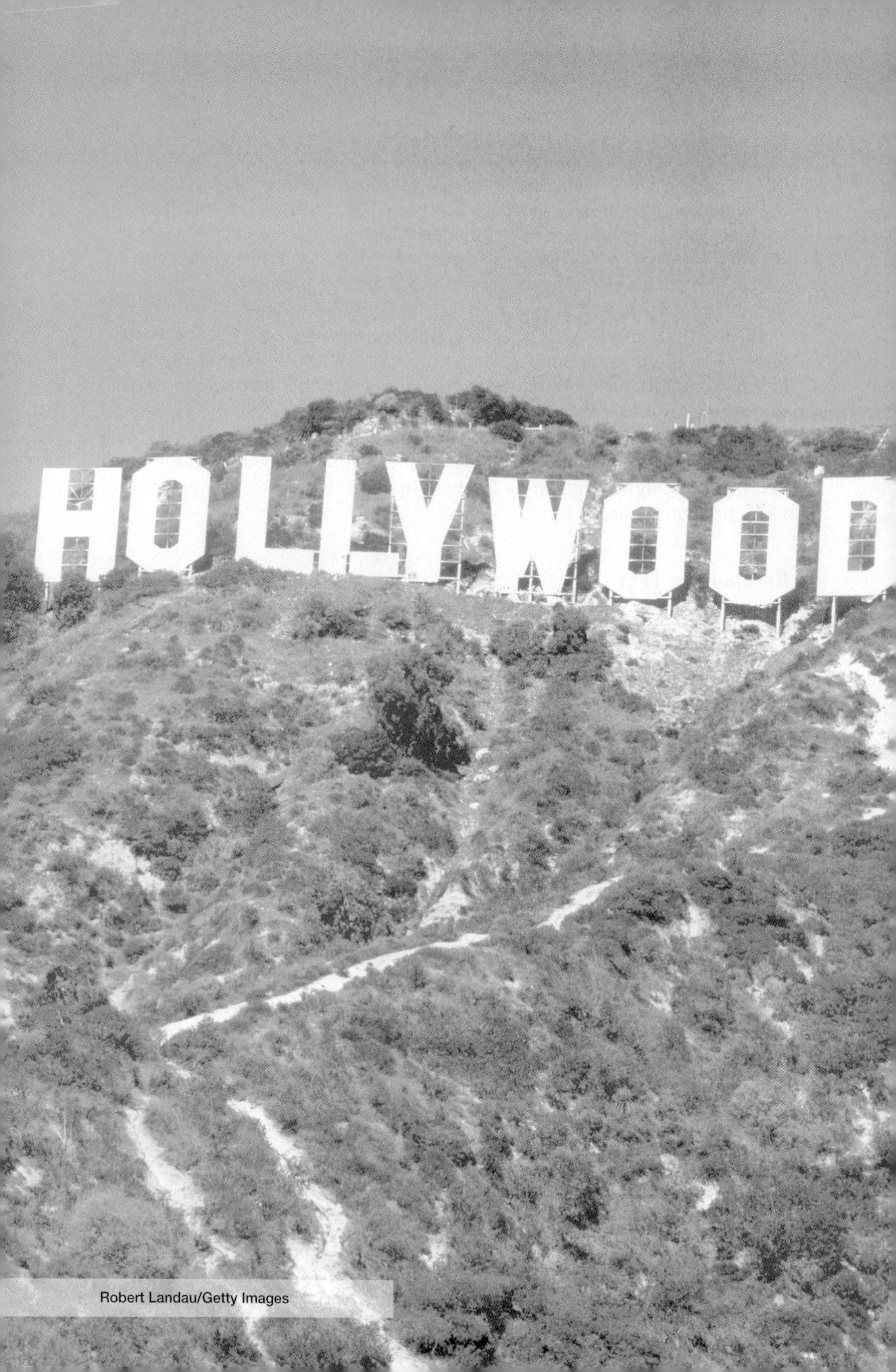

Robert Landau/Getty Images

4

THE HOLLYWOOD SIGN
The Culture of American Film

For Godzilla's Sake!

It's a strange day in Hollywood when a gigantically destructive monster is cast as the *hero* of a movie. But that is exactly what happened when, in 2014, Gareth Edwards brought out the thirtieth installment in the never-ending Godzilla saga, reconstructing the iconic dragon/dinosaur as humanity's last hope against even more fearsome beasties. While this was not the first time that Godzilla had been so cast (in both Japanese and American versions of the story), Edwards's *Godzilla* offers a particularly instructive lesson in cinematic semiotics.

Performing a semiotic analysis of *Godzilla* would appear to be a disarmingly easy task. After all, the marketers of the film went out of their way to state explicitly what the film "means." Even the description on the film's DVD package declares that "this spectacular adventure pits Godzilla, the world's most famous monster, against malevolent creatures that, bolstered by humanity's scientific arrogance, threaten our very existence." And just in case we miss the point, Edwards himself announced in a Comic-Con interview that "Godzilla is definitely a representation of the wrath of nature. We've taken it very seriously and the theme is man versus nature and Godzilla is certainly the nature side of it. You can't win that fight. Nature's always going to win and that's what the subtext of our movie is about. He's the punishment we deserve." And so, that would seem to wrap it all up — except that a careful semiotic reading of the movie reveals that this isn't what it's about at all. So let's look again.

Remember that a semiotic analysis takes us from the **denotation** of a sign to its **connotative significance** by situating it in a **historically informed system of associated and differentiated signs**. Using **abductive** reasoning, and keeping in mind the **overdetermined** nature of most cultural **signifiers**, the semiotic analysis arrives at an interpretation. We can do that here by beginning with a denotational plot summary of the movie: what it *shows*.

Although it takes some time to become clear to the viewer, the story concerns the discovery of a prehistoric species of subterranean monsters called MUTOs (for Massive Unidentified Terrestrial Organisms) who thrive on nuclear radiation. The dawning of the atomic age has drawn them to the surface to snack on all the nice nuclear goodies available in such facilities as atomic power plants and nuclear waste dumps, and the main action of the film begins (after setting up a backstory from fifteen years earlier) with a MUTO destroying a Japanese nuclear reactor, which just happens to be under surveillance by a shadowy international research organization called Monarch. This group has been monitoring a heretofore dormant Godzilla, who apparently has been sleeping under the reactor but awakes when the MUTO attacks. After trashing the power plant, the MUTO (a winged male) takes off to hook up with a wingless female MUTO on the U.S. mainland (after a catastrophic stopover in Hawaii), and a young U.S. Navy lieutenant, who happens to be the son of the head engineer of the now defunct Japanese reactor whose personal story opens the film, gets caught up in the mess and joins the attempt to stop the MUTOs. As the U.S. military helplessly attempts (and fails) to stop them, the MUTOs create a nest for hundreds of soon-to-hatch monsters (enough to destroy the solar system, it would seem) in San Francisco. But Godzilla — who is somehow able to hear and understand the MUTO's "language" as they communicate with each other (across the Pacific Ocean) — decides for reasons of his own (yes, Godzilla is a "he" this time around) that he should pursue the MUTOs and destroy them. In the end, he does and then swims off into the sunset as the survivors of a devastated San Francisco cheer him on, while the naval lieutenant is reunited with his beautiful wife and child, who have miraculously escaped the destruction thanks to Godzilla's intervention. While we have omitted some details very much worth pursuing in a longer treatment of the movie, this is its basic denotative setup.

The next step is to construct a system of associations and differences. As a giant reptilian monster, Godzilla can be associated with a larger **archetypal** phylum of monsters that includes medieval dragons, sea monsters, and other giant creatures that emerge from the natural world to threaten humanity. Such monsters, and their stories, have always signified a human apprehension that nature is hostile and must be conquered, and the monster characteristically is slain by a hero (or group of heroes) who thus restores human hegemony over the natural world.

It is therefore significant that when the Japanese creators of the first Godzilla story used this ancient archetype, they introduced a certain *difference*. For while the original Godzilla was certainly a monster and a threat to

A still of Godzilla from the 2014 movie.

humanity who had to be defeated, her existence as the result of nuclear bomb testing could nevertheless be traced to human, not natural, causes. This shifting of the blame, so to speak, from nature to culture, is of especial importance as we look further at the system to which *Godzilla* belongs. For in addition to its archetypal associations, *Godzilla* has cinematic ones. As a member of the monster movie subcategory of the larger action-thriller film genre, it can be associated with a long film history that usually casts the monster as a force to be destroyed. So the fact that, in this version of the film, the monster is the destroyer of much worse monsters and actually saves humanity introduces a second difference — one that is also crucial to understanding the semiotic significance of the film. And when we relate this difference to the one introduced in the 1954 origin story, we can see an emerging counterstory to the usual man versus nature narrative, one in which man, not nature, is the problem.

Such a shift is a clear reflection of a growing historical apprehension that human activity, from the industrial revolution onward, is the real threat to human, and even planetary, survival. Guided by the comments made by the film's director, writers, and actors, we see that *Godzilla* can unquestionably be linked with a great many contemporary movies (like the *Avatar* films) wherein it is man's destructive threat to nature, rather than the other way around, that is at stake. Indeed, as a Monarch scientist in the movie tells an American admiral who is fighting the MUTOs, since human "arrogance" against nature is responsible for the MUTO mess, only nature (in the form of Godzilla) can restore the "balance." To a certain extent, then, *Godzilla* is a signifier of an ever-growing (especially in the era of climate change) apprehension that humanity is making a shambles of the earth. That certainly is the view of the movie's creators and performers, and it is certainly what the movie *says* in its own dialogue. But, as is so often the case with commercial entertainment, there's a hitch, a contradiction, to consider, and we have to dig deeper to find it.

The key to the matter lies in looking not at what the movie *says* about itself but at what it *does*. And this is what *Godzilla* does: It depicts a symbolic creature of the nuclear age (Godzilla = Nature) destroying other creatures (the MUTOs), who are no less "natural" than he is. Thus, the film's final image of the joyful reunion of the naval lieutenant and his family, which Godzilla has made possible, is fundamentally reassuring. Because the real "message" of the movie is that no matter how much humans may damage the earth, nature itself will fix everything. It's like saying "don't worry about global warming, because mother nature will clean up the mess before it gets completely out of hand."

If the movie were more honest, however, the MUTOs would have won. And Godzilla, as a co-creation of the nuclear age getting revenge on humanity (as Edwards claims), would have been on the MUTOs's side. But if the movie had done that, it wouldn't have grossed three quarters of a billion dollars, and that's the real significance here. For when performing a semiotic analysis of popular culture, you must never lose sight of the fact that popular culture exists to produce profits, and uplifting movies produce much higher profits than downers. An apocalyptic image of Godzilla and the MUTOs teaming up to trash the world would have been a downer indeed. So, *Godzilla* instead panders to its audience's desire to see the characters it most identifies with (the handsome naval lieutenant and his adorable family) live happily ever after, at the same time reassuring everyone that although humanity may have messed up the planet, ultimately benign forces (somehow, somewhere) will take care of everything.

The Culture Industry

Filmmakers have been providing Americans with entertainments that have both reflected and shaped their desires for over a century. Long before the advent of TV, movies offered viewers the glamour, romance, and sheer excitement that modern life seems to deny. So effective have movies been in molding audience desire that such early cultural critics as Theodor Adorno and Max Horkheimer[1] accused them of being part of a vast, Hollywood-centered "culture industry" whose products successfully distracted their audiences from the inequities of modern life and, thus, effectively maintained the social status quo under capitalism by drawing everyone's attention away from it.

More recent analysts, however, are far less pessimistic. Indeed, for many cultural studies "populists," films, along with the rest of popular culture, can represent a kind of mass resistance to the political dominance — or what is often called the *hegemony* — of the social and economic powers-that-be. For such critics, films can provide utopian visions of a better world, stimulating their viewers to imagine how their society might be improved, and so, perhaps, inspiring them to go out and do something about it.

---

[1] **Theodor Adorno** (1903–1969) and **Max Horkheimer** (1895–1973) authored *Dialectic of Enlightenment* (1947), a book whose analyses included a scathing indictment of the culture industry. — EDS.

Whether you believe that films distract us from the real world or inspire us to imagine a better one, their central place in contemporary American culture demands interpretation, for their impact goes well beyond the movie theater or Netflix rental. Far from being mere entertainments — as our reading of *Godzilla* demonstrates — movies constitute a profound part of our everyday lives, with every film festival and award becoming big news, and each major release becoming the talk of the country. Just think of the pressure you might feel to discuss the latest film sensation among your friends. Consider how, if you decide to save a few bucks, not watch the latest hit, and wait for the DVD release or to watch it online, you can lose face and be seriously on the social outs. No, nothing is frivolous about the movies. You've been watching them all your life: Now's the time to start thinking about them semiotically.

Interpreting the Signs of American Film

Interpreting a movie or a group of movies is not unlike interpreting a television program or group of programs. Again, you should suspend your personal feelings and aesthetic judgments about your subject. As with any semiotic analysis, your goal is to interpret the cultural significance of your topic, not to give it a thumbs-up or a thumbs-down. Thus, you may find it more rewarding to interpret films that promise to be culturally meaningful than to simply examine your favorite flick. Determining whether a film is culturally meaningful in the prewriting stage, of course, may be a hit-or-miss affair; you may find that your first choice does not present any particularly interesting grounds for interpretation. That's why it can be helpful to consider reasons a particular movie is special, such as enormous popularity or widespread critical attention. Of course, cult favorites, while often lacking in critical or popular attention, can also be signs pointing toward their self-selected audiences and thus are strong candidates for analysis. Academy Award nominees are also reliable as cultural signs.

Your interpretation of a movie or group of movies should begin with a construction of the *system* in which it belongs — that is, those movies, past and present, with which it can be *associated*. While tracing those associations,

---

Discussing the Signs of Film

In any given year, one film may dominate the Hollywood box office, becoming a blockbuster that captures that public's cinematic imagination. In class, discuss which film would be your choice as this year's top hit. Then analyze the film semiotically. Why has *this* film so successfully appealed to so many moviegoers?

be on the lookout for striking *differences* from films that are otherwise like what you are analyzing, because those differences are what often reveal the significance of your subject.

Archetypes are useful features for film analysis as well. An archetype is anything that has been repeated in storytelling from ancient times to the present. There are character archetypes, such as the wise old man, represented by such figures as Yoda and Gandalf, and plot archetypes, such as the heroic quest, which is the archetypal backbone of films like *The Lord of the Rings* trilogy. All those male buddy films — from *Butch Cassidy and the Sundance Kid* to *Lethal Weapon* to *Men in Black* — hark back to archetypal male-bonding stories as old as *The Epic of Gilgamesh* (from the third millennium B.C.E.) and the *Iliad*, while Cruella de Vil from *101 Dalmatians* is sister to the Wicked Witch of the West, Snow White's evil stepmother, and every other witch or crone dreamed up by the patriarchal imagination. All those sea monsters, from Jonah's "whale" to Moby-Dick to the great white shark in *Jaws*, are part of the same archetypal phylum, and every time a movie hero struggles to return home after a long journey — Dorothy to Kansas, Lassie to Timmy — a story as old as Exodus and the *Odyssey* is retold.

Hollywood is well aware of the enduring appeal of archetypes (see Linda Seger's selection in this chapter for a how-to description of archetypal script-writing), and director George Lucas's reliance on the work of anthropologist Joseph Campbell in his creation of the *Star Wars* saga is well known. But it's not always the case that either creators or consumers are consciously aware of the archetypes before them. Part of a culture's collective unconscious, archetypal stories can send messages that their audiences only subliminally understand. A heavy dosage of male-bonding films in a given Hollywood season, for instance, can send the unspoken cultural message that a man can't really make friends with a woman and that women are simply the sexual reward for manly men. Similarly, too many witches in a given Hollywood season can send the antifeminist message that there are too many bitches. Conversely, the modification of an archetype, as in the *female*-bonding film *Thelma and Louise*, can signify a feminist emergence.

Repetition with a Difference

Just as movies frequently repeat ancient archetypal character and plot types, they also may refer to other movies and modern cultural artifacts in what is referred to as a **postmodern** manner. Postmodernism is, in effect, both a historical period and an attitude. As a historical period, postmodernism refers to the culture that emerged during the advent of twentieth-century mass media, one obsessed with electronic imagery and the products of mass culture. As an attitude, postmodernism rejects the values of the past, not to support new values but instead to ironize value systems as such. Thus, in the postmodern worldview, our traditional hierarchical distinctions valuing high culture

---

Exploring the Signs of Film

In your journal, list your favorite movies. Then consider your list: What does it say about you? What **cultural mythologies** do the movies tend to reflect, and why do you think those myths appeal to you? What signs particularly appeal to your emotions? What sort of stories about human life do you most respond to?

---

over low culture, say, or creativity over imitation, tend to get flattened out. What was once viewed in terms of an oppositional hierarchy (origination is opposed to emulation and is superior to it) is reconceived and deconstructed. Postmodern artists, accordingly, tend to reproduce, with an ironic or parodic twist, already-existing cultural images in their work, especially if they can be drawn from mass culture and mass society. Roy Lichtenstein's cartoon canvases, for instance, parody popular comic strips, and Andy Warhol's *Campbell's Soup Cans* repeats the familiar labels of the Campbell Soup Company — thus mixing high culture and mass culture in a new, nonoppositional, relation.

To put this another way, the postmodern worldview holds that it is no longer possible or desirable to create new images; rather, one surveys the vast range of available images that mass culture has to offer, and repeats them, but with a difference. Postmodern filmmakers accordingly allude to existing films in their work, as in the final scene of Tim Burton's *Batman*, which directly alludes to Alfred Hitchcock's *Vertigo*, or Oliver Stone and Quentin Tarantino's *Natural Born Killers*, which recalls *Bonnie and Clyde*. Such allusions to, and repetitions of, existing cultural images in postmodern cinema are called *double-coding*, because of the way that the postmodern artifact simultaneously refers to existing cultural **codes** and recasts them in new contexts. The conclusion of *Batman*, for example, while echoing *Vertigo*'s climactic scene, differs dramatically in its significance, turning from Hitchcock's tragedy to Burton's quasi-farce.

Movies as Metaphors

Sometimes movies can also be seen as metaphors for larger cultural concerns. Consider the classic B-movies of the 1950s. Whenever some "blob" threatened to consume New York or some especially toxic slime escaped from a laboratory, the suggestion that science — especially nuclear science — was threatening to destroy the world filled the theater along with the popcorn fumes. And if it wasn't science that was the threat, Cold War filmmakers could scare us with communism, as in films such as *Invasion of the Body Snatchers,*

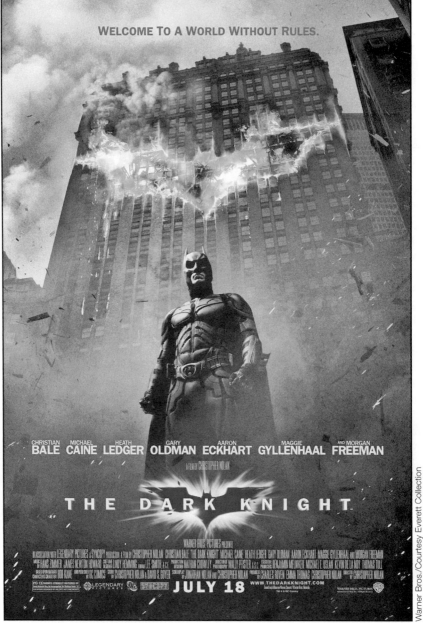

Reading Film Online

Most major films released in the United States have their own Web sites. You can find them listed online under the film's title or in print ads for the film. Select a current film, log on to the Web site, and analyze it semiotically. What images are used to attract your interest in the film? What interactive strategies, if any, are used to increase your commitment to the film? If you've seen the movie, how does the site's presentation of it compare with your experience of viewing it? Alternatively, analyze the posters designed to attract attention to a particular film; a useful resource is the Movie Poster Page (www.musicman.com/mp/mp.html).

---

with its metaphorical depiction of a town in which everyone looked the same but had really been taken over by aliens. "Beware of your neighbors," the movie seemed to warn. "They could be commies."

In such ways, an entire film can be a kind of metaphor, but you can find many smaller metaphors at work in the details of a movie as well. Early film-makers, for example, put a tablecloth on the table in dining scenes to signify that the characters at the table were good, decent people (you can find such a metaphor in Charlie Chaplin's *The Kid*, where an impoverished tramp who can't afford socks or a bathrobe still has a nice tablecloth on the breakfast table). Sometimes a director's metaphors have a broad political significance, as at the end of the Rock Hudson / James Dean / Elizabeth Taylor classic *Giant*, where the parting shot presents a tableau of a white baby goat standing next to a black baby goat, which is juxtaposed with the image of a white baby standing in a crib side by side with a brown baby. Since the human babies are both the grandchildren of the film's protagonist (one of whose sons has married a Mexican woman, the other an Anglo), the goats are added to under-score metaphorically (if rather heavy-handedly) the message of racial reconciliation that the director wanted to send.

Reading a film, then, is much like reading a novel. Both are texts filled with intentional and unintentional signs, metaphors, and archetypes, and both are cultural signifiers. The major difference is in their medium of expression. Literary texts are cast entirely in written words; films combine verbal language, visual imagery, and sound effects. Thus, we perceive literary and cinematic texts differently, for the written sign is perceived in a linear fashion that relies on one's cognitive and imaginative powers, while a film primarily targets the senses: One sees and hears (and sometimes even smells!). That film is such a sensory experience often conceals its textuality. One is tempted to sit back and go with the flow, to say that it's only entertainment and doesn't have to "mean" anything at all. But even the most cartoonish cinematic entertainment can harbor a rather profound cultural significance. Our analysis of *Godzilla* that leads off this chapter is intended to show how. Now it's your turn.

The Readings

Robert B. Ray's "The Thematic Paradigm" begins this chapter, revealing how American cinema has mediated some of this country's most profound cultural contradictions through its portrayals of "official" and "outlaw" heroes. A set of paired readings follows, with Christine Folch analyzing the cultural differences that make sci-fi and fantasy movies all the rage in America but nothing special in India, while Abraham Riesman takes on two of America's favorite fantasy characters and the cultural overtones of their ongoing conflict. Linda Seger next provides a how-to guide for creating the kind of archetypal characters that made *Star Wars* one of the most popular movies of all time. The next three readings address the representation of racial identity in film. Matt Zoller Seitz offers a critical exposé of cinema's "'Magical Negro': a saintly African-American character who acts as a mentor to a questing white hero," and Helena Andrews compares the critical reactions to *The Butler* and *The Help*, revealing that complicated attitudes toward race and gender have affected how the two films have been received. Jessica Hagedorn then surveys a tradition of American filmmaking that stereotypes Asian women as either tragic or trivial. Taking a social-class-based approach to the codes of American cinema, Michael Parenti notes the caste biases inherent in such popular hits as *Pretty Woman*, and Michael Agresta surveys the rise and fall of the once-mighty Western, a genre that even *The Lone Ranger* (not to mention Johnny Depp) was unable to save as America comes to terms with its own history. David Denby concludes the chapter with an explanation for why generations of teenagers flock to all those jocks-and-cheerleaders-versus-the-nerds movies.

ROBERT B. RAY
The Thematic Paradigm

Usually we consider movies to be merely entertainment, but as Robert B. Ray demonstrates in this selection from his book *A Certain Tendency of the Hollywood Cinema* (1985), American films have long reflected fundamental patterns and contradictions in our society's myths and values. Whether in real life or on the silver screen, Ray explains, Americans have always been ambivalent about the value of civilization, celebrating it through official heroes like George Washington and Jimmy Stewart, while at the same time questioning it through outlaw heroes like Davy Crockett and Huck Finn. Especially when presented together in the same film, these two hero types help mediate America's ambivalence, providing a mythic solution. Ray's analyses show how the movies are rich sources for cultural interpretation. Robert B. Ray is a professor of English at the University of Florida at Gainesville.

The dominant tradition of American cinema consistently found ways to overcome dichotomies. Often, the movies' reconciliatory pattern concentrated on a single character magically embodying diametrically opposite traits. A sensitive violinist was also a tough boxer (*Golden Boy*); a boxer was a gentle man who cared for pigeons (*On the Waterfront*). A gangster became a coward because he was brave (*Angels with Dirty Faces*); a soldier became brave because he was a coward (*Lives of a Bengal Lancer*). A war hero was a former pacifist (*Sergeant York*); a pacifist was a former war hero (*Billy Jack*). The ideal was a kind of inclusiveness that would permit all decisions to be undertaken with the knowledge that the alternative was equally available. The attractiveness of Destry's refusal to use guns (*Destry Rides Again*) depended on the tacit understanding that he could shoot with the best of them, Katharine Hepburn's and Claudette Colbert's revolts against conventionality (*Holiday*, *It Happened One Night*) on their status as aristocrats.

Such two-sided characters seemed particularly designed to appeal to a collective American imagination steeped in myths of inclusiveness. Indeed, in creating such characters, classic Hollywood had connected with what Erik Erikson has described as the fundamental American psychological pattern:

> The functioning American, as the heir of a history of extreme contrasts and abrupt changes, bases his final ego identity on some tentative combination of dynamic polarities such as migratory and sedentary, individualistic and standardized, competitive and co-operative, pious and free-thinking, responsible and cynical, etc. . . .
>
> To leave his choices open, the American, on the whole, lives with two sets of "truths."[1]

[1] Erik H. Erikson, *Childhood and Society* (New York: Norton, 1963), p. 286.

The movies traded on one opposition in particular, American culture's traditional dichotomy of individual and community that had generated the most significant pair of competing myths: the outlaw hero and the official hero.[2] Embodied in the adventurer, explorer, gunfighter, wanderer, and loner, the outlaw hero stood for that part of the American imagination valuing self-determination and freedom from entanglements. By contrast, the official hero, normally portrayed as a teacher, lawyer, politician, farmer, or family man, represented the American belief in collective action, and the objective legal process that superseded private notions of right and wrong. While the outlaw hero found incarnations in the mythic figures of Davy Crockett, Jesse James, Huck Finn, and all of Leslie Fiedler's "Good Bad Boys" and Daniel Boorstin's "ring-tailed roarers," the official hero developed around legends associated with Washington, Jefferson, Lincoln, Lee, and other "Good Good Boys."

An extraordinary amount of the traditional American mythology adopted by Classic Hollywood derived from the variations worked by American ideology around this opposition of natural man versus civilized man. To the extent that these variations constituted the main tendency of American literature and legends, Hollywood, in relying on this mythology, committed itself to becoming what Robert Bresson has called "the Cinema."[3] A brief description of the competing values associated with this outlaw hero–official hero opposition will begin to suggest its pervasiveness in traditional American culture.

1. *Aging*: The attractiveness of the outlaw hero's childishness and propensity to whims, tantrums, and emotional decisions derived from America's cult of childhood. Fiedler observed that American literature celebrated "the notion that a mere falling short of adulthood is a guarantee of insight and even innocence." From Huck to Holden Caulfield, children in American literature were privileged, existing beyond society's confining rules. Often, they set the plot in motion (e.g., *Intruder in the Dust*, *To Kill a Mockingbird*), acting for the adults encumbered by daily affairs. As Fiedler also pointed out, this image of childhood "has impinged upon adult life itself, has become a 'career' like everything else in America,"[4] generating stories like *On the Road* or *Easy Rider* in which adults try desperately to postpone responsibilities by clinging to adolescent lifestyles.

While the outlaw heroes represented a flight from maturity, the official heroes embodied the best attributes of adulthood: sound reasoning and judgment, wisdom and sympathy based on experience. Franklin's

---

[2]Leading discussions of the individual–community polarity in American culture can be found in *The Contrapuntal Civilization: Essays Toward a New Understanding of the American Experience*, ed. Michael Kammen (New York: Crowell, 1971). The most prominent analyses of American literature's use of this opposition remain Leslie A. Fiedler's *Love and Death in the American Novel* (New York: Stein and Day, 1966) and A. N. Kaul's *The American Vision* (New Haven: Yale University Press, 1963).

[3]Robert Bresson, *Notes on Cinematography*, trans. Jonathan Griffin (New York: Urizen Books, 1977), p. 12.

[4]Leslie A. Fiedler, *No! In Thunder* (New York: Stein and Day, 1972), pp. 253, 275.

Autobiography and *Poor Richard's Almanack* constituted this opposing tradition's basic texts, persuasive enough to appeal even to outsiders (*The Great Gatsby*). Despite the legends surrounding Franklin and the other Founding Fathers, however, the scarcity of mature heroes in American literature and mythology indicated American ideology's fundamental preference for youth, a quality that came to be associated with the country itself. Indeed, American stories often distorted the stock figure of the Wise Old Man, portraying him as mad (Ahab), useless (Rip Van Winkle), or evil (the Godfather).

2. *Society and Women*: The outlaw hero's distrust of civilization, typically represented by women and marriage, constituted a stock motif in American mythology. In his *Studies in Classic American Literature*, D. H. Lawrence detected the recurring pattern of flight, observing that the Founding Fathers had come to America "largely to get *away*. . . . Away from what? In the long run, away from themselves. Away from everything."[5] Sometimes, these heroes undertook this flight alone (Thoreau, *Catcher in the Rye*); more often, they joined ranks with other men: Huck with Jim, Ishmael with Queequeg, Jake Barnes with Bill Gorton. Women were avoided as representing the very entanglements this tradition sought to escape: society, the "settled life," confining responsibilities. The outlaw hero sought only uncompromising relationships, involving either a "bad" woman (whose morals deprived her of all rights to entangling domesticity) or other males (who themselves remained independent). Even the "bad" woman posed a threat, since marriage often uncovered the clinging "good" girl underneath. Typically, therefore, American stories avoided this problem by killing off the "bad" woman before the marriage could transpire (*Destry Rides Again, The Big Heat, The Far Country*). Subsequently, within the all-male group, women became taboo, except as the objects of lust.

The exceptional extent of American outlaw legends suggests an ideological anxiety about civilized life. Often, that anxiety took shape as a romanticizing of the dispossessed, as in the Beat Generation's cult of the bum, or the characters of Huck and "Thoreau," who worked to remain idle, unemployed, and unattached. A passage from Jerzy Kosinski's *Steps* demonstrated the extreme modern version of this romanticizing:

> I envied those [the poor and the criminals] who lived here and seemed so free, having nothing to regret and nothing to look forward to. In the world of birth certificates, medical examinations, punch cards, and computers, in the world of telephone books, passports, bank accounts, insurance plans, wills, credit cards, pensions, mortgages and loans, they lived unattached.[6]

In contrast to the outlaw heroes, the official heroes were preeminently worldly, comfortable in society, and willing to undertake even those

[5]D. H. Lawrence, *Studies in Classic American Literature* (New York: Viking/Compass, 1961), p. 3. See also Fiedler's *Love and Death in the American Novel* and Sam Bluefarb's *The Escape Motif in the American Novel: Mark Twain to Richard Wright* (Columbus: Ohio State University Press, 1972).

[6]Jerzy Kosinski, *Steps* (New York: Random House, 1968), p. 133.

public duties demanding personal sacrifice. Political figures, particularly Washington and Lincoln, provided the principal examples of this tradition, but images of family also persisted in popular literature from *Little Women* to *Life with Father* and *Cheaper by the Dozen*. The most crucial figure in this tradition, however, was Horatio Alger, whose heroes' ambition provided the complement to Huck's disinterest. Alger's characters subscribed fully to the codes of civilization, devoting themselves to proper dress, manners, and behavior, and the attainment of the very things despised by the opposing tradition: the settled life and respectability.[7]

3. *Politics and the Law*: Writing about "The Philosophical Approach of the Americans," Tocqueville noted "a general distaste for accepting any man's word as proof of anything." That distaste took shape as a traditional distrust of politics as collective activity, and of ideology as that activity's rationale. Such a disavowal of ideology was, of course, itself ideological, a tactic for discouraging systematic political intervention in a nineteenth-century America whose political and economic power remained in the hands of a privileged few. Tocqueville himself noted the results of this mythology of individualism which "disposes each citizen to isolate himself from the mass of his fellows and withdraw into the circle of family and friends; with this little society formed to his taste, he gladly leaves the greater society to look after itself."[8]

This hostility toward political solutions manifested itself further in an ambivalence about the law. The outlaw mythology portrayed the law, the sum of society's standards, as a collective, impersonal ideology imposed on the individual from without. Thus, the law represented the very thing this mythology sought to avoid. In its place, this tradition offered a natural law discovered intuitively by each man. As Tocqueville observed, Americans wanted "to escape from imposed systems ... to seek by themselves and in themselves for the only reason for things ... in most mental operations each American relies on individual effort and judgment" (p. 429). This sense of the law's inadequacy to needs detectable only by the heart generated a rich tradition of legends celebrating legal defiance in the name of some "natural" standard: Thoreau went to jail rather than pay taxes, Huck helped Jim (legally a slave) to escape, Billy the Kid murdered the sheriff's posse that had ambushed his boss, Hester Prynne resisted the community's sexual mores. This mythology transformed all outlaws into Robin Hoods, who "correct" socially unjust laws (Jesse James, Bonnie and Clyde, John Wesley Harding). Furthermore, by customarily portraying the law as the tool of villains (who used it to revoke mining claims, foreclose on mortgages, and disallow election results — all on legal technicalities), this mythology betrayed a profound pessimism about the individual's access to the legal system.

[7]See John G. Cawelti, *Apostles of the Self-Made Man: Changing Concepts of Success in America* (Chicago: University of Chicago Press, 1965), pp. 101–23.

[8]Alexis de Tocqueville, *Democracy in America,* ed. J. P. Mayer, trans. George Lawrence (Garden City, N.Y.: Anchor/Doubleday, 1969), pp. 430, 506. Irving Howe has confirmed Tocqueville's point, observing that Americans "make the suspicion of ideology into something approaching a national creed." *Politics and the Novel* (New York: Avon, 1970), p. 337.

If the outlaw hero's motto was "I don't know what the law says, but I do know what's right and wrong," the official hero's was "We are a nation of laws, not of men," or "No man can place himself above the law." To the outlaw hero's insistence on private standards of right and wrong, the official hero offered the admonition, "You cannot take the law into your own hands." Often, these official heroes were lawyers or politicians, at times (as with Washington and Lincoln), even the executors of the legal system itself. The values accompanying such heroes modified the assurance of Crockett's advice, "Be sure you're right, then go ahead."

In sum, the values associated with these two different sets of heroes contrasted markedly. Clearly, too, each tradition had its good and bad points. If the extreme individualism of the outlaw hero always verged on selfishness, the respectability of the official hero always threatened to involve either blandness or repression. If the outlaw tradition promised adventure and freedom, it also offered danger and loneliness. If the official tradition promised safety and comfort, it also offered entanglements and boredom.

The evident contradiction between these heroes provoked Daniel Boorstin's observation that "never did a more incongruous pair than Davy Crockett and George Washington live together in a national Valhalla." And yet, as Boorstin admits, "both Crockett and Washington were popular heroes, and both emerged into legendary fame during the first half of the nineteenth century."[9]

The parallel existence of these two contradictory traditions evinced the general pattern of American mythology: the denial of the necessity for choice. In fact, this mythology often portrayed situations requiring decision as temporary aberrations from American life's normal course. By discouraging commitment to any single set of values, this mythology fostered an ideology of improvisation, individualism, and ad hoc solutions for problems depicted as crises. American writers have repeatedly attempted to justify this mythology in terms of material sources. Hence, Irving Howe's "explanation":

> It is when men no longer feel that they have adequate choices in their styles of life, when they conclude that there are no longer possibilities of honorable maneuver and compromise, when they decide that the time has come for "ultimate" social loyalties and political decisions—it is then that ideology begins to flourish. Ideology reflects a hardening of commitment, the freezing of opinion into system. . . . The uniqueness of our history, the freshness of our land, the plenitude of our resources—all these have made possible, and rendered plausible, a style of political improvisation and intellectual free-wheeling.[10]

Despite such an account's pretext of objectivity, its language betrays an acceptance of the mythology it purports to describe: "honorable maneuver and compromise," "hardening," "freezing," "uniqueness," "freshness," and "plenitude" are all assumptive words from an ideology that denies its own status.

[9]Daniel J. Boorstin, *The Americans: The National Experience* (New York: Random House, 1965), p. 337.

[10]*Politics and the Novel,* p. 164.

Furthermore, even granting the legitimacy of the historians' authenticating causes, we are left with a persisting mythology increasingly discredited by historical developments. (In fact, such invalidation began in the early nineteenth century, and perhaps even before.)

The American mythology's refusal to choose between its two heroes went beyond the normal reconciliatory function attributed to myth by Lévi-Strauss. For the American tradition not only overcame binary oppositions; it systematically mythologized the certainty of being able to do so. Part of this process involved blurring the lines between the two sets of heroes. First, legends often brought the solemn official heroes back down to earth, providing the sober Washington with the cherry tree, the prudent Franklin with illegitimate children, and even the upright Jefferson with a slave mistress. On the other side, stories modified the outlaw hero's most potentially damaging quality, his tendency to selfish isolationism, by demonstrating that, however reluctantly, he would act for causes beyond himself. Thus, Huck grudgingly helped Jim escape, and Davy Crockett left the woods for three terms in Congress before dying in the Alamo for Texas independence. In this blurring process, Lincoln, a composite of opposing traits, emerged as the great American figure. His status as president made him an ex officio official hero. But his Western origins, melancholy solitude, and unaided decision-making all qualified him as a member of the other side. Finally, his ambivalent attitude toward the law played the most crucial role in his complex legend. As the chief executive, he inevitably stood for the principle that "we are a nation of laws and not men"; as the Great Emancipator, on the other hand, he provided the prime example of taking the law into one's own hands in the name of some higher standard.

Classic Hollywood's gallery of composite heroes (boxing musicians, rebellious aristocrats, pacifist soldiers) clearly derived from this mythology's rejection of final choices, a tendency whose traces Erikson detected in American psychology:

> The process of American identity formation seems to support an individual's ego identity as long as he can preserve a certain element of deliberate tentativeness of autonomous choice. The individual must be able to convince himself that the next step is up to him and that no matter where he is staying or going he always has the choice of leaving or turning in the opposite direction if he chooses to do so. In this country the migrant does not want to be told to move on, nor the sedentary man to stay where he is; for the life style (and the family history) of each contains the opposite element as a potential alternative which he wishes to consider his most private and individual decision.[11]

The reconciliatory pattern found its most typical incarnation, however, in one particular narrative: the story of the private man attempting to keep from being drawn into action on any but his own terms. In this story, the reluctant hero's ultimate willingness to help the community satisfied the official values.

[11] *Childhood and Society,* p. 286.

But by portraying this aid as demanding only a temporary involvement, the story preserved the values of individualism as well.

Like the contrasting heroes' epitomization of basic American dichotomies, the reluctant hero story provided a locus for displacement. Its most famous version, for example, *Adventures of Huckleberry Finn*, offered a typically individualistic solution to the nation's unresolved racial and sectional anxieties, thereby helping to forestall more systematic governmental measures. In adopting this story, Classic Hollywood retained its censoring power, using it, for example, in *Casablanca* to conceal the realistic threats to American self-determination posed by World War II.

Because the reluctant hero story was clearly the basis of the Western, American literature's repeated use of it prompted Leslie Fiedler to call the classic American novels "disguised westerns."[12] In the movies, too, this story appeared in every genre: in Westerns, of course (with *Shane* its most schematic articulation), but also in gangster movies (*Angels with Dirty Faces*, *Key Largo*), musicals (*Swing Time*), detective stories (*The Thin Man*), war films (*Air Force*), screwball comedy (*The Philadelphia Story*), "problem pictures" (*On the Waterfront*), and even science fiction (the Han Solo character in *Star Wars*). *Gone with the Wind*, in fact, had two selfish heroes who came around at the last moment, Scarlett (taking care of Melanie) and Rhett (running the Union blockade), incompatible only because they were so much alike. The natural culmination of this pattern, perfected by Hollywood in the 1930s and early 1940s, was *Casablanca*. Its version of the outlaw hero–official hero struggle (Rick versus Laszlo) proved stunningly effective, its resolution (their collaboration on the war effort) the prototypical Hollywood ending.

The reluctant hero story's tendency to minimize the official hero's role (by making him dependent on the outsider's intervention) suggested an imbalance basic to the American mythology: Despite the existence of both heroes, the national ideology clearly preferred the outlaw. This ideology strove to make that figure's origins seem spontaneous, concealing the calculated, commercial efforts behind the mythologizing of typical examples like Billy the Kid and Davy Crockett. Its willingness, on the other hand, to allow the official hero's traces to show enables Daniel Boorstin to observe of one such myth, "There were elements of spontaneity, of course, in the Washington legend, too, but it was, for the most part, a self-conscious product."[13]

The apparent spontaneity of the outlaw heroes assured their popularity. By contrast, the official values had to rely on a rational allegiance that often wavered. These heroes' different statuses accounted for a structure fundamental to American literature, and assumed by Classic Hollywood: a split between the moral center and the interest center of a story. Thus, while the typical Western contained warnings against violence as a solution, taking the law into one's own hands, and moral isolationism, it simultaneously

20

---

[12]*Love and Death in the American Novel*, p. 355.
[13]*The Americans: The National Experience*, p. 337.

glamorized the outlaw hero's intense self-possession and willingness to use force to settle what the law could not. In other circumstances, Ishmael's evenhanded philosophy paled beside Ahab's moral vehemence, consciously recognizable as destructive.

D. H. Lawrence called this split the profound "duplicity" at the heart of nineteenth-century American fiction, charging that the classic novels evinced "a tight mental allegiance to a morality which all [the author's] passion goes to destroy." Certainly, too, this "duplicity" involved the mythology's pattern of obscuring the necessity for choosing between contrasting values. Richard Chase has put the matter less pejoratively in an account that applies equally to the American cinema:

> The American novel tends to rest in contradictions and among extreme ranges of experience. When it attempts to resolve contradictions, it does so in oblique, morally equivocal ways. As a general rule it does so either in melodramatic actions or in pastoral idylls, although intermixed with both one may find the stirring instabilities of "American humor."[14]

Or, in other words, when faced with a difficult choice, American stories resolved it either simplistically (by refusing to acknowledge that a choice is necessary), sentimentally (by blurring the differences between the two sides), or by laughing the whole thing off.

READING THE TEXT

1. In your own words, describe the two basic hero types in American cinema that Ray describes.
2. How do these two hero types relate to America's "psychological pattern" (para. 2)?
3. Explain why, according to Ray, the outlaw hero typically mistrusts women.
4. Define what Ray means by the "reluctant hero" (para. 17).

READING THE SIGNS

1. What sort of hero is Jyn Erso in *Rogue One: A Star Wars Story* (2016) or Rey in *Star Wars: Episode VII—The Force Awakens* (2015)? Write an essay in which you apply Ray's categories of hero to your chosen character, supporting your argument with specific references to the film.
2. In class, brainstorm on the board official and outlaw heroes you've seen in movies. Then categorize these heroes according to characteristics they share (such as race, gender, profession, or social class). What patterns emerge in your categories, and what is the significance of those patterns?
3. **CONNECTING TEXTS** Ray focuses on film, but his categories of hero can be used as a critical framework to analyze other media, including television. What

[14]Richard Chase, *The American Novel and Its Tradition* (Garden City, N.Y.: Anchor/Doubleday, 1957), p. 1.

kinds of heroes are the heroes in *Game of Thrones*? To develop your ideas, consult Emily Nussbaum's "The Aristocrats: The Graphic Arts of *Game of Thrones*" (p. 274).

4. Cartoon television series like *The Simpsons* and *Archer* feature characters that don't readily fit Ray's two main categories of hero. Invent a third type of hero to accommodate such characters.

5. In class, brainstorm a list of female heroes from film and television. Then try to categorize them according to Ray's article. Do the characters easily fit the categories Ray mentions, or do they seem to be mismatches? Do you feel a need to create an additional category? If so, what would it be?

FANTASY AND FILM

CHRISTINE FOLCH

Why the West Loves Sci-Fi and Fantasy: A Cultural Explanation

Hollywood loves sci-fi and fantasy; Bollywood doesn't. Just why the Indian movie industry (which is the world's largest) is so uninterested in fantasy is an anthropological question that Christine Folch sets out to answer in this *Atlantic* analysis. The key, Folch believes, lies in history, a history that in the West has included a post-Enlightenment reign of scientific rationalism that has led to a general disenchantment with things-as-they-are, which fantasy strives to reverse by "re-enchant[ing] the world." Experiencing a different kind of history without this disenchantment, Indians, Folch suggests, feel no need for cinematic fantasy, so Bollywood doesn't bother much with it. Christine Folch is an assistant professor of anthropology at Duke University.

Hollywood's had a long love affair with sci-fi and fantasy, but the romance has never been stronger than it is today. A quick glance into bookstores, television lineups, and upcoming films shows that the futuristic and fantastical is everywhere in American pop culture. In fact, of Hollywood's top earners since 1980, a mere eight have *not* featured wizardry, space or time travel, or apocalyptic destruction caused by aliens/zombies/Robert Downey Jr.'s acerbic wit. Now, with *Man of Steel*, it appears we will at last have an effective reboot of the most important superhero story of them all.

These tales of mystical worlds and improbable technological power appeal universally, right? Maybe not. Bollywood, not Hollywood, is the largest movie industry in the world. But only a handful of its top hits of the last four decades have dealt with science fiction themes, and even fewer are fantasy or horror. American films in those genres make much of their profits abroad, but they tend to underperform in front of Indian audiences.

This isn't to say that there aren't folk tales with magic and mythology in India. There are. That makes their absence in Bollywood and their overabundance in Hollywood all the more remarkable. Whereas Bollywood takes quotidian family dramas and imbues them with spectacular tales of love and wealth found-lost-regained amidst the pageantry of choreographed dance pieces, Hollywood goes to the supernatural and futurism. It's a sign that longing for mystery is universal, but the taste for science fiction and fantasy is cultural.

Cultural differences are fascinating because even as we learn about others, we learn about ourselves. As an anthropologist, I want to flip this conversation: Why are *we* so into science fiction and fantasy? Nineteenth-century German sociologist Max Weber had a useful theory about this: The answer may be that we in the West are "disenchanted." The world in which we live feels explainable, predictable, and boring. Weber posited that because of modern science, a rise in secularism, an impersonal market economy, and government administered through bureaucracies rather than bonds of loyalty, Western societies perceived the world as knowably rational and systematic, leading to a widespread loss of a sense of wonder and magic. Because reality is composed of processes that can be identified with a powerful-enough microscope or calculated with a fast-enough computer, so Weber's notion of disenchantment goes, there is no place for mystery. But this state of disenchantment is a difficult one because people seem to *like* wonder.

And so we turn to science fiction and fantasy in an attempt to re-enchant the world. Children and childhood retain mystery, and so one tactic has been to take fairytales and rewrite them for adults and here we get the swords and sorcery of modern fantasy. Another strategy was to reinsert the speculative unknown into the very heart of scientific processes. But just because *we* have mined myth for magic—and, remember, even what we define as *myth* would have been called *religion* two millennia earlier (and the very fact that we think those two terms equivalent is also cultural)—does not mean that this fills the same need for wonder elsewhere.

India has developed many of the same features as America: a capitalist economy, an enormous bureaucratic government, and cutting-edge scientific expertise. But its intellectual history is different. Weber's argument is much more nuanced and substantive than the cursory description I have given here, but, in sum, disenchantment is rooted in the intellectual tradition of the 18th-century European Enlightenment with its struggles over the place of religion versus rationality. The aftermath of that contest in the West was to relegate the supernatural mysterious to a lower position than material-based reason. The key point is that this is a particular moment in cultural history, not some necessary and universal stage of human societal "development." Similarly, for that reason, I'd guess Japan's vibrant tradition of the supernatural in its anime, and China's recent taste for American FX spectacles, results from those countries' specific cultural contexts rather than from disenchantment. (And some of the ways the West looks to the non-West for re-enchantment are another, Orientalist can of worms best left for a different day.)

Anyone looking to debunk cultural explanations for the American/Indian sci-fi gap might point out that Hollywood has had the big-budget, dragons-and-droids market flooded for years. Perhaps Bollywood, for commercial reasons, doesn't want to jump in. Average production costs for American superhero blockbusters hover around $200 million these days, and audiences have come to expect the computer-generated spectacle that kind of money buys. But . . . *Star Wars* was made for $11 million in 1977 (less than $40 million now) and 25 percent of *Iron Man 3*'s $200 million budget was Robert Downey Jr.'s salary. Surely there's enough technical expertise and financial muscle in India to digitize a realistic Mars landing when the country's space program is on track to launch a real spacecraft (unmanned) to the red planet this upcoming November.

What about the fact that American blockbusters make tons of money worldwide? For films like *Avatar* and *The Hobbit*, foreign sales equal or exceed domestic U.S. sales. But India, the world's ninth-largest economy and second-most populous country, does not even rank in the top 12 foreign markets for the genre. The list of those markets reads like the attendees of a G-8 summit (plus some key trading partners): the United Kingdom, Japan, France, Germany, Italy, Mexico, Brazil, Spain, South Korea, Russia, Australia, and China. *Avatar* (2009) set the high-water mark for India, where South Asian audiences purchased $24 million worth of tickets—about 10 percent of foreign ticket sales worldwide. But for most science fiction, countries with smaller GDPs than India (Australia, Mexico, South Korea) are higher consumers. Of *Avengers'* (2012) $888 million worldwide, $12 million came from India; *Iron Man 3* is on track with similar numbers; and, to their credit, Indian audiences contributed a paltry $2.8 million to *Transformers 3*'s $434 million. Fantasy fares much worse. *The Hobbit* (2012) made $714 million worldwide; it took home $1.8 million in India. That is barely more than Croatia's $1.4 million.

The simplest conclusion to draw from this is that Bollywood doesn't produce science fiction and fantasy because Indian audiences aren't as keen on it. Local cultural production doesn't just result from economic wherewithal; desires and needs also matter. And desires and needs are cultural. This sometimes feels hard to accept because desires and needs feel so *natural*. Often we think that the way we live is normal and not cultural; this is what anthropologists call "tacit ethnocentrism," when we are not *trying* to be prejudiced, but we have unquestioned assumptions that somehow we are the normal human baseline and others somehow deviate from that.

Hollywood continues to make science fiction and fantasy movies   10
because disenchantment creates a demand for these stories, but disenchantment predates Hollywood. We were journeying ten thousand leagues under
the sea or scarcely surviving a war of the worlds before the film industry
began. If the uptick of *Hunger Games*–inspired archery lessons and the CDC's
humorous-but-practical Zombie Preparedness Guide are any indication, this
is not going away any time soon. Re-enchantment delivers something more
important than escapism or entertainment. Through its promise of a world
of mystery and wonder, it offers the hope that we haven't seen all that
there is.

READING THE TEXT

1. Explain in your own words Max Weber's notion of "disenchantment"
   (para. 4).
2. What is Folch's explanation for why Western film audiences find the supernatural and futurism appealing?
3. According to Folch, what are the cultural reasons Indian film audiences are
   not "keen on" science fiction and fantasy?
4. What was the Enlightenment, and how did it affect Western consciousness?
5. What does Folch mean by the anthropological term "tacit ethnocentrism"
   (para. 9)?

READING THE SIGNS

1. Research the last ten years of American movies, and determine how many of
   the most successful films were fantasies. Use your findings to write your own
   argument about why fantasy films appeal to American audiences, basing your
   claims on an analysis of particular movies.
2. Write an essay in which you support, refute, or modify the claim that the rise
   of fantasy films in America reflects market forces pandering to immature cinematic tastes.
3. Watch a Bollywood film such as *Dhoom 3* (2013), the all-time most popular Indian film, or *Dear Zindagi* (2016). In an essay, analyze the nature of its
   appeal to Indian audiences, using Folch's selection as a critical framework.
   What cultural needs and desires does the film seem to satisfy?
4. Folch claims that "Bollywood takes quotidian family dramas and imbues
   them with spectacular tales of love and wealth found-lost-regained amidst
   the pageantry of choreographed dance pieces" (para. 3). In an essay, compare an Indian film like *Devdas* (2002) with an American movie such as *My
   Big Fat Greek Wedding* (2002). How do the films you select depict family and
   interpersonal relations? What cultural explanations can you offer for your
   observations?

ABRAHAM RIESMAN

What We Talk about When We Talk about Batman and Superman

Frenemies since 1940, Batman and Superman have coexisted in a complex relationship ever since DC Comics cloned the Caped Crusader from the superhero DNA of the Man of Steel. But, Abraham Riesman asks, why do we so often want to see them fighting each other? What it comes down to, Riesman argues in this historical interpretation of the men in spandex, is that they each stand for different ways of "how to do good," with Superman (reflecting "an era of buoyant, blinkered consensus") "operating on hope and inspiration," and Batman—only fully emerging from Superman's shadow in the troubled 1970s and 1980s—depending upon "fear and intimidation." So it really matters that every time the two have come to grips in the past fifteen years or so, the Dark Knight has always been getting the upper hand: darkness over light. A parable for our times. Abraham Riesman is a writer and editor at *New York Magazine*.

Are Batman and Superman allies or rivals, at their core? They're definitely not *enemies*, and that's only partly because they're both superheroes. For long stretches, particularly when the characters were new, they had a deeply chummy relationship, with Batman like a non-superpowered Superman — a lesser, but cheerful, do-gooder who also fought for truth, justice, and the American way. (It was kind of adorable, with Batman almost acting like a kid who smilingly looked up on his star-athlete older brother.)

And yet, for the past 30 years, the relationship has been punctuated by a series of spectacular fights — a gruesome tussle over ideology in 1986's graphic novel *Batman: The Dark Knight Returns*, a dramatic dust-up due to mind control in the 2003 comic-book story line "Hush," and, of course, an upcoming gladiator match in this weekend's big-screen tentpole *Batman v Superman: Dawn of Justice*. At this point, nobody really remembers that early, sunny friendship — when it comes to superheroes, pure friendship's boring. Batman and Superman are both, of course, good guys, but what we so often want to see is them fighting.

But why? Why are fans so desperate to see superheroes in conflict that they urge superhero writers to employ absurd narrative contrivances like mind control or alternate universes to make happen what would otherwise be vanishingly unlikely fights (a tactic used well over a dozen times in the history of Batman-Superman tales)? One big answer is no answer at all—who *wouldn't* want to see them fight? Every comics geek's inner adolescent is perpetually asking, *What's the point of having two heroes if you aren't also going to game out who'd win?* As comics critic Chris Sims put it in a column on the topic, "When you have characters and all you see them doing is winning, it's natural to wonder who would win harder if they ever had to compete. For that question, Superman and Batman make the perfect contenders."

But we also want to see them fight because, to an unusual degree even for comic books, the fights *mean* something. That is, they are about something—or some *things*. Namely: how to make a better world, with Superman operating through hope and inspiration, and Batman through fear and intimidation. As the villain Lex Luthor puts it in the new movie, it's "god versus man, day versus night."

Let's start with "god versus man." Superman is an alien—which is to say, celestial—creature, born on another planet but here completely alone, completely singular in his powers, which have at times included feats like reversing the spin of the Earth to turn back time. Batman is not just a man but a broken one, who inhabits a broken universe, his parents killed by a petty criminal and raised in an era of rapid urban decay—"an old-money billionaire, a human, an orphan who has seen the worst of the world and let it all but turn him to stone," in the words of critic Meg Downey. Superman, by contrast, "is a farm boy, an alien, raised with a stable adoptive family, who has seen the worst of the world and let it teach him a profound sense of empathy."

Which leads us to "day versus night." Superman has faith that humanity will tend toward goodness if you give it trust and hope; Batman lacks that faith and believes the world only gets in line if you grab it by the throat and never let go. The former spends his contemplative moments hoping for the best; the latter spends those moments vigilantly preparing for the worst. But this contrast isn't just characterological; it's also historical. The icons were created almost simultaneously, but Superman is unmistakably a figure of his early years—the 1940s and 1950s, an era of buoyant, blinkered wartime and postwar consensus (at least as it might have been felt by most white, boyish comic-book readers), when it seemed appropriate to deploy a godlike do-gooder to do things like help cats out of trees or return purses to de-pursed Metropolis women. (One of his early nicknames was the Man of Tomorrow, after all.) Batman came of age later, beginning in the 1970s, the era of American malaise and urban decay, using cynicism as a weapon for good and training his sights on a Gotham City so broken it often looked like a war zone (often fighting super-criminals who hoped not just to plunder the city but overturn any lingering faith its denizens had in the virtue of compassion and social order). Which of these two worldviews provides the better way to live a good and productive life? You can do both, of course—just as you can love both characters and write them in such a way where they get along with one another. But readers don't just want that—readers want to see the conflict.

5

And, in a real-world sense, most of them are on one side. Today, Batman is a far more popular character than Superman, and he typically wins whenever they go toe-to-toe in a story — which is, of course, ridiculous, considering he's just an earthling, but that only makes it all the more remarkable as a reflection of reader preferences and prejudices. Outside of comics and movies, too, his worldview predominates, in the form of a perennially apocalyptic vision of the near future. In all ways, Batman is winning in the battle of Batman vs. Superman, which is especially strange given how little New York today, say, looks like the Gotham of *The Dark Knight Returns*. But we've been living so long in Batman's universe that it can be hard to remember his worldview didn't always have the upper hand.

They began as friends — almost as doubles. Superman was created by Cleveland cartoonists Jerry Siegel and Joe Shuster and debuted in 1938 in the pages of *Action Comics* No. 1. At first, Superman only barely resembled the big blue Boy Scout we know today: He smirked while punching out slumlords, domestic abusers, and loan sharks and he seemed relatively unconcerned with preserving individual human life. He was, as Superman historian Glen Weldon puts it in his exhaustive and fascinating *Superman: The Unauthorized Biography*, a "bully for peace."

He was also an instant sensation. DC Comics knew it had a hit on its hands, but wanted a bigger one — which means they needed their star to be as family-friendly as possible. As comics historian Gerard Jones recounts in his chronicle of the era, *Men of Tomorrow: Geeks, Gangsters, and the Birth of the Comic Book*, DC exec Jack Liebowitz saw the nascent Man of Steel as "something that could be built and sustained here, a kind of entertainment that kids liked better than pulps and would continue to if given reason to keep coming back." Accordingly, in 1940, he and editor Whitney Ellsworth drew up a pristine code of conduct for superheroes that, among other tenets, forbade DC heroes from knowingly killing. It was not unlike the onset of the Hays Code in Hollywood, and by the time U.S. soldiers were being sent off to war in 1942, Superman had become cheery, lovable, and status quo-respecting.

Those were not adjectives you could use to describe the initial depictions 10 of Batman. He was first published in DC's 1939 comic *Detective Comics* No. 27, the creation of Bob Kane and Bill Finger. At first, he was a "weird figure of the dark" and an "avenger of evil," as one of the early stories put it. Unlike Superman, he had no special powers other than being exceedingly wealthy. He was more or less a rip-off of pulp hero The Shadow and spent his time in the darkness, attacking — and occasionally even murdering — evildoers. But, like Superman, he was also an instant smash — which meant the same image-buffering fate. In his new history of Batman, *The Caped Crusade: Batman and the Rise of Nerd Culture,* Weldon tells of newspaper editorials and church bulletins railing against dark, violent comic books.

As a result, the editorial leadership pushed Batman out of the shadows, making him brighter and poppier, and even turning the weird loner into a kind of doting father figure to a scrappy young ward named Robin (a relationship that could've really gotten dark and weird in different hands). "Adding Robin was no mere cosmetic tweak," writes Weldon, "it was a fundamental and permanent change that placed Batman in a new role of protector and provider." He stopped killing. He worked cheerfully with the Gotham police. He walked around in broad daylight. The Batman and Superman brands were more or less in sync.

Of course, Superman was a much more natural family-friendly sell than Batman, because comics writers couldn't quite eliminate all of the darkness from the character of the Dark Knight, as later they'd have trouble trying to turn Superman into something approaching an antihero: One of these characters was a benevolently powerful space-god, the other a weirdo orphan wearing bat ears. This probably, at least in part, explains Superman's bigger stature through the 1940s—his persona was a near-perfect vessel for imperious American confidence and social order. But Batman had his clean-cut pitch, too: He may not have had superpowers, but he was a kind of icon of self-improvement, since he had willed himself to reach the peak of human physical potential (well, willed and spent) and had fought a delightful gallery of enemies.

Oddly enough, it took DC a long time to figure out that these guys were two great tastes that could taste great together. Superman and Batman first appeared in an image together on the cover of a 1940 promotional tie-in comic for that year's World's Fair, but the interior pages showed no story where the two of them interacted. In 1941, there was a comic in which they stood side by side to help with a fund-raising drive for war orphans, but they had no dialogue with each other. That same year, they started appearing alongside one another on the covers of a new comics series called *World's Finest*, and on those covers, you saw them wordlessly playing baseball or going skiing—but once you opened the comic, you saw no stories where they actually hung out.

Superhero fiction has been a trans-media enterprise for longer than many give it credit for, and the genius notion of having Batman and Superman actually solve crimes together—as opposed to just convention-bid in tandem—apparently didn't materialize until a 1945 episode of Superman's spin-off radio show, *The Adventures of Superman*. Their first printed co-narrative came in *Superman* No. 76, published in 1952. There, Bruce Wayne and Clark Kent—who had no knowledge of each other's secret superhero-ing—found themselves in the same cabin on a cruise ship. When some criminals start a massive fire, Bruce turns out the cabin's light to change into his costume, and Clark takes the opportunity to do the same. But suddenly, they get caught in the act by light from the flames passing through the porthole. "Why—why, you're *Superman!*" Batman exclaims. "And you, Bruce Wayne ... you're *Batman!*" Superman counters. "No time to talk this over now, *Superman!*" Batman says as they rush out of the cabin.

Their ensuing adventure set a template for the way they'd interact for   15
the next 20-odd years: They complete each other and accentuate each
other's different power-sets while having the same squeaky-clean tone and
goals. Readers rarely saw a true ideological conflict between the two, and
Batman subscribed to the Superman-ish notion that good can always triumph over evil, so long as we live clean lives and partner up with fellow
do-gooders. The only difference between them was their skill sets. "They
had Batman be the master technician and Superman be the big jock," says
Weldon. "Batman would be the ultimate brain and Superman would come
over to Gotham for help on a case because *It's just too hard for me to figure!*"
Occasionally, the two would have friendly contests (for example, No. 76 saw
them performing feats of strength to win their respective cities the right to
host an electronics convention), and they would occasionally challenge each
other for the betterment of each (in No. 149, Batman and Superman each
use an amnesia machine on themselves so they can try to re-discover
each other's secret identities).

There were also real conflicts, though typically they unfolded under odd
circumstances. "The logic of that time was heavily driven by covers," says
comics historian and longtime DC executive Paul Levitz. You wanted to grab
lucrative young eyeballs with insane vignettes on the front of a comic book
and "two heroes fighting was a classically successful cover." The story on the
inside was of secondary importance, largely built up to satisfy what was on
the front. Irwin Donenfeld, the executive vice president of DC throughout
much of the late '50s and early '60s, was particularly fond of this tactic, so
you got nutso covers like that of *World's Finest* No. 109, in which a flying (!)
Batman throws a massive cinderblock at Superman while a horrified Robin
gazes at them and thinks to himself, *The sorcerer's spell that's been cast over*
Batman *is forcing him to fight* Superman *— and now he has* super-powers *to
do it with!* Such stories satisfied a fannish desire to see the two fight, but
what made them even more exciting was how perverse they were — there's
no way, after all, that these two would ever *really* have a problem with one
another, right? And, whatever the fun of seeing them fight, you never had to
worry too much about a permanent rupture: There was always some wacky
explanation, like mind control, mistaken identity, or simply explaining that
the tale was an "imaginary story," wholly removed from normal continuity.
The chummy status quo would always return by the next issue. The gods
were in their heaven, all was right with the world.

It was only in the '70s and '80s that Batman truly emerged from Superman's shadow, and it's hard to avoid the impression that the Dark Knight was
a product of that time (just as Superman was a product of the mid-century).
This was a period shadowed by the assassinations of two Superman-like
symbols of hope — Robert F. Kennedy and Martin Luther King, Jr. Cities from
coast to coast erupted into vicious race riots. A sitting president was tied to
an insidious crime and resigned on live television. We lost a war for the first

time and the economy skidded into an oil-slicked slowdown. At the cinema, audiences wanted heroes that were less like John Wayne and more like Dirty Harry.

In comics, they got one. For the first time since that brief window of grim violence in his earliest stories, the Dark Knight was dark again. That was a real reversal, given the deep, Technicolor imprint left by the '60s *Batman* TV show, which may be the clearest depiction of the soft-focus Batman of the Superman era (what could possibly have been at stake in that always-sunny playhouse Gotham?). The Batman comics, in a bid for brand synergy, got similarly goofy. But viewers grew tired of the show quickly, turning it from a brief hit into a canceled failure and cultural punch line and spawning a wave of angry fan letters asking DC's higher-ups to revise the character. One such letter, published in the pages of *Batman* No. 210: "Batman is a creature of the night. [He] prowls the streets of Gotham and retains an aura of mystery," it read. "Get the super-hero out, and the detective in!"

Batman comics were ailing in sales, so DC's leadership was willing to give it a shot. Under the guidance of editor Julius "Julie" Schwartz, upstart writer/ artist team Denny O'Neil and Neal Adams were put in charge of *Batman*. As O'Neil recalls it, "I walked into Julie's office and he offered me *Batman* like this: 'We're going to keep publishing *Batman*, obviously, but we're not gonna do the camp thing anymore. Whaddaya got, my boy?' What I thought was this: we'll go back to 1939." O'Neil looked to Batsy's grim origin story for inspiration: "You've got this dark guy who's seen his parents killed and he spends his life symbolically avenging that death," he says. "That version of Batman seems to be the one that's right." O'Neil and Adams opted to have Batman scowl instead of smile, go out in the darkness and eschew the light, and meditate on how few people he could truly trust. "Superman has more faith in the system," says comics critic Ardo Omer. "Batman was created because the system failed him and continued to fail Gotham."

Batman was a much more natural icon of 1970s angst and anomie, but the darker turn in comics also came to Metropolis, where Superman's virtues — once taken as self-evident — were being questioned in his own sto- ries. O'Neil was brought on to write Superman tales, too, and felt it was no longer interesting to read about a perfect man who did only good. "The essence of fantasy melodrama is conflict," O'Neil says. "You've got a guy who, at his strongest and most powerful, could blow out a sun! How are you going to create conflict for that guy?" DC's leadership agreed. Through vari- ous in-story machinations, his powers were weakened for a while. But more important, doubting Superman became the order of the day. A 1972 tale penned by Elliot S. Maggin was boldly titled "Must There Be a Superman?" and saw the Man of Tomorrow realizing that he can't fix structural problems like poverty and oppression. "You stand so proud, *Superman*," read the opening narration, "in your *strength* and your *power* — with a pride that has found its way into the soul of every man who has stood above other men! But as with all men of *power*, you must eventually question yourself and your *use* of that *power*." Wait, were we talking about Kal-El of Krypton, or the United States of America?

As Americans began to distrust power, so too did Batman begin to distrust Superman. They still fought side by side in the pages of *World's Finest* and on the roster of DC's premier super-team, the Justice League, but there were cracks in the façade. In 1973's *World's Finest* No. 220, written by Bob Haney and drawn by Dick Dillin, the two are trying to crack a case, and the Kryptonian is turning up his nose at their villain's quest for "*illegal revenge*." "*I* can understand revenge," Batman says with a condescending scowl. "I took it myself against Joe Chill, my parents' killer! It's a human emotion — revenge! Trouble with you, friend, is *you're* not human!" The ticked-off Superman punches a tree and asks, "*Who's* not human!?"

An ascendant Batman and Batman-ist worldview made concrete conflict almost inevitable, and matters came to a boiling point in 1983's *Batman and the Outsiders* No. 1, written by Mike W. Barr and drawn by Jim Aparo. During a meeting of the Justice League, Batman declares that he's had enough of the Superman-led squad's law-abiding approach to saving the world. He says he's going to break international regulations to rescue someone and when Superman tries to stop him, a furious Batman slaps his old friend's hand away and says he's resigning. Superman tries to appeal to the better angels of Batman's nature: "We've always served as an *example* to the others —" But the Dark Knight cuts him off. "I never asked for that, Superman!" he barks. "I never wanted men to *imitate* me — only *fear* me!"

Nowhere was their ideological conflict more pointed than in the most famous Batman story ever told, which is also the greatest Batman-Superman fight story ever told: writer/artist Frank Miller's 1986 masterwork *The Dark Knight Returns*. It's a dense tale set in a dystopian Gotham City tattooed with graffiti and beset by violent youths. Miller had been living in New York during its Koch-era nadir, getting mugged and seeing the tabloids scream about urban decay and the vigilantism of men like Bernhard Goetz. When Miller was commissioned to write a Batman tale, he decided to make Bruce Wayne what he called a "god of vengeance" — a pretty good description of Dirty Harry, actually, or other iconic antiheroes, like Travis Bickle and Rambo, who had already passed into American myth. "If he fights," Miller wrote in his notes for Batman, "it's in a way that leaves them too roughed up to talk." His ideal Batman "plays more on guilt and PRIMAL fears."

The result was, indeed, steeped in primal fear. In *The Dark Knight Returns*, an aging Bruce comes out of retirement and goes on a *Death Wish*-esque crusade to clean up the streets by any means necessary. He has also come to hate the sunshiny outlook of Superman, a figure who — in Miller's depiction — has a naïve faith that it's morning in America. Miller's Superman has made a Faustian pact with the government, taking orders from President Reagan. (Well, he's not technically *called* Reagan, but any reader will recognize the fictional commander-in-chief's wrinkled smile and folksy chatter.) "I gave them my *obedience*," Clark thinks to himself while destroying some

Soviet weaponry. "No, I *don't* like it. But I get to save lives — and the *media* stays quiet." When Batman leads an army of vigilantes during a night of chaos in Gotham, Superman is ordered to take down his erstwhile ally.

The fight that followed was the most perversely inventive one in the canon. Superman arrives in Gotham and Batman completely beats the shit out of him. As it turns out, Superman may be strong, but Batman has two advantages: wealth and paranoia. His distrust of the Metropolis Marvel led him to come up with a cunning plan in preparation for the battle, and he can throw as many toys into it as he likes. He fires missiles at Superman; he wears a massive battle-suit that he plugs into the city's electrical grid, then punches Superman *hard*; he has a pal hit the Man of Steel with some synthetic Kryptonite (Superman's historic weakness); and he ultimately wins, knocking Superman to a standstill. All the while, he takes pride in hurting Superman and meditates on their differing worldviews. "You sold us out, Clark," he thinks to himself. "Just like your *parents* taught you to. *My* parents taught me a *different* lesson — lying on this *street — shaking* in deep *shock — dying* for no reason at *all —* they showed me that the world only makes *sense* when you *force* it to."

A similar exchange punctuates writer/artist John Byrne's miniseries *The Man of Steel*, another influential recast of the Batman-Superman relationship, published the same year as *The Dark Knight Returns* (though less well-known). Issue No. 3 chronicled a wholly rebooted version of the heroes' first meeting, devoid of the charming cruise-ship meet-up. Instead, the two of them, early in their careers, join together to catch a criminal — but they immediately question each other's approach to the task. Batman beats up a lowlife thug in an alleyway for information; Superman finds Batman right afterward and calls him an "outlaw" and an "inhuman monster." They decide to focus on taking down the villain, and, as they part ways, they reach a tense détente. "Well, I still won't say I fully approve of your methods, Batman," Superman says, flying away, "and I'm going to be keeping an eye on you, to make certain you don't *blow it* for the rest of us ... but *good luck*."

But let's get back to *The Dark Knight Returns.* "In political terms, Superman would be a conservative and Batman would be a radical," Miller said when I interviewed him a few months ago. Miller himself identifies as a libertarian, so his protagonist's distrust of power makes all the sense in the world. But the political question of the book is, in my view, only a symptom of a larger philosophical matter. This Batman is utterly without faith in anything beyond his immediate control. Sure, he can trust his butler, his sidekick, and his weaponry — but that's about it. Everyone and everything else needs to be throttled and bent into shape, in order to wrestle with a world otherwise almost beyond repair. What's more, Batman hates Superman because Superman *does* have faith: faith in the government, faith in Reaganite prosperity, faith that Batman might be able to see reason and give up. In Batman's eyes, these are failings.

No one had ever before attempted to show these two being in such opposition, and so filled with bloodlust. But the crazy experiment was a massive success. For the first time, Batman comics started consistently outselling Superman ones, but the transformation went beyond mere sales. "It's difficult to overstate the influence *The Dark Knight Returns* has had on comics and the culture that has risen around them," Weldon writes. Thanks to Miller, the vision of Batman as a pitch-black bruiser and schemer was carved into the rock of superhero fandom. In 1989, Tim Burton's *Batman* hit theaters and, while it lacked the deep gothic mood of later screen hits like the influential *Batman: The Animated Series* and Christopher Nolan films that followed, it offered many of the dark, angry pleasures that *Dark Knight Returns* had surfaced — and it was a box-office smash unlike anything a DC character had ever seen.

Very few tales since then have dared to put the two heroes so viciously at odds as they were in *Dark Knight*, but every story of conflict since is shadowed by Miller's and Byrne's characterizations. In 1988's Batman story line "A Death in the Family" — written by Jim Starlin and drawn by Jim Aparo — Robin is brutally murdered by the Joker and a complicated diplomatic situation makes any Bat-revenge legally tricky. Clark flies in to tell Bruce to stay in line: "There's nothing you can do here," he says. Bruce fires off a massive punch to Clark's jaw, which of course doesn't even bruise the Man of Steel. "Feel better now?" Superman asks, frowning.

Even when they got along, after *Dark Knight*, there was often a steely   30
sense that things *could* go awry between them. A 1990 Batman-Superman crossover story called "Dark Knight Over Metropolis" dealt with the theft of a ring made out of Kryptonite, and at the end, Supes opts to give the ring to Batsy for safekeeping, just in case someone evil ever takes over Superman's mind and he needs to be taken down. "I want the means to stop me," Clark says, "to be in the hands of a man I can trust with my life." It's a sweet moment, but also a grim one. Indeed, for all the talk of trust, Superman was dourly preparing for the worst and acting out of fear. In other words, much as Batman had acted like Superman in the middle of the century, we had somehow entered a world where Superman was acting like Batman.

Perhaps more important, the Batman mentality — paranoid, fatalistic, violent — was setting the pace for superhero fiction generally. Superman was killed by a rampaging monster in 1992. One year later, a brutal villain snapped Bruce Wayne's spine, and a younger, more vicious successor took over the Bat-mantle. Superman came back from the dead and the original Batman took back the cape and cowl, but they still fought increasingly apocalyptic threats that required harsh pragmatism to beat. The best-selling comics across the industry in the early- to mid-'90s were violent and oozing with themes as dark as the colors. America wasn't as decrepit and frightening as it had been in prior decades, especially in its cities, but in an age of increasing cynicism, Batman felt far more *au courant* than the Metropolis Marvel.

As a new century dawned, conflicts between the two became more frequent in comics and, in nearly every one, Batman kept winning.

There was 2000's Justice League story line "Tower of Babel," written by Mark Waid and drawn by Howard Porter, in which we learned that Batman had detailed and brilliant plans to take down every member of the League, just in case — including Superman. There was the 2003 alternate-history tale *Superman: Red Son*, written by Mark Millar and drawn by Dave Johnson and Kilian Plunkett, which imagined a world where Kal-El of Krypton landed in the Soviet Union and became a Stalinist dictator — only to be challenged by an anarchist Russian Batman who uses his superior wit to knock the snot out of Soviet Supes before killing himself with a suicide bomb. There was that same year's *Batman* No. 612, written by Jeph Loeb and drawn by Jim Lee, where Batman uses that old Kryptonite ring to knock a mind-controlled Superman onto his butt. There were 2014's *Batman* Nos. 35 and 36, written by Scott Snyder and drawn by Greg Capullo, wherein Superman gets mind-controlled yet again and Batsy spits a tiny pellet of Kryptonite-like material into Supes's eye to put him down. "Who wins in a fight?" Batman muses to himself in that last story. "The answer is always the same. Neither of us."

It's a nice rhetorical flourish, but in the real world, Batman *is* winning. Not only do creators nowadays think stories work better when he comes out on top, but he also outsells Superman on the comics stands and — much more important — at the box office. Way back in the earliest days of big-budget superhero filmmaking, 1978's *Superman: The Movie* was a sensation — but its sequels showed massively declining returns and that incarnation of the franchise was canned after 1987's loathed *Superman IV: The Quest for Peace*. Two years later, Batman struck big with the afore-mentioned Burton flick, which got two hit sequels: 1992's *Batman Returns* and 1995's *Batman Forever*. The failure of 1997's *Batman & Robin* put DC Comics-based movies in the wilderness for a while, but it was Batman who led them back to the Promised Land. Christopher Nolan's *Batman Begins* hit theaters in 2005 and was a surprise critical success, but the real action came with its two sequels. *The Dark Knight* and *The Dark Knight Rises* each made more than a billion dollars worldwide — numbers that were unthink-able for a superhero flick just a decade earlier. As many film critics noted, in the age of the War on Terror, this Batman seemed to be the hero we deserved.

Superman, on the other hand, couldn't get airborne. Bryan Singer's *Superman Returns* hit theaters in 2006 and it was as sunny, colorful, and hopeful as you'd want a Superman story to be. But Warner Bros. was disap-pointed in its performance and cancelled plans for a sequel. After years of failed proposals, a new Superman movie finally hit theaters in 2013: Zack Snyder's *Man of Steel*. It was a hit, raking in $668 million worldwide and giving Warner the confidence to use it as the starting point for its new DC Comics-based "shared universe" of interconnected films, the next of which is *Batman v Superman*. But at what price to his soul did Superman get this box-office victory? *Man of Steel* is a very dark movie. The visuals play out with gritty, color-drained filters. Superman spends much of the movie moping over a dead parent and wondering what the point of everything is. In the end, he has a horrifically violent battle with a fellow Kryptonian that levels Metropolis. He even grimly concludes that the only way to end that fight is to kill his rival (something the comics versions of Superman *and* Batman never do). The whole endeavor shows us a Superman who is brooding, angry, and pessimistic. In other words, it seems like the only way to do a successful Superman movie is to make it feel like a Batman movie. With *Batman v Superman,* they've just made another one.

The Batman perspective has some things going for it, of course: The world can indeed look pretty dark, as our collective anxieties and casually apocalyptic political mood testify daily. But it is also not the 1970s or '80s anymore, and new threats like ISIS and climate change aside, the urban hellscapes which gave rise to the Dark Knight are distant memories at this point. Which does make you wonder: How much is the cynicism of Batman a logical response to a terrifying future, and how much a self-perpetuating worldview with a locomotive logic of its own? And then there's the cost to comic-book *narrative*: If Batman and Superman are going to keep fighting, could we maybe let the Man of Steel win? Because if the political worldview of superhero fiction is going to hang in the balance with each battle, the least we could ask for is a little genuine suspense about which one of the do-gooders is going to come out on top.

READING THE TEXT

1. Summarize in your own words the history of the relationship between Batman and Superman, as Riesman presents it.

2. According to Riesman, how do Batman and Superman's fictional characters reflect cultural periods in real-life history?

3. Why does Riesman call *The Dark Knight Returns* (1986) "the greatest Batman-Superman-fight story ever told" (para. 23)?

4. In the Batman-Superman fight, which character does Riesman believe is "winning" in recent years, and why?

READING THE SIGNS

1. **CONNECTING TEXTS** In class, form teams and debate Riesman's opening question: "Are Batman and Superman allies or rivals, at their core?" (para. 1). To develop your ideas, consult Robert B. Ray's "The Thematic Paradigm" (p. 303). Use the class debate as a brainstorming session for an essay in which you propose your own response to Riesman's question.

2. Write an essay in which you support, refute, or complicate Frank Miller's contention that "in political terms, Superman would be a conservative and Batman would be a radical" (para. 27).

3. Write an essay in which you analyze the rise of superheroes, like Deadpool, who do not "do good." What does the popularity of such characters suggest about the mood of American society today?

4. In an essay, analyze a current female superhero such as Wonder Woman. To what extent is her mission "to do good," or is her heroism manifested in other ways? In what ways might her gender affect her creators' construction of her mission?

LINDA SEGER

Creating the Myth

> To be a successful screenwriter, Linda Seger suggests in this selection from *Making a Good Script Great* (1987), you've got to know your archetypes. Seger reveals the secret behind the success of such Hollywood creations as *Star Wars's* Luke Skywalker and tells you how you can create such heroes yourself. In this how-to approach to the cinema, Seger echoes the more academic judgments of such semioticians of film as the late Umberto Eco—that the road to popular success in mass culture is paved with cultural myths and clichés. A script consultant and author, Seger has also given professional seminars on filmmaking around the world.

All of us have similar experiences. We share in the life journey of growth, development, and transformation. We live the same stories, whether they involve the search for a perfect mate, coming home, the search for fulfillment, going after an ideal, achieving the dream, or hunting for a precious treasure. Whatever our culture, there are universal stories that form the basis for all our particular stories. The trappings might be different, the twists and turns that create suspense might change from culture to culture, the particular characters may take different forms, but underneath it all, it's the same story, drawn from the same experiences.

Many of the most successful films are based on these universal stories. They deal with the basic journey we take in life. We identify with the heroes because we were once heroic (descriptive) or because we wish we could do what the hero does (prescriptive). When Joan Wilder finds the jewel and saves her sister, or James Bond saves the world, or Shane saves the family from the evil ranchers, we identify with the character, and subconsciously recognize the story as having some connection with our own lives. It's the same story as the fairy tales about getting the three golden hairs from the devil, or finding the treasure and winning the princess. And it's not all that different a story from the caveman killing the woolly beast or the Roman slave gaining his freedom through skill and courage. These are our stories—personally and collectively—and the most successful films contain these universal experiences.

Some of these stories are "search" stories. They address our desire to find some kind of rare and wonderful treasure. This might include the search for outer values such as job, relationship, or success; or for inner values such as respect, security, self-expression, love, or home. But it's all a similar search.

Some of these stories are "hero" stories. They come from our own experiences of overcoming adversity, as well as our desire to do great and special acts. We root for the hero and celebrate when he or she achieves the goal because we know that the hero's journey is in many ways similar to our own.

We call these stories *myths*. Myths are the common stories at the root of   5
our universal existence. They're found in all cultures and in all literature, ranging from the Greek myths to fairy tales, legends, and stories drawn from all of the world's religions.

A myth is a story that is "more than true." Many stories are true because one person, somewhere, at some time, lived it. It is based on fact. But a myth is more than true because it is lived by all of us, at some level. It's a story that connects and speaks to us all.

Some myths are true stories that attain mythic significance because the people involved seem larger than life, and seem to live their lives more intensely than common folk. Martin Luther King, Jr., Gandhi, Sir Edmund Hillary, and Lord Mountbatten personify the types of journeys we identify with, because we've taken similar journeys—even if only in a very small way.

Other myths revolve around make-believe characters who might capsulize for us the sum total of many of our journeys. Some of these make-believe characters might seem similar to the characters we meet in our dreams. Or they might be a composite of types of characters we've met.

In both cases, the myth is the "story beneath the story." It's the universal pattern that shows us that Gandhi's journey toward independence and Sir Edmund Hillary's journey to the top of Mount Everest contain many of the same dramatic beats. And these beats are the same beats that Rambo takes to set free the MIAs, that Indiana Jones takes to find the Lost Ark, and that Luke Skywalker takes to defeat the Evil Empire.

In *Hero with a Thousand Faces*, Joseph Campbell traces the elements that   10
form the hero myth. In their own work with myth, writer Chris Vogler and seminar leader Thomas Schlesinger have applied this criteria to *Star Wars*. The myth within the story helps explain why millions went to see this film again and again.

The hero myth has specific story beats that occur in all hero stories. They show who the hero is, what the hero needs, and how the story and character interact in order to create a transformation. The journey toward heroism is a process. This universal process forms the spine of all the particular stories, such as the *Star Wars* trilogy.

The Hero Myth

1. In most hero stories, the hero is introduced in ordinary surroundings, in a mundane world, doing mundane things. Generally, the hero begins as a non-hero; innocent, young, simple, or humble. In *Star Wars*, the first time we see Luke Skywalker, he's unhappy about having to do his chores, which consist of picking out some new droids for work. He wants to go out and have fun. He wants to leave his planet and go to the Academy, but he's stuck. This is the setup of most myths. This is how we meet the hero before the call to adventure.

2. Then something new enters the hero's life. It's a catalyst that sets the story into motion. It might be a telephone call, as in *Romancing the Stone*, or the German attack in *The African Queen*, or the holograph of Princess Leia in *Star Wars*. Whatever form it takes, it's a new ingredient that pushes the hero into an extraordinary adventure. With this call, the stakes are established, and a problem is introduced that demands a solution.

3. Many times, however, the hero doesn't want to leave. He or she is a reluctant hero, afraid of the unknown, uncertain, perhaps, if he or she is up

Star Wars, 1977.

to the challenge. In *Star Wars*, Luke receives a double call to adventure. First, from Princess Leia in the holograph, and then through Obi-Wan Kenobi, who says he needs Luke's help. But Luke is not ready to go. He returns home, only to find that the Imperial Stormtroopers have burned his farmhouse and slaughtered his family. Now he is personally motivated, ready to enter into the adventure.

4. In any journey, the hero usually receives help, and the help often comes from unusual sources. In many fairy tales, an old woman, a dwarf, a witch, or a wizard helps the hero. The hero achieves the goal because of this help, and because the hero is receptive to what this person has to give.

There are a number of fairy tales where the first and second sons are sent to complete a task, but they ignore the helpers, often scorning them. Many times they are severely punished for their lack of humility and unwillingness to accept help. Then the third son, the hero, comes along. He receives the help, accomplishes the task, and often wins the princess.

In *Star Wars*, Obi-Wan Kenobi is a perfect example of the "helper" character. He is a kind of mentor to Luke, one who teaches him the Way of the Force and whose teachings continue even after his death. This mentor character appears in most hero stories. He is the person who has special knowledge, special information, and special skills. This might be the prospector in *The Treasure of the Sierra Madre*, or the psychiatrist in *Ordinary People*, or Quint in *Jaws*, who knows all about sharks, or the Good Witch of the North who gives Dorothy the ruby slippers in *The Wizard of Oz*. In *Star Wars*, Obi-Wan gives Luke the light saber that was the special weapon of the Jedi Knight. With this, Luke is ready to move forward and do his training and meet adventure.

5. The hero is now ready to move into the special world where he or she will change from the ordinary into the extraordinary. This starts the hero's transformation, and sets up the obstacles that must be surmounted to reach the goal. Usually, this happens at the first Turning Point of the story, and leads into Act Two development. In *Star Wars*, Obi-Wan and Luke search for a pilot to take them to the planet of Alderaan, so that Obi-Wan can deliver the plans to Princess Leia's father. These plans are essential to the survival of the Rebel Forces. With this action, the adventure is ready to begin.

6. Now begin all the tests and obstacles necessary to overcome the enemy and accomplish the hero's goals. In fairy tales, this often means getting past witches, outwitting the devil, avoiding robbers, or confronting evil. In Homer's *Odyssey*, it means blinding the Cyclops, escaping from the island of the Lotus-Eaters, resisting the temptation of the singing Sirens, and surviving a shipwreck. In *Star Wars*, innumerable adventures confront Luke. He and his cohorts must run to the *Millennium Falcon*, narrowly escaping the Stormtroopers before jumping into hyperspace. They must make it through the meteor shower after Alderaan has been destroyed. They must evade capture on the Death Star, rescue the Princess, and even survive a garbage crusher.

7. At some point in the story, the hero often hits rock bottom. He often 20
has a "death experience," leading to a type of rebirth. In *Star Wars*, Luke
seems to have died when the serpent in the garbage-masher pulls him under,
but he's saved just in time to ask R2D2 to stop the masher before they're
crushed. This is often the "black moment" at the second turning point, the
point when the worst is confronted, and the action now moves toward the
exciting conclusion.

8. Now, the hero seizes the sword and takes possession of the treasure.
He is now in charge, but he still has not completed the journey. Here Luke
has the Princess and the plans, but the final confrontation is yet to begin.
This starts the third-act escape scene, leading to the final climax.

9. The road back is often the chase scene. In many fairy tales, this is the
point where the devil chases the hero and the hero has the last obstacles to
overcome before really being free and safe. His challenge is to take what he
has learned and integrate it into his daily life. He *must* return to renew the
mundane world. In *Star Wars*, Darth Vader is in hot pursuit, planning to blow
up the Rebel Planet.

10. Since every hero story is essentially a transformation story, we need
to see the hero changed at the end, resurrected into a new type of life. He
must face the final ordeal before being "reborn" as the hero, proving his
courage and becoming transformed. This is the point, in many fairy tales,
where the Miller's Son becomes the Prince or the King and marries the Princess. In *Star Wars*, Luke has survived, becoming quite a different person
from the innocent young man he was in Act One.

At this point, the hero returns and is reintegrated into his society. In *Star
Wars*, Luke has destroyed the Death Star, and he receives his great reward.

This is the classic "Hero Story." We might call this example a *mission* or *task* 25
myth, where the person has to complete a task, but the task itself is not the
real treasure. The real reward for Luke is the love of the Princess and the safe,
new world he had helped create.

A myth can have many variations. We see variations on this myth in
James Bond films (although they lack much of the depth because the hero
is not transformed), and in *The African Queen*, where Rose and Allnutt must
blow up the *Louisa*, or in *Places in the Heart*, where Edna overcomes obstacles to achieve family stability.

The *treasure myth* is another variation on this theme, as seen in
Romancing the Stone. In this story, Joan receives a map and a phone call
which forces her into the adventure. She is helped by an American bird-
catcher and a Mexican pickup-truck driver. She overcomes the obstacles of
snakes, the jungle, waterfalls, shootouts, and finally receives the treasure,
along with the "prince."

Whether the hero's journey is for a treasure or to complete a task,
the elements remain the same. The humble, reluctant hero is called to an
adventure. The hero is helped by a variety of unique characters. S/he must

overcome a series of obstacles that transform him or her in the process, and then face the final challenge that draws on inner and outer resources.

The Healing Myth

Although the hero myth is the most popular story, many myths involve healing. In these stories, some character is "broken" and must leave home to become whole again.

The universal experience behind these healing stories is our psychological need for rejuvenation, for balance. The journey of the hero into exile is not all that different from the weekend in Palm Springs, or the trip to Hawaii to get away from it all, or lying still in a hospital bed for some weeks to heal. In all cases, something is out of balance and the mythic journey moves toward wholeness. 30

Being broken can take several forms. It can be physical, emotional, or psychological. Usually, it's all three. In the process of being exiled or hiding out in the forest, the desert, or even the Amish farm in *Witness*, the person becomes whole, balanced, and receptive to love. Love in these stories is both a healing force and a reward.

Think of John Book in *Witness*. In Act One, we see a frenetic, insensitive man, afraid of commitment, critical and unreceptive to the feminine influences in his life. John is suffering from an "inner wound" which he doesn't know about. When he receives an "outer wound" from a gunshot, it forces him into exile, which begins his process of transformation.

At the beginning of Act Two, we see John delirious and close to death. This is a movement into the unconscious, a movement from the rational, active police life of Act One into a mysterious, feminine, more intuitive world. Since John's "inner problem" is the lack of balance with his feminine side, this delirium begins the process of transformation.

Later in Act Two, we see John beginning to change. He moves from his highly independent lifestyle toward the collective, communal life of his Amish hosts. John now gets up early to milk the cows and to assist with the chores. He uses his carpentry skills to help with the barn building and to complete the birdhouse. Gradually, he begins to develop relationships with Rachel and her son, Samuel. John's life slows down and he becomes more receptive, learning important lessons about love. In Act Three, John finally sees that the feminine is worth saving, and throws down his gun to save Rachel's life. A few beats later, when he has the opportunity to kill Paul, he chooses a nonviolent response instead. Although John doesn't "win" the Princess, he has nevertheless "won" love and wholeness. By the end of the film, we can see that the John Book of Act Three is a different kind of person from the John Book of Act One. He has a different kind of comradeship with his fellow police officers, he's more relaxed, and we can sense that somehow, this experience has formed a more integrated John Book.

Combination Myths

Many stories are combinations of several different myths. Think of *Ghostbusters*,   35
a simple and rather outrageous comedy about three men saving the city of
New York from ghosts. Now think of the story of "Pandora's Box." It's about
the woman who let loose all manner of evil upon the earth by opening a box
she was told not to touch. In *Ghostbusters*, the EPA man is a Pandora figure. By
shutting off the power to the containment center, he inadvertently unleashes
all the ghosts upon New York City. Combine the story of "Pandora's Box" with
a hero story, and notice that we have our three heroes battling the Marshmal-
low Man. One of them also "gets the Princess" when Dr. Peter Venkman finally
receives the affections of Dana Barrett. By looking at these combinations, it is
apparent that even *Ghostbusters* is more than "just a comedy."

Tootsie is a type of reworking of many Shakespearean stories where a
woman has to dress as a man in order to accomplish a certain task. These
Shakespearean stories are reminiscent of many fairy tales where the hero
becomes invisible or takes on another persona, or wears a specific disguise to hide his or her real qualities. In the stories of "The Twelve Dancing
Princesses" or "The Man in the Bearskin," disguise is necessary to achieve a
goal. Combine these elements with the transformation themes of the hero
myth where a hero (such as Michael) must overcome many obstacles to his
success as an actor and a human being. It's not difficult to understand why
the *Tootsie* story hooks us.

Archetypes

A myth includes certain characters that we see in many stories. These characters are called *archetypes*. They can be thought of as the original "pattern"
or "character type" that will be found on the hero's journey. Archetypes take
many forms, but they tend to fall within specific categories.

Earlier, we discussed some of the helpers who give advice to help the
hero—such as the *wise old man* who possesses special knowledge and often
serves as a mentor to the hero.

The female counterpart of the wise old man is the *good mother*. Whereas
the wise old man has superior knowledge, the good mother is known for
her nurturing qualities, and for her intuition. This figure often gives the hero
particular objects to help on the journey. It might be a protective amulet, or
the ruby slippers that Dorothy receives in *The Wizard of Oz* from the Good
Witch of the North. Sometimes in fairy tales it's a cloak to make the person
invisible, or ordinary objects that become extraordinary, as in "The Girl of
Courage," an Afghan fairy tale about a maiden who receives a comb, a whet-
stone, and a mirror to help defeat the devil.

Many myths contain a *shadow figure*. This is a character who is the   40
opposite of the hero. Sometimes this figure helps the hero on the journey;

other times this figure opposes the hero. The shadow figure can be the negative side of the hero which could be the dark and hostile brother in "Cain and Abel," the stepsisters in "Cinderella," or the Robber Girl in "The Snow Queen." The shadow figure can also help the hero, as the whore with the heart of gold who saves the hero's life, or provides balance to his idealization of woman.

Many myths contain *animal archetypes* that can be positive or negative figures. In "St. George and the Dragon," the dragon is the negative force which is a violent and ravaging animal, not unlike the shark in *Jaws*. But in many stories, animals help the hero. Sometimes there are talking donkeys, or a dolphin which saves the hero, or magical horses or dogs.

The *trickster* is a mischievous archetypical figure who is always causing chaos, disturbing the peace, and generally being an anarchist. The trickster uses wit and cunning to achieve his or her ends. Sometimes the trickster is a harmless prankster or a "bad boy" who is funny and enjoyable. More often, the trickster is a con man, as in *The Sting*, or the devil, as in *The Exorcist*, who demanded all the skills of the priest to outwit him. The "Till Eulenspiegel" stories revolve around the trickster, as do the Spanish picaresque novels. Even the tales of Tom Sawyer have a trickster motif. In all countries, there are stories that revolve around this figure, whose job it is to outwit.

"Mythic" Problems and Solutions

We all grew up with myths. Most of us heard or read fairy tales when we were young. Some of us may have read Bible stories, or stories from other religions or other cultures. These stories are part of us. And the best way to work with them is to let them come out naturally as you write the script.

Of course, some filmmakers are better at this than others. George Lucas and Steven Spielberg have a strong sense of myth and incorporate it into their films. They both have spoken about their love of the stories from childhood, and of their desire to bring these types of stories to audiences. Their stories create some of the same sense of wonder and excitement as myths. Many of the necessary psychological beats are part of their stories, deepening the story beyond the ordinary action-adventure.

Myths bring depth to a hero story. If a filmmaker is thinking only about the action and excitement of a story, audiences might fail to connect with the hero's journey. But if the basic beats of the hero's journey are evident, a film will often inexplicably draw audiences, in spite of critics' responses to the film.

Take *Rambo*, for instance. Why was this violent, simple story so popular with audiences? I don't think it was because everyone agreed with its politics. I do think Sylvester Stallone is a master at incorporating the American myth into his filmmaking. That doesn't mean it's done consciously. Somehow he is naturally in sync with the myth, and the myth becomes integrated into his stories.

Clint Eastwood also does hero stories, and gives us the adventure of the myth and the transformation of the myth.... Eastwood's films have given more attention to the transformation of the hero, and have been receiving more serious critical attention as a result.

All of these filmmakers—Lucas, Spielberg, Stallone, and Eastwood—dramatize the hero myth in their own particular ways. And all of them prove that myths are marketable.

Application

It is an important part of the writer's or producer's work to continually find opportunities for deepening the themes within a script. Finding the myth beneath the modern story is part of that process.

To find these myths, it's not a bad idea to reread some of Grimm's fairy   50 tales or fairy tales from around the world to begin to get acquainted with various myths. You'll start to see patterns and elements that connect with our own human experience.

Also, read Joseph Campbell and Greek mythology. If you're interested in Jungian psychology, you'll find many rich resources within a number of books on the subject. Since Jungian psychology deals with archetypes, you'll find many new characters to draw on for your own work.

With all of these resources to incorporate, it's important to remember that the myth is not a story to force upon a script. It's more a pattern which you can bring out in your own stories when they seem to be heading in the direction of a myth.

As you work, ask yourself:

Do I have a myth working in my script? If so, what beats am I using of the hero's journey? Which ones seem to be missing?

Am I missing characters? Do I need a mentor type? A wise old man? A wizard? Would one of these characters help dimensionalize the hero's journey?

Could I create new emotional dimensions to the myth by starting my character as reluctant, naïve, simple, or decidedly "unheroic"?

Does my character get transformed in the process of the journey?

Have I used a strong three-act structure to support the myth, using the first turning point to move into the adventure and the second turning point to create a dark moment, or a reversal, or even a "near-death" experience?

Don't be afraid to create variations on the myth, but don't start with the myth itself. Let the myth grow naturally from your story. Developing myths is part of the rewriting process. If you begin with the myth, you'll find your writing becomes rigid, uncreative, and predictable. Working with the myth in the rewriting process will deepen your script, giving it new life as you find the story within the story.

READING THE TEXT

1. How does Seger define the "hero myth" (para. 11), and what are its typical stages?

2. In your own words, explain what Seger means by "the healing myth" (para. 29).

3. What is an "archetype" in film (para. 37)?

READING THE SIGNS

1. Seger is writing to aspiring screenwriters. How does her status as an industry insider affect her description of heroic archetypes?

2. **CONNECTING TEXTS**　Focusing on gender issues, compare Seger's formulation of heroes with Robert B. Ray's in "The Thematic Paradigm" (p. 303). To what extent do Seger and Ray adequately explain the role of women—and men— in movies?

3. **CONNECTING TEXTS**　Review Michael Parenti's "Class and Virtue" (p. 354), and write an essay identifying the myths behind the modern stories *Pretty Woman* (1990), *Juno* (2007), or *Don't Breathe* (2016).

4. Watch *The BFG* (2016) or a segment of the *Lord of the Rings* trilogy, and write an essay in which you explain the myths and archetypal characters the film includes. How might archetypal and mythic patterns explain the film's success?

5. Seger recommends that aspiring screenwriters read Grimm's fairy tales for inspiration. You can find them online. Read some of Grimm's tales, and then write an argument assessing the suitability of such tales as inspiration for films today.

6. Watch one of the *Hunger Games* films, focusing particularly on character types. In an essay, analyze the film's use of archetypes. To what extent does it replicate, reinvent, or otherwise complicate archetypal characters?

MATT ZOLLER SEITZ

The Offensive Movie Cliché That Won't Die

You've seen a satirical portrayal of him on *The Simpsons*, in the guise of Bleeding Gums Murphy, and he has appeared quite seriously in such movies as *The Legend of Bagger Vance*, *The Green Mile*, and *Legendary*. He's the "Magical Negro": "a saintly African American character who acts as a mentor to a questing white hero" in many recent movies. First identified as such by Spike Lee, as Matt Zoller Seitz observes in this critique of the character, the "Magical Negro" has his roots in such figures as Uncle Remus and Bill "Bojangles" Robinson, and his persistence in American popular culture can be read as a signifier of a larger cultural negotiation in which, Seitz argues, white America, finding itself no longer in complete control of the cultural and political agenda, is trying to strike a "deal." Matt Zoller Seitz is a freelance critic and film editor and the founder of the online publication *The House Next Door.*

"You always know the right things to say," says Cal Chetley (Devon Graye), the high school wrestler hero of *Legendary*, in conversation with Harry "Red" Newman (Danny Glover), a local fisherman.

The hero seems bewildered and delighted as he says this. He's about to compete in an important match, reeling from melodramatic blows. When Harry shows up out of nowhere to give Cal a pep talk, the stage is set for a *Rocky*-style, go-the-distance ending. But if Cal had thought about Harry in terms of pop culture stereotypes, he could have answered his own implied question: *How come you're always there when I need you, even though I barely know you?* Harry seems to stand apart from the rest of the community, even though he's a familiar and beloved part of it. The only character who speaks to Harry directly is Cal, and their conversations are always about Cal and his well-being. He's such the benevolent guardian angel figure that the cynical viewer half-expects him to be revealed as a figment of Cal's imagination.

He's not imaginary. He's a "Magical Negro": a saintly African American character who acts as a mentor to a questing white hero, who seems to be disconnected from the community that he adores so much, and who often seems to have an uncanny ability to say and do exactly what needs to be said or done in order to keep the story chugging along in the hero's favor.

We have Spike Lee to thank for popularizing this politically incorrect but very useful term. Lee used it in a 2001 appearance at college campuses. He was blasting a then-recent wave of such characters, played by the likes of Cuba Gooding Jr., in *What Dreams May Come* (a spirit guide helping Robin Williams rescue his wife from Hell), Will Smith in *The Legend of Bagger Vance* (a sherpa-on-the-green, mentoring Matt Damon's golfer), Laurence Fishburne in *The Matrix* (Obi-Wan to Keanu Reeves' Luke Skywalker), and Michael Clarke Duncan in *The Green Mile* (a gentle giant on death row whose touch heals white folks' illnesses).

The word choice is deliberately anachronistic—"negro" started to fall out 5 of fashion about forty years ago. But that's why it's so devastating. The word "negro" was a transitional word that fell between the white-comforting "colored" and the more militantly self-determined and oppositional "black." It asked for dignity and autonomy without going that extra step asserting that it existed anyway, with or without white America's approval. "Negro" fits the sorts of characters that incensed Lee. Even though the movies take pains to insist that the African American character is as much a flesh-and-blood person as the white hero, the relationship is that of a master and servant. And not a *real* servant, either: one that really, truly lives to serve, has no life to speak of beyond his service to Da Man, and never seems to trouble himself with doubts about the cause to which he's devoting his time and energy. "How is it that black people have these powers but they use them for the benefit of white people?" Lee asked sarcastically.

The Magical Negro character (or as Lee called him, the "super-duper magical negro") wasn't invented in the 1990s. He's been around for at least a hundred years, accumulating enough examples (from Uncle Remus in *Song of the South* through the clock-keeper played by Bill Cobbs in *The Hudsucker Proxy*) to merit snarky lists, an entry in the urban dictionary, and a

A scene from *The Green Mile*.

detailed Wikipedia page (turns out Stephen King's fiction has been a Magical Negro factory). The term gained an even wider audience when a candidate to chair the Republican National Committee mailed out a song titled "Barack the Magic Negro," with lyrics to the tune of the Peter, Paul and Mary hit. Outraged liberals focused on the surface racism encoded in the song title, ignoring the possibility that the song, however lead-footed in its humor, was rooted in something real.

What got lost in the flap over the song was the phrase's relevance to Obama's candidacy: There was (among Democrats, at least) a widespread sense that replacing George W. Bush with the Illinois senator would send a definitive signal that everything was different now, that it was time to rebuild, repair, rejuvenate, and move forward, not just toward a post-Bush society, but a post-racial one. It was an absurd hope, one that Obama himself seemed to resist endorsing at first, only to relent and begin publicly playing up his pioneer status as the first not-entirely-Caucasian man to pursue and then win the Democratic presidential nomination. Frequent *Salon* commenter David Ehrenstein tackled this subject in a memorable 2007 *Los Angeles Times* piece that called Obama a "magic negro" almost a year before that RNC ditty appeared. Likening Obama to a spiritual descendant of the noble, kindhearted, often sexless black men portrayed by pioneering leading man Sidney Poitier, he wrote, "Like a comic-book superhero, Obama is there to help, out of the sheer goodness of a heart we need not know or understand. For as with all Magic Negroes, the less real he seems, the more desirable he becomes."

Suffice to say Obama's election triggered a paroxysm of paranoia, insecurity, and rage in roughly half the population (maybe more, if polls on immigration and the Park51 project are to be believed). These flare-ups of privilege (wherein an almost entirely white sector of the populace descended from once-despised immigrants embraces the idea that "we" have to protect or reclaim "our" country from "them") cast retrospective light on the Magical Negro resurgence, which flowered in earnest during the last Democratic administration and has been going full-steam ever since.

Between demographers' projections of a twenty-first-century majority-minority swap, Clinton's unprecedented (un-presidented?) comfort with African American culture (which he made official during the 1992 campaign, in an effective bit of pandering stagecraft, by playing sax on *The Arsenio Hall Show*), and hip-hop's supplanting rock as the country's unofficial national soundtrack, there was a sense, even in the pre-Internet era, that the white man either wasn't in control anymore or soon wouldn't be. Whitey was just going to have to deal.

Things haven't played out quite so simply, of course. In every aspect of quality of life that can be measured, nonwhite folks have always tended to be worse off than whites. That hasn't changed in the aughts, and the recession/depression has hit black men especially hard.

10

Looking back over the last twenty years' worth of cultural and demographic unrest, the M. N. phenomenon seems a form of psychological jujitsu—one that takes a subject that some white folks find unpleasant or even troubling to ponder (justifiably resentful black people's status in a country that, fifty years after the start of the modern civil rights struggle, is still run by, and mostly for, whites) and turns it into a source of gentle reassurance. Do "they" hate us? Oh, no! In fact, deep down they want "us" to succeed, and are happy to help "us" succeed, as long as we listen well and are polite. That's why Whoopi Goldberg put her life on hold to help Demi Moore get in touch with her dead boyfriend in *Ghost*, and Jennifer Hudson lived to serve Sarah Jessica Parker in the first *Sex and the City* movie. And it's why Danny Glover's character—one of but a few black men in an otherwise white town—takes such a keen interest in the life of a bantamweight high school wrestler who has apparently lived in the same town with Harry his entire life and recognizes him as a local eccentric, yet never bothered to get to know him before now.

People that enjoyed *Legendary* may say I'm being unfair to Harry, that there's more to him than Magical Negro-hood. And yes, it's true, at the end—spoiler alert!—we're told that he's not just a gravel-voiced sweetheart who likes to hang out by the local creek, catching fish and dispensing words of wisdom. He's actually quite influential—not *literally* magical, but nevertheless demi-godlike in his influence over the town and its history. But the specifics of Harry's character don't refute the label; quite the contrary. The revelation of Harry's influence is a nifty trick, one that's common in nearly all movies featuring nonwhite mentor / sidekick / deus ex machina characters. It seems appealing enough in the abstract. But it's weak soup when you look at such a character's role in the totality of the story.

Danny Glover, arguably one of cinema's most versatile and likable character actors, gets to play something close to God (he even narrates the story and turns out to have had a hand in three generations of local lives). But he doesn't get a good scene with anybody but the hero, doesn't get even the intimation of a private life, and barely speaks to anyone in the town that supposedly adores and respects him. Like the clock-tender in *The Hudsucker Proxy*, the HIV-stricken painter/saint from *In America*, and Ben Vereen's characters in *Pippin* and *All That Jazz*, Harry's aura of omnipotence is compensation for being shut out of the movie. It's a screenwriter's distraction that obscures the character's detachment from the heart of the narrative—and the character's essentially decorative nature. Like the hot-tempered black police captain who demands the maverick white detective's badge and the stern black woman judge who dresses down the kooky but irresponsible white heroine and warns her to get her life together, the Magical Negro is a glorified walk-on role, a narrative device with a pulse. The M. N. doesn't really drive the story, but is a glorified hood ornament attached to the end of a car that's being driven by white society, vigorously turning a little steering wheel that's not attached to anything.

READING THE TEXT

1. In your own words, define the term "Magical Negro" (para. 3). Why is it considered "anachronistic" (para. 5)?

2. What evidence does Seitz offer to suggest that the Danny Glover character in *Legendary* is a Magical Negro?

3. Why did some commentators dub Barack Obama, who was not a cinematic character, a Magical Negro during the 2008 presidential race?

4. Characterize Seitz's tone in this selection. In what ways does it affect your response to his argument?

READING THE SIGNS

1. **CONNECTING TEXTS**   Write your own interpretation of the representation of African American characters in *Legendary*, *Ghost*, *Sex and the City*, *All That Jazz*, or another film that Seitz refers to. To develop your ideas, consult Michael Omi's "In Living Color: Race and American Culture" (p. 462). To what extent do the characters in the film you've selected display traits of "overt" or "inferential" racism, as Omi describes those concepts?

2. **CONNECTING TEXTS**   Both the Magical Negro and the black domestic servant are exaggerated versions of racial stereotypes. In class, compare and contrast these stereotypes. What underlying myths regarding racial difference do they display? Use your discussion to jump-start your own essay about the extent to which these stereotypes perpetuate racial myths. To develop your ideas, read Helena Andrews's "*The Butler* versus *The Help*: Gender Matters" (p. 341).

3. Seitz attributes the recurrence of the Magical Negro stereotype, in part, to concern about changing demographics whereby Caucasians would no longer be the dominant ethnic group in America. Considering today's political landscape, what signs do you see that support or complicate this explanation? Be sure to consider national voting patterns, particularly in the 2016 presidential election.

4. Seitz comments parenthetically that "Stephen King's fiction has been a Magical Negro factory" (para. 6). Read at least one King novel that includes African American characters. Write an essay in which you support, refute, or modify this assertion.

5. Seitz is critical of the Magical Negro stereotype, but it has been argued that this particular representation of African Americans is a positive response to accusations that this demographic group too often is portrayed with overtly negative, violent stereotypes. Write an essay in which you evaluate this argument, taking care to base your claims on an analysis of specific films and characters.

6. Using Seitz's article as a critical framework, analyze the depiction of African American characters in a film such as *Suicide Squad* (2016) or *Birth of a Nation* (2016). To what extent does the film you select reinforce, redefine, or complicate mainstream depictions of African Americans?

HELENA ANDREWS
The Butler *versus* The Help: *Gender Matters*

Though both movies shared much, including commercial success, *The Butler*, in Helena Andrews's words, was critically "toasted," while "*The Help* was trashed." Finding the critical dichotomy grounded in gender biases that undervalue "women's work" — the lead character in *The Help* is a maid — Andrews situates *The Butler* in a system of recent films featuring black men that give the benefit of the doubt to their lead characters, even as black actresses are still criticized for playing "mammy"-like roles. Helena Andrews is a contributing editor at *The Root*, where this article first appeared, and the author of *Bitch Is the New Black* (2011).

Like many of the films in the "it's complicated" historical-fiction genre, *Lee Daniels' The Butler* uses broad strokes to paint a decidedly unpretty picture — the cinematic equivalent of an Instagram filter.

But despite the artistic liberties and Forrest Gump–like rendering of the life of White House butler Cecil Gaines — based upon the true story of Eugene Allen — in its first week out *The Butler* has seemed to bob and weave past the reflexive reproof such movies usually attract.

Almost immediately, I noticed the stark difference in tone between critical discussion of *The Butler* and another similarly entitled film, *The Help*. Whereas this most recent film, jam-packed with big first names like Oprah, Cuba and Forest, has been toasted, *The Help* was trashed.

Early criticism of *The Help* — starring Viola Davis, who was nominated for an Academy Award for her leading role as Aibileen, a maid — was swift and unrelenting. As part of her publicity blitz in the lead up to the film's release and the ensuing awards season, Davis spent as much time defending her choice to play Aibileen as she did promoting the film.

In an interview with newsman Tavis Smiley — who pointedly told Davis and her co-star, Octavia Spencer, "I want you to win, but I'm ambivalent about what you are winning for" — Davis had to explain herself. 5

"The black artist cannot live in a place, in a revisionist place. The black artist can only tell the truth about humanity, and humanity is messy, people are messy," said Davis. At this point the actress had had a lot of practice being on the defense.

"I've been under assault that the maid, the mammy, is a tired image, to which I respond and have responded that I created a character, a human being, and this is an important story to tell. It's an important dialogue to have," said Davis in an interview with the *Wall Street Journal* right before the 2011 awards season.

None of Davis' defensive tactics have been necessary for Forest Whitaker during the full-court publicity press for *The Butler*.

While on ABC's *The View*, Whitaker said early positive responses to the film had been "universal." In an interview with the *New York Times*, the actor was asked about his methods, how he was able to convey his character's "pride and struggle," and not why he'd decided to take on such a role. *Rolling Stone* film critic Peter Travers asked Whitaker in an interview about the research involved in playing Cecil Gaines.

So far the most popular sentiment from the film — repeated in several   10 interviews — is the notion that black domestics serving white families were, in fact, subversive.

"Just by their presence, by their dignity, by their dedication to their work, they were able to move things forward," explained Whitaker on *Good Morning America*.

This is a radical shift in thought when applied to the debate about the lack of nonstereotypical roles in mainstream Hollywood. From Hattie McDaniel onward, the debate about whether or not black actors and actresses (along with screenwriters, directors and producers) should ever play the roles of the maid or the butler has been ongoing. Davis couldn't escape the backlash for her role in *The Help* in 2011, but just two years later Whitaker has.

The most obvious difference between Davis' Aibileen and Whitaker's Cecil is the characters' gender. Then comes the issue of class and access. Aibileen is a maid in a middle-class enclave in Jackson, Miss., serving up chicken salad and changing diapers. Cecil is a tuxedoed butler at the most famous address in the United States, serving tea in fine china to the leaders of the free world. They both wear the uniform. They both wear two faces.

But Aibileen's world is dominated by women. She does "women's work" — cleaning, cooking, care-giving. Cecil, though just as invisible, occupies space crowded by men. He's "in service" and "serving his country," as President Ronald Reagan (played by Alan Rickman) puts it.

I don't think it's too far of a stretch to think that for most — despite the   15 effusive testaments to the legacy of maids delivered by Oprah and the film's director, Lee Daniels — the role of the maid, no matter how dignified, is still considered less significant. It's a story that audiences, especially black ones, believe has been told before.

To be fair, *The Help* and *The Butler* are two distinct narratives. The white characters, though presidents and first ladies they may be, are ancillary to Cecil's story. *The Butler* is woven around Cecil's life. By contrast, in *The Help*, Aibileen's story is tightly tied to those of the white women around her, a narrative device that didn't sit well with some because it reinforces the notion that black women's stories cannot stand on their own.

Still, the onslaught of accolades for the recent batch of films starring black men in historically complicated roles, from Jamie Foxx's Django to Whitaker's Cecil and Chiwetel Ejiofor's Solomon Northup in the upcoming *12 Years a Slave*, says something about how films featuring black actresses in similarly uncomfortable roles are perceived. And in a creative landscape where Harriet Tubman gets a "sex tape" instead of a starring role, I'm not sure if it says something good.

READING THE TEXT

1. Summarize in your own words how the critical response to *The Butler* and *The Help* differed, in Andrews's estimation.

2. What does Viola Davis mean by saying, "The black artist cannot live ... in a revisionist place" (para. 6)?

3. What evidence does Andrews provide to support her contention that attitudes toward gender and class have influenced the different responses to these two films?

4. Define in your own words the "mammy" (para. 7) role in films.

READING THE SIGNS

1. Analyze reviews of *The Butler* and *The Help* (using a site like Rotten Tomatoes), and write an essay in which you support, refute, or complicate Andrews's claims about the critical reception of these films. Alternatively, read reviews of another film focused on African American characters, such as *12 Years a Slave* (2013), and analyze their response to the portrayal of blacks in the film.

2. **CONNECTING TEXTS**   Andrews refers to an ongoing "debate about whether or not black actors and actresses (along with screenwriters, directors and producers) should ever play the roles of the maid or the butler" (para. 12). In an argumentative essay, present your own position in this debate, being sure to ground your claims in an analysis of specific characters. To develop your ideas, read Michael Omi's "In Living Color: Race and American Culture" (p. 462) and Matt Zoller Seitz's "The Offensive Movie Cliché That Won't Die" (p. 335).

3. **CONNECTING TEXTS**   Andrews suggests that attitudes toward class also influenced viewers' responses to *The Help* and *The Butler*. Adopting the perspective of Michael Parenti in "Class and Virtue" (p. 354), conduct your own analysis of how the two films use class-based signs to shape their characters' identities.

4. Using Andrews's essay as a critical framework, analyze the role of the female protagonists in the TV program *Devious Maids*. To what extent do you think the program perpetuates class and racial stereotypes?

Lee Daniels' The Butler

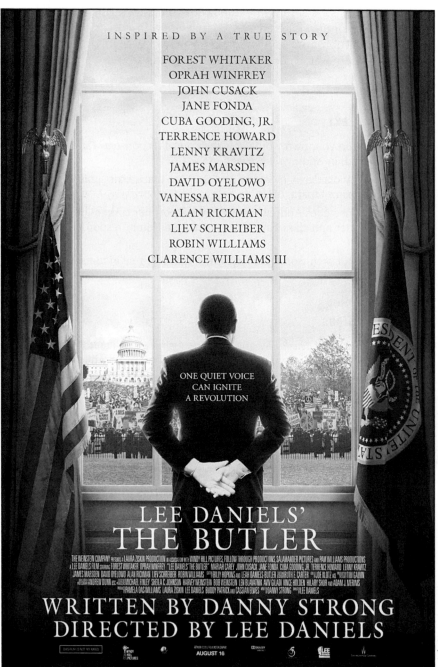

READING THE SIGNS

1. Based on this poster for *Lee Daniels' The Butler*, how would you characterize the subject matter of this film? Does the poster make you want to see the film? Why or why not?

2. If you have read Helena Andrews's "*The Butler* versus *The Help*: Gender Matters" (p. 341), then you already know a little bit about the plot of this film, the story of an African American White House butler. In your opinion, how is the central figure in the poster (the butler of the film's title) portrayed in the poster? What are we supposed to think about this character from the poster alone?

3. Judging from this poster for *The Butler*, who in your opinion is the intended audience for this film? Why? What elements in this poster appeal to that intended audience?

4. Consider the caption on this poster: "One quiet voice can ignite a revolution." In your opinion, is this caption effective as a teaser? Why or why not? How is the language in this caption designed to stoke interest in the film?

JESSICA HAGEDORN

Asian Women in Film: No Joy, No Luck

Why do movies always seem to portray Asian women as tragic victims of history and fate? Jessica Hagedorn asks in this essay, which originally appeared in *Ms.* Even such movies as *The Joy Luck Club*, based on Amy Tan's breakthrough novel that elevated Asian American fiction to best-seller status, reinforce old stereotypes of the powerlessness of Asian and Asian American women. A screenwriter and novelist, Hagedorn calls for a different kind of storytelling that will show Asian women as powerful controllers of their own destinies. Jessica Hagedorn's publications include the novels *Dogeaters* (1990), and *Toxicology* (2011).

Pearl of the Orient. Whore. Geisha. Concubine. Whore. Hostess. Bar Girl. Mamasan. Whore. China Doll. Tokyo Rose. Whore. Butterfly. Whore. Miss Saigon. Whore. Dragon Lady. Lotus Blossom. Gook. Whore. Yellow Peril. Whore. Bangkok Bombshell. Whore. Hospitality Girl. Whore. Comfort Woman. Whore. Savage. Whore. Sultry. Whore. Faceless. Whore. Porcelain. Whore. Demure. Whore. Virgin. Whore. Mute. Whore. Model Minority. Whore. Victim. Whore. Woman Warrior. Whore. Mail-Order Bride. Whore. Mother. Wife. Lover. Daughter. Sister.

As I was growing up in the Philippines in the 1950s, my fertile imagination was colonized by thoroughly American fantasies. Yellowface variations on the exotic erotic loomed larger than life on the silver screen. I was mystified and enthralled by Hollywood's skewed representations of Asian women: sleek, evil goddesses with slanted eyes and cunning ways, or smiling, sarong-clad South Seas "maidens" with undulating hips, kinky black hair, and white skin darkened by makeup. Hardly any of the "Asian" characters were played by Asians. White actors like Sidney Toler and Warner Oland played "inscrutable Oriental detective" Charlie Chan with taped eyelids and a singsong, chop suey accent. Jennifer Jones was a Eurasian doctor swept up in a doomed "interracial romance" in *Love Is a Many Splendored Thing*. In my mother's youth, white actor Luise Rainer played the central role of the Patient Chinese Wife in the 1937 film adaptation of Pearl Buck's novel *The Good Earth*. Back then, not many thought to ask why; they were all too busy being grateful to see anyone in the movies remotely like themselves.

Cut to 1960: *The World of Suzie Wong*, another tragic East/West affair. I am now old enough to be impressed. Sexy, sassy Suzie (played by Nancy Kwan) works out of a bar patronized by white sailors, but doesn't seem bothered by any of it. For a hardworking girl turning nightly tricks to support her baby, she manages to parade an astonishing wardrobe in damn near every scene, down to matching handbags and shoes. The sailors are also strictly Hollywood, sanitized and not too menacing. Suzie and all the other prostitutes in this movie are cute, giggling, dancing sex machines with hearts of gold. William Holden plays an earnest, rather prim, Nice Guy painter seeking inspiration in The Other. Of course, Suzie falls madly in love with him. Typically, she tells him, "I not important," and "I'll be with you until you say — Suzie, go away." She also thinks being beaten by a man is a sign of true passion and is terribly disappointed when Mr. Nice Guy refuses to show his true feelings.

Next in Kwan's short-lived but memorable career was the kitschy 1961 musical *Flower Drum Song*, which, like *Suzie Wong*, is a thoroughly American commercial product. The female roles are typical of Hollywood musicals of the times: women are basically airheads, subservient to men. Kwan's counterpart is the Good Chinese Girl, played by Miyoshi Umeki, who was better playing the Loyal Japanese Girl in that other classic Hollywood tale of forbidden love, *Sayonara*. Remember? Umeki was so loyal, she committed double suicide with actor Red Buttons. I instinctively hated *Sayonara* when I first saw it as a child; now I understand why. Contrived tragic resolutions were the only way Hollywood got past the censors in those days. With one or two exceptions, somebody in these movies always had to die to pay for breaking racial and sexual taboos.

Until the recent onslaught of films by both Asian and Asian American filmmakers, Asian Pacific women have generally been perceived by Hollywood with a mixture of fascination, fear, and contempt. Most Hollywood movies either trivialize or exoticize us as people of color and as women. Our intelligence is underestimated, our humanity overlooked, and our diverse cultures treated as interchangeable. If we are "good," we are childlike, 5

submissive, silent, and eager for sex (see France Nuyen's glowing performance as Liat in the film version of *South Pacific*) or else we are tragic victim
types (see *Casualties of War*, Brian De Palma's graphic 1989 drama set in
Vietnam). And if we are not silent, suffering doormats, we are demonized
dragon ladies — cunning, deceitful, sexual provocateurs. Give me the
demonic any day — Anna May Wong as a villain slithering around in a slinky
gown is at least gratifying to watch, neither servile nor passive. And she
steals the show from Marlene Dietrich in Josef von Sternberg's *Shanghai
Express*. From the 1920s through the 1930s, Wong was our only female
"star." But even she was trapped in limited roles, in what filmmaker Renee
Tajima has called the dragon lady / lotus blossom dichotomy.

Cut to 1985: There is a scene toward the end of the terribly dishonest but
weirdly compelling Michael Cimino movie *Year of the Dragon* (cowritten by
Oliver Stone) that is one of my favorite twisted movie moments of all time.
If you ask a lot of my friends who've seen that movie (especially if they're
Asian), it's one of their favorites too. The setting is a crowded Chinatown
nightclub. There are two very young and very tough Jade Cobra gang girls in
a shoot-out with Mickey Rourke, in the role of a demented Polish American
cop who, in spite of being Mr. Ugly in the flesh — an arrogant, misogynistic
bully devoid of any charm — wins the "good" Asian American anchorwoman
in the film's absurd and implausible ending. This is a movie with an actual
disclaimer as its lead-in, covering its ass in advance in response to antici-
pated complaints about "stereotypes."

My pleasure in the hard-edged power of the Chinatown gang girls in *Year
of the Dragon* is my small revenge, the answer to all those Suzie Wong "I want
to be your slave" female characters. The Jade Cobra girls are mere background to the white male foreground/focus of Cimino's movie. But long after
the movie has faded into video-rental heaven, the Jade Cobra girls remain
defiant, fabulous images in my memory, flaunting tight metallic dresses and
spiky cock's-comb hairdos streaked electric red and blue.

Mickey Rourke looks down with world-weary pity at the unnamed Jade
   Cobra girl (Doreen Chan) he's just shot who lies sprawled and bleeding
   on the street: "You look like you're gonna die, beautiful."
JADE COBRA GIRL: "Oh yeah? [blood gushing from her mouth] I'm proud of
   it."
ROURKE: "You are? You got anything you wanna tell me before you go,
   sweetheart?"
JADE COBRA GIRL: "Yeah. [pause] Fuck you."

Cut to 1993: I've been told that like many New Yorkers, I watch movies with the right side of my brain on perpetual overdrive. I admit to being
grouchy and overcritical, suspicious of sentiment, and cynical. When a critic
like Richard Corliss of *Time* magazine gushes about *The Joy Luck Club* being
"a fourfold *Terms of Endearment*," my gut instinct is to run the other way.
I resent being told how to feel. I went to see the 1993 eight-handkerchief

Anna May Wong.

movie version of Amy Tan's bestseller with a group that included my ten-year-old daughter. I was caught between the sincere desire to be swept up by the turbulent mother-daughter sagas and my own stubborn resistance to being so obviously manipulated by the filmmakers. With every flashback came tragedy. The music soared; the voice-overs were solemn or wistful; tears, tears, and more tears flowed on-screen. Daughters were reverent; mothers carried dark secrets.

I was elated by the grandness and strength of the four mothers and the luminous actors who portrayed them, but I was uneasy with the passivity of the Asian American daughters. They seemed to exist solely as receptors for

Michelle Yeoh, *Tomorrow Never Dies*, 1997.

their mothers' amazing life stories. It's almost as if by assimilating so easily into American society, they had lost all sense of self.

In spite of my resistance, my eyes watered as the desperate mother played by Kieu Chinh was forced to abandon her twin baby girls on a country road in war-torn China. (Kieu Chinh resembles my own mother and her twin sister, who suffered through the brutal Japanese occupation of the Philippines.) So far in this movie, an infant son had been deliberately drowned, a mother played by the gravely beautiful France Nuyen had gone catatonic with grief, a concubine had cut her flesh open to save her dying mother, an insecure daughter had been oppressed by her boorish Asian American husband, another insecure daughter had been left by her white husband, and so on. ... The overall effect was numbing as far as I'm concerned, but a man sitting two rows in front of us broke down sobbing. A Chinese Filipino writer even more grouchy than me later complained, "Must ethnicity only be equated with suffering?"

Because change has been slow, *The Joy Luck Club* carries a lot of cultural baggage. It is a big-budget story about Chinese American women, directed by a Chinese American man, cowritten and coproduced by Chinese American women. That's a lot to be thankful for. And its box office success proves that an immigrant narrative told from female perspectives can have mass appeal. But my cynical side tells me that its success might mean only one thing in Hollywood: more weepy epics about Asian American mother-daughter relationships will be planned.

That the film finally got made was significant. By Hollywood standards (think white male; think money, money, money), a movie about Asian Americans even when adapted from a bestseller was a risky proposition. When I asked a producer I know about the film's rumored delays, he simply said, "It's still an *Asian* movie," surprised I had even asked. Equally interesting was director Wayne Wang's initial reluctance to be involved in the project; he told the *New York Times*, "I didn't want to do another Chinese movie."

Maybe he shouldn't have worried so much. After all, according to the media, the nineties are the decade of "Pacific Overtures" and East Asian chic. Madonna, the pop queen of shameless appropriation, cultivated Japanese high-tech style with her music video "Rain," while Janet Jackson faked kitschy orientalia in hers, titled "If." Critical attention was paid to movies from China, Japan, and Vietnam. But that didn't mean an honest appraisal of women's lives. Even on the art house circuit, filmmakers who should know better took the easy way out. Takehiro Nakajima's 1992 film *Okoge* presents one of the more original film roles for women in recent years. In Japanese, "okoge" means the crust of rice that sticks to the bottom of the rice pot; in pejorative slang, it means fag hag. The way "okoge" is used in the film seems a reappropriation of the term; the portrait Nakajima creates of Sayoko, the so-called fag hag, is clearly an affectionate one. Sayoko is a quirky, self-assured woman in contemporary Tokyo who does voice-overs for cartoons, has a thing for Frida Kahlo paintings, and is drawn to a gentle young gay man named Goh. But the other women's roles are disappointing, stereotypical "hysterical females" and the movie itself turns conventional halfway through. Sayoko sacrifices herself to a macho brute Goh desires, who rapes her as images of Frida Kahlo paintings and her beloved Goh rising from the ocean flash before her. She gives birth to a baby boy and endures a terrible life of poverty with the abusive rapist. This sudden change from spunky survivor to helpless, victimized woman is baffling. Whatever happened to her job? Or that arty little apartment of hers? Didn't her Frida Kahlo obsession teach her anything?

Then there was Tiana Thi Thanh Nga's *From Hollywood to Hanoi*, a self-serving but fascinating documentary. Born in Vietnam to a privileged family that included an uncle who was defense minister in the Thieu government and an idolized father who served as press minister, Nga (a.k.a. Tiana) spent her adolescence in California. A former actor in martial arts movies and fitness teacher ("Karaticize with Tiana"), the vivacious Tiana decided to make a record of her journey back to Vietnam.

From Hollywood to Hanoi is at times unintentionally very funny. Tiana   15
includes a quick scene of herself dancing with a white man at the Metropole hotel in Hanoi, and breathlessly announces: "That's me doing the tango with Oliver Stone!" Then she listens sympathetically to a horrifying account of the My Lai massacre by one of its few female survivors. In another scene, Tiana cheerfully addresses a food vendor on the streets of Hanoi: "Your hairdo is so pretty." The unimpressed, poker-faced woman gives a brusque, deadpan reply: "You want to eat, or what?" Sometimes it is hard to tell the difference between Tiana Thi Thanh Nga and her Hollywood persona: The real Tiana still seems to be playing one of her B-movie roles, which are mainly fun because they're fantasy. The time was certainly right to explore postwar Vietnam from a Vietnamese woman's perspective; it's too bad this film was done by a Valley Girl.

Nineteen ninety-three also brought Tran Anh Hung's *The Scent of Green Papaya*, a different kind of Vietnamese memento — this is a look back at the peaceful, lush country of the director's childhood memories. The film opens in Saigon, in 1951. A willowy ten-year-old girl named Mui comes to work for a troubled family headed by a melancholy musician and his kind, stoic wife. The men of this bourgeois household are idle, pampered types who take naps while the women do all the work. Mui is male fantasy: She is a devoted servant, enduring acts of cruel mischief with patience and dignity; as an adult, she barely speaks. She scrubs floors, shines shoes, and cooks with loving care and never a complaint. When she is sent off to work for another wealthy musician, she ends up being impregnated by him. The movie ends as the camera closes in on Mui's contented face. Languid and precious, *The Scent of Green Papaya* is visually haunting, but it suffers from the director's colonial fantasy of women as docile, domestic creatures. Steeped in highbrow nostalgia, it's the arty Vietnamese version of *My Fair Lady* with the wealthy musician as Professor Higgins, teaching Mui to read and write.

And then there is Ang Lee's tepid 1993 hit, *The Wedding Banquet* — a clever culture-clash farce in which traditional Chinese values collide with contemporary American sexual mores. The somewhat formulaic plot goes like this: Wai-Tung, a yuppie landlord, lives with his white lover, Simon, in a chic Manhattan brownstone. Wai-Tung is an only child and his aging parents in Taiwan long for a grandchild to continue the family legacy. Enter Wei-Wei, an artist who lives in a grungy loft owned by Wai-Tung. She slugs tequila straight from the bottle as she paints and flirts boldly with her young, uptight landlord, who brushes her off. "It's my fate. I am always attracted to handsome gay men," she mutters. After this setup, the movie goes downhill, all edges blurred in a cozy nest of happy endings. In a refrain of Sayoko's plight in *Okoge*, a pregnant, suddenly complacent Wei-Wei gives in to family pressures — and never gets her life back.

"It takes a man to know what it is to be a real woman."
— SONG LILING in *M. Butterfly*

Ironically, two gender-bending films in which men play men playing women reveal more about the mythology of the prized Asian woman and the superficial trappings of gender than most movies that star real women. The slow-moving *M. Butterfly* presents the ultimate object of Western male desire as the spy / opera diva Song Liling, a Suzie Wong / Lotus Blossom played by actor John Lone with a five o'clock shadow and bobbing Adam's apple. The best and most profound of these forays into crossdressing is the spectacular melodrama *Farewell My Concubine*, directed by Chen Kaige. Banned in China, *Farewell My Concubine* shared the prize for Best Film at the 1993 Cannes Film Festival with Jane Campion's *The Piano*. Sweeping through fifty years of tumultuous history in China, the story revolves around the lives of two male Beijing Opera stars and the woman who marries one of them. The three characters make an unforgettable triangle, struggling over love, art, friendship, and politics against the bloody backdrop of cultural upheaval. They are as capable of casually betraying each other as they are of selfless, heroic acts. The androgynous Dieyi, doomed to play the same female role of concubine over and over again, is portrayed with great vulnerability, wit, and grace by male Hong Kong pop star Leslie Cheung. Dieyi competes with the prostitute Juxian (Gong Li) for the love of his childhood protector and fellow opera star, Duan Xiaolou (Zhang Fengyi).

Cheung's highly stylized performance as the classic concubine-ready-to-die-for-love in the opera within the movie is all about female artifice. His sidelong glances, restrained passion, languid stance, small steps, and delicate, refined gestures say everything about what is considered desirable in Asian women — and are the antithesis of the feisty, outspoken woman played by Gong Li. The characters of Dieyi and Juxian both see suffering as part and parcel of love and life. Juxian matter-of-factly says to Duan Xiaolou before he agrees to marry her: "I'm used to hardship. If you take me in, I'll

wait on you hand and foot. If you tire of me, I'll ... kill myself. No big deal."
It's an echo of Suzie Wong's servility, but the context is new. Even with her
back to the wall, Juxian is not helpless or whiny. She attempts to manipulate
a man while admitting to the harsh reality that is her life.

Dieyi and Juxian are the two sides of the truth of women's lives in most   20
Asian countries. Juxian in particular — wife and ex-prostitute — could be
seen as a thankless and stereotypical role. But like the characters Gong Li
has played in Chinese director Zhang Yimou's films, *Red Sorghum*, *Raise the
Red Lantern*, and especially *The Story of Qiu Ju*, Juxian is tough, obstinate,
sensual, clever, oafish, beautiful, infuriating, cowardly, heroic, and banal.
Above all, she is resilient. Gong Li is one of the few Asian Pacific actors
whose roles have been drawn with intelligence, honesty, and depth. Nevertheless, the characters she plays are limited by the possibilities that exist for
real women in China.

"Let's face it. Women still don't mean shit in China," my friend Meel-
ing reminds me. What she says so bluntly about her culture rings painfully
true, but in less obvious fashion for me. In the Philippines, infant girls aren't
drowned, nor were their feet bound to make them more desirable. But sons
were and are cherished. To this day, men of the bourgeois class are coddled
and prized, much like the spoiled men of the elite household in *The Scent
of Green Papaya*. We do not have a geisha tradition like Japan, but physical
beauty is overtreasured. Our daughters are protected virgins or primed as
potential beauty queens. And many of us have bought into the image of the
white man as our handsome savior: G.I. Joe.

Buzz magazine recently featured an article entitled "Asian Women / L.A.
Men," a report on a popular hangout that caters to white men's fantasies of
nubile Thai women. The lines between movies and real life are blurred. Male
screenwriters and cinematographers flock to this bar-restaurant, where the
waitresses are eager to "audition" for roles. Many of these men have been
to Bangkok while working on film crews for Vietnam War movies. They've
come back to L.A., but for them, the movie never ends. In this particular
fantasy the boys play G.I. Joe on a rescue mission in the urban jungle, saving the whore from herself. "A scene has developed here, a kind of R-rated
Cheers," author Alan Rifkin writes. "The waitresses audition for sitcoms. The
customers date the waitresses or just keep score."

Colonization of the imagination is a two-way street. And being enshrined
on a pedestal as someone's Pearl of the Orient fantasy doesn't seem so
demeaning, at first; who wouldn't want to be worshipped? Perhaps that's
why Asian women are the ultimate wet dream in most Hollywood movies;
it's no secret how well we've been taught to play the role, to take care of
our men. In Hollywood vehicles, we are objects of desire or derision; we
exist to provide sex, color, and texture in what is essentially a white man's
world. It is akin to what Toni Morrison calls "the Africanist presence" in literature. She writes: "Just as entertainers, through or by association with blackface, could render permissible topics that otherwise would have been taboo,

so American writers were able to employ an imagined Africanist persona to articulate and imaginatively act out the forbidden in American culture." The same analogy could be made for the often titillating presence of Asian women in movies made by white men.

Movies are still the most seductive and powerful of artistic mediums, manipulating us with ease by a powerful combination of sound and image. In many ways, as females and Asians, as audiences or performers, we have learned to settle for less — to accept the fact that we are either decorative, invisible, or one dimensional. When there are characters who look like us represented in a movie, we have also learned to view between the lines, or to add what is missing. For many of us, this way of watching has always been a necessity. We fill in the gaps. If a female character is presented as a mute, willowy beauty, we convince ourselves she is an ancestral ghost — so smart she doesn't have to speak at all. If she is a whore with a heart of gold, we claim her as a tough feminist icon. If she is a sexless, sanitized, boring nerd, we embrace her as a role model for our daughters, rather than the tragic whore. And if she is presented as an utterly devoted saint suffering nobly in silence, we lie and say she is just like our mothers. Larger than life. Magical and insidious. A movie is never just a movie, after all.

READING THE TEXT

1. Summarize in your own words Hagedorn's view of the traditional images of Asian women as presented in American film.

2. What is the chronology of Asian women in film that Hagedorn presents, and why do you think she gives us a historical overview?

3. Why does Hagedorn say that the film *The Joy Luck Club* "carries a lot of cultural baggage" (para. 11)?

4. What sort of images of Asian women does Hagedorn imply that she would prefer to see?

READING THE SIGNS

1. Watch *The Joy Luck Club*, and write an essay in which you support, refute, or modify Hagedorn's interpretation of the film. Alternatively, view another film featuring Asian characters, such as *Better Luck Tomorrow* or *Gran Torino*, or a TV show with Asian characters, such as *Fresh off the Boat,* and use Hagedorn's article as a critical framework to evaluate your choice's representation of Asian characters.

2. **CONNECTING TEXTS** In class, form teams and debate the proposition that Hollywood writers and directors have a social responsibility to avoid stereotyping ethnic characters. To develop your team's arguments, brainstorm films that depict various ethnicities, and then discuss whether the portrayals are damaging or benign. You might also consult Michael Omi's "In Living Color: Race and American Culture" (p. 462).

3. Study a magazine that targets Asian American readers, such as *Tea*, *Hyphen*, or *Yolk*. Then write an essay in which you analyze whether Asian women in the magazine fit the stereotypes that Hagedorn describes, keeping in mind the magazine's intended readership (businessmen, twentysomethings of both sexes, and so forth).

4. **CONNECTING TEXTS**   Watch one of the gender-bending films Hagedorn mentions (such as *M. Butterfly*), and write your own analysis of the gender roles portrayed in the film. To develop your ideas, consult Aaron Devor's "Gender Role Behaviors and Attitudes" (p. 474).

5. Few American films have featured Asian characters as protagonists. Watch an exception to this trend, *Harold & Kumar Go to White Castle* (2004), and write a semiotic analysis of the racial depictions in this film. To what extent does this film replicate or avoid the stereotypes Hagedorn discusses?

MICHAEL PARENTI

Class and Virtue

In 1993, a movie called *Indecent Proposal* presented a story in which a billionaire offers a newly poor middle-class woman a million dollars if she'll sleep with him for one night. In Michael Parenti's terms, what was really indecent about the movie was the way it showed the woman falling in love with the billionaire, thus making a romance out of a class outrage. But the movie could get away with it, partly because Hollywood has always conditioned audiences to root for the 1 percent and to ignore the inequities of class privilege. In this selection from *Make-Believe Media: The Politics of Entertainment* (1992), Parenti argues that Hollywood has long been in the business of representing the interests of the ruling classes. Whether it is forgiving the classist behavior in *Pretty Woman* or glamorizing the lives of the wealthy, Hollywood makes sure its audiences leave the theater thinking you can't be too rich. Michael Parenti is a writer who lectures widely at university campuses around the country. His most recent book, *Profit Pathology and Other Indecencies* (2015), continues to explore the impact of class power on social and political life.

Class and Virtue

The entertainment media present working people not only as unlettered and uncouth but also as less desirable and less moral than other people. Conversely, virtue is more likely to be ascribed to those characters whose speech and appearance are soundly middle- or upper-middle class.

Even a simple adventure story like *Treasure Island* (1934, 1950, 1972) manifests this implicit class perspective. There are two groups of acquisitive persons searching for a lost treasure. One, headed by a squire, has money enough to hire a ship and crew. The other, led by the rascal Long John Silver, has no money — so they sign up as part of the crew. The narrative implicitly assumes from the beginning that the squire has a moral claim to the treasure, while Long John Silver's gang does not. After all, it is the squire who puts up the venture capital for the ship. Having no investment in the undertaking other than their labor, Long John and his men, by definition, will be "stealing" the treasure, while the squire will be "discovering" it.

To be sure, there are other differences. Long John's men are cutthroats. The squire is not. Yet, one wonders if the difference between a bad pirate and a good squire is itself not preeminently a matter of having the right amount of disposable income. The squire is no less acquisitive than the conspirators. He just does with money what they must achieve with cutlasses. The squire and his associates dress in fine clothes, speak an educated diction, and drink brandy. Long John and his men dress slovenly, speak in guttural accents, and drink rum. From these indications alone, the viewer knows who are the good guys and who are the bad. Virtue is visually measured by one's approximation to proper class appearances.

Sometimes class contrasts are juxtaposed within one person, as in *The Three Faces of Eve* (1957), a movie about a woman who suffers from multiple personalities. When we first meet Eve (Joanne Woodward), she is a disturbed, strongly repressed, puritanically religious person, who speaks with a rural, poor-Southern accent. Her second personality is that of a wild, flirtatious woman who also speaks with a rural, poor-Southern accent. After much treatment by her psychiatrist, she is cured of these schizoid personalities and emerges with a healthy third one, the real Eve, a poised, self-possessed, pleasant woman. What is intriguing is that she now speaks with a cultivated, affluent, Smith College accent, free of any low-income regionalism or ruralism, much like Joanne Woodward herself. This transformation in class style and speech is used to indicate mental health without any awareness of the class bias thusly expressed.

Mental health is also the question in *A Woman under the Influence* (1974), 5 the story of a disturbed woman who is married to a hard-hat husband. He cannot handle — and inadvertently contributes to — her emotional deterioration. She is victimized by a spouse who is nothing more than an insensitive, working-class bull in a china shop. One comes away convinced that every unstable woman needs a kinder, gentler, and above all, more *middle-class* hubby if she wishes to avoid a mental crack-up.

Class prototypes abound in the 1980s television series *The A-Team*. In each episode, a Vietnam-era commando unit helps an underdog, be it a Latino immigrant or a disabled veteran, by vanquishing some menacing force such as organized crime, a business competitor, or corrupt government officials. As always with the make-believe media, the A-Team does good work on an individualized rather than collectively organized basis, helping particular victims by thwarting particular villains. The A-Team's leaders are two white males of privileged background. The lowest ranking members of the team, who do none of the thinking nor the leading, are working-class palookas. They show they are good with their hands, both by punching out the bad guys and by doing the maintenance work on the team's flying vehicles and cars. One of them, "B.A." (bad ass), played by the African American Mr. T., is visceral, tough, and purposely bad-mannered toward those he doesn't like. He projects an image of crudeness and ignorance and is associated with the physical side of things. In sum, the team has a brain (the intelligent white leaders) and a body with its simpler physical functions (the working-class characters), a hierarchy that corresponds to the social structure itself.[1]

Sometimes class bigotry is interwoven with gender bigotry, as in *Pretty Woman* (1990). A dreamboat millionaire corporate raider finds himself all alone for an extended stay in Hollywood (his girlfriend is unwilling to join him), so he quickly recruits a beautiful prostitute as his playmate of the month. She is paid three thousand dollars a week to wait around his super-posh hotel penthouse ready to perform the usual services and accompany him to business dinners at top restaurants. As prostitution goes, it is a dream gig. But there is one cloud on the horizon. She is low-class. She doesn't know which fork to use at those CEO power feasts, and she's bothersomely fidgety, wears tacky clothes, chews gum, and, y'know, doesn't talk so good. But with some tips from the hotel manager, she proves to be a veritable Eliza Doolittle in her class metamorphosis. She dresses in proper attire, sticks the gum away forever, and starts picking the right utensils at dinner. She also figures out how to speak a little more like Joanne Woodward without the benefit of a multiple personality syndrome, and she develops the capacity to sit in a poised, wordless, empty-headed fashion, every inch the expensive female ornament.

She is still a prostitute but a classy one. It is enough of a distinction for the handsome young corporate raider. Having liked her because she was charmingly cheap, he now loves her all the more because she has real polish and is a more suitable companion. So suitable that he decides to do the right thing by her: set her up in an apartment so he can make regular visits at regular prices. But now she wants the better things in life, like marriage, a nice house, and, above all, a different occupation, one that would allow her to use less of herself. She is furious at him for treating her like, well, a prostitute. She decides to give up her profession and get a high school diploma

---

[1] Gina Marchetti, "Class, Ideology and Commercial Television: An Analysis of *The A-Team*," *Journal of Film and Video* 39, Spring 1987, pp. 19–28.

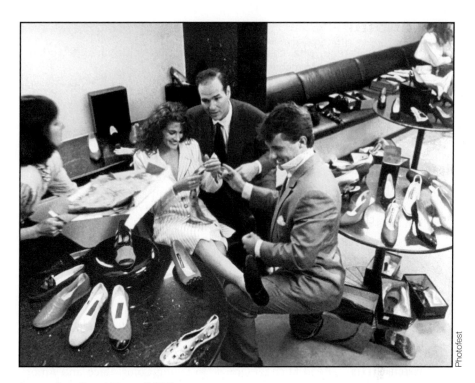

A scene from *Pretty Woman* (1990).

so that she might make a better life for herself — perhaps as a filing clerk or receptionist or some other of the entry-level jobs awaiting young women with high school diplomas.[2]

After the usual girl-breaks-off-with-boy scenes, the millionaire prince returns. It seems he can't concentrate on making money without her. He even abandons his cutthroat schemes and enters into a less lucrative but supposedly more productive, caring business venture with a struggling old-time entrepreneur. The bad capitalist is transformed into a good capitalist. He then carries off his ex-prostitute for a lifetime of bliss. The moral is a familiar one, updated for post-Reagan yuppiedom: A woman can escape from economic and gender exploitation by winning the love and career advantages offered by a rich male. Sexual allure goes only so far unless it develops a material base and becomes a class act.[3]

[2]See the excellent review by Lydia Sargent, *Z Magazine*, April 1990, pp. 43–45.
[3]Ibid.

READING THE TEXT

1. According to Parenti, what characteristics are typically attributed to working-class and upper-class film characters?

2. How does Parenti see the relationship between "class bigotry" and "gender bigotry" (para. 7) in *Pretty Woman*?

3. What relationship does Parenti see between mental health and class values in films?

READING THE SIGNS

1. Watch *Wall Street*, *Unstoppable*, or *The Fighter*, and analyze the class issues that the movie raises. Alternatively, watch an episode of *Shark Tank*, and perform the same sort of analysis.

2. Do you agree with Parenti's interpretation of *Pretty Woman*? Write an argumentative essay in which you defend, challenge, or complicate his reading of the film.

3. **CONNECTING TEXTS**   Read Aaron Devor's "Gender Role Behaviors and Attitudes" (p. 474). How would Devor explain the gender bigotry that Parenti finds in *Pretty Woman*?

4. Watch the 1954 film *On the Waterfront* with your class. How are labor unions and working-class characters portrayed in that film? Does the film display the class bigotry that Parenti describes?

5. **CONNECTING TEXTS**   Read Michael Omi's "In Living Color: Race and American Culture" (p. 462). Then write an essay in which you create a category of cinematic racial bigotry that corresponds to Parenti's two categories of class and gender bigotry. What films have you seen that illustrate your new category?

MICHAEL AGRESTA

How the Western Was Lost—and Why It Matters

The Western, once one of Hollywood's favorite and most reliable film genres, is in trouble. With such highly promoted box-office disappointments as *The Lone Ranger* (2013) and *Cowboys & Aliens* (2011), among others, the Western just isn't what it was. In this analysis of both the genre and the particular example of *The Lone Ranger*, Michael Agresta sets out to determine what happened. The trouble, primarily, is history, because while the Western is all about history, that history, in Agresta's words, has become "embarrassing to us." The conquest of the West was a messy, and racist, process, so toxic a subject that any film that takes it on has to use extraordinary measures (as, for example, transporting it to another planet, like *Avatar*'s Pandora) to save it. Hi-ho, Silver, away! A freelance writer on popular culture and the arts, Michael Agresta has written for such publications as *Slate*, the *Wall Street Journal*, and the *Atlantic*, where this selection originally appeared.

The Lone Ranger's failure at the box office earlier this month not only dealt a blow to mega-budget Hollywood blockbusters, Johnny Depp's career, and Disney. The Jerry Bruckheimer–Gore Verbinski flop — which cost a reported $250 million to make and brought in just $50 million opening on a holiday weekend — also may mark a decisive chapter in the sad story of how the Western was lost.

Since the dawn of film, the Western has been one of the great, durable movie genres, but its audience seems to be finally drying up. *The Lone Ranger* is the third Western to flop in four summers, and the most expensive, capping a trend set by *Cowboys & Aliens* and *Jonah Hex*. (Remember them? Exactly.) Western fans are getting older and whiter with respect to the overall population, and as any Republican political consultant will tell you, that doesn't bode well for the future. Other, newer genres like superhero movies and fighting-robot flicks have cowboy movies outgunned with younger generations and international audiences.

Now the genre finds itself in the ironic position of needing a hero to save it, and quick. If *The Lone Ranger* goes down in history as the last of the big-budget oaters, it'll be a sad milestone for moviemaking — and for America. For a century plus, we have relied on Westerns to teach us our history and reflect our current politics and our place in the world. We can ill afford to lose that mirror now, especially just because we don't like what we see staring back at us.

Westerns provide many timeless pleasures — tough guy heroes, action set pieces on horseback, adventures in magnificent landscapes, good triumphing over evil. It's all there already in arguably the first narrative film ever made, *The Great Train Robbery.*

But to discuss Westerns as if they just boiled down to heroic stories of 5 saving the homestead from savages, tracking the bad guy through the wilderness, or finding the treasure in the mountains would be to miss the real meaning of the genre. Westerns have earned their place at the heart of the national culture and American iconography abroad because they've provided a reliable vehicle for filmmakers to explore thorny issues of American history and character. In the enduring examples of the genre, the real threat to the homestead, we learn, is an economic system that is being rigged for the wealthy, or the search for the bad guy becomes a search for meaning in a culture of violent retribution, or the treasure of the Sierra Madre is a diabolical mirage of the American dream.

Through the past century of Western movies, we can trace America's self-image as it evolved from a rough-and-tumble but morally confident outsider in world affairs to an all-powerful sheriff with a guilty conscience. After World War I and leading into World War II, Hollywood specialized in tales of heroes taking the good fight to savage enemies and saving defenseless settlements in the process. In the Great Depression especially, as capitalism and American exceptionalism came under question, the cowboy hero was often mistaken for a criminal and forced to prove his own worthiness — which he inevitably did. Over the '50s, '60s, and '70s however, as America enforced its dominion over half the planet with a long series of coups, assassinations, and increasingly dubious wars, the figure of the cowboy grew darker and more complicated. If you love Westerns, most of your favorites are probably from this era — *Shane, The Searchers, Butch Cassidy and the Sundance Kid, McCabe & Mrs. Miller*, the spaghetti westerns, etc. By the height of the Vietnam protest era, cowboys were antiheroes as often as they were heroes.

The dawn of the 1980s brought the inauguration of Ronald Reagan and the box-office debacle of the artsy, overblown *Heaven's Gate*. There's a sense of disappointment to the decade that followed, as if the era of revisionist Westerns had failed and a less nuanced patriotism would have to carry the day. Few memorable Westerns were made in the '80s, and Reagan himself proudly associated himself with an old-fashioned, pre-Vietnam cowboy image. But victory in the Cold War coincided with a revival of the genre, including the revisionist strain, exemplified in Clint Eastwood's career-topping *Unforgiven*. A new, gentler star emerged in Kevin Costner, who scored a postcolonial megahit with *Dances with Wolves*. Later, in the 2000s, George W. Bush reclaimed the image of the cowboy for a foreign policy far less successful than Reagan's, and the genre retreated to the art house again.

Under the presidency of Barack Obama, there has been a short-lived Western revival that would seem to match America's tentative new moral authority. If the genre in this era can be said to have a unifying aim, it's to divest itself and its audiences of a strictly white, male, heterosexual perspective on history, and by extension on present day conflicts. *Cowboys & Aliens* is a cynical attempt at a post-racial Western — just take the Indians out of the equation so we can be good guys again! — but with more sincerity. *True Grit, Django Unchained*, and now *The Lone Ranger* have all put non-male, non-white perspectives front and center. (Two other notable movies from the past 15 years, the wonderful *Brokeback Mountain* and the awful *Wild Wild West*, also fit this model.) It's worth pointing out, however, that all of these examples (except *Brokeback Mountain*) were directed by white men, and *The Lone Ranger* has Tonto played by an actor with only the slightest claim to American Indian ancestry.

Although end-of-year prestige movies like *True Grit* and *Django Unchained* have broken through to achieve critical acclaim, Oscars, and substantial return on investment, the Obama era has not been kind to newfangled Westerns that aimed for large audiences. Exacerbating the problem is the rejection of cowboy movies by international audiences, particularly the Chinese. So even as filmmakers have become more interested in incorporating a diversity of viewpoints, they have hit against what appears a global demographic ceiling. It's another reason why *The Lone Ranger* will probably be the last attempt to build a true summer tent-pole in the genre.

Armie Hammer and Johnny Depp in *The Lone Ranger* (2013).

Nobody likes a weak ending, and this is especially true for cowboy movies. A   10
sad outcome we can accept, even the death of a genre, but at least let our hero
meet his challenge, fulfill his destiny, stand his (or her) ground. Watching *The
Lone Ranger* slink off into the sunset, it's hard to feel any sense of resolution
for the Western.

It's always difficult to diagnose the reason for a movie's success or failure. Did the audience dislike what *The Lone Ranger* tried to do, or the fact
that it executed its aims poorly? Since it bombed definitively on opening
weekend (long before China got a look at it, too) it seems safest to base
conclusions in part on the movie's advertising and the media storylines surrounding its release.

Three contributing factors stand out. First, there was some coverage
of an outcry about racism in Depp's portrayal of Tonto, which conceivably
made audiences less comfortable laughing along with the pidgin English.
Second, advertising leaned heavily on the association with the *Pirates of the
Caribbean* franchise, touting the movie as a family-friendly adventure yarn,
but word quickly spread that *The Lone Ranger* was not safe for kids. Finally,
the 149-minute runtime can't have helped.

The irony is that the very factors that helped make *The Lone Ranger*
a bomb also helped make it much more interesting than typical summer
fare. (Mild spoilers follow.) The runtime ballooned because the filmmakers
wouldn't dispense with a time-consuming framing story that shows Depp's

Tonto, in old-man makeup and a historically inappropriate headdress, wilting away inside a Museum of Natural History–style display called "The Noble Savage in His Native Habitat." The scenes deemed unsafe for children included two graphic depictions of American Indian genocide. The character of Tonto came to the filmmakers with heavy racist baggage, and, rather than tossing him out altogether, they took on the challenge of trying to carry that baggage while walking the tightrope of commenting on a stereotype through the performance of that same stereotype.

This is not to say that any of these bold moves are executed adeptly. The framing story never goes anywhere; the Indian genocide scenes are distastefully incidental to the plot, especially one scene of mass slaughter that provides the heroes cover to get out of a pickle; Depp's winking performance is still fundamentally problematic, as if he or any other white actor had done a modern Mr. Bojangles, blackface and all, and tried to get actual laughs out of it.

Still, in simple terms, *The Lone Ranger* went there. And there. And over 15
there. *The Lone Ranger* did not fail for being timid. In this cautious, sequel-dominated era of summer movies, that's a recommendation in itself. Even if they weren't particularly clever about it, Verbinski and his collaborators deserve credit for engaging critically with the history involved, both the 19th-century Indian massacres and the legacy of racism from the early 20th-century source material.

This is also a tribute to the genre. The ground rules of the Western more or less forced Verbinski and company into that treacherous territory. They could make, say, a movie about Caribbean pirates without addressing the slave trade, even though such pirates often held slaves as cargo. That's fine, because pirate movies are about gold, not slaves. Everyone knows that. Westerns, on the contrary, are traditionally about cowboys and Indians, or at least homesteaders and land and railroad barons, the kinds of men who built the cities we live in today.

It's the task of Westerns to address that history, even as decade by decade that history becomes more and more embarrassing to us. In theory, it's a beautiful thing, though in practice it means cowboy movies are easy to bungle, because by now they all take place on contested ground. Every Western must find its own way to reconcile itself to the founding contradictions of America. A certain kind of escapism becomes impossible.

Unless, of course, we stop making and watching Westerns. The genres that currently rule the box office do other things well — sci-fi movies can address the ecological crisis and challenges of new technology, for instance, and superhero movies can provide never-ending glosses on the core myth of American exceptionalism — but none are particularly engaged with history, especially pre–World War II. And none can boast the richness of symbolic language developed by Westerns over the course of a century at the heart of film culture.

It would be a terrible thing to give up on that language, especially now, in the wake of *The Lone Ranger*'s failure. Isn't there anyone, perhaps a female or non-white director, capable of making a great mass-audience Western for the Obama era? Or, if it's too late for that, then for whatever era comes next? If neither, here's hoping that filmmakers will keep trying at the art-house level and on cable television.

The other great theme of the Western, after that of the conquering of native   20 peoples and the establishment of civilization in the desert, is that of loss and of nostalgia for a certain way of life — the early freedoms of the West, the idea of riding across an unfenced landscape, the infinite possibilities of the frontier. That "West," of course, is already gone, fallen, conquered. It has been for decades, even though holding onto some sense of it seems crucial to our identity as Americans. Movie Westerns have been tracking that loss for a century.

Now, as *The Lone Ranger* leaves theaters this month, that sense of loss begins to expand to cowboy movies themselves. The train is leaving the station, and the thing we rely on to help make sense of ourselves in the world is tied to the tracks. Is there a hero on the horizon?

READING THE TEXT

1. Why does Agresta say that the Western has been "a reliable vehicle for film-makers to explore thorny issues of American history and character" (para. 5)?

2. In your own words, trace the history of the American Western, as Agresta describes it.

3. What does the term "American exceptionalism" (para. 18) mean?

4. In what ways have modern Westerns changed the motifs and patterns of classic Westerns?

5. According to Agresta, why was 2013's *The Lone Ranger* a box-office failure?

READING THE SIGNS

1. Watch *The Lone Ranger*, and write an essay in which you take on Agresta's contention that "the very factors that helped make *The Lone Ranger* a bomb also helped make it much more interesting than typical summer fare" (para. 13).

2. **CONNECTING TEXTS**   Watch one of the films that Agresta mentions, such as *Django Unchained* (2012) or *Brokeback Mountain* (2005), and write a semiotic analysis of the film's depiction of race relations. To develop your ideas, read Michael Omi's "In Living Color: Race and American Culture" (p. 462).

3. Write a semiotic analysis of a recent Western, such as *Hell or High Water* (2016), *The Magnificent Seven* (2016), or *The Dark Tower* (2017). In what ways does it resemble a conventional Western? How does it differ? Alternatively, write an essay that asks the same questions of the TV show *The Walking Dead*.

4. **CONNECTING TEXTS**   Both Agresta and Christine Folch ("Why the West Loves Sci-Fi and Fantasy: A Cultural Explanation," p. 311) offer cultural explanations for what Americans find most compelling in films. Write an essay in which you synthesize their views, developing your own cultural explanations as well.

DAVID DENBY

High-School Confidential: Notes on Teen Movies

Face it: High school for most of us is one extended nightmare, a long-playing drama starring cheerleaders and football players who sneer at the mere mortals who must endure their haughty reign. So it's little wonder that, as David Denby argues in this *New Yorker* essay from 1999, teen movies so often feature loathsome cheerleaders and football stars who, one way or another, get theirs in this ever-popular movie genre. Indeed, Denby asks, "Who can doubt where Hollywood's twitchy, nearsighted writers and directors ranked — or feared they ranked — on the high-school totem pole?" Nerds at the bottom, where else, like the millions of suffering kids who flock to their films. Denby is a staff writer and film critic for the *New Yorker*.

The most hated young woman in America is a blonde — well, sometimes a redhead or a brunette, but usually a blonde. She has big hair flipped into a swirl of gold at one side of her face or arrayed in a sultry mane, like the magnificent pile of a forties movie star. She's tall and slender, with a waist as supple as a willow, but she's dressed in awful, spangled taste: her outfits could have been put together by warring catalogues. And she has a mouth on her, a low, slatternly tongue that devastates other kids with such insults as "You're vapor, you're Spam!" and "Do I look like Mother Teresa? If I did, I probably wouldn't mind talking to the geek squad." She has two or three friends exactly like her, and together they dominate their realm — the American high school as it appears in recent teen movies. They are like wicked princesses, who enjoy the misery of their subjects. Her coronation, of course, is the senior prom, when she expects to be voted "most popular" by her class. But, though she may be popular, she is certainly not liked, so her power is something of a mystery. She is beautiful and rich, yet in the end she is preëminent because. . . she is preëminent, a position she works to maintain with Joan Crawford–like tenacity. Everyone is afraid of her; that's why she's popular.

She has a male counterpart. He's usually a football player, muscular but dumb, with a face like a beer mug and only two ways of speaking — in a conspiratorial whisper, to a friend; or in a drill sergeant's sudden bellow. If her weapon is the snub, his is the lame but infuriating prank — the can of Sprite emptied into a knapsack, or something sticky, creamy, or adhesive deposited in a locker. Sprawling and dull in class, he comes alive in the halls and in the cafeteria. He hurls people against lockers; he spits, pours, and sprays; he has a projectile relationship with food. As the crown prince, he claims the best-looking girl for himself, though in a perverse display of power he may invite an outsider or an awkward girl — a "dog" — to the prom, setting her up for some special humiliation. When we first see him, he is riding high, and virtually the entire school colludes in his tyranny. No authority figure — no teacher or administrator — dares correct him.

Thus the villains of the recent high-school movies. Not every American teen movie has these two characters, and not every social queen or jock shares all the attributes I've mentioned. (Occasionally, a handsome, dark-haired athlete can be converted to sweetness and light.) But as genre figures these two types are hugely familiar; that is, they are a common memory, a collective trauma, or at least a social and erotic fantasy. Such movies of the past year [1999] as *Disturbing Behavior*, *She's All That*, *Ten Things I Hate about You*, and *Never Been Kissed* depend on them as stock figures. And they may have been figures in the minds of the Littleton shooters, Eric Harris and Dylan Klebold, who imagined they were living in a school like the one in so many of these movies — a poisonous system of status, snobbery, and exclusion.

Do genre films reflect reality? Or are they merely a set of conventions that refer to other films? Obviously, they wouldn't survive if they didn't provide emotional satisfaction to the people who make them and to the audiences who watch them. A half century ago, we didn't need to see ten Westerns a year in order to learn that the West got settled. We needed to see it settled ten times a year in order to provide ourselves with the emotional gratifications of righteous violence. By drawing his gun only when he was provoked, and in the service of the good, the classic Western hero transformed the gross tangibles of the expansionist drive (land, cattle, gold) into a principle of moral order. The gangster, by contrast, is a figure of chaos, a modern, urban person, and in the critic Robert Warshow's formulation he functions as a discordant element in an American society devoted to a compulsively "positive" outlook. When the gangster dies, he cleanses viewers of their own negative feelings.

High-school movies are also full of unease and odd, mixed-up emotions. 5 They may be flimsy in conception; they may be shot in lollipop colors, garlanded with mediocre pop scores, and cast with goofy young actors trying to make an impression. Yet this most commercial and frivolous of genres harbors a grievance against the world. It's a very specific grievance, quite different from the restless anger of such fifties adolescent-rebellion movies as *The Wild One*, in which someone asks Marlon Brando's biker "What are you rebelling against?" and the biker replies "What have you got?" The fifties teen outlaw was against anything that adults considered sacred. But no movie teenager now revolts against adult authority, for the simple reason that adults have no authority. Teachers are rarely more than a minimal, exasperated presence, administrators get turned into a joke, and parents are either absent or distantly benevolent. It's a teen world, bounded by school, mall, and car, with occasional moments set in the fast-food outlets where the kids work, or in the kids' upstairs bedrooms, with their pinups and rack stereo systems. The enemy is not authority; the enemy is other teens and the social system that they impose on one another.

The bad feeling in these movies may strike grownups as peculiar. After all, from a distance American kids appear to be having it easy these days. The teen audience is facing a healthy job market; at home, their parents are stuffing the den with computers and the garage with a bulky SUV. But most teens aren't thinking about the future job market. Lost in the eternal swoon of late adolescence, they're thinking about their identity, their friends, and their clothes. Adolescence is the present-tense moment in American life. Identity and status are fluid: abrupt, devastating reversals are always possible. (In a teen movie, a guy who swallows a bucket of cafeteria coleslaw can make himself a hero in an instant.) In these movies, accordingly, the senior prom is the equivalent of the shoot-out at the O.K. Corral; it's the moment when one's worth as a human being is settled at last. In the rather pedestrian new comedy *Never Been Kissed*, Drew Barrymore, as a twenty-five-year-old newspaper reporter, goes back to high school pretending to be a student, and immediately falls into her old, humiliating pattern of trying to impress the good-looking rich kids. Helplessly, she pushes for approval, and even gets herself chosen prom queen before finally coming to her senses. She finds it nearly impossible to let go.

Genre films dramatize not what happens but how things feel — the emotional coloring of memory. They fix subjectivity into fable. At actual schools, there is no unitary system of status; there are many groups to be a part of, many places to excel (or fail to excel), many avenues of escape and self-definition. And often the movies, too, revel in the arcana of high-school cliques. In last summer's *Disturbing Behavior*, a veteran student lays out the cafeteria ethnography for a newcomer: Motorheads, Blue Ribbons, Skaters, Micro-geeks ("drug of choice: Stephen Hawking's *A Brief History of Time* and a cup of jasmine tea on Saturday night"). Subjectively, though, the social system in *Disturbing Behavior* (a high-school version of *The Stepford Wives*) and in the other movies still feels coercive and claustrophobic: humiliation is the most vivid emotion of youth, so in memory it becomes the norm.

The movies try to turn the tables. The kids who cannot be the beautiful ones, or make out with them, or avoid being insulted by them — these are the heroes of the teen movies, the third in the trio of character types. The female outsider is usually an intellectual or an artist. (She scribbles in a diary, she draws or paints.) Physically awkward, she walks like a seal crossing a beach, and is prone to drop her books and dither in terror when she stands before a handsome boy. Her clothes, which ignore mall fashion, scandalize the social queens. Like them, she has a tongue, but she's tart and grammatical, tending toward feminist pungency and precise diction. She may mask her sense of vulnerability with sarcasm or with Plathian rue (she's stuck in the bell jar), but even when she lashes out she can't hide her craving for acceptance.

The male outsider, her friend, is usually a mass of stuttering or giggling sexual gloom: he wears shapeless clothes; he has an undeveloped body, either stringy or shrimpy; he's sometimes a Jew (in these movies, still the generic outsider). He's also brilliant, but in a morose, preoccupied way that suggests masturbatory absorption in some arcane system of knowledge. In a few special cases, the outsider is not a loser but a disengaged hipster, either saintly or satanic. (Christian Slater has played this role a couple of times.) This outsider wears black and keeps his hair long, and he knows how to please women. He sees through everything, so he's ironic by temperament and genuinely indifferent to the opinion of others — a natural aristocrat, who transcends the school's contemptible status system. There are whimsical variations on the outsider figure, too. In the recent *Rushmore*, an obnoxious teen hero, Max Fischer (Jason Schwartzman), runs the entire school: he can't pass his courses but he's a dynamo at extracurricular activities, with a knack for staging extraordinary events. He's a con man, a fund-raiser, an entrepreneur — in other words, a contemporary artist.

In fact, the entire genre, which combines self-pity and ultimate vindica-   10
tion, might be called "Portrait of the Filmmaker as a Young Nerd." Who can doubt where Hollywood's twitchy, nearsighted writers and directors ranked — or feared they ranked — on the high-school totem pole? They are still angry, though occasionally the target of their resentment goes beyond the jocks and cheerleaders of their youth. Consider this anomaly: the young actors and models on the covers of half the magazines published in this country, the shirtless men with chests like burnished shields, the girls smiling, glowing, tweezed, full-lipped, full-breasted (but not too full), and with skin so honeyed that it seems lacquered — these are the physical ideals embodied by the villains of the teen movies. The social queens and jocks, using their looks to dominate others, represent an American barbarism of beauty. Isn't it possible that the detestation of them in teen movies is a veiled strike at the entire abs-hair advertising culture, with its unobtainable glories of perfection? A critic of consumerism might even see a spark of revolt in these movies. But only a spark.

My guess is that these films arise from remembered hurts which then get recast in symbolic form. For instance, a surprising number of the outsider heroes have no mother. Mom has died or run off with another man; her child, only half loved, is ill equipped for the emotional pressures of school. The motherless child, of course, is a shrewd commercial ploy that makes a direct appeal to the members of the audience, many of whom may feel like outsiders, too, and unloved, or not loved enough, or victims of some prejudice or exclusion. But the motherless child also has powers, and will someday be a success, an artist, a screenwriter. It's the wound and the bow all over again, in cargo pants.

As the female nerd attracts the attention of the handsomest boy in the senior class, the teen movie turns into a myth of social reversal — a Cinderella fantasy. Initially, his interest in her may be part of a stunt or a trick: he is leading her on, perhaps at the urging of his queenly girlfriend. But his gaze lights her up, and we see how attractive she really is. Will she fulfill the eternal American fantasy that you can vault up the class system by removing your specs? She wants her prince, and by degrees she wins him over, not just with her looks but with her superior nature, her essential goodness. In the male version of the Cinderella trip, a few years go by, and a pale little nerd (we see him at a reunion) has become rich. All that poking around with chemicals paid off. Max Fischer, of *Rushmore*, can't miss being richer than Warhol.

So the teen movie is wildly ambivalent. It may attack the consumerist ethos that produces winners and losers, but in the end it confirms what it is attacking. The girls need the seal of approval conferred by the converted jocks; the nerds need money and a girl. Perhaps it's no surprise that the outsiders can be validated only by the people who ostracized them. But let's not be too schematic: the outsider who joins the system also modifies it, opens it up to the creative power of social mobility, makes it bend and laugh, and perhaps this turn of events is not so different from the way things work in the real world, where merit and achievement stand a good chance of trumping appearance. The irony of the Littleton shootings is that Klebold and Harris, who were both proficient computer heads, seemed to have forgotten how the plot turns out. If they had held on for a few years they might have been working at a hip software company, or have started their own business, while the jocks who oppressed them would probably have wound up selling insurance or used cars. That's the one unquestionable social truth the teen movies reflect: geeks rule.

There is, of course, a menacing subgenre, in which the desire for revenge turns bloody. Thirty-one years ago, Lindsay Anderson's semi-surrealistic *If . . .* was set in an oppressive, class-ridden English boarding school, where a group of rebellious students drive the school population out into a courtyard and open fire on them with machine guns. In Brian De Palma's 1976 masterpiece *Carrie*, the pale, repressed heroine, played by Sissy Spacek, is courted at last by a handsome boy but gets violated — doused with pig's blood — just as she is named prom queen. Stunned but far from powerless, Carrie uses her telekinetic powers to set the room afire and burn down the school. *Carrie* is the primal school movie, so wildly lurid and funny that it exploded the clichés of the genre before the genre was quite set: The heroine may be a wrathful avenger, but the movie, based on a Stephen King book, was clearly a grinning-gargoyle fantasy. So, at first, was *Heathers*, in which Christian Slater's satanic outsider turns out to be a true devil. He and his girlfriend (played by a very young Winona Ryder) begin gleefully knocking off the rich, nasty girls and the jocks, in ways so patently absurd that their revenge seems a mere wicked dream. I think it's unlikely that these movies had a direct effect on the actions of the Littleton shooters, but the two boys would surely have recognized the emotional world of *Heathers* and *Disturbing Behavior* as their own. It's a place where feelings of victimization join fantasy, and you experience the social élites as so powerful that you must either become them or kill them.

But enough. It's possible to make teen movies that go beyond these fixed 15 polarities — insider and outsider, blond-bitch queen and hunch-shouldered nerd. In Amy Heckerling's 1995 comedy *Clueless*, the big blonde played by Alicia Silverstone is a Rodeo Drive clotheshorse who is nonetheless possessed of extraordinary virtue. Freely dispensing advice and help, she's almost ironically good — a designing goddess with a cell phone. The movie offers a sunshiny satire of Beverly Hills affluence, which it sees as both absurdly swollen and generous in spirit. The most original of the teen comedies, *Clueless* casts away self-pity. So does *Romy and Michele's High School Reunion* (1997), in which two gabby, lovable friends, played by Mira Sorvino and Lisa Kudrow, review the banalities of their high-school experience so knowingly that they might be criticizing the teen-movie genre itself. And easily the best American film of the year so far is Alexander Payne's *Election*, a high-school movie that inhabits a different aesthetic and moral world altogether from the rest of these pictures. *Election* shreds everyone's fantasies and illusions in a vision of high school that is bleak but supremely just. The movie's villain, an overachieving girl (Reese Witherspoon) who runs for class president, turns out to be its covert heroine, or, at least, its most poignant character. A cross between Pat and Dick Nixon, she's a lower-middle-class striver who works like crazy and never wins anyone's love. Even when she's on top, she feels excluded. Her loneliness is produced not by malicious cliques but by her own implacable will, a condition of the spirit that may be as comical and tragic as it is mysterious. *Election* escapes all the clichés; it graduates into art.

READING THE TEXT

1. Describe in your own words the stereotypical male and female villains common in teen movies.
2. What does Denby mean by the comment, "Adolescence is the present-tense moment in American life" (para. 6)?
3. What sort of characters are typically the heroes in teen films, in Denby's view?
4. In what ways does a Cinderella fantasy influence teen films?
5. What is the "menacing subgenre" (para. 14) of teen movies?

READING THE SIGNS

1. Using Denby's description of stock character types in teen movies as your critical framework, analyze the characters in a teen TV program, such as *The Carrie Diaries*, *Awkward*, or *90210*. Do you see the same conventions at work? How do you account for any differences you might see?
2. In class, brainstorm a list of current teen films. Then, using the list as evidence, write an essay in which you assess the validity of Denby's claim: "The enemy [in teen films] is not authority; the enemy is other teens and the social system that they impose on one another" (para. 5).
3. Watch *The Perks of Being a Wallflower* (2012), and write an essay in which you argue whether it can be categorized as a teen film, at least as Denby defines the genre.
4. Denby asks, "Do genre films reflect reality? Or are they merely a set of conventions that refer to other films?" (para. 4). Write an essay in which you propose your own response to these questions, using as evidence your high school experience and specific teen films. In addition, you can consider as evidence teen-based TV programs such as *Glee* or a film such as *The Edge of Seventeen* (2016).

PAY ATTENTION WHILE WALKING

YOUR FACEBOOK STATUS UPDATE CAN WAIT.

  Metropolitan Etiquette Authority

5

THE CLOUD
Semiotics and the New Media

The New Panopticon

In the summer of 2016, someone hacked into the e-mail server of the Democratic National Committee, scoring another coup for WikiLeaks and igniting fireworks at the Democrats' presidential nominating convention. In the same season, a live-streamed video appeared on Facebook, broadcasting the death of Philando Castile, a black resident of St. Paul, Minnesota who had been pulled over by the police for a minor traffic violation, and was then shot and killed while his fiance narrated what happened. Meanwhile, Edward Snowden, the former National Security Agency (NSA) subcontractor who revealed in 2013 that the NSA had been collecting and storing data related to just about every phone call and Internet transaction made in America for years, remained on the lam.

In other words, it was business as usual in the strange new world of digital technology, an era when such corporate titans as Google, Facebook, and Apple are mining user data and selling that information to anyone willing to pay for it, and ordinary citizens post to Twitter, YouTube, Snapchat, and innumerable other social media sites both the trivial and monumental events of their daily experiences. For good or ill, such a constant state of surveillance indicates that there's a price to pay for all the pleasures and conveniences of the digital age. That price is our privacy, whether it's seized by the government on behalf of national security, personally broadcast to reveal social injustices, or sold for the benefit of businesses that want to know what we're doing so they can more efficiently market goods and services to us. In one way or another, the new media are transforming America into what the late Michel Foucault called a "Panopticon": a society in which everything we do is being monitored, as in a prison.

And yet, that isn't the way that many, if not most, people see it. Rather — especially for those who have spent their lives within the digital era — their smartphones, tablets, e-readers, laptops, and even desktops are not merely sources of pleasure or convenience. They are necessities, required not only for work, school, and play, but for existence itself. Who cares if someone's watching as long as the connection is still up, and you can remain enveloped in the vast, round-the-clock social network in which no one ever has to be alone? It isn't a Panopticon; it's a global village that's revolutionizing human life all over the world.

So which is it: prison or village? An abuse of power or a triumph of social evolution? Like all technological interventions — such as the automobile or television — that have made an indelible impact on society, digital technology is not easy to assess, but there may be no subject as important to think about semiotically in an era when the new media are expanding into every corner of our lives with a velocity that some think will soon become infinite. Indeed, your analyses of the new media could well begin with questions just like these.

The Global Hive

Grasping the impact of the new media isn't made any easier by the conflicting signals that have been sent by media history itself. In 1962, when Marshall McLuhan launched the modern era of media studies with his groundbreaking book *The Gutenberg Galaxy*, the situation looked pretty straightforward. At the time, television, cinema, radio, and stereos were the dominant electronic media, so it was only natural that McLuhan would focus on the shift he saw taking place from a **text**, or print-based, **culture** to an aural and **image**-based culture. Such a culture would mark a radical change in consciousness, he predicted, a departure from the logical form of thinking fostered by the linear structure of alphabetic writing and a return, of sorts, to a more ancient oral/visual consciousness in what he was the first to call the "global village."

With the rise of the Internet and related digital technologies, however, McLuhan's predictions have become considerably complicated. While digital technology, too, is an electronic medium saturated with visual images and aural content, it has also brought the (digitally) printed word back into **popular culture** and consciousness. Indeed, before the full blossoming of the Internet as we know it today, word processing and, subsequently, print-based e-mail constituted the leading edge of the digital revolution. And with the rise of the blogosphere in the 1990s, not to mention the online posting of such traditional print media as newspapers, magazines (does anyone remember "zines"?), and fiction (does anyone remember "hypertexts"?) and the rise of texting (often at the expense of telephonic talking), the digital proliferation of print appeared to refute one of McLuhan's most fundamental observations about media history. Indeed, things seemed to be going *back* to Gutenberg.

With the decline of MySpace — which in its heyday tended to be plastered with visual imagery and aural content — at the hands of Facebook, which made printed text the dominant feature on the screen "page," this return of the font appeared to be closer to accomplishment. Sure, there was still YouTube, but Facebook was really getting much of the attention.

But while it's far too early to predict the eventual demise of Facebook, a new trend is appearing, a differential shift in the high-speed history of digital culture. This **difference** involves the emergence of such sites as Twitter (still print based but reduced to a kind of digital shorthand) and Tumblr, which, in its presentation of "microblogs," is heavy on uploaded images and light on printed text. Facebook, for its part, has largely supplanted the much more text-based world of the original blogging site, and individual Facebook pages can be filled with photos and videos in a kind of semi-return to the MySpace era. Add the continued popularity of YouTube and newer, but firmly established sites, like Instagram, Snapchat, Pinterest, and Flickr, devoted to the uploading of an endless image stream contributed by a ubiquitous arsenal of iPhones, Droids, Galaxys, and other devices, and you have a veritable tsunami of pixels, not fonts.

The ability to upload your own images instantly with the same device that took the pictures has further enhanced the "village-like" nature of the cloud in a socially profound manner as well. We call it "sharing," but it's more than that, because the tendency to post images of your personal experiences even as you experience them is an expression and intensification of what sociologists call the "heterodirectedness" of our culture. A heterodirected society is one in which members live their lives predominantly in relation to others, constantly seeking their approval and recognition. In contrast with the autonomous individualist, who isn't concerned with what others think, the heterodirected person lives within a social web where everyone is in contact with everyone else, not only sharing with others but ultimately judging them. It is not unlike the premodern experience of small-town or village life, where everyone knew everyone else, but now, thanks to new technologies, the scale is global, with people all over the world living their lives in relation to the often-anonymous others who share their experiences via those tiny digital boxes that they can never seem to put down.

So maybe it's premature to rule McLuhan out entirely. Perhaps the global village has arrived in the form of a global hive, a buzzing crowd of digitally connected Netizens who appear to be unable to let go for a few minutes to concentrate on an actual here-and-now as they hook up with a virtual elsewhere.

Of course, you hardly need to be told about how digital technology has revolutionized the ways in which people communicate with each other and consume entertainment. You don't need to be told about the latest social networking sites. Indeed, even if we try to identify what those sites are, by the time this book is published that information would be dated, as we discovered when composing the Introduction to our initial chapter on digital technology for the sixth edition of *Signs of Life in the U.S.A.* At that time, MySpace was the 800-pound gorilla of social networking, with hundreds of millions of mostly youthful members. Facebook was an outlier, something for some college students in the Northeast and a few adults. But by the time the sixth edition appeared, Facebook had become a worldwide behemoth, and MySpace was on the way out.

So, when considering the semiotics of digital technology and social media, the point is not to identify what's hot and what's not; instead, you should explore the cultural significance of "digitality." Consider for a moment the basic setup, the experiential situation of online communication through social media sites. They weren't always called "social media," by the way. In the early days of the Internet, they were called "chat rooms."

Whose Space?

The first chat rooms were rather primitive places. Austere, you might say, with no images, music, or decoration of any kind, just plain text boxes where words materialized as if from out of nowhere. Visiting such places was a bit of an adventure, a pioneering voyage into cyberspace and the uncharted expanses of the electronic frontier.

Until the advent of the now-ubiquitous smartphone and tablet, these excursions were carried out indoors, in homes and offices via stationary desktop computers. Today, of course, thanks to mobile devices, the journey can be taken anywhere — into the street, the classroom, a club, a park, a restaurant, an airport — literally everywhere. Yet, either way, via desktop or smartphone, navigating the cloud through an ever-expanding number of social networking sites disrupts some very ancient codes governing the use of social space, deconstructing not only the old demarcations between public and private space but the meaning of social experience itself.

Consider for a moment an ordinary public road: It isn't just a ribbon of asphalt; it's a complex structure of codes for pedestrians. These codes tell you that you may walk down the street, but must stick to the side (or sidewalk if there is one), and that it's best to stay to the right to avoid oncoming foot traffic. If there are private houses on the street, you may approach the front door, but you're not supposed to cut through the yard, and you're certainly not allowed to enter without permission. You may enter the public space of a store, shopping center, or post office, but you probably need to pay to enter a museum, and you must pass through a security checkpoint if you are entering a courthouse or an airline terminal.

Now consider your own physical personal space: There, you set the rules. You determine who enters it and what can be done there. You might actually write out the rules that govern your space (as in posting a NO SMOKING sign), but those rules are more likely to be obeyed if you are personally present. Indeed, the most basic personal space rule is that no unauthorized person should be in it when you are absent.

The spaces of everyday life, both public and private, are, in short, packed with codes that we violate or ignore at our peril. These codes all originate in the way that people define their territories. A *territory* is a space that has been given meaning through having been claimed by an individual or group of individuals. Unclaimed, unmarked space is socially meaningless, but put up a building or a fence and the uncircumscribed landscape becomes a bounded territory, a human habitat with its own rules for permitted and unpermitted behavior. Anyone unaware of those rules can't survive for long in human society.

But what sort of territory is a social media site, and what rules govern it? In a sense, it's a place where its users are all hosts and guests simultaneously, with the rules accordingly being quite confusing. A host is hospitable; a guest is polite and follows the host's guidance. But with no one in the cloud being entirely host or entirely guest, things can easily go wrong. You don't insult people in their own homes, but online flaming occurs all too often. Indeed, many sites and forums where people socialize and communicate are described as being like the Wild West — a wide-open space known for its lack of clear rules of conduct and the way in which it challenged traditional conceptions of social space. The result has been a blurring of the traditional lines between the uses of public and private space and, with that, much confusion about how to behave in the essentially public arena of digital communication. Just read responses people make in the feedback or comments sections of popular Web sites like YouTube. Certainly, the old rules about public courtesy no longer apply.

This is one reason so many people flocked to Facebook. Since everyone is the administrator of his or her Facebook page, it feels like you are in control there, that your Facebook page is like your own home: a private space whose rules you control. But it really isn't. Not only does Facebook periodically change how its privacy protections work, but the company can, and does, overstep those protections all the time to sell your information to virtually anyone who wants it, and the company will give it to the government as well. So even though your Facebook page may feel private and controllable, it's actually quite public — as all too many Facebook users have learned to their distress.

Or consider the very common phenomenon of someone (perhaps yourself) in an ostensibly public setting — say, sitting with a group of friends — while engaging in an essentially private activity on a mobile device. Whether texting, tweeting, posting to Instagram, updating your Facebook page, or doing any one of an almost-unlimited number of online activities, you have, once again, turned a public social space into a private one, moving back and forth

---

Exploring the Signs of the Cloud

If you have a Facebook page, describe it in your journal and discuss why you designed it as you did. What signs did you choose to communicate your identity, and why? Did you deliberately avoid including some signs? If so, why? If you chose not to join Facebook or another such site, why did you make that choice?

---

between what were once separate spheres (after all, you can share what you are doing on your Galaxy, or even put it aside for a moment and talk to the people around you) as if there were no difference between them.

Thus, one way or another, the private/public divide is being undone, and the old rules governing the use of social space are becoming obsolete. This is all happening so quickly that not only is it easy to take for granted, but there hasn't been sufficient time to constitute new rules to take the place of the old ones. Given that society cannot function without such codes, this change is of profound social significance, a problem that cannot be addressed without first realizing that it exists.

Shame on You

The newest wrinkle in the ongoing digital deconstruction of the boundary between public and private can be found in the fast-growing phenomenon of public "shaming." Made especially notorious by the case of a Playboy model using her smartphone to "body shame" a naked woman in a gym shower in 2016, the habit of posting images and other information to the Internet in order to embarrass, humiliate, or harm those whose actions, or even just personal appearance, offends someone is now breaking down the barrier between the public administration of justice and private acts of vigilantism. That is, while all of us can probably identify instances of atrocious behavior that profoundly disturb us and for which we desire retribution, a society in which such desires can go unrestrained by systems of justice founded in the public sphere is ever in danger of descending into a chaos of private vengeance. This may seem paradoxical — after all, Internet shaming is a highly public act. But by taking upon themselves the privilege to determine who is "guilty" of some sort of "crime" and then to mete out "justice" to the perpetrator, shamers are rather like vigilantes: private citizens who co-opt the powers of a publicly controlled and regulated justice system.

Thus, while it can feel good to join a public shaming of someone who has done something awful, there's a larger significance that is often overlooked. Although some have compared shaming to the public pillories of the past, this is not an accurate comparison because howsoever inadequate the legal protections were for those condemned to the pillory, there was at least some legal control over the punishment. The privately constructed pillories of the modern shamer have no such limits and are expressions, instead, of mob rule.

The Medium Is the Barrier

The ease with which digital technology has been adapted to the will of the mob can be attributed, at least in part, to the profound way that life in the cloud is impairing our capacity to understand fully the feelings of other people. This empathy gap, which has been often noted by researchers, has been promoted by the way we interact not with people in the cloud but with electronic devices and their mediating software. While the invention of the telephone began to disrupt person-to-person communication in the nineteenth century, today's social media greatly magnify the possibilities of socializing in the absence of anyone being physically present. You can tweet to the whole world, but no one is necessarily listening. You can have thousands of Facebook "friends" without meeting any of them face to face. You can even "tweet with the stars," though the chances that any celebrity tweeter will know who you are, or care, are tiny. Often, then, that sense of intimacy with others in the cloud is, in reality, an illusion, especially given the way that people can stage-manage their online profile. How, in such conditions, can you know for certain whether those profiles of "friends" whom you have never met are accurate or true?

Thus, the lack of actual spatial proximity in digital communication produces what could be called a "proxemic disruption" within human history. **Proxemics**, a field loosely related to semiotics, is the study of how we communicate with others in face-to-face situations, including such means as body language, facial expression, and tone of voice. Because these social cues are absent in the cloud, social communication itself is being revolutionized in ways that are not yet entirely clear. Certainly, there has been a loss of civility due to the proxemic disruption, because the threat of direct retaliation for rude or insulting behavior that exists in face-to-face communication no longer exists, while the possibility for misunderstanding has also increased. Indeed, a phenomenon known as "Poe's Law" — which refers to the difficulty of determining whether or not someone is being ironic in the cloud — is a particularly striking example of how the lack of physical contact can lead to less, not more, effective communication, despite the apparently limitless opportunities for social interaction that the cloud provides.

What is more, much of the communication that does take place in the cloud is either a form of shorthand or simply an exchange of pictures. Then there's the fact that those whom you allow to "speak" on your Facebook page more often than not do not speak at all: They just give you a thumbs-up. And if people say anything you don't like, you can silence them. This is profoundly different from traditional communication among peers, which cannot be individually controlled and requires much more complete verbalization. In some

---

Discussing the Signs of the Cloud

Critics of online social networking sites have expressed concern that excessive online networking will diminish participants' ability to socialize normally in face-to-face environments. In class, discuss the legitimacy of this concern, drawing upon your personal experiences with social networking.

---

ways, then, communication in the cloud has become a highly segregated activity where only those who already agree with each other are allowed to "speak," and they don't have to say much because everyone already agrees.

The upshot of this new form of socializing includes not only an increasing polarization of American society into hostile camps who speak only to each other, but also a declining capacity to socialize with others in a nonvirtual setting. Studies of the phenomenon reveal increasing numbers of people who need instruction in how to go about arranging a live date with another person or who attend digital "rehab" programs to teach them how to interact with the real world.

A Bridge over Troubled Waters

On the flip side of this apparently antisocial tendency of life in the cloud are such phenomena as "crowd funding," which can bring people together to help others in trouble, and the more basic fact that life in the cloud doesn't *feel* antisocial to the innumerable people who "live" there. In fact, it feels all-inclusive, like a vast buzzing hive of closely related "friends." Clearly, part of the appeal of the new media is that they make people feel connected, with family, with friends, and with online communities that may be based on little more than shared interests — instantly postable to sites like Pinterest that encourage the passing around of information like a vast chain letter — but that can be very real communities all the same. Human beings are social animals, after all, but nothing in our genes says that those with whom we socialize have to be physically present. The addictive nature of digital technology, the way that its users suffer something like drug withdrawal when they are deprived of it, is a powerful testimony to the deep appeal of socializing in the cloud. Whether this compelling draw of digital socializing will eventually lead to a whole new definition of "society," a new way of relating to other people, is anyone's guess at this point. But there is no doubt that it has become a very effective way of making money for those who control the networks. And that leads us to our final semiotic question.

Top-Down after All?

Traditionally, the **mass media** have been structured in a top-down manner, with corporate elites providing passive **consumers** with the news, entertainments, and products that they consume, along with the advertisements that promote them. But now the top-down news has turned into a bottom-up conversation in which anyone can become a pundit, while newspapers and online news sites invite input from their readers. Broadband Internet access has turned video creativity over to the masses in such a way that you no longer have to be a famous director or producer to present your own television shows or films to a wide audience, and you don't have to be an authorized critic to respond, with YouTube, Rotten Tomatoes, and related sites offering unlimited opportunities to critique what you find there. In short, what was once a passive and vicarious media experience for consumers is now active and participatory.

Another way of putting this is that, until recently, our relationship with the mass media has been more or less a one-way street. Those with the power to control the media (TV networks, radio stations, movie studios, newspaper owners, corporate sponsors with advertising dollars to spend) have broadcast their signals to us (TV and radio programs, films, newspapers, and ads), and we have passively received them, without being able to answer back. The late semiologist and sociologist Jean Baudrillard (1929–2007) regarded this situation as one of the essential conditions of **postmodern** times and used it as a basis for his analyses of contemporary society. But today, much of the mass media now actively elicits responses from their audiences, and consumers are able to create and disseminate their own media content. Indeed, an ordinary news story can be remixed into memes that go viral and become news stories of their own, like the "Bed Intruder Song" in 2010, which turned an interview with the brother of a victim of sexual assault into an international sensation. It thus certainly appears that something post-postmodern is emerging beyond Baudrillard's perceptions.

But while the new media are definitely opening up channels for democratic communication and expression that previously did not exist, they have also created new elites whose wealth and power depend upon their ability to exploit the mass of people who use the technologies they offer. We have already referred here to the price we all have to pay for personal privacy thanks to the panoptic capabilities of digital technology, but there is also the way that technology tycoons can monopolize daily life and shut down older, predigital forms of commerce and professional activity. We're referring here to the assaults on "brick-and-mortar" retailing via online shopping sites, print journalism via online news outlets, and face-to-face education via massive open online courses (MOOCs) as just three prominent examples.

What has made the creation of the new media elites possible, in part, has been the consumer expectation (and demand) that "information should be free." While consumers do not balk at paying for the tangible commodities they purchase online, most do feel that such intangible commodities as education, music, and written texts should be accessible without cost. Already trained by commercial TV and radio to expect free content, American consumers were immediately receptive to the similar business models of the new media, taking for granted the free use of online services, not realizing that those services have a cost and that they aren't really free at all. Thus, traditional media (like newspapers) that both paid for their operational expenses and gained a profit by charging customers directly are losing their consumer base, while the new media titans that have found ways to monetize their operations without any direct out-of-pocket costs to consumers are replacing them.

At the same time, once-populist, user-generated sites have tended to become dominated by social and corporate elites very quickly. Twitter is an example. Although it's still a site where anyone can tweet (if he or she is a registered user, that is) and remains a premier source of breaking news stories from the people who experience them first, the major news corporations now present news stories in the form of tweets from their reporters in the field, while politicians (with Donald Trump being an especially successful example) employ the platform as a springboard to public office.

And so we have a paradox: Top-down has met bottom-up in a cloud that is at once democratic and hierarchical, your space and corporate space. The democratic, user-generated spaces in the cloud are simultaneously revolutionary and business as usual. Users pass around their own content (often not self-created), but they do so on sites that are owned by huge corporations that require registration so that their services can be profitable. More importantly, in the **context** of a socioeconomic system in and through which vast amounts of wealth are being shifted upward into the hands of a corporate elite, along with their highly educated upper-middle-class workforce that is increasingly centered in information technology, the indications are that the overall outcome of the digtal revolution may be an intensification of socioeconomic inquality, not a solution to it. Somehow, the future doesn't seem to be what it used to be.

In the famous 1984 Super Bowl commercial that introduced the Macintosh, Apple Computer promised that the future was going to belong to the people, not to rigid, profit-seeking corporate powers. Web 1.0 and Web 2.0 were both built, in large part, by people who believed in this vision of a sort of anticorporate utopia. But that isn't what is happening at all. The Macintosh ad, after all, featured a big screen with an image of Big Brother hectoring a room full of hypnotized viewers. Is that so very different from the constant spectacle of the CEOs of Apple, Google, Facebook, and other digital titans standing on a stage to deliver the word on their next big device or service? Or from the billions of people who compulsively stare into their digital devices, knowing that those devices are looking back at the behest of corporate elites who want to use their information to profit from and to control their behavior?

We are all living in the midst of a gigantic social experiment that presents us with paradoxes all the way down. At once democratic and a major

Reading the Cloud

YouTube allows users to create their own "television" content, or video channels, yet the site is also filled with content taken from corporate or commercial media sources, such as TV clips, concert footage, music videos, and the like. Conduct a survey of YouTube content to estimate the ratio of user-created content to postings of professional performers by corporate or commercial sources. Analyze and interpret your results semiotically. What are the implications of your findings for the bottom-up versus top-down debate over Web 2.0 "democracy"?

enabler of socioeconomic inequality, a place of intense sociability and antisocial anomie, of altruism and vigilantism, convenience and crime, the cloud is a very complicated thing indeed. Often uncritically celebrated as a status-quo-extinguishing "disruption," the brave new world of digital technology is easy to take at its own valuation, but the profound differences that it has introduced into our lives call for semiotic disruption. That is what this chapter is for.

The Readings

The International Center for Media and the Public Agenda begins this chapter with a report indicating that our penchant for digital toys may be literally addictive. A set of paired readings follows, with Ronald J. Deibert going deep inside the cloud to reveal how our every move there is accessible "to third parties beyond our control," and Joseph Turow exploring the brave new world of data mining, whereby advertisers target their ads by following you around on the Internet. Erin Lee is next with a college journalism piece on social media activism, suggesting mixed opinions on its real-world efficacy, while Brian Dunning concludes that it's all just useless "slacktivism." Brooke Gladstone's graphic essay literally illustrates the ways in which the Internet plays back to its users whatever they already believe, and it's followed by John Herrman's case study on how Facebook has effectively made itself into a gigantic echo chamber of one-sided political viewpoints. Timothy B. Lee then shows how the economics of online games such as *Pokémon Go* are crowding out local retailers and "increasingly transforming America into two parallel economies": the digital haves and the digital have-nots, while Nancy Jo Sales provides a kind of history of the selfie, connecting the Kodak Instamatics of the 1960s to the Instagram culture of the present. Next, danah boyd reveals the surprising racial coding that separates rival social networking sites Facebook and MySpace and that has led to the near demise of the latter. S. Craig Watkins concludes the chapter with an exploration of the racial evolution of #Black Twitter.

INTERNATIONAL CENTER FOR MEDIA AND THE PUBLIC AGENDA

Students Addicted to Social Media

It's official: The use of digital technology is addictive, or so concludes a 2010 study by the International Center for Media and the Public Agenda at the University of Maryland. After two hundred University of Maryland students willingly gave up their digital devices for twenty-four hours, journalism professor Susan D. Moeller found them virtually traumatized by the experience. Indeed, as one student wrote, "Texting and IM-ing my friends gives me a constant feeling of comfort. … When I did not have those two luxuries, I felt quite alone and secluded from my life. Although I go to a school with thousands of students, the fact that I was not able to communicate with anyone via technology was almost unbearable." Maybe iPhones should come with a warning from the Surgeon General?

American college students today are addicted to media, describing their feelings when they have to abstain from using media in literally the same terms associated with drug and alcohol addictions: *In withdrawal, Frantically craving, Very anxious, Extremely antsy, Miserable, Jittery, Crazy*.

A new study out today from the International Center for Media and the Public Agenda (ICMPA) at the University of Maryland concludes that most college students are not just unwilling, but functionally unable to be without their media links to the world. "I clearly am addicted and the dependency is sickening," said one student in the study. "I feel like most people these days are in a similar situation, for between having a BlackBerry, a laptop, a television, and an iPod, people have become unable to shed their media skin."

The new ICMPA study, "24 Hours: Unplugged," asked 200 students at the College Park campus to give up all media for 24 hours. After their 24 hours of abstinence, the students were then asked to blog on private class Web sites about their experiences: to report their successes and admit to any failures. The 200 students wrote more than 110,000 words: in aggregate, about the same number of words as a 400-page novel.

Without Digital Ties, Students Feel Unconnected Even to Those Who Are Close By

"We were surprised by how many students admitted that they were 'incredibly addicted' to media," noted the project director Susan D. Moeller, a journalism professor at the University of Maryland and the director of the

International Center for Media and the Public Agenda which conducted the study. "But we noticed that what they wrote at length about was how they hated losing their personal connections. Going without media meant, in their world, going without their friends and family."

"The students did complain about how boring it was to go anywhere and do anything without being plugged into music on their MP3 players," said Moeller. "And many commented that it was almost impossible to avoid the TVs on in the background at all times in their friends' rooms. But what they spoke about in the strongest terms was how their lack of access to text messaging, phone calling, instant messaging, e-mail, and Facebook, meant that they couldn't connect with friends who lived close by, much less those far away."

"Texting and IM-ing my friends gives me a constant feeling of comfort," wrote one student. "When I did not have those two luxuries, I felt quite alone and secluded from my life. Although I go to a school with thousands of students, the fact that I was not able to communicate with anyone via technology was almost unbearable."

The student responses to the assignment showed not just that 18–21-year-old college students are constantly texting and on Facebook — with calling and e-mail distant seconds as ways of staying in touch, especially with friends — but that students' lives are wired together in such ways that opting out of that communication pattern would be tantamount to renouncing a social life.

News: Accessed via Connections with Friends & Family

Very few students in the study reported that they regularly watched news on television or read a local or national newspaper (although a few said they regularly read *The Diamondback*, the University of Maryland student newspaper). They also didn't mention checking mainstream media news sites or listening to radio news while commuting in their cars. Yet student after student demonstrated knowledge of specific news stories. How did they get the information? In a disaggregated way, and not typically from the news outlet that broke or committed resources to a story. "To be entirely honest I am glad I failed the assignment," wrote one student, "because if I hadn't opened my computer when I did I would not have known about the violent earthquake in Chile from an informal blog post on Tumblr."

"Students expressed tremendous anxiety about being cut off from information," observed Ph.D. student Raymond McCaffrey, a former writer and editor at *The Washington Post*, and a current researcher on the study. "One student said he realized that he suddenly 'had less information than everyone else, whether it be news, class information, scores, or what happened on *Family Guy*.'"

"They care about what is going on among their friends and families and   10
even in the world at large," said McCaffrey. "But most of all they care about
being cut off from that instantaneous flow of information that comes from
all sides and does not seem tied to any single device or application or
news outlet."

That's the real takeaway of this study for journalists: Students showed
no significant loyalty to a news program, news personality or even news
platform. Students have only a casual relationship to the originators of
news, and in fact rarely distinguished between news and more general
information.

While many in the journalism profession are committing significant
resources to deliver content across media platforms — print, broadcast,
online, mobile — the young adults in this study appeared to be generally
oblivious to branded news and information. For most of the students reporting in the study, information of all kinds comes in an undifferentiated wave
to them via social media. If a bit of information rises to a level of interest, the student will pursue it — but often by following the story via "uncon-
ventional" outlets, such as through text messages, their e-mail accounts,
Facebook, and Twitter.

Students said that only the most specific or significant news events — for
example, a medal event at the Olympics — merited their tuning in to a
mainstream outlet. Even news events that students cared about were often
accessed via their personal interactions. To learn about the Maryland vs.
Virginia Tech basketball game, for example, one student told of "listening
to someone narrate the game from a conversation they were having on
their own phone" (although he would have preferred watching it on TV) and
another student told of calling her father to learn more about the earthquake
in Chile.

Study Background

The University of Maryland is a large state university campus, and the
class, *JOUR 175: Media Literacy*, that undertook this 24-hour media-free
assignment, is a "core course" for the entire student body — which means
it enrolls undergraduate students across majors. It is, in short, a class of
200 students, characterized by a diversity of age, race, ethnicity, religion,
and nationality. According to the assignment, students had to go media-
free for a full day (or had to try to go media-free), but they were allowed to
pick which 24 hours in a nine-day period, from February 24–March 4. By
coincidence that period saw several major news events, including the earthquake in Chile on February 27, and the close of the Vancouver Olympics on
February 28.

According to separately obtained demographic data on the student class,   15
75.6 percent of the students in JOUR 175 self-identify as Caucasian/White,
9.4 percent as Black, 6.3 percent as Asian, 1.6 percent as Latino, 3.1 percent
as Mixed Race, and 3.9 percent as Other. Students who self-reported themselves as non-American said they were from China, South Korea, Sri Lanka,
and Ethiopia. Women outnumbered men, 55.9 percent to 44.1 percent.

44.1 percent of the class reported that their parents or guardians earned
over $100,000 or more; 28.3 percent reported that their parents or guard-
ians earned between $75–$100,000; 22 percent reported coming from a
household with an income between $50–75,000; and 5.5 percent reported
that their families' income was between $25–50,000.

40.9 percent of the students who responded to the demographic survey reported that they were first-year students, 40.9 percent reported that
they were sophomores, 11 percent reported that they were juniors, and
7.1 percent reported that they were seniors or beyond. Most students
reported their ages as between 18–21; the average class age was 19.5.

When asked about what types of media devices they own, 43.3 percent
of the students reported that they had a "smart phone" (e.g., a BlackBerry or
an iPhone), and 56.7 percent said they did not.

Prof. Susan Moeller led the study research team, and the six teaching
assistants for the course acted as researchers/authors, conducting a qualita-
tive content analysis of the student responses. Those six TAs, all Ph.D. students in the Philip Merrill College of Journalism, were: Ms. EunRyung Chong,
Mr. Sergei Golitsinski, Ms. Jing Guo, Mr. Raymond McCaffrey, Mr. Andrew
Nynka, and Ms. Jessica Roberts.[1]

READING THE TEXT

1. What are the symptoms of addiction to social media, according to the
   International Center for Media and the Public Agenda study conducted at the
   University of Maryland?
2. What can journalists learn from this study?
3. What is the primary reason the students in this study use digital media?
4. In your own words, how can people's reliance on social media be considered
   an "addiction"?

READING THE SIGNS

1. Write a journal entry in which you reflect upon your own use of text messaging, social media, and other forms of electronic media. Why do you use such
   media? Would you consider yourself "addicted"? If you do not use them, or do
   so rarely, why is that your preference?

[1] The study is available online at http://www.withoutmedia.wordpress.com.

2. Conduct a similar experiment in your class, having everyone give up their use of all digital media for twenty-four hours. Then use your course Web site to blog about your experiences (or discuss them in class). To what extent does your experiment replicate the results of the University of Maryland study? If your results differ, how do you account for that difference?

3. Write an essay that assesses students' reliance on text messaging and social media as their primary source for news of the world rather than mainstream news sources. You might base your essay on interviews with acquaintances about which news sources they typically rely on.

4. Do some research on the clinical definition of "addiction," and then write an essay in which you argue whether reliance on electronic media can accurately be classified as addictive.

THE DIGITAL PANOPTICON

RONALD J. DEIBERT

Black Code: Surveillance, Privacy, and the Dark Side of the Internet

The Internet is like the Force: It has a dark side and a light side, and the two go hand in hand. For while, as Ronald J. Deibert notes in this exposé of the many dangers of the Internet, "social networking, cloud computing, and mobile forms of connectivity are convenient and fun . . . they are also a dangerous brew," enabling unidentified third parties to track us "in time and space with a degree of precision that would make tyrants of past days envious." And there isn't very much that we can do about it because our entire lives — from our bank accounts to our elections — are now so entwined in cyberspace that there is little about us that cannot be tracked and hacked. Oh, Brave New World indeed! Ronald J. Deibert is professor of Political Science and Director of the Citizen Lab at the Munk School of Global Affairs, University of Toronto. He is the author of *Black Code: Surveillance, Privacy, and the Dark Side of the Internet* (2013), from which this selection is taken.

Look around you. Do you see anyone peering into their smartphone? How many times have you checked your email today? Have you searched for a wifi café to do so? How many people have you texted? Maybe you're a contrarian, don't own a smartphone. You find all this "connectivity" to be a social menace that isolates people from the world around them, as they stare endlessly into the glow of their computer screens, or engage in loud conversations with invisible others as they walk down the street gesticulating. If your date answers that cellphone call all is lost, you think. The digital revolution is not all that it's cracked up to be, you say, and you resist it.

Good luck with that.

Even those of you who resist or fear cyberspace sense that we are in the midst of an onslaught. And we are! You resist initially because it is drawing you in, inevitably. Whether you like it or not, to remain part of civil society you have to deal with it. Cyberspace is everywhere. By the end of 2012 there were more mobile devices on the planet than people: cellphones, laptops, tablets, gaming consoles, even Internet-connected cars. Some estimates put the number of Internet-connected devices now at 10 billion. Cyberspace has become what researchers call a "totally immersive environment," a phenomenon that cannot be avoided or ignored, increasingly embedded in societies rich and poor, a communications arena that does not discriminate. Connectivity in Africa, for instance, grows at some 2,000 percent a year.[1] While the digital divide remains deep, it's shrinking fast, and access to cyberspace is growing much faster than good governance over it. Indeed, in many regions rapid connectivity is taking place in a context of chronic underemployment, disease, malnutrition, environmental stress, and failed or failing states.

Cyberspace is now an unavoidable reality that wraps our planet in a complex information and communications skin. It shapes our actions and choices and relentlessly drives us all closer together, drives us even towards those whom, all things being equal, we would rather keep at a distance. A shared space, a global commons, the public square writ large. You've heard all the ecstatic metaphors used by enthusiasts and your thoughts turn elsewhere. "Hell is other people," Jean-Paul Sartre famously wrote in *No Exit*, and now teeming billions of them are potentially in your living room, or at least in your email inbox, that silent assassin. You cherish your privacy.

Of course, there have been previous revolutions in communications   5
technology that have upset the order of things and caused outrage and celebration. The alphabet, the invention of writing, the development of the printing press, the telegraph, radio, and television come to mind. But one of the many things that distinguishes cyberspace is the speed by which it has spread (and continues to spread). Those other technological innovations no doubt changed societies but in an "immersive" sense only over many generations, and more locally than not. Cyberspace, on the other hand, has connected two-thirds of the world — has joined, that is, more than 4 billion people in a single communications environment — in less than twenty years.

---

[1] Information on Internet connectivity and growth rates is collected at Internet World Stats: Usage and Population Statistics, http://www.Internetworldstats.com/stats.htm.

And it is moving onward, accelerating in fact, bringing legions into its fold each and every day.

The amount of digital information now doubles every year, and the "information superhighway" might be best described as continuous exponential growth, more on-ramps, more data, all the time, faster, more immediate, more accessible, its users always on, always connected. This speed and volume make getting a handle on the big picture difficult, and the truth is — a hideous truth, especially for those of you who think of yourselves as "off the grid," somehow away from the connected world, and proudly disconnected — is that no one is immune. Let's imagine for a moment that you don't own a computer, have never sent an email or text, and don't know what "app" means. The thing that informs you, that prepares you for cocktail parties and other gatherings, is mainstream or "old" media — newspapers, radio, and TV. Look closely at this "old media": How much of it is now "informed by," even directed by, "new media," by thousands, even millions, of "citizen journalists," unpaid, unaccountable, but with cellphone cameras permanently at the ready, documenting events as they happen in real time, unfiltered, and, perhaps, unreliable. The other truth is that no one really knows what this hurricane will leave behind or where it will take us. We're just struggling to hang on.

Another chief difference between then and now is that today, through cyberspace, it is us, the users, who create the information, do the connect-ing, and sustain and grow this unique communications and technological ecosystem. Save for the telephone, previous communications revolutions required a certain passivity on the part of consumers. There was little or no interactivity. We turned on the radio and listened, watched television happy to tune out and not to have to respond. The information provided, even the news of the day, simply washed over us. (We might get a call from a ratings agency, might be polled, might write a letter to the editor, but in the main we were passive recipients not active participants.) Cyberspace is wholly dif-ferent, and potentially far more egalitarian. It is the lonely man in a café clicking away, the mother out for dinner with friends discreetly contacting her kids, the armed militant in Mogadishu, the criminal in Moscow, as much as it is anyone or any institution in particular, who feed the machine, cause it to grow, to envelop us further. While it is difficult to pin down a constantly moving target, this much can be said: it is peculiar to cyberspace that we, the users, shape it as much as we are shaped by it. We are at it every day, every night, transforming it all the while. Cyberspace is what we make of it. It is ours. We need to remember this before it slips through our grasp.

This remains the issue. One of the extraordinary — and for many liberating — things about cyberspace is that while massive and hugely profit-able corporations like Apple and Google have made it possible and accessible (virtually) to all, they don't actually control it. Indeed, while having seeded the terrain, Apple, Google, and other gigantic corporations might have no greater control over cyberspace than those of us operating alone, at home, at our computer screens. This generative quality changes everything, causes grave concern, causes many to demand that cyberspace be brought under control.

It's difficult not to marvel at the extraordinary benefits of cyberspace. To be able to publish anything and have it immediately reach a potential world-wide audience represents a democratization of communications that philosophers and science fiction writers have dreamed about for centuries. Families continents apart now share in each other's daily struggles and triumphs. Physicians connect with patients thousands of kilometres away, in real time. Through vast aggregations of data we can now predict when disease outbreaks are likely to occur, and take precautionary measures. We can pinpoint our exact longitude and latitude, identify the nearest wifi hotspot, and notify a friend that we are, well, nearby and would like to meet.

But there is a dark side to all this connectivity: malicious threats that are   10 growing from the inside out, a global disease with many symptoms that is buttressed by disparate and mutually reinforcing causes. Some of these forces are the unintended by-products of the digital universe into which we have thrust ourselves, mostly with blind acceptance. Others are more sinister, deliberate manipulations that exploit newly discovered vulnerabilities in cyberspace. Together they threaten to destroy the fragile ecosystem we have come to take for granted.

Social networking, cloud computing, and mobile forms of connectivity are convenient and fun, but they are also a dangerous brew. Data once stored on our actual desktops and in filing cabinets now evaporates into the "cloud," entrusted to third parties beyond our control. Few of us realize that data stored by Google, even data located on machines in foreign jurisdictions, are subject to the U.S.A. Patriot Act because Google is headquartered in the United States and the Act compels it to turn over data when asked to do so, no matter where it is stored.[2] (For this reason, some European countries are debating laws that will ban public officials from using Google and/or other cloud computing services that could put their citizens' personal information at risk.) Mobile connectivity and social networking might give us instant awareness of each other's thoughts, habits, and activities, but in using them we have also entrusted an unprecedented amount of information about ourselves to private companies. We can now be tracked in time and space with a degree of precision that would make tyrants of days past envious — all by our own consent. Mobile devices are what Harvard's Jonathan Zittrain, author of *The Future of the Internet*, calls

---

[2]The official title of the Patriot Act is "Uniting and Strengthening America by Providing Appropriate Tools Required to Intercept and Obstruct Terrorism (USA PATRIOT) Act of 2001." The full Act can be found at http://www.gpo.gov/fdsys/pkg/PLAW-107publ56/pdf/PLAW-107publ56 .pdf. See also "USA Patriot Act," Electronic Privacy Information Center, http://epic.org/privacy /terrorism/usapatriot/default.html.

"tethered appliances": they corral us into walled gardens controlled by others, with unknown repercussions.[3]

These technological changes are occurring alongside a major demographic shift in cyberspace. The Internet may have been born in the West but its future will almost certainly be decided elsewhere. North Americans and Europeans make up less than 25 percent of Internet users, and the West in general is almost at saturation point. Asia, on the other hand, comprises nearly 50 percent of the world's Internet population (the most by region), and only 28 percent of its people are online (next to last by region). Some of the fastest growth is happening among the world's weakest states, in zones of conflict where authoritarianism (or something close), mass youth unemployment, and organized crime prevail. How burgeoning populations in Africa, Asia, the Middle East, and Latin America will use and shape cyberspace is an open question.

The young "netizens" who launched the Arab Spring were born into a world of satellite broadcasts, mobile phones, and Internet cafés. They were plugged into the digital world and able to exploit viral networks in ways difficult for authorities to anticipate or control. Meanwhile, perhaps the most innovative users of social networking and mobile technologies in Latin America today are the drug cartels, which use these tools to instill fear in citizens and lawmakers, intimidate journalists, and suppress free speech. To understand how and in what ways cyberspace will be used in the years to come we need to analyze innovation from the global South and East, from users in cities like Tegucigalpa, Nairobi, and Shanghai, the new centres of gravity for cyberspace.

And then there is cyber crime, a part of cyberspace since the origins of the Internet, but now explosive in terms of its growth and complexity. The economy of cyber crime has morphed from isolated acts by lone "basement" criminals into a highly professionalized transnational enterprise worth billions annually. Every day, security companies must review thousands of new samples of malicious software. Botnets that can be used for distributed denial-of-service (DDOS) attacks against any target can be rented from public forums and websites for less than $100.[4] Some even offer 24/7 technical help. Freely available spyware used to infiltrate networks has now become commonplace, a mass commodity. As a result, the people who maintain network security for governments, banks, and other businesses face a continuous onslaught of cyber-crime attacks.

Cyberspace has evolved so quickly that organizations and individuals   15 have yet to adopt proper security practices and policies. We have created a

---

[3]Jonathan Zittrain warns about the shift towards "tethered appliances" in *The Future of the Internet and How to Stop It* (New Haven: Yale University Press, 2008).

[4]A price list of illicit products and services sold in the Russian cyber crime underground is documented in this Trend Micro report: Max Goncharov, "Russian Underground 101," *Trend Micro*, 2012, http://www.trendmicro.com/cloud-content/us/pdfs/security-intelligence/white-papers/wp-russian-underground-101.pdf.

hyper-media environment characterized by constant innovation from the edges, extensive social sharing of data, and mobile networking from multiple platforms and locations, and in doing so, we have unintentionally opened ourselves up to multiple opportunities for criminal exploitation. Cyber crime thrives partly because of a lack of controls, because the criminals themselves can reap a digital harvest from across the globe and hide in jurisdictions with lax law enforcement and regulations. Furthermore, it moves at the speed of electrons, while international law enforcement moves at the speed of bureaucratic institutions. It is almost routine now to hear about cyber criminals living openly in places like St. Petersburg, Russia, and exalted as tech entrepreneurs, not the digital thugs that they are.

No doubt, cyber crime is a major nuisance, a shadowy, unregulated economy that costs decent folks dearly, but even more disturbing is how cyber crime, espionage, sabotage, and even warfare appear to be blurring together. Almost daily, there are breaches against government departments, private companies, or basic infrastructure. The Citizen Lab has investigated several of these cases, two of which we documented in our reports, *Tracking GhostNet* and *Shadows in the Cloud*. The victims, all compromised by China-based perpetrators, included major defence contractors, global media outlets, government agencies, ministries of foreign affairs, embassies, and international organizations like the United Nations.

How far down this road have we gone? A 2012 *New York Times* report revealed that the United States and Israel were responsible for the Stuxnet virus, which sabotaged Iranian nuclear enrichment facilities in June 2010. While the two countries remained mum about the charge, they did not deny it. The incident represents the first time governments have tacitly acknowledged responsibility for a cyber attack on the critical infrastructure of another country, a de facto act of war through cyberspace.

The techniques used in these state-based breaches and attacks are indistinguishable from those used by cyber criminals. Indeed, Stuxnet has been described as a "Frankenstein" of existing cyber-crime methods and tradecraft, and many now see cyber crime as a strategic vector for state-based and corporate espionage. Hidden in the shadows of low-level thuggery and cyber crime for cash, in other words, are more serious and potentially devastating operations, like acts of sabotage against critical infrastructure. Now perilously networked together, such infrastructure is especially vulnerable to cyber attacks: our smart grids, financial sectors, nuclear enrichment facilities, power plants, hospitals, and government agencies are all there for the taking. And this is happening at a time when militaries, criminal organizations, militants, and any individual with an axe to grind are refining capabilities to target and disrupt those networks. Cyberspace has become a battleground, a ground zero, for geopolitical contests and armed struggle.

Cyber crime is much more than a persistent nuisance. It has become a key risk factor for governments and businesses. The consequences of this exploding threat are numerous and wide-ranging and have led to greater and greater pressures for state regulation and intervention. Proliferating cyber crime and espionage have vaulted cyber security to the top of the international political agenda and brought about a sea change in the way that governments approach cyberspace. Where once the dominant descriptor of Internet regulation was "hands off," today the talk is all about control, the necessary assertion of state power, and, increasingly, geopolitical contestation over cyberspace itself.

The OpenNet Initiative (ONI), a project in which the Citizen Lab partici- 20 pates and that documents Internet content filtering worldwide, notes that roughly 1 billion Internet users live in countries (over forty of them) that regularly censor the Internet. States have become adept at content-control regulations, mostly downloading responsibilities to the private sector to police the Internet on their behalf, but some governments have gone further, engaging in offensive operations on their own, including disabling opposition websites through DDOS or other attacks, and/or using pro-government bloggers to flood (and sometimes disable) the information space.

Although conventional wisdom has long maintained that authoritarian regimes would wither in the face of the Internet (and some in the Middle East and North Africa appear to have done so), many have turned the domain to their advantage. Tunisia and Egypt may have succumbed to Facebook-enabled protestors, but China, Vietnam, Syria, Iran, Belarus, and others have successfully employed second- and third-generation control techniques to penetrate and immobilize opposition groups and cultivate a climate of fear and self-censorship. These states are winning cyberspace wars. For them "Internet freedom" is just another excuse for state control.

It would be wrong, however, to see the growing assertion of state power in cyberspace as coming only from authoritarian regimes. As Stuxnet suggests, cyberspace controls, in fact, are being driven and legitimized just as much by liberal democratic countries. Many liberal democratic governments have enacted or are proposing Internet content-filtering laws, mostly, they say, to clamp down on copyright infringements, online child pornography, or other content deemed objectionable, hateful, or likely to incite violence. Many have also pushed for new surveillance powers, downloading responsibilities for the collection of data onto the private sector while relaxing judicial oversight around the sharing of information with law enforcement and intelligence agencies. They are also developing offensive information operations. The United States and many other Western governments now speak openly about the need to fight (and win) wars in this domain.

Not surprisingly new companies have sprouted up to serve the growing pressure to "secure" cyberspace, a growth industry now worth tens of billions of dollars annually. Countries that censor the Internet have usually relied on products and services developed by Western manufacturers: Websense in Tunisia, Fortinet in Burma, SmartFilter in Saudi Arabia, Tunisia, Oman, and the United Arab Emirates. Filtering and surveillance devices manufactured by Blue Coat Systems, an American firm, have been found operating on public networks in Afghanistan, Bahrain, Burma, China, Egypt, India, Indonesia, Iraq, Kenya, Kuwait, Lebanon, Malaysia, Nigeria, Qatar, Russia, Saudi Arabia, Singapore, South Korea, Syria, Thailand, Turkey, and Venezuela — a list that includes some of the world's most notorious human rights abusers. Netsweeper, a Canadian company, sells censorship products and services to ISPs across the Middle East and North Africa, helping regimes there block access to human rights information, basic news, information about alternative lifestyles, and opinion critical of the regimes. In 2012, dissidents in the United Arab Emirates and Bahrain were shown, during interrogations where they were arrested and beaten, transcripts of their private chats and emails, their computers obviously compromised by their own government security agencies. Those agencies didn't use an off-the-shelf piece of cybercrime spyware to do the job; rather, they employed a high-grade commercial network intrusion kit sold to them by British and Italian companies.

American, Canadian, and European firms that used to brag about connecting individuals and wiring the world are now turning those wires into secret weapons of war and repression. Suddenly, policy-makers are being given tools they never before imagined: advanced deep packet inspection, content filtering, social network mining, cellphone tracking, and computer network exploitation and attack capabilities.

This is not the way it was supposed to be.   25

As the imperatives to regulate, secure, and control cyberspace grow, we risk degrading (even destroying) what made cyberspace unique in the first place. In the face of urgent issues and real threats, policy-makers may be tempted to lower the bar for what is seen as acceptable practice or, worse, throw the baby out with the bath water. Before extreme solutions are adopted we must address the core value that underpins cyberspace itself: ensuring that it remains secure, but also open and dynamic, a communications system for citizens the world over.

READING THE TEXT

1. What are the differences between "old" and "new" media, according to Deibert, and why do those differences matter?

2. Summarize in your own words the dangers that Deibert sees in the proliferation of new media.

3. What is the significance of the Stuxnet virus of 2010, in Deibert's view?

4. What is Deibert's attitude toward the growth of cybersecurity firms, especially those that do business overseas?

5. Study Deibert's use of the second person in this selection. What effect does it have on your response to his ideas?

READING THE SIGNS

1. In your journal, reflect on your own experience with new media. What participatory media do you engage in, and why? If you avoid such media, what are
   the reasons behind your behavior?

2. **CONNECTING TEXTS**   In class, form teams and debate the proposition that the
   benefits of the information superhighway outweigh the potential dangers that
   Deibert describes. To develop your ideas, consult "The Cloud: Semiotics and
   the New Media" (p. 371) and Joseph Turow's "The Daily You: How the New
   Advertising Industry Is Defining Your Identity and Your Worth" (below).

3. Write an essay in which you analyze the rhetorical and argumentative strategies that Deibert employs in this selection, including the use of concession,
   the consideration of contrary positions, and direct address to the reader. How
   do techniques such as these contribute to the overall effectiveness of Deibert's
   argument?

4. **CONNECTING TEXTS**   Both Diebert and Joseph Turow ("The Daily You: How the
   New Advertising Industry Is Defining Your Identity and Your Worth," below)
   analyze the potential abuses and dangers of an Internet-driven world. In an
   essay, compare and contrast their essays. Which do you find a more effective
   argument, and why?

THE DIGITAL PANOPTICON

| JOSEPH TUROW

The Daily You: How the New Advertising Industry Is Defining Your Identity and Your Worth

It's called "data mining": the practice by which such digital media
giants as Google and Facebook track every move by Internet users
and sell that information to marketers who use it to construct advertisements that are tailor-made for their recipients. In this selection
from his book *The Daily You* (2013), Joseph Turow describes how this
world of digital profiling and personalized marketing works. If his revelation "creeps you out," Turow explains, you are not alone. Joseph
Turow is the Robert Lewis Shayon Professor of Communication at the
University of Pennsylvania's Annenberg School.

At the start of the twenty-first century, the advertising industry is guiding
one of history's most massive stealth efforts in social profiling. At this point
you may hardly notice the results of this trend. You may find you're getting
better or worse discounts on products than your friends. You may notice

that some ads seem to follow you around the internet. Every once in a while a website may ask you if you like a particular ad you just received. Or perhaps your cell phone has told you that you will be rewarded if you eat in a nearby restaurant where, by the way, two of your friends are hanging out this very minute.

You may actually like some of these intrusions. You may feel that they pale before the digital power you now have. After all, your ability to create blogs, collaborate with others to distribute videos online, and say what you want on Facebook (carefully using its privacy settings) seems only to confirm what marketers and even many academics are telling us: that consumers are captains of their own new-media ships.

But look beneath the surface, and a different picture emerges. We're at the start of a revolution in the ways marketers and media intrude in — and shape — our lives. Every day most if not all Americans who use the internet, along with hundreds of millions of other users from all over the planet, are being quietly peeked at, poked, analyzed, and tagged as they move through the online world. Governments undoubtedly conduct a good deal of snooping, more in some parts of the world than in others. But in North America, Europe, and many other places, companies that work for marketers have taken the lead in secretly slicing and dicing the actions and backgrounds of huge populations on a virtually minute-by-minute basis. Their goal is to find out how to activate individuals' buying impulses so they can sell us stuff more efficiently than ever before. But their work has broader social and cultural consequences as well. It is destroying traditional publishing ethics by forcing media outlets to adapt their editorial content to advertisers' public-relations needs and slice-and-dice demands. And it is performing a highly controversial form of social profiling and discrimination by customizing our media content on the basis of marketing reputations we don't even know we have.

Consider a fictional middle class family of two parents with three children who eat out a lot in fast-food restaurants. After a while the parents receive a continual flow of fast-food restaurant coupons. Data suggest the parents, let's call them Larry and Rhonda, will consistently spend far more than the coupons' value. Additional statistical evaluations of parents' activities and discussions online and off may suggest that Larry and Rhonda and their children tend toward being overweight. The data, in turn, result in a small torrent of messages by marketers and publishers seeking to exploit these weight issues to increase attention or sales. Videos about dealing with overweight children, produced by a new type of company called content farms, begin to show up on parenting websites Rhonda frequents. When Larry goes online, he routinely receives articles about how fitness chains emphasize weight loss around the holidays. Ads for fitness firms and diet pills typically show up on the pages with those articles. One of Larry and Rhonda's sons, who is fifteen years old, is happy to find a text message on his phone that invites him to use a discount at an ice cream chain not too far from his house. One of their daughters, by contrast, is mortified when she receives texts inviting her to a diet program and an ad on her Facebook page inviting her to a clothing store for hip, over-sized women. What's more, people keep sending her Twitter messages about weight loss. In the meantime, both Larry and Rhonda are getting ads from check-cashing services and payday-loan companies. And Larry notices sourly on auto sites he visits that the main articles on the home page and the ads throughout feature entry-level and used models. His bitterness only becomes more acute when he describes to his boss the down-market Web he has been seeing lately. Quite surprised, she tells him she has been to the same auto sites recently and has just the opposite impression: many of the articles are about the latest German cars, and one home-page ad even offered her a gift for test-driving one at a dealer near her home.

This scenario of individual and household profiling and media customi- 5
zation is quite possible today. Websites, advertisers, and a panoply of other companies are continuously assessing the activities, intentions, and back-grounds of virtually everyone online; even our social relationships and com-ments are being carefully and continuously analyzed. In broader and broader ways, computer-generated conclusions about who we are affect the media content — the streams of commercial messages, discount offers, informa-tion, news, and entertainment — each of us confronts. Over the next few decades the business logic that drives these tailored activities will transform the ways we see ourselves, those around us, and the world at large. Govern-ments too may be able to use marketers' technology and data to influence what we see and hear.

From this vantage point, the rhetoric of consumer power begins to lose credibility. In its place is a rhetoric of esoteric technological and statistical knowledge that supports the practice of social discrimination through pro-filing. We may note its outcomes only once in a while, and we may shrug when we do because it seems trivial — just a few ads, after all. But unless we try to understand how this profiling or reputation-making process works and what it means for the long term, our children and grandchildren will bear the full brunt of its prejudicial force.

The best way to enter this new world is to focus on its central driv-ing force: the advertising industry's media-buying system. Media buying involves planning and purchasing space or time for advertising on outlets as diverse as billboards, radio, websites, mobile phones, and newspapers. For decades, media buying was a backwater, a service wing of advertising agencies that was known for having the lowest-paying jobs on Madison Ave-nue and for filling those jobs with female liberal arts majors fresh out of college. But that has all changed. The past twenty years have seen the rise of "media agencies" that are no longer part of ad agencies, though they may both be owned by the same parent company. Along with a wide array of satellite companies that feed them technology and data, media agencies have become magnets for well-remunerated software engineers and financial statisticians of both sexes.

In the United States alone, media-buying agencies wield more than $170 billion of their clients' campaign funds; they use these funds to purchase space and time on media they think will advance their clients' marketing aims. But in the process they are doing much more. With the money as leverage, they are guiding the media system toward nothing less than new ways of thinking about and evaluating audience members and defining what counts as a successful attempt to reach them. Traditionally, marketers have used media such as newspapers, magazines, radio, billboards, and television to reach out to segments of the population through commercial messages. These advertisers typically learned about audience segments from survey companies that polled representative portions of the population via a variety of methods, including panel research. A less prestigious direct-marketing business has involved contacting individuals by mail or phone. Firms have rented lists of public data or purchase information that suggests who might be likely customers.

The emerging new world is dramatically different. The distinction between reaching out to audiences via mass media and by direct-response methods is disappearing. Advertisers in the digital space expect all media firms to deliver to them particular types of individuals — and, increasingly, *particular* individuals — by leveraging a detailed knowledge about them and their behaviors that was unheard of even a few years ago. The new advertising strategy involves drawing as specific a picture as possible of a person based in large part on measurable physical acts such as clicks, swipes, mouseovers, and even voice commands. The strategy uses new digital tracking tools like cookies and beacons as well as new organizations with names like BlueKai, Rapleaf, Invidi, and eXelate. These companies track people on websites and across websites in an effort to learn what they do, what they care about, and who their friends are. Firms that exchange the information often do ensure that the targets' names and postal addresses remain anonymous — but not before they add specific demographic data and lifestyle information. For example:

- Rapleaf is a firm that claims on its website to help marketers "customize your customers' experience." To do that, it gleans data from individual users of blogs, internet forums, and social networks. It uses ad exchanges to sell the ability to reach those people. Rapleaf says it has "data on 900 + million records, 400 + million consumers, [and] 52 + billion friend connections." Advertisers are particularly aware of the firm's ability to predict the reliability of individuals (for example, the likelihood they will pay their mortgage) based on Rapleaf's research on the trustworthiness of the people in those individuals' social networks.

- A company called Next Jump runs employee discount and reward programs for about one-third of U.S. corporate employees. It gets personal information about all of them from the human relations departments of the companies and supplements that information with transactional data from the manufacturers it deals with as well as from credit companies. Armed with this combination of information, Next Jump can predict what people want and what they will pay for. It also generates a "UserRank" score for every employee based on how many purchases a person has made and how much he or she has spent. That score plays an important role in determining which employee gets what product e-mail offers and at what price.

- A firm called The Daily Me already sells an ad and news personalization technology to online periodicals. If a *Boston Globe* reader who reads a lot of soccer sports news visits a *Dallas Morning News* site, the Daily Me's technology tells the *Dallas Morning News* to serve him soccer stories. Moreover, when an ad is served along with the story, its text and photos are instantly configured so as to include soccer terms and photos as part of the advertising pitch. A basketball fan receiving an ad for the same product will get language and photos that call out to people with hoop interests.

These specific operations may not be in business a few years from now. ₁₀ In the new media-buying environment, companies come and go amid furious competition. The logic propelling them and more established firms forward, though, is consistent: the future belongs to marketers and media firms — *publishers*, in current terminology — that learn how to find and keep the most valuable customers by surrounding them with the most persuasive media materials. Special online advertising exchanges, owned by Google, Yahoo!, Microsoft, Interpublic, and other major players, allow publishers to auction and media agencies to "buy" individuals with particular characteristics, often in real time. That is, it is now possible to buy the right to deliver an ad to a person with specific characteristics at the precise moment that that person loads a Web page. In fact, through an activity called cookie matching, . . . an advertiser can actually bid for the right to reach an individual whom the advertiser knows from previous contacts and is now tracking around the Web. Moreover, the technology keeps changing. Because consumers delete Web cookies and marketers find cookies difficult to use with mobile devices, technology companies have developed methods to "fingerprint" devices permanently and allow for persistent personalization across many media platforms.

The significance of tailored commercial messages and offers goes far beyond whether or not the targeted persons buy the products. Advertisements and discounts are status signals: they alert people as to their social position. If you consistently get ads for low-priced cars, regional vacations, fast-food restaurants, and other products that reflect a lower-class status, your sense of the world's opportunities may be narrower than that of someone who is feted with ads for national or international trips and luxury products. Moreover, if like Larry and Rhonda you happen to know that your colleague is receiving more ads for the luxury products than you are, and more and better discounts to boot, you may worry that you are falling behind in society's estimation of your worth.

In fact, the ads may signal your opportunities actually *are* narrowed if marketers and publishers decide that the data points — profiles — about you across the internet position you in a segment of the population that is relatively less desirable to marketers because of income, age, past-purchase behavior, geographical location, or other reasons. Turning individual profiles into individual evaluations is what happens when a profile becomes a reputation. Today individual marketers still make most of the decisions about which particular persons matter to them, and about how much they matter. But that is beginning to change as certain publishers and data providers — Rapleaf and Next Jump, for example — allow their calculations of value to help advertisers make targeting decisions. In the future, these calculations of our marketing value, both broadly and for particular products, may become routine parts of the information exchanged about people throughout the media system.

The tailoring of news and entertainment is less advanced, but it is clearly under way. Technologies developed for personalized advertising and coupons point to possibilities for targeting individuals with personalized news and entertainment. Not only is this already happening, the logic of doing that is becoming more urgent to advertisers and publishers. Advertisers operate on the assumption that, on the internet as in traditional media, commercial messages that parade as soft (or "human interest") news and entertainment are more persuasive than straightforward ads. Publishers know this too, and in the heat of a terrible economic downturn even the most traditional ones have begun to compromise long-standing professional norms about the separation of advertising and editorial matter. And in fact many of the new online publishers — companies, such as Demand Media, that turn out thousands of text and video pieces a day — never really bought into the old-world ideas about editorial integrity anyway. What this means is that we are entering a world of intensively customized content, a world in which publishers and even marketers will package personalized advertisements with soft news or entertainment that is tailored to fit both the selling needs of the ads and the reputation of the particular individual.

The rise of digital profiling and personalization has spawned a new industrial jargon that reflects potentially grave social divisions and privacy issues. Marketers divide people into *targets* and *waste*. They also use words like *anonymous* and *personal* in unrecognizable ways that distort and drain them of their traditional meanings. If a company can follow your behavior in the digital environment — an environment that potentially includes your mobile phone and television set — its claim that you are "anonymous" is meaningless. That is particularly true when firms intermittently add off-line information such as shopping patterns and the value of your house to their online data and then simply strip the name and address to make it "anonymous." It matters little if your name is John Smith, Yesh Mispar, or 3211466. The persistence of information about you will lead firms to act based on what they know, share, and care about you, whether you know it is happening or not.

All these developments may sound more than a little unsettling; *creeped* 15 *out* is a phrase people often use when they learn about them. National surveys I have conducted over the past decade consistently suggest that although people know companies are using their data and do worry about it, their understanding of exactly how the data are being used is severely lacking. That of course shouldn't be surprising. People today lead busy, even harried, lives. Keeping up with the complex and changing particulars of data mining is simply not something most of us have the time or ability to do. There are many great things about the new media environment. But when companies track people without their knowledge, sell their data without letting them know what they are doing or securing their permission, and then use those data to decide which of those people are targets or waste, we have a serious social problem. The precise implications of this problem are not yet clear. If it's allowed to persist, and people begin to realize how the advertising industry segregates them from and pits them against others in the ads they get, the discounts they receive, the TV-viewing suggestions and news stories they confront, and even the offers they receive in the supermarket, they may begin to suffer the effects of discrimination. They will likely learn to distrust the companies that have put them in this situation, and they may well be incensed at the government that has not helped to prevent it. A comparison to the financial industry is apt. Here was an industry engaged in a whole spectrum of arcane practices that were not at all transparent to consumers or regulators but that had serious negative impact on our lives. It would be deeply unfortunate if the advertising system followed the same trajectory.

Despite valiant efforts on the part of advocacy groups and some federal and state officials, neither government rulings nor industry self-regulation has set policies that will address these issues before they become major sources of widespread social distress. Part of the reason for the lack of action may be that neither citizens nor politicians recognize how deeply embedded in American life these privacy-breaching and social-profiling activities are. Few individuals outside advertising know about the power of the new media-buying system: its capacity to determine not only what media firms do but how we see ourselves and others. They don't know that that system is working to attach marketing labels to us based on the clicks we make, the conversations we have, and the friendships we enjoy on websites, mobile devices, iPads, supermarket carts, and even television sets. They don't know that the new system is forcing many media firms to sell their souls for ad money while they serve us commercial messages, discounts, and, increasingly, news and entertainment based on our marketing labels. They don't realize that the wide sharing of data suggests that in the future marketers and media firms may find it useful to place us into personalized "reputation silos" that surround us with worldviews and rewards based on labels marketers have created reflecting our value to them. Without this knowledge, it is hard to even begin to have broad-based serious discussions about what society and industry should do about this sobering new world: into the twenty-first century the media-buying system's strategy of social discrimination will increasingly define how we as individuals relate to society — not only how much we pay but what we see and when and how we see it.

READING THE TEXT

1. In your own words, describe how the methods digital media agencies use to ascertain consumer behavior differ from traditional consumer research strategies used at least twenty years ago.

2. Describe in a paragraph what Turow means by the "advertising industry's media-buying system" (para. 7).

3. According to this selection, how are digitally obtained profiles of individuals and households translated into personalized advertising?

4. Make a list of the advantages and problems of digital marketing strategies.

5. What assumptions does Turow make about his readers' likely responses to his indictment of the digital mining of personal information? How do those assumptions shape your response to his argument?

READING THE SIGNS

1. Write a letter to the hypothetical couple Larry and Rhonda, whom Turow describes as being surprised and bitter about the precise profiling of their household by media marketers. Can you offer any suggestions about how to avoid being so profiled?

2. In class, hold a debate on whether marketers' mining of personal information and creation of specific consumer profiles are advantageous or problematic for the consumer (do not consider whether this strategy benefits the marketers or their clients). For the former position, your argument might focus on the advantages of customized "content"; for the latter, your argument might focus on the creation of social distinctions and/or privacy concerns. After the debate, write an essay in which you advance your own argument about this question.

3. As Turow explains, the majority of consumers do not realize that their Internet activities are mined for commercial reasons. Write an essay in which you support, oppose, or complicate the proposition that for-profit data miners such as Google should pay, in money or services, users whom they monitor for information that they then sell.

4. In an essay, analyze semiotically the Web site of one of the data-tracking companies that Turow mentions, such as TowerData (formerly Rapleaf) or Next Jump, or the Web site of an online advertising exchange such as those owned by Google and Yahoo. What signs appear on the Web site (especially the home page) that indicate whose interests the company serves?

5. In his conclusion, Turow expresses a desire for "broad-based serious discussions about what society and industry should do about this sobering new world." He continues, "Into the twenty-first century the media-buying system's strategy of social discrimination will increasingly define how we as individuals relate to society — not only how much we pay but what we see and when and how we see it" (para. 16). In an essay, respond to Turow's concerns. To what extent do you see media buying and data mining as contradicting traditional American social values?

ERIN LEE
How Effective Is Social Media Activism?

The good news is that, thanks to digital social media, political activism is easier to inspire than ever before. The bad news is that clicking a "Like" button doesn't really accomplish anything, or does it? In this survey of social media activism, Dartmouth College student journalist Erin Lee presents two sides of the question, observing how, on the one hand, the #OscarsSoWhite Twitter campaign did have a real effect on the way the Academy nominates its Oscar award candidates, but on the other, the "'only way to make a democracy work is to get off social media and do things in the real world.'" Perhaps you might want to investigate the question further by retweeting this article.

As Shonda Rhimes wrapped up her insightful Dartmouth commencement speech back in 2014, she slipped in a little zinger admonishing social media activism — "A hashtag is not helping."

"Hashtags are very pretty on Twitter," she said. "But a hashtag is not a movement. A hashtag does not make you Dr. King. A hashtag does not change anything. It's a hashtag. It's you, sitting on your butt, typing on your computer and then going back to binge-watching your favorite show." Rhimes went on to encourage her young, Ivy League audience to instead go out and do something. But is Shonda right?

April Reign, creator of the hashtag #OscarsSoWhite, said she has seen the power of social media and the influence that "hashtag activism" can have.

She created #OscarsSoWhite in response to the lack of racial diversity in the 2016 Oscar nominations, sparking a national sensation. Mainstream media picked up the hashtag, and some celebrities announced they would boycott the Oscars in protest. The Academy of Motion Picture Arts and Sciences eventually said it would make significant changes to its voting requirements and governing structure to work towards increasing the diversity of its membership. "I think we can credit the conversations stemming from the hashtag and the issues behind it to making system change for the first time in the 80 year history of the Academy," Reign said.

She said that young activists often use social media as a way to communicate, organize and raise awareness, citing the Black Lives Matter movement's active use of hashtags. "We're connected more by the internet than by a personal relationship or a geography," she said. "Those who think hashtags don't work or that young millennials are apathetic really haven't spent a lot of time being a part of that, because it does exist and it is successful."

Kevin Bui '17 said social media works as a forum to share articles and contribute to a greater social conversation. "I want to put a certain message out there through my social media and state what I believe about certain issues," Bui said. "The majority of people won't care, but what it can do is help challenge the people who do care to think about things in a new way or different way." Bui added that many young people are unaware of current social and political issues, which is something social media can help solve. "I do think in general the current generation is more resistant to change and activism because the structural inequality we see today isn't as blatant," Bui said. "A lot of people think we have already achieved equality, which I don't think is true."

Columbia University journalism professor Todd Gitlin said that historically, college students are generally not socially and politically active because they have other more immediate priorities. "Most students at most times are apathetic in that whatever they think or think they think, they have other priorities besides stepping up and doing political work," he said. "With the exception of episodic excitements, only a small percentage of students participate in any kind of political activity." Robert Wright '18, a Dartmouth organizer for Bernie Sanders' campaign, noted that many students are not as politically active because they are not immediately affected by policy changes. "A lot of young people are already jaded and feel like no matter what they do nothing big is going to change," he said.

Gitlin said he believes social media does not make a difference in levels of student activism, as many high points in student activism, such as the anti-Vietnam war movement in the 1960s, occurred before the advent of social media and the Internet. "It could even be argued that social media makes it easier to pull people out to a single action," he said. "It also inflates the feeling that the movement is already on top of its environment, that it's got momentum." Gitlin added that popular social media-driven movements,

5

such as President Barack Obama's 2008 campaign or the Occupy Wall Street movement, tend to be short-term moments that can distract from enduring efforts. "Social media are like wisps of oxygen — they get people excited but then they wear out," he said.

However, Alcides Velasquez, communications professor at Pontificia Universidad Javeriana in Bogotá, Colombia, wrote in an email that his research shows social media does have a mobilizing effect among young adults, though the degree varies depending on the type of social media activity. He said social media can make college students feel like they have a greater ability to effect change in the real world. "Political uses of social media among college students increases how capable young people feel about achieving their own political objectives," he said. Velasquez said movements generated on social media do not often result in concrete, institutional change, though some do turn into offline movements. Perceptions of efficacy, social resources and the level of cohesion of the group all play a role into how successful a movement becomes, he said.

Avi Sholkoff, a first year student at the University of Michigan, wrote a *Huffington Post* article advocating for hashtag activism in the midst of the 2014 uproar over events in Ferguson, Missouri. In an interview, he said social media can amplify awareness of issues, which sometimes translates to more legitimate action. He cited the ALS Ice Bucket Challenge as a social media campaign that raised a significant amount of money for a cause, moving beyond the confines of the internet. "Something I've learned in years with technology is that technology is a tool and not a toy," Sholkoff said. "Social media can be fun, but it also is a tool to educate and advocate."

Wright, who started the "Dartmouth Students and Staff for Bernie" 10 Facebook group, said social media was an effective way to reach out to large groups of people, though it is more of a "means to an end." The goal is to use social media to help recruit people to campaign door-to-door, phone bank and actually vote, he said.

"The only way to make a democracy work is to get off social media and do things in the real world," he said.

READING THE TEXT

1. Summarize in your own words the benefits social media activism can effect, as Lee describes them.

2. What does Todd Gitlin mean by claiming that "social media are like wisps of oxygen" (para. 7)?

3. Why are young people particularly drawn to social media activism, as opposed to other kinds, according to this selection?

4. How would you characterize Lee's own attitude toward hashtag activism? Does she take a position herself?

READING THE SIGNS

1. **CONNECTING TEXTS**   In class, form teams and debate the controversy over hashtag activism that Lee outlines, with one team presenting the skepticism that Shonda Rhimes expresses in her commencement speech and the other supporting April Reign's defense of such political activity. To develop your ideas, consult Brian Dunning's "Slacktivism: Raising Awareness" (below) and S. Craig Watkins's "The Evolution of #Black Twitter" (p. 445). Use the class debate as a jumping-off point for an essay in which you argue your own views on the matter.

2. In an essay, write your own response to Todd Gitlin's assertion that social media activism "inflates the feeling that [a] movement is already on top of its environment" (para. 7). Support your ideas by referencing the history of particular hashtag campaigns, such as #OscarsSoWhite or #BringBackOurGirls.

3. Write an argument that supports, contradicts, or complicates Keven Bui's assertion that "the current generation is more resistant to change and activism because the structural inequality we see today isn't as blatant.... A lot of people think we have already achieved equality" (para. 5).

4. **CONNECTING TEXTS**   Compare Lee's selection with Brian Dunning's "Slacktivism: Raising Awareness" (below), focusing on their use of argumentative and persuasive strategies. Which author do you find more effective, and why?

BRIAN DUNNING

Slacktivism: Raising Awareness

For Brian Dunning, the jury is in: Social media activism is nothing more than useless "slacktivism," and he's against it. Indeed, he declares that "I hereby, officially, expand the definition of slacktivism to include not only 'Like' buttons, online petitions, retweets, and other such desktop actions; but also to include any activism of *any* sort for a cause that you did not research personally and thoroughly enough to determine its validity." Surveying such slacktivist failures as the *Kony 2012* YouTube video campaign, Dunning throws down the gauntlet in this podcast and blog post from skeptoid.com. Brian Dunning is a science writer and the host and producer of the podcast *Skeptoid: Critical Analysis of Pop Phenomena*.

"Slacktivism" is a portmanteau of slacker activism. Everyone likes to think they are being an activist. The Internet is bursting at the seams with ways to make this easy: click a Facebook "Like" button; sign an online petition;

retweet a shocking photograph. Such forms of armchair activism almost never accomplish anything. At their best, most of them are wastes of your time; a pointless click of the mouse. But at their worst, they can steal millions of dollars from armchair activists who are persuaded to donate actual money to what they're told is some useful cause.

I remember a day in the 1980s when I was driving through a depressed area of Los Angeles, and there was a billboard advertising "Speak Out Against Racism," with a 976 phone number. These are premium rate phone numbers where the owner receives a portion of the caller's bill for the call. Out of curiosity, I noted the number and called it later, and all it was was a solicitation for you to leave your thoughts about racism, and then you could speak for however long you wanted, into the recording. There was no indication that anyone was even listening to the recorded messages; in fact, I doubt anyone did anything but collected their monthly check for the calls and took it to the bank. It was an early version of what we now call slacktivism; a malicious one at that, because someone was making money off people who thought they were doing something useful.

Today, an example of slacktivism is more likely to be benign. The online petition is very common. Online petitions are not generally binding on anyone, so they carry essentially no weight at all. But they're an easy way to make people think they're accomplishing something, so companies like Change.org offer them by the hundreds of thousands; Google currently lists about three quarters of a million petitions on that site alone. Perhaps once in a long while, a petition will garner enough signatures to persuade a reporter to write an article that a company may respond to from a public relations perspective; but more often, these are not productive. One such example was a petition demanding that PepsiCo remove brominated vegetable oil from their products. Known as BVO, this oil has many uses including non-food applications, like virtually every compound found in virtually every food. Thus, it's really easy to scare people with. "This food contains a chemical used in flame retardant!" shouted the petition. Not a problem, but because of the negative publicity, PepsiCo announced they'd remove it.

Slacktivism is also commonly used to promote deliberate hoaxes, in addition to the ignorant paranoia to which PepsiCo responded. Twitter is often used to spread misinformation in a shocking way that prompts many people to respond. In 2014, a photograph was circulated that showed a laboratory with a lot of cats strapped into frightening-looking racks. The caption said "Retweet if you say NO to animal testing." Over 5,000 people spread the shocking message, with cries of "vivisection" and all sorts of horrors, apparently unaware that it was a photo that had, at some point, been deliberately misattributed by a hoaxer who got it from the Gainseville Sun news website. The cats in the picture had been seized from an abusive hoarder, and were being spayed and neutered by veterinary students at the University of Florida to prepare them for adoption to start new lives.

Perhaps the most dramatic example of how slacktivism can be mere 5 exploitation was the famous *Kony 2012* viral video which came out on YouTube in March 2012. It was a 30-minute shockumentary film about the fugitive African warlord Joseph Kony, whose cult-like guerrilla army is called the Lord's Resistance Army, and basically goes around Africa raping, pillaging, and murdering. Within weeks *Kony 2012* became the most successful viral video ever, getting over 100 million views in its first six days. Incredibly, a Pew Research Center poll found that 58 percent of young adults in the United States had heard of the video, comparable to your average major studio motion picture. The movie's call to action? Send money now — but not to African law enforcement, to the filmmakers themselves.

Let's look at two red flags: How massive of a financial exploitation this was for the filmmakers, and how staggeringly useless it was so far as having anything to do with stopping Kony.

Kony 2012 was made by an American charity called Invisible Children, whose mission statement shown in their tax return for the fiscal year in which they produced the movie was:

> *Invisible Children uses film, creativity, and social action to end the use*
> *of child soldiers in Joseph Kony's rebel war and restore RLA-affected*
> *communities in Central Africa to peace and prosperity — and in doing*
> *so — to create a successful grassroots movement that can help end war*
> *permanently.*

If I might paraphrase: We make YouTube videos that we hope will end war. And just what did *Kony 2012* do for Invisible Children's YouTube production bank account? By the end of their fiscal year, which ended on June 30, about four months after the movie came out, they reported gross receipts of $31.9 million dollars. All of it was donations made by people who watched their movies. They reported no grants or other sources of income.

According to their mission statement, your donations were not used to stop Kony; they were used to make more movies *about* stopping Kony. Is that really where you had hoped your donation was going? But they did make the followup movie. They made *Kony 2012: Part II — Beyond Famous,* but chances are you never heard of that one. The hype was over by that point. Invisible Children's tax returns, which are public information since they are a charity, show that they spent $15.5 million in 2012. Quite a budget, considering that *Kony 2012: Part II — Beyond Famous* was only 20 minutes long, and took one month to produce. I would like to have been a guest at that production's catering table.

So, clearly, persuading people that donating to their online video turned 10 out to be little more than financial exploitation. But let's examine our second red flag. Was raising awareness about Kony a useful thing to do?

No, it was not, most assuredly. Law enforcement had been on Kony's case for nearly a decade before the YouTube movie. *Forbes Magazine* had listed him on their "World's Most Wanted" in 2008 alongside Osama bin Laden, and in 2011 alongside Ayman alZawahiri. In 2005, Kony was indicted by the International Criminal Court for crimes against humanity. Uganda and the African Union had been actively engaged in finding Kony for a long time.

Even the United States had already been involved in the fight against Kony. Four years before the movie, US President George W. Bush authorized Operation Lightning Thunder directing the United States Africa Command to provide assistance to the Ugandan military in its fight against Kony. Two years before the movie, President Barack Obama signed the Lord's Resistance Army Disarmament and Northern Uganda Recovery Act, and six months before the movie he sent 100 combat troops to Africa to directly find and disarm Kony. By no means was there any need to "raise awareness" among the people whose job it was to be aware of Kony.

Kony 2012 was slacktivism at its very worst. It took a world issue that, while unknown to most Western people on the street, was very well known to everyone involved with it; and with the message of "raising awareness" it unnecessarily took millions of dollars from people who believed their money was going to be used to solve a problem, as if nobody had ever thought to try and solve it before.

The whole idea of "raising awareness" is used far too often to justify practically anything and everything. People ask "But isn't it good to raise awareness of issue X or issue Y," and I say, no, it's not always a good thing to do. We should only spend money raising awareness when the target audience consists of the people who are in a position to actually do something about the issue, but aren't because they're unaware of it. Raising awareness of Joseph Kony among 100 million American students did nothing for the Ugandan military teams who have been engaged full-time in fighting him since 2004. Raising awareness of something like breast cancer is almost always pointless; the only people I can think of who aren't aware of it are pre-Kindergarten, and aren't likely to make sizable donations to research.

Raising awareness with Facebook "Like" buttons certainly does no harm, 15 but it's called slacktivism for a reason. By doing it, you're slacking. You're only making yourself feel good. If you really care about the issue, find out what group is actually out there on the ground working to solve it, find out what their real needs are, and do whatever it takes. Probably it involves writing a check. If you can't afford to give, and you feel that clicking the "Like" button is better than doing nothing at all, then first trouble yourself to research if this issue is even real. My whole job here at *Skeptoid* is basically learning to separate what's real from what's not, and in my experience, I've found that most online slacktivism campaigns (and I do mean "most") are bogus. They're based on bad information, bad science, and are hoaxes as often as not.

As an example, let's say your big passion is animal welfare. What are you likely to do when someone sends you a picture similar to the one of cats being spayed and neutered in an apparent chamber of vivisection horrors? That campaign of misinformation *harms* your cause. *It makes you a less effective activist.* Slacktivism is not just ineffective, it is counterproductive.

I hereby, officially, expand the definition of slacktivism to include not only "Like" buttons, online petitions, retweets, and other such desktop actions; but also to include any activism of *any* sort for a cause that you did not research personally and thoroughly enough to determine its validity.

Keep in mind that causes like being opposed to human slavery are not really all that revolutionary. It's not exactly a courageous act of defiance to say "People should not be enslaved." That's something nearly everyone agrees with. When you see a photo or story online of something that appears to be way over the line of what the average person would do, your red flag of skepticism should go way up. Maybe it's true as reported, but chances are better than even that the story or picture is misattributed, exaggerated, or otherwise wrong. Research it and find out. Clear the misinformation out of your cause. Be a good activist, never a slacktivist.

READING THE TEXT

1. Define in your own words what Dunning means by "slacktivism."

2. Why does Dunning consider *Kony 2012* "slacktivism at its very worst" (para. 13)?

3. Explain how, in Dunning's view, slacktivism can be "counterproductive" (para. 16).

4. Characterize Dunning's tone here. How does it affect your response to his argument?

READING THE SIGNS

1. Write an essay in which you support, refute, or modify Dunning's charge that *Kony 2012* was "little more than financial exploitation" (para. 10). Be sure to include in your argument an analysis of the film itself.

2. In an essay, write your own evaluation of the effectiveness of online petitions and "Like" buttons that are in service of a social or political cause. To develop your ideas, interview acquaintances who are regular participants in such awareness-raising campaigns, focusing on both their motives for doing so and their sense of such actions' effectiveness.

3. **CONNECTING TEXTS**   Adopting Dunning's perspective on slacktivism, write a response to S. Craig Watkins's "The Evolution of #Black Twitter" (p. 445). How would he assess Watkins's claim, for instance, that "'#IfTheyGunned-MeDown' was not a passive form of civic engagement. It was aware of and

contested public discourses about race, demanded social justice, and changed the behavior of news editors across the country" (para. 13).

4. **CONNECTING TEXTS**   In "Inside Facebook's (Totally Insane, Unintentionally Gigantic, Hyperpartisan) Political-Media Machine" (p. 415), John Hermann outlines the ease with which Facebook news feeds can be manipulated by a politically motivated organization. Given his revelations, and Dunning's views on social media activism, write an essay in which you assess the extent to which the efficacy of online activism may be compromised by such news feeds. To develop your essay, visit some online news feeds and scrutinize them for evidence of fake news or other misinformation about social causes.

5. In an essay, compare slacktivism to "public shaming," both of which are individuals' uses of social media to draw attention to a cause or event. Be sure to ground your discussion in particular examples of social media activism and public shaming.

BROOKE GLADSTONE

Influencing Machines: The Echo Chambers of the Internet

Now that graphic novels are receiving the same scholarly attention and respect as traditional publications, why shouldn't there be graphic cultural studies texts? Oh wait, there already are. Joining such books as the Pantheon *For Beginners* series, Brooke Gladstone presents here, in graphic form, a lecture on the phenomenon of the niche-media "echo chamber" effect: i.e., the way that highly segmented media outlets play back to their customers exactly the worldview that they already have, effectively hardening existing ideological divisions in the country as Americans construct conflicting realities. Gladstone's pithy presentation can help explain Donald Trump's takeover of the Republican Party and victory in the 2016 presidential election, as well as the reason why it is so hard to get anywhere in discussions of such serious issues as global climate change and abortion. Brooke Gladstone is the host and managing editor of the National Public Radio newsmagazine, *On the Media*, and the author of *The Influencing Machine: Brooke Gladstone on the Media* (2012), from which this selection is taken.

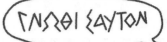

BACK BEFORE THERE WERE MEDIA OUTLETS, an ancient

traveler noted a fateful warning carved on the temple of the Oracle of
Delphi (a notorious newsmaker). It read: "Know thyself."

Now the media cover the world like cloudy water. We have to
consciously filter it. In an era when everything is asserted and anything
denied, we really need to know who we are and how our brains work.

Humans run on emotion, assumption, and impulse. We can't function
on logic alone. People who can't feel pleasure or preference because of damage to the orbital
prefrontal cortex are paralyzed by the simple decisions most of us make effortlessly every day.
The blue pen or the black pen? Mary or Sue? Any choice—whether of a mate or a breakfast
cereal—engulfs them in a quicksand of pros and cons.

But emotion, assumption, and impulse also allow us to weave cozy cocoons of
unexamined prejudice and received wisdom. They shield us from the pain of unwelcome
information. William James once said that "the greatest enemy of any one of our truths may
be the rest of our truths." So you have to ask yourself . . . well, here's how James Fitzjames
Stephen framed the key questions back in 1873 . . .

What do you think of yourself?
What do you think of the world?... They
are riddles of the Sphinx, and in some way or other
we must deal with them. If we decide to leave them
unanswered, that is a choice; if we waver in our
answer, that, too, is a choice: but whatever choice
we make, we make it at our peril...

We stand on a mountain pass in
the midst of whirling snow and blinding mist
through which we get glimpses now and then of paths
which may be deceptive. If we stand still we shall be
frozen to death. If we take the wrong road we shall
be dashed to pieces. We do not certainly know
whether there is any right one.
What must we do?

Many say that the Internet's ability to link like-minded souls everywhere fosters the creation of virtually impermeable echo chambers.

The echo chambers give rise to cybercascades: when a "fact" sent by one person spreads in a geometric progression to others until millions of people around the world potentially believe it.

Cut off from dissenters, the chambers fill with an unjustified sense of certainty. It's called **incestuous amplification**, a term first applied to isolated military planners who base their strategies on flawed assumptions.

Incestuous amplification can occur in any sphere, even without the Internet. But it helps.

Real estate bubble? Fuggedabboutit!

Hint: When you hear a group of guys called "Masters of the Universe," **run!**

Cass Sunstein cites many studies showing how people who talk only to like-minded others grow more extreme. They **marginalize the moderates**...

...and **demonize** dissenters. The greatest danger of echo chambers is unjustified **extremism**. It's an ongoing **threat** to our **democracy**.

READING THE TEXT

1. According to Gladstone, how do media today mirror back to their consumers their existing political and worldviews?

2. Define in your own words the terms "echo chamber" and "incestuous amplification" (p. 413).

3. Why does Gladstone say the "the technology that expands our worldview can also diminish it" (p. 414)?

READING THE SIGNS

1. Write a rhetorical analysis of the effect of the graphic presentation that Gladstone uses to make her points.

2. Write a brief essay that presents the same message that Gladstone is conveying. Then compare your prose version with her graphic design. What different effects do they have on a reader? Share your essay with the class.

3. **CONNECTING TEXTS**   In an essay, discuss the extent to which the echo chamber effect influenced the 2016 presidential election. To develop your ideas, you might consult John Hermann's "Inside Facebook's (Totally Insane, Unintentionally Gigantic, Hyperpartisan) Political-Media Machine" (below), Jessica Contrera's "Most Young People Don't Vote. Condescending to Them Isn't Helping." (p. 190), and Lilliana Mason's "Why Are Americans So Angry This Election Season?" (p. 510).

4. Write an essay in response to Gladstone's question "How do we develop intellectually or morally if we can evade encounters with the unfamiliar, the unwelcome, and the unimagined?" (p. 414).

JOHN HERRMAN

Inside Facebook's (Totally Insane, Unintentionally Gigantic, Hyperpartisan) Political-Media Machine

John Herrman's in-depth analysis of the way in which Facebook has come to dominate not only the dissemination of the news in America, but exactly what news individual Facebook subscribers receive, is a case study in the "echo chamber" effect of contemporary news consumption. Revealing the ways in which Facebook employs the same data mining techniques that it uses to construct consumer profiles for marketing purposes, Herrman shows how your Facebook news feed can become "bluer" or "redder," depending upon the kinds of comments that appear on your page. For with such third-party sources as the Liberty Alliance promoting ideological news content on Facebook in essentially the same way that consumer products merchandisers market their goods on social media, the inevitable outcome is the construction of a myriad of ideological closed circuits — with those within the circuit "sharing" the same ever-expanding messages. And there's no way out of the situation, Herrman concludes, for "Facebook's primacy is a foregone conclusion, and the question of Facebook's relationship to political discourse is absurd — they're one and the same." John Herrman is a David Carr fellow at the *New York Times*.

Open your Facebook feed. What do you see? A photo of a close friend's child. An automatically generated slide show commemorating six years of friendship between two acquaintances. An eerily on-target ad for something you've been meaning to buy. A funny video. A sad video. A recently live video. Lots of video; more video than you remember from before. A somewhat less-on-target ad. Someone you saw yesterday feeling blessed. Someone you haven't seen in 10 years feeling worried.

And then: A family member who loves politics asking, "Is this really who we want to be president?" A co-worker, whom you've never heard talk about politics, asking the same about a different candidate. A story about Donald Trump that "just can't be true" in a figurative sense. A story about Donald Trump that "just can't be true" in a literal sense. A video of Bernie Sanders speaking, overlaid with text, shared from a source you've never seen before, viewed 15 million times. An article questioning Hillary Clinton's honesty; a headline questioning Donald Trump's sanity. A few shares that go a bit too far: headlines you would never pass along yourself but that you might tap, read and probably not forget.

Maybe you've noticed your feed becoming bluer; maybe you've felt it becoming redder. Either way, in the last year, it has almost certainly become more intense. You've seen a lot of media sources you don't recognize and a lot of posts bearing no memorable brand at all. You've seen politicians and celebrities and corporations weigh in directly; you've probably seen posts from the candidates themselves. You've seen people you're close to and people you're not, with increasing levels of urgency, declare it is now time to speak up, to take a stand, to set aside allegiances or hangups or political correctness or hate.

Facebook, in the years leading up to this election, hasn't just become nearly ubiquitous among American internet users; it has centralized online news consumption in an unprecedented way. According to the company, its site is used by more than 200 million people in the United States each month, out of a total population of 320 million. A 2016 Pew study found that 44 percent of Americans read or watch news on Facebook. These are approximate exterior dimensions and can tell us only so much. But we can know, based on these facts alone, that Facebook is hosting a huge portion of the political conversation in America.

The Facebook product, to users in 2016, is familiar yet subtly expansive. Its algorithms have their pick of text, photos and video produced and posted by established media organizations large and small, local and national, openly partisan or nominally unbiased. But there's also a new and distinctive sort of operation that has become hard to miss: political news and advocacy pages made specifically for Facebook, uniquely positioned and cleverly engineered to reach audiences exclusively in the context of the news feed. These are news sources that essentially do not exist outside of Facebook, and you've probably never heard of them. They have names like Occupy Democrats; The Angry Patriot; US Chronicle; Addicting Info; RightAlerts; Being Liberal; Opposing Views; Fed-Up Americans; American News; and hundreds more. Some of these pages have millions of followers; many have hundreds of thousands.

Using a tool called CrowdTangle, which tracks engagement for Facebook pages across the network, you can see which pages are most shared, liked and commented on, and which pages dominate the conversation around election topics. Using this data, I was able to speak to a wide array of the activists and entrepreneurs, advocates and opportunists, reporters and hobbyists who together make up 2016's most disruptive, and least understood, force in media.

Individually, these pages have meaningful audiences, but cumulatively, their audience is gigantic: tens of millions of people. On Facebook, they rival the reach of their better-funded counterparts in the political media, whether corporate giants like CNN or the *New York Times*, or openly ideological web operations like Breitbart or Mic. And unlike traditional media organizations, which have spent years trying to figure out how to lure readers out of the Facebook ecosystem and onto their sites, these new publishers are happy to live inside the world that Facebook has created. Their pages are accommodated but not actively courted by the company and are not a major part of its public messaging about media. But they are, perhaps, the purest expression of Facebook's design and of the incentives coded into its algorithm — a system that has already reshaped the web and has now inherited, for better or for worse, a great deal of America's political discourse.

In 2006, when Mark Zuckerberg dropped out of college to run his rapidly expanding start-up, Mark Provost was a student at Rogers State University in Claremore, Okla., and going through a rough patch. He had transferred restlessly between schools, and he was taking his time to graduate; a stock-picking hobby that grew into a promising source of income had fallen apart. His outlook was further darkened by the financial crisis and by the years of personal unemployment that followed. When the Occupy movement began, he quickly got on board. It was only then, when Facebook was closing in on its billionth user, that he joined the network.

Now 36, Provost helps run US Uncut, a left-leaning Facebook page and website with more than 1.5 million followers, about as many as MSNBC has, from his apartment in Philadelphia. (Sample headlines: "Bernie Delegates

Want You to See This DNC Scheme to Silence Them" and "This Sanders Delegate Unleashing on Hillary Clinton Is Going Absolutely Viral.") He frequently contributes to another popular page, The Other 98%, which has more than 2.7 million followers.

Occupy got him on Facebook, but it was the 2012 election that showed   10 him its potential. As he saw it, that election was defined by social media. He mentioned a set of political memes that now feel generationally distant: Clint Eastwood's empty chair at the 2012 Republican National Convention and Mitt Romney's debate gaffe about "binders full of women." He thought it was a bit silly, but he saw in these viral moments a language in which activists like him could spread their message.

Provost's page now communicates frequently in memes, images with overlaid text. "May I suggest," began one, posted in May 2015, when opposition to the Trans-Pacific Partnership was gaining traction, "the first 535 jobs we ship overseas?" Behind the text was a photo of Congress. Many are more earnest. In an image posted shortly thereafter, a photo of Bernie Sanders was overlaid with a quote: "If Germany, Denmark, Sweden and many more provide tuition-free college," read the setup, before declaring in larger text, "we should be doing the same." It has been shared more than 84,000 times and liked 75,000 more. Not infrequently, this level of zeal can cross into wishful thinking. A post headlined "Did Hillary Clinton Just Admit on LIVE TV That Her Iraq War Vote Was a Bribe?" was shared widely enough to merit a response from Snopes, which called it "quite a stretch."

This year, political content has become more popular all across the platform: on homegrown Facebook pages, through media companies with a growing Facebook presence and through the sharing habits of users in general. But truly Facebook-native political pages have begun to create and refine a new approach to political news: cherry-picking and reconstituting the most effective tactics and tropes from activism, advocacy and journalism into a potent new mixture. This strange new class of media organization slots seamlessly into the news feed and is especially notable in what it asks, or doesn't ask, of its readers. The point is not to get them to click on more stories or to engage further with a brand. The point is to get them to share the post that's right in front of them. Everything else is secondary.

While Web publishers have struggled to figure out how to take advantage of Facebook's audience, these pages have thrived. Unburdened of any allegiance to old forms of news media and the practice, or performance, of any sort of ideological balance, native Facebook page publishers have a freedom that more traditional publishers don't: to engage with Facebook purely on its terms. These are professional Facebook users straining to build media companies, in other words, not the other way around.

From a user's point of view, every share, like or comment is both an act of speech and an accretive piece of a public identity. Maybe some people want to be identified among their networks as news junkies, news curators or as some sort of objective and well-informed reader. Many more people simply want to share specific beliefs, to tell people what they think or, just as important, what they don't. A newspaper-style story or a dry, matter-of-fact headline is adequate for this purpose. But even better is a headline, or meme, that skips straight to an ideological conclusion or rebuts an argument.

Rafael Rivero is an acquaintance of Provost's who, with his twin brother, 15 Omar, runs a page called Occupy Democrats, which passed three million followers in June. This accelerating growth is attributed by Rivero, and by nearly every left-leaning page operator I spoke with, not just to interest in the election but especially to one campaign in particular: "Bernie Sanders is the Facebook candidate," Rivero says. The rise of Occupy Democrats essentially mirrored the rise of Sanders's primary run. On his page, Rivero started quoting text from Sanders's frequent email blasts, turning them into Facebook-ready memes with a consistent aesthetic: colors that pop, yellow on black. Rivero says that it's clear what his audience wants. "I've probably made 10,000 graphics, and it's like running 10,000 focus groups," he said. (Clinton was and is, of course, widely discussed by Facebook users: According to the company, in the last month 40.8 million people "generated interactions" around the candidate. But Rivero says that in the especially engaged, largely oppositional left-wing-page ecosystem, Clinton's message and cautious brand didn't carry.)

Because the Sanders campaign has come to an end, these sites have been left in a peculiar position, having lost their unifying figure as well as their largest source of engagement. Audiences grow quickly on Facebook but can disappear even more quickly; in the case of left-leaning pages, many had accumulated followings not just by speaking to Sanders supporters but also by being intensely critical, and often utterly dismissive, of Clinton.

Now that the nomination contest is over, Rivero has turned to making anti-Trump content. A post from earlier this month got straight to the point: "Donald Trump is unqualified, unstable and unfit to lead. Share if you agree!" More than 40,000 people did.

"It's like a meme war," Rivero says, "and politics is being won and lost on social media."

In retrospect, Facebook's takeover of online media looks rather like a slow-motion coup. Before social media, web publishers could draw an audience one of two ways: through a dedicated readership visiting its home page or through search engines. By 2009, this had started to change. Facebook had more than 300 million users, primarily accessing the service through desktop browsers, and publishers soon learned that a widely shared link could produce substantial traffic. In 2010, Facebook released widgets that publishers could embed on their sites, reminding readers to share, and these tools were widely deployed. By late 2012, when Facebook passed a billion users, referrals from the social network were sending visitors to publishers' websites at rates sometimes comparable to Google, the web's previous de facto distribution hub. Publishers took note of what worked on Facebook and adjusted accordingly.

This was, for most news organizations, a boon. The flood of visitors 20 aligned with two core goals of most media companies: to reach people and to make money. But as Facebook's growth continued, its influence was intensified by broader trends in internet use, primarily the use of smart-phones, on which Facebook became more deeply enmeshed with users' daily routines. Soon, it became clear that Facebook wasn't just a source of readership; it was, increasingly, where readers lived.

Facebook, from a publisher's perspective, had seized the web's means of distribution by popular demand. A new reality set in, as a social-media net-work became an intermediary between publishers and their audiences. For media companies, the ability to reach an audience is fundamentally altered, made greater in some ways and in others more challenging. For a dedicated Facebook user, a vast array of sources, spanning multiple media and indus-tries, is now processed through the same interface and sorting mechanism, alongside updates from friends, family, brands and celebrities.

From the start, some publishers cautiously regarded Facebook as a resource to be used only to the extent that it supported their existing busi-nesses, wary of giving away more than they might get back. Others embraced it more fully, entering into formal partnerships for revenue sharing and video production, as the *New York Times* has done. Some new-media start-ups, most notably BuzzFeed, have pursued a comprehensively Facebook-centric production-and-distribution strategy. All have eventually run up against the same reality: A company that can claim nearly every internet-using adult as a user is less a partner than a context — a self-contained marketplace to which you have been granted access but which functions according to rules and incentives that you cannot control.

The news feed is designed, in Facebook's public messaging, to "show people the stories most relevant to them" and ranks stories "so that what's most important to each person shows up highest in their news feeds." It is a framework built around personal connections and sharing, where value is both expressed and conferred through the concept of engagement. Of course, engagement, in one form or another, is what media businesses have always sought, and provocation has always sold news. But now the incen-tives are literalized in buttons and written into software.

Any sufficiently complex system will generate a wide variety of results, some expected, some not; some desired, others less so. On July 31, a Facebook page called Make America Great posted its final story of the day. "No Media Is Telling You About the Muslim Who Attacked Donald Trump, So We Will . . .," read the headline, next to a small avatar of a pointing and yell-ing Trump. The story was accompanied by a photo of Khizr Khan, the father of a slain American soldier. Khan spoke a few days earlier at the Democratic National Convention, delivering a searing speech admonishing Trump for his comments about Muslims. Khan, pocket Constitution in hand, was juxta-posed with the logo of the Muslim Brotherhood in Egypt. "It is a sad day in

America," the caption read, "where we the people must expose the TRUTH because the media is in the tank for 1 Presidential Candidate!"

Readers who clicked through to the story were led to an external web-   25
site, called Make America Great Today, where they were presented with a brief write-up blended almost seamlessly into a solid wall of fleshy ads. Khan, the story said — between ads for "(1) Odd Trick to 'Kill' Herpes Virus for Good" and "22 Tank Tops That Aren't Covering Anything" — is an agent of the Muslim Brotherhood and a "promoter of Islamic Shariah law." His late son, the story suggests, could have been a "Muslim martyr" working as a double agent. A credit link beneath the story led to a similar-looking site called Conservative Post, from which the story's text was pulled verbatim. Conservative Post had apparently sourced its story from a longer post on a right-wing site called Shoebat.com.

Within 24 hours, the post was shared more than 3,500 times, collecting a further 3,000 reactions — thumbs-up likes, frowning emoji, angry emoji — as well as 850 comments, many lengthy and virtually all impassioned. A modest success. Each day, according to Facebook's analytics, posts from the Make America Great page are seen by 600,000 to 1.7 million people. In July, articles posted to the page, which has about 450,000 followers, were shared, commented on or liked more than four million times, edging out, for example, the Facebook page of *USA Today*.

Make America Great, which inhabits the fuzzy margins of the political Facebook page ecosystem, is owned and operated by a 35-year-old online marketer named Adam Nicoloff. He started the page in August 2015 and runs it from his home outside St. Louis. Previously, Nicoloff provided web services and marketing help for local businesses; before that, he worked in restaurants. Today he has shifted his focus to Facebook pages and websites that he administers himself. Make America Great was his first foray into political pages, and it quickly became the most successful in a portfolio that includes men's lifestyle and parenting.

Nicoloff's business model is not dissimilar from the way most publishers use Facebook: build a big following, post links to articles on an outside website covered in ads and then hope the math works out in your favor. For many, it doesn't: Content is expensive, traffic is unpredictable and website ads are both cheap and alienating to readers. But as with most of these Facebook-native pages, Nicoloff's content costs comparatively little, and the sheer level of interest in Trump and in the type of inflammatory populist rhetoric he embraces has helped tip Nicoloff's system of advertising arbitrage into serious profitability. In July, visitors arriving to Nicoloff's website produced a little more than $30,000 in revenue. His costs, he said, total around $8,000, partly split between website hosting fees and advertising buys on Facebook itself.

Then, of course, there's the content, which, at a few dozen posts a day, Nicoloff is far too busy to produce himself. "I have two people in the

Philippines who post for me," Nicoloff said, "a husband-and-wife combo." From 9 a.m. Eastern time to midnight, the contractors scour the internet for viral political stories, many explicitly pro-Trump. If something seems to be going viral elsewhere, it is copied to their site and promoted with an urgent headline. (The Khan story was posted at the end of the shift, near midnight Eastern time, or just before noon in Manila.) The resulting product is raw and frequently jarring, even by the standards of this campaign. "There's No Way I'll Send My Kids to Public School to Be Brainwashed by the LGBT Lobby," read one headline, linking to an essay ripped from Glenn Beck's The Blaze; "Alert: UN Backs Secret Obama Takeover of Police; Here's What We Know …," read another, copied from a site called The Federalist Papers Project. In the end, Nicoloff takes home what he jokingly described as a "doctor's salary" — in a good month, more than $20,000.

Terry Littlepage, an internet marketer based in Las Cruces, N.M., has taken this model even further. He runs a collection of about 50 politically themed Facebook pages with names like The American Patriot and My Favorite Gun, which push visitors to a half-dozen external websites, stocked with content aggregated by a team of freelancers. He estimates that he spends about a thousand dollars a day advertising his pages on Facebook; as a result, they have more than 10 million followers. In a good month, Littlepage's properties bring in $60,000.

Nicoloff and Littlepage say that Trump has been good for business, but each admits to some discomfort. Nicoloff, a conservative, says that there were other candidates he preferred during the Republican primaries but that he had come around to the nominee. Littlepage is also a recent convert. During the primaries, he was a Cruz supporter, and he even tried making some left-wing pages on Facebook but discovered that they just didn't make him as much money.

In their angry, cascading comment threads, Make America Great's followers express no such ambivalence. Nearly every page operator I spoke to was astonished by the tone their commenters took, comparing them to things like torch-wielding mobs and sharks in a feeding frenzy. No doubt because of the page's name, some Trump supporters even mistake Nicoloff's page for an official organ of the campaign. Nicoloff says that he receives dozens of messages a day from Trump supporters, expecting or hoping to reach the man himself. Many, he says, are simply asking for money.

Many of these political news pages will likely find their cachet begin to evaporate after Nov. 8. But one company, the Liberty Alliance, may have found a way to create something sustainable and even potentially transformational, almost entirely within the ecosystem of Facebook. The Georgia-based firm was founded by Brandon Vallorani, formerly of Answers in Genesis, the organization that opened a museum in Kentucky promoting a literal biblical creation narrative. Today the Liberty Alliance has around 100 sites in its network, and about 150 Facebook pages, according to Onan Coca, the company's 36-year-old editor in chief. He estimates their cumulative follower count to be at least 50 million. Among the company's partners are the former congressman Allen West, the 2008 election personality Joe the Plumber, the conservative actor Kirk Cameron and the former "Saturday Night Live" cast member Victoria Jackson. Then there are Liberty's countless news-oriented pages, which together have become an almost ubiquitous presence on right-leaning political Facebook in the last few years. Their names are instructive and evocative: Eagle Rising; Fighting for Trump; Patriot Tribune; Revive America; US Herald; The Last Resistance.

A dozen or so of the sites are published in-house, but posts from the company's small team of writers are free to be shared among the entire network. The deal for a would-be Liberty Alliance member is this: You bring the name and the audience, and the company will build you a prefab site, furnish it with ads, help you fill it with content and keep a cut of the revenue. Coca told me the company brought in $12 million in revenue last year. (The company declined to share documentation further corroborating his claims about followers and revenue.)

Because the pages are run independently, the editorial product is varied. But it is almost universally tuned to the cadences and styles that seem to work best on partisan Facebook. It also tracks closely to conservative Facebook media's big narratives, which, in turn, track with the Trump campaign's messaging: Hillary Clinton is a crook and possibly mentally unfit; ISIS is winning; Black Lives Matter is the real racist movement; Donald Trump alone can save us; the system — all of it — is rigged. Whether the Liberty Alliance succeeds or fails will depend, at least in part, on Facebook's algorithm. Systemic changes to the ecosystem arrive through algorithmic adjustments, and the company recently adjusted the news feed to "further reduce clickbait headlines." 35

For now, the network hums along, mostly beneath the surface. A post from a Liberty Alliance page might find its way in front of a left-leaning user who might disagree with it or find it offensive, and who might choose to engage with the friend who posted it directly. But otherwise, such news exists primarily within the feeds of the already converted, its authorship obscured, its provenance unclear, its veracity questionable. It's an environment that's at best indifferent and at worst hostile to traditional media brands; but for this new breed of page operator, it's mostly upside. In front of largely hidden and utterly sympathetic audiences, incredible narratives can take shape, before emerging, mostly formed, into the national discourse.

Consider the trajectory of a post from August, from a Facebook page called Patriotic Folks, the headline of which read, "Spread This: Media Rigging the Polls, Hiding New Evidence Proving Trump Is Winning." The article cited a litany of social-media statistics highlighting Trump's superior engagement numbers, among them Trump's Facebook following, which is nearly twice as large as Clinton's. "Don't listen to the lying media — the only legitimate attack they have left is Trump's poll numbers," it said. "Social media proves the GOP nominee has strong foundation and a firm backing."

The story spread across this right-wing Facebook ecosystem, eventually finding its way to Breitbart and finally to Sean Hannity's "Morning Minute," where he read through the statistics to his audience.

Before Hannity signed off, he posed a question: "So, does that mean anything?" It's a version of the question that everyone wants to answer about Facebook and politics, which is whether the site's churning political warfare is actually changing minds — or, for that matter, beginning to change the political discourse as a whole. How much of what happens on the platform is a reflection of a political mood and widely held beliefs, simply captured in a new medium, and how much of it might be created, or intensified, by the environment it provides? What is Facebook doing to our politics?

Appropriately, the answer to this question can be chosen and shared on Facebook in whichever way you prefer. You might share this story from the *New York Times Magazine*, wondering aloud to your friends whether our democracy has been fundamentally altered by this publishing-and-advertising platform of unprecedented scale. Or you might just relax and find some memes to share from one of countless pages that will let you air your political id. But for the page operators, the question is irrelevant to the task at hand. Facebook's primacy is a foregone conclusion, and the question of Facebook's relationship to political discourse is absurd — they're one and the same. As Rafael Rivero put it to me, "Facebook is where it's all happening."

READING THE TEXT

1. How do Facebook news feeds differ from traditional news sources, according to Herrman?

2. Explain in your own words how Facebook determines what will appear in your news feeds.

3. Summarize how, according to Herrman, Mark Provost uses Facebook to promote his political agenda.

4. What Facebook-related strategies did Adam Nicoloff and Terry Littlepage use to encourage the election of Donald Trump in 2016?

5. What significance does Herrman find in the growth of Liberty Alliance?

READING THE SIGNS

1. If you have a Facebook page, analyze a week's worth of news feeds that you receive. What do your results reveal about Facebook's profile of you? To what extent do you think that profile is accurate? Alternatively, study the news feeds of relatives or acquaintances, and prepare a political profile based on your Facebook information alone. What response do the profiles' subjects have to your results?

2. **CONNECTING TEXTS** Read Brooke Gladstone's "Influencing Machines: The Echo Chambers of the Internet" (p. 410). Adopting her perspective, write an essay

in which you assess the applicability of the term "echo chamber" to describe Facebook's news feed practices.

3. **CONNECTING TEXTS**   In class, brainstorm ways that an ordinary citizen can try to escape the echo chamber effects of digital media. Use the class's results to formulate an essay that evaluates the extent to which digital technology is threatening the free flow of information that has long been considered a cornerstone of a democratic society. To develop your ideas, consult Ronald J. Deibert's "Black Code: Surveillence, Privacy, and the Dark Side of the Internet" (p. 386).

4. **CONNECTING TEXTS**   Write an essay that argues your response to Herrman's question "What is Facebook doing to our politics?" (para. 38). To develop your ideas, consult the Introduction to Chapter 7, "American Paradox: Culture, Conflict, and Contradiction in the U.S.A." (p. 515) and Lilliana Mason's "Why Are Americans So Angry This Election Season?" (p. 510).

TIMOTHY B. LEE

Pokémon Go *Is Everything That Is Wrong with Late Capitalism*

For a while in the summer of 2016, it looked like everyone on Earth was playing *Pokémon Go*, Nintendo's latest release of its gaming mega-sensation. And that, Timothy B. Lee argues in this economic analysis of the phenomenon, is exactly the problem. For the economics of online gaming tend to redistribute wealth away from those parts of the world that do not have a large digital footprint to those that do. And that is why the economies of such places as San Francisco and Santa Monica, California are booming, while much of the Midwest and the South stagnates. Ironically, then, even as everyone plays the same game, the social results are different, with some regions of America leaping ahead, and others falling far behind, producing a nation very much at odds with itself. Timothy B. Lee is a senior editor at Vox.com, where this selection originally appeared.

In July 2016, two things happened that will have long-lasting impact on American society and the global economy. First, the yield on the ten-year Treasury fell to a record low of 1.366 percent. Second, Nintendo released *Pokémon Go*, a mobile game that in a matter of days has become a viral sensation. These two developments are more closely connected than it might seem at first glance. Obviously, it would be ridiculous to claim that *Pokémon Go* is singlehandedly responsible for recent macroeconomic trends. But technology-based products like *Pokémon Go* explain a lot about the current state of the global economy.

If you were looking to have fun with some friends 50 years ago, you might have gone to a bowling alley. Maybe you would have hung out at a diner or gone to the movies. These were all activities that involved spending a certain amount of money in the local economy. That created opportunities for adults in your town to start and run small businesses. It also meant that a teenager who wanted to find a summer job could find one waiting tables or taking tickets at the movie theater.

You can spend money on *Pokémon Go* too. But the economics of the game are very different. When you spend money on items in the *Pokémon Go* world, it doesn't go into the pocket of a local Pokémon entrepreneur — it goes into the pockets of the huge California and Japan-based global companies that created *Pokémon Go*. There are, of course, some good things about this. *Pokémon Go* can be a much more affordable hobby than going to a bowling alley or the movies. In fact, you don't have to spend any money on it. And the explosion of options made possible by online platforms creates real value — the average teenager has vastly more options for games to play, movies to watch, and so forth than at any time in American history.

But the *Pokémon Go* economy also has some real downsides. One has to do with regional inequality. Nintendo and its partners are rumored to be earning more than $1 million per day from *Pokémon Go*. That money is flowing away from small and medium cities and toward big technology companies concentrated in big cities. And obviously *Pokémon Go* isn't the only example of this. Amazon is doing something similar in the retail industry, diverting business away from local retailers and sucking cash into its corporate headquarters in Seattle. Companies like Google, Facebook, and Vox Media are drawing ad dollars that previously went to local newspapers and television stations.

Of course, America has always had geographic industry clusters that [5] sold products nationwide — think about the Detroit auto business or the Hollywood movie industry. But there was an important difference: Major twentieth-century industries tended to generate a lot of opportunities in communities where their product was sold. A film might be made in Hollywood, but local people all over America had to build and operate movie theaters. Cars might be made in Detroit, but people all over the country had to run auto dealerships and car repair shops.

In contrast, a lot of internet-based businesses are so ethereal that they barely create any jobs in most markets. Smartphone platforms have created some jobs making apps, but app makers don't have to live in any particular location. In practice, they tend to be heavily concentrated in the same big cities as most other technology jobs. The result is that the internet economy is increasingly transforming America into two parallel economies. Cities on the receiving end of *Pokémon Go*–style money gushers are booming so much that acute housing shortages are causing rents to skyrocket. The rest of the country has barely seen an economic recovery at all.

In the twentieth century, new industries tended to create a lot of demand for capital. It took a lot of cash to build assembly lines and movie studios, of course. But beyond that, thousands of people all over the country would go to their local banks to finance the construction of movie theaters, auto dealerships, and so forth. This meant that people with capital to lend could almost always find people eager to borrow it to finance new business ventures. This, in turn, made the job of America's central bank, the Federal Reserve, relatively easy. Anytime the Fed wanted to boost growth, it could cut interest rates and get a burst of entrepreneurs starting new businesses.

But the *Pokémon Go* economy is different. Nintendo and its partners obviously needed to invest some cash in hiring programmers and designers to build the game. But the sums involved here are tiny compared with the cost of building a new car assembly line. And *Pokémon Go* seems unlikely to produce very many opportunities for complementary local businesses. People play on their smartphones, so there's no need for Pokémon cyber cafes. Smartphones are too cheap for smartphone repair shops to be a good business. And this seems to have severed the traditional link between capital accumulation and economic growth. Since 2008, the US economy has been awash in cheap capital. In a few places, especially Silicon Valley, that has created bubble-like conditions where every crazy idea seems to get funding.

Yet the total sums being invested in these areas are a fraction of the overall capital people have available to invest. And in the rest of the country, people are struggling to find any productive investment ideas. So interest rates keep falling as people increasingly despair of finding ways to get high returns from their savings. Ultimately, this situation hurts everyone, because it shows up as a shortfall of overall demand. Slow growth outside of big cities means that customers have less money to spend on games like *Pokémon Go*.

The success of *Pokémon Go* points to two big areas where policymakers 10 ought to change their approach. One is to relax housing policy to allow more people to move to areas where high-tech products are made. While the average resident of Kansas City or Baltimore might not have the skills to create the next great mobile game, he or she probably could find work as a schoolteacher, nurse, or construction worker in San Francisco or New York — but only if he or she is allowed to live within commuting distance of technology workers.

The other is to think harder about managing demand. There may be more that central banks can do to boost demand. If that doesn't work, then more direct income redistribution may be called for — taxing rich people in high-growth areas to fund expanded government services, wage subsidies, or even cash payments to people in slower-growing parts of the country.

READING THE TEXT

1. What connection does Lee see between the larger economy and games like *Pokémon Go*?

2. In your own words, what does Lee mean by "parallel economies" (para. 6)?

3. How do Internet-related businesses differ from America's traditional "geographic industry clusters" (para. 5), in Lee's view?

4. What solutions to economic disparities created by "the *Pokémon Go* economy" does Lee suggest?

READING THE SIGNS

1. In your journal, describe your typical recreational activities and hobbies. Where do they occur? In public places like movie theatres or coffeeshops? Or in private locations, such as your home or dorm room? How does your recreational behavior reflect what Lee calls "the *Pokémon Go* economy"?

2. In an essay, propose your own solutions to the problems of regional economic inequality that Lee outlines, including in your discussion an assessment of those that he presents.

3. Lee claims that the *Pokémon Go* economy "hurts everyone, because it shows up as a shortfall of overall demand" (para. 9). In class, brainstorm how the *Pokémon Go* economy may affect college students in particular, considering especially that they will be entering the workforce after graduation. Use the class discussion as a springboard for your own essay that examines the impact of Internet-based business on millennials.

4. Lee focuses more on *Pokémon Go*'s economic consequences than on it as a game. In an essay, conduct a semiotic analysis of the *Pokémon Go* game, trying to account for its popularity in American culture, especially among the young. You might base your essay in part on interviews conducted with *Pokémon Go* fans; in addition, you might consult the Introduction to this chapter, "The Cloud: Semiotics and the New Media" (p. 371).

NANCY JO SALES

From the Instamatic to Instagram: Social Media and the Secret Lives of Teenagers

For anyone who thinks that Instagram invented the selfie, Nancy Jo Sales has news for you: The selfie was effectively invented in the 1960s, when the Kodak Corporation released the Instamatic as a camera for teenage girls who "want to show off their pretty clothes and who they're friends with." An ethnographic study of how today's teenage girls use Instagram to construct and promote themselves on the Internet, Sales's text shows how digital culture hasn't really changed anything fundamentally; it has only made it a lot easier, and faster, for girls to send "'really hot pictures of [themselves] even though [they] don't look like that in real life.'" Nancy Jo Sales is the author of *American Girls: Social Media and the Secret Lives of Teenagers* (2016), from which this selection is taken.

Behind the Lens

Kids started having their own cameras, en masse, in the 1960s. Kodak Instamatics, which came out in 1963, were inexpensive ($16) and easy to use, durable and small, the perfect size to fit in a child's pocket or the upper tray of a footlocker on its way to summer camp. The Instagram logo, in a conscious nod, echoes the look of the early Instamatics — a dark stripe on top, metallic on the bottom, with a round flat lens and viewfinder in the middle. The logo was nostalgic, also a confident announcement of how this new mobile app would continue to popularize photography as successfully as its symbolic predecessor. More than 50 million Instamatics were sold between 1963 and 1970, making it then the best-selling camera of all time. Between its launch in 2010, by two male Silicon Valley software engineers who met at Stanford, and 2015, Instagram gained over 400 million active users worldwide, more people than live in America, according to its own statistics.

Instamatics were also one of the first cameras marketed directly to girls. In 1932, Kodak had come out with a camera for boys, its Boy Scout Brownie (a variation on its popular Brownie camera, introduced in 1900), appealing to male youths who fancied themselves living adventurous lives as campers and explorers, near heroic lives which deserved documentation. With the Instamatic, Kodak realized it had a vast new demographic to target: teen girls. But the pitch was very different. It said that girls could use cameras to become popular.

Teenagers of both sexes were experiencing the rapid cultural changes under way in the '60s, but the lives of girls especially were transforming. They were more sexually liberated than girls in the past, as well as more sexualized by the media and advertising, and they were more independent. More of them either worked part-time or had access to their parents' disposable incomes in a strong economy — they had money to spend, with which they were buying more of the clothes and makeup that were relentlessly marketed to them. You can almost hear the unrepentant sexist Don Draper, of *Mad Men*, working up the Kodak pitch: "Why do girls want cameras?

They're sentimental, they're vain, they want to be popular, they want to show off their pretty clothes and who they're friends with. They want to make memories. And they want to look good in those memories."

Kodak sold its Instamatics to girls in ads infused with an aura of nostalgia (which Draper once described as "delicate, but potent"). An ad in *Seventeen* in 1968 urged girls to buy Instamatics before they returned to high school after summer vacation: *"What you're going back to deserves a great camera,"* said the tagline. "You can just imagine what's coming up," read the copy. "Homecoming parade. Games. Dances. Old friends and new faces. It makes sense to have a great camera. And it makes sense for it to be one of our Kodak Instamatic cameras. . . . It's one back-to-school outfit you really ought to have." It was as if a girl could relate to a technological device only if it offered the same advantages as a miniskirt.

The layout for the ad was accompanied by two candid-looking shots, 5 one of a pretty blond girl dressed as a cheerleader; she's surrounded by five basketball-player boys after a championship game. Their proud coach wields a trophy; they won. The girl is kissing one of the boys on the cheek; he seems to be the team's cute captain. The other photo shows the girl with this same boy; now it's prom night and she's wearing a virginal white dress and gloves. Her hair is in ringlets, a corsage is pinned to the strap of her gown; she's beaming. The boy, standing beside her, is looking suave in a white tux.

The message: cameras were tools for creating an idealized self, and pictures were a kind of self-promotion. And the ideal girl (in Kodak's view, a pretty, blond white girl) would have the attention of boys. If only everybody could see how popular she was.

Instagram gave girls that opportunity. The way many girls use the app is not so different from how girls have been taught to use photography for decades. The difference now lies in the chance to show the whole world one's beauty, boyfriends, special moments, and clothes, not just the other kids in school. And with that broadcasting power comes an enormous thrill: the chance to become not just popular, but actually famous. Famous for just being you.

"I think it's more of a challenge for you to go on a reality show and get people to fall in love with you for being you," Kim Kardashian told Barbara Walters on her *10 Most Fascinating People* special. Walters didn't point out that reality shows are actually scripted entertainment, and Kim didn't mention it, either.

Montclair, New Jersey

Valley Road runs through the center of Upper Montclair, the tonier section of town. The buildings there are quaint and small, many of them in the Tudor style familiar to suburbs of New York. The Dunkin' Donuts is like any other in the chain, with a logoed pink-and-orange sign showing a steaming cup of coffee. Through the window, on a Friday afternoon, you could see the place was teeming with middle-school-age kids, some standing on a couch by the window, bouncing and gesticulating.

Riley, Sophia, and Victoria approached the doughnut store tentatively.   10

"I'm not going in, I can't go in," Riley said, moving against the wall of the building so she would not be seen by anyone inside.

"Really?" said Sophia. "It's okay. It's all dying down."

"No, it isn't," Riley said. She was suddenly breathing rapidly. "I feel like I'm having an anxiety attack. Is this an anxiety attack?" she asked, her voice becoming high and thin.

Sophia and Victoria stared at her with concern, not knowing what to do.

"I know someone who gets them," Sophia said helpfully. "She takes   15 medicine."

Later Riley's mother told me Riley suffered from an anxiety disorder and was being treated with medication. "Sometimes I wonder whether that is why they attack her," her mother said, "because they know she's fragile."

"You go in first," Riley said. "What if Danny's in there? What if Zack's in there? What if they take pictures of me?" And then: "Get me a strawberry doughnut with sprinkles."

Sophia and Victoria ventured inside the store. They didn't often go in the Dunkin' Donuts on a Friday afternoon. That was when the popular kids — "the cliquey kids and thotty," or slutty, "girls in the shortest shorts" — congregated to "try and act cool," said Sophia.

Victoria and Sophia were not part of this crowd, as Riley was, or perhaps once had been. In fact, Sophia said that Riley had "shunned" her at times during that school year. "She gets influenced by other kids," Sophia said. "But she's my friend, so I'm going to stick by her. With social media it's really hard to know who your true friends are, and this is how you know, how someone treats you when everyone hates you."

Inside the store, there were around twenty kids, and all of them seemed   20 to be screaming. They sat on the brown-and-orange vinyl booths in front of half-empty boxes of doughnuts; they stood in clusters in the aisles, talking close up in one another's faces. There were boys in sweatpants and T-shirts, long shorts and sports jerseys, powdered sugar on their cheeks and lips; there were girls in short shorts and tank tops and crop tops, hands on hips.

There were three girls taking a selfie together, all doing the duckface, smizing — a word coined by former Victoria's Secret supermodel Tyra Banks for "smiling with your eyes."

They vamped for the camera, then peered into the screen, checking the photo.

"Oh, we look hot!" one of them exclaimed. "Post it!"

Kids were talking, yelling:

"Oh my God, she's so fake."

"So fake." 25

"I love your Instagram. You have good feed."

"I know."

"She gets like three hundred likes on every picture. I'm like, Stop it."

At Victoria's house, a white clapboard Colonial house, the girls were joined by another friend, Melinda, age thirteen; she was a girl from their school, white, with streaked blond hair, wearing shorts, a blue button-down, and Converse. Her mother was a university professor and her father a film editor. "I am so excited to be talking about this, because we never talk about social media, we just live on it," she said.

The girls sat around the dining room table eating their doughnuts and 30 the brownies Victoria's mother had left for them on a plate. Victoria's mother was picking up her little sister at soccer practice. The dining room was lined with windows looking out on a deep backyard where you could see round-breasted robins hopping in the grass.

The girls filled Melinda in on Riley's difficulty outside the Dunkin' Donuts.

"I can't believe I had an anxiety attack over this," Riley moaned. "I got afraid someone would post something about me if I went in there. That's what social media is doing. It's anxiety-causing and depressing."

"It causes so much drama," Sophia agreed, her mouth full of brownie. "You don't know how much drama I have over my phone."

"With girls our age, so much drama happens over social networking," Melinda told me. "Probably more stuff happens on my phone than in real life."

"I feel like we're living in a second world," Riley said. "There's a real 35 world and a second world," on social media.

As they started talking about all this, they became urgent and intense. They began talking fast, raising their voices, interrupting and overlapping one another.

"All we talk about all day is what's happening on our phones, but we never talk about how *weird* that is," Sophia said.

"I spend so much time on Instagram looking at people's pictures and sometimes I'll be like, Why am I spending my time on this? And yet I keep doing it," said Melinda.

"If I go on my phone to look at Snapchat," Riley said, "I go on it for like an hour, like a really long time, I lose track."

"The minute I start my homework I have to have my phone by me," 40 Sophia said, "to see what my friends are texting or if they're sending me texts, and then I'm automatically in a conversation. It's like someone is constantly tapping you on the shoulder, and you have to look. It's distracting."

All of them said they were in one or more group chats of four to eight friends and that they sent or received "hundreds" of texts a day. "Oh my God, at least three hundred," Sophia said. "I get a text, and it's like, *Oooooh*, I have to check that, like, Oh my God, what are they saying? I don't want to miss anything. I'll be like, Mom, it's really important drama, I have to solve it! But sometimes it'll be like nothing, like what kind of chips you eat.

"But I *need* my phone," Sophia added, "I can't survive without it. I stay up all night looking at my phone."

"Two weeks ago I really annoyed my parents by going on my phone too much, so my punishment was I had to delete my Instagram app on my phone for a week," Melinda said. "By the end of the week I was stressing, like, What if I am losing followers?"

"I've always wanted to delete my Instagram," Sophia said, "but then I think, I look so good in all my photos."

She logged on to her Instagram account to show me her page: it was 45 picture after picture of her face, all with the same mysterious, come-hither expression.

"The classic Sophia selfie, bite-tongue smile," she said with a laugh. "It's my brand."

All of them said they had Photoshopped their pictures and edited them with special filters and apps — especially their selfies. "I've darkened my lips and made my eyebrows on fleek," meaning on point, Sophia said. "I never post the first selfie I take. Sometimes it takes like seventy tries.

"Every time I post a selfie," she went on, "I need to check who's commenting — like, Oh my God, I'm getting so many comments. People are like, 'Oh my God gorgeous,' and you feel good about yourself. I'm so happy when I get likes. We're all obsessed with how many likes we get. Everyone says, I get no likes, I get no likes, but everyone says that even if they *get* likes — it never feels like enough. I feel like I'm brainwashed into wanting likes."

What was striking in hearing them talk about this was how conscious they were of what they were doing, their awareness of the inauthenticity of the self they presented on social media.

"It's funny it's called a 'selfie,'" Riley said, "because half the time it 50 doesn't even look like you. So you're getting people to like this picture of you that isn't even real."

The acquiring of likes has become a major theme in corporate marketing, of course; companies invest serious money in studying how to get social media users to like and tweet and post about their products. Social media users have become the most powerful of advertisers, taking word of mouth to a whole new level. For a *Frontline* segment in 2014, "Generation Like," technology writer Douglas Rushkoff went to Montclair to talk to teenagers about their role in building brands. "When a kid likes something online," Rushkoff said on-air, "a product or a brand or a celebrity, it becomes part of the identity that they broadcast to the world, the way a T-shirt or a bedroom poster defined me when I was a teen. For kids today, you are what you like. . . . And guess what? Getting people to be 'all about' something is big business." Including the business of social media itself — the more active users are, the more data about them social media companies can collect, and the higher they are valued, as they can then sell the data to other companies. "That's why companies need kids to stay online, clicking and liking and tweeting," Rushkoff told a group of Montclair high school students.

But the *Frontline* segment didn't touch upon why kids seek likes for themselves — or how their methods often mirror the very techniques companies use to market brands. The girls in Montclair said, for example, that they planned what time of day they posted, trying to hit prime times for getting likes — another central tenet of social media marketing. On the *Frontline* segment, *New York Times* writer Brooks Barnes talked about the "day by day, hour by hour" social media marketing strategy he witnessed in covering the marketing of *The Hunger Games* in 2012: "The goal is to create a controlled brushfire online."

"I always find a good time to post," Melinda said. "You don't want to post in the middle of the night when no one sees it. I was on vacation and there was a time difference, so I would literally stay up to two in the morning so I could post pictures at a certain time so more people here would like them. My mom was like, What are you doing?"

Melinda and Victoria told of how they had gone to a Katy Perry concert together and posted on Instagram almost identical pictures of Perry performing onstage, but Melinda's pictures had gotten more likes, because she had posted them at a more desirable time.

"I thought it meant people liked Melinda better," Victoria said.   55

"Oh, no, it's just because of when I posted," Melinda reassured her. "I'm obsessed with getting more likes than other people — I'm always comparing myself to see how many likes my photo got. I'll post a picture on Instagram and immediately start checking."

The captions that went with their posts were also a source of forethought, sometimes requiring a groupthink, like a brainstorming session on *Mad Men* — how to make them sound witty and clever?

"I work so hard on my captions," Riley said. "Everyone has that one group chat where they're like, Oh my God, help me with my captions, what should my caption be?"

The location of their photos was a crucial consideration as well. "I go to the woods to get really artsy lighting and stuff," said Sophia.

"You'll ask the people in your group chat, Should this be my location? 60 What should I do?" said Riley.

"You get more likes if you're someplace cool," Melinda explained.

"It's called 'good feed,'" Sophia said, "if you take good photos and use filters and a VSCO Cam," a spiffy camera and editing app, "and like, have like really good captions."

They said the most admired style of feed among their friends was the one they called "artsy" or "aesthetic." The "aesthetic" aesthetic evolved in the late 2000s with the 2007 advent of Tumblr and other sites devoted to the posting of one's own art, as well as aggregated images of art and fashion and photography. It's used to describe a sense that social media posting *is* art — or can be art, if it's "aesthetic" enough. (Not to be confused with, although perhaps related to, the "New Aesthetic" concept introduced by British artist and writer James Bridle in 2011 to describe the response to technology by artists working in the digital age.)

"You can, like, post a picture of your cereal," Sophia said, "but you have to make it aesthetic."

"Aesthetic" looks, aesthetically, like a manifestation of hipster style, as   65
exemplified by Sofia Coppola's *The Virgin Suicides*, with a dose of *Rookie* and *Real Simple* magazines. "Aesthetic" Instagrams show pictures of filtered pastel skies, girls with expressions bathed in ennui, vintage-looking buildings in black-and-white, and minimalistic bowls of steel-cut oats.

"People say, 'That's so my aesthetic,'" Sophia said. "And it means literally anything that they like. Like, you could say, 'Cheerios are so my aesthetic.'"

By 2015 "aesthetic" so dominated online culture it was already being satirized. *"Is it aesthetic? Is it aesthetic?"* asked teenage singer Ben J. Pierce (KidPOV) in his satirical "The Aesthetic Song" on YouTube. *"Put a bagel on a blanket — is it aesthetic?"*

"It's so much pressure to make your Instagram aesthetic," Victoria said with a groan. "You can't really do anything *wrong*. And if you do, people could laugh at you, like, Oh, look at her Instagram, it's so not aesthetic — it's so *basic*."

("Basic" was another thing entirely — basically the opposite of "aesthetic," referring to girls who were behind the trends, the purchasers of too-obvious brands, from Gap to Gucci.)

"How you look is all anybody cares about anymore," Sophia insisted,   70
becoming a bit agitated. "Being beautiful nowadays is seen as way better than being smart. It's terrible. Like if you're a supermodel on Instagram, everyone loves you. Like I do this, too, so I can't judge: if I find a supermodel on Instagram, I'll comment like, I love you so much. Even though they haven't done anything to help the world and they're literally just standing there looking pretty. People love them just 'cause they're beautiful. And like, being smart — no one cares about that. If people aren't pretty nowadays, they're done with their life. Like, Oh my God, I'm not pretty, I can't live life."

"The new word is 'goals,'" Sophia went on. "Everyone says 'goals.' You find a really pretty girl on Instagram and you're like, '*Goals.*' Goals to have my eyebrows like hers, goals to have my lips like hers, goals to have my hair like hers. You'll see on Instagram comments like, 'My goal is to look like her.' Think about it. That's a *goal*? No one cares about being smart anymore. If you're beautiful everyone will love you."

The other girls had stopped eating the brownies.

"But it's fun to post really hot pictures of yourself even though you don't look like that in real life," Sophia said with a toss of her head. "'Cause when I take a really pretty selfie, people will be like, Oh, gorgeous."

READING THE TEXT

1. Sales begins the selection with a description of the Kodak Instamatic camera, introduced in 1963. How does this historical reference situate her later discussion of social media engagement among some teens today?

2. Summarize in your own words the tone of the conversational interchange among the teens whom Sales describes in a donut store on pages 430–32.

3. Why does Sales consider teens' desire for more social media "likes" a matter of concern?

4. Much of this selection is based on transcripts that Sales produced from interviews with young women. How does this primary evidence work to affect your response to her article?

READING THE SIGNS

1. In your journal, write a response to the young woman whom Sales quotes as saying "How you look is all anybody cares about anymore. . . . And like, being smart — no one cares about that" (para. 70). If you can connect with her sentiments, explore why; if you do not, what advice would you give this person?

2. In class, brainstorm "goals" that students have, and then compare them to the goals Sales mentions in her essay. How do you account for similarities or differences between your class and Sales's interviewees, beyond the fact that the latter were pre-college age? Use the class discussion as a basis for your own essay in which you argue for what constitutes identifying "goals" among your cohort/peers.

3. **CONNECTING TEXTS**   Read "Students Addicted to Social Media" (p. 382), and use its discussion as a critical framework for an argument about the extent to which the girls whom Sales interviewed can be considered suffering from digital addiction.

4. In an essay, support, oppose, or qualify the proposition that young teens' use of social media should be strictly monitored by adults. Alternatively, adopt the perspective of an adult (a parent, say, or teacher), and write a letter to the girls in this selection informing them of the potential benefits and dangers of the ways in which they use social media.

5. **CONNECTING TEXTS**   Write an essay in which you argue whether social media encourage teens, like those whom Sales interviews, to adopt traditional codes of gendered behavior. To develop your ideas, you might consult danah boyd's "It's Complicated: MySpace vs. Facebook" (next page); although boyd does not focus on gender, she does make a parallel argument that social media reinforce economic and racial inequalities.

6. Visit the Facebook or Instagram sites of several acquaintances, and do a semiotic reading of the digitial image they construct for themselves. What signs do they use to create that image, and what messages about their identities are they sending to the world? Do you observe a discrepancy between the acquaintances' online profile and their real-life identity?

DANAH BOYD

It's Complicated: MySpace vs. Facebook

Once upon a time, almost everyone was on MySpace. Oh, there was
Friendster and Facebook, but Facebook was for networking adults
and a few Ivy League college students. Then, suddenly, everyone
was on Facebook. Well, not everyone, of course, and in this study
of the shift from MySpace to Facebook, danah boyd explains what
happened. Interviewing numerous Facebook users, boyd concludes
that a good deal of racial and class snobbery was involved in the
shift from one platform to another. So maybe the world of social networking isn't really drawing people together after all; it may only be
reproducing ancient conflicts and divisions. A principal researcher at
Microsoft Research and research assistant professor in media, culture,
and communication at New York University, boyd is the author of *It's
Complicated: The Social Lives of Networked Teens* (2014).

Segregation in Everyday Life

In the United States, racism is pervasive, if not always visible. Class politics intertwine with race, adding another dimension to existing social divisions. Teens are acutely aware of the power of race and class in shaping
their lives, even if they don't always have nuanced language to talk about
it; furthermore, just because teens live in a culture in which racism is ever
present doesn't mean that they understand how to deal with its complexities
or recognize its more subtle effects. Some don't realize how a history of racism shapes what they observe. Heather, a white sixteen-year-old from Iowa,
told me,

> I don't want to sound racist, but it is the black kids a lot of times that
> have the attitudes and are always talking back to the teachers, getting in
> fights around the school, starting fights around the school. I mean yeah,
> white kids of course get into their fights, but the black kids make theirs
> more public and so it's seen more often that oh, the black kids are such
> troublemakers.

In examining high school dynamics in the 1980s, linguist Penelope Eckert
argued that schools are organized by social categories that appear on the surface to be about activities but in practice are actually about race and class.[1]
I noticed this as I went through the rosters of various sports teams at a school

[1] Eckert, *Jocks and Burnouts*.

in North Carolina. At first, when I asked students about why different sports seemed to attract students of one race exclusively, they told me that it was just what people were into. Later, one white boy sheepishly explained that he liked basketball but that, at his school, basketball was a black sport and thus not an activity that he felt comfortable doing. As a result of norms and existing networks, the sports teams in many schools I visited had become implicitly coded and culturally divided by race. Many teens are reticent to challenge the status quo.

Even in schools at which teens prided themselves on being open-minded, I found that they often ignorantly reproduced racial divisions. For example, in stereotypical fashion, teens from more privileged backgrounds would point to having friends of different races as "proof" of their openness.[2] When I asked about racial divisions in more privileged schools or in schools situated in progressive communities, I regularly heard the postracial society mantra, with teens initially telling me that race did not matter in friend groups at their school. And then we'd log in to their Facebook or MySpace page and I would find clues that their schools were quite segregated. For example, I'd find that friend networks within diverse schools would be divided by race. When I'd ask teens to explain this, they'd tell me that the divisions I was seeing were because of who was in what classes or who played what sport, not realizing that racial segregation played a role in those aspects of school life, too.

While on a work trip in Colorado, I met a group of privileged teens who were in town because their parents were at the meeting I was attending. Bored with the adult conversations, I turned to the teens in a casual manner. I started talking with Kath, a white seventeen-year-old who attended an east coast private school renowned for its elite student body and its phenomenal diversity program. Our casual conversation turned to race dynamics in schools; she was a passionate, progressive teen who took the issue of race seriously. Curious to see how this played out in her community, I asked her if we could visit her Facebook page together. I offered her my computer, and she gleefully logged into her account. Given the small size of her school, I wasn't surprised that she was friends with nearly everyone from her grade and many students from other grades. I asked her to show me her photos so that we could look at the comments on them. Although her school had recruited students from diverse racial and ethnic backgrounds, most of those who had left comments on her profile were white. I pointed this out

[2]The tendency for people to downplay racism by talking about how they have friends of different races is so common that it is a frame through which people look at cross-race connections. In the 2012 book *Some of My Best Friends Are Black*, Tanner Colby describes the challenges of racial integration in the United States through four different case studies. In a more comedic treatment of the same issue, comedian Baratunde Thurston dedicates an entire chapter in *How to Be Black* to "how to be the black friend." He offers entertaining advice to black readers on how they can make white people feel comfortable by taking concrete steps to be a "good" black friend.

to her and asked her to bring up profiles of other students in her grade from different racial and ethnic backgrounds. In each case, the commenters were predominantly of the same broad racial or ethnic background as the profile owner. Kath was stunned and a bit embarrassed. In her head, race didn't matter at her school. But on Facebook people were spending their time interacting with people from similar racial backgrounds.

When I analyzed friending patterns on social network sites with youth,   5
I consistently found that race mattered. In large and diverse high schools where teens didn't befriend everyone in their school, their connections alone revealed racial preference. In smaller diverse schools, the racial dynamics were more visible by seeing who commented on each other's posts or who appeared tagged together in photographs. Only when I visited schools with low levels of diversity did race not seem to matter in terms of online connections. For example, in Nebraska, I met a young Muslim woman of Middle Eastern descent in a mostly white school. She had plenty of friends online and off, and not surprisingly, all were white. Of course, this did not mean that she was living in a world where ethnic differences didn't matter. Her classmates posted many comments about Middle Eastern Muslim terrorists on Facebook with caveats about how she was different.

Birds of a feather flock together, and personal social networks tend to be homogeneous, as people are more likely to befriend others like them.[3] Sociologists refer to the practice of connecting with like-minded individuals as *homophily*. Studies have accounted for homophily in sex and gender, age, religion, education level, occupation, and social class. But nowhere is homophily more strongly visible in the United States than in the divides along racial and ethnic lines. The reasons behind the practice of homophily and the resultant social divisions are complex, rooted in a history of inequality, bigotry, oppression, and structural constraints in American life.[4]

It's easy to lament self-segregation in contemporary youth culture, but teens' choice to connect to people like them isn't necessarily born out of their personal racist beliefs. In many cases, teens reinforce homophily in order to cope with the racist society in which they live. In *Why Are All the Black Kids Sitting Together in the Cafeteria?* psychologist Beverly Tatum argues that self-segregation is a logical response to the systematized costs of racism. For teens who are facing cultural oppression and inequality, connecting along lines of race and ethnicity can help teens feel a sense of belonging, enhance identity development, and help them navigate systematic racism. Homophily isn't simply the product of hatred or prejudice. It is also a mechanism of safety. Seong, a seventeen-year-old from Los Angeles, echoed this sentiment when she told me, "In a way we connect more 'cause we see each other and we're like, oh." Familiarity mattered to Seong because, as

[3]For a discussion of homophily, including how American society is divided along racial and ethnic lines, see McPherson, Smith-Lovin, and Cook, "Birds of a Feather."
[4]See Lin, "Inequality in Social Capital."

a Korean immigrant, she feels isolated and confused by American norms that seem very foreign to her. She doesn't want to reject her non-Korean peers, but at times, she just wants to be surrounded by people who understand where she comes from. Still, teens' willingness to accept — and thus *expect* — self-segregation has problematic roots and likely contributes to ongoing racial inequality.[5]

Race-based dynamics are a fundamental part of many teens' lives — urban and suburban, rich and poor. When they go online, these fraught dynamics do not disappear. Instead, teens reproduce them. Although the technology makes it possible *in principle* to socialize with anyone online, in practice, teens connect to the people that they know and with whom they have the most in common.

MySpace vs. Facebook

In a historic small town outside Boston, I was sitting in the library of a newly formed charter school in the spring of 2007. One of the school's administrators had arranged for me to meet different students to get a sense of the school dynamics. Given what I knew about the school, I expected to meet with a diverse group of teens, but I found myself in a series of conversations with predominantly white, highly poised, academically motivated teens who were reluctant to talk about the dynamics of inequality and race at their school.

After I met a few of her peers, Kat, a white fourteen-year-old from a   10 comfortable background, came into the library, and we started talking about the social media practices of her classmates. She made a passing remark about her friends moving from MySpace to Facebook, and I asked to discuss the reasons. Kat grew noticeably uncomfortable. She began simply, noting that "MySpace is just old now and it's boring." But then she paused, looked down at the table, and continued. "It's not really racist, but I guess you could say that. I'm not really into racism, but I think that MySpace now is more like ghetto or whatever." Her honesty startled me so I pressed to learn more. I asked her if people at her school were still using MySpace and she hesitantly said yes before stumbling over her next sentence. "The people who use MySpace — again, not in a racist way — but are usually more like ghetto and hip-hop rap lovers group." Probing a little deeper, Kat continued to stare at and fiddle with her hands as she told me that everyone who was still using MySpace was black, whereas all of her white peers had switched to Facebook.[6]

---

[5]Bonilla-Silva, *Racism Without Racists*.

[6]For a more detailed analysis of the division that emerged in the 2006-2007 school year between Facebook and MySpace, see boyd, "White Flight in Networked Publics?" Craig Watkins also documents the racialized tension between these sites in his work on youth and social media. Watkins, *The Young and the Digital*.

During the 2006–2007 school year, when MySpace was at its peak in popularity with American high school students, Facebook started to gain traction. Some teens who had never joined MySpace created accounts on Facebook. Others switched from MySpace to Facebook. Still others eschewed Facebook and adamantly stated that they preferred MySpace. The presence of two competing services would not be particularly interesting if it weren't for the makeup of the participants on each site. During that school year, as teens chose between MySpace and Facebook, race and class were salient factors in describing which teens used which service. The driving force was obvious: teens focused their attention on the site where their friends were socializing.[7] In doing so, their choices reified the race and class divisions that existed within their schools. As Anastasia, a white seventeen-year-old from New York, explained in a comment she left on my blog:

> My school is divided into the "honors kids," (I think that is self-explanatory), the "good not-so-honors kids," "wangstas," (they pretend to be tough and black but when you live in a suburb in Westchester you can't claim much hood), the "latinos/hispanics," (they tend to band together even though they could fit into any other groups) and the "emo kids" (whose lives are alllllways filled with woe). We were all in MySpace with our own little social networks but when Facebook opened its doors to high schoolers, guess who moved and guess who stayed behind.... The first two groups were the first to go and then the "wangstas" split with half of them on Facebook and the rest on MySpace.... I shifted with the rest of my school to Facebook and it became the place where the "honors kids" got together and discussed how they were procrastinating over their next AP English essay.

When I followed up with Anastasia, I learned that she felt as though it was taboo to talk about these dynamics. She stood by her comment but also told me that her sister said that she sounded racist. Although the underlying segregation of friendship networks defined who chose what site, most teens didn't use the language of race and class to describe their social network site preference. Some may have recognized that this was what was happening, but most described the division to me in terms of personal preference.

My interviews with teens included numerous descriptive taste-based judgments about each site and those who preferred them. Those who relished MySpace gushed about their ability to "pimp out" their profiles with "glitter," whereas Facebook users viewed the resultant profiles as "gaudy," "tacky," and "cluttered." Facebook fans relished the site's aesthetic minimalism, while MySpace devotees described Facebook profiles as "boring," "lame," "sterile," and "elitist." Catalina, a white fifteen-year-old from Austin, told me that Facebook is better because "Facebook just seems more clean to me." What Catalina saw as cleanliness, Indian-Pakistani seventeen-year-old

---

[7]As Siân Lincoln points out in *Youth Culture and Private Space*, teenagers use whatever platform their friends use, even if they personally prefer other platforms.

Anindita from Los Angeles labeled "simple." She recognized the value of simplicity, but she preferred the "bling" of MySpace because it allowed her to express herself.

In differentiating Facebook and MySpace through taste, teens inadvertently embraced and reinforced a host of cultural factors that are rooted in the history of race and class. Taste is not simply a matter of personal preference; it is the product of cultural dynamics and social structure. In *Distinction*, philosopher Pierre Bourdieu describes how one's education and class position shape perceptions of taste and how distinctions around aesthetics and tastes are used to reinforce class in everyday life. The linguistic markers that teens use to describe Facebook and MySpace — and the values embedded in those markers — implicitly mark class and race whether teens realize it or not.

Just as most teens believe themselves to be friends with diverse groups of people, most teens give little thought to the ways in which race and class connect to taste. They judge others' tastes with little regard to how these tastes are socially constructed. Consider how Craig, a white seventeen-year-old from California, differentiated MySpace and Facebook users through a combination of social and cultural distinctions:

> The higher castes of high school moved to Facebook. It was more cultured, and less cheesy. The lower class usually were content to stick to MySpace. Any high school student who has a Facebook will tell you that MySpace users are more likely to be barely educated and obnoxious. Like Peet's is more cultured than Starbucks, and Jazz is more cultured than bubblegum pop, and like Macs are more cultured than PC's, Facebook is of a cooler caliber than MySpace.

In this 2008 blog post entitled "Myface; Spacebook," Craig distinguished between what he saw as highbrow and lowbrow cultural tastes, using consumption patterns to differentiate classes of people and describe them in terms of a hierarchy. By employing the term "caste," Craig used a multicultural metaphor with ethnic and racial connotations that runs counter to the American ideal of social mobility. In doing so, he located his peers in immutable categories defined by taste.

Not all teens are as articulate as Craig with regard to the issue of taste and class, but most recognized the cultural distinction between MySpace and Facebook and marked users according to stereotypes that they had about these sites. When Facebook became more broadly popular, teens who were early adopters of Facebook started lamenting the presence of "the MySpace people." Again, Craig described this dynamic:

> Facebook has become the exact thing it tried to destroy. Like Anikin Skywalker, who loved justice so much, and he decided to play God as Darth Vader, Facebook has lost its identity and mission. It once was the

cool, cultured thing to do, to have a Facebook, but now its the same. Girls have quizzes on their Facebooks: "Would you like to hook up with me? Yes, No" without a shred of dignity or subtlety. Again, I must scroll for 5 minutes to find the comment box on one's Facebook. The vexation of bulletins of MySpace are now replaced by those of applications. It alienated its "cultured" crowd by the addition of these trinkets.

From Craig's perspective, as Facebook became popular and mainstream, it, too, became lowbrow. The cultural distinction that existed during the 2006–2007 school year had faded, and now both sites felt "uncivilized" to Craig. He ended his post with a "desperate" plea to Google to build something "cultured."

In differentiating MySpace and Facebook as distinct cultural spaces and associating different types of people with each site, teens used technology to reinforce cultural distinctions during the time in which both sites were extraordinarily popular. These distinctions, far from being neutral, are wedded to everyday cultural markers. In constituting an "us" in opposition to "them," teens reinforce social divisions through their use of and attitudes toward social media. Even as teens espouse their tolerance toward others with respect to embodied characteristics, they judge their peers' values, choices, and tastes along axes that are rooted in those very characteristics.

The racial divide that these teens experienced as they watched their classmates choose between MySpace and Facebook during the 2006–2007 school year is one that happens time and again in technology adoption. In some cases, white teens use different technologies than teens of color. For example, Black and Latino urban youth embraced early smartphones like the Sidekick, but the device had limited traction among Asian, white, and suburban youth. In other cases, diverse populations adopt a particular tool, but practices within the service are divided along race and class lines. Such was the case in 2013 on both Facebook and Twitter, where teens' linguistic and visual conventions — as well as their choice of apps — were correlated with their race.[8]

People influence the technology practices of those around them. Because of this, the diffusion of technology often has structural features that reflect existing social networks. As teens turn to social media to connect with their friends, they consistently reproduce networks that reflect both the segregated realities of everyday life and the social and economic inequalities that exist within their broader peer networks. Teens go online to hang out with

---

[8]Black and African American individuals are overrepresented on Twitter compared to their participation online more generally. Scholars have begun analyzing a practice known colloquially as "Black Twitter," referring both to the significant presence of black users as well as how practices and norms in Twitter appear to differ across race lines. See Brock, "From the Blackhand Side"; and Florini, "Tweets, Tweeps, and Signifyin'."

their friends, and given the segregation of American society, their friends are quite likely to be of the same race, class, and cultural background.

READING THE TEXT

1. How, according to boyd's research, do digital choices reflect existing racial and class divisions?
2. What does the term "postracial society mantra" (para. 3) mean, as boyd uses it?
3. What does the sociological term "homophily" (para. 6) mean?
4. Summarize in your own words the racial "friending patterns on social network sites" (para. 5) that boyd discovered in her research.

READING THE SIGNS

1. In your journal, discuss why you prefer MySpace, Facebook, or another social networking site. What is your view of sites that you do not use? If you do not use any social networking sites, discuss why you are not attracted to them.
2. Write an essay in which you support, refute, or complicate boyd's assertion that "in differentiating MySpace and Facebook as distinct cultural spaces and associating different types of people with each site, teens used technology to reinforce cultural distinctions.... In constituting an 'us' in opposition to 'them,' teens reinforce social divisions through their use of and attitudes toward social media" (para. 16). To develop evidence for your argument, you might interview some peers who use social media and, as boyd did in her research, review your interviewee's social media pages and the photos posted there. Do you see any racial, gender, or class patterns?
3. Watch the movie *The Social Network* (2009), and write a paper arguing for or against the proposition that the prestige of Facebook's Harvard origins has been a significant cause of its rise in popularity and the decline of MySpace.
4. Conduct a class debate in which you address boyd's conclusion that "as teens turn to social media to connect with their friends, they consistently reproduce networks that reflect both the segregated realities of everyday life and the social and economic inequalities that exist within their broader peer networks" (para. 18). To develop your ideas, consult the Introduction to this chapter. Use the debate as a jumping-off point for your own essay that responds to her conclusion.
5. Write a comparative essay that analyzes today's Facebook and MySpace. Do the appearances of the sites continue to reflect teenager Craig's opinion that Facebook "was more cultured, and less cheesy" than MySpace (para. 14)? Alternatively, compare two other social networking sites, such as Instagram and Tumblr.

S. CRAIG WATKINS

The Evolution of #Black Twitter

Perhaps it all concluded with the shooting of Michael Brown in Ferguson, Missouri: the final overcoming of the cultural narrative that bespoke a digital divide that excluded blacks and Latinos from the world of social media. Indeed, as S. Craig Watkins notes in this analysis of the rise of #Black Twitter, by 2013 the interconnectivity between mobile digital devices and social media outlets had reversed previous trends to find 25 percent of African Americans on Twitter to only 16 percent of online whites. The result has been a transformation of American politics, Watkins reports, with black social activism via handheld digital devices eclipsing such traditional measures of political participation as newspaper subscriptions, party affiliation, and vote casting — which can help to explain the rapid rise of the Black Lives Matter movement. S. Craig Watkins is a professor of Radio-TV-Film at the University of Texas at Austin and the author of *The Young and the Digital: What the Migration to Social Network Sites, Games, and Anytime, Anywhere Media Means for our Future* (2010).

The fatal shooting of eighteen-year-old Michael Brown in Ferguson, Missouri began dominating the national headlines instantly. One of the biggest factors, as *Newsweek*'s Elijah Wolfson points out, was the use of social media by the residents of Ferguson as well as those sympathetic to the concerns about hyper-aggressive police tactics. Speaking about Ferguson, MSNBC's Chris Hayes told a *New York Times* reporter, "this story was put on the map, driven, and followed on social media more so than any story I can remember since the Arab spring."

Amidst the surge of social media a number of journalists reported on what they perceived to be a new phenomenon, "Black Twitter." The use of the term can be problematic insofar as it tends to frame Black Twitter as a monolith practice. How a black teen trying to make it in his or her local hip hop network uses Twitter, for example, will vary significantly from how a black researcher interested in public health will use the platform. Black Twitter is a dynamic set of practices that are not only marked by race but also by class, gender, geography, social experience, and varying degrees of social capital (i.e., social networks) and cultural capital (i.e., style, linguistic practices, and prestige).

A Brief History of Black Twitter

Starting around 2007 the convergence of mobile devices and social media began to upset the traditional digital divide narrative.The old narrative constructed African Americans and Latinos, for example, as largely technology poor and disconnected, literally and figuratively, from the hyper-connected world of networked media.Since 2009 research from the Pew Internet & American Life Project, the Kaiser Family Foundation, Nielsen, and the Connected Learning Research Network clearly illustrate a turning point in the technology practices of blacks and Latinos.Twitter is a notable example.

Between 2010 and 2012 the percentage of Americans using Twitter doubled. In the U.S., young people and African Americans led the user growth of the micro blogging service. As of 2013 25 percent of online African Americans used Twitter compared to sixteen percent of online whites.

Young African Americans drive Black Twitter. They were likely the first among American youth to adopt the platform at scale. When I started interviewing black and Latino teens in 2007/2008 about their social media practices — two things stood out. First, the adoption of mobile was decisive. Second, they were beginning to show some affinity for platforms like Twitter even when most industry insiders and tech reporters were openly confused about why teens — get this — were not using Twitter.

The teens that I interviewed were using the mobile versions of Twitter to share their thoughts and daily experiences with peers and experiment with their social identities and new modes of creative expression. Today, according to Twitter, 78 percent of active users are on mobile. To the extent that early (circa 2008) Black Twitter skewed heavily toward youth it comes as no surprise that much of their engagement with the platform was fueled by their interests in popular culture. Hip hop stars were among the first wave of celebrities to realize social media's potential for brand management, connecting with fans, and content distribution. By 2008, just one year after Twitter's take-off at SXSW Interactive 2007, hip hop icons like Questlove (joined 2008), Talib Kweli Greene (joined 2008), and Common (joined 2008) were building their presence on the site.

No population in the U.S. was more poised for the rise of mobile-based social media than young African Americans and Latinos. For a variety of social and economic reasons practically all of their social media use was via a handheld device. This made them, in the words of E. Everett Rogers, early adopters of mobile social media in the U.S. This ran counter to the dominant digital divide narrative. Early adopter status in the tech consumer world is a source of prestige, cultural power, and, historically, has been associated with white, middle-class, college educated white males. But the face of early adopter status in the convergence between social and mobile media was unlike any experts could have predicted.

5

Power Users & Powerful Users

When analyzing social media it is important to make a distinction between "power users" and "powerful users." The former is a reference to *frequency* of use whereas the latter is a reference to *currency* in use. Much of early Black Twitter use might be best characterized as "power use," African American youth were among the heaviest users of Twitter in terms of time spent, tweets posted, or top-trending hashtags. Whereas 40 percent of young African Americans (ages 18–29) use Twitter about 29 percent of their white counterparts do. This explains why over the years African American related tweets — everything from "yo mama so black ..." jokes to Twitter streams related to TV shows watched in black households — have trended high on the platform. As far back as 2008 and 2009, black-inflected topics began trending on Twitter much to the dismay of some whites who expressed annoyance. It was tantamount to having an exclusive neighborhood invaded by unwanted visitors.

Power use, however, should not be conflated with powerful use. Powerful use is the degree to which use carries weight and influence in, for example, the political, policy, or pop culture realm. The power of Twitter resides in its brevity and speed of communication, the networks it can tap, and the content it can spread. But not all networks, tweets, or content are equal. Whereas most observations of Black Twitter tend to construct African Americans as power users there is rarely a consideration of them as powerful users. This, however, is changing as Black Twitter evolves.

#IfTheyGunnedMeDown"

Two days after the death of Michael Brown the hashtag "IfTheyGunned- 10
MeDown" began trending on Twitter. The hashtag was a creative, critical, and communal response among young people to the image of Mr. Brown circulated by the major news media organizations. Some suggested that the peace sign that he flashed in the photo could be interpreted as a gang sign, a suggestion that Mr. Brown was a menace to society. Black youth across the U.S. "joined" "#IfTheyGunnedMeDown," posting a surge of photos that countered the trope of black criminality.

"#IfTheyGunnedMeDown" did three things. First, it changed the images that the press used to characterize Michael Brown. Subsequent images showed him in close-ups, smiling, wearing headphones, or in cap and gown. If the initial photo or even the video of the convenience store robbery implied villainy, the latter images suggest greater complexity and humanity. Second, the hashtag put news media organizations on notice that they were being watched, scrutinized, and held accountable for the narratives that they constructed. Finally, social media use by Ferguson residents played a role in redirecting the arc of the story and the ensuing conversation about race and inequality in the U.S.

"#IfTheyGunnedMeDown" was not a passive form of civic engagement. It was aware of and contested public discourses about race, demanded social justice, and changed the behavior of news editors across the country. The collective action was a powerful experience for many young people and is certain to nourish their sense of civic efficacy or the feeling that their voice matters.

Social Media: The CNN of Black America

Back in the 1990s Public Enemy's Chuck D famously called rap music "the CNN of Black America." I once asked him what he meant by that statement. He explained that rap music was journalistic in tone and was, in effect, young black America's window onto the world. A generation later the political and journalistic attributes of #Ferguson embody this vision in tangible form. The daily deluge of videos and pictures from the streets of Ferguson became the raw materials that helped to reframe public and policy discourse. The media are now interrogating the militarization of our police force and Congress is holding hearings. (Militarization of the local police is not new, see, for example, Mike Davis.)

#Ferguson signals a noteworthy element in the social media repertoire of black youth and demonstrates how "power use" can transform into "powerful use." Twitter hashtags and photos are a common feature of youth social media engagement and everyday life. In general, these elements of social media are more likely to intersect with young people's personal, peer, and pop culture interests. However, through those practices young people cultivate creative skills, communication practices, and currencies that can turn decisively political. In the wake of the Michael Brown shooting those same modes of social media engagement were used to engage news media organizations and public discourse about race, the vulnerability of black bodies, and the use of force by law enforcement. This is what some researchers refer to as the 'latent capacity' of social media. That is, the idea that the kinds of social media literacies that young people are cultivating in their peer-driven networks — making and sharing memes, photos, videos, and other storytelling genres — can transition from pop culture engagement to political engagement.

In their survey of young people, researchers Cathy Cohen and Joseph Kahne found that young people use social media to engage in civic and political action. They call this participatory politics. The use of Twitter by Ferguson's African American community in the wake of Mr. Brown's death 15 is a rich case study of participatory politics in action. Conversations among African Americans about racism, injustice, or inequality are not new. So, while Twitter has not necessarily changed black civic and political speech, it has altered the scale of "black talk" and, consequently, its capacity for impact.

Political scientists measure political participation along metrics such as reading the newspaper, affiliation with a political party, attending a town hall meeting, or casting a vote. But the use of social media to report, live-stream, critique, and mobilize gives rise to a whole new generation of civic actors and civic acts that we are just beginning to recognize. #Ferguson illuminates how Black Twitter has evolved into a diverse and dynamic terrain of social media practice that belies the very label used to describe it. As the events in Ferguson began to heat up an NBC correspondent on the ground tweeted, "as powerful as our press have been through years of our democracy, social media raises temp on public officials like never before." This is the chief role of political engagement and an emergent aspect of Black Twitter: to make those in authority responsive to the needs of the people. Social media will not be the primary reason change may one day come to cities like Ferguson but it is almost certain to play a role in any transformation that takes place.

READING THE TEXT

1. Explain in your own words why Watkins finds the term "Black Twitter" to be "problematic" (para. 2).

2. What does Watkins mean by "dominant digital divide narrative" (para. 7), and how does he debunk that narrative?

3. In Watkins's view, how has the use of social media among blacks and Latinos evolved since 2007?

4. According to Watkins, what is the difference between "power users" and "powerful users" (para. 8–9)?

READING THE SIGNS

1. **CONNECTING TEXTS** Adopting Watkins's perspective on blacks' use of social media, write a response to danah boyd's position ("It's Complicated: MySpace versus Facebook," p. 437) that social media use among young people tends to reinforce the racial and class status quo.

2. Visit another high-profile social media site, such as Snapchat or Instagram, and study the demographic patterns that you see among a sample of users. Rely on these observations as evidence for an essay in which you support, refute, or complicate Watkins's claim that "no population in the U.S. was

more poised for the rise of mobile-based social media than young African Americans and Latinos" (para. 7).

3. **CONNECTING TEXTS**   Survey students on your campus, preferably those of different ethnicities, about their use of social media and engagement in political activism. Then use your results to support an assessment that "the kinds of social media literacies that young people are cultivating in their peer-driven networks … can transition from pop culture engagement to political engagement" (para. 14). To develop your ideas, consult Erin Lee ("How Effective Is Social Media Activism?," p. 402) and Brian Dunning ("Slacktivism: Raising Awareness," p. 405).

4. Watkins credits Black Twitter for changing public awareness about the Michael Brown shooting in Ferguson, Missouri. Research the online discussions of a subsequent shooting involving police or the ambush of law enforcement officers in Dallas, Texas, in 2016. Use your findings to develop an argument about the efficacy of social media activism in the particular incident you select.

Navigating On- and Off-line Lives

AFP/Getty Images

READING THE SIGNS

1. How often on a daily basis do you encounter stickers, signs, or posters like this one, which asks you to link up some sort of real-world experience with

your social media account? What types of things are you most likely to "like," and why?

2. Think about all the companies, services, and entertainments that you've "liked." What inferences might a stranger make about you based on these "likes"? How do they contribute to a fuller picture of "you" on social media?

3. **CONNECTING TEXTS**   Write an essay in which you argue whether or not signs like this one are a part of what Timothy B. Lee called "the Internet economy" (p. 426).

6

MY SELFIE, MY SELF

Identity and Ideology in the New Millennium

It's Not So Transparent

Being trans is more than meets the eye.

Just ask Caitlyn Jenner, who spent her entire adult life as one of the world's most famous male athletes and media celebrities before her announcement, at age 66, that she had really been a woman in spirit all along. Alongside such popular cultural phenomena as *Transparent*, the Amazon Studios comedy that brought the transgender experience to mainstream TV, and the Obama administration's directive to American public schools to allow transgender students "access to such [restroom] facilities consistent with their gender identity," Jenner's announcement helped bring to the forefront an identity issue that had long lingered at the margins of American culture. Indeed, the second decade of the new millennium could itself be identified as the time when the trans community came out of the shadows.

But then, this decade has also been a time when questions about human identity have become especially prominent, as racial, sexual, gender, class, and religious identities have all played major roles in America's political life and popular culture. Intersecting with the profound challenges to traditional identity formation offered by the Internet, such classifications today have assumed a status that is at once both fluid and adamant, changing shape according to the circumstances in which they appear. In other words, the question of identity itself has no simple answer, and in this chapter we will explore its many dimensions and how they bear upon our culture.

Who Are You?

You are not your self-portrait, but if you are at all like the hundreds of millions of people who own smartphones, it's quite likely that you have presented yourself to the world by way of a digital image taken, quite literally, at arm's length: your selfie. And since that image has the power to define who you are to an incalculable number of people the world over, you may have very carefully constructed it before posting it to Instagram or Snapchat or LinkedIn or wherever. "Here I am," says your selfie. "This is me, my unique self." But, in truth, a selfie cannot tell anyone much about who you are, and, paradoxically enough, one selfie really looks quite like another, often featuring the same poses and facial expressions framed within the strict limits imposed by a tiny camera held less than two feet from your face. So, you have to go beyond your selfie to let other people know who you are, but that's a lot more difficult, isn't it? Who are you, anyway?

We like to think, especially in America where individualism is such a prized **mythology**, that our identity is completely within our control, autonomous and self-constructed. But it isn't that simple, because a large part of who you are is shaped socially and externally from your many experiences in life. Your social **class**, for example, influences what life experiences you may (or may not) have had, and these experiences powerfully affect your consciousness and sense of self. Your race, too, has a strong effect; because we have not yet created a post-racial society, the way people treat you is affected by your ethnicity and influences how you identify yourself. And your religion, gender, and sexual orientation, too, profoundly affect your experience and identity.

It's easy to forget the many ways our identities began to be formed in childhood, and all human cultures have their ways of influencing that process. Traditionally, your family, your country, and your religion have played the most prominent role in shaping your identity, but in an entertainment culture like ours, popular culture increasingly performs this task.

Just think of all those children's television programs you may have watched even before you could walk or talk. When America's (and, increasingly, the world's) children spend hours in front of a TV set (which has been called "the great pacifier"), watching programs whose plots and characters subtly communicate to them how to behave — from appropriate gender roles to appropriate professional careers — the role of popular culture in shaping personal identity can be enormous. And at the same time that children are exposed to all that television, they are also absorbing a great deal of advertising. These ads are carefully constructed not only to shape children as consumers when they grow up but also to "brand" them as consumers of the products they see advertised, in the expectation of a lifetime of brand loyalty. Much the same can happen with kiddie flicks, which so often inculcate traditional social norms even as they dazzle young viewers' eyes with today's technological wizardry.

The products you consume in your youth can also have a powerful effect on your sense of identity. Your favorite clothing styles, for example, are not only personal forms of expression but **signs** of your identification with the various youth cohorts who share your tastes. In a sense, using **consumption** as a badge of your identity can be considered a form of self-stereotyping (have you ever pegged someone as a "skater" or a "geek"?), but if we are the ones adopting the signs, it doesn't feel like stereotyping. Rather, it feels like choice. And choice, as the example of Caitlyn Jenner illustrates, has come to disrupt one of the most rigid sets of identity constructors within the human experience: the **gender codes** that have traditionally defined our identities as gendered subjects.

Gender Codes

A **gender code** is a culturally constructed **system** that prescribes the appropriate roles and behaviors for men and women in society. Assuming both a continuity between your biological sex and your gender awareness or identity, as well as a normative heterosexual orientation, such codes tell you how to conduct yourself as a male or a female. At least in traditional Western codes we find maxims such as these: *Boys don't cry; girls wear makeup. Boys are aggressive; girls are passive. Boys play sports; girls are cheerleaders. Men go out to work; women stay at home and raise children.* The list is long, and it has shaped your gender identity since your birth.

But challenges by transgender people to the assumption that biological sexual identity determines psychological gender identity have disrupted the authority of the traditional codes, leading to a multiplicity of possible identities that can be chosen rather than received. The popularity of such reality TV programs as *RuPaul's Drag Race* and the aforementioned *Transparent* are striking signs of this disruption of the old gender codes.

Similarly, disruptions of the heteronormative assumptions that have traditionally governed sexual identity are also changing the cultural landscape. The success of TV shows like *Modern Family*, the increasing number of athletes and politicians coming out to their fans and constituents, and the growing number of Americans who endorse same-sex marriage all signify an emerging acceptance of the freedom to differ from mainstream notions of sexual identity and desire.

But this is not to say that traditional gender codes have disappeared from popular culture. They're still very much at work and are particularly evident in advertising campaigns. Consider, for example, a famous campaign for Axe grooming products. **Denotatively,** Axe is simply a perfume, but since the traditional gender codes specify that perfume is a woman's product, the marketing of Axe fragrances is designed to **connote** a hypermasculine identity for its male consumers. Thus, like Brut before it, Axe products are given

---

Exploring the Signs of Gender

In your journal, explore the expectations about gender roles that you grew up with. What gender norms were you taught by your family or the media, either overtly or implicitly? Have you ever had any conflicts with your parents over "natural" gender roles? If so, how did you resolve them? Do you think your gender-related expectations today are the same as those you had when you were a child?

---

a name traditionally associated with such masculine-coded traits as violence and aggression. One particularly striking Axe ad featured a swarm of passionate women running frantically toward a beach where a single man stands dousing himself in Axe fragrance, reinforcing the gender-coded belief that an unmarried man should "score" as often as possible (a woman who behaves in the same way can be called all kinds of unpleasant names).

Similarly, products (especially cosmetics) aimed at women play up the traditional gender-coded prescription that a woman's primary concern should be to attract the gaze of a man — that is, to look beautiful. This is so glaringly obvious in women's magazines that it has stimulated its own backlash in the well-known Dove "Campaign for Real Beauty." But, while the campaign does feature more ordinary models than do other beauty product ads, it does not abandon the focus on physical attractiveness that the traditional code demands — and, it might also be pointed out, the same company that constructed the Dove campaign is also behind the Axe line of products.

Maybe things haven't changed so much after all.

Postfeminist or Third Wave?

American popular culture, through its endless images of eroticized female bodies, continues to tell girls and women that their primary identities lie in their ability to be sexually attractive to men — a concept that's particularly challenging to cultural theory. For, given the attempts of the feminist movement in the 1970s to challenge such messages — which are reflections of what journalist Ariel Levy has called a "raunch culture" — the current era might seem to be more postfeminist than feminist when it comes to female identity in America. That is, some of the current signs (for instance, the notorious performance of Miley Cyrus at the 2013 MTV Video Music Awards ceremony) suggest that America may have abandoned feminist goals and reverted to the most conservative of gender-coded prescriptions.

But it may not be that simple. For many women who embrace what is often called third-wave feminism, the confident display of their sexuality is actually empowering rather than degrading, a taking charge rather than a knuckling under — an attitude that was behind the immense popularity among women of the TV hit *Sex and the City* and similar books, movies, and TV series, like *Girls*. Third-wave feminists regard themselves as representing an evolution within the women's movement itself, not a movement away from it, arguing that being proud of her body and using it to get what she wants is part of a woman's empowerment and a valid identity choice. More traditional feminists are not persuaded by this argument, however, and point out that, by focusing their attention on their bodies rather than their minds, women may subject themselves to the tyranny of a youth-worshipping culture that will reject them once they are past the peak of their sexually appealing years. It is no accident that the vast majority of the images of women we see in popular culture are of very young women. There are a lot more Betty Boops than Betty Whites.

The Space for Race

The emergence of the Black Lives Matter movement in the wake of a series of police shootings of black men and women has made it quite clear that the claim America had entered a "post-racial" era with the election of its first black president was strikingly premature. And Spike Lee's announcement that he would not attend the 2016 Academy Awards ceremony — a tweet that launched the #OscarsSoWhite movement — made it equally clear that racial identity was still very much at issue in American popular culture. While television series like *Scandal* and *Orange Is the New Black* seek to address such issues head on, a long history of negative stereotyping of African Americans, Asian Americans, Native Americans, and Latin Americans in American entertainment continues to make the representation of racial minorities a highly sensitive subject. Complaints about the character of Jar Jar Binks in the *Star Wars* saga, for example, were based upon a perception that it perpetrated a derisive stereotype of Afro-Caribbean culture, while even *Avatar*, with its sympathetic depiction of a nonwhite society under siege by white invaders, has been compared to *Dances with Wolves* as yet another example of a stereotypical story in which a group of nonwhites needs a white hero to lead them. And, in 2013, Disney's box-office failure with *The Lone Ranger* was also attributed, at least in part, to its revival of the always racially problematic character of Tonto.

But while the representation of race in popular culture is still a politically potent topic, certain changes in racial identity itself are altering the landscape. With increasing numbers of Americans identifying themselves as being of mixed race (while Barack Obama identified himself as "Black, African Am., or

---

Discussing the Signs of Race

Demographers predict that, by the middle of the twenty-first century, America will no longer have any racial or ethnic majority population. In class, discuss what effects this may have on Americans' sense of this country's history, culture, and identity.

Negro" on his 2010 census form, he could have chosen "mixed race" as well), the traditional racial categories, like those of gender, are in a state of flux. Indeed, even the term "minority" is approaching obsolescence in a country that will have no racial majority by midcentury.

The Great Divide

More subtly, but arguably just as profoundly, your social class also shapes your identity. But unlike such identifying categories as race and gender, class has historically been underplayed, even denied, as a component in American life. Obscured by the mythology of the American dream, which promises an opportunity for upward social mobility to everyone, class has been the great blind spot in American history ever since Michel-Guillaume-Saint-Jean de Crèvecoeur (an eighteenth-century French aristocrat who wrote glowingly of his experiences in America) declared that America was a land of economic equality that had transcended Europe's great gulf between rich and poor.

The inability of Americans to recognize the role that social class plays (and has always played) in their lives was dramatically altered in the wake of the Great Recession that broke over America like a tidal wave after the near-meltdown of our economy in 2008. Movements like Occupy Wall Street, which famously divided America into "the 99 percent" and "the 1 percent," have finally brought class to the forefront, empowering the near-successful run of Bernie Sanders for the Democratic presidential nomination in 2016, even as the gap between rich and poor continues to widen and the middle class continues to shrink.

But so pertinacious are cultural mythologies that the America of vast class differences is still not very visible in popular culture. The movie *Batman: The Dark Knight Rises* certainly alluded to the class divide in 2012, but, as a number of critics noted at the time, it characterized the class revolution of Bane and company as brutally terroristic, thus potentially undermining those with a serious desire to promote class equality. Generally, one can argue that while American popular culture is eager to present itself as progressive about race and gender, it is not so eager to reveal the effects of class inequality — which

Denis Poroy/AP Images

Science fiction fans wear elaborate costumes at the annual Comic-Con convention.

is not very surprising when so many members of the entertainment industry belong to that 1 percent.

Be Whatever You Want to Be

Race, class, and gender form a triad of identifiers that are especially prominent in **cultural studies**, but there are plenty of signs indicating the emergence of a new, highly fluid and individualistic mode of identity formation in American culture: the self-constructions that appear on social media sites and apps, from LinkedIn to Facebook, Instagram to Snapchat, Twitter to Tumblr, and everything in between and beyond. In short, in the digital era, the emphasis is often on self-promotion, not demographic classification.

That's because on the Internet, you can be pretty much what you want to be. From online gaming sites (like *World of Warcraft*), where you can adopt a host of identities, to Facebook profiles, where you can present to the world an idealized version of yourself, the Internet has revolutionized the traditional restrictions on identity formation. With no one able to see you in person, you can adopt whatever personae you like, exchanging identities as if you were changing your clothes. Such freedom to present yourself in whatever way you like has been a fundamental appeal of the Internet from its beginnings.

But just as the Internet creates the opportunity for self-making, it also offers users the possibility of disguise — a masked *non-identity* that seems to unleash some of our most antisocial tendencies. Consider the crowd-sourced nastiness of the comments sections on most Web sites; you will find the same aggression, vile language, trolls, and hostility, no matter what the topic. This "keyboard courage" is made possible by the anonymity that the Internet confers upon its users, who feel emboldened to say things that they would not say face-to-face because nonvirtual society has ways of policing itself that the Internet does not (a lot of rude comments on the Internet would get their posters punched out if delivered in person; others would get them fired).

Paradoxically, then, the Internet offers to its users a kind of non-identity in its offer of anonymity. And since identification is also a form of social control (think of your driver's license — it is your photo ID, and without it you cannot legally drive your car or board a commercial airplane), the outbursts that fill the Internet are signifiers not only of all the conflict out there but also of a resentment against the restrictions that come with social identity. Such resentment bears a close relation to that fundamental American mythology of individualism, which can be found at work so often in American culture, for it is our individualism that guides our cherishing of our liberty. The possibility of escaping identity, of having a non-identity, offers an immense freedom — even if that freedom is expressed only as a license to rant in public.

The Supermarket of IDs

But let's look again at your ability to construct your own online identity. You pay a price for the self-making you can do on the Internet. As you advertise yourself, the social networking site on which you do so is mining your data to sell to others who want to advertise to you. Rather than setting up your own Web page — which is what people did in the Internet's early days — you build your social networking identity upon mass-produced platforms that offer ease and convenience in exchange for your life details. Ironically, your identity is a **commodity** for sale, and you sold it without having had any choice in the matter if you want to live in the cloud.

Reading Identity Online

Many Internet sites are devoted to the culture of a particular ethnicity, gender, or cultural subgroup. Visit several such sites and survey the breadth of information available within them. Is there any information that you wish would appear online but could not find? Do you find any material problematic?

In short, identity itself has become a commodity in America. The mining of our private information can be very disturbing to members of a society in which individualism and independence are so highly valued, but it is routinely shrugged off by consumers who are pleased to have advertising tailored to their online profiles. This isn't very surprising in a consumer culture wherein people have been trained from the cradle to *identify* themselves as consumers.

And so we come full circle to what it really means to live in a consumer society and why the study and understanding of popular culture, so much of which is involved with consumption, is important. Although one American tradition, a mythology that goes back to the roots of this nation, clings desperately to a sense of individualism within a **mass culture**, another more recent development — the advent of consumerism — is taking that all away. At a time when Americans are demonstrating a desire for greater and greater personal choice in who they are, it's getting harder and harder to be someone in a mass society that has put identity up for sale. After all, even Caitlyn Jenner, having been there and done that, can now shop at redbubble.com and buy her own "Call Me Caitlyn" T-shirt.

And so can you.

The Readings

Michael Omi's historical survey of racial stereotyping in American entertainment opens this chapter, providing an essential foundation for the analysis of race in popular culture. A set of paired readings by Aaron Devor and Deborah Blum follows, with Devor analyzing the ways men and women manipulate the signs by which we traditionally communicate our gender identity, and Blum indicating that biology *does* play a role in gender identity formation and that we can best understand the gender gap by looking at both the cultural and the physiological determinants of human behavior. Michael Hulshof-Schmidt is next with a meditation on the complications that arise when anyone tries to pin down an all-inclusive label for the queer community, while Kevin Jennings's personal memoir chronicles his struggles with growing up gay in conflict with his family's traditionalist construction of male identity. Samantha Raphelson then turns to the history of generational labeling, revealing how much of what goes into identifying this generation or that one is simply done for marketing purposes. Rachel Lowry follows with a news feature on millennials who "may be suffering from an identity crisis" because their online profiles and their more authentic selves can radically differ, while Brittney Cooper critiques the white-washing of American film and TV. Lilliana Mason concludes the readings with a scholarly study of the ways in which group identity formation has been powering the extraordinary divisiveness behind the 2016 presidential campaign.

MICHAEL OMI

In Living Color: Race and American Culture

Though many like to think that racism in America is a thing of the past, Michael Omi argues that racism is a pervasive feature in our lives, one that is both overt and inferential. Using race as a sign by which we judge a person's character, inferential racism invokes deep-rooted stereotypes, and as Omi shows in his survey of American film, television, and music, our popular culture is hardly immune from such stereotyping. Indeed, when ostensibly "progressive" programs like *Saturday Night Live* can win the National Ethnic Coalition of Organizations' "Platinum Pit Award" for racist stereotyping in television, and shock jocks such as Howard Stern command big audiences and salaries, one can see popular culture has a way to go before it becomes color-blind. The author of *Racial Formation in the United States: From the 1960s to the 1990s* (with Howard Winant, 1986, 1994), Michael Omi is a professor of comparative ethnic studies at the University of California, Berkeley.

In February 1987, Assistant Attorney General William Bradford Reynolds, the nation's chief civil rights enforcer, declared that the recent death of a black man in Howard Beach, New York, and the Ku Klux Klan attack on civil rights marchers in Forsyth County, Georgia, were "isolated" racial incidences. He emphasized that the places where racial conflict could potentially flare up were "far fewer now than ever before in our history," and concluded that such a diminishment of racism stood as "a powerful testament to how far we have come in the civil rights struggle."[1]

Events in the months following his remarks raise the question as to whether we have come quite so far. They suggest that dramatic instances of racial tension and violence merely constitute the surface manifestations of a deeper racial organization of American society — a system of inequality which has shaped, and in turn been shaped by, our popular culture.

In March, the NAACP released a report on blacks in the record industry entitled "The Discordant Sound of Music." It found that despite the revenues generated by black performers, blacks remain "grossly underrepresented" in the business, marketing, and A&R (Artists and Repertoire) departments of major record labels. In addition, few blacks are employed as managers, agents, concert promoters, distributors, and retailers. The report concluded that:

---

[1]Reynolds's remarks were made at a conference on equal opportunity held by the Bar Association in Orlando, Florida. *The San Francisco Chronicle* (February 7, 1987). Print.

The record industry is overwhelmingly segregated and discrimination is rampant. No other industry in America so openly classifies its operations on a racial basis. At every level of the industry, beginning with the separation of black artists into a special category, barriers exist that severely limit opportunities for blacks.[2]

Decades after the passage of civil rights legislation and the affirmation of the principle of "equal opportunity," patterns of racial segregation and exclusion, it seems, continue to characterize the production of popular music.

The enduring logic of Jim Crow is also present in professional sports. In April, Al Campanis, vice president of player personnel for the Los Angeles Dodgers, explained to Ted Koppel on ABC's *Nightline* about the paucity of blacks in baseball front offices and as managers. "I truly believe," Campanis said, "that [blacks] may not have some of the necessities to be, let's say, a field manager or perhaps a general manager." When pressed for a reason, Campanis offered an explanation which had little to do with the structure of opportunity or institutional discrimination within professional sports:

[W]hy are black men or black people not good swimmers? Because they don't have the buoyancy. . . .They are gifted with great musculature and various other things. They're fleet of foot. And this is why there are a lot of black major league ballplayers. Now as far as having the background to become club presidents, or presidents of a bank, I don't know.[3]

Black exclusion from the front office, therefore, was justified on the basis of biological "difference."

The issue of race, of course, is not confined to the institutional arrangements   5
of popular culture production. Since popular culture deals with the symbolic realm of social life, the images which it creates, represents, and disseminates contribute to the overall racial climate. They become the subject of analysis and political scrutiny. In August, the National Ethnic Coalition of Organizations bestowed the "Golden Pit Awards" on television programs, commercials, and movies that were deemed offensive to racial and ethnic groups. *Saturday Night Live*, regarded by many media critics as a politically "progressive" show, was singled out for the "Platinum Pit Award" for its comedy skit "Ching Chang," which depicted a Chinese storeowner and his family in a derogatory manner.[4]

These examples highlight the *overt* manifestations of racism in popular culture — institutional forms of discrimination which keep racial minorities out of the production and organization of popular culture, and the crude racial caricatures by which these groups are portrayed. Yet racism in popular

---

[2]Economic Development Department of the NAACP, "The Discordant Sound of Music (A Report on the Record Industry)," (Baltimore, Maryland: The NAACP, 1987), pp. 16–17. Print.
[3]Campanis's remarks on *Nightline* were reprinted in *The San Francisco Chronicle* (April 9, 1987). Print.
[4]Ellen Wulfhorst, "TV Stereotyping: It's the 'Pits,'" *The San Francisco Chronicle* (August 24, 1987). Print.

culture is often conveyed in a variety of implicit, and at times invisible, ways. Political theorist Stuart Hall makes an important distinction between *overt* racism, the elaboration of an explicitly racist argument, policy, or view, and *inferential* racism, which refers to "those apparently naturalized representations of events and situations relating to race, whether 'factual' or 'fictional,' which have racist premises and propositions inscribed in them as a set of *unquestioned assumptions*." He argues that inferential racism is more widespread, common, and indeed insidious since "it is largely *invisible* even to those who formulate the world in its terms."[5]

Race itself is a slippery social concept which is paradoxically both "obvious" and "invisible." In our society, one of the first things we notice about people when we encounter them (along with their sex/gender) is their *race*. We utilize race to provide clues about *who* a person is and *how* we should relate to her/him. Our perception of race determines our "presentation of *self*," distinctions in status, and appropriate modes of conduct in daily and institutional life. This process is often unconscious; we tend to operate off of an unexamined set of *racial beliefs*.

Racial beliefs account for and explain variations in "human nature." Differences in skin color and other obvious physical characteristics supposedly provide visible clues to more substantive differences lurking underneath. Among other qualities, temperament, sexuality, intelligence, and artistic and athletic ability are presumed to be fixed and discernible from the palpable mark of race. Such diverse questions as our confidence and trust in others (as salespeople, neighbors, media figures); our sexual preferences and romantic images; our tastes in music, film, dance, or sports; indeed our very ways of walking and talking are ineluctably shaped by notions of race.

Ideas about race, therefore, have become "common sense" — a way of comprehending, explaining, and acting in the world. This is made painfully obvious when someone disrupts our common sense understandings. An encounter with someone who is, for example, racially "mixed" or of a racial/ethnic group we are unfamiliar with becomes a source of discomfort for us, and momentarily creates a crisis of racial meaning. We also become disoriented when people do not act "black," "Latino," or indeed "white." The content of such stereotypes reveals a series of unsubstantiated beliefs about who these groups are, what they are like, and how they behave.

The existence of such racial consciousness should hardly be surprising. ¹⁰ Even prior to the inception of the republic, the United States was a society shaped by racial conflict. The establishment of the Southern plantation economy, Western expansion, and the emergence of the labor movement, among other significant historical developments, have all involved conflicts over the definition and nature of the *color line*. The historical results have

---

[5]Stuart Hall, "The Whites of Their Eyes: Racist Ideologies and the Media," in George Bridges and Rosalind Brunt, eds., *Silver Linings* (London: Lawrence and Wishart, 1981), pp. 36–37. Print.

been distinct and different groups have encountered unique forms of racial oppression — Native Americans faced genocide, blacks were subjected to slavery, Mexicans were invaded and colonized, and Asians faced exclusion. What is common to the experiences of these groups is that their particular "fate" was linked to historically specific ideas about the significance and meaning of race.[6] Whites defined them as separate "species," ones inferior to Northern European cultural stocks, and thereby rationalized the conditions of their subordination in the economy, in political life, and in the realm of culture.

A crucial dimension of racial oppression in the United States is the elaboration of an ideology of difference or "otherness." This involves defining "us" (i.e., white Americans) in opposition to "them," an important task when distinct racial groups are first encountered, or in historically specific periods where preexisting racial boundaries are threatened or crumbling.

Political struggles over the very definition of who an "American" is illustrate this process. The Naturalization Law of 1790 declared that only free *white* immigrants could qualify, reflecting the initial desire among Congress to create and maintain a racially homogeneous society. The extension of eligibility to all racial groups has been a long and protracted process. Japanese, for example, were finally eligible to become naturalized citizens after the passage of the Walter-McCarran Act of 1952. The ideological residue of these restrictions in naturalization and citizenship laws is the equation within popular parlance of the term "American" with "white," while other "Americans" are described as black, Mexican, "Oriental," etc.

Popular culture has been an important realm within which racial ideologies have been created, reproduced, and sustained. Such ideologies provide a framework of symbols, concepts, and images through which we understand, interpret, and represent aspects of our "racial" existence.

Race has often formed the central themes of American popular culture. Historian W. L. Rose notes that it is a "curious coincidence" that four of the "most popular reading-viewing events in all American history" have in some manner dealt with race, specifically black/white relations in the south.[7] Harriet Beecher Stowe's *Uncle Tom's Cabin*, Thomas Ryan Dixon's *The Clansman* (the inspiration for D. W. Griffith's *The Birth of a Nation*), Margaret Mitchell's *Gone with the Wind* (as a book and film), and Alex Haley's *Roots* (as a book and television miniseries) each appeared at a critical juncture in American race relations and helped to shape new understandings of race.

Emerging social definitions of race and the "real American" were reflected in American popular culture of the nineteenth century. Racial and ethnic stereotypes were shaped and reinforced in the newspapers, 15

---

[6]For an excellent survey of racial beliefs see Thomas F. Gossett, *Race: The History of an Idea in America* (New York: Shocken, 1965). Print.

[7]W. L. Rose, *Race and Religion in American Historical Fiction: Four Episodes in Popular Culture* (Oxford: Clarendon, 1979). Print.

magazines, and pulp fiction of the period. But the evolution and ever-increasing sophistication of visual mass communications throughout the twentieth century provided, and continue to provide, the most dramatic means by which racial images are generated and reproduced.

Film and television have been notorious in disseminating images of racial minorities which establish for audiences what these groups look like, how they behave, and, in essence, "who they are." The power of the media lies not only in their ability to reflect the dominant racial ideology, but in their capacity to shape that ideology in the first place. D. W. Griffith's aforementioned epic *Birth of a Nation*, a sympathetic treatment of the rise of the Ku Klux Klan during Reconstruction, helped to generate, consolidate, and "nationalize" images of blacks which had been more disparate (more regionally specific, for example) prior to the film's appearance.[8]

In television and film, the necessity to define characters in the briefest and most condensed manner has led to the perpetuation of racial caricatures, as racial stereotypes serve as shorthand for scriptwriters, directors, and actors. Television's tendency to address the "lowest common denominator" in order to render programs "familiar" to an enormous and diverse audience leads it regularly to assign and reassign racial characteristics to particular groups, both minority and majority.

Many of the earliest American films deal with racial and ethnic "difference." The large influx of "new immigrants" at the turn of the century led to a proliferation of negative images of Jews, Italians, and Irish which were assimilated and adapted by such films as Thomas Edison's *Cohen's Advertising Scheme* (1904). Based on an old vaudeville routine, the film featured a scheming Jewish merchant, aggressively hawking his wares. Though stereotypes of these groups persist to this day,[9] by the 1940s many of the earlier ethnic stereotypes had disappeared from Hollywood. But, as historian Michael Winston observes, the "outsiders" of the 1890s remained: "the ever-popular Indian of the Westerns; the inscrutable or sinister Oriental; the sly, but colorful Mexican; and the clowning or submissive Negro."[10]

In many respects the "Western" as a genre has been paradigmatic in establishing images of racial minorities in film and television. The classic scenario involves the encircled wagon train or surrounded fort from which whites bravely fight off fierce bands of Native American Indians. The point

---

[8]Melanie Martindale-Sikes, "Nationalizing 'Nigger' Imagery through *Birth of a Nation*," paper prepared for the 73rd Annual Meeting of the American Sociological Association (September 4–8, 1978) in San Francisco.

[9]For a discussion of Italian, Irish, Jewish, Slavic, and German stereotypes in film, see Randall M. Miller, ed., *The Kaleidoscopic Lens: How Hollywood Views Ethnic Groups* (Englewood, N.J.: Jerome S. Ozer, 1980). Print.

[10]Michael R. Winston, "Racial Consciousness and the Evolution of Mass Communications in the United States," *Daedalus*, vol. III, No. 4 (Fall 1982). Print.

of reference and viewer identification lies with those huddled within the circle — the representatives of "civilization" who valiantly attempt to ward off the forces of barbarism. In the classic Western, as writer Tom Engelhardt observes, "the viewer is forced behind the barrel of a repeating rifle and it is from that position, through its gun sights, that he receives a picture history of Western colonialism and imperialism."[11]

Westerns have indeed become the prototype for European and American   20
excursions throughout the Third World. The cast of characters may change, but the story remains the same. The "humanity" of whites is contrasted with the brutality and treachery of nonwhites; brave (i.e., white) souls are pitted against the merciless hordes in conflicts ranging from Indians against the British Lancers to Zulus against the Boers. What Stuart Hall refers to as the imperializing "white eye" provides the framework for these films, lurking outside the frame and yet seeing and positioning everything within; it is "the unmarked position from which . . . 'observations' are made and from which, alone, they make sense."[12]

Our "common sense" assumptions about race and racial minorities in the United States are both generated and reflected in the stereotypes presented by the visual media. In the crudest sense, it could be said that such stereotypes underscore white "superiority" by reinforcing the traits, habits, and predispositions of nonwhites which demonstrate their "inferiority." Yet a more careful assessment of racial stereotypes reveals intriguing trends and seemingly contradictory themes.

While all racial minorities have been portrayed as "less than human," there are significant differences in the images of different groups. Specific racial minority groups, in spite of their often interchangeable presence in films steeped in the "Western" paradigm, have distinct and often unique qualities assigned to them. Latinos are portrayed as being prone toward violent outbursts of anger; blacks as physically strong, but dim-witted; while Asians are seen as sneaky and cunningly evil. Such differences are crucial to observe and analyze. Race in the United States is not reducible to black/white relations. These differences are significant for a broader understanding of the patterns of race in America, and the unique experience of specific racial minority groups.

It is somewhat ironic that *real* differences which exist within a racially defined minority group are minimized, distorted, or obliterated by the media. "All Asians look alike," the saying goes, and indeed there has been little or no attention given to the vast differences which exist between, say, the Chinese and Japanese with respect to food, dress, language, and culture. This blurring within popular culture has given us supposedly Chinese

---

[11]Tom Engelhardt, "Ambush at Kamikaze Pass," in Emma Gee, ed., *Counterpoint: Perspectives on Asian America* (Los Angeles: Asian American Studies Center, UCLA, 1976), p. 270. Print.
   [12]Hall, "Whites of Their Eyes," p. 38. Print.

characters who wear kimonos; it is also the reason why the fast-food restaurant McDonald's can offer "Shanghai McNuggets" with teriyaki sauce. Other groups suffer a similar fate. Professor Gretchen Bataille and Charles Silet find the cinematic Native American of the Northeast wearing the clothing of the Plains Indians, while living in the dwellings of Southwestern tribes:

> The movie men did what thousands of years of social evolution could not do, even what the threat of the encroaching white man could not do; Hollywood produced the homogenized Native American, devoid of tribal characteristics or regional differences.[13]

The need to paint in broad racial strokes has thus rendered "internal" differences invisible. This has been exacerbated by the tendency for screenwriters to "invent" mythical Asian, Latin American, and African countries. Ostensibly done to avoid offending particular nations and peoples, such a subterfuge reinforces the notion that all the countries and cultures of a specific region are the same. European countries retain their distinctiveness, while the Third World is presented as one homogeneous mass riddled with poverty and governed by ruthless and corrupt regimes.

While rendering specific groups in a monolithic fashion, the popular cultural imagination simultaneously reveals a compelling need to distinguish and articulate "bad" and "good" variants of particular racial groups and individuals. Thus each stereotypic image is filled with contradictions: The bloodthirsty Indian is tempered with the image of the noble savage; the *bandido* exists along with the loyal sidekick; and Fu Manchu is offset by Charlie Chan. The existence of such contradictions, however, does not negate the one-dimensionality of these images, nor does it challenge the explicit subservient role of racial minorities. Even the "good" person of color usually exists as a foil in novels and films to underscore the intelligence, courage, and virility of the white male hero.

Another important, perhaps central, dimension of racial minority stereotypes is sex/gender differentiation. The connection between race and sex has traditionally been an explosive and controversial one. For most of American history, sexual and marital relations between whites and nonwhites were forbidden by social custom and by legal restrictions. It was not until 1967, for example, that the U.S. Supreme Court ruled that antimiscegenation laws were unconstitutional. Beginning in the 1920s, the notorious Hays Office, Hollywood's attempt at self-censorship, prohibited scenes and subjects which dealt with miscegenation. The prohibition, however, was not evenly applied in practice. White men could seduce racial minority women, but white women were not to be romantically or sexually linked to racial minority men.

Women of color were sometimes treated as exotic sex objects. The sultry Latin temptress — such as Dolores Del Rio and Lupe Velez — invariably

25

---

[13]Gretchen Bataille and Charles Silet, "The Entertaining Anachronism: Indians in American Film," in Randall M. Miller, ed., *Kaleidoscopic Lens*, p. 40. Print.

had boyfriends who were white North Americans; their Latino suitors were portrayed as being unable to keep up with the Anglo-American competition. From Mary Pickford as Cho-Cho San in *Madame Butterfly* (1915) to Nancy Kwan in *The World of Suzie Wong* (1961), Asian women have often been seen as the gracious "geisha girl" or the prostitute with a "heart of gold," willing to do anything to please her man.

By contrast, Asian men, whether cast in the role of villain, servant, side-kick, or kung fu master, are seen as asexual or, at least, romantically unde-sirable. As Asian American studies professor Elaine Kim notes, even a hero such as Bruce Lee played characters whose "single-minded focus on perfect-ing his fighting skills precludes all other interests, including an interest in women, friendship, or a social life."[14]

The shifting trajectory of black images over time reveals an interesting dynamic with respect to sex and gender. The black male characters in *The Birth of a Nation* were clearly presented as sexual threats to "white womanhood." For decades afterward, however, Hollywood consciously avoided portraying black men as assertive or sexually aggressive in order to minimize controversy. Black men were instead cast as comic, harmless, and nonthreatening figures exemplified by such stars as Bill "Bojangles" Robinson, Stepin Fetchit, and Eddie "Rochester" Anderson. Black women, by contrast, were divided into two broad character types based on color categories. Dark black women such as Hattie McDaniel and Louise Beavers were cast as "dowdy, frumpy, dumpy, overweight mammy figures"; while those "close to the white ideal," such as Lena Horne and Dorothy Dandridge, became "Hollywood's treasured mulattoes" in roles emphasizing the tragedy of being of mixed blood.[15]

It was not until the early 1970s that tough, aggressive, sexually assertive black characters, both male and female, appeared. The "blaxploitation" films of the period provided new heroes (e.g., *Shaft*, *Superfly*, *Coffy*, and *Cleopatra Jones*) in sharp contrast to the submissive and subservient images of the past. Unfortunately, most of these films were shoddy productions which did little to create more enduring "positive" images of blacks, either male or female.

In contemporary television and film, there is a tendency to present and equate racial minority groups and individuals with specific social problems. Blacks are associated with drugs and urban crime, Latinos with "illegal" immigration, while Native Americans cope with alcoholism and tribal conflicts. Rarely do we see racial minorities "out of character," in situations removed from the stereotypic arenas in which scriptwriters have tradition-ally embedded them. Nearly the only time we see young Asians and Latinos   30

[14]Elaine Kim, "Asian Americans and American Popular Culture," in Hyung-Chan Kim, ed., *Dictionary of Asian American History* (New York: Greenwood, 1986), p. 107. Print.

[15]Donald Bogle, "A Familiar Plot (A Look at the History of Blacks in American Movies)," *The Crisis*, Vol. 90, No. 1 (January 1983), p. 15. Print.

of either sex, for example, is when they are members of youth gangs, as *Boulevard Nights* (1979), *Year of the Dragon* (1985), and countless TV cop shows can attest to.

Racial minority actors have continually bemoaned the fact that the roles assigned them on stage and screen are often one-dimensional and imbued with stereotypic assumptions. In theater, the movement toward "blind casting" (i.e., casting actors for roles without regard to race) is a progressive step, but it remains to be seen whether large numbers of audiences can suspend their "beliefs" and deal with a Latino King Lear or an Asian Stanley Kowalski. By contrast, white actors are allowed to play anybody. Though the use of white actors to play blacks in "black face" is clearly unacceptable in the contemporary period, white actors continue to portray Asian, Latino, and Native American characters on stage and screen.

Scores of Charlie Chan films, for example, have been made with white leads (the last one was the 1981 *Charlie Chan and the Curse of the Dragon Queen*). Roland Winters, who played Chan in six features, was once asked to explain the logic of casting a white man in the role of Charlie Chan: "The only thing I can think of is, if you want to cast a homosexual in a show, and you get a homosexual, it'll be awful. It won't be funny . . . and maybe there's something there."[16]

Such a comment reveals an interesting aspect about myth and reality in popular culture. Michael Winston argues that stereotypic images in the visual media were not originally conceived as representations of reality, nor were they initially understood to be "real" by audiences. They were, he suggests, ways of "coding and rationalizing" the racial hierarchy and interracial behavior. Over time, however, "a complex interactive relationship between myth and reality developed, so that images originally understood to be unreal, through constant repetition began to *seem* real."[17]

Such a process consolidated, among other things, our "common sense" understandings of what we think various groups should look like. Such presumptions have led to tragicomical results. Latinos auditioning for a role in a television soap opera, for example, did not fit the Hollywood image of "real Mexicans" and had their faces bronzed with powder before filming because they looked too white. Model Aurora Garza said, "I'm a real Mexican and very dark anyway. I'm even darker right now because I have a tan. But they kept wanting to make my face darker and darker."[18]

Historically in Hollywood, the fact of having "dark skin" made an actor 35 or actress potentially adaptable for numerous "racial" roles. Actress Lupe Velez once commented that she had portrayed "Chinese, Eskimos, Japs,

[16]Frank Chin, "Confessions of the Chinatown Cowboy," *Bulletin of Concerned Asian Scholars*, Vol. 4, No. 3 (Fall 1972). Print.

[17]Winston, "Racial Consciousness," p. 176. Print.

[18]*The San Francisco Chronicle* (September 21, 1984). Print.

squaws, Hindus, Swedes, Malays, and Japanese."[19] Dorothy Dandridge, who was the first black woman teamed romantically with white actors, presented a quandary for studio executives who weren't sure what race and nationality to make her. They debated whether she should be a "foreigner," an island girl, or a West Indian.[20] Ironically, what they refused to entertain as a possibility was to present her as what she really was, a black American woman.

The importance of race in popular culture is not restricted to the visual media. In popular music, race and race consciousness have defined, and continue to define, formats, musical communities, and tastes. In the mid-1950s, the secretary of the North Alabama White Citizens Council declared that "Rock and roll is a means of pulling the white man down to the level of the Negro."[21] While rock may no longer be popularly regarded as a racially subversive musical form, the very genres of contemporary popular music remain, in essence, thinly veiled racial categories. "R & B" (Rhythm and Blues) and "soul" music are clearly references to *black* music, while Country & Western or heavy metal music are viewed, in the popular imagination, as *white* music. Black performers who want to break out of this artistic ghettoization must "cross over," a contemporary form of "passing" in which their music is seen as acceptable to white audiences.

The airwaves themselves are segregated. The designation "urban contemporary" is merely radio lingo for a "black" musical format. Such categorization affects playlists, advertising accounts, and shares of the listening market. On cable television, black music videos rarely receive airplay on MTV, but are confined instead to the more marginal BET (Black Entertainment Television) network.

In spite of such segregation, many performing artists have been able to garner a racially diverse group of fans. And yet, racially integrated concert audiences are extremely rare. Curiously, this "perverse phenomenon" of racially homogeneous crowds takes place despite the color of the performer. Lionel Richie's concert audiences, for example, are virtually all-white, while Teena Marie's are all-black.[22]

Racial symbols and images are omnipresent in popular culture. Commonplace household objects such as cookie jars, salt and pepper shakers, and ashtrays have frequently been designed and fashioned in the form of racial caricatures. Sociologist Steve Dublin in an analysis of these objects found that former tasks of domestic service were symbolically transferred onto these commodities.[23] An Aunt Jemima–type character, for example, is

---

[19]Quoted in Allen L. Woll, "Bandits and Lovers: Hispanic Images in American Film," in Miller, ed., *Kaleidoscopic Lens*, p. 60. Print.

[20]Bogle, "Familiar Plot," p. 17.

[21]Dave Marsh and Kevin Stein, *The Book of Rock Lists* (New York: Dell, 1981), p. 8. Print.

[22]*Rock & Roll Confidential*, No. 44 (February 1987), p. 2. Print.

[23]Steven C. Dublin, "Symbolic Slavery: Black Representations in Popular Culture," *Social Problems*, Vol. 34, No. 2 (April 1987). Print.

used to hold a roll of paper towels, her outstretched hands supporting the item to be dispensed. "Sprinkle Plenty," a sprinkle bottle in the shape of an Asian man, was used to wet clothes in preparation for ironing. Simple commodities, the household implements which help us perform everyday tasks, may reveal, therefore, a deep structure of racial meaning.

A crucial dimension for discerning the meaning of particular stereotypes and   40
images is the *situation context* for the creation and consumption of popular culture. For example, the setting in which "racist" jokes are told determines the function of humor. Jokes about blacks where the teller and audience are black constitute a form of self-awareness; they allow blacks to cope and "take the edge off" of oppressive aspects of the social order which they commonly confront. The meaning of these same jokes, however, is dramatically transformed when told across the "color line." If a white, or even black, person tells these jokes to a white audience, it will, despite its "purely" humorous intent, serve to reinforce stereotypes and rationalize the existing relations of racial inequality.

Concepts of race and racial images are both overt and implicit within popular culture — the organization of cultural production, the products themselves, and the manner in which they are consumed are deeply structured by race. Particular racial meanings, stereotypes, and myths can change, but the presence of a *system* of racial meanings and stereotypes, of racial ideology, seems to be an enduring aspect of American popular culture.

The era of Reaganism and the overall rightward drift of American politics and culture has added a new twist to the question of racial images and meanings. Increasingly, the problem for racial minorities is not that of misportrayal, but of "invisibility." Instead of celebrating racial and cultural diversity, we are witnessing an attempt by the right to define, once again, who the "real" American is, and what "correct" American values, mores, and political beliefs are. In such a context, racial minorities are no longer the focus of sustained media attention; when they do appear, they are cast as colored versions of essentially "white" characters.

The possibilities for change — for transforming racial stereotypes and challenging institutional inequities — nonetheless exist. Historically, strategies have involved the mobilization of political pressure against an offending institution(s). In the late 1950s, for instance, "Nigger Hair" tobacco changed its name to "Bigger Hare" due to concerted NAACP pressure on the manufacturer. In the early 1970s, Asian American community groups successfully fought NBC's attempt to resurrect Charlie Chan as a television series with white actor Ross Martin. Amidst the furor generated by Al Campanis's remarks cited at the beginning of this essay, Jesse Jackson suggested that a boycott of major league games be initiated in order to push for a restructuring of hiring and promotion practices.

Partially in response to such action, Baseball Commissioner Peter Ueberroth announced plans in June 1987 to help put more racial minorities in management roles. "The challenge we have," Ueberroth said, "is to manage change without losing tradition."[24] The problem with respect to the issue of race and popular culture, however, is that the *tradition* itself may need to be thoroughly examined, its "common sense" assumptions unearthed and challenged, and its racial images contested and transformed.

READING THE TEXT

1. Describe in your own words the difference between "overt racism" and "inferential racism" (para. 6).
2. Why, according to Omi, is popular culture so powerful in shaping America's attitudes toward race?
3. Why does Omi identify many attitudes toward race as "common sense" (para. 34), and what is his judgment about such ideas?
4. What relationship does Omi see between gender and racial stereotypes?
5. How did race relations change in America during the 1980s, in Omi's view?

READING THE SIGNS

1. In class, brainstorm stereotypes, both positive and negative, attributed to specific racial groups. Then discuss the possible sources of these stereotypes. In what ways have they been perpetuated in popular culture, including film, TV, advertising, music, and consumer products? What does your discussion reveal about popular culture's influence on our most basic ways of seeing the world?
2. Using Omi's essay as your critical framework, write an essay in which you explore how the film *12 Years a Slave* (2013) may reflect or redefine American attitudes toward racial identity and race relations. Alternatively, watch *Fruitvale Station* (2013), *Mi Familia* (1995), *Aloha* (2015), or another film that addresses race relations.
3. Study an issue of a magazine targeted to a specific ethnic readership, such as *Essence*, *Ebony*, *Latina*, or *Jade*, analyzing both its articles and advertising. Then write an essay in which you explore the extent to which the magazine accurately reflects that ethnicity or, in Omi's words, appeals to readers as "colored versions of essentially 'white' characters" (para. 42).
4. Omi claims that "in contemporary television and film, there is a tendency to present and equate racial minority groups and individuals with specific social problems" (para. 30). In class, brainstorm films and TV shows that have characters that are ethnic minorities; pick one example and watch it. Does Omi's claim apply to that example, or does it demonstrate different patterns of racial representation?
5. Watch the film *Avatar* (2009) and then, using Omi's categories of "overt" and "inferential" racism, write your own analysis of the race relations in this movie.

[24]*The San Francisco Chronicle* (June 13, 1987). Print.

AARON DEVOR

Gender Role Behaviors and Attitudes

"Boys will be boys, and girls will be girls": Few of our cultural mythologies seem as natural as this one. But in this exploration of the gender signals that traditionally tell what a "boy" or "girl" is supposed to look and act like, Aaron Devor shows how these signals are not "natural" at all but instead are cultural constructs. While the classic cues of masculinity — aggressive posture, self-confidence, a tough appearance — and the traditional signs of femininity — gentleness, passivity, strong nurturing instincts — are often considered "normal," Devor explains that they are by no means biological or psychological necessities. Indeed, he suggests, they can be richly mixed and varied, or to paraphrase the old Kinks song "Lola," "Boys can be girls and girls can be boys." Devor is professor of sociology, former dean of graduate studies, and the founder and academic director of the Transgender Archives at the University of Victoria and author of *Gender Blending: Confronting the Limits of Duality* (1989), from which this selection is excerpted.

Gender Role Behaviors and Attitudes

The clusters of social definitions used to identify persons by gender are collectively known as "femininity" and "masculinity." Masculine characteristics are used to identify persons as males, while feminine ones are used as signifiers for femaleness. People use femininity or masculinity to claim and communicate their membership in their assigned, or chosen, sex or gender. Others recognize our sex or gender more on the basis of these characteristics than on the basis of sex characteristics, which are usually largely covered by clothing in daily life.

These two clusters of attributes are most commonly seen as mirror images of one another with masculinity usually characterized by dominance and aggression, and femininity by passivity and submission. A more evenhanded description of the social qualities subsumed by femininity and masculinity might be to label masculinity as generally concerned with egoistic dominance and femininity as striving for cooperation or communion.[1]

---

[1] Eleanor Maccoby, *Social Development: Psychological Growth and the Parent-Child Relationship* (New York: Harcourt, 1980), p. 217. Egoistic dominance is a striving for superior rewards for oneself or a competitive striving to reduce the rewards for one's competitors even if such action will not increase one's own rewards. Persons who are motivated by desires for egoistic dominance not only wish the best for themselves but also wish to diminish the advantages of others whom they may perceive as competing with them.

Characterizing femininity and masculinity in such a way does not portray the two clusters of characteristics as being in a hierarchical relationship to one another but rather as being two different approaches to the same question, that question being centrally concerned with the goals, means, and use of power. Such an alternative conception of gender roles captures the hierarchical and competitive masculine thirst for power, which can, but need not, lead to aggression, and the feminine quest for harmony and communal well-being, which can, but need not, result in passivity and dependence.

Many activities and modes of expression are recognized by most members of society as feminine. Any of these can be, and often are, displayed by persons of either gender. In some cases, cross-gender behaviors are ignored by observers, and therefore do not compromise the integrity of a person's gender display. In other cases, they are labeled as inappropriate gender role behaviors. Although these behaviors are closely linked to sexual status in the minds and experiences of most people, research shows that dominant persons of either gender tend to use influence tactics and verbal styles usually associated with men and masculinity, while subordinate persons, of either gender, tend to use those considered to be the province of women.[2] Thus it seems likely that many aspects of masculinity and femininity are the result, rather than the cause, of status inequalities.

Popular conceptions of femininity and masculinity instead revolve around hierarchical appraisals of the "natural" roles of males and females. Members of both genders are believed to share many of the same human characteristics, although in different relative proportions; both males and females are popularly thought to be able to do many of the same things, but most activities are divided into suitable and unsuitable categories for each gender class. Persons who perform the activities considered appropriate for another gender will be expected to perform them poorly; if they succeed adequately, or even well, at their endeavors, they may be rewarded with ridicule or scorn for blurring the gender dividing line.

The patriarchal gender schema currently in use in mainstream North American society reserves highly valued attributes for males and actively supports the high evaluation of any characteristics which might inadvertently become associated with maleness. The ideology underlying the schema postulates that the cultural superiority of males is a natural outgrowth of the innate predisposition of males toward aggression and dominance, which is assumed to flow inevitably from evolutionary and biological sources. Female attributes are likewise postulated to find their source in innate predispositions acquired in the evolution of the species. Feminine characteristics are thought to be intrinsic to the female facility for

5

---

[2]Judith Howard, Philip Blumstein, and Pepper Schwartz, "Sex, Power, and Influence Tactics in Intimate Relationships," *Journal of Personality and Social Psychology* 51 (1986), pp. 102–9; Peter Kollock, Philip Blumstein, and Pepper Schwartz, "Sex and Power in Interaction: Conversational Privileges and Duties," *American Sociological Review* 50 (1985), pp. 34–46.

childbirth and breastfeeding. Hence, it is popularly believed that the social position of females is biologically mandated to be intertwined with the care of children and a "natural" dependency on men for the maintenance of mother-child units. Thus the goals of femininity and, by implication, of all biological females are presumed to revolve around heterosexuality and maternity.[3]

Femininity, according to this traditional formulation, "would result in warm and continued relationships with men, a sense of maternity, interest in caring for children, and the capacity to work productively and continuously in female occupations."[4] This recipe translates into a vast number of proscriptions and prescriptions. Warm and continued relations with men and an interest in maternity require that females be heterosexually oriented. A heterosexual orientation requires women to dress, move, speak, and act in ways that men will find attractive. As patriarchy has reserved active expressions of power as a masculine attribute, femininity must be expressed through modes of dress, movement, speech, and action which communicate weakness, dependency, ineffectualness, availability for sexual or emotional service, and sensitivity to the needs of others.

Some, but not all, of these modes of interrelation also serve the demands of maternity and many female job ghettos. In many cases, though, femininity is not particularly useful in maternity or employment. Both mothers and workers often need to be strong, independent, and effectual in order to do their jobs well. Thus femininity, as a role, is best suited to satisfying a masculine vision of heterosexual attractiveness.

Body postures and demeanors which communicate subordinate status and vulnerability to trespass through a message of "no threat" make people appear to be feminine. They demonstrate subordination through a minimizing of spatial use: People appear feminine when they keep their arms closer to their bodies, their legs closer together, and their torsos and heads less vertical than do masculine-looking individuals. People also look feminine when they point their toes inward and use their hands in small or childlike gestures. Other people also tend to stand closer to people they see as feminine, often invading their personal space, while people who make frequent appeasement gestures, such as smiling, also give the appearance of femininity. Perhaps as an outgrowth of a subordinate status and the need to avoid conflict with more socially powerful people, women tend to excel over

---

[3]Nancy Chodorow, *The Reproduction of Mothering: Psychoanalysis and the Sociology of Gender* (Berkeley: U of California P, 1978), p. 134.

[4]Jon K. Meyer and John E. Hoopes, "The Gender Dysphoria Syndromes: A Position Statement on So-Called 'Transsexualism,'" *Plastic and Reconstructive Surgery* 54 (Oct. 1974), pp. 444–51.

Rearing children is work typically done by women, but not always.

men at the ability to correctly interpret, and effectively display, nonverbal communication cues.[5]

Speech characterized by inflections, intonations, and phrases that convey nonaggression and subordinate status also make a speaker appear more feminine. Subordinate speakers who use more polite expressions and ask more questions in conversation seem more feminine. Speech characterized by sounds of higher frequencies are often interpreted by listeners as feminine, childlike, and ineffectual.[6] Feminine styles of dress likewise display subordinate status through greater restriction of the free movement of the body, greater exposure of the bare skin, and an emphasis on sexual characteristics. The more gender distinct the dress, the more this is the case.

Masculinity, like femininity, can be demonstrated through a wide variety 10 of cues. Pleck has argued that it is commonly expressed in North American

[5]Erving Goffman, *Gender Advertisements* (New York: Harper, 1976); Judith A. Hall, *Non-Verbal Sex Differences: Communication Accuracy and Expressive Style* (Baltimore: Johns Hopkins UP, 1984); Nancy M. Henley, *Body Politics: Power, Sex and Non-Verbal Communication* (Englewood Cliffs, N.J.: Prentice, 1979); Marianne Wex, *"Let's Take Back Our Space": "Female" and "Male" Body Language as a Result of Patriarchal Structures* (Berlin: Frauenliteraturverlag Hermine Fees, 1979).

[6]Karen L. Adams, "Sexism and the English Language: The Linguistic Implications of Being a Woman," in *Women: A Feminist Perspective*, 3rd ed., ed. Jo Freeman (Palo Alto, Calif.: Mayfield, 1984), pp. 478–91; Hall, pp. 37, 130–37.

society through the attainment of some level of proficiency at some, or all, of the following four main attitudes of masculinity. Persons who display success and high status in their social group, who exhibit "a manly air of toughness, confidence, and self-reliance" and "the aura of aggression, violence, and daring," and who conscientiously avoid anything associated with femininity are seen as exuding masculinity.[7] These requirements reflect the patriarchal ideology that masculinity results from an excess of testosterone, the assumption being that androgens supply a natural impetus toward aggression, which in turn impels males toward achievement and success. This vision of masculinity also reflects the ideological stance that ideal maleness (masculinity) must remain untainted by female (feminine) pollutants.

Masculinity, then, requires of its actors that they organize themselves and their society in a hierarchical manner so as to be able to explicitly quantify the achievement of success. The achievement of high status in one's social group requires competitive and aggressive behavior from those who wish to obtain it. Competition which is motivated by a goal of individual achievement, or egoistic dominance, also requires of its participants a degree of emotional insensitivity to feelings of hurt and loss in defeated others, and a measure of emotional insularity to protect oneself from becoming vulnerable to manipulation by others. Such values lead those who subscribe to them to view feminine persons as "born losers" and to strive to eliminate any similarities to feminine people from their own personalities. In patriarchally organized societies, masculine values become the ideological structure of the society as a whole. Masculinity thus becomes "innately" valuable and femininity serves a contrapuntal function to delineate and magnify the hierarchical dominance of masculinity.

Body postures, speech patterns, and styles of dress which demonstrate and support the assumption of dominance and authority convey an impression of masculinity. Typical masculine body postures tend to be expansive and aggressive. People who hold their arms and hands in positions away from their bodies, and who stand, sit, or lie with their legs apart — thus maximizing the amount of space that they physically occupy — appear most physically masculine. Persons who communicate an air of authority or a readiness for aggression by standing erect and moving forcefully also tend to appear more masculine. Movements that are abrupt and stiff, communicating force and threat rather than flexibility and cooperation, make an actor look masculine. Masculinity can also be conveyed by stern or serious facial expressions that suggest minimal receptivity to the influence of others, a characteristic which is an important element in the attainment and maintenance of egoistic dominance.[8]

---

[7]Joseph H. Pleck, *The Myth of Masculinity* (Cambridge, Mass.: MIT P, 1981), p. 139.
[8]Goffman; Hall; Henley; Wex.

Speech and dress which likewise demonstrate or claim superior status are also seen as characteristically masculine behavior patterns. Masculine speech patterns display a tendency toward expansiveness similar to that found in masculine body postures. People who attempt to control the direction of conversations seem more masculine. Those who tend to speak more loudly, use less polite and more assertive forms, and tend to interrupt the conversations of others more often also communicate masculinity to others. Styles of dress which emphasize the size of upper body musculature, allow freedom of movement, and encourage an illusion of physical power and a look of easy physicality all suggest masculinity. Such appearances of strength and readiness to action serve to create or enhance an aura of aggressiveness and intimidation central to an appearance of masculinity. Expansive postures and gestures combine with these qualities to insinuate that a position of secure dominance is a masculine one.

Gender role characteristics reflect the ideological contentions underlying the dominant gender schema in North American society. That schema leads us to believe that female and male behaviors are the result of socially directed hormonal instructions which specify that females will want to have children and will therefore find themselves relatively helpless and dependent on males for support and protection. The schema claims that males are innately aggressive and competitive and therefore will dominate over females. The social hegemony of this ideology ensures that we are all raised to practice gender roles which will confirm this vision of the nature of the sexes. Fortunately, our training to gender roles is neither complete nor uniform. As a result, it is possible to point to multitudinous exceptions to, and variations on, these themes. Biological evidence is equivocal about the source of gender roles; psychological androgyny is a widely accepted concept. It seems most likely that gender roles are the result of systematic power imbalances based on gender discrimination.[9]

READING THE TEXT

1. List the characteristics that Devor describes as being traditional conceptions of "masculinity" and "femininity" (para. 1).

2. What relationship does Devor see between characteristics that are considered masculine and feminine?

3. How does Devor explain the cultural belief in the "superiority" (para. 5) of males?

4. How, in Devor's view, do speech and dress communicate gender roles?

[9]Howard, Blumstein, and Schwartz; Kollock, Blumstein, and Schwartz.

Reading the Signs

1. In small groups that identify as the same gender, brainstorm lists of traits that you consider to be masculine and feminine, and then have each group write its list on the board. Compare the lists produced by male and female groups. What patterns of differences or similarities do you see? To what extent do the traits presume a heterosexual orientation? How do you account for your results?

2. Study the speech patterns, styles of dress, and other nonverbal cues communicated by your friends during a social occasion, such as a party, trying not to reveal that you are observing them for an assignment. Then write an essay in which you analyze these cues used by your friends. To what extent do your friends enact the traditional gender codes Devor describes?

3. **CONNECTING TEXTS**   Study a popular magazine such as *Vanity Fair*, *Rolling Stone*, or *Maxim* for advertisements depicting men and women interacting with each other. Then write an essay in which you interpret the body postures of the models, using Devor's selection as your framework for analysis. How do males and females typically stand? To what extent do the models enact stereotypically masculine or feminine stances? To develop your essay, consult Steve Craig's "Men's Men and Women's Women" (p. 167).

4. **CONNECTING TEXTS**   Devor argues that female fashion traditionally has restricted body movement while male styles of dress usually allow freedom of movement. In class, discuss whether this claim is still true today, being sure to consider a range of clothing types (such as athletic wear, corporate dress, party fashion, and so forth). Use the class discussion as a jumping off point for your own essay on this topic. To develop your ideas, consult Jia Tolentino's "How 'Empowerment' Became Something for Women to Buy" (p. 180), Anna Keszeg's "What Their Clothes Tell Us about Those Girls" (p. 243), and Mariah Burton Nelson's "I Won. I'm Sorry." (p. 553).

PERFORMING GENDER

DEBORAH BLUM

The Gender Blur: Where Does Biology End and Society Take Over?

There's an old argument over whether nature or nurture is more important in determining human behavior. Nowhere is this argument more intense than in gender studies, where proponents of the social construction of gender identities are currently exploring the many ways in which our upbringing shapes our behavior. But after watching her two-year-old son emphatically choose to play only with carnivorous dinosaur toys and disdainfully reject the "wimpy" vegetarian variety, Deborah Blum decided that nurture couldn't be all that there was to it. Exploring the role of biology in the determination of human behavior, Blum argues that both nature and nurture have to be taken into account if we are to understand gender differences. A Pulitzer Prize–winning professor of journalism at the University of Wisconsin at Madison, Blum is the author of several books, including *Sex on the Brain: The Biological Differences between Men and Women* (1997) and *The Poisoner's Handbook: Murder and the Birth of Forensic Medicine in Jazz Age New York* (2010).

I was raised in one of those university-based, liberal elite families that politicians like to ridicule. In my childhood, every human being — regardless of gender — was exactly alike under the skin, and I mean exactly, barring his or her different opportunities. My parents wasted no opportunity to bring this point home. One Christmas, I received a Barbie doll and a softball glove. Another brought a green enamel stove, which baked tiny cakes by the heat of a lightbulb, and also a set of steel-tipped darts and competition-quality dartboard. Did I mention the year of the chemistry set and the ballerina doll?

It wasn't until I became a parent — I should say, a parent of two boys — that I realized I had been fed a line and swallowed it like a sucker (barring the part about opportunities, which I still believe). This dawned on me during my older son's dinosaur phase, which began when he was about two-and-a-half. Oh, he loved dinosaurs, all right, but only the blood-swilling carnivores. Plant-eaters were wimps and losers, and he refused to wear a T-shirt marred by a picture of a stegosaur. I looked down at him one day, as he was snarling around my feet and doing his toddler best to gnaw off my right leg, and I thought: This goes a lot deeper than culture.

Raising children tends to bring on this kind of politically incorrect reaction. Another friend came to the same conclusion watching a son determinedly bite his breakfast toast into the shape of a pistol he hoped would blow away — or at least terrify — his younger brother. Once you get past the guilt part — Did I do this? Should I have bought him that plastic allosaur with the oversized teeth? — such revelations can lead you to consider the far more interesting field of gender biology, where the questions take a different shape: Does love of carnage begin in culture or genetics, and which drives which? Do the gender roles of our culture reflect an underlying biology, and, in turn, does the way we behave influence that biology?

The point I'm leading up to — through the example of my son's innocent love of predatory dinosaurs — is actually one of the most straightforward in this debate. One of the reasons we're so fascinated by childhood behaviors is that, as the old saying goes, the child becomes the man (or woman, of course). Most girls don't spend their preschool years snarling around the house and pretending to chew off their companion's legs. And they — mostly — don't grow up to be as aggressive as men. Do the ways that we amplify those early differences in childhood shape the adults we become? Absolutely. But it's worth exploring the starting place — the faint signal that somehow gets amplified.

"There's plenty of room in society to influence sex differences," says 5 Marc Breedlove, a behavioral endocrinologist at the University of California at Berkeley and a pioneer in defining how hormones can help build sexually different nervous systems. "Yes, we're born with predispositions, but it's society that amplifies them, exaggerates them. I believe that — except for the sex differences in aggression. Those [differences] are too massive to be explained simply by society."

Aggression does allow a straightforward look at the issue. Consider the following statistics: Crime reports in both the United States and Europe record between ten and fifteen robberies committed by men for every one by a woman. At one point, people argued that this was explained by size difference. Women weren't big enough to intimidate, but that would change, they predicted, with the availability of compact weapons. But just as little girls don't routinely make weapons out of toast, women — even criminal ones — don't seem drawn to weaponry in the same way that men are. Almost twice as many male thieves and robbers use guns as their female counterparts do.

Or you can look at more personal crimes: domestic partner murders. Three-fourths of men use guns in those killings; 50 percent of women do. Here's more from the domestic front: In conflicts in which a woman killed a man, he tended to be the one who had started the fight — in 51.8 percent of the cases, to be exact. When the man was the killer, he again was the likely first aggressor, and by an even more dramatic margin. In fights in which women died, they had started the argument only 12.5 percent of the time.

Enough. You can parade endless similar statistics but the point is this: Males are more aggressive, not just among humans but among almost all species on earth. Male chimpanzees, for instance, declare war on neighboring troops, and one of their strategies is a warning strike: They kill females and infants to terrorize and intimidate. In terms of simple, reproductive genetics, it's an advantage of males to be aggressive: You can muscle your way into dominance, winning more sexual encounters, more offspring, more genetic future. For the female — especially in a species like ours, with time for just one successful pregnancy a year — what's the genetic advantage in brawling?

Thus the issue becomes not whether there is a biologically influenced sex difference in aggression — the answer being a solid, technical "You betcha" — but rather how rigid that difference is. The best science, in my opinion, tends to align with basic common sense. We all know that there are extraordinarily gentle men and murderous women. Sex differences are always generalizations: they refer to a behavior, with some evolutionary rationale behind it. They never define, entirely, an individual. And that fact alone should tell us that there's always — even in the most biologically dominated traits — some flexibility, an instinctive ability to respond, for better and worse, to the world around us.

This is true even with physical characteristics that we've often assumed 10 are nailed down by genetics. Scientists now believe height, for instance, is only about 90 percent heritable. A person's genes might code for a six-foot-tall body, but malnutrition could literally cut that short. And there's also some evidence, in girls anyway, that children with stressful childhoods tend to become shorter adults. So while some factors are predetermined, there's evidence that the prototypical male/female body design can be readily altered.

It's a given that humans, like most other species — bananas, spiders, sharks, ducks, any rabbit you pull out of a hat — rely on two sexes for reproduction. So basic is that requirement that we have chromosomes whose primary purpose is to deliver the genes that order up a male or a female. All other chromosomes are numbered, but we label the sex chromosomes with the letters X and Y. We get one each from our mother and our father, and the basic combinations are these: XX makes female, XY makes male.

There are two important — and little known — points about these chromosomal matches. One is that even with this apparently precise system, there's nothing precise — or guaranteed — about the physical construction of male and female. The other point makes that possible. It appears that sex doesn't matter in the early stages of embryonic development. We are unisex at the point of conception.

If you examine an embryo at about six weeks, you see that it has the ability to develop in either direction. The fledgling embryo has two sets of ducts — Wolffian for male, Muellerian for female — an either/or structure, held in readiness for further development. If testosterone and other androgens are released by hormone-producing cells, then the Wolffian ducts develop into the channel that connects penis to testes, and the female ducts wither away.

Without testosterone, the embryo takes on a female form; the male ducts vanish and the Muellerian ducts expand into oviducts, uterus, and vagina. In other words, in humans, anyway (the opposite is true in birds), the female is the default sex. Back in the 1950s, the famed biologist Alfred Jost showed that if you castrate a male rabbit fetus, choking off testosterone, you produce a completely feminized rabbit.

We don't do these experiments in humans — for obvious reasons — but 15 there are naturally occurring instances that prove the same point. For instance: In the fetal testes are a group of cells, called Leydig cells, that make testosterone. In rare cases, the fetus doesn't make enough of these cells (a defect known as Leydig cell hypoplasia). In this circumstance we see the limited power of the XY chromosome. These boys have the right chromosomes and the right genes to be boys; they just don't grow a penis. Obstetricians and parents often think they see a baby girl, and these children are routinely raised as daughters. Usually, the "mistake" is caught about the time of puberty, when menstruation doesn't start. A doctor's examination shows the child to be internally male; there are usually small testes, often tucked within the abdomen. As the researchers put it, if the condition had been known from the beginning, "the sisters would have been born as brothers."

Just to emphasize how tricky all this body-building can get, there's a peculiar genetic defect that seems to be clustered by heredity in a small group of villages in the Dominican Republic. The result of the defect is a failure to produce an enzyme that concentrates testosterone, specifically for building the genitals. One obscure little enzyme only, but here's what happens without it: You get a boy with undescended testes and a penis so short and stubby that it resembles an oversized clitoris.

In the mountain villages of this Caribbean nation, people are used to it. The children are usually raised as "conditional" girls. At puberty, the secondary tide of androgens rises and is apparently enough to finish the construction project. The scrotum suddenly descends, the phallus grows, and the child develops a distinctly male body — narrow hips, muscular build, and even slight beard growth. At that point, the family shifts the child over from daughter to son. The dresses are thrown out. He begins to wear male clothes and starts dating girls. People in the Dominican Republic are so familiar with this condition that there's a colloquial name for it: *guevedoces*, meaning "eggs (or testes) at twelve."

It's the comfort level with this slip-slide of sexual identity that's so remarkable and, I imagine, so comforting to the children involved. I'm positive that the sexual transition of these children is less traumatic than the abrupt awareness of the "sisters who would have been brothers." There's a message of tolerance there, well worth repeating, and there are some other key lessons, too.

These defects are rare and don't alter the basic male-female division of our species. They do emphasize how fragile those divisions can be. Biology allows flexibility, room to change, to vary and grow. With that comes room for error as well. That it's possible to live with these genetic defects, that they don't merely kill us off, is a reminder that we, male and female alike, exist on a continuum of biological possibilities that can overlap and sustain either sex.

Marc Breedlove points out that the most difficult task may be separating   20 how the brain responds to hormones from how the brain responds to the *results* of hormones. Which brings us back, briefly, below the belt: In this context, the penis is just a result, the product of androgens at work before birth. "And after birth," says Breedlove, "virtually everyone who interacts with that individual will note that he has a penis, and will, in many instances, behave differently than if the individual was a female."

Do the ways that we amplify physical and behavioral differences in childhood shape who we become as adults? Absolutely. But to understand that, you have to understand the differences themselves — their beginning and the very real biochemistry that may lie behind them.

Here is a good place to focus on testosterone — a hormone that is both well-studied and generally underrated. First, however, I want to acknowledge that there are many other hormones and neurotransmitters that appear to influence behavior. Preliminary work shows that fetal boys are a little more active than fetal girls. It's pretty difficult to argue socialization at that point. There's a strong suspicion that testosterone may create the difference.

And there are a couple of relevant animal models to emphasize the point. Back in the 1960s, Robert Goy, a psychologist at the University of Wisconsin at Madison, first documented that young male monkeys play much more roughly than young females. Goy went on to show that if you manipulate testosterone level — raising it in females, damping it down in males — you can reverse those effects, creating sweet little male monkeys and rowdy young females.

Is testosterone the only factor at work here? I don't think so. But clearly we can argue a strong influence, and, interestingly, studies have found that girls with congenital adrenal hypoplasia — who run high in testosterone — tend to be far more fascinated by trucks and toy weaponry than most little girls are. They lean toward rough-and-tumble play, too. As it turns out, the strongest influence on this "abnormal" behavior is not parental disapproval, but the company of other little girls, who tone them down and direct them toward more routine girl games.

And that reinforces an early point: If there is indeed a biology to sex differences, we amplify it. At some point — when it is still up for debate — we   25

Shoppers gather at the opening of an American Girl doll store in Colorado.

Andy Cross/The Denver Post/Getty Images

gain a sense of our gender, and with it a sense of "gender-appropriate" behavior.

Some scientists argue for some evidence of gender awareness in infancy, perhaps by the age of twelve months. The consensus seems to be that full-blown "I'm a girl" or "I'm a boy" instincts arrive between the ages of two and three. Research shows that if a family operates in a very traditional, Beaver Cleaver kind of environment, filled with awareness of and association with "proper" gender behaviors, the "boys do trucks, girls do dolls" attitude seems to come very early. If a child grows up in a less traditional family, with an emphasis on partnership and sharing — "We all do the dishes, Joshua" — children maintain a more flexible sense of gender roles until about age six.

In this period, too, relationships between boys and girls tend to fall into remarkably strict lines. Interviews with children find that three-year-olds say that about half their friendships are with the opposite sex. By the age of five, that drops to 20 percent. By seven, almost no boys or girls have, or will admit to having, best friends of the opposite sex. They still hang out on the same playground, play on the same soccer teams. They may be friendly, but the real friendships tend to be boy-to-boy or girl-to-girl.

There's some interesting science that suggests that the space between boys and girls is a normal part of development; there are periods during which children may thrive and learn from hanging out with peers of the same sex. Do we, as parents, as a culture at large, reinforce such separations? Is the pope Catholic? One of my favorite studies looked at little boys who asked for toys. If they asked for a heavily armed action figure, they got the soldier about 70 percent of the time. If they asked for a "girl" toy, like a baby doll or a Barbie, their parents purchased it maybe 40 percent of the time. Name a child who won't figure out how to work *that* system.

How does all this fit together — toys and testosterone, biology and behavior, the development of the child into the adult, the way that men and women relate to one another?

Let me make a cautious statement about testosterone: It not only has 30 some body-building functions, it influences some behaviors as well. Let's make that a little less cautious: These behaviors include rowdy play, sex drive, competitiveness, and an in-your-face attitude. Males tend to have a higher baseline of testosterone than females — in our species, about seven to ten times as much — and therefore you would predict (correctly, I think) that all of those behaviors would be more generally found in men than in women.

But testosterone is also one of my favorite examples of how responsive biology is, how attuned it is to the way we live our lives. Testosterone, it turns out, rises in response to competition and threat. In the days of our ancestors, this might have been hand-to-hand combat or high-risk hunting endeavors. Today, scientists have measured testosterone rise in athletes preparing for a game, in chess players awaiting a match, in spectators following a soccer competition.

If a person — or even just a person's favored team — wins, testosterone continues to rise. It falls with a loss. (This also makes sense in an evolutionary perspective. If one was being clobbered with a club, it would be extremely unhelpful to have a hormone urging one to battle on.) Testosterone also rises in the competitive world of dating, settles down with a stable and supportive relationship, climbs again if the relationship starts to falter.

It's been known for years that men in high-stress professions — say, police work or corporate law — have higher testosterone levels than men in the ministry. It turns out that women in the same kind of strong-attitude professions have higher testosterone than women who choose to stay home. What I like about this is the chicken-or-egg aspect. If you argue that testosterone influenced the behavior of those women, which came first? Did they have high testosterone and choose the law? Or did they choose the law, and the competitive environment ratcheted them up on the androgen scale? Or could both be at work?

And, returning to children for a moment, there's an ongoing study by Pennsylvania researchers, tracking that question in adolescent girls, who are being encouraged by their parents to engage in competitive activities that were once for boys only. As they do so, the researchers are monitoring, regularly, two hormones: testosterone and cortisol, a stress hormone. Will these hormones rise in response to this new, more traditionally male environment? What if more girls choose the competitive path; more boys choose the other? Will female testosterone levels rise, male levels fall? Will that wonderful, unpredictable, flexible biology that we've been given allow a shift, so that one day, we will literally be far more alike?

We may not have answers to all those questions, but we can ask them, and we can expect that the answers will come someday, because science clearly shows us that such possibilities exist. In this most important sense, sex differences offer us a paradox. It is only through exploring and understanding what makes us different that we can begin to understand what binds us together. 35

READING THE TEXT

1. What effect do Blum's opening personal anecdotes have on the persuasiveness of her argument?

2. What evidence does Blum offer to support her contention that males are naturally more aggressive than females?

3. How does testosterone affect human behavior, according to Blum?

4. What does the term "'conditional' girls" (para. 17) mean for some members of a rural area in the Dominican Republic, and what significance does Blum attribute to this status?

5. In Blum's view, how do the cultural choices that humans make, such as engaging in sports or other competitive activities, affect hormone balances?

READING THE SIGNS

1. In your journal, reflect on the way your upbringing shaped your sense of appropriate gender behavior. Do you recall any patterns of preferring some toys over others? What media influences might have affected your attitudes?

2. **CONNECTING TEXTS**   Blum's selection challenges the common cultural studies position that gender behavior is socially constructed. Write an essay in which you defend, qualify, or reject Blum's point of view. To develop your ideas, consult Aaron Devor's "Gender Role Behaviors and Attitudes" (p. 474), Michael Hulshof-Schmidt's "What's in an Acronym?" (p. 489), and Kevin Jennings's "American Dreams" (p. 492).

3. Write an essay describing how you would raise a boy to counteract his stereotypical tendencies to aggressive behavior. Alternatively, describe how you would raise a girl to avoid the common stereotypes associated with females.

4. Visit the library, and investigate recent research on the possible genetic basis for homosexuality. Then write an essay in which you extend Blum's argument for the biological basis of gendered behavior to sexual orientation. Alternatively, research the current scientific literature on transgenderism.

Gender Identity Online

Noah Berger/AP Images

1. In February 2014, Facebook made headlines when it expanded its number of gender categories to more than fifty, including "pangender," "gender fluid," and "transgender." This photo shows Facebook software engineer Brielle Harrison demonstrating the new options for gender identity, and the original caption for this photo indicated that she planned to switch her identifier to "Trans Woman." How does such a move by Facebook challenge traditional ideas of gender identity?

2. Visit your Facebook page and explore these gender identity labels yourself. Pick a few and research them. How do they differ from one another? Why do you think Facebook chose to add so many fine variations in gender identity for users to choose from?

MICHAEL HULSHOF-SCHMIDT

What's in an Acronym? Parsing the LGBTQQIP2SAA Community

As Michael Hulshof-Schmidt puts it in this entry from his personal blog *Social Justice For All*, "Most oppressed and minority communities have struggled with finding a descriptor that they feel embraces them and that they can embrace." This act of finding a name has been especially challenging for the queer community, which, by its own philosophy, resists the reductionist act of labeling human beings and behavior. Providing a succinct overview of the problem, Hulshof-Schmidt describes the difficulties that have cropped up in the ongoing attempt to be adequately inclusive, illustrating how full inclusiveness can result in some pretty complicated acronyms. Not to worry, however, Hulshof-Schmidt concludes, because "in the long run, the intent matters more than the label." Michael Hulshof-Schmidt is an instructor in the School of Social Work at Portland State University.

Every few months another online debate flares up about exactly what the LGBT community should call itself. Generally speaking, most people default to LGBT (or GLBT, with a slight majority favoring the L-first version). This explicitly calls out key components of a diverse group: Lesbian, Gay, Bisexual, Transgender. As shorthand goes, it's fairly effective, recognizing the spectrum of sexual orientation and gender identity in four simple letters. Of course, it can't please everyone, and like most compromises, leaves plenty of people feeling unheard.

Four other forms of shorthand see frequent use in the media and on the Internet. Many people opt simply for "gay." Unfortunately, that leaves out any aspect of the community that doesn't identify explicitly with same-sex attraction. It also traditionally applies to men, resulting in sexist language, however unintentional.

Opponents of the community typically use "the homosexual community" which manages to be gender neutral but also leaves out significant populations (although those populations may be just as happy not to get attention from these groups.) The more academic term "sexual minorities" is also used. Although this has broader meaning it also draws focus to the word "sexual," avoidance of which resulted in the use of the word "gay" in the first place. Members of the LGBT community don't want to be defined strictly by possible behavior, but as complex, fully realized human beings. In an America with a strong puritanical streak — even today — the word "sexual" still has too much power to stigmatize.

Many activists have reclaimed the word "queer" as a preferred descriptor. Taking back the word from the bullies and foes is a way to regain power. This is much like *Bitch* magazine co-opting a frequent slur as a way to raise feminist activists above their oppressors. For many, however, the scars from being called "queer" are too deep and too fresh to choose it as an identity. So what's a diverse, inclusion-inclined community to do?

Over time, a number of other additions have been suggested to the LGBT acronym. The most common is Q, signifying "questioning" to recognize that many people are uncertain about their sexual orientation or gender identity (or both). Some also use the Q for queer. At full throttle, the letters wind up something like LGBTQQIP2SAA — Lesbian, Gay, Bisexual, Transgender, 5

- Two Q's to cover both bases (queer and questioning);
- I for Intersex, people with two sets of genitalia or various chromosomal differences;
- P for Pansexual, people who refuse to be pinned down on the Kinsey scale;
- 2S for Two-Spirit, a tradition in many First Nations that considers sexual minorities to have both male and female spirits;
- A for Asexual, people who do not identify with any orientation; and
- A for Allies, recognizing that the community thrives best with loving supporters, although they are not really part of the community itself.

That manages to be pretty inclusive, but it's also pretty unwieldy.

Labels are tricky things. Most oppressed and minority communities have struggled with finding a descriptor that they feel embraces them and that they can embrace. The evolution of Negro to Colored to Black to

African-American shows a clear transition from outside labels to a community claiming its own identity, although many within the community object to African-American. The journey from Indians to Native Americans to First Nations is similar, with many outside the community being unfamiliar with the latter designation. The transition from handicapped to disabled was successful (and codified in law) but the attempt to destigmatize to "differently abled" was just too awkward to find common usage.

It's that kind of awkwardness that stymies the best attempts to find the magic LGBT label. The problem stems from the best of intentions, inclusion. People are complex, with multiple identities. Everyone has a sexual orientation, gender identity, race, religion (or lack thereof), ethnicity, and many other components. It's laudable for the LGBT community to recognize that there is strength in working together and to try to find a descriptor that shows that intent. In the long run, the intent matters more than the label. Rather than take umbrage at a less than fully inclusive LGBTQ — which at least shows good intent — let's focus on the work we need to do together to make this a better place for everyone.

READING THE TEXT

1. What explanation does Hulshof-Schmidt offer for the controversy in the LGBT community over what to call itself?
2. Summarize in your own words the reasons "gay," "queer," "homosexual communities," and "sexual minorities" can be considered problematic terms, according to Hulshof-Schmidt.
3. How does the debate about what to call the LGBT community mirror similar struggles that other minority groups have faced, according to Hulshof-Schmidt?
4. What does Hulshof-Schmidt mean by saying that, by adopting the term "queer" or "bitch," one is "taking back the word from the bullies and foes" (para. 4)?

READING THE SIGNS

1. In an essay, propose your own candidate for a label to describe the LGBT community. In class, share your suggested labels. What patterns do you see in the class's proposals?
2. Select one of the other minority groups that Hulshof-Schmidt mentions, and research the history of labels that have been attached to it. Use your research as the basis of an essay in which you argue whether the most current nomenclature constitutes the best label for the group.
3. Visit your school's Web site, and analyze the language used to describe the minority groups that Hulshof-Schmidt discusses in his selection. You might pay particular attention to sections that discuss student groups and academic departments. Use your findings as evidence in an essay in which you assess the extent to which your school achieves the goal of inclusiveness that Hulshof-Schmidt recommends without being "unwieldy" (para. 5).

KEVIN JENNINGS

American Dreams

When Ellen DeGeneres became the first television star to come out of the closet on prime-time TV, gay men and lesbians around the country celebrated what appeared to be a major step forward for one of America's most marginalized communities. But the firestorm of protest that also attended Ellen's coming-out equally demonstrated just how far homosexuals have to go before winning full acceptance into American society. In this personal narrative (first published in 1994) of what it means to grow up gay in America, Kevin Jennings reveals the torment endured by a child forced to conceal his difference from everyone around him, especially his own parents. With years of self-denial and one suicide attempt behind him, Jennings shows how he eventually came to accept himself as he is and in so doing achieved his own version of the American dream. Kevin Jennings is founder of the Gay, Lesbian, and Straight Education Network (GLSEN) and served as the assistant deputy secretary for the Office of Safe and Drug-Free Schools at the U.S. Department of Education from 2009–2011. He is now the Executive Director of the Arcus Foundation.

When I was little, I honestly thought I would grow up to be the president. After all, I lived in a land of opportunity where anyone, with enough determination and hard work, could aspire to the highest office in the land. I planned to live out the American Dream.

I realized, however, that something was amiss from an early age. I grew up in the rural community of Lewisville, North Carolina, just outside the city of Winston-Salem. As you might guess from the city's name, Winston-Salem, Winston-Salem makes its living from the tobacco industry: It was cigarettes that propelled local conglomerate RJR-Nabisco to its status as one of the world's largest multinational corporations. Somehow this rising tide of prosperity never lapped at our doors, and the Jennings family was a bitter family indeed. Poor whites descended from Confederate veterans, we eagerly sought out scapegoats for our inexplicable failure to "make it" in the land of opportunity. My uncles and cousins joined the Ku Klux Klan, while my father, a fundamentalist minister, used religion to excuse his prejudices — against blacks, against Jews, against Catholics, against Yankees, against Communists and liberals (basically the same thing, as far as he was concerned), and, of course, against gays. Somehow the golden rule of "Do unto others as you would have them do unto you" never made it into his gospel. Instead, I remember church services filled with outbursts of paranoia, as we were warned about the evils of those whom we (incorrectly) held responsible for our very real oppression. I grew up believing that there was a Communist plot undermining our nation, a Jewish conspiracy controlling the banks and the media, and that black men — whom I unself-consciously referred to as "niggers" — spent their days plotting to rape white women. In case this seems like a history lesson on the Stone Age, please consider that I was born in 1963 and graduated from high school in 1981. Hardly the ancient past!

My father's profession as a traveling minister never left much money for luxuries like college tuition. Nevertheless, my mother was determined that I, her last chance, was going to make good on the Dream that had been denied to her and to my four older siblings — that one of her children would be the first member of our extended family ever to go to college. Not that it was going to be easy: my father died when I was eight, and my mother went to work at McDonald's (the only job she could get with her limited credentials). Every penny was watched carefully; dinner was often leftover quarter-pounders that she didn't have to pay for. I'm the only person I know who sees the Golden Arches, takes a bite, and thinks, "Mmm, just like Mom used to make!"

Throughout high school, I was determined to make it, determined to show my mother — and myself — that the American Dream really could come true. I worked hard and got ahead, earning a scholarship to Harvard after I had remade myself into the image of what I was told a successful person was like. Little did I realize at that point the price I was paying to fit in.

The first thing to go was any sign of my Southern heritage. As I came into contact with mainstream America, through high school "gifted and talented" programs and, later, at college in Massachusetts, I began to realize that we Southerners were different. Our home-cooked meals — grits, turnip greens, red-eye gravy — never seemed to show up in frozen dinners, and if a character on television spoke with a Southern accent, that immediately identified him or her as stupid or as comic relief. As the lesbian writer Blanche Boyd put it:

> When television programs appeared, a dreadful truth came clear to me: Southerners were not normal people. We did not sound like normal people . . . [and] what we chose to talk about seemed peculiarly different also. I began to realize we were hicks. Television took away my faith in my surroundings. I didn't want to be a hick. I decided to go North, where people talked fast, walked fast, and acted cool. I practiced talking like the people on television. . . . I became desperate to leave the South.

Like Blanche Boyd, I deliberately erased my accent and aped the false monotone of television newscasters. I never invited college friends home to North Carolina for fear they might meet my family and realize they were worthless, ignorant hicks — which is how I'd come to view those whom I loved. I applied to colleges on the sole criterion that they not be in the South. I ran as far from Lewisville, North Carolina, as I could.

Michael Springer/Getty Images

LGBTQ protestors march in favor of ordaining and consecrating the Rev. Gene Robinson, the first openly gay Bishop in the Anglican church.

But there were some things about myself I could not escape from or change, no matter how hard I tried — among them the fact that I am gay.

I had always known I was gay, even before I had heard the word or knew what it meant. I remember that at age six or seven, the "adult" magazines that so fascinated my older brothers simply didn't interest me at all, and I somehow knew that I'd better hide this feeling from them. As I grew older and began to understand what my feelings meant, I recoiled in horror from myself. After all, my religious upbringing as a Southern Baptist had taught me that gay people were twisted perverts destined for a lifetime of eternal damnation.

Being as set as I was on achieving the American Dream, I was not about to accept the fact that I was gay. Here is where I paid the heaviest price for my Dream. I pursued what I thought was "normal" with a vengeance in high school, determined that, if the spirit was weak, the flesh would be more willing at the prospect of heterosexuality. I dated every girl I could literally get my hands on, earning a well-deserved reputation as a jerk who tried to see how far he could get on the first date. I attacked anyone who suggested that gay people might be entitled to some rights, too, and was the biggest teller of fag jokes at Radford High. But what I really hated was myself, and this I couldn't escape from, no matter how drunk or stoned I got, which I was doing on an almost daily basis by senior year.

That was also the year I fell in love for the first time, with another boy in my class. It turned out he was gay, too, and we made love one night in late May. I woke up the next morning and realized that it was true — I really was a fag after all. I spent that day trying to figure out how I was going to live the American Dream, which seemed impossible if I was homosexual. By nightfall I decided it *was* impossible, and without my Dream I couldn't see a reason why I'd want to be alive at all. I went to my family's medicine cabinet, took the new bottle of aspirin out, and proceeded to wash down 140 pills with a glass of gin. I remember the exact number — 140 — because I figured I could only get down about ten at one swallow, so I carefully counted out fourteen little stacks before I began. Thanks to a friend who got to me in time, I didn't die that night. My story has a happy ending — but a lot of them don't. Those moments of desperation helped me understand why one out of every three gay teens tries to commit suicide.

At Harvard, the most important lessons I learned had little to do with   10
Latin American or European history, which were my majors. Instead, I learned the importance of taking control of my own destiny. I met a great professor who taught me that as long as I stayed in the closet, I was accepting the idea that there was something wrong with me, something that I needed to hide. After all, as my favorite bisexual, Eleanor Roosevelt, once said, "No one can make you feel inferior without your consent." By staying closeted, I was consenting to my own inferiority. I realized that for years, I had let a Dream — a beautiful, seductive, but ultimately false Dream — rule my life. I had agreed to pay its price, which was the rejection of my family, my culture, and eventually myself. I came to understand that the costs of the Dream far outweighed its rewards. I learned that true freedom would be mine only when I was able to make my own decisions about what I wanted out of life instead of accepting those thrust upon me by the Dream. Since I made that realization, I have followed my own path instead of the one I had been taught was "right" all my life.

Once I started down this new path, I began to make some discoveries about the society in which I was raised, and about its notions of right and wrong. I began to ask many questions, and the answers to these questions were not always pleasant. Why, for example, did my mother always earn less than men who did the same exact work? Why did I learn as a child that to cheat someone was to "Jew" them? Why was my brother ostracized when he fell in love with and later married a black woman? Why did everyone in my family work so hard and yet have so little? I realized that these inequalities were part of the game, the rules of which were such that gays, blacks, poor people, women, and many others would always lose to the wealthy white heterosexual Christian men who have won the Presidency forty-two out of forty-two times. Those odds — 100 percent — are pretty good ones to bet on. No, I discovered that true freedom could not be achieved by a Dream that calls on us to give up who we are in order to fit in and become "worthy" of power. Holding power means little if women have to become masculine "iron ladies" to get it, if Jews have to "Americanize" their names, if blacks have to learn to speak so-called Standard English (though we never acknowledge *whose* standard it is), or if gays and lesbians have to hide what everyone else gets to celebrate — the loves of their lives.

Real freedom will be ours when the people around us — and when we ourselves — accept that we, too, are "real" Americans, and that we shouldn't have to change to meet anyone else's standards. In 1924, at age twenty-two, the gay African American poet Langston Hughes said it best, in his poem "I, Too":

> Tomorrow,
> I'll be at the table
> When company comes.
> Nobody'll dare
> Say to me,
> "Eat in the kitchen,"
> Then.
> Besides,
> They'll see how beautiful I am
> And be ashamed —
> I, too, am America.

By coming out as a gay man and demanding my freedom, I realize that I have done the most American thing of all. And while I have come a long way since the days when I dreamed of living in the White House, I have discovered that what I'm fighting for now is the very thing I thought I'd be fighting for if I ever became President — "liberty and justice for all."

READING THE TEXT

1. According to Jennings, how did his Southern upbringing influence his goals for the future?

2. Why did Jennings feel he had to eschew his Southern heritage?

3. In what ways did Jennings deny to himself his sexual orientation, and why did he do so?

4. In your own words, trace the evolution of Jennings's understanding of the American dream as he grew up.

5. What is the relationship between the excerpt from Langston Hughes's "I, Too" and Jennings's story?

READING THE SIGNS

1. In your journal, write your own account of how you responded to normative gender codes as a high school student. To what extent did you feel pressure to conform to or to renounce traditional expectations — or to do both?

2. Jennings describes his early attempts to deny his sexual orientation. In class, discuss how other minority or underprivileged groups — ethnic minorities, women, the disabled — sometimes try to erase their identities. What social and cultural forces motivate such self-denial? Use the discussion as a springboard for an essay in which you explore why one might be motivated to do so.

3. In class, brainstorm two lists: films or TV shows that reinforce heterosexuality as normative and those that present homosexuality positively. Then compare your lists. What conclusions do you draw about popular culture's influence on American gender codes?

4. **CONNECTING TEXTS** In an essay, discuss how Jennings might respond to the TV program *The Outs*. To develop your ideas, read John Sherman's "The New Normative: Queer Politics in *The Outs*" (p. 259).

SAMANTHA RAPHELSON

From GIs to Gen Z (Or Is It iGen?): How Generations Get Nicknames

As if there weren't enough labels that pigeon-hole your identity, there are always those generational tags that lump together millions of people simply on the basis of their birth year. In this feature story, Samantha Raphelson surveys the history of demographic identification, focusing on the emerging monikers for the post-millennial generation: there's "Generation Z, plurals, Generation Wii — but iGeneration seems to be winning," Raphelson reports. But no matter which label sticks, it will be soon appropriated by Madison Avenue to keep on selling the goods. Samantha Raphelson is a digital news intern for NPR.org.

Nobody likes to be labeled. We especially hated labels back in high school, when we were forced into one of several groups: jocks, nerds, theater kids, freaks and so on.

Now imagine categorizing people based on the years they were born: the GI generation, Generation X, baby boomers, millennials.

When we label generations, that's exactly what we do, except the groups are much larger than one high school's cliques. Who names generations, what do these names mean, and how do we avoid stereotyping a group of people that can span decades?

"Baby Busters" Goes Bust

"On the one hand I would say that obviously what a generation is does not 5
necessarily have anything to do with its name," says Neil Howe, a historian
who coined the term "millennial generation" in the 1991 book *Generations*,
which he co-authored with the late William Strauss. "Sometimes these names
are very random and contingent on the year."

Which is how Howe and Strauss invented the name millennials: "We
thought that an upbeat name would be good because of the changing
way they were being raised. They would be the first to graduate high
school in the year 2000, so the name millennial instantly came to mind,"
Howe says.

The naming of generations was not always so obvious. In fact, Generation X, the name for those born between 1965 and 1980, did not exist while
Howe and Strauss were writing *Generations*. They were originally called the
baby busters because birth rates decreased after the previous generation,
the baby boomers.

"Labels that derive from the previous generation don't tend to stick,"
says Jean Twenge, a psychology professor at San Diego State University and
author of *Generation Me: Why Today's Young Americans Are More Confident,
Assertive, Entitled — and More Miserable Than Ever Before.*

The Generation X label first appeared in a Robert Capa photo essay
on young adults coming of age after World War II. The name resurfaced
in 1964, when a London publication did a series on British youth culture,
which eventually became a book called *Generation X*. And when a young
Billy Idol was looking for a band name in the mid-1970s, he remembered
the book from his childhood and claimed the title.

Generation X wasn't the preferred label until Douglas Coupland's 1991 10
book, *Generation X: Tales for an Accelerated Culture*, explained that the letter
"X" was meant to signify his generation's desire not to be defined.

"We were this unknown, disaffected generation," says Matt Carmichael,
journalist and author of *Buyographics: How Demographic and Economic
Changes Will Reinvent the Way Marketers Reach Consumers.*

Before Generation X, there were the baby boomers, named to describe
the economic boom after World War II and, later, the rise in fertility rates.
Even the U.S. Census Bureau uses the name, Howe says.

"It may have stuck partially because their adolescence and young adulthood was tumultuous, so the idea of it being a boom had some resonance,"
Twenge says.

Other generations were named to describe individuals' collective
attitudes and behaviors. The silent generation were too young to see action
in World War II but were too old to take part in the Summer of Love.

"Cautious and conformist, they act like middle-aged adults even though 15
they're only 22," explains Howe, adding that this label first appeared in a
November 1961 *Time* article.

But this characterization of the silent generation wasn't realized until
well after the fact, says Carmichael.

"A good generational name will take that into account — that you can
ascribe the meanings as you need them," he says.

That was sort of how it worked with the GI generation, fighters in World
War II, the group that came before the silents. Journalist Tom Brokaw wrote
a book called *The Greatest Generation* about them. Howe says they are sometimes referred to as the swing generation because of their jazz music.

Journalists and magazine editors aren't the only competitors in the generational naming race. Advertising executives label generations in order to,
in theory, better reach these large groups of people.

"In terms of market research, marketers and brands like being able to 20
have labels to describe people," Carmichael says. "It helps to be able to communicate with them and to them."

In a 1993 *Advertising Age* editorial, the term Generation Y was used to
describe what is now known as the millennial generation. But by 2005, it
became clear that *Ad Age*'s analysis of Gen Y was completely misguided.

"We were both kind of talking about the same kids, but there was a different interpretation," Howe says. "Gen Y painted a portrait of this generation of kids that were extreme radicalized versions of Generation X, and we
said no, they aren't like that at all. If you look at the data on this, they are
completely the opposite with risktaking."

In 2012, the trade magazine accepted defeat.

"Generation Y was a placeholder until we found out more about them,"
says Carmichael, who used to write for *Ad Age*. "In many ways it's not a better name, but I think that millennial at least gives you the sense that it's a
turning point — that there is something different going on within this generation and that they are living in times that are kind of a turning point as well."

The problem marketers often tackle is that not everyone identifies with 25
the label chosen for their generation.

"The labels help companies and the labels help media," says Erica
Williams Simon, a social impact and communications strategist. "The labels
help people who are trying to reach young people, but they're completely
irrelevant to young people. The labels do nothing to shape our identity.
Labels are pretty much irrelevant because your life experience is what
shapes and defines you."

She adds that a downside to generational labels is that they can lead
to stereotypes — cue all the research about millennials being technology-
obsessed and self-involved.

What Will The "I" Stand For?

Despite this, experts are still debating what to call the generation after the millennials. There are a few names floating around — Generation Z, plurals, Generation Wii — but iGeneration seems to be winning.

Simon says choosing iGen will exclude a lot of people.

"If we identify the next generation solely by technology we're forgetting   30 about the low-income young people who don't have the access to technology that higher-income young people have," she says. "It's very hard to label something in a way that reflects everyone's experience."

Carmichael still likes iGen because it leaves room for interpretation.

"I also like the idea that the 'i' could be any number of things: It could be for interactive, it could be for international, it could be for something we haven't thought of yet, but in 10 years when we know this generation, we can say, 'Now the 'i' stands for this,'" he says.

READING THE TEXT

1. In your own words, summarize the history of generational naming in America, as Raphelson presents it.

2. What, according to Raphelson, will the post-millennial generation be called, and why?

3. What roles do marketing and advertising play in generational identification?

4. In your own words, why did "Generation Y" have a short life span?

READING THE SIGNS

1. In class, discuss possible responses to Raphelson's question: "How do we avoid stereotyping a group of people that can span decades?" (para. 3). Use the discussion as a springboard for an essay in which you propose your own response to her question.

2. Interview your parents, grandparents, or others of an older generation about the generational label that is typically applied to their group. To what extent do they find it suits their sense of personal identity? Use your interview results as evidence for an essay in which you support, oppose, or complicate the definition of their generation as Raphelson describes it.

3. **CONNECTING TEXTS**   In an essay, support, refute, or modify Erica Williams Simon's assertion that "labels help people who are trying to reach young people, but they're completely irrelevant to young people. The labels do nothing to shape our identity" (para. 26). To develop your ideas, consult Jessica Contrera's "Most Young People Don't Vote. Condescending to Them Isn't Helping" (p. 190) and Rachel Lowry's "Straddling Online and Offline Profiles, Millennials Search for Identity" (p. 501).

4. **CONNECTING TEXTS**   Journalist Matt Carmichael claims that "marketers . . . like being able to have labels to describe people. . . . It helps to be able to

communicate with them and to them" (para. 20). In an essay, support, refute, or qualify the proposition that Carmichael's claim is an overly benign reading of marketers' tendency to categorize consumers. To develop your ideas, consult James B. Twitchell's "What We Are to Advertisers" (p. 163) and Joseph Turow's "The Daily You: How the New Advertising Industry Is Defining Your Identity and Your Worth" (p. 394).

RACHEL LOWRY
Straddling Online and Offline Profiles, Millennials Search for Identity

It's hard to know who you really are when everyone counsels you to market yourself on such social networking sites as LinkedIn and Facebook, which is pretty much the fate of most of the people who belong to the generation of millennials. And so, as Rachel Lowry reports in this feature for *Deseret News*, a lot of millennials, who have spent their entire lives with digital technology and self-hyped social media profiles, have begun to wonder just who their authentic selves really are. Sometimes it's best just to find some time to be alone, but that's not easy to do when you're online all the time. So maybe it's time to turn that smartphone off, once in a while, so you can look for yourself. Rachel Lowry works on the photography blog for *TIME* magazine.

Twenty-year-old Mariah Hanaike waits in the disconcerting silence of a temporary employment agency lobby in Redwood City, Calif. Though the interview has not yet begun, Hanaike said she knows she is being scrutinized before she shakes the hand of a potential employer. "You know the person you're going to meet is somewhere close in the building preparing for you, maybe by looking you up on Facebook or Googling your name, possibly reading an embarrassing entry about you on your mom's blog or being surprised to not find you on LinkedIn," said Hanaike. "I can't just be myself where and when I want because anything I do has the potential to end up on some site somewhere where anyone can look at it and judge. I feel like I need to water down who I am."

Millennials, the term given for those born between 1980 and 2000, may be suffering from an identity crisis as they search for their authentic self. According to a recent online study, one out of four millennials say they can only be their true self when alone. As today's twenty-somethings create online identities to market themselves professionally, as well as socially, some fear that the disparity between the two can prevent a young person from finding authentic self-definition.

Living Life Publicly

As today's younger generation navigates the transition to adulthood, reconciling between online and offline identities can be difficult.

Nearly 25 percent of all millennials say they can only be their true self when alone, Belgium researcher Joeri Van den Bergh found. In his book, *Millennials: How Cool Brands Stay Hot, Branding to Generation Y*, Van den Bergh argues that authenticity is key for brands to connect with millennials. "The key concept behind authenticity is to stay true to yourself, so we wanted to know when millennials stay true to themselves," he said.

Van den Bergh asked 4,056 people, ages 15 to 25, when they felt they were or weren't being authentic online or offline, with friends, parents, partners or employers. Identity, he found, was strongly influenced by the back-and-forth of these two spheres. "Millennials are pre-wired to achieve and create success stories in their lives," Van den Bergh said. "They would rather blow up some stories or pretend they are having fun on Instagram and Facebook than admit they had a boring night out to the friends and immediate social circle." This can alter authenticity in identity, Van den Bergh found. Only half of the millennials surveyed believe themselves to be authentic and real. "[It's] a response to the social society in which private moments are rare and everything is transparent and in the open on social media," Van den Bergh said.

For Victor Ruiz, 25, a student at Utah State University, social media perpetuates the problem. "We live in a capitalist society," Ruiz said. "People don't want to be singled out, especially in a negative way, so they will try to make themselves look better and good to impress. They would try to make their online pages look as though they are living the American dream and not expose weakness." It's a "fluffy portrayal of reality," said 27-year-old Angie Rideout, a hairstylist in Salt Lake City. "It shows what we value, how we spend our time, and who we spend our time with."

If you don't participate online, you risk being uninvolved and out of touch, said Hanaike, who is also attending LDS Business College in Salt Lake City. "Nobody will show you to others for you, so you will be voiceless and unseen." Hanaike said online media can be detrimental to her offline identity. "I am perfectly capable of representing myself without a domain name or URL," she said. "But I do not have that option. My freedom is definitely being infringed upon. I can't just be myself where and when I want because literally anything I do has the potential to end up on some site somewhere where anyone can look at it and judge."

5

Twenty-three-year-old Braden Bissegger, a student at LDS Business College, agrees. "You're required to define yourself to be involved: Build a Facebook page and Twitter account and post your thoughts and show the world who you are," Bissegger said. "But what if that's inaccurate? What if we are all purporting to be something we're not? Yes, we are certainly in an identity crisis."

Linking In

Hanaike is one of 80 million millennials, ages 18 to 24, in the U.S., many of whom are competing for the job market, according to a 2010 U.S. Census Bureau report. How to get a leg up? Many say self-promotion through online media can be huge. "It's standard procedure for hiring managers to check out your Facebook, Twitter, and LinkedIn profiles," wrote Jenna Goudreau in a recent *Forbes* article. "Simply sifting through job postings and sending out applications en masse was never a good route to success, and is even less so now," wrote Phyllis Korkki, an employment editor for the *New York Times*. "One of the most important questions that many job seekers can ask these days is this: How searchable am I?"

Professional self-branding and social networking is necessary no matter what the economy looks like, according to David Lake, a 25-year-old marketer in Lindon. "When tools like these are available you can either keep up with the times and use them for your benefit, or you can let others take advantage of the opportunity," Lake said. "The days of a paper resume and a blind interview are over. With social media platforms and personal websites, interviewers can know a lot about who you are before the interview even starts." 10

For many millennials, however, self-branding can bleed into narcissism or the creation of a false persona. "It is upsetting to think that an employer can base their decision to hire me on who I appear to be on online media. That is not the person that they are hiring," said Hanaike. "I don't want to appear narcissistic when I talk to a potential employer," said Duncan Purser, 25, a student of managerial financial accounting. "But with the way applying for jobs goes in today's technological work, you have to promote yourself and continually go for presence."

Thoren Williams, a 22-year-old studying accounting at LDS Business College, agrees. "If you don't update your LinkedIn when applying for jobs, your personality doesn't come through on social media platforms and it can seem as if you don't have one," Williams said. "Potential employers may assume they know what type of an employee you would be because they've checked out your resume on LinkedIn."

It's almost necessary to be a little bit narcissistic, Hanaike said. "If you want to get noticed, or if you want someone to see your qualifications, you have to show them, lest you get swept away with the tide." For Hanaike, this can lead to a disparity between online and offline identity.

Reconciling Identities

So how do you reconcile the two identities and maintain a true center?

For Mutual Leonard, a 29-year-old actuarial analyst living in Salt Lake   15 City, culture can be a strong source of identity. "Mormons with pioneer heritage, for example, say 'My grandmother walked across the plains. I'm not giving up my religion for anything. This is my identity.'" Leonard said culture prepares youth for adulthood, preparing boys to be men through priesthood duties in a church, or hunting for your first kill as initiation into a tribe. "Psychologically, you need that kind of a thing," he said, noting that identity requires an outward focus. "You will establish identity as soon as you focus on something beyond yourself."

Katie Greer, a nation-wide Internet and technology safety trainer, recommends tolerance. "I could follow someone's entire day online, seeing when they wake up, eat, what they wear, and the traffic they hit," said Greer. "Perhaps we should lift our eyes from our screens more often and live the lives we are purporting." Reconciliation, Greer said, requires creating an identity worth owning up to online. "I'm 30 years old and it's really bizarre to think of all the things in my life that have formed my identity: Soccer, politics, clubs, sports, friends," Greer said. "I worked really hard to prove who I was, for myself, my friends, my family, the colleges I've applied to. Can I just put all that effort into saying I am something I'm not online? It's kind of like cheating." The things today's twenty-somethings do can later define you, Greer warned. Being cautious about what one posts online can avoid false labels and assumptions.

Millennials, themselves, are learning how to create a consistent identity across the many platforms before them. "I meet people who seem to be in a sort of fog because they are so focused on Facebook and getting likes," Bissegger said. "But then I've also seen many people who are not trying to boast or brag about themselves, but trying to show how they are contributing to something or giving of themselves and social media is one of their most effective platforms." In fact, those who are able to see social media as a means of getting beyond yourself are the ones who are confident in their identity, Hanaike said. "We've been given a lot of crap, as millennials, but if we want our future to be something significant and if we want our lives to be great, we have to have self-confidence," she said. "It takes a certain level of self-awareness to think I am going to provide something for the community and the world that no one else is, so that I can do the best job of doing this. That is the antithesis of an identity crisis."

For David Lake, the two platforms can actually enhance one's identity both online and offline. "Facebook and other social networks give a voice and confidence to many people that didn't previously have either of those things," Lake said. "They might be shy or naturally lacking in confidence. Now that they have a stage to project their voice, we really get to see who those people are."

READING THE TEXT

1. Summarize in your own words Lowry's explanation for why millennials feel that they are losing touch with their essential selves.

2. What does researcher Joeri Van den Bergh mean by saying, "Millennials are pre-wired to achieve and create success stories in their lives" (para. 5)?

3. Why does interviewee Mutual Leonard claim that culture can ground one's sense of identity?

4. In your own words, explain how concerns about future job prospects can affect millennials' profiles on social networking sites such as Facebook and LinkedIn.

READING THE SIGNS

1. In a journal entry, describe how you might have profiled yourself on a social networking site. Did you try to "improve" your self-image, or did you just describe yourself as accurately as you could? Then consider why you chose that profile. If you have not constructed a social media profile, discuss why you preferred to avoid that venue.

2. **CONNECTING TEXTS** In an essay, explore how the job-related stress that Lowry discusses supports or deviates from the proposition that social media control our lives more than users control social media. As evidence, you might interview some upper-division students who are contemplating entering the job market and ask them about their social media profiles. To develop your ideas, read Joseph Turow's "The Daily You: How the New Advertising Industry Is Defining Your Identity and Your Worth" (p. 394).

3. Lowry suggests that millennials feel pressured by job counselors, teachers, and parents to use social media to market themselves. But young people are also influenced by their peers. In an essay, evaluate the influence adults and peers have on engagement with social media. In your essay, you should base your analysis on interviews with social media users, perhaps analyzing how they behaved in high school and in college.

4. **CONNECTING TEXTS** Lowry elucidates some ways that online communication can be problematic. Brainstorm various ways that Facebook and other sites have affected millennials' sense of and projection of identity. Then use your thoughts to support an essay in which you argue your own position on how social media affect young people's sense of identity. For further ideas, consult

"Students Addicted to Social Media" by the International Center for Media and the Public Agenda (p. 382), Nancy Jo Sales's "From the Instamatic to Instagram: Social Media and the Secret Lives of Teenagers" (p. 428), and danah boyd's "It's Complicated: MySpace vs. Facebook" (p. 437).

BRITTNEY COOPER

Hollywood's Post-Racial Mirage: How Pop Culture Got Gentrified

With America's "post-racial" moment now appearing to be something with a great future behind it, a great deal of assessment of the current racial climate on TV and film is taking place, and as far as Brittney Cooper is concerned, the outlook is cloudy at best. For as Cooper argues in this *Salon* essay, while there has been a recent diversification effort in Hollywood, American television is still *less* diverse than it was in the 1990s, and the movies seem, in Cooper's words, to be captivated by "the idea that progress means black people's lives can fit into traditional white narratives." Wanting to see more movies and more TV series devoted to black actors performing in roles shaped by their specifically African American experience, Cooper calls for a Hollywood aesthetic of difference rather than sameness, celebrating the different stories to be told in a multi-racial America. Brittney Cooper teaches Women's and Gender Studies and Africana Studies at Rutgers University and is a contributing writer at *Salon*.

The increase of colorblind casting in sci-fi television shows like *The Walking Dead* and *Sleepy Hollow* suggests that a "post-racial revolution" is being televised, according to a writer at CNN. John Blake especially celebrates shows like *Arrow*, which have a diverse racial cast and manage in many instances to avoid stereotypes. Certainly, I agree with Blake that television is slowly but surely diversifying in ways that it simply has not been diverse over the last decade. (ABC's *Scandal* has a diverse cast, a black female lead, and is one of the most popular shows on television. It is certainly a personal favorite.)

But I'm not sure post-racialism is a thing to want, that it should be our goal.

First, although television seems to be changing, we should not forget that 20 years ago television was more diverse. When we tell ourselves these post-racial fantasies of progress, we act like more black people cast in roles that have traditionally gone to white people is progress. Second, we act as though this is the best definition of diversity. I came of age in the 1990s, where there were several black shows that populated the landscape of my adolescence — *The Cosby Show, The Fresh Prince of Bel-Air, Martin, In Living Color, Living Single, Sister Sister, The Parent 'Hood, The Wayans, Smart Guy, Hanging With Mr. Cooper,* and *Family Matters.* As a little kid, I watched *227* and *Amen.* All of these shows were spread out over a combination of minor networks like UPN and the WB and the traditional major networks.

Slowly by the late 1990s all black shows were being outsourced to the minor networks. Then those networks consolidated, with UPN and the WB becoming the CW, and then the CW decided in the late 2000s to move from an "urban programming format." The same thing is true of the movie industry. In the 1990s, there were black movies — black gangsta movies, black love movies, black family movies. *Boyz N the Hood, Love Jones,* and *Soul Food* are representative classic black movies of the era. By the mid-2000s, the only person able to command an impressive box office showing was Tyler Perry.

Commitment to racial diversity on the big and small screens has always been fickle.   5

Now the tide is changing as black actors are being asked to do black versions of white movies like *About Last Night* or the thinly veiled mashup of *The Hangover* and *Bridesmaids,* that will be *Think Like a Man, Too.* I have seen or plan to see these movies, because I like seeing people who look like me on the big screen. But I'm bothered by the idea that progress means black people's lives can fit into traditional white narratives. Why are black stories particular, but white stories universal? Surely this is not the best definition of diversity.

And it certainly is not progress. It's more like the gentrification of media, being marketed to us as progress. Under the logic of gentrification, both the physical kind and this new mediated kind, those of us who harken back to a prior moment when people of color could live and work and be represented on their own terms are seen as barriers to progress. Even though we are made to witness the systematic removal of people of color from posts and property that they have labored for generations to have access to, we are supposed to be impressed when these new social and geographical formations allow token participation by people of color, who are viewed as having crossover appeal. To be clear, crossing over means that despite your color, white people like you. It's an ugly truth, but we should tell it. And given the racist audience backlash to the casting of *The Hunger Games* character Rue as black and to the new version of *Annie* starring African-American Quvenzhané Wallis, I'm not sure we should actually believe this optimistic narrative of post-racial revolution.

In fact, the backlash toward these young black characters is more in line with a recent finding from the Cooperative Children's Book Center, that of 3,200 children's books published in 2013, only 93 were about black characters. To this day, I keep a list of children's stories that feature black girl protagonists, so that my friends with daughters can have culturally relevant books for their children.

African-American author Walter Dean Myers penned a response to the children's book study in the *New York Times*. I didn't even know people wrote children's books about African-Americans until I stumbled upon a whole shelf of Mr. Myers' books one lazy summer when my mother left me at the library all day. I eagerly brought home a copy of the teenage love story *Motown and Didi*, which remains a favorite to this day, alongside a stack of books that included stories about the Box Car Children and the Sweet Valley Twins. My personal favorite was Baby Sitters Club books, but those only came out once a month, and I usually had devoured them by the second day after purchase. And while the characters were mostly white, part of being a voracious-reading black kid in the '90s meant you learned to relate to white children, and to identify with the "universality" of their narratives.

I also vividly remember my joy at seeing and eagerly purchasing a copy   10
of Myers' *The Mouse Rap* in 1992. Though I preferred stories with female protagonists, the chocolate black boy on the cover, who had dreams of being a rapper, appealed to me.

As a young black girl growing up in a predominantly white environment, race mattered. Despite my attempts to mimic the cultural habits and speaking styles of my white counterparts, a journey to racial self-awareness that got me mercilessly teased by my black counterparts, I was never going to be white and didn't especially want to be. Like other children, I wanted to fit in and not be bullied. Reading children's and young adult stories with black characters helped me to imagine other ways to be black besides the sometimes limiting representations that I saw in my immediate environment. Those black stories also affirmed my nerd self, letting me know that white children didn't have a monopoly on smarts, and that I didn't have to jettison blackness to embrace nerd-dom. Seeing ourselves represented, not as devoid of race but as shaped by and deeply influenced by race, matters. To have race not as a biological but as a social condition is not a bad thing. We all do.

And until all of us — white people included — grapple with what this means, until we can tell the truth honestly about it, our swift desire to get to a post-racial future will remain a gilded project, and one steeped in dishonesty.

That kind of dishonesty will have us doing as John Blake did, invoking the work of Octavia Butler, an African-American sci-fi author, to make the case for post-racialism. I think Butler would take deep issue with being read into a genealogy of post-racial cultural production. She thought that black life provided the ground upon which to explore questions of dystopic futures, life after armageddon, and other forms of relationship to the human body, to African-American history, and to the time-space continuum. Blackness is central, rather than incidental to her work.

For the young black time-traveling teens in Kiese Laymon's *Long Division*, their Mississippi-inflected, crooked-letter blackness is central to who they understand themselves to be. These characters, and African-Americans more generally, to disagree with Harlem Renaissance thinker George Schuyler, are not simply "lampedblack Anglo-Saxons," dropped into the middle of an Ebony version of *A Wrinkle in Time*.

Butler, Myers and Laymon show us black possibility through their fear-   15
less engagement with what it means to be both human and black. The stories they tell, the movies and shows that could be made from those stories, are far better models for diversity than our current infatuation with colorblind casting.

Post-racism, not post-racialism, should be our goal. To be American means we are deeply shaped by narratives of race, culture, and power. And celebrating our multiculturalism is not a bad thing. But multiculturalism and post-racialism are not the same. In their most ideal states, one recognizes the power, possibility and gifts of our differences and uses those truths to connect us. The other — the latter — erases the salience of those differences and attempts to use the lie of sameness to connect us. As ever, the question for us remains, what kind of nation do we want to be?

READING THE TEXT

1. Describe in your own words what the term "post-racialism" (para. 2) means.

2. Summarize the history of black TV programing from the 1990s to the present, as Cooper describes it.

3. What does Cooper mean by saying the current appearance of racial diversity in TV and film is "like the gentrification of media, being marketed to us as progress" (para. 7)?

4. Characterize Cooper's tone and inclusion of personal references. How do they affect your response as a reader?

READING THE SIGNS

1. Cooper notes the value of "culturally relevant books" (para. 8) for children. In your journal, reflect on the importance to you as a child of books and toys that reflected your own ethnic background. Did you think about such matters, or did your parents encourage you to do so?

2. In an essay, support, refute, or modify Cooper's contention that post-racialism in TV and film is problematic. Be sure to demonstrate your argument with references to programs or films that depict black and other minority characters.

3. Watch one of the TV shows of the 1990s that Cooper mentions she viewed in her adolescence (see para. 3). Study the depictions of black characters and those of other ethnicities. To what extent do you share Cooper's implicit endorsement of those representations of race?

4. Watch an episode of *Scandal*, and do a semiotic reading of the representation of racial identity of the show's characters. Would you identify the show as "post-racial"? Does your reading offer any insights into why the show has been popular?

5. **CONNECTING TEXTS**   In an essay, write a response to Cooper's assertion that "crossing over means that despite your color, white people like you. It's an ugly truth, but we should tell it" (para. 7). To develop your ideas, consult Matt Zoller Seitz's "The Offensive Movie Cliché That Won't Die" (p. 335) and Helena Andrews's "*The Butler* versus *The Help*: Gender Matters" (p. 341).

LILLIANA MASON

Why Are Americans So Angry This Election Season?

Throughout the 2016 presidential election campaign, a lot of American voters were seeing red, and they didn't have to come from so-called "red states" to feel that way. As Lilliana Mason argues in this opinion piece for the *Washington Post*, much of that anger came from our human tendency to identify ourselves according to the group in which we feel we most belong, and by 2016 those groups had divided along racial and religious lines. Thus, Mason observes, "Republicans tend toward Christian and white identities, and Democrats tend toward non-religious and non-white identities. With these highly aligned identities, people tend to be more sensitive to threats from outsiders, reacting with higher levels of anger than those with cross-cutting identities." Presenting the results of her experimental research to support this claim, Mason indicates that anger is likely to be a critical emotion in American politics for years to come. Lilliana Mason is an assistant professor in the Department of Government and Politics at the University of Maryland.

In the 2016 presidential race, we hear a lot about anger. Voters are angry about the economy, about race, about the "establishment." But knowing what voters are angry about doesn't necessarily tell us why they are angry. There may be logical reasons, but there may also be a more basic, primal force.

My recent research focuses on one such force: the enduring power of group identity. In particular, the growing "sorting" of the American electorate along partisan, religious and racial lines has created the conditions for the anger and intolerance that have been so obvious this year. Belonging to a social group is intimately connected to our individual sense of esteem. Without social identities, we are alone in the world, and our losses make us losers. With social identities, we have groups whose victories can dampen and even eclipse our own personal failures, and possibly buttress our self-esteem in situations when we need it. These identities can provoke prejudice against outsiders who we must compete with. Of course, we typically identify with more than one group. We are members of a political party, race, a religion, a class, a gender, a town, and any other group that you could possibly call "we." Particularly important, then, is whether these identities "go together" or are in tension with each other. When these identities do go together — when they are "sorted" — most of the members of one group are (or are believed to be) also members of another group.

This sorting is what has been happening among Americans. Partisan identities have become increasingly aligned with religious and racial identities. Republicans tend toward Christian and white identities, and Democrats tend toward non-religious and non-white identities. With these highly aligned identities, people tend to be more sensitive to threats from outsiders, reacting with higher levels of anger than those with cross-cutting identities.

In research forthcoming in *Public Opinion Quarterly*, I find two pieces of evidence that corroborate this pattern. First, the electorate as a whole has grown angrier about their electoral opponents, and more proud of their own candidates, since the 1980s. Americans are increasingly taking sides and becoming emotionally engaged during election season. Second, I conducted an experiment in which I threatened the status of either a party or a system of beliefs. The threats were artificial blog posts in which partisan bloggers from the opposing side predicted the defeat of a party (Republicans or Democrats) or a set of liberal or conservative policies.

For example, in the blog post that threatened a Democrat's partisan iden- 5
tity, the blog post said "We're going to defeat the hardcore socialist Obama, we are raising more money than Democrats, our Congressional candidates are in safer seats, and Democrats have obviously lost Americans' trust." The equivalent blog post for Republicans said: "Obama will easily win re-election against whatever lunatic the Republicans run, we are raising more money than Republicans, our Congressional candidates are in safer seats, and Republicans have obviously lost Americans' trust."

In both cases, those whose racial, religious, and partisan identities were well-sorted were more likely to react angrily to both types of threat, compared to those whose identities were not sorted. Strong partisans were emotionally engaged by the party-based messages, while strong ideologues were emotionally engaged by the issue-based messages. But only the alignment between partisan, religious, and racial identities predicted emotional reactions to all of the messages.

In this election, recent polls suggest that Republicans with well-sorted identities are more likely to support Donald Trump. His candidacy has been notable for its reliance on anger and "winning" — a message well-tailored to activating emotions and social identities.

Taken together, all of these findings suggest that we shouldn't expect Americans to be any less angry any time soon. The poorly sorted, cross-cutting identities that can act as an emotional dampener are increasingly rare. There are simply fewer people in the "unflappable" portion of the population. We are left with an increasingly volatile electorate.

READING THE TEXT

1. According to Mason, what are the psychological benefits of belonging to a group?
2. In your own words, what does Mason mean by "sorted" (para. 2) identities?
3. Describe the evidence that Mason advances to support her argument.
4. What relationship does Mason establish between belonging to a group and Americans' increasing political anger?

READING THE SIGNS

1. In your journal, reflect on your own sense of group identity. Which groups do you align yourself with? To what extent is your allegiance to these groups "sorted," or do you belong in what Mason terms the "'unflappable' portion of the population" (para. 8)?
2. It is not common for cultural studies arguments to be supported by formal experimental evidence. In class, discuss Mason's experiment that posted artificial blogs to Republican and Democratic readers. How persuasive do you find her evidence?
3. **CONNECTING TEXTS**   Reflecting on the outcome of the 2016 presidential election, write an essay in which you refute, challenge, or complicate Mason's argument about the reasons the American electorate seemed so angry. To develop your ideas, consult Jeffrey Fleishman's "How an Angry National Mood Is Reflected in Pop Culture" (p. 531) and Jim Tankersley's "Why the Upper Middle Class Might Be the Real Target of Today's Anger" (p. 536).

4.   **CONNECTING TEXTS**   Mason concludes her selection with this nod to the future: "We are left with an increasingly volatile electorate" (para. 8). In an essay, write your assessment of this prediction, keeping in mind that demographic changes in America will continue to redefine who the electorate is. To develop your ideas, consult Samantha Raphelson's "From GIs to Gen Z (Or Is It iGen?): How Generations Get Nicknames" (p. 497).

7

AMERICAN PARADOX

Culture, Conflict, and Contradiction in the U.S.A.

Six Contradictions That Count

In October 2009, James Arthur Ray, a self-help guru whose books and seminars promised material well being and financial success to those who followed his own particular brand of New Age philosophy, conducted a "Spiritual Warrior" retreat in the Arizona desert. This retreat included fasting, isolation, and a culminating sweat lodge ritual that resulted in the deaths of three people who had paid upward of $10,000 to participate. The ensuing fallout from the disaster led to a prison term for Ray, as well as to the destruction of his business empire. It also cast a glaring light upon a fundamental contradiction within American culture, a paradoxical embrace of fundamentally opposed cultural **mythologies** that, when analyzed in the **context** of an entire **system** of related contradictions, can help us to understand the many conflicts and controversies that divide Americans today into often hostile camps and that are reflected throughout our popular and political culture.

We can begin our exploration of these contradictions with a list of six especially significant ones. Although other cultural contradictions than these could be explored (can you think of any?), these six constitute the most prominent on the current social and popular cultural scene. And although they can often be found intermixing with each other in confoundedly complicated ways, we can categorize and describe them each as follows:

1. America's contradictory history of spiritual religiosity alongside money-worshipping materialism;

2. America's contradictory history of Puritanical sexual repression alongside sexual commodification;

3. America's contradictory history of individualism alongside social and consumer conformity;

4. America's contradictory history of egalitarian populism alongside economic elitism;

5. America's contradictory history of freedom alongside chattel slavery and its aftermath;

6. America's contradictory history as a land of immigrants alongside anti-immigrant nativism.

Dying for Dollars: Spiritual Materialism

Let's start with our first contradiction. Adapting spiritual practices to materialistic ends is a strikingly American tradition that can be explained by the dual trajectories of our nation's founding. Combining the spiritual strivings of the Massachusetts Bay Puritans — who sought to build a sanctified "City upon a Hill" in the New World — and the get-rich-quick goals of the Virginia Company of London — which underwrote the settlement at Jamestown — American history has always involved a paradoxical coexistence between the spirit and the profit motive. Indeed, the American Revolution itself was simultaneously a materialistic tax revolt and a spiritual expression of the value of freedom. But if you really want to get a grasp of the matter, consider the American Christmas, which celebrates that most holy day in the Christian calendar via a spending spree that not even the Grinch has been able to curtail.

It is in this context that we can understand how Americans can spend enormous amounts of money to attend spiritual retreats designed to help them make enormous amounts of money. Or how the Tea Party could bring together both evangelical Christians and tax protesters. And it can also help us understand how Americans who may be outraged by the public expression of human sexuality can create beauty pageants for six-year-old girls.

Toddlers and Tiaras: Sexual Repression Meets the Profit Motive

Prior to the sexual revolution of the 1960s and 1970s, the prevailing sexual mythology in America could be characterized as one of modesty and repression. Clearly reflected in Hollywood's Hays Code, which restricted the sexual content of movies from the 1930s onward, this Puritanical streak in the American character led many people to disapprove of the sexual energy of rock and roll in the 1950s and, notoriously, caused broadcasters to film Elvis Presley from the waist up when he first performed on *The Ed Sullivan Show* (they objected to the King's vigorous pelvic gyrations). Within the terms of this mythology, humanity's fundamental sexual instincts must be controlled through prohibitions on premarital sex and channeled into state-approved heterosexual marital relationships.

But in the wake of the "Summer of Love" in 1967, a sexual revolution swept America, one that has tipped the balance toward an ever-freer expression of sexuality in popular culture and everyday life, while instigating a social and political backlash that has animated American politics from the days of the Moral Majority to the present. In the midst of this conflict between two sexual **ideologies**, we can find the paradoxical existence of such reality TV programs as TLC's *Toddlers and Tiaras*, which survived the *Here Comes Honey Boo Boo* years to return to the airwaves in 2016. The existence of child beauty contests is actually doubly paradoxical, because not only do they sexualize young children, but the fans of such contests tend to be the sort of people who lean to the sexually repressive side of the American ideological spectrum. But this paradox can be explained by the fact that a lot of money can be made in such spectacles — for the contestants, for the pageants' producers, and for TLC — and so we find spiritual Puritanism being outweighed by a money-worshipping profit motive.

The commodification of human sexuality in America, of course, goes far beyond such phenomena as toddler beauty pageants: It permeates our entire popular culture. And here we find one of the places in which different cultural contradictions can get tangled up with each other to produce especially paradoxical results. For while the tradition of sexual repression in America is closely tied to our Puritanical religious history, America's modern-day Puritans tend to be avid supporters of unrestricted capitalism and so have not been opposing sexual expression (at least not *heterosexual* expression) as energetically as in the past. The striking **difference**, then, between the sexually repressive 1950s and the sexually commodified present is thus a sign of a decline of the old spiritual-Puritanical preeminence in American culture in favor not only of sexual freedom but of untrammeled sexual profiteering.

The Pokémon Paradox: Individualism in a Mass Consumer Society

Then there is the contradiction between America's proud tradition of individualism and its total immersion into mass consumption. A strikingly contemporary signifier of this conflict can be found in one of the lesser news items to appear in the traumatic summer of 2016 — when every day seemed to bring word of another terror attack, police shooting, or police ambush — an announcement in the *Concord Journal* that the town fire station had been designated as a *Pokémon Go* character location. Taken by itself, this was hardly significant; after all, with the release of the wildly popular augmented reality game, the entire world had been populated with Pokémon awaiting capture at

Do Not Pokémon and Drive.

innumerable gaming sites. But what made this site significant was its address: 209 Walden Street, Concord, Massachusetts, a location less than a mile from both Walden Pond and the Old North Bridge — the former location a living symbol of one of America's greatest experiments in self-reliant individualism, and the latter where Emerson's "shot heard round the world" effectively inaugurated the American Revolution. This is to say, 209 Walden Street happens to share the name of the quiet pond that a young Concord eccentric named Henry David Thoreau made famous over a century and half ago, evoking a proudly individualistic tradition that played a major role in the decisions that led to that fire fight at the Old North Bridge which, in turn, led to the founding of the United States of America. And to this day, individualism is one of our most cherished cultural identities.

But this individualism stands in striking contrast to such phenomena as *Pokémon Go*, a digitally mass produced game simultaneously played by millions and millions of players in a gigantic act of mass consumption. Henry David Thoreau would not have played *Pokémon Go*: After all, he was the man who encouraged those who could to march to the beat of a different drummer. But in a consumer society that cherishes its individualism, mass consumption itself can be marketed as an expression of individualistic rebellion. As a global producer of mass-produced sneakers once put it in a marketing campaign: "Reeboks Let U.B.U." And so, individualism meets its opposite in consumerism and is swamped by it.

The 1 Percent: American Populism versus Elitism

Our fourth contradiction can be dramatically illustrated by Donald Trump's successful campaign for the presidency in 2016, whereby a self-proclaimed billionaire became the voice of working- and middle-class Americans who felt left behind by the American dream. This paradoxical development was compounded by the fact that, by 2016, the socioeconomic divide in America between rich and poor, 1 percent and 99 percent, upper-middle /upper class and everyone else, had been widening to Grand Canyon proportions in the post-Great Recession lead-up to the campaign. Thus, even as the American middle and lower-middle classes appeared to be moving ever closer to the brink of extinction, a large swath of that demographic was voting Trump.

The explanation for this paradox is, as in so many other cases, **overdetermined**, involving racial as well as economic components (we'll get back to race in a moment). But for now, we can see how the paradox of the Trump constituency reflects that contradiction in American society, which has always juxtaposed such egalitarian values as Abraham Lincoln's cherished celebration of a society "of the people, by the people, and for the people" alongside a ferocious success ethic that urges us to rise above the crowd and "go for the gold." Distracted by the American dream — the cultural mythology that promises the opportunity for upward social mobility for all — Americans have traditionally tended to ignore, or even deny, that there is any contradiction at all, thus ignoring the fact of class inequality in America. Believing in social mobility, Americans have seen society as a kind of moving escalator, not a tiered set of social classes.

The Great Recession has done much to shatter that old complacency, and both the Sanders and the Trump campaigns in 2016 were insurgencies against a society that has been tipped ever further in favor of the ruling class. But how, at least for Republican voters, did that insurgency come to be expressed by support for a member of the ruling class? Part of the answer to that question lies in the fact that it has happened before, indeed, almost two centuries ago, when the vast uprising of Jacksonian democracy — the nineteenth-century electoral insurgency of the "common man" — was borne on the shoulders of a plantation-owning aristocrat. Thomas Jefferson, too, who so famously celebrated the "common man," was himself a member of the plantation aristocracy. The paradoxical combination of egalitarian populism and plutocratic elitism runs deep in America, leading to such apparently contradictory phenomena as billionaire-led populism.

But, to get back to race, we can see that Andrew Jackson and Thomas Jefferson were also *slave-owning* aristocrats, and that Donald Trump's appeal was racial as well as social — all of which raises the shadow of yet another fundamental American contradiction, one that by the summer of 2016 was the most volatile and controversial of all.

Oscars So White: The Enduring Legacy of Slavery

When Spike Lee launched the Oscar boycott heard round the Academy in 2016, his was but one of a multitude of expressions of racial frustration in the land, spurred on by a sequence of shootings that included such now-famous victims as Trayvon Martin and Michael Brown, the massacre at the Emanuel African Methodist Episcopal Church in Charleston, and police being gunned down in the streets of Dallas and Baton Rouge. Putting an end to the hope that the election of Barack Obama signaled the beginning of a "post-racial" society, this resurgence of racial conflict, which many compared to the more violent years of the 1960s, was expressed not only by the rise of such movements as Black Lives Matter but also by the votes of many white voters who saw Donald Trump as their voice.

But once again America had been there before, in fact had always been there — precisely because of what is probably the most profound, and paradoxical, contradiction of them all in our history: the fact that we are a nation founded on the principle of the equality of all people, and that many of the men who declared that principle in 1776 were also slave owners who wrote slavery into the Constitution. Four score and seven years later, the nation was in the midst of a Civil War because of this unresolved contradiction, a racial dissociation that is now roiling America in ways that go beyond the legacies of slavery.

The Statutes of Liberty: Immigration Controversy in the Land of Immigrants

And this brings us to our sixth contradiction. The racial reverberations of the Trump campaign were related less to the history of slavery than they were to the controversies over Latin American and Muslim immigration. But this too was hardly new in a nation of immigrants that has always experienced nativistic opposition to immigration. Today, when all people of European descent are regarded as being of the same race, it's hard to fathom how race could have had anything to do with American opposition to Irish, German, eastern European, and southern European immigrants in the nineteenth century. But race was, indeed, at the heart of the matter. The country saw Anglo Saxons feeling racially superior to Irish, German, Italian, Greek, Polish, Jewish, and Estonian immigrants, indeed, to any Europeans from non-northern European countries, just as anti-immigrant sentiment today cannot be divided from racial attitudes toward Asian, Latin American, and Middle Eastern newcomers. In short, here is another case where different cultural contradictions get tangled up together, with our racial history playing a direct role in our paradoxical immigrant history, and the two histories together producing volatile social conditions and conflicts.

As you contemplate the cultural contradictions that we have been discussing so far, you may be thinking that while they are national in scope, they are regional in expression. That is, one side of the various controversies that erupt from these cultural contradictions tends to be embraced by people in certain identifiable regions in the country, while the other side is embraced by people in equally identifiable regions. You know what these regions are: they are the red states and the blue states, signifiers of a divided country that can help us interpret a great deal of what happens in contemporary America.

What's Red and Blue and Mad All Over?

Long before the Trump campaign effectively brought the whole matter into the open, the legacy of our many cultural contradictions was already visible in the red state/blue state electoral divide that was first officially noted after the 2000 presidential election. At the time, electoral maps coded the states that voted Republican in red and the states that voted Democratic in blue. Since then, it has become common to refer to "red state" and "blue state" regions of America, with the former generally considered conservative, and the latter liberal or progressive. Although these terms run the risk of stereotyping, red and blue states do tend to take different sides in relation to America's cultural and ideological conflicts, reflecting their opposing positions on some very fundamental American values.

These differences are readily apparent in our popular culture. Consider such dichotomies in the world of popular music as hip-hop versus country, or rhythm-and-blues versus heavy metal. In television, the fans of, say, *Duck Dynasty* differ from the devotees of *Game of Thrones*, while the split between Fox News and MSNBC viewers is notorious. It's easy to take such oppositions for granted, but they have not always been the case in American entertainment. In the ideologically divided 1960s, for example, the majority of Americans still watched the same national news programs (with Walter Cronkite assuming the status of a kindly Uncle-in-Chief), the same TV shows (on just three commercially sponsored networks), and listened to radio stations whose formats included everything from the Beatles to the Beach Boys, Sinatra to the Supremes, acid rock to soul, and Jimi Hendrix to Bobbie Gentry. Now, by contrast, in the niche-marketed world of modern entertainment, consumers not only have innumerable choices tailored to their personal tastes, they can also customize their consumption according to their own ideological preferences, creating self-confirming echo chambers that ensure that they never have to listen to anyone with whom they disagree.

The outcome of such choices is that popular culture does not simply reflect the conflicts and contradictions in American society; it amplifies them. With the two leading political parties — Democrat and Republican — falling further and further apart, their voters hold not only different ideological values but different visions of just what America is. The land whose motto has long been *e pluribus unum* is becoming a site of discord and division. And there is little-to-no likelihood that popular culture will be able to harmonize the dissonant chords within our country today when it is so much more profitable to exacerbate them.

The Readings

Barbara Ehrenreich opens the chapter with an explanation of how America's essential optimism is often in contradiction to the realities that get us into trouble. Jeffrey Fleishman and Jim Tankersley follow with a set of paired readings that take up where Chapter 6 leaves off, exploring the ways that an angry national mood is reflected throughout our popular culture and how class conflict may be at the bottom of it all. George Packer is next with a trenchant look at today's celebrities, an exclusive "superclass" of entertainers and corporate executives whose cultural and economic power stands in blatant contrast to America's egalitarian values. Alfred Lubrano's reflection on the personal disruptions in moving out of the working class through higher education reveals some of the contradictions within our class-based society, while Randall Kennedy explores the contradictions inherent in racial profiling. Next, Mariah Burton Nelson's essay on the predicament of women athletes points out the mixed cultural pressures that women must negotiate when they enter the world of competitive sports. Wade Graham concludes the chapter with an analysis of the contradictions inherent in the current "green cities" movement, arguing that "despite the rhetoric of reconciling the city with nature, today's green urban dream is too often about bringing a technologically controlled version of nature into the city and declaring the problem solved."

BARBARA EHRENREICH
Bright-Sided

Americans, as a rule, tend to look on the bright side of things, cherishing an essential optimism that has made America a fertile breeding ground for visionaries and entrepreneurs. But being blind to the dark side of reality — the risks and dangers that can upset the sunniest of plans — can cause us to be "bright-sided" by them, in Barbara Ehrenreich's memorable phrase, like a quarterback who didn't see that defensive tackle approaching. And so it was for America between 2001–2006, when home buyers, bankers, and investors alike saw nothing but a future of ever-increasing home values, only to hit the dirt in a crushing recession, the effects of which continue to plague us to this day. Not wishing to cast a cloud on America's sunny disposition, Ehrenreich nevertheless believes that America could be a better, indeed happier, place, if it can only "recover from the mass delusion that is positive thinking." Barbara Ehrenreich is a social analyst and the author of many books, including *Bright-Sided: How the Relentless Promotion of Positive Thinking Is Undermining America* (2009), from which this selection is taken.

Americans are a "positive" people. This is our reputation as well as our self-image. We smile a lot and are often baffled when people from other cultures do not return the favor. In the well-worn stereotype, we are upbeat, cheerful, optimistic, and shallow, while foreigners are likely to be subtle, world-weary, and possibly decadent. American expatriate writers like Henry James and James Baldwin wrestled with and occasionally reinforced this stereotype, which I once encountered in the 1980s in the form of a remark by Soviet émigré poet Joseph Brodsky to the effect that the problem with Americans is that they have "never known suffering." (Apparently he didn't know who had invented the blues.) Whether we Americans see it as an embarrassment or a point of pride, being positive — in affect, in mood, in outlook — seems to be engrained in our national character.

Who would be churlish or disaffected enough to challenge these happy features of the American personality? Take the business of positive "affect," which refers to the mood we display to others through our smiles, our greetings, our professions of confidence and optimism. Scientists have found that the mere act of smiling can generate positive feelings within us, at least if the smile is not forced. In addition, good feelings, as expressed through our words and smiles, seem to be contagious: "Smile and the world smiles with you." Surely the world would be a better, happier place if we all greeted one another warmly and stopped to coax smiles from babies — if only through the well-known social psychological mechanism of "mood contagion." Recent studies show that happy feelings flit easily through social networks, so that one person's good fortune can brighten the day even for only distantly connected others.[1]

Furthermore, psychologists today agree that positive feelings like gratitude, contentment, and self-confidence can actually lengthen our lives and improve our health. Some of these claims are exaggerated, as we shall see, though positive feelings hardly need to be justified, like exercise or vitamin supplements, as part of a healthy lifestyle. People who report having positive feelings are more likely to participate in a rich social life, and vice versa, and social connectedness turns out to be an important defense against depression, which is a known risk factor for many physical illnesses. At the risk of redundancy or even tautology, we can say that on many levels, individual and social, it is *good* to be "positive," certainly better than being withdrawn, aggrieved, or chronically sad.

So I take it as a sign of progress that, in just the last decade or so, economists have begun to show an interest in using happiness rather than just the gross national product as a measure of an economy's success. Happiness is, of course, a slippery thing to measure or define. Philosophers have debated what it is for centuries, and even if we were to define it simply as a greater frequency of positive feelings than negative ones, when we ask people if they are happy we are asking them to arrive at some sort of average over many moods and moments. Maybe I was upset earlier in the day but then was cheered up by a bit of good news, so what am I really? In one well-known psychological experiment, subjects were asked to answer a questionnaire on life satisfaction—but only after they had performed the apparently irrelevant task of photocopying a sheet of paper for the experimenter. For a randomly chosen half of the subjects, a dime had been left for them to find on the copy machine. As two economists summarize the results, "Reported satisfaction with life was raised substantially, by the discovery of the coin on the copy machine—clearly not an income effect."[2]

In addition to the problems of measurement, there are cultural differences in how happiness is regarded and whether it is even seen as a virtue. Some cultures, like our own, value the positive affect that seems to signal internal happiness; others are more impressed by seriousness, self-sacrifice, or a quiet willingness to cooperate. However hard to pin down, though, happiness is somehow a more pertinent metric for well-being, from a humanistic perspective, than the buzz of transactions that constitute the GDP.

Surprisingly, when psychologists undertake to measure the relative happiness of nations, they routinely find that Americans are not, even in prosperous times and despite our vaunted positivity, very happy at all.

5

---

[1] "Happiness Is 'Infectious' in Network of Friends: Collective — Not Just Individual — Phenomenon," *ScienceDaily*, Dec. 5, 2008, http://www.sciencedaily.com/releases/2008/12/081205094506.htm.

[2] Daniel Kahneman and Alan B. Krueger, "Developments in the Measurement of Subjective Well-Being," *Journal of Economic Perspectives* 20 (2006): 3–24.

A recent meta-analysis of over a hundred studies of self-reported happiness worldwide found Americans ranking only twenty-third, surpassed by the Dutch, the Danes, the Malaysians, the Bahamians, the Austrians, and even the supposedly dour Finns.[3] In another potential sign of relative distress, Americans account for two-thirds of the global market for antidepressants, which happen also to be the most commonly prescribed drugs in the United States. To my knowledge, no one knows how antidepressant use affects people's responses to happiness surveys: Do respondents report being happy because the drugs make them feel happy or do they report being unhappy because they know they are dependent on drugs to make them feel better? Without our heavy use of antidepressants, Americans would likely rank far lower in the happiness rankings than we currently do.

When economists attempt to rank nations more objectively in terms of "well-being," taking into account such factors as health, environmental sustainability, and the possibility of upward mobility, the United States does even more poorly than it does when only the subjective state of "happiness" is measured. The Happy Planet Index, to give just one example, locates us at 150th among the world's nations.[4]

How can we be so surpassingly "positive" in self-image and stereotype without being the world's happiest and best-off people? The answer, I think, is that positivity is not so much our condition or our mood as it is part of our ideology — the way we explain the world and think we ought to function within it. That ideology is "positive thinking," by which we usually mean two things. One is the generic content of positive thinking — that is, the positive thought itself — which can be summarized as: Things are pretty good right now, at least if you are willing to see silver linings, make lemonade out of lemons, etc., and things are going to get a whole lot better. This is optimism, and it is not the same as hope. Hope is an emotion, a yearning, the experience of which is not entirely within our control. Optimism is a cognitive stance, a conscious expectation, which presumably anyone can develop through practice.

The second thing we mean by "positive thinking" is this practice, or discipline, of trying to think in a positive way. There is, we are told, a practical reason for undertaking this effort: Positive thinking supposedly not only makes us feel optimistic but actually makes happy outcomes more likely. If you expect things to get better, they will. How can the mere process of thinking do this? In the rational explanation that many psychologists would offer today, optimism improves health, personal efficacy, confidence, and resilience, making it easier for us to accomplish our goals. A far less rational theory also runs rampant in American ideology — the idea that our thoughts can, in some mysterious way, directly affect the physical world. Negative

---

[3]"Psychologist Produces the First-Ever 'World Map of Happiness,'" *ScienceDaily,* Nov. 14, 2006, http://www.sciencedaily.com/releases/2006/11/061113093726.htm.

[4]http://rankingamerica.wordpress.com/2009/01/11/the-us-ranks-150th-in-planet-happiness/, Jan. 11,2009.

thoughts somehow produce negative outcomes, while positive thoughts realize themselves in the form of health, prosperity, and success. For both rational and mystical reasons, then, the effort of positive thinking is said to be well worth our time and attention, whether this means reading the relevant books, attending seminars and speeches that offer the appropriate mental training, or just doing the solitary work of concentration on desired outcomes — a better job, an attractive mate, world peace.

There is an anxiety, as you can see, right here in the heart of American 10 positive thinking. If the generic "positive thought" is correct and things are really getting better, if the arc of the universe tends toward happiness and abundance, then why bother with the mental effort of positive thinking? Obviously, because we do not fully believe that things will get better on their own. The practice of positive thinking is an effort to pump up this belief in the face of much contradictory evidence. Those who set themselves up as instructors in the discipline of positive thinking — coaches, preachers, and gurus of various sorts — have described this effort with terms like "self-hypnosis," "mind control," and "thought control." In other words, it requires deliberate self-deception, including a constant effort to repress or block out unpleasant possibilities and "negative" thoughts. The truly self-confident, or those who have in some way made their peace with the world and their destiny within it, do not need to expend effort censoring or otherwise controlling their thoughts. Positive thinking may be a quintessentially American activity, associated in our minds with both individual and national success, but it is driven by a terrible insecurity.

Americans did not start out as positive thinkers — at least the promotion of unwarranted optimism and methods to achieve it did not really find articulation and organized form until several decades after the founding of the republic. In the Declaration of Independence, the Founding Fathers pledged to one another "our lives, our fortunes, and our sacred honor." They knew that they had no certainty of winning a war for independence and that they were taking a mortal risk. Just the act of signing the declaration made them all traitors to the crown, and treason was a crime punishable by execution. Many of them did go on to lose their lives, loved ones, and fortunes in the war. The point is, they fought anyway. There is a vast difference between positive thinking and existential courage.

Systematic positive thinking began, in the nineteenth century, among a diverse and fascinating collection of philosophers, mystics, lay healers, and middle-class women. By the twentieth century, though, it had gone mainstream, gaining purchase within such powerful belief systems as nationalism and also doing its best to make itself indispensable to capitalism. We don't usually talk about American nationalism, but it is a mark of how deep it runs that we apply the word "nationalism" to Serbs, Russians, and others, while believing ourselves to possess a uniquely superior version called "patriotism." A central tenet of American nationalism has been the belief that the United States is "the greatest nation on earth" — more dynamic, democratic, and prosperous than any other nation, as well as technologically superior. Major religious leaders, especially on the Christian right, buttress this conceit with the notion that Americans are God's chosen people and that America is the designated leader of the world — an idea that seemed to find vivid reinforcement in the fall of Communism and our emergence as the world's "lone superpower." That acute British observer Godfrey Hodgson has written that the American sense of exceptionalism, which once was "idealistic and generous, if somewhat solipsistic," has become "harder, more hubristic." Paul Krugman responded to the prevailing smugness in a 1998 essay entitled "American the Boastful," warning that "if pride goeth before a fall, the United States has one heck of a come-uppance in store."[5]

But of course it takes the effort of positive thinking to imagine that America is the "best" or the "greatest." Militarily, yes, we are the mightiest nation on earth. But on many other fronts, the American score is dismal, and was dismal even before the economic downturn that began in 2007. Our children routinely turn out to be more ignorant of basic subjects like math and geography than their counterparts in other industrialized nations. They are also more likely to die in infancy or grow up in poverty. Almost everyone acknowledges that our health care system is "broken" and our physical infrastructure crumbling. We have lost so much of our edge in science and technology that American companies have even begun to outsource their research and development efforts. Worse, some of the measures by which we do lead the world should inspire embarrassment rather than pride: We have the highest percentage of our population incarcerated, and the greatest level of inequality in wealth and income. We are plagued by gun violence and racked by personal debt.

While positive thinking has reinforced and found reinforcement in American national pride, it has also entered into a kind of symbiotic relationship with American capitalism. There is no natural, innate affinity between capitalism and positive thinking. In fact, one of the classics of sociology, Max Weber's *Protestant Ethic and the Spirit of Capitalism*, makes a still impressive case for capitalism's roots in the grim and punitive outlook of Calvinist Protestantism, which required people to defer gratification and resist all pleasurable temptations in favor of hard work and the accumulation of wealth.

But if early capitalism was inhospitable to positive thinking, "late" capitalism, or consumer capitalism, is far more congenial, depending as it does on the individual's hunger for *more* and the firm's imperative of *growth*. The consumer culture encourages individuals to want more — cars, larger homes, television sets, cell phones, gadgets of all kinds — and positive thinking is ready at hand to tell them they deserve more and can have it if they really want it and are willing to make the effort to get it. Meanwhile, in a competitive business world, the companies that manufacture these goods and provide the paychecks that purchase them have no alternative but to grow. If you don't steadily increase market share and profits, you risk being driven out of business or swallowed by a larger enterprise. Perpetual growth,

15

[5]Godfrey Hodgson, *The Myth of American Exceptionalism* (New Haven: Yale University Press, 2009), 113; Paul Krugman, "America the Boastful," *Foreign Affairs,* May–June 1998.

whether of a particular company or an entire economy, is of course an absurdity, but positive thinking makes it seem possible, if not ordained.

In addition, positive thinking has made itself useful as an apology for the crueler aspects of the market economy. If optimism is the key to material success, and if you can achieve an optimistic outlook through the discipline of positive thinking, then there is no excuse for failure. The flip side of positivity is thus a harsh insistence on personal responsibility: If your business fails or your job is eliminated, it must be because you didn't try hard enough, didn't believe firmly enough in the inevitability of your success. As the economy has brought more layoffs and financial turbulence to the middle class, the promoters of positive thinking have increasingly emphasized this negative judgment: to be disappointed, resentful, or downcast is to be a "victim" and a "whiner."

But positive thinking is not only a water carrier for the business world, excusing its excesses and masking its follies. The promotion of positive thinking has become a minor industry in its own right, producing an endless flow of books, DVDs, and other products; providing employment for tens of thousands of "life coaches," "executive coaches," and motivational speakers, as well as for the growing cadre of professional psychologists who seek to train them. No doubt the growing financial insecurity of the middle class contributes to the demand for these products and services, but I hesitate to attribute the commercial success of positive thinking to any particular economic trend or twist of the business cycle. America has historically offered space for all sorts of sects, cults, faith healers, and purveyors of snake oil, and those that are profitable, like positive thinking, tend to flourish.

At the turn of the twenty-first century, American optimism seemed to reach a manic crescendo. In his final State of the Union address in 2000, Bill Clinton struck a triumphal note, proclaiming that "never before has our nation enjoyed, at once, so much prosperity and social progress with so little internal crisis and so few external threats." But compared with his successor, Clinton seemed almost morose. George W. Bush had been a cheerleader in prep school, and cheerleading — a distinctly American innovation — could be considered the athletically inclined ancestor of so much of the coaching and "motivating" that has gone into the propagation of positive thinking. He took the presidency as an opportunity to continue in that line of work, defining his job as that of inspiring confidence, dispelling doubts, and pumping up the national spirit of self-congratulation. If he repeatedly laid claim to a single adjective, it was "optimistic." On the occasion of his sixtieth birthday, he told reporters he was "optimistic" about a variety of foreign policy challenges, offering as an overview, "I'm optimistic that all problems will be solved." Nor did he brook any doubts or hesitations among his close advisers. According to Bob Woodward, Condoleezza Rice failed to express some of her worries because, she said, "the president almost demanded optimism. He didn't like pessimism, hand-wringing or doubt."[6]

[6] 2000 State of the Union Address, Jan. 27, 2000, http://www.washingtonpost.com/wpsrv /politics/special/states/docs/sou00.htm; Geoff Elliott, "Dubya's 60th Takes the Cake," *Weekend Australian,* July 8, 2006; Woodward, quoting Rice, *Meet the Press* transcript, Dec. 21, 2008, http://today.msnbc.msn.com/id/28337897/.

Then things began to go wrong, which is not in itself unusual but was a possibility excluded by America's official belief that things are good and getting better. There was the dot-com bust that began a few months after Clinton's declaration of unprecedented prosperity in his final State of the Union address, then the terrorist attack of September 11, 2001. Furthermore, things began to go wrong in a way that suggested that positive thinking might not guarantee success after all, that it might in fact dim our ability to fend off real threats. In her remarkable book, *Never Saw It Coming: Cultural Challenges to Envisioning the Worst*, sociologist Karen Cerulo recounts a number of ways that the habit of positive thinking, or what she calls optimistic bias, undermined preparedness and invited disaster. She quotes *Newsweek* reporters Michael Hirsch and Michael Isikoff, for example, in their conclusion that "a whole summer of missed clues, taken together, seemed to presage the terrible September of 2001."[7] There had already been a terrorist attack on the World Trade Center in 1993; there were ample warnings, in the summer of 2001, about a possible attack by airplane, and flight schools reported suspicious students like the one who wanted to learn how to "fly a plane but didn't care about landing and takeoff." The fact that no one — the FBI, the INS, Bush, or Rice — heeded these disturbing cues was later attributed to a "failure of imagination." But actually there was plenty of imagination at work — imagining an invulnerable nation and an ever-booming economy — there was simply no ability or inclination to imagine the worst.

A similar reckless optimism pervaded the American invasion of Iraq. Warnings about possible Iraqi resistance were swept aside by leaders who promised a "cakewalk" and envisioned cheering locals greeting our troops with flowers. Likewise, Hurricane Katrina was not exactly an unanticipated disaster. In 2002, the New Orleans *Times-Picayune* ran a Pulitzer Prize-winning series warning that the city's levees could not protect it against the storm surge brought on by a category 4 or 5 hurricane. In 2001, *Scientific American* had issued a similar warning about the city's vulnerability.[8] Even when the hurricane struck and levees broke, no alarm bells went off in Washington, and when a New Orleans FEMA official sent a panicky e-mail to FEMA director Michael Brown, alerting him to the rising number of deaths and a shortage of food in the drowning city, he was told that Brown would need an hour to eat his dinner in a Baton Rouge restaurant.[9] Criminal negligence or another "failure of imagination"? The truth is that Americans had been working hard for decades to school themselves in the techniques of positive thinking, and these included the reflexive capacity for dismissing disturbing news.

The biggest "come-uppance," to use Krugman's term, has so far been the financial meltdown of 2007 and the ensuing economic crisis. By the late

20

---

[7]Quoted in Karen A. Cerulo, *Never Saw It Coming: Cultural Challenges to Envisioning the Worst* (Chicago: University of Chicago Press, 2006), 18.

[8]Cerulo, *Never Saw It Coming,* 239.

[9]Hope Yen, "Death in Streets Took a Back Seat to Dinner," *Seattle Times,* Oct. 25, 2005.

first decade of the twenty-first century, positive thinking had become ubiquitous and virtually unchallenged in American culture. It was promoted on some of the most widely watched talk shows, like *Larry King Live* and the *Oprah Winfrey Show*; it was the stuff of runaway best sellers like the 2006 book *The Secret*; it had been adopted as the theology of America's most successful evangelical preachers; it found a place in medicine as a potential adjuvant to the treatment of almost any disease. It had even penetrated the academy in the form of the new discipline of "positive psychology," offering courses teaching students to pump up their optimism and nurture their positive feelings. And its reach was growing global, first in the Anglophone countries and soon in the rising economies of China, South Korea, and India.

But nowhere did it find a warmer welcome than in American business, which is, of course, also global business. To the extent that positive thinking had become a business itself, business was its principal client, eagerly consuming the good news that all things are possible through an effort of mind. This was a useful message for employees, who by the turn of the twenty-first century were being required to work longer hours for fewer benefits and diminishing job security. But it was also a liberating ideology for top-level executives. What was the point in agonizing over balance sheets and tedious analyses of risks — and why bother worrying about dizzying levels of debt and exposure to potential defaults — when all good things come to those who are optimistic enough to expect them?

I do not write this in a spirit of sourness or personal disappointment of any kind, nor do I have any romantic attachment to suffering as a source of insight or virtue. On the contrary, I would like to see more smiles, more laughter, more hugs, more happiness and, better yet, joy. In my own vision of utopia, there is not only more comfort, and security for everyone — better jobs, health care, and so forth — there are also more parties, festivities, and opportunities for dancing in the streets. Once our basic material needs are met — in my utopia, anyway — life becomes a perpetual celebration in which everyone has a talent to contribute. But we cannot levitate ourselves into that blessed condition by wishing it. We need to brace ourselves for a struggle against terrifying obstacles, both of our own making and imposed by the natural world. And the first step is to recover from the mass delusion that is positive thinking.

READING THE TEXT

1. What contradictions have psychological studies found between Americans' valuing of happiness and well-being and their actual state of happiness?

2. When did positive thinking begin to be a cultural trait of Americans, according to Ehrenreich?

3. What is the relationship, in Ehrenreich's view, between positive thinking and capitalism?

4. How, according to Ehrenreich, has positive thinking contributed to recent and current American problems and catastrophes?

5. Examine Ehrenreich's rhetorical strategies. Why does she outline, early in her essay, the reasons that a positive attitude can be beneficial? What effect does that discussion have on your response to her essay?

READING THE SIGNS

1. Conduct a class debate over the proposition that positive thinking led Americans, especially politicians, to be naïvely optimistic in not anticipating recent national events despite plenty of warning signs. You might focus on the civic disaster wrought on New Orleans by Hurricane Katrina in 2005, the 2015 terrorist attacks in San Bernardino, CA, or pundits' inability to predict that Donald Trump would carry traditionally democratic states like Wisconsin in the 2016 presidential election.

2. **CONNECTING TEXTS**   Read or reread Laurence Shames's "The More Factor" (p. 76). Adopting Ehrenreich's argument about Americans' predilection for positive thinking, write an essay in which you explain why "the hunger for more," as Shames puts it, is so prevalent in American culture.

3. **CONNECTING TEXTS**   Read or reread Neal Gabler's "The Social Networks" (p. 240), and write an essay in which you argue whether the ever-present friendships and sense of close community that Gabler identifies in some TV shows reflect the sort of positive thinking that Ehrenreich describes. Be sure to base your argument on a close reading of at least one show that Gabler mentions that fits this category of programming.

4. Read Rhonda Byrne's *The Secret* and write an analysis of how it reflects the American cult of positive thinking. Alternatively, do such an analysis of one of the many books in the *Chicken Soup for the Soul* series or Louise L. Hay's *You Can Heal Your Life*.

5. **CONNECTING TEXTS**   Adopting Ehrenreich's point of view, enter a conversation with Erin Lee ("How Effective Is Social Media Activism?," p. 402) and Brian Dunning ("Slacktivism: Raising Awareness," p. 405) about the potential efficacy of social media activism. What advice might she give Lee and Dunning?

THE CONSEQUENCES OF CONTRADICTIONS

JEFFREY FLEISHMAN
How an Angry National Mood Is Reflected in Pop Culture

When the going gets tough, the tough get angry, or so one might conclude from the vast array of edgy entertainments that we find today in American popular culture. Threatened by globalization, economic malaise, and international terrorism, Americans are strikingly anxious these days. And so, as Jeffrey Fleishman writes in this survey of American anger and the arts, "We get Batman and Superman — once the extensions of our better selves — battling each other in a grim rain; the take-no-prisoners TV commentaries of Samantha Bee and John Oliver; abrasive, if clever, comics like Amy Schumer; rage and betrayal in Beyoncé's *Lemonade*; meth and degradation in *Breaking Bad*; beheadings, dragons, torture and wars for supremacy in *Game of Thrones*." America has been through tough times before, Fleishman notes, but then we had artists like Woody Guthrie and Bob Dylan to mediate the anger. Now, in the era of social mediated echo chambers and niche marketing, there seems to be no common vision to contain the rage. The result is, in Fleishman's conclusion, only more rage. Jeffrey Fleishman is a senior writer on film, art, and culture for the *Los Angeles Times*.

Our screens and phones fume with righteousness. Our superheroes have forsaken us and our fictions pale against our headlines. Social media taunts have poisoned our political discourse and disfigured our reality. We have become an angry, fractious lot, a *Game of Thrones* for a digitized and unsettled century.

Much of our vexation arises from the insecurities of white working and middle classes threatened by a country reimagined by Wall Street, globalization, technology and changing demographics. The backlash has agitated racial tensions and identity politics that played out in the presidential campaigns of Donald Trump and Bernie Sanders but also reverberated beyond our borders to a world shaken by financial crises, Britain's vote to exit from the European Union, waves of Syrian refugees and terrorist attacks in Paris, Brussels, Baghdad, and San Bernardino.

Visceral and at times frightening narratives are running through our popular culture. We get Batman and Superman — once the extensions of our better selves — battling each other in a grim rain; the take-no-prisoners TV commentaries of Samantha Bee and John Oliver; abrasive, if clever, comics like Amy Schumer; rage and betrayal in Beyonce's *Lemonade*; meth and degradation in *Breaking Bad*; beheadings, dragons, torture and wars for supremacy in *Game of Thrones*.

Ta-Nehisi Coates' *Between the World and Me*, bestselling meditation on being a black man in America, is, along with Kendrick Lamar's Grammy-winning "The Blacker the Berry," among the most profound expressions on anger and disillusionment around race. Two of last year's most heralded films reflected fury that, while set in the recent past, connects with the current political turmoil: *The Big Short* was an examination of the greed and hubris that led to the 2008 financial collapse, calling out a Wall Street culture that has become a target of populist politics, while *Straight Outta Compton* reminded audiences of the LAPD's brutal history with minority communities as new police shootings of African Americans set off disturbances across the nation.

Such works reflect the darker elements of our natures at a time when   5
our realities seem more perilous than our make-believes. The canon of art is
to make sense of seminal times, to pull insight from extremity and find universal meaning in uproar — that's what powered much of pop culture
through turbulent times like the Vietnam War or the Great Depression. But
our anger today in the arts is aimed at narrower audiences and amplified
through social media and appears more pulse-pounding and instantaneous
than in past decades.

Our predilections both in popular culture and politics have increasingly
turned tribal, as if a once-common language has broken into coded dialects
that separate us from the other. Our entertainment options, many of them
self-produced on Facebook, Snapchat, and YouTube, are plugged into multiple platforms. Our invective is searing, and our common ground is shrinking
in a competitive and raucous media landscape that refracts and fuels our
worst instincts.

Where are the broader signposts and what are the cultural descendants of
Neil Young's "Ohio" or Jimi Hendrix's assaultive rendition of the "Star-Spangled
Banner"? Where is Bob Dylan's "The Times They Are a Changin'" or Marvin
Gaye's "What's Going On"? Where are Archie Bunker's rants, Paddy Chayef-
sky's screenplay for *Network* or Norman Mailer's *The Armies of the Night*?

"Art is so fragmented. We're off in our own ghettos," said Charles
Randolph, who co-wrote the screenplay for *The Big Short*. He added that
social media and other outlets offer few galvanizing touchstones, such as the
original 1977 television miniseries *Roots* (not this year's remake, which had
a fraction of the original's audience), that resonate across race, economic
class, and culture.

"I don't see the traditional players coming along and doing what
they do," he said. "But you also don't see younger artists articulating the
universal anger.

"Why hasn't any artist done the job of a crazy politician from New York?"   10
Randolph said in reference to Donald Trump, the presumptive Republican
nominee who has channeled and amplified widespread dismay with public
and financial institutions. Trump will headline what is expected to be a
messy convention in Cleveland that begins Monday.

Artistic Dilemma

Writers and artists have long faced dilemmas on tapping into the zeitgeist.
Some suggest art should arise immediately from the times it is articulating;
others say art and popular culture best define landmark moments through a
dispassionate prism of time and distance.

Philip Roth, in a 1961 essay, was perplexed over how to decipher a nation
entering a decade of turmoil: "The American writer in the middle of the 20th
century has his hands full in trying to understand, and then describe, and

then make credible much of the American reality. It stupefies, it sickens, it infuriates, and finally it is even a kind of embarrassment to one's own meager imagination. The actuality is continually outdoing our talents, and the culture tosses up figures almost daily that are the envy of any novelist."

Even the most socially attuned artists would have been hard-pressed over the last year to conjure anything as dramatic or revealing as the moods and faces at rallies for Trump and Sanders. The presidential campaign, notably during the Republican primary, has given us populist passions in a real-time mash-up of a *Saturday Night Live* skit and an updating of novelist's Robert Penn Warren's political masterwork, *All the King's Men*.

"I'll say this about Trump: Anger is an addiction. We like it. The brain likes it. And now you've got a country full of addicts," Paul Simon was quoted as saying by *Billboard* magazine. "And the media and certain politicians are the dealers. So everybody's angry all the time, and they're all juiced up. I'm not saying there's nothing to be angry about. What I'm saying is, you can't make a calm decision when somebody's got you in a rage."

One wonders how Archie Bunker would view today's America from his [15] living room in Queens. A bigot and a racist who wore white socks with black shoes, Archie (Carroll O'Connor) was the embattled everyman of the 1970s groundbreaking television sitcom *All in the Family*. With his flag-pin patriotism, Archie, as politically incorrect as a man could be, clung to a past that was vanishing around him. But everyone knew the joke was on him; his insufferability allowed him our sympathy, or if not that, at least our understanding. It's hard to imagine that attitude of amused tolerance for a character like Archie today.

But Archie's was a time when much of American popular culture was distilled through three TV channels, a dial of radio stations, family-owned movie houses, newspapers, and weekly magazines. Today talk radio, reality shows, and legions of blogs tap into and stoke anger.

The era of hashtags and selfies has given rise to political expression and art that are instant and fiercely personal. Facts matter less than egos; swift thumbs and eviscerating texts have little time for context. A similar reckoning for cultural and political forces roiled civil rights protests and anti-Vietnam War marches of the 1960s but, except for certain pockets including the South, there were moments of shared purpose amid the many convulsions.

"Bobby Kennedy sat with Cesar Chavez. You had Woodstock and a racially multicultural effort that was the impulse of the '60s," said Dawn Porter, documentary film director of *Gideon's Army* and *Trapped*. "But today we're more separate and you have to cross a line. It is very dangerous. People at Trump rallies, it's pretty scary stuff. I don't see someone [an artist or musician] speaking to a multiracial audience. It's odd. I can't see a Trump supporter sitting with a person from Black Lives Matter. Who would be their headliner?"

Art has illuminated pivotal moments and forced evaluations throughout American history. The Depression-era photographs of poor families taken by Margaret Bourke-White, Walker Evans, and Dorothea Lange captured the public's imagination. Woody Guthrie's folk song "This Land Is Your Land," written in 1940 and released years later, was a blistering counterpoint to Irving Berlin's "God Bless America." Playwright Arthur Miller's *Death of a Salesman* resonated with the cruelty and tragedy of the American dream in the immediate post-World War II years.

This year's two big Tony winners reflect these separate realities. The multicultural cast of the Broadway sensation *Hamilton*, a musical about founding father Alexander Hamilton, embodies the nation's diversity. Playing not far away is *The Humans*, a potent rendering of the dashed expectations of the white middle class, including a line that crystallizes our economic fears: "Don't cha think it should cost less to be alive?"

Different fears are realized in Ayad Akhtar's Pulitzer Prize-winning *Disgraced,* just finishing its run at the Mark Taper Forum, about the stewing torment of a Pakistani American lawyer torn between his Muslim ancestry and his Western aspirations. In a recent interview, Akhtar said he was struck by how much the dramatic language of the theater has often been eclipsed by the knives-out vernacular of the real world.

"I wrote the play in 2010 and I didn't think that that kind of degradation of rhetoric could exist anywhere but the theater," he said. "But now we're living in a world where what's happening on stage is not all that controversial. It's happening everywhere, all the time, about shifts in American life."

Our rage these days often cuts deeper than our sense of humor. There are fewer agreed-upon pathways that allow us to examine together our transgressions, foibles, prejudices, and fears. Our shared humanity has been demarcated on smaller and smaller screens that often brim more with quicksilver judgment than open-mindedness. The lines have hardened. The terrain is vast and splintered, and as the lyrics of Lamar's "The Blacker the Berry" suggest, self-loathing may bristle beneath the rancor:

"I mean, it's evident that I'm irrelevant to society / That's what you're telling me, penitentiary would only hire me / Curse me till I'm dead / Church me with your fake prophesyzing that I'mma be just another slave in my head / Institutionalize manipulation and lies / Reciprocation of freedom only live in your eyes / You hate me don't you? / I know you hate me just as much as you hate yourself."

READING THE TEXT

1. To what causes does Fleishman attribute the current angry national mood?
2. What differences does Fleishman find between the anger expressed in 1960s popular culture and that of today, and how does he explain those differences?

3. How have social media contributed to the current national mood, in Fleishman's view?

4. In what particular ways does current popular culture reflect American anger and anxiety, according to Fleishman?

READING THE SIGNS

1. Watch one of the films that Fleishman mentions, such as *Straight Outta Compton* or *The Big Short*, and write your own analysis of its depiction of anger and rage at the political status quo. Alternatively, watch a TV program like *Game of Thrones*.

2. Fleishman claims that artists in the past could present a common vision during hard times. Research the work of one of the artists he mentions, such as Margaret Bourke-White, Walker Evans, or Arthur Miller, focusing on how that artist responded to national tragedy. Write an essay in which you explain how those artists were signs of their times, just as Fleishman says that today's angry artists reflect today's mood.

3. Watch an episode or two of *All in the Family*, and write an essay that responds to Fleishman's musing comment: "One wonders how Archie Bunker would view today's America" (para. 15).

4. In class, form teams and debate the artists' dilemma that Fleishman poses: "Some suggest art should arise immediately from the times it is articulating; others say art and popular culture best define landmark moments through a dispassionate prism of time and distance" (para. 11). Each team should base its arguments on specific artists and their work.

THE CONSEQUENCES OF CONTRADICTIONS

| JIM TANKERSLEY

Why the Upper Middle Class Might Be the Real Target of Today's Anger

A funny thing happened on the way to the economic "recovery" from the Great Recession: While the economic lot of the middle, lower-middle, and working classes declined, the wealth of the upper-middle class (along with the 1 percent) continued to grow, as it had been since the 1980s. This is why, Jim Tankersley explains in this Wonkblog for the *Washington Post*, America today hosts such a healthy market for luxury goods, even as the vast majority of Americans struggle. And it is also why we see so much anger in the land. As Tankersley summarizes the views of economist Stephen Rose, the "poor and the middle class are not so much angry at the top 1 percent . . . as they are at the upper middle class — the people who used to be middle class like them but who now live in nicer houses and drive sports cars and . . . maybe look down on the workers left behind in their rise." Such are the paradoxes of social mobility in the land of opportunity. Jim Tankersley covers economic policy for the *Washington Post.*

Stephen Rose is an economist who writes often about income inequality and the size of the middle class, and as all good researchers do, he began his latest project with a question. Why, he wondered, does Mercedes-Benz advertise on television?

It was a simple way of asking why luxury brands focus resources on appealing to a mass audience of U.S. consumers, particularly at a time when technology is making it easier to micro-target the very rich. The answer, his research found, is that there might be more buying power in a particular group of consumers — people he calls the upper middle class — than other economists have estimated.

"What's happening," Rose said, "is that's where the money is."

Rose defines the upper middle class as households earning the equivalent of $100,000 to $349,999 a year for a family of three, in 2014 dollars. (For a single worker, that equivalent works out to just less than $58,000 a year.)

In his new paper, released Tuesday by the Urban Institute, Rose argues   5
that the upper middle class swelled to include a significantly larger share of U.S. workers in 2014 than it did in 1979 — and that in that time, the economy delivered much faster income gains to those upper-middle-class workers, and to very rich workers, than for everyone else.

The upper middle class grew from just less than 13 percent of the U.S. population in 1979 to nearly 30 percent in 2014, Rose found by using census data. He attributes the trend to increasing returns to higher education and advanced skills in an evolving economy.

In that time, the middle class, the lower middle class and the poor, as he defines them, all shrunk as a share of the population; the share of the super-rich boomed.

Nearly all of that movement occurred during the mid-1980s, under President Ronald Reagan, and in the late 1990s, under President Bill Clinton, Rose's numbers suggest. The research shows little shift in the composition of the income groupings since the dawn of the 21st century.

Still, Rose's finding is far more optimistic than others have reported, including the Pew Research Center, which warned in December that the middle class (defined differently from how Rose does) has shrunk by more than 10 percentage points as a share of the population since 1971. Rose's previous work has also drawn criticism from some inequality researchers, such as the economist Dean Baker, who say it overstates the gains for middle-class workers over the past several decades.

It's easy to quibble with Rose's boundaries for the income groups in this   10
analysis; the cut-off for "upper middle class" falls around the 95th percentile
of household incomes, according to the Census Bureau, making it sound a
lot more like "rich" than any form of middle class.

But Rose's secondary finding may well draw agreement from economists concerned about rising inequality. He shows that the rich and the
upper middle class, to a smaller degree, captured an increasing share of the
gains from economic growth over that 35 year span. In 1979, the bottom
three groups earned 70 percent of all income in the country, he estimates.
By 2014, that share had dropped below 40 percent.

Rose sees, in these figures, a new explanation for today's political
turmoil and a new prism for the inequality debate. The poor and the middle
class are not so much angry at the top 1 percent, he says, as they are at the
upper middle class — the people who used to be middle class like them but
who now live in nicer houses and drive sports cars and, Rose says, maybe
look down on the workers left behind in their rise.

"It's bittersweet," he said of the findings, "in a sense that it looks to be
a good thing — everyone's moving up! Who could be against it?" The downside, he added, is the elevation of a group of people "who are different from
the people below them, and notice it, and the people below them resent it."

The resented class, he said, are the folks who can drive off with that new
Mercedes from the TV.

READING THE TEXT

1. In your own words, how have class divisions in America changed since 1979?

2. Why, according to economist Stephen Rose, are poor and middle-class
   Americans angry at the upper-middle class but not the upper class?

3. How do the references to TV ads for Mercedes-Benz serve to illustrate Stephen
   Rose's overall point about class differences and hostility?

4. Tankersley relies on economic data to propose his answer to the question posed
   in his title. How do the statistics he presents affect your response to this selection?

READING THE SIGNS

1. **CONNECTING TEXTS**   Tankersley, Lilliana Mason ("Why Are Americans So Angry
   This Election Season?," p. 510), and Jeffrey Fleishman ("How an Angry
   National Mood Is Reflected in Pop Culture," p. 531) all propose explanations
   for the current contentious zeitgeist in America but base their essays on different sorts of evidence. Synthesize their explanations, and write an essay that
   proposes your own overarching argument for why Americans seem so angry.

2. **CONNECTING TEXTS**   America's most popular entertainers and athletes belong to
   the economic 1 percent (or wealthier), but Americans rarely reflect their anger
   at them. In an essay, propose your explanation for Americans' tolerance for
   the super-rich, being sure to refer to particular celebrities as examples. To

develop your ideas about Americans' attitudes toward class, you might consult Jack Solomon's "Masters of Desire: The Culture of American Advertising" (p. 152) and George Packer's "Celebrating Inequality" (below).

3. Write an essay in which you support, challenge, or complicate the proposition that the growing inequality that economist Stephen Rose outlines played a significant role in the 2016 election of Donald Trump — even though Trump himself is a member of the very rich.

GEORGE PACKER
Celebrating Inequality

"Our age is lousy with celebrities," George Packer quips in this 2013 essay for the *New York Times*, and it's only getting worse. Indeed, in tough times like today's, when the gap between the rich and the poor yawns ever wider, celebrities loom larger on the social horizon than they have in more equitable times, overshadowing the rest of us. And we're not just talking about entertainers. Indeed, as Packer notes, they include entrepreneurs, bankers, computer engineers, real estate developers, media executives, journalists, politicians, scientists, and even chefs. And as the new celebrity deities gobble up whatever opportunities are left in America, Packer believes, America itself is turning backward to the days of the Jazz Age and Jay Gatsby. So, meet the new celebrity gods; same as the old celebrity gods — or "something far more perverse." George Packer is a staff writer for the *New Yorker* and the author of numerous books, including the National Book Award–winning *The Unwinding: An Inner History of the New America* (2013).

The Roaring '20s was the decade when modern celebrity was invented in America. F. Scott Fitzgerald's *The Great Gatsby* is full of magazine spreads of tennis players and socialites, popular song lyrics, movie stars, paparazzi, gangsters, and sports scandals — machine-made by technology, advertising, and public relations. Gatsby, a mysterious bootlegger who makes a meteoric ascent from Midwestern obscurity to the palatial splendor of West Egg, exemplifies one part of the celebrity code: it's inherently illicit. Fitzgerald intuited that, with the old restraining deities of the 19th century dead and his generation's faith in man shaken by World War I, celebrities were the new household gods.

What are celebrities, after all? They dominate the landscape, like giant monuments to aspiration, fulfillment, and overreach. They are as intimate as they are grand, and they offer themselves for worship by ordinary people searching for a suitable object of devotion. But in times of widespread opportunity, the distance between gods and mortals closes, the monuments shrink closer to human size, and the centrality of celebrities in the culture recedes. They loom larger in times like now, when inequality is soaring and trust in institutions — governments, corporations, schools, the press — is falling.

The Depression that ended Fitzgerald's Jazz Age yielded to a new order that might be called the Roosevelt Republic. In the quarter-century after World War II, the country established collective structures, not individual monuments, that channeled the aspirations of ordinary people: state universities, progressive taxation, interstate highways, collective bargaining, health insurance for the elderly, credible news organizations.

One virtue of those hated things called bureaucracies is that they oblige everyone to follow a common set of rules, regardless of station or background; they are inherently equalizing. Books like William H. Whyte's *The Organization Man* and C. Wright Mills's *White Collar* warned of the loss of individual identity, but those middle-class anxieties were possible only because of the great leveling. The "stars" continued to fascinate, especially with the arrival of TV, but they were not essential. Henry Fonda, Barbara Stanwyck, Bette Davis, Jimmy Stewart, Perry Como, Joe DiMaggio, Jack Paar, Doris Day and Dick Clark rose with Americans — not from them — and their successes and screw-ups were a sideshow, not the main event.

Our age is lousy with celebrities. They can be found in every sector of 5 society, including ones that seem less than glamorous. We have celebrity bankers (Jamie Dimon), computer engineers (Sergey Brin), real estate developers / conspiracy theorists (Donald J. Trump), media executives (Arianna Huffington), journalists (Anderson Cooper), mayors (Cory A. Booker), economists (Jeffrey D. Sachs), biologists (J. Craig Venter) and chefs (Mario Batali).

There is a quality of self-invention to their rise: Mark Zuckerberg went from awkward geek to the subject of a Hollywood hit; Shawn Carter turned into Jay-Z; Martha Kostyra became Martha Stewart, and then *Martha Stewart Living*. The person evolves into a persona, then a brand, then an empire, with the business imperative of grow or die — a process of expansion and commodification that transgresses boundaries by substituting celebrity for institutions. Instead of robust public education, we have Mr. Zuckerberg's "rescue" of Newark's schools. Instead of a vibrant literary culture, we have Oprah's book club. Instead of investments in public health, we have the Gates Foundation. Celebrities either buy institutions, or "disrupt" them.

After all, if you *are* the institution, you don't need to play by its rules. Mr. Zuckerberg's foundation myth begins with a disciplinary proceeding at Harvard, which leads him to drop out and found a company whose motto is "Move fast and break things." Jay-Z's history as a crack dealer isn't just a hard-luck story — it's celebrated by fans (and not least himself) as an early sign of hustle and smarts. Martha Stewart's jail time for perjury merely proved that her will to win was indomitable. These new celebrities are all more or less start-up entrepreneurs, and they live by the hacker's code: ask forgiveness, not permission.

The obsession with celebrities goes far beyond supermarket tabloids, gossip Web sites and reality TV. It obliterates old distinctions between high and low culture, serious and trivial endeavors, profit making and philanthropy, leading to the phenomenon of being famous for being famous. An activist singer (Bono) is given a lucrative role in Facebook's initial public offering. A patrician politician (Al Gore) becomes a plutocratic media executive and tech investor. One of America's richest men (Michael R. Bloomberg) rules its largest city.

This jet-setting, Davos-attending crowd constitutes its own superclass, who hang out at the same TED talks, big-idea conferences and fund-raising galas, appear on the same talk shows, invest in one another's projects, wear one another's brand apparel, champion one another's causes, marry and cheat on one another. *The New Digital Age,* the new guide to the future by Eric Schmidt and Jared Cohen of Google, carries blurbs from such technology experts as Henry A. Kissinger and Tony Blair. The inevitable next step is for Kim Kardashian to sit on the board of a tech start-up, host a global-poverty-awareness event, and write a book on behavioral neuroscience.

This new kind of celebrity is the ultimate costume ball, far more exclusive and decadent than even the most potent magnates of Hollywood's studio era could have dreamed up. Their superficial diversity dangles before us the myth that in America, anything is possible — even as the American dream quietly dies, a victim of the calcification of a class system that is nearly hereditary.

As mindless diversions from a sluggish economy and chronic malaise, the new aristocrats play a useful role. But their advent suggests that, after decades of widening income gaps, unequal distributions of opportunity and reward, and corroding public institutions, we have gone back to Gatsby's time — or something far more perverse. The celebrity monuments of our age have grown so huge that they dwarf the aspirations of ordinary people, who are asked to yield their dreams to the gods: to flash their favorite singer's corporate logo at concerts, to pour open their lives (and data) on Facebook, to adopt Apple as a lifestyle. We know our stars aren't inviting us to think we can be just like them. Their success is based on leaving the rest of us behind.

READING THE TEXT

1. In your own words, trace the evolution of the celebrity from the 1920s to the post-World War II era to today, as Packer describes it.

2. What does Packer mean when he asserts that today a celebrity "evolves into a persona, then a brand, then an empire, with the business imperative of grow or die" (para. 6)?

3. Why does Packer consider today's celebrities their "own superclass" (para. 9)?

4. What relation does Packer find between the plethora of celebrities today and economic conditions?

5. Why does Packer say that America today is returning to the ethos of the Jazz Age (or, perhaps, becoming even worse)?

READING THE SIGNS

1. In class, discuss the meanings of the terms "celebrities" and "heroes." Using that conversation as a starting point, write an essay that argues for your own definition of the two terms, taking care to delineate distinctions between them. Be sure to ground your discussion in real-life examples of both categories, as Packer does in his essay.

2. As Packer mentions, one kind of current celebrity is the person who is "famous for being famous" (para. 8). In class, brainstorm a list of current such celebrities and discuss what they have in common. Use this discussion to jump-start your own essay on what this sort of fame signifies about the values and world-view of modern America.

3. Write an essay in which you support, refute, or complicate Packer's claim that "this new kind of celebrity is the ultimate costume ball. . . . Their superficial diversity dangles before us the myth that in America, anything is possible" (para. 10). To develop your ideas, consult the introduction to this chapter.

4. Select one of the recent celebrities whom Packer mentions, such as Martha Stewart or Bono, and research the public relations surrounding the individual. Use your findings to endorse, refute, or modify Packer's contention that "these new celebrities are all more or less start-up entrepreneurs, and they live by the hacker's code: ask forgiveness, not permission" (para. 7).

5. In your journal, ruminate about which celebrities you admire and why. Then, in an essay, subject one or two of your choices to Packer's critique of today's celebrities. Do they survive his accusation that they "have grown so huge that they dwarf the aspirations of ordinary people, who are asked to yield their dreams to the gods" (para. 11)? Alternatively, if you do not admire any celebrities, write an essay in which you explain why, basing your comments on examples of particular "celebrity monuments of our age" (para. 11).

ALFRED LUBRANO

The Shock of Education: How College Corrupts

One of America's most fundamental contradictions lies at the heart of the American dream itself. That is, America's promise of social mobility compels those who begin at the bottom to abandon their origins in order to succeed, which entails giving up a part of one-self and leaving one's home behind. It can be a wrenching transition, and in this reflection on what it means to achieve the dream, Alfred Lubrano describes the strain of moving between two worlds, relating both his own experiences moving from working-class Brooklyn to an Ivy League school and those of other working-class "Straddlers" who moved into the middle class. The son of a bricklayer, Lubrano is a journalist and National Public Radio commentator. He is the author of *Limbo: Blue-Collar Roots, White-Collar Dreams* (2004), from which this selection is taken.

College is where the Great Change begins. People start to question the blue-collar take on the world. Status dissonance, the sociologists call it. Questions arise: Are the guys accurate in saying people from such-and-such a race are really so bad? Was Mom right when she said nice girls don't put out? Suddenly, college opens up a world of ideas — a life of the mind — abstract and intangible. The core blue-collar values and goals — loyalty to family and friends, making money, marrying, and procreating — are supplanted by stuff you never talked about at home: per-sonal fulfillment, societal obligation, the pursuit of knowledge for knowledge's sake, and on and on. One world opens and widens; another shrinks.

There's an excitement and a sadness to that. The child, say Sennett and Cobb, is deserting his past, betraying the parents he is rising above, an unavoidable result when you're trying to accomplish more with your life than merely earning a paycheck.[1] So much will change between parent and child, and between peers, in the college years. "Every bit of learning takes you further from your parents," says Southwest Texas State University history professor Gregg Andrews, himself a Straddler. "I say this to all my freshmen to start preparing them." The best predictor of whether you're going to have problems with your family is the distance between your education and your parents', Jake Ryan says. You may soon find yourself with nothing to talk to your folks or friends about.

---

[1] Richard Sennett and Jonathan Cobb, *The Hidden Injuries of Class* (New York: Alfred A. Knopf, 1972), 131.

This is the dark part of the American story, the kind of thing we work to hide. Mobility means discomfort, because so much has to change; one can't allow for the satisfactions of stasis: You prick yourself and move, digging spurs into your own hide to get going, forcing yourself to forget the comforts of the barn. In this country, we speak grandly of this metamorphosis, never stopping to consider that for many class travelers with passports stamped for new territory, the trip is nothing less than a bridge burning.

Fighting Self-Doubt

When Columbia plucked me out of working-class Brooklyn, I was sure they had made a mistake, and I remained convinced of that throughout most of my time there. My high school was a gigantic (4,500 students) factory; we literally had gridlock in the halls between classes, kids belly to back between history and English class. A teacher once told me that if every one of the reliable corps of truant students actually decided to show up to class one day, the school could not hold us all. (We were unofficially nicknamed "the Italian Army." When our football guys played nearby New Utrecht, which boasted an equivalent ethnic demographic, kids dubbed the game the "Lasagna Bowl.") Lafayette High School roiled with restless boys and girls on their way to jobs in their parents' unions or to secretaries' desks. How could you move from that to an elite college?

At night, at home, the difference in the Columbia experiences my father and I were having was becoming more evident. The family still came together for dinner, despite our disparate days. We talked about general stuff, and I learned to self-censor. I'd seen how ideas could be upsetting, especially when wielded by a smarmy freshman who barely knew what he was talking about. No one wanted to hear how the world worked from some kid who was first learning to use his brain; it was as unsettling as riding in a car with a new driver. When he taught a course on Marx, Sackrey said he used to tell his students just before Thanksgiving break not to talk about "this stuff at the dinner table" or they'd mess up the holiday. Me mimicking my professors' thoughts on race, on people's struggle for equality, or on politics didn't add to the conviviality of the one nice hour in our day. So I learned to shut up.

After dinner, my father would flip on the TV in the living room. My mom would grab a book and join him. And I'd go looking for a quiet spot to study. In his autobiography, *Hunger of Memory: The Education of Richard Rodriguez*, the brilliant Mexican-American Straddler, writer, and PBS commentator invokes British social scientist Richard Hoggart's "scholarship boys," finding pieces of himself in them. Working-class kids trying to advance in life, the scholarship boys learned to withdraw from the warm noise of the gathered

5

family to isolate themselves with their books.[2] (Read primarily as a memoir of ethnicity and — most famously — an anti–affirmative action tract, the book is more genuinely a dissertation on class. At a sidewalk café in San Francisco, Rodriguez himself tells me how often his book is miscatalogued.) Up from the immigrant working class, Rodriguez says in our interview, the scholarship boy finds himself moving between two antithetical places: home and school. With the family, there is intimacy and emotion. At school, one learns to live with "lonely reason." Home life is in the now, Rodriguez says; school life exists on an altogether different plane, calm and reflective, with an eye toward the future.

The scholarship boy must learn to distance himself from the family circle in order to succeed academically, Rodriguez tells me. By doing this, he slowly loses his family. There's a brutality to education, he says, a rough and terrible disconnect. Rodriguez says he despised his parents' "shabbiness," their inability to speak English. "I hated that they didn't know what I was learning," he says. He thought of D. H. Lawrence's *Sons and Lovers*, and of Paul Morel, the coal miner's son. Lawrence is a model for Rodriguez, in a way. Rodriguez remembers the scene in which the son watches his father pick up his schoolbooks, his rough hands fingering the volumes that are the instruments separating the two men. Books were establishing a disharmony between the classroom and Rodriguez's house. Preoccupation with language and reading is an effeminacy not easily understood by workers. "It sears your soul to finally decide to talk like your teacher and not your father," Rodriguez says. "I'm not talking about anything less than the grammar of the heart."

Myself, I studied in the kitchen near the dishwasher because its white noise drowned out the television. As long as the wash cycle ran, I could not hear Mr. T and the A-Team win the day. I did not begrudge my father his one indulgence; there wasn't much else that could relax him. He was not a drinker. TV drained away the tumult and hazard of his Columbia day [he was a bricklayer]. My own room was too close to the living room. My brother's small room was too crowded for both of us to study in. You never went in your parents' bedroom without them in it, inviting you. When the dishes were clean and the kitchen again too quiet to beat back the living room noise, I'd go downstairs to my grandparents' apartment. If they were both watching the same TV show on the first floor, then the basement was free. Here was profound and almost disquieting silence. I could hear the house's systems rumble and shake: water whooshing through pipes, the oil burner powering on and off, and the refrigerator humming with a loud efficiency.

---

[2]Richard Rodriguez, *Hunger of Memory: The Education of Richard Rodriguez* (New York: Bantam Books, 1983), 46. Rodriguez himself quotes from Richard Hoggart, *The Uses of Literacy* (London: Chatto and Windus, 1957), chap. 10.

Down in the immaculate redwood-paneled kitchen/living room, which sometimes still smelled of the sausages and peppers my grandfather may have made that night (my grandparents cooked and ate in their basement, something that never seemed unusual to us), I was ninety minutes from my school and two floors below my family in a new place, underscoring my distance from anything known, heightening my sense of isolation — my limbo status. I read Homer, Shakespeare, and Molière down there. I wrote a paper on landscape imagery in Dante's *Inferno*. In my self-pitying, melodramatic teenager's mind, I thought I had been banished to a new, lonely rung of hell that Dante hadn't contemplated.

By 11 p.m., I'd go back upstairs. My mother would be in bed, my father asleep on his chair. I'd turn off the TV, which awakened my dad. He'd walk off to bed, and I'd study for a couple more hours. His alarm would go off before 5 a.m., and he'd already be at Columbia by the time I woke up at 6:30. That's how our Ivy League days ended and began. When my father was done with Columbia, he moved on to another job site. When I was done with Columbia, I was someone else. I'd say I got the better deal. But then, my father would tell you, that was always the plan. . . .

Macbeth and Other Foolishness

Middle-class kids are groomed for another life. They understand, says Patrick Finn, why reading *Macbeth* in high school could be important years down the road. Working-class kids see no such connection, understand no future life for which digesting Shakespeare might be of value. Very much in the now, working-class people are concerned with immediate needs. And bookish kids are seen as weak.

Various education studies have shown that schools help reinforce class. 10 Teachers treat the working class and the well-to-do differently, this work demonstrates, with the blue-collar kids getting less attention and respect. It's no secret, education experts insist, that schools in poorer areas tend to employ teachers who are less well-trained. In these schools, the curriculum is test-based and uncreative. Children are taught, essentially, to obey and fill in blanks. By fourth grade, many of the children are bored and alienated; nothing in school connects to their culture. Beyond that, many working-class children are resistant to schooling and uncooperative with teachers, experts say. They feel pressure from other working-class friends to not participate and are told that being educated is effeminate and irrelevant. Educators have long understood that minority children have these problems, says Finn. But they rarely understand or see that working-class white kids have similar difficulties. "So we're missing a whole bunch of people getting screwed by the education systems," he says.

In our conversations, Finn explains that language is a key to class. In a working-class home where conformity is the norm, all opinions are dictated by group consensus, by what the class says is so. There's one way to do everything, there's one way to look at the world. Since all opinions are shared, there's never a need to explain thought and behavior. You talk less. Language in such a home, Finn says, is implicit.

Things are different in a middle-class home. There, parents are more willing to take the time to explain to little Janey why it's not such a good idea to pour chocolate sauce on the dog. If Janey challenges a rule of the house, she's spoken to like an adult, or at least not like a plebe at some military school. (Working-class homes are, in fact, very much like the military, with parents barking orders, Straddlers tell me. It's that conformity thing again.) There is a variety of opinions in middle-class homes, which are more collaborative than conformist, Finn says. Middle-class people have a multiviewed take on the world. In such a home, where one needs to express numerous ideas and opinions, language is by necessity explicit.

When it's time to go to school, the trouble starts. The language of school — of the teachers and the books — is explicit. A child from a working-class home is at a huge disadvantage, Finn says, because he's used to a narrower world of expression and a smaller vocabulary of thought. It's little wonder that kids from working-class homes have lower reading scores and do less well on SATs than middle-class kids, Finn says.

In high school, my parents got me a tutor for the math part of the SATs, to bolster a lackluster PSAT score. That sort of thing happens all the time in middle-class neighborhoods. But we were setting precedent among our kind. Most kids I knew from the community were not taking the SATs, let alone worrying about their scores. If you're from the middle class, you do not feel out of place preparing for college. Parents and peers help groom you, encourage you, and delight in your progress. Of course, when you get to freshman year, the adjustments can be hard on anyone, middle-class and working-class kids alike. But imagine going through freshman orientation if your parents are ambivalent — or hostile — about your being there, and your friends aren't clear about what you're doing.

It was like that for my friend Rita Giordano, forty-five, also a journalist, 15 also from Brooklyn. Her world, like mine, was populated by people who thought going from 60th to 65th Streets was a long journey. So when Rita took sojourns into Greenwich Village by herself on Saturday mornings as a teenager, she made sure not to tell any of her friends. It was too oddball to have to explain. And she'd always come back in time to go shopping with everyone. She couldn't figure out why she responded to the artsy vibe of the Village; she was just aware that there were things going on beyond the neighborhood. When it came time for college, she picked Syracuse University because it was far away, a new world to explore. That bothered her friends, and she'd have to explain herself to them on trips back home. "What do you do up there?" they asked her. "Don't you get homesick?" Suddenly, things felt awkward among childhood friends who had always been able to talk. "It was confusing to come home and see people thinking that you're not doing what they're doing, which meant you're rejecting them," said Rita, a diminutive, sensitive woman with large, brown eyes. " 'Don't they see it's still me?' I wondered. I started feeling like, how do I coexist in these two worlds, college and home? I mean, I could talk to my girlfriends about what color gowns their bridesmaids would wear at their fantasy weddings. But things like ambition and existential questions about where you fit in the world and how you make your mark — we just didn't go there."

And to make matters more complicated, there was a guy. Rita's decision to go to Syracuse didn't sit well with the boyfriend who was probably always going to remain working class. "In true Brooklyn fashion, he and his friends decided one night they were going to drive four hundred miles to Syracuse to bring me back, or whatever. But on the way up, they totaled the car and my boyfriend broke his leg. He never got up there, and after that, the idea of him bringing me to my senses dissipated."

Another Straddler, Loretta Stec, had a similar problem with a blue-collar lover left behind. Loretta, a slender thirty-nine-year-old English professor at San Francisco State University with delicate features and brown hair, needed to leave the commotion of drugs and friends' abortions and the repressed religious world of Perth Amboy, New Jersey, for the calm life of the mind offered by Boston College. The only problem was Barry. When Loretta was seventeen, she and Barry, an older construction worker, would ride motorcycles in toxic waste dumps. He was wild and fine — what every working-class girl would want. But Loretta knew life had to get better than Perth Amboy, so she went off to Boston. Barry and she still got together, though. They even worked on the same taping crew at a construction site during the summer between Loretta's freshman and sophomore years. But the differences between them were growing. All the guys on the job — Barry included — thought it was weird that Loretta would read the *New York Times* during lunch breaks. "What's with that chick?" people asked.

By the time Loretta returned to Boston for her second year, she knew she was in a far different place than Barry. The working class was not for her. Hanging around with this guy and doing construction forever — it sounded awful. "I was upwardly mobile, and I was not going to work on a construction crew anymore," Loretta says. She tried to break it off, but Barry roared up I-95 in a borrowed car to change her mind. Loretta lived in an old Victorian with middle-class roommates who had never met anyone like Barry. When he showed up with a barking Doberman in tow, she recalled he was screaming like Stanley Kowalski in *A Streetcar Named Desire* that he wanted Loretta back. The women became terrified. Loretta was able to calm first Barry, then her roommates. Afterward, the couple went to listen to some music. In a little place on campus, a guitar trio started performing a Rolling

Stones song. Suddenly, Barry turned to Loretta and began scream-singing about wild horses not being able to drag him from her, really loud, trying to get her to see his resolve. "People were wondering who was this guy, what's his deal?" Loretta says. "It pointed out the clash between my new world and the old. You don't do stuff like that. It was embarrassing, upsetting, and confusing. I didn't want to hurt him. But I knew it wasn't going to work for me." They walked around campus, fighting about things coming to an end. At some point, she recalls, Barry noticed that a college student with a nicer car than his — Loretta can't remember exactly what it was — had parked behind his car, blocking him. Already ramped up, Barry had a fit and smashed a headlight of the fancy machine with a rock. There Loretta was, a hundred feet from her campus Victorian, newly ensconced in a clean world of erudition and scholarship, far from the violence and swamps of central Jersey. Her bad-boy beau, once so appealing, was raving and breathing hard, trying to pull her away from the books, back down the turnpike to the working class.

"That was really the end of it," Loretta says. "I couldn't have a guy around who was going to act like that. He was wild and crazy and I was trying to make my way." Barry relented, and left Loretta alone. They lost touch, and Loretta later learned that Barry had died, the cause of death unknown to her. It was such a shock.

READING THE TEXT

1. What is your response to Lubrano's title, and why do you think he chose it for his essay?
2. Summarize in your own words the difference between Lubrano's high school and college experiences.
3. What does Richard Rodriguez mean by saying, "There's a brutality to education" (para. 6)?
4. Why did Lubrano avoid discussing his Columbia University experiences with his family?
5. How does child rearing differ in blue-collar and in middle-class families, in Lubrano's view? What evidence does he advance to support his claims?

READING THE SIGNS

1. In your journal, reflect on the effects — positive or negative — that attending college may have had on your relationship with your family and high school friends. How do you account for any changes that may have occurred?
2. In an argumentative essay, support, challenge, or complicate Gregg Andrews's statement that "every bit of learning takes you further from your parents" (para. 1).
3. Write a synthesis of the personal tales of Lubrano, Loretta Stec, and Rita Giordano. Then use your synthesis as the basis of an essay in which you explain how their collective experiences combine to demonstrate Lubrano's

position that "for many class travelers with passports stamped for new territory, the trip is nothing less than a bridge burning" (para. 2).

4. Interview students from both blue-collar and middle- or upper-class backgrounds about the effect that attending college has had on their relationship with their family and high school friends. Use your findings to support your assessment of Lubrano's position that college can create divisions between blue-collar students and their families but that it tends not to have that effect on other classes.

5. Analyze Lubrano's use of evidence and quotations. Who is quoted directly? Who is quoted indirectly? What sources and experts are consulted? Use your observations for support in an argumentative essay in which you analyze what Lubrano's article implies about expertise and authority.

RANDALL KENNEDY
Blind Spot

Racial profiling has been a hot-button issue in recent years, eliciting such sardonic condemnations as the claim that for many Americans it has become a crime to be caught "driving while black." Randall Kennedy enters the controversy here from an unusual angle, finding a fundamental contradiction in the positions of both supporters and opponents of racial profiling. With supporters of racial profiling asserting the rights of the community over those of the individual, while at the same time endorsing the rights of the individual over those of the community when it comes to affirmative action, and opponents of racial profiling doing just the reverse, it is time, Kennedy suggests, for both sides to listen to what the other has to say. This selection originally appeared in the April 2002 issue of the *Atlantic*. Randall Kennedy is the Michael R. Klein Professor of Law at Harvard Law School.

What is one to think about "racial profiling"? Confusion abounds about what the term even means. It should be defined as the policy or practice of using race as a factor in selecting whom to place under special surveillance: if police officers at an airport decide to search Passenger A because he is twenty-five to forty years old, bought a first-class ticket with cash, is flying cross-country, and is apparently of Arab ancestry, Passenger A has been subjected to racial profiling. But officials often prefer to define racial profiling as being based *solely* on race; and in doing so they are often seeking to preserve their authority to act against a person *partly* on the basis of race. Civil rights activists, too, often define racial profiling as solely race-based; but their aim is to arouse their followers and to portray law-enforcement officials in as menacing a light as possible.

The problem with defining racial profiling in the narrow manner of these strange bedfellows is that doing so obfuscates the real issue confronting Americans. Exceedingly few police officers, airport screeners, or other authorities charged with the task of foiling or apprehending criminals act solely on the basis of race. Many, however, act on the basis of intuition, using race along with other indicators (sex, age, patterns of past conduct) as a guide. The difficult question, then, is not whether the authorities ought to be allowed to act against individuals on the basis of race alone; almost everyone would disapprove of that. The difficult question is whether they ought to be allowed to use race *at all* in schemes of surveillance. If, indeed, it is used, the action amounts to racial discrimination. The extent of the discrimination may be relatively small when race is only one factor among many, but even a little racial discrimination should require lots of justification.

The key argument in favor of racial profiling, essentially, is that taking race into account enables the authorities to screen carefully and at less expense those sectors of the population that are more likely than others to contain the criminals for whom officials are searching. Proponents of this theory stress that resources for surveillance are scarce, that the dangers to be avoided are grave, and that reducing these dangers helps everyone — including, sometimes especially, those in the groups subjected to special scrutiny. Proponents also assert that it makes good sense to consider whiteness if the search is for Ku Klux Klan assassins, blackness if the search is for drug couriers in certain locales, and Arab nationality or ethnicity if the search is for agents of al-Qaeda.

Some commentators embrace this position as if it were unassailable, but under U.S. law racial discrimination backed by state power is presumptively illicit. This means that supporters of racial profiling carry a heavy burden of persuasion. Opponents rightly argue, however, that not much rigorous empirical proof supports the idea of racial profiling as an effective tool of law enforcement. Opponents rightly contend, also, that alternatives to racial profiling have not been much studied or pursued. Stressing that racial profiling generates clear harm (for example, the fear, resentment, and alienation felt by innocent people in the profiled group), opponents of racial profiling sensibly question whether compromising our hard-earned principle of antidiscrimination is worth merely speculative gains in overall security.

A notable feature of this conflict is that champions of each position ⁵ frequently embrace rhetoric, attitudes, and value systems that are completely at odds with those they adopt when confronting another controversial instance of racial discrimination — namely, affirmative action. Vocal supporters of racial profiling who trumpet the urgency of communal needs when discussing law enforcement all of a sudden become fanatical individualists when condemning affirmative action in college admissions and the labor market. Supporters of profiling, who are willing to impose what amounts to a racial tax on profiled groups, denounce as betrayals of "color blindness" programs that require racial diversity. A similar turnabout can be seen on the part of many of those who support affirmative action. Impatient with talk of communal needs in assessing racial profiling, they very often have no difficulty with subordinating the interests of individual white candidates to the purported good of the whole. Opposed to race consciousness in policing, they demand race consciousness in deciding whom to admit to college or select for a job.

The racial-profiling controversy — like the conflict over affirmative action — will not end soon. For one thing, in both cases many of the contestants are animated by decent but contending sentiments. Although exasperating, this is actually good for our society; and it would be even better if participants in the debates acknowledged the simple truth that their adversaries have something useful to say.

READING THE TEXT

1. Summarize in your own words the contradiction Kennedy finds in the controversies over racial profiling and affirmative action.

2. Why does Kennedy say that definitions of racial profiling are marked by "confusion" (para. 1)?

3. Why does Kennedy call opponents and supporters of racial profiling "strange bedfellows" (para. 2)?

4. Why do you think Kennedy finds "the decent but contending sentiments" at the heart of the racial profiling controversy to be "good for our society" (para. 6)?

READING THE SIGNS

1. Kennedy finds a contradiction between opposing racial profiling and promoting affirmative action. Write an essay in which you support, refute, or modify his stance. Do you see any areas of common ground in the two positions?

2. Write a journal entry in which you reflect on an experience in which you believe you were singled out because of your appearance, ethnicity, gender, or other physically obvious characteristic. How did you respond at the time, and would you respond the same way today? Alternatively, write about a friend who had such an experience.

3. Write an essay in which you explore the relative claims of the rights of the individual and the rights of the community in modern American culture. To what extent do those claims reflect a fundamental contradiction in American social ideology?

4. In the debates over both racial profiling and affirmative action, the discussions tend to presume that determining ethnic identity is a simple matter. Do some research on the topic of racial and biracial identity and write an essay in which you explore the implications that mixed-race backgrounds and cultural practices such as claiming may have for these debates.

MARIAH BURTON NELSON

I Won. I'm Sorry.

Athletic competition, when you come right down to it, is about winning, which is no problem for men, whose gender codes tell them that aggression and domination are admirable male traits. But "how can you win, if you're female?" Mariah Burton Nelson asks, when the same gender codes insist that women must be feminine, "not aggressive, not victorious." And so women athletes, even when they do win, go out of their way to signal their femininity by dolling themselves up and smiling a lot. Beauty and vulnerability seem to be as important to today's female athlete as brawn and gold medals, Nelson complains, paradoxically contradicting the apparent feminist gains that women athletes have made in recent years. A former Stanford University and professional basketball player, Mariah Burton Nelson is the author of *We Are All Athletes* (2002) and *Making Money on the Sidelines* (2008). She is vice president for innovation and planning at the American Society of Association Executives. This piece originally appeared in *Self* magazine.

When Sylvia Plath's husband, Ted Hughes, published his first book of poems, Sylvia wrote to her mother: "I am so happy that HIS book is accepted FIRST. It will make it so much easier for me when mine is accepted. . . ."

After Sylvia killed herself, her mother published a collection of Sylvia's letters. In her explanatory notes, Aurelia Plath commented that from the time she was very young, Sylvia "catered to the male of any age so as to bolster his sense of superiority." In seventh grade, Aurelia Plath noted, Sylvia was pleased to finish second in a spelling contest. "It was nicer, she felt, to have a boy first."

How many women still collude in the myth of male superiority, believing it's "nicer" when boys and men finish first? How many of us achieve but only in a lesser, smaller, feminine way, a manner consciously or unconsciously designed to be as nonthreatening as possible?

Since I'm tall, women often talk to me about height. Short women tell me, "I've always wanted to be tall — but not as tall as you!" I find this amusing, but also curious. Why not? Why not be six-two?

Tall women tell me that they won't wear heels because they don't want   5
to appear taller than their husbands or boyfriends, even by an inch. What are these women telling me — and their male companions? Why do women regulate their height in relation to men's height? Why is it still rare to see a woman who is taller than her husband?

Women want to be tall enough to feel elegant and attractive, like models. They want to feel respected and looked up to. But they don't want to be so tall that their height threatens men. They want to win — to achieve, to reach new heights — but without exceeding male heights.

How can you win, if you're female? Can you just do it? No. You have to play the femininity game. Femininity by definition is not large, not imposing, not competitive. Feminine women are not ruthless, not aggressive, not victorious. It's not feminine to have a killer instinct, to want with all your heart and soul to win — neither tennis matches nor elected office nor feminist victories such as abortion rights. It's not feminine to know exactly what you want, then go for it.

Femininity is about appearing beautiful and vulnerable and small. It's about winning male approval.

One downhill skier who asked not to be identified told me the following story: "I love male approval. Most women skiers do. We talk about it often. There's only one thing more satisfying than one of the top male skiers saying, 'Wow, you are a great skier. You rip. You're awesome.'

Serena Williams at Wimbledon.

AP Images/Noah Berger

"But it's so fun leaving 99 percent of the world's guys in the dust — oops,"   10
she laughs. "I try not to gloat. I've learned something: If I kick guys' butts
and lord it over them, they don't like me. If, however, I kick guys' butts then
act 'like a girl,' there is no problem. And I do mean girl, not woman.
Nonthreatening."

Femininity is also about accommodating men, allowing them to feel
bigger than and stronger than and superior to women, not emasculated by
them.

Femininity is unhealthy, obviously. It would be unhealthy for men to act
passive, dainty, obsessed with their physical appearance, and dedicated to
bolstering the sense of superiority in the other gender, so it's unhealthy for
women too. These days, some women are redefining femininity as strong, as
athletic, as however a female happens to be, so that "feminine" becomes synonymous with "female." Other women reject both feminine and masculine
terms and stereotypes, selecting from the entire range of human behaviors instead of limiting themselves to the "gender-appropriate" ones. These
women smile only when they're happy, act angry when they're angry, dress
how they want to. They cling to their self-respect and dignity like a life raft.

But most female winners play the femininity game to some extent,
using femininity as a defense, a shield against accusations such as bitch,
man-hater, lesbian. Feminine behavior and attire mitigate against the affront
of female victory, soften the hard edges of winning. Women who want to
win without losing male approval temper their victories with beauty, with
softness, with smallness, with smiles.

In the fifties, at each of the Amateur Athletic Union's women's basketball
championships, one of the players was crowned a beauty queen. (This still
happens at Russian women's ice hockey tournaments.) Athletes in the
All-American Girls Baseball League of the forties and fifties slid into base
wearing skirts. In 1979, professional basketball players with the California
Dreams were sent to John Robert Powers' charm school. Ed Temple, the
legendary coach of the Tennessee State Tigerbelles, the team that produced
Wilma Rudolph, Wyomia Tyus, Willye White, Madeline Manning, and countless other champions, enforced a dress code and stressed that his athletes
should be "young ladies first, track girls second."

Makeup, jewelry, dress, and demeanor were often dictated by the male   15
coaches and owners in these leagues, but to some extent the players played
along, understanding the trade-off: in order to be "allowed" to compete, they
had to demonstrate that they were, despite their "masculine" strivings, real
("feminine") women.

Today, both men and women wear earrings, notes Felshin, "but the
media is still selling heterosexism and 'feminine' beauty. And if you listen
carefully, in almost every interview" female athletes still express apologetic
behavior through feminine dress, behavior, and values.

Florence Griffith-Joyner, Gail Devers, and other track stars of this modern era dedicate considerable attention to portraying a feminine appearance.

Basketball star Lisa Leslie has received more attention for being a model than for leading the Americans to Olympic victory. Steffi Graf posed in bikinis for the 1997 *Sports Illustrated* swimsuit issue. In a Sears commercial, Olympic basketball players apply lipstick, paint their toenails, rock babies, lounge in bed, and pose and dance in their underwear. Lisa Leslie says, "Everybody's allowed to be themselves. Me, for example, I'm very feminine."

In an Avon commercial, Jackie Joyner Kersee is shown running on a beach while the camera lingers on her buttocks and breasts. She tells us that she can bench-press 150 pounds and brags that she can jump farther than "all but 128 men." Then she says: "And I have red toenails." Words flash on the screen: "Just another Avon lady." Graf, Mary Pierce, Monica Seles, and Mary Jo Fernandez have all played in dresses. They are "so much more comfortable" than skirts, Fernandez explained. "You don't have to worry about the shirt coming up or the skirt being too tight. It's cooler, and it's so feminine."

"When I put on a dress I feel different — more feminine, more elegant, more ladylike — and that's nice," added Australia's Nicole Bradtke: "We're in a sport where we're throwing ourselves around, so it's a real asset to the game to be able to look pretty at the same time."

Athletes have become gorgeous, flirtatious, elegant, angelic, darling — and the skating commentators' favorite term: "vulnerable." Some think this is good news: proof that femininity and sports are compatible. "There doesn't have to be such a complete division between 'You're beautiful and sexy' and 'you're athletic and strong,'" says Linda Hanley, a pro beach volleyball player who also appeared in a bikini in the 1997 *Sports Illustrated* swimsuit issue.

Athletes and advertisers reassure viewers that women who compete are still willing to play the femininity game, to be cheerleaders. Don't worry about us, the commercials imply. We're winners but we'll still look pretty for you. We're acting in ways that only men used to act but we'll still act how you want women to act. We're not threatening. We're not lesbians. We're not ugly, not bad marriage material. We're strong but feminine. Linguists note that the word "but" negates the part of the sentence that precedes it.

There are some recent examples of the media emphasizing female power in an unambiguous way. "Women Muscle In," the *New York Times Magazine* proclaimed in a headline. The *Washington Post* wrote, "At Olympics, Women Show Their Strength." And a new genre of commercials protests that female athletes are NOT cheerleaders, and don't have to be. Olympic and pro basketball star Dawn Staley says in a Nike commercial that she plays basketball "for the competitiveness" of it. "I need some place to release it. It just builds up, and sports is a great outlet for it. I started out playing with the guys. I wasn't always accepted. You get criticized, like: 'You need to be in the kitchen. Go put on a skirt.' I just got mad and angry and went out to show them that I belong here as much as they do."

Other commercials tell us that women can compete like conquerors. A Nike ad called "Wolves" shows girls leaping and spiking volleyballs while a voice says, "They are not sisters. They are not classmates. They are not friends. They are not even the girls' team. They are a pack of wolves. Tend to your sheep." Though the athletes look serious, the message sounds absurd. When I show this commercial to audiences, they laugh. Still, the images do depict the power of the volleyball players: their intensity, their ability to pound the ball almost through the floor. The script gives the players (and viewers) permission not to be ladylike, not to worry about whether their toenails are red.

But in an American Basketball League commercial, the Philadelphia Rage's female basketball players are playing rough; their bodies collide. Maurice Chevalier sings, "Thank heaven for little girls." The tag line: "Thank heaven, they're on our side."

Doesn't all this talk about girls and ladies simply focus our attention on femaleness, femininity, and ladylike behavior? The lady issue is always there in the equation: something to redefine, to rebel against. It's always present, like sneakers, so every time you hear the word *athlete* you also hear the word *lady* — or feminine, or unfeminine. It reminds me of a beer magazine ad from the eighties that featured a photo of Olympic track star Valerie Brisco-Hooks. "Funny, she doesn't look like the weaker sex," said the print. You could see her impressive muscles. Clearly the intent of the ad was to contrast an old stereotype with the reality of female strength and ability. But Brisco-Hooks was seated, her legs twisted pretzel style, arms covering her chest. But in that position, Brisco-Hooks didn't look very strong or able. In the line, "Funny, she doesn't look like the weaker sex," the most eye-catching words are funny, look, weaker, and sex. Looking at the pretzel that is Valerie, you begin to think that she looks funny. You think about weakness. And you think about sex.

When she was young, Nancy Kerrigan wanted to play ice hockey with her older brothers. Her mother told her, "You're a girl. Do girl things."

Figure skating is a girl thing. Athletes in sequins and "sheer illusion sleeves" glide and dance, their tiny skirts flapping in the breeze. They achieve, but without touching or pushing anyone else. They win, but without visible signs of sweat. They compete, but not directly. Their success is measured not by confrontation with an opponent, nor even by a clock or a scoreboard. Rather, they are judged as beauty contestants are judged: by a panel of people who interpret the success of the routines. Prettiness is mandatory. Petite and groomed and gracious, figure skaters — like cheerleaders, gymnasts, and aerobic dancers — camouflage their competitiveness with niceness and prettiness until it no longer seems male or aggressive or unseemly.

The most popular sport for high school and college women is basketball. More than a million fans shelled out an average of $15 per ticket in 1997, the inaugural summer of the Women's National Basketball Association. But the most televised women's sport is figure skating. In 1995 revenue from skating shows and competitions topped six hundred million dollars. In the seven months between October 1996 and March 1997, ABC, CBS, NBC, Fox,

ESPN, TBS, and USA dedicated 162.5 hours of programming to figure skating, half of it in prime time. Kerrigan earns up to three hundred thousand dollars for a single performance.

Nearly 75 percent of the viewers of televised skating are women. The average age is between twenty-five and forty-five years old, with a household income of more than fifty thousand dollars. What are these women watching? What are they seeing? What's the appeal?

Like golf, tennis, and gymnastics, figure skating is an individual sport 30 favored by white people from the upper classes. The skaters wear cosmetics, frozen smiles, and revealing dresses. Behind the scenes they lift weights and sweat like any serious athlete, but figure skating seems more dance than sport, more grace than guts, more art than athleticism. Figure skating allows women to compete like champions while dressed like cheerleaders.

In women's figure skating, smiling is part of "artistic expression." In the final round, if the competitors are of equal merit, artistry weighs more heavily than technique. Midori Ito, the best jumper in the history of women's skating, explained a weak showing at the 1995 world championships this way: "I wasn't 100 percent satisfied. . . . I probably wasn't smiling enough."

The media portray female figure skaters as "little girl dancers" or "fairy tale princesses" (NBC commentator John Tesh); as "elegant" (Dick Button); as "little angels" (Peggy Fleming); as "ice beauties" and "ladies who lutz" (*People* magazine). Commentators frame skaters as small, young, and decorative creatures, not superwomen but fairy-tale figments of someone's imagination.

After Kerrigan was assaulted by a member of Tonya Harding's entourage, she was featured on a *Sports Illustrated* cover crying "Why me?" When she recovered to win a silver medal at the Olympics that year, she became "America's sweetheart" and rich to boot. But the princess turned pumpkin shortly after midnight, as soon as the ball was over and she stopped smiling and started speaking. Growing impatient during the Olympic medal ceremony while everyone waited for Baiul, Kerrigan grumbled, "Oh, give me a break, she's just going to cry out there again. What's the difference?"

What were Kerrigan's crimes? She felt too old to cavort with cartoon characters. Isn't she? She expressed anger and disappointment — even bitterness and bad sportsmanship — about losing the gold. But wasn't she supposed to want to win? What happens to baseball players who, disappointed about a loss, hit each other or spit on umpires? What happens to basketball players and football players and hockey players who fight? Men can't tumble from a princess palace because we don't expect them to be princesses in the first place, only athletes.

Americans fell out of love with Kerrigan not because they couldn't adore 35 an athlete who lacked grace in defeat, but because they couldn't adore a female athlete who lacked grace in defeat.

Female politicians, lawyers, and businesswomen of all ethnic groups also play the femininity game. Like tennis players in short dresses, working women seem to believe it's an asset to look pretty (but not too pretty) while throwing themselves around. The female apologetic is alive and well in corporate boardrooms, where women say "I'm sorry, maybe someone else already stated this idea, but . . ." and smile while they say it.

When Newt Gingrich's mother revealed on television that Newt had referred to Hillary Clinton as a bitch, how did Hillary respond? She donned a pink suit and met with female reporters to ask how she could "soften her image." She seemed to think that her competitiveness was the problem and femininity the solution.

So if you want to be a winner and you're female, you'll feel pressured to play by special, female rules. Like men, you'll have to be smart and industrious, but in addition you'll have to be "like women": kind, nurturing, accommodating, nonthreatening, placating, pretty, and small. You'll have to smile. And not act angry. And wear skirts. Nail polish and makeup help, too.

READING THE TEXT

1. Summarize in your own words the contradictory messages about appropriate gender behavior that women athletes must contend with, according to Nelson.

2. Nelson begins her article with an anecdote about poet Sylvia Plath. How does this opening frame her argument about women in sports?

3. What is the "femininity game" (para. 7), in Nelson's view, and how do the media perpetuate it?

4. What sports are coded as "feminine," according to Nelson, and why?

READING THE SIGNS

1. Watch a women's sports event on television, such as an LPGA match, analyzing the behavior and appearance of the athletes. Use your observations as evidence in an essay in which you assess the validity of Nelson's claims about the contradictory gender role behaviors of female athletes.

2. If you are a female athlete, write a journal entry exploring whether you feel pressure to act feminine and your responses to that pressure. If you are not a female athlete, reflect on the behavior and appearance of women athletes on your campus. Do you see signs that they are affected by the femininity game?

3. Obtain a copy of a magazine that focuses on women's sports, such as *Sports Illustrated Women,* or visit an online magazine such as sportsister.com or womensportreport.com. Analyze the articles and the ads in the magazine, noting models' and athletes' clothing, physical appearance, and speech patterns. Using Nelson's argument as a critical framework, write an essay in which you analyze whether the magazine perpetuates traditional gender roles or presents sports as an avenue for female empowerment.

4. Interview women athletes on your campus, and ask them whether they feel pressured by the femininity game. Have they been accused of being lesbians or bitches simply because they are athletes? Do they feel pressure to be physically attractive or charming? Do you see any correlation between an athlete's

sport and her responses? Use your observations as the basis of an argument about the influence of traditional gender roles on women athletes at your school.

WADE GRAHAM

Are We Greening Our Cities, or Just Greenwashing Them?

We may be living in the headiest times for ecologically sensitive architecture since Buckminster Fuller's 1960s. Indeed, among architectural visionaries, as Wade Graham writes in this feature for the *Los Angeles Times*, the "goal is even bigger: 'eco-cities' that will leapfrog the last century's flawed development patterns and deliver us in stylish comfort to a low-carbon, green future." It all sounds very nice, and Graham is on board with the sentiment, but he can't help noting how such a "green" project as Apple's new "spaceship campus" is "by any measure a huge, complex, massively resource-intensive and incredibly expensive ($5 billion) folly, achievable only by one of the richest corporations on Earth." That's not to mention the size of its parking lot for the 13,000 commuters who work there. So much for dreams of Arcadia in the techno future. Wade Graham is a writer, historian, and landscape designer and the author of *Dream Cities: Seven Urban Ideas That Shape the World* (2016).

Architecture and urban design are in the throes of a green fever dream: Everywhere you look there are plans for "sustainable" buildings, futuristic eco-cities, even vertical aquaponic farms in the sky, each promising to redeem the ecologically sinful modern city and bring its inhabitants back into harmony with nature. This year, two marquee examples are set to open: Bjarke Ingels' Via 57 West in New York, a 32-story luxury-apartment pyramid enfolding a garden, and the Louvre Abu Dhabi, by Jean Nouvel, a complex shielded from the harsh climate of the Arabian Peninsula by an enormous white dome. The dreamers' goal is even bigger: "eco-cities" that will leapfrog the last century's flawed development patterns and deliver us in stylish comfort to a low-carbon, green future.

In part, the dream reflects a pragmatic push for energy efficiency, recycled materials and lower carbon emissions — a competition rewarded with LEED certification in silver, gold or platinum. But it also includes a remarkable effort to turn buildings green — almost literally — by covering them in plants.

Green roofs are sprouting on Wal-Marts and green walls festooned with ferns and succulents in Cubist patterns appear on hotels, banks, museums — even at the mall, as I found on a recent trip to the Glendale Galleria in Los Angeles.

All of this is surely a good idea, at some level: trying to repair some of the damage our lifestyle has done to the planet by integrating nature into what have been, especially in the modern era, wasteful, harsh, alienating, concrete urban deserts. But, despite the rhetoric of reconciling the city with nature, today's green urban dream is too often about bringing a technologically controlled version of nature into the city and declaring the problem solved, rather than looking at the deeper causes of our current environmental and urban discontents.

Greening the city is not a new ideal. Ancient Romans waxed lyrical about Arcadia, a mythical bucolic escape from the ills of urban life: money-making, crime, pollution, disease and, of course, luxury and the moral turpitude that goes with it. City-dwellers have always been sensitive to the charge that the metropolis is guilty of a special kind of iniquity, which bars it from grace, and must be cleansed. (Remember Sodom and Gomorrah.) The corollary belief that the green countryside fosters all that is pure and wholesome is a foundational myth of Western culture. It is why, when most people amass enough filthy lucre, they move to the suburbs and cultivate a large, useless lawn, as if the greensward alone could buy them salvation.

Since Plato's *Republic*, visionaries have described the ideal human community as something less like a city and more like a big, well-ordered farm. Think of Charles Fourier's utopian phalanxes, the Shaker settlements, Frank Lloyd Wright's proposed Broadacre City, Soviet collectives, Israeli kibbutzes or the innumerable 19th and 20th century "garden cities" strewn around the American and European landscapes. A more modest contemporary form is perhaps the Brooklyn Grange, the hipsterish but messianic urban farm outfit that grows bespoke salad greens hydroponically on several rented New York City rooftops for environmentally conscious urbanites. It is undoubtedly a beneficial enterprise, but, given the realities of high urban land values and labor costs, such a model is unlikely to replace the world's nearly 6 million square miles of horizontal farms.

Today's signature eco-building, Apple's "spaceship" campus now under construction in Silicon Valley, designed by the British architect Norman Foster, is a good example of the shortcomings of the green dream. Though we are assured it will be sustainable, energy efficient, and "slim" — preserving 80 percent of its 175-acre site for landscaping, it is by any measure a huge, complex, massively resource-intensive and incredibly expensive ($5 billion) folly, achievable only by one of the richest corporations on Earth. What is more damning is that, at the end of the day, it will be just another appendage of suburban sprawl, a white-collar workplace located next to a freeway, dependent on vast garages (even if most of them are tastefully buried) for its 13,000 commuters — and thus with no smaller environmental footprint than a conventional office park.

A look at the green dream's origins is revealing. The Louvre Abu Dhabi, Apple's spaceship and another new Silicon Valley "campus," Google's planned complex to be covered in transparent tenting that it says will "blur the difference between our buildings and nature," are direct descendants of the work of the American visionary R. Buckminster Fuller and his Japanese partner, Shoji Sadao. In 1960, Fuller and Sadao proposed building a two-mile-wide, transparent geodesic dome over Midtown Manhattan. It would eliminate bad weather and the cost of heating and cooling separate buildings. It wasn't built, but other, lesser domed environments were, all over the world, and these helped spawn a global epidemic of drawing-board futuristic eco-cities.

Among the movement's avatars were Paolo Soleri, whose projected Utopia, Arcosanti, only amounted to a few, odd concrete structures in the Arizona desert, and the Japanese Metabolists of the 1960s and '70s, whose plans for massive floating city-farms and modular megastructures in the sky were outlandish. (They nevertheless directly influenced the development of undersea exploration modules, offshore oil platforms and the International Space Station.) Indeed, Foster was a student and later a collaborator of Fuller and Sadao, and his masterpieces — the Gherkin in London and the remade Reichstag in Berlin, to name just two of scores — are essentially climate-controlled domes, carefully modeled on his teachers' earlier work.

These projects are, then, really the fulfillment of a set of blue-sky dreams from the Dr. Strangelove era — where every cinematic space colony contained a domed conservatory and keeping the plants in the greenhouse alive was all that stood between humans and disaster. In the end, those dreams are not about reintegrating society with nature, but leaving Earth itself behind for an engineered habitat under the dome, in the sky, or at least on the roof.

Like driving an $85,000 Tesla, designing a perfect green building or 10 eco-city isn't enough to save the world. Although our buildings, like our cars, have been woefully inefficient environmentally, architecture isn't responsible in any meaningful way for humanity's disastrous environmental impacts, nor can it hope to solve them alone. An economic system based on the destruction of nature and the shifting of real costs onto those less fortunate and onto the future, is the real problem. No dome can protect us from our own profligacy and improvidence, nor can any number of hydroponic lettuce farms blunt the damage being done to real nature, or what is left of it, on planet Earth.

Instead of making "nature" into an urban lifestyle accessory, architects and planners must work to design better relationships between the parts of our cities and nature, and to promote just relationships between the people in them. The work of this year's Pritzker Prize winner, the Chilean architect Alejandro Aravena, is a case in point. He is less interested in making technologically impressive buildings than in collaborating with residents themselves to design low-cost, efficient housing solutions for the urban working class, especially in the wake of natural disasters. It is a more productive path forward than planting shrubs on skyscrapers.

READING THE TEXT

1. In your own words, explain what Graham means by "green fever dream" (para. 1).

2. According to Graham, what is the history of the ideal of environmentally friendly cities?

3. What does Graham mean by claiming that many twentieth-century attempts at green building design are "the fulfillment of a set of blue-sky dreams from the Dr. Strangelove era" (para. 9)? What is his justification for that claim?

4. What more environmentally sensitive alternative would Graham prefer to the current green building fad?

5. How does Graham use concession, history, and specific examples to support his overall argument?

READING THE SIGNS

1. In class, brainstorm ways in which your campus has attempted to become more environmentally sustainable. Then, focusing on a few of these strategies, write an essay in which you assess whether they are indeed environmentally effective or, as Graham puts it, examples of "greenwashing." Share your essays with the class, and then together with other students, brainstorm — and act on — ways in which your campus could improve its environmental footprint.

2. Advocates of a high-tech future often claim that technology can solve our environmental problems. In an essay, evaluate this position, considering past instances of technology's success or failure in solving real-life problems.

3. **CONNECTING TEXTS**   How might Julia B. Corbett ("A Faint Green Sell: Advertising and the Natural World," p. 209) and Michael Pollan ("Supermarket Pastoral," p. 96) respond to Graham's lament that "today's green urban dream is too often about bringing a technologically controlled version of nature into the city and declaring the problem solved, rather than looking . . . deeper (para. 3)? Use a close reading of Corbett's and Pollan's essays as the basis of your response.

4. Several authors in this textbook — not simply Graham but also Michael Pollan, Thomas Frank, Jia Tolentino, Brooke Gladstone, and Barbara Ehrenrich, among others, and the chapter introductions — explore the ways in which a seemingly positive image or constructive social movement, in fact, may be not supporting its original cause. Read two or three of these authors and synthesize how positive images may in fact derail the causes that their devotees advance. Then, in your own essay, explore why people find easy answers to be so attractive and propose your own solution to encourage them to be more critical thinkers about American society and popular culture.

GLOSSARY

abduction (n.)   A form of logical inference, first proposed by Charles Sanders Peirce, by which one seeks the most likely explanatory hypothesis or cause for a phenomenon. For example, the most likely explanation for the fact that in teen horror movies the first victims of the murderous monster are the cheerleader and the football player is that the majority of the teen audience enjoys the imaginative revenge of seeing snooty high school types done in.

archetype (n.)   A recurring character type or plot pattern found in literature, mythology, and popular culture. Sea monsters like Jonah's whale and Moby-Dick are archetypes, as are stories that involve long sea journeys or descents into the underworld.

canon (n.)   Books or works that are considered essential to a literary tradition, as the plays of Shakespeare are part of the canon of English literature.

class (n.)   A group of related objects or people. Those who share the same economic status in a society are said to be of the same social class: for example, working class, middle class, upper class. Members of a social class tend to share similar interests and political viewpoints.

code (n.)   A system of **signs** or values that assigns meanings to the elements that belong to it. Thus, a traffic code defines a red light as a "stop" signal and a green light as a "go," while a fashion code determines whether an article of clothing is stylish. To *decode* a system is to figure out its meanings, as in interpreting the tattooing and body-piercing fads.

commodification (n.)   The transforming of an abstraction or behavior into a product for sale. For example, selling mass-produced hamburgers as an expression of rule-breaking defiance and individualism.

connotation (n.)   The meaning suggested by a word, as opposed to its objective reference, or **denotation**. Thus, the word *flag* might connote (or suggest) feelings of patriotism, while it literally denotes (or refers to) a pennant-like object.

consumption (n.)   The use of products and services, as opposed to their production. A *consumer culture* is one that consumes more than it produces. As a consumer culture, for example, America uses more goods than it manufactures, which results in a trade deficit with those *producer cultures* (such as China) with which America trades.

context (n.)   The environment in which a **sign** can be interpreted. In the context of a college classroom, for example, T-shirts, jeans, and sneakers are interpreted as ordinary casual dress. Wearing the same outfit in the context of a job interview at an investment bank would be interpreted as meaning that you're not serious about wanting the job.

cultural studies (n.)   The academic study of ordinary, everyday culture rather than **high culture**. See also **culture**; **culture industry**; **mass culture**; **popular culture**.

culture (n.)   The overall system of values and traditions shared by a group of people. Not exactly synonymous with *society*, which can include numerous cultures within its boundaries, a culture encompasses the worldviews of those who belong to it. Thus, the United States, which is a multicultural society, includes the differing worldviews of people of African, Asian, Latin American, Native American, and European descent. See also **cultural studies**; **culture industry**; **high culture**; **mass culture**; **popular culture**.

culture industry (n.)   The commercial forces behind the production of **mass culture** or entertainment. See also **cultural studies**; **culture**; **high culture**; **mass culture**; **popular culture**.

denotation (n.)   The particular object or class of objects to which a word refers. Contrast with **connotation**.

discourse (n.)   The words, concepts, and presuppositions that constitute the knowledge and understanding of a particular community, often academic or professional.

dominant culture (n.)   The group within a **multicultural** society whose traditions, values, and beliefs are held to be normative, as the European tradition is the dominant culture in the United States.

Eurocentric (adj.)   Related to a worldview founded on the traditions and history of European culture, usually at the expense of non-European cultures.

function (n.)   The utility of an object, as opposed to its cultural meaning. Spandex or Lycra shorts, for example, have a functional value for cyclists because they're lightweight and aerodynamic. On the other hand, such shorts are a general fashion item for both men and women because of their cultural meaning, not their function. Many noncyclists wear spandex to project an image of hard-bodied fitness, sexiness, or just plain trendiness, for instance.

gender (n.)   One's sexual identity and the roles that follow from it, as determined by the norms of one's culture rather than by biology or genetics. The assumption that women should be foremost in the nurturing of children is a gender norm; the fact that only women can give birth is a biological phenomenon.

high culture (n.)   The products of the elite arts, including classical music, literature, drama, opera, painting, and sculpture. See also **cultural studies**; **culture**; **culture industry**; **mass culture**; **popular culture**.

icon (n.), **iconic** (adj.)   In **semiotics**, a **sign** that visibly resembles its referent, as a photograph looks like the thing it represents. More broadly, an icon is someone (often a celebrity) who enjoys a commanding or representative place in popular culture. Beyoncé is a music video icon. Contrast with **symbol**.

ideology (n.)   The beliefs, interests, and values that determine one's interpretations or judgments and that are often associated with one's social class. For example, in the ideology of modern business, a business is designed to produce profits, not social benefits.

image (n.)   Literally, a pictorial representation; more generally, the identity that one projects to others through such things as clothing, grooming, speech, and behavior.

mass culture (n.)   A subset of **popular culture** that includes the popular entertainments that are commercially produced for widespread consumption. See also **cultural studies**; **culture**; **culture industry**; **high culture**.

mass media (n. pl.)   The means of communication, often controlled by the **culture industry**, that include newspapers, popular magazines, radio, television, film, and the Internet.

multiculturalism (n.), **multicultural** (adj.)   In American education, the movement to incorporate the traditions, history, and beliefs of the United States' non-European cultures into a traditionally *monocultural* (or single-culture) curriculum dominated by European thought and history.

mythology (n.)   The overall framework of values and beliefs incorporated in a given cultural system or worldview. Any given belief within such a structure — like the belief that "a woman's place is in the home" — is called a *myth*.

overdetermination (n.)   Originally a term from Freudian psychoanalytic theory to describe the multiple causes of a psychological affect, overdetermination more generally describes the multiplicity of possible causes for any social phenomenon. Combined with abductive reasoning, overdetermination is a key element in **semiotic** interpretation. See also **abduction**.

politics (n.)   Essentially, the practice of promoting one's interests in a competitive social environment. Not restricted to electioneering; there may be office politics, classroom politics, academic politics, and sexual politics.

popular culture (n.)   That segment of a **culture** that incorporates the activities of everyday life, including the consumption of consumer goods and the production and enjoyment of mass-produced entertainments. See also **cultural studies; culture industry; high culture; mass culture**.

postmodernism (n.), **postmodern** (adj.)   The worldview behind some contemporary literature, art, music, architecture, and philosophy that rejects traditional attempts to make meaning out of human history and experience. For the *postmodern* artist, art does not attempt to create new explanatory myths or **symbols** but rather recycles or repeats existing images, as does the art of Andy Warhol.

proxemics (n.)   The study of human uses of space in interactions with other humans, including body language, facial expression, distance between subjects, gestures, and so on.

semiotics (n.)   In short, the study of **signs**. Synonymous with *semiology*, semiotics is concerned with both the theory and the practice of interpreting linguistic, cultural, and behavioral sign systems. One who practices *semiotic analysis* is called a *semiotician* or *semiologist*.

sign (n.)   Anything that bears a meaning. Words, objects, images, and forms of behavior are all signs whose meanings are determined by the particular **codes**, or **systems**, in which they appear.

symbol (n.), **symbolic** (adj.)   A **sign**, according to semiotician Charles Sanders Peirce, whose significance is arbitrary. The meaning of the word *bear*, for example, is arbitrarily determined by those who use it. Contrast with **icon**.

system (n.)   The **code**, or network, within which a **sign** functions and so achieves its meaning through its associational and differential relations with other signs. The English language is a sign system, as is a fashion code.

text (n.)   A complex of **signs**, which may be linguistic, imagistic, behavioral, and/or musical, that can be read or interpreted.

ACKNOWLEDGMENTS

Michael Agresta, "How the Western Was Lost — and Why It Matters," as first published in *The Atlantic Magazine*. Used with permission from the author.

Helena Andrews, "The Butler versus The Help: Gender Matters," *The Root*, August 23, 2013. Copyright © 2013 by The Root. Used with permission.

Chris Arning, "What Can Semiotics Contribute to Packaging Design?" Copyright © Creative Semiotics. Used with permission.

Deborah Blum, "The Gender Blur: Where Does Biology End and Society Take Over?" from Utne Reader, Sept.–Oct.1998. Copyright © 1998 by Deborah Blum. Reprinted by permission of International Creative Management, Inc.

danah boyd, excerpt from *It's Complicated: MySpace vs. Facebook*. Copyright © 2014 by danah boyd. Reprinted by permission of Yale University Press.

Patti Schifter Caravello, "Judging Quality on the Web" by Patti Schifter Caravello, UCLA Research Library. Reprinted with permission.

Jessica Contrera, "Most Young People Don't Vote — Condescending to Them Doesn't Help," *The Washington Post*, August 30.

Brittney Cooper, "Hollywood's post-racial mirage: How pop-culture got gentrified," *Salon*, March 25, 2014. Copyright © 2014 Salon. This article first appeared in *Salon .com*, at https://www.salon.com. An online version remains in the Salon Archives. Used with permission.

Julia B. Corbett, "A Faint Green Sell: Advertising and the Natural World," from *Enviropop: Studies in Environmental Rhetoric and Popular Cultures*, eds. Mark Meister & Phyllis M. Japp, pp. 81–94. Copyright © 2002 by Mark Meister and Phyllis M. Japp. Reproduced with permission of ABC-CLIO, LLC; permission conveyed through Copyright Clearance Center, Inc.

Steve Craig, "Men's Men and Women's Women: How TV Commercials Portray Gender to Different Audiences," from *Issues and Effects of Mass Communication: Other Voices* by Steve Craig. Reprinted by permission of the author.

Claire Miye Stanford, "You've Got the Wrong Song: *Nashville* and Country Music Feminism." This article was originally published in *The Los Angeles Review of Books* (www.lareviewofbooks.org). Copyright © 2013 Los Angeles Review of Books. Used with permission.

Jim Tankersley, "Why the Upper Middle Class Might Be the Real Target," *The Washington Post*, June 21, 2016.

Jia Tolentino, "How 'Empowerment' Became Something for Women to Buy," *The New York Times,* April 12, 2016.

Joseph Turow, "Introduction," from *The Daily You: How the New Advertising Industry Is Defining Your Identity and Your Worth* by Joseph Turow. Copyright © 2012 by Joseph Turow. Reprinted by permission of Yale University Press.

James B. Twitchell, "What We Are to Advertisers," from *Lead Us into Temptation: The Triumph of American Materialism* by James B. Twitchell. Copyright © 1999 by James B. Twitchell. Reprinted by permission of the author.

S. Craig Watkins, "The Evolution of #Black Twitter," *dmlcentral.com*, September 22, 2014. Used with permission from the author.

INDEX OF AUTHORS AND TITLES